Communicating Christ Cross-Culturally

—————— 2nd Edition ——————

An Introduction to Missionary Communication

David J. Hesselgrave

ZondervanPublishingHouse
Academic and Professional Books
Grand Rapids, Michigan

A Division of HarperCollins*Publishers*

Communicating Christ Cross-Culturally, 2nd ed.
Copyright © 1991 by David J. Hesselgrave

Requests for information should be addressed to:
Zondervan Publishing House
Grand Rapids, Michigan 49530

Library of Congress Cataloging-in-Publication Data

Hesselgrave, David J.
Communicating Christ cross-culturally / David J. Hesselgrave. – 2nd ed.
p.   cm.
Includes bibliographical references and indexes.
ISBN 0-310-36811-1
1. Communication – Religious aspects – Christianity.
2. Communication. 3. Missions.   I. Title.
BV4319.H47   1991
261 – dc20   90-47323
                                                                        CIP

Edited by Gerard Terpstra
Designed by Jan M. Ortiz
Figures by Louise Bauer

Printed in the United States of America

99 00 01 02 /DC/ 20 19 18 17 16 15 14 13 12 11

Communicating Christ
Cross-Culturally
—————2nd Edition—————

To the memory of my
Father and Mother
Albertus Roy and Selma Johnson Hesselgrave
whose highest joy was to commend their
children to Christian faith and service

CONTENTS

FIGURES

FOREWORD TO THE FIRST EDITION

This volume is no offer of "three snappy sessions on instant communication." It is the serious work of a gifted scholar. Not only the professional missiologist in his classroom and study but also the student eagerly preparing for mission service, the troubled missionary facing daily pressures of communicating the gospel in alien cultures, and the overworked executive plotting strategies for his denominational task force or mission society will all profit immensely from the treasury of wisdom amassed in this book. On every page the author reflects, though quite unobtrusively, a mastery of the vast literature that has grown up around the intersection of the new science of communication skills, cross-cultural communication, and missiology. For the sake of the professional missionary, practicing the art of cross-cultural communication and crying for help, Dr. Hesselgrave also draws richly from his own years as a practicing church planter seeking to communicate the Christian gospel across a cultural barrier. Best of all, he practices what he preaches; and, in spite of a studied determination never to be superficial or frothy, he manages to communicate beautifully as he unfolds the complex problems of communication theory and works toward practical solutions.

This volume displays many excellences, not the least of which is a broad empirical approach to the issues raised by the interface of communication and mission. Seldom does Dr. Hesselgrave ride personal hobbies. He presents alternative viewpoints fairly and draws widely from all related disciplines to secure the light that each in turn throws upon the issue at hand. His conclusions, therefore, are broadly informed and usually reliable and very convincing.

In a way almost unique among recent writers on this subject, Dr. Hesselgrave combines both theological wisdom and scientific knowledge. On the one hand, he evidences a complete fidelity to the full authority of Scripture; on the other, he also displays a keen sensitivity to the insights of science. He is no less rigorously loyal to the one than to the other and seeks to mold the result into a coherent and comprehensive whole that is eminently practical. In one sense, this may be the unique contribution of the volume. Its readers are getting the best of both worlds—solid theological substance without trimmings and the latest and richest fruits of scholarly research without adulteration. Moreover, the whole is set rather firmly within historical and philosophical frameworks.

In this volume, then, Dr. Hesselgrave provides church and classroom with a rich treasury of wisdom—the ripe fruit of many years as a working missionary and now a decade and a half as a scholar in the study and in the classroom. I predict that *Communicating Christ Cross-Culturally* will prove a trustworthy guide for those seeking the best way to translate the gospel meaningfully from one culture to another. It will also stimulate missiologists to a new and higher level of research in communication theory. And it will provide a data-bank of great value for the working missionary and the mission strategist.

KENNETH S. KANTZER
Editor, *Christianity Today*

FOREWORD TO THE REVISED EDITION

This revised edition of Dr. David Hesselgrave's great work *Communicating Christ Cross-Culturally* updates the original edition and interacts with the most recent literature on this increasingly important topic. The original edition went through fifteen printings and, very deservedly, has come to be one of the most widely used textbooks on Christian cross-cultural communication. The revisions in this new edition are extensive and carry on the high level of discussion maintained throughout the original edition, taking into account, for example, the current discussion on the relationship between form and function and the enormous body of literature that has sprung up recently on contextualization. To enhance the volume's usefulness for students, Dr. Hesselgrave has added an extensive bibliography on various aspects of cross-cultural communication.

This revision of *Communicating Christ Cross-Culturally* is superb. It raises a great book into a unique category, undoubtedly the finest book on this topic available today.

KENNETH S. KANTZER
Director of the Ph.D. Program
Trinity Evangelical Divinity School
and Dean of *Christianity Today*'s
Theological Institute

PREFACE TO THE REVISED EDITION

Whether we focus on Christian missions, the discipline known as missiology, or communication theory itself, much has transpired since the first edition of this book came off the press in 1978. Therefore, on the one hand, it has not only been advisable to undertake this revision, it has also been necessary. On the other hand, many of the basic considerations are much the same today and will remain so into the future. So an affirmation of, and continuity with, that which was written previously is both warranted and desirable.

Over the period of about fifteen years, some fifteen printings of this book have appeared. Its ministry has been far beyond what I anticipated in the middle 1970s. Teachers, students, and practitioners from all parts of the world have expressed appreciation. Not a few have said that it has been used of God to enhance their ministry. And one missionary couple from Africa, whose influence and outreach have become little short of phenomenal, journeyed all the way to Deerfield to explain how our great God used this book to keep them on the field and redirect their strategy. No Christian author could ask for more than that the God of all wisdom and grace thus use his sincere but inadequate literary efforts. To God be the glory!

It is appropriate that I express gratitude to all who have in any way aided me in the publication of this revision of *Communicating Christ Cross-Culturally*. To my esteemed colleague Kenneth S. Kantzer, who once again has contributed the Foreword; to my assistant Kent Carle, who put the bibliography in final form; to my wife, Gertrude, and my children, especially my daughter, Sheryl Kroeker, who prepared the indexes, their spouses, and their children, all of whom continue to provide the kind of help and inspire the kind of hope that allow me to concentrate on the writing enterprise; to faculty colleagues whose ideas stimulate continued reflection; to the staff at Zondervan Publishing House who work with me; and to all who have in any way encouraged me—to all of these I direct my heartfelt thanks.

As in the first edition, I continue to use the masculine pronoun and the word *man* in a generic sense rather than resort to the alternatives. Given the limitations of the English language, this approach seems to be a small price to pay for a more straightforward style.

It is appropriate also that I repeat here a portion of the Preface to the first edition. There I wrote, "If the Christian mission were something to be played, communication would be the name of the game. As it is, the Christian mission is serious business—the King's business! In it missionaries have ambassadorial rank. Their special task is to cross cultural and other boundaries in order to communicate Christ. That is a tremendously rewarding endeavor. But it is also an unusually demanding one."

That still being true, may our commissioning Lord be pleased to use this book in a still greater way to enable his ambassadors to represent him and his kingdom effectively and well.

Part I

COMMUNICATION AND MISSION

Chapter 1

Communication, The Missionary Problem Par Excellence

John listened intently as the chapel speaker repeated his basic thesis with arresting cogency and conviction. In his message the speaker had demonstrated that world evangelization is not only commanded in the Scriptures but is also logically possible. "We can evangelize the world—now!" he declared. To John it seemed so forceful, and even simple, really. If thousands would be willing to go—right now! There seemed to be no doubt. We *could* evangelize the world if we would just "go and tell."

Thirty years later John boarded a plane en route to a missionary convention for Christian young people. In anticipation of counseling inquiring youth, he reflected upon his own experience on the field. He recalled how eager some of the people—especially the young—had been to hear his message. He recalled the frustration of trying to get his message across, first through an interpreter and then, haltingly, by speaking the new language himself. He remembered how complicated his task had become as he settled in one place to instruct the believers and, with God's help, mold them into a church. Name after name, face after face, crisis after crisis came to his mind: the struggle to understand the personal problems of those people, problems at once so similar and so very different from those of his experience; the emergence of Christian leaders and viable congregations; the hours in the study, with small groups, in the pulpit and platform, and behind a microphone; the furloughs and research at the university to master materials relevant to his target culture.

Time passed quickly. After a few minutes with a book on missionary strategy and a brief conversation with an affable seat partner, John arrived at his destination.

That night John found himself in a youth rally that was fairly bursting with youthful enthusiasm. After some rousing songs and a series of five-minute reports from the fields, the speaker began his message with carefully articulated words: "Young people, we can evangelize the world now, by the end of this decade. . . ."

Although it is obvious that we must pick and choose according to our purpose, *any* one-word or one-phrase summary of our missionary task in the world runs the risk of reductionism. However, the question we must face is this: Do we hasten the accomplishment of our mission by repeatedly referring to it in terms of its narrowest dimension?

Let the reader not misunderstand. The word evangelize *(euangelizō)* is used some fifty-four times in the New Testament; evangel or gospel *(euangelion)* is used seventy-six times; and evangelist *(euangelistēs)* is used three times. These are good words. They are biblical words. And we *are* to evangelize the world. We *can* evangelize the world. We *must* evangelize the world. The world *will be* evangelized. But more must be said about the matter.

The danger of reductionism is seen in the English theologian C. H. Dodd's resort to another primary word, proclaim *(kēryssō)*, and its related forms proclamation *(kērygma)* and herald *(kēryx)*, in order to sum up the New Testament mission and message. Michael Green rightly takes issue with Dodd and insists that *kēryssō* is but one of *three* great words used in the New Testament in this connection, the others being the previously mentioned *euangelizō* and *martyreō* (bear witness). Green urges a careful consideration of all three terms in order that a "broader-based understanding of the early Christian gospel" might emerge.[1] Green's point is well taken. But in order to understand the scope of the task it is instructive to examine still other New Testament words used in connection with the apostolic ministry of the church:

1. Syncheō (confound)—Acts 9:22
2. Symbibazō (prove)—Acts 9:22
3. Diēgeomai (describe)—Acts 9:27
4. Syzēteō (argue)—Acts 9:29
5. Laleō (talk)—Acts 9:29
6. Dialegomai (reason with)—Acts 18:4
7. Peithō (persuade)—Acts 18:4
8. Noutheteō (admonish, warn)—Acts 20:31
9. Katēcheō (inform, instruct)—Acts 21:21, 24
10. Deomai (beg, beseech)—2 Cor. 5:20
11. Elenchō (reprove)—2 Tim. 4:2
12. Epitimaō (rebuke)—2 Tim. 4:2
13. Parakaleō (exhort, urge)—1 Peter 2:11

We will return to some of these words at various points in our discussion. I list them here to support my contention that if we desire to succinctly summarize our missionary task, one of the best words available to us is the word *communication*. In view of the challenges and questions currently facing the church, this is the term Hendrik Kraemer settles on in order to put the task in a "wider and deeper setting."

> One of the most important effects of this trend set in motion by the attempt to rediscover the marching orders of the Church is the new awakening of evangelistic responsibility to the world in many Churches. But here bewilderment begins. At the very moment a Church commences to turn away from the introversion in which it is steeped by its acceptance of being primarily an established institution, and looks at its real field, the world, a new realism awakens. Innumerable questions immediately assail such a

[1]Michael Green, *Evangelism in the Early Church* (Grand Rapids: Eerdmans, 1970), 48.

Church, such questions as: What am I? To what purpose am I? Am I fulfilling this purpose? Where and how do I live? In a ghetto, or in living contact with the world? Does the world listen when I speak to it, and if not, why not? Am I really proclaiming the gospel, or am I not? Why has such a wall of separation risen between the world and what I must stand for? Do I know the world in which people live, or do I not? Why am I evidently regarded as a residue of a world that belongs irrevocably to the past? How can I find a way to speak again with relevancy and authority, transmitting "the words of eternal life" entrusted to me?

Amidst the welter of such questions, engendered by a newly awakened apostolic consciousness, communication has become a problem with which the Churches everywhere are wrestling. Apparently one could express it as well in a different way and inquire after the best and most appropriate methods of evangelism. But that is not right. In that case we would have done better by giving to our discussion the title "The Problem of Evangelism." The word "communication" puts the problem in a far wider and deeper setting.[2]

I too want to explore the missionary "problem" in its larger dimensions. As a matter of fact, even the word "communication" does not do justice to biblical prescriptions and descriptions having to do with the missionary task, but it does get nearer to the heart of it. Let me say, then, that in this book we will concern ourselves with communicating Christ across cultural barriers to the various peoples of the world. I will assume a commitment to Christ, the Holy Scriptures, and world evangelization. The primary focus will be on the relationship between Christian communication and world cultures.

[2]Hendrik Kraemer, *The Communication of the Christian Faith* (Philadelphia: Westminster, 1956), 10–11.

Chapter 2

Man, The Communicating Creature

Communication is fundamental to human beings. To be sure, they are not the only creatures of God that can communicate. But they are the only creatures on earth who can put communication in the form of symbols that have no relationship to their referents aside from that which the human mind assigns to them. Moreover, transcending time and space, human beings can transfer information to others in remote places or to those who will yet be born.

Of all the miracles related in the first chapters of Genesis, some of the most significant must be implied in those simple and sublime verses having to do with language and communication (italics are mine in each case):

> And God created man in His own image, in the image of God He created him; male and female He created them. And God blessed them; and God *said* to them (Gen. 1:27–28).
>
> And the Lord God *commanded* the man, saying (Gen. 2:16).

And the man *gave names* to all the cattle, and to the birds of the sky, and to every beast of the field (Gen. 2:20).

Now the serpent was more crafty than any beast. . . . And he *said* to the woman, "Indeed, has God *said* (Gen. 3:1).

And they heard the sound of the Lord God walking in the garden in the cool of the day, . . . Then the Lord God *called* to the man, and *said* to him, "Where are you?" (Gen. 3:8–9).

One of the most disastrous calamities to result from man's early rebellion against God was the disruption of that state described in Genesis 11:1: "Now the whole earth used the same language and the same words." Think of the potential of that state of affairs! But, of course, having almost unlimited potential for mutual understanding and peace, humanity also had unimaginable potential for uniting the forces of evil. In their fallen state it was the latter potential that they exploited, and as a result God imposed a kind of cultural quarantine upon them: "Come, let Us go down and there confuse their language, that they may not understand one another's speech" (Gen. 11:7).

All students of communication can appreciate the conclusion of a man who has reflected as deeply on the human predicament as Kenneth Burke who said that our problem is Babel![1] And they can at least understand the concern of Sir Maurice Mawby for *community* when he says,

You know, the greatest thing for the world would be a common language. I'd adopt any religion, it doesn't matter to me. . . . Man's not a solitary [sic], he can't live alone, so he has to learn how to live with his fellow humans.[2]

Neither Burke nor Mawby get to the root of the problem, however, because they do not recognize the intransigent

[1]Kenneth Burke, *A Grammar of Motives and a Rhetoric of Motives* (Cleveland: World, Meridian, 1962), 547.

[2]Sir Maurice Mawby, "Australia and Asia," *The Asia Magazine*, September 24, 1972, 26.

insistence of people to turn a deaf ear to heaven. It is possible for people to begin to understand and appreciate what *could* take place when they really communicate with one another. However, that the divine-human relationship must be restored before true communication *will* take place is something they do not understand. As Professor Kraemer writes:

> But, as the Bible is the record of the acts of God's revelation toward the *re*-creation, the *re*-storement of man in his *normal* (from the divine point of view) existence, the indispensable complement of Gen., ch. 11 is Acts, ch. 2. In this last chapter the condition of language in human life appears to be of paramount significance, because, when the full power of the Holy Spirit reigns, in other words, when the divine-human dialogue is restored, the confusion of languages disappears and there is full communication again. Fall and redemption, Babel and Pentecost are the hidden factors behind language and communication. The story of Acts, ch. 2, indicates with the realism that is peculiar to the Bible the fact that humanity, since this event of Pentecost, remains pending between fall and redemption, Babel and Pentecost, because of our own attitude of lack of faith.[3]

The significance of Kraemer's words is apparent, not only in the theology of the events to which he refers and in the history of people and nations, but in the philosophy of language and the science of communication as well.

Thus when we review the philosophy of language, our attention is drawn to Confucius, who attempted a moral, social, and religious reconstruction through the proper use of words (especially as they relate to the statuses and roles of persons), as implied in his theory of the "rectification of names." In the West, the brilliant mind of Socrates grappled with the correct meaning of words, as every student of philosophy knows. Subsequently, various philosophies of language have been woven into the very fabric of man's

[3]Hendrik Kraemer, *Communication of the Christian Faith* (Philadelphia: Westminster, 1956), 66.

intellectual quest. For example, in our day Susanne K. Langer sees the preoccupation with symbols (i.e., "arbitrary sounds and marks") as a distinguishing feature of the arts and sciences as well as philosophy. Since she, like Burke and Mawby, reckons apart from the consequences of the Fall, she sees this preoccupation with symbols and their meanings as a precursor of a brighter future. "Perhaps it [the philosophical study of symbols] holds the seed of a new intellectual harvest to be reaped in the next season of human understanding," she writes.[4]

When we review the science of communication, our attention is drawn first to the likes of Aristotle, Cicero, and Quintilian. These ancients, of course, thought of communication more in terms of an *art*, its theory being termed rhetoric and its practice being called oratory. Aristotle defined rhetoric as the art of discovering in every case the "available means of *persuasion*." The persuader was successful to the degree to which he actually brought the audience to "right" belief and action.[5] Belief and actions that were "right," of course, were not easily defined. In our day, Kenneth Burke basically agrees with Aristotle but prefers the word *identification* as a key term because he sees rhetoric and communication as compensatory to the division of humanity into competing camps— each camp with its own language.[6] I. A. Richards insists that the emphasis should be on *listening*, which includes analyzing the causes of misunderstanding and positing remedies. In his view persuasion and disputation feed the combative impulse and "can put us in mental blinders and make us take another man's words in the ways in which we can down him with the least trouble."[7]

At the very beginning of our study, therefore, let true

[4]Susanne K. Langer, *Philosophy in a New Key* (New York: New American Library of World Literature, Mentor, 1948), 33.
[5]*Rhetoric and the Poetics of Aristotle*, trans. W. Thys Roberts and Ingram Bewater (New York: Malen Library, 1954), 19–24.
[6]Burke, *Grammar of Motives*, 543–83.
[7]I. A. Richards, *A Philosophy of Rhetoric* (New York: Oxford University Press, 1936), 24–25.

Christians humbly bow before their Creator in thanksgiving for the wisdom and knowledge he has vouchsafed to them in Christ. Christ came to make possible the understanding and oneness of which philosophers of language, scientists of communication, and ordinary people everywhere alternately dream and despair. But Christians ought not be smug nor complacent in their knowledge of Christ, for he has given them a commission to disciple the nations. Therefore they must still learn if they are to teach, if they are to *communicate Christ across cultures!*

Chapter 3

The Legacy of Rhetoric to Christian Communication

To the ancients of such places as Athens, Rome, and Alexandria rhetoric represented the highest of intellectual achievement because it entailed both consummate learning and persuasive skills. To the average person today it probably means little more than flowery or inflated speech. But students of communication, homiletics, and debate will be aware of the fact that even today we have a great indebtedness to those learned ancients, both within and without the church, whose writings have informed these arts across the intervening centuries and still do so today.

RHETORIC AND HOMILETICS

The literary parentage of the sermon as we know it today is still to be found in the ancient schools of rhetoric. As Michael Green has explained, for more than 150 years the early church knew nothing of "set addresses following certain homiletical patterns within the four walls of a church."[1]

---

[1]Michael Green, *Evangelism in the Early Church* (Grand Rapids: Eerdmans, 1970), 194.

Rather, there was "the greatest variety in the type and content of evangelistic preaching."[2] When sermonizing began to develop as an "art," it was informed by rhetoric. Augustine is a case in point.

Augustine was a brilliant, ambitious pagan young man from North Africa who, while still comparatively young, climbed the ladder of success to the honored profession of *rhetor* (legal orator). Called to be the *rhetor* of Milan, Italy, he went to hear the eloquence of the renowned Ambrose, who had captivated the minds and hearts of thousands from his Milan pulpit. Convicted and converted, and baptized by Ambrose on Easter, 387, Augustine returned to Hippo in North Africa to become one of the most penetrating and influential theologians the church has ever produced.

About the time Augustine was ordained as Bishop of Hippo in the year 396, he undertook the writing of the work *On Christian Doctrine*. The question he faced head-on in that work was a most significant one. Christendom was the arena of the struggle between orthodoxy and heresy—a struggle that culminated in the Council of Chalcedon in 451. The various perversions of orthodox doctrine tended to reflect one strain or another of the pagan ideological heritage. The task to which Augustine set himself was basically twofold: (1) to define Christian doctrine in such a way as to preserve its exclusive character and sift out pagan accretions; and (2) to effect a rapprochement between revelational truth and those aspects of pagan intellectual achievement not inherently antagonistic to that truth.

In the work itself, Augustine has various ways of referring to the second part of his task. One of the classic statements of the problem is his well-known analogy in the conclusion of Book II. At the time of the Exodus, the Egyptians possessed not only the idols and accoutrements of pagan religion with which the Israelites refused to have anything to do, but also clothing, and vases and ornaments of gold and silver, which the Israelites took with them to put to their own use. In view

[2]Ibid.

of this, Augustine decided concerning his basic problem that the amount of useful information obtainable from history, "number," disputation, and philosophy is small when compared to that derivable from the Scriptures. Yet "gold from Egypt is still gold," and for that reason it should be used to the best possible advantage by the church. Augustine, therefore, believed and taught his students that wherever they may find truth, it is the Lord's.[3]

The "gold from Egypt" that Augustine imports for use in *On Christian Doctrine* is in large measure of the rhetorical variety. Book IV in the larger work has been aptly called "the first manual of Christian rhetoric."[4] The entire work, however, is devoted to achieving Augustine's overall objectives by aiding students in the determination of both the content and the form of the Christian sermon. Noting this, James Murphy quotes Augustine as follows:

> There are two things necessary to the treatment of the Scripture: A way of discovering *(modus inveniendi)* those things which are to be understood, and a way of expressing to others *(modus proferendi)* what we have learned.[5]

The first three books of *On Christian Doctrine* are concerned with the former of these essentials, and the fourth is concerned with the latter. Thus while being everywhere true to Scripture, Augustine imports "Egyptian gold" and utilizes it in the course of orthodox Christianity by teaching the basics of the sermonic form of Christian communication.

This process continues today. Lloyd Perry has analyzed 68 books on homiletics written in America between the years 1834 and 1954.[6] In these books he discovered 205 references to

---

[3]Augustine, *On Christian Doctrine*, trans. D. W. Robertson, Jr. (New York: Liberal Arts, 1958), II.18, p. 28.

[4]James J. Murphy, "Augustine and the Debate About a Christian Rhetoric," *Quarterly Journal of Speech* 46 (December 1960): 408.

[5]Ibid.

[6]Lloyd Perry, "Trends and Emphases in the Philosophy, Materials and Methodology of American Protestant Homiletical Education as Established by

Cicero, 103 to Aristotle, 101 to Quintilian, 53 to Fenelon, 50 to Plato, and a significant number of additional references to Whately and Campbell, the well-known British exponents of the classical approach to rhetoric and homiletics. Perry laments the recent trend away from explicit citings of the classical rhetoricians in contemporary textbooks on homiletics. He notes that this trend has been accompanied by an increased emphasis on the *philosophy of preaching* and less and less emphasis on the *methodology of sermonizing.*[7]

It would seem that when it comes to the practical art of sermon building and sermon delivery, contemporary homileticians would be well advised to pay close attention to the insights of the ancient exponents of rhetoric!

RHETORIC AND COMMUNICATION THEORY IN ITS LARGER DIMENSIONS

Homileticians are not alone in devoting attention to rhetorical theory. Various scholars with interests in intracultural and intercultural communication theory, both within and without the church, are giving increased attention to it. And in doing so, they are reinforcing its function and widening its significance. I will be referring to some of their conclusions in more depth as I proceed, but a brief sampling here will illustrate what I have in mind.

1. Aristotle defined rhetoric as the art of discovering in any instance the available means of persuasion. Although modern scholars tend to agree with that thrust, they usually increase its scope. Donald C. Bryant defines rhetoric as "the rationale of informative and persuasive discourse."[8] Douglas Ehninger finds even that definition overly confining and suggests that "current practice is to extend it to encompass all

a Study of Selected Trade and Textbooks Published Between 1834–1954" (Ph.D. dissertation, Northwestern University, 1961).
    [7]Ibid., 407.
    [8]Donald C. Bryant, "Rhetoric: Its Function and Scope," *Quarterly Journal of Speech*, 1953.

of the ways in which, and all of the ends for which, symbols of any sort may be used to affect another's mind."[9]

2. At a 1983 conference at the Catholic University of America, Jean Dietz Moss, William A. Wallace, and others addressed themselves to the widespread difficulty that contemporary speakers and writers have in "getting to the heart of the matter and setting it forth cogently."[10] They concentrated on the adaptation and application of classical rhetorical techniques with a view to introducing more of them into instruction at the university level.[11]

3. George R. Bramer,[12] Richard E. Young, Alton L. Becker, and Kenneth Pike[13] have made comparative studies of modern "Rogerian rhetoric" (the cooperative search for truth) as over against the classical style of argumentation (which tended to be more confrontational). Despite their differing conclusions, they agree that much is to be learned from the classical rhetoricians.

4. In recent writings of translation theory, linguistic experts such as Eugene A. Nida and William Reyburn give concerted emphasis to those features of language structure and style that they identify as being rhetorical (e.g., parallelism, hyperbole, irony, chiasm, rhetorical questions, personification) and thereby reawaken interest in linguistic forms and many of the question with which the classicists are concerned.[14]

5. In post–World War II years, a variety of communication

[9]Quoted by Cecil A. Blake, "Rhetoric and Intercultural Communication," in *Handbook of Intercultural Communication*, ed. Molefi Kete Asante, Eileen Newmark, and Cecil A. Blake (Beverly Hills: Sage Publications, 1979), 86.

[10]Jean Dietz Moss, ed., *Rhetoric and Praxis: The Contribution of Classical Rhetoric to Practical Reasoning* (Washington, D.C.: The Catholic University of America Press, 1986), Preface, vii.

[11]Ibid.

[12]Cf. George R. Bramer, "Right Rhetoric: Classical Roots for Contemporary Aims in Writing" in Moss, *Rhetoric and Praxis*, 135–56.

[13]Cf. Richard E. Young, Alton L. Becker, and Kenneth Pike, *Rhetoric: Discovery and Change* (New York: Harcourt, Brace and World, 1970).

[14]Cf. Eugene A. Nida and William D. Reyburn, *Meaning Across Cultures* (Maryknoll, N.Y.: Orbis, 1981).

scholars—including William S. Howell,[15] Robert T. Oliver,[16] and John C. Condon, Jr.[17]—have widened our horizons so as to take into account differences between cultures. As a result we no longer think of rhetoric in the singular as though the principles of Western rhetoric, whether ancient or modern, were always and everywhere applicable. Rather, we think in terms of "multiple rhetorics" and extend our understanding of communication by undertaking the study of "comparative rhetoric" and "ethno-rhetoric."

A perusal of the expanding bibliography of books on intercultural communication reveals that the subject has been approached from a variety of perspectives and disciplines. This is true of Christian works as well as others. The perspectives provided by each discipline—whether linguistics (as in the case of Eugene A. Nida), anthropology (Marvin K. Mayers, Charles H. Kraft), comparative religion (Hendrik Kraemer), or marketing (James F. Engel)—serve us well, provided they do not blind us to the insights of other disciplines or the truth of Scripture.

The basic approach taken in this book is informed by communication and rhetorical theory. As such it is eclectic, as was classical rhetoric, drawing from a wide variety of disciplines with the recognition that "gold from Egypt is still gold." After all, there is much knowledge that is not contained in the Bible. And even though that knowledge may not be essential for "life and godliness," it can be pressed into kingdom service. At the same time, we must recognize that essential knowledge is contained in Scripture. Whatever does not conform to Scripture needs to be identified and dispensed with. That too is a part of our task because such "knowledge" is not Egyptian "gold" at all. It is "fool's gold"!

---

[15]William S. Howell, "Theoretical Directions for Intercultural Communication" in Asante et al., *Handbook of Intercultural Communication*, 23–42.

[16]Robert T. Oliver, *Culture and Communication* (Springfield, Ill.: Charles C. Thomas, 1962).

[17]John C. Condon and Fathi Yousef, *An Introduction to Intercultural Communication* (Indianapolis: Bobbs Merrill Educational Publishing, 1975).

Chapter 4

Perspectives From the Science of Communication

Concerning our understanding of communication, Melvin DeFleur makes the following confession:

> The communication process is utterly fundamental to all our psychological and social processes. Without repetitively engaging in acts of communication with our fellows, none of us could develop the mental processes and social nature that distinguishes us from other forms of life. Without language systems and other important tools of communication, we could not carry on the thousands of organized group activities and lead our interdependent lives. Yet in spite of the awesome importance of the communication process to every human being, every group, and every society, we know less about it than we do about the life cycle of the bat or the chemical composition of the sediment on the ocean floor.[1]

Though DeFleur's statement borders on hyperbole, it has enough truth in it to humble us when we attempt an

---

[1] Melvin L. DeFleur, *Theories of Mass Communication*, 2nd ed. (New York: David McKay, 1970), 76.

explanation of so remarkable a phenomenon as communication. And it reminds us that communication as a science is still in its infancy.

A BASIC MODEL OF THE COMMUNICATION PROCESS

Aristotle viewed communication in relationship to three points of reference: the speaker, the speech, and the audience. These served well as a framework for one of the most influential works on communication ever conceived.[2] In more recent times a variety of more complex models have been introduced in an effort to understand the communication process better. For example, Kenneth Burke interprets communication experiences as *dramas*. The analytic tool of his "dramatistic" approach is the "pentad"—act, scene, agent, agency, and purpose.[3] Based largely on the work of Eric Berne,[4] a *game model* is sometimes used to analyze communication events, particularly those having to do with the give and take of political and economic negotiations. In this case, communication is usually described in terms of conflict, strategies, points, score, winning, losing, and so forth. But far and away the most widely used model is the *cybernetic model* growing out of telecommunication and computer technology. (The word *cybernetics* was coined by Norbert Wiener and has to do with the comparative study of the human nervous system and electronic information systems.) Building on Wiener's work,[5] Claude Shannon and Warren Weaver constructed a model of communication containing such elements as a sender, receiver, channel, code, encoder, decoder, noise, and feedback.[6]

[2] I refer, of course, to Aristotle's *Rhetoric*.
[3] Burke, *A Grammar of Motives and a Rhetoric of Motives* (Cleveland: World, Meridian Books, 1962), 547.
[4] Eric Berne, *Games People Play* (New York: Grove, 1964).
[5] Norbert Wiener, *The Human Use of Human Beings* (Boston: Houghton Mifflin, 1954).
[6] This discussion is based on the proposals of Claude E. Shannon and Warren Weaver, *The Mathematical Theory of Communication* (Urbana: University of Illinois Press, 1949).

Many variations of this model appear in the literature; so, although we propose to introduce some unique features as we proceed, our basic model of the communication process will be familiar to many of our readers (see figure 1).

Figure 1

COMMUNICATION

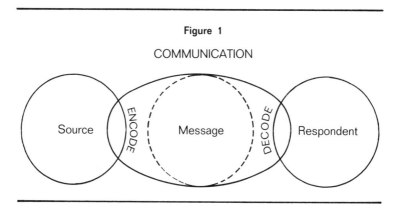

It will be immediately apparent that "source" corresponds to Aristotle's "speaker"; however, "source" is a more general term and for that reason better suits our needs. Similarly, "respondent" (or "receptor") has a somewhat enlarged meaning but corresponds to "audience." "Message," of course, corresponds to "speech."

Only two components in our initial model, then, are entirely new. *Encoding* involves the utilization of mind and body to put the message, which previously existed only in the form of ideas and impulses within the source, into some kind of a coded system such as the French language, Indian smoke signals, or the beat of the talking drums of Africa. By the same token, *decoding* reverses the process and turns the code back into a message.

It is important to note that "*the* message" never exists in the sense of having an independent existence. Much misunderstanding would be averted if we could but grasp the fact that in a primary sense messages are in human beings—in sources and receptors. Only in a secondary sense are they in

41

codes—that is, in words or pictures or acts. (I will discuss this problem in greater depth in chapter 5.)

As much as we might desire simplicity, we must address ourselves to various factors that, while complicating our initial model, also serve to make it more understandable and useful.

PRIMARY, SECONDARY, AND TERTIARY SOURCES

We must first take into account the fact that not all sources communicate messages that are their own in the sense that they originate them or are completely free to modify them. Aldous Huxley's short story "Green Tunnels" contains a message that he obviously wanted to communicate. When a high school teacher in a class in the interpretation of literature undertakes to explain Huxley's intended message, it must be understood that the message being discussed is not the teacher's message.

Similarly, the prophets and apostles repeatedly claim to be speaking for God in such a way that it is his word they are communicating. Theologians theorize as to how the personality, background, and communication skills of the particular prophet or apostle came into play in the inspiration of Scripture. In any case, the missionary who has a high (biblical) view of inspiration identifies the words of the prophets and apostles as *God's* Word and undertakes to communicate *God's* message to others. In this sense the missionary is a secondary source and is obligated to communicate that message as clearly and faithfully as possible. This means that he must study both the author's message and the original audience with great seriousness. He can adjust the form of the message, amplify, bring out certain truths, and, in general, introduce the message as he deems best; but, insofar as possible, he must adhere to the original content. For this reason the missionary cannot be held ultimately accountable for his success or lack of it (as people understand success) as long as he is faithful to the biblical message.

Of couse, when the missionary speaks of his own conversion or recounts the way in which God has forgiven, blessed, and otherwise directed him, he becomes a primary source. These experiences are uniquely his and therefore become a mighty testimony to the grace of God with which respondents in any culture can identify to a significant degree.

When Paul wrote these oft-quoted words: "The things which you have heard from me in the presence of many witnesses, these entrust to faithful men, who will be able to teach others also" (2 Tim. 2:2), he was referring to still another type of source, which we will call "tertiary." Speaking as an apostle, Paul was saying that his gospel did not consist merely of his insight, opinion, or wisdom. He had received it by revelation directly from the Lord (cf. Gal. 1:6–12). He had passed it on to Timothy. Now Timothy was to select and train faithful men who would communicate it to still others. Now, if God is thought of as the primary Source in this process, then Paul was the secondary source and Timothy and his adepts become tertiary sources. If, in line with what I have said above about the prophetic and apostolic calling, we think of Paul's gospel as being at one and the same time God's gospel *and* Paul's gospel, then Timothy becomes a secondary source and his adepts become tertiary sources.

Whether the source of the Christian message in a given situation will be thought of as primary, secondary, or tertiary will be a matter of definition and context. What is of fundamental importance in Christian communication is that we keep a clear distinction between divine revelation and human experience, intuition, insight, interpretation, and opinion—whether ours or someone else's. It is the message of divine revelation that must be passed on from person to person, from the people of one culture to the people of another culture, and from generation to generation.

RESPONDENTS AND THEIR RESPONSES

It is axiomatic that Christians who are concerned about fulfilling the Great Commission will have a fundamental concern for the integrity of the gospel message and for its acceptance. But, as I have indicated, communication is not primarily "station to station." It is "person to person" and "people to people." In the modern world we have become increasingly aware of individual and "people group" differences, and we have analyzed these differences in a variety of ways. Of course, the principle of audience adaptation as such is not new. The New Testament Gospels present ways of presenting the message of Christ to different audiences. Earlier, Aristotle had much to say about audiences, the importance of recognizing whether they were friendly or hostile, and the necessity of adjusting one's speech accordingly.

The contemporary cybernetic model we are employing here uses terms like *respondent* or *receptor*, encourages a variety of respondent analyses, and insists on respondent-oriented communication. Therefore we will be analyzing respondents, not only in classical or even biblical terms, but also in terms of recent anthropological, sociological, and psychological studies. As we do so, it will be well to keep in mind that effective communication by its very nature is, as Charles Kraft terms it, "receptor-oriented."[7] The more we can learn about our receptors (or respondents), the more successful we will be in informing and persuading them, provided, of course, that we use that information in "molding" the gospel message.

THE ENCODING AND DECODING PROCESSES

I said that encoding consists of putting the message into some kind of coded system for the benefit of a respondent and that decoding has to do with turning the code back into a message. Although we have been thinking in terms of written and spoken language codes, there are numerous other types of codes, as we will see. Before we do, it would be well to

[7]Charles H. Kraft, *Communication Theory for Christian Witness* (Nashville: Abingdon, 1983), 107.

consider some ideas that shed light on the encoding and decoding processes.

First, central to the processes of encoding and decoding is the concept of *symbol*. One of the unique abilities of human beings is the ability to assign meaning to elements of a code that otherwise have no meaning. It is to this feature of coded systems that the Spanish philosopher J. L. Aranguren calls attention when he identifies any medium of transmission as a *sign* that has no meaning in and of itself.[8] Usually, however, this feature is thought of as being unique to *symbols*, which are then contrasted with signs. Eugene Nida's understanding is helpful in this regard. He says that signs "indicate the existence of a particular thing, event, or condition within a context."[9] Symbols, however, can be understood "apart from the immediate context or stimuli."[10] Nida does not mean that contexts are not important in the interpretation of symbols but that the meaning of a symbol is not bound by its context. Rather, a symbol is "an instrument by which we label and manipulate our conceptions."[11] He goes on to explain that a *pure symbol* (e.g., the word *death*) does not partake of the properties of its referent. An *iconic symbol* (e.g., the cross as a symbol of Christ's death) does partake of the properties of its referent. Another way of distinguishing symbols is in terms of whether or not they are convertible from one symbol system into another. *Discursive symbols* are convertible into linguistic discourse (e.g., mathematical formulae can be put into language). *Presentational symbols*, such as the lines of Michelangelo's frescoes in the Sistine Chapel or the stirring chords of Hayden's oratorio *The Creation*, cannot be fully translated into language.

Distinctions such as these not only clarify our thinking, they also serve to point up the fact that, although lesser

---

[8]Jose L. Aranguren, *Human Communication*, trans. Francis Partridge (New York: McGraw-Hill, 1967), 23–26.

[9]Eugene A. Nida, *Message and Mission: The Communication of the Christian Faith* (New York: Harper & Row, 1960), 65.

[10]Ibid.

[11]Ibid., 66.

creatures can communicate, of all the creatures God placed on earth the only *symbolizing* creation is humankind.

Second, communication involves both a code and the encoding/decoding processes. People may encode messages without reference to a respondent. For example, a housewife may talk when no one else is present simply to relieve boredom or break the silence. A professor may articulate his thesis when no one is around just to clarify the issues in his own mind. But communication has not taken place because in neither case is a decoding respondent present.

Again, people may perceive some sort of meaning apart from any code as such. For example, a forest ranger scans the horizon to see if there is smoke. Smoke would be a *sign* of fire. But communication is not involved because neither an encoder nor a code is involved. Of course, several centuries ago an Indian standing on the same spot as the forest ranger might have decoded smoke on the horizon as meaning "The enemy is approaching from the West. Make preparation for war." In that case a code, an encoder, and a decoder were all involved. Communication occurred.

The word *communication* comes from the Latin word *communis* (common). *We must establish a "commonness" with someone to have communication. The "commonness" is to be found in mutually shared codes.*

Third, human communication is only partially effective even in the most ideal of circumstances. Why? Because the "commonness" between encoder and decoder is not complete. Differences in enculturation, personality, experiences, interest, short- and long-term memory, and much else always impinge upon the encoding and decoding processes. The result is that respondents seldom, if ever, decode exactly the same message as the one encoded by the source. Thus, though we speak of such things as "discovering the author's intent" and "replicating the impact of a message on the original audience"—and in common parlance often say "I understand" and "I see"—it is well to keep in mind that effective communication is not easily achieved and miscommunication is not easy to avoid.

VERBAL AND NONVERBAL CODES

In the process of communication, then, a source encodes messages by putting them into verbal *or* nonverbal codes that must be available to the respondent if true communication is to take place. *Verbal communication* means that the message has been put into one form or another of a *language* code. A language basically consists of a series of linguistic symbols and a system for their arrangement. *Linguistic symbols* are units of speech to which groups of people have assigned a commonality of meaning. The symbols themselves are essentially arbitrary. For example, "storm" could be "morst" and stand for the same phenomenon if enough communicators agreed on that meaning.

Verbal communication is usually thought of as existing in two forms, the spoken and the written; but it should be remembered that spoken language takes precedence. Written language is based on the spoken, not vice versa. Both spoken and written symbols are characterized by arbitrariness and adaptability. For example, not only could the English word "storm" be replaced by "morst" (as spelled as well as pronounced), but it can also be written in shorthand or Braille.

Some intriguing questions present themselves for consideration at this point. For example, what about the intonation and stress that are so important in encoding oral messages? These range from the highly codified nine tones of Cantonese to a very gutteral *nyet* of an irate Russian to the stress on "you" that can be put in the English sentence "I mean *you!*" The tonal system of Cantonese is an indispensable part of the language code. When a Cantonese choir sings unfamiliar songs, it is often necessary to *speak* the words before *singing* them; otherwise the meaning of the lyrics would be lost in the tones that constitute the melody. It is obvious that the tones in spoken Cantonese are a part of the language code just as the written ideographs convey information apart from the phonetic significance assigned to them. The gutteral quality of the Russian *nyet* and the English stress on "*you,*" above, are not as clearly a part of language as such, though they may be studied in the linguistic context. They are usually included in a special category called *paralanguage*[12]—a category that includes pitch, rate, rhythm, pacing, and voice tension as well as volume and inflection.

Nonverbal communication involves the encoding of a message by means of some code other than a linguistic one. Social scientists have identified some twenty to twenty-five of these, including *silent language* (gesture, "proper" behavior, and the use of space, time, and color to communicate); the so-called *universal language* of music and the plastic arts; artifacts, ritual, and drama; and *image projection* (such things as the reputation, attitude, knowledge, clothing, and the status of the source). We might say that we communicate nonverbally through our "being" (what we *are* and what we are *perceived to be*) and through our "behavior" (what we *do* with our bodies and temporal-spatial materials). (Semiotics [semeiotics] is the study of signs or, more specifically, of nonverbal codes.)

As compared to verbal communication, nonverbal communication assigns lesser importance to *denotative meaning*, (i.e., "pointing meaning") than it does to connotative meaning (i.e., suggestive significance). Nonverbal communication tends to be suggestive and intensional and plays a supportive role due to the nature of nonverbal codes. For example, codes of "correct behavior" as described by custom, and codes that govern "good music," "good dress," and "fine drama," may be very complex and relatively flexible. But the importance of these nonverbal codes would be difficult to overestimate.

COMMUNICATION CHANNELS AND MEDIA

Communicationists use various designations for the means whereby messages are conveyed from sources to respondents. The term *channel* is quite often used when interpersonal communication is in view and emphasis is

[12]The stress on "you" is usually conveyed in written English by italicizing, underlining, or capitalization as in the sign KEEP OUT! THIS MEANS YOU!

48

placed on auditory channels (for sounds), visual channels (for sight), olfactory channels (for odors), thermal channels (for temperature), and epidermal channels (for touch). In our electric age mass communication has assumed tremendous significance in communication theory and practice, and as a consequence much attention has been given to "media." The importance (and complexity) attached to the various media is revealed in Wilbur Shramm's classification system. He makes a distinction between four generations of instructional media, for example: first-generation media include charts, maps, graphs, written materials, models, demonstrations, and dramatizations; second-generation media include printed textbooks, workbooks, and tests; third-generation media include photographs, slides, film strips, silent motion pictures, recordings, sound motion pictures, radio and television; and fourth-generation media include programmed instruction, language laboratories, and electronic digital computers.[13]

Obviously, in this book we will be concerned with both "channels" and "media" in the senses in which these terms are used in the previous paragraph. For present purposes, however, I will largely confine the discussion to "media" and use the term much as Schramm and others use it to refer to the means whereby messages in both verbal and nonverbal codes are conveyed to respondents. In place of Schramm's somewhat complicated classification I will use a rather simple dichotomy. The designation *simple media* will refer to written autographs, original diagrams, basic models, dance, drama, speeches, sermons, and the like. *Syndetic media* will refer to books, film, radio, television, mass meetings, small group dialogue, and the like—in short, those media that use simple media in various combinations, that extend them in time and space in order to convey a message to a wider audience, and that require multiple communication skills in the encoding and decoding processes. The distinction is not hard and fast. It may come down to categorizing on the basis

[13]Wilbur Schramm, *Mass Media and National Development* (Stanford: Stanford University Press, 1964), 141–42.

of a particular use of the medium and the perspective of the analyst.

Generally speaking, Schramm's first-generation media are simple media and his second-, third-, and fourth-generation media are syndetic in this dichotomy. But the reader should note that I am extending the meaning of the word "media" beyond its usual limits in order to include face-to-face conversation, formal and informal speeches, and gesture behavior in the case of our simple-media category. This is done to facilitate comparative analysis. Usually simple and syndetic media will be easily differentiated. Sometimes, as I said, the distinction becomes blurred, and categorization becomes a matter of one's perspective and preference.

In any case, missionaries must divest themselves forever of the naïve notion that the gospel message as decoded by respondents is the same irrespective of how it is conveyed to the world—whether by book, magazine, radio, television, film, sound recording, tract, chalk artistry, or drama. Perhaps no fiction has had wider currency in Western missions than the idea that if you put a gospel message into any of these media at one end, it will come out the other end as the same gospel message.

FEEDBACK

Everyone who has had experience with microphones and amplifying systems will be familiar with the annoyance of feedback. What happens is quite simple. The sound of the speaker's voice (or whatever sound may be involved) enters the microphone and is transmitted into electrical impulses that in turn activate voice coils in the speaker and send intensified sound waves into the air. Depending upon many factors—including the positioning of the microphone and the speaker, the volume of the amplified sound, and the acoustical qualities of the building—the amplified sound may well return to the microphone and itself be amplified. In this way a circularity of "sound, amplified sound, reamplified sound" is set up, and this can become deafening.

Figure 2

THE PROCESS OF COMMUNICATION

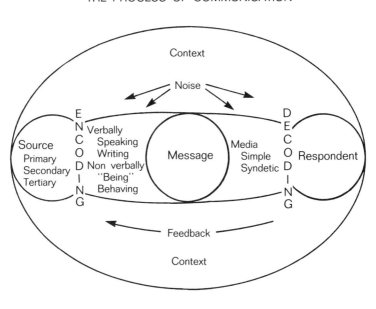

Something analogous to this occurs in the process of communication. My earliest recollection of communication by telephone is that it involved several requirements. First, there was a certain combination of rings before the call was "ours." Second, one had to be careful as to what was said on the telephone, for in a very short period of time everyone in the neighborhood would "hear the message." Third, one was never absolutely quiet while "talking on the telephone": it seemed necessary to assure the speaker at the other end of the wire that the contraption was still working and the listener was "getting the message." The listener always kept up an intermittent "I see," "Is that right?" "Yes," "Oh, no," or "Louder, please!" as appropriate.

Modern technology has all but eliminated the first two of these requirements. It has made the third requirement somewhat less critical as far as telephone conversations are concerned. But we may safely assume that technology will never completely satisfy the need for response, for true communication is always two-way. Whether we are engaged in interpersonal or mass communication, there is always the need to know that someone is listening, that the listener is thinking, and, indeed, *what* he or she is thinking. This response may be a simple "Hmm" in interpersonal communication or it may be the response to letter week or a high Nielsen Rating in the case of a radio broadcast. It may be positive or negative. But feedback is important to effective communication. Good communicators pay attention to it and make necessary compensations.

One of the problems with a good deal of contemporary sermonizing is that it is monological or one-way from preacher to congregation, with very little attention to audience analysis and response. Effective preachers learn to preach "dialogically" in the sense that they anticipate audience questions and reaction; are alert to feedback in the forms of attention, restlessness, and so forth; and adjust their sermonic communication accordingly. And some preachers are discovering the advantages of scheduling occasions when full dialogue can be employed—when members of the audience can raise questions, voice objections, provide illustrations, or whatever—concurrent with the sermon delivery.

NOISE

The communication process is not limited to factors that are intended or thought out. Street sounds, room temperature, idiosyncratic behavior on the part of certain individuals— these and innumerable other factors can affect communication adversely. They are often subsumed under the category of "noise" in communication theory, though noise in the usual sense may not be involved. Communication can be aided by reducing the influence of "noise" as much as possible.

COMMUNICATION AND CONTEXT

Finally, we must see the importance of context or setting to communication. Take some of the random bits of verbal communication that are common at a baseball game: "The pitcher was hit very hard"; "Two men died on base"; "Murder the umpire"; "We wuz robbed"; and "The scalpers had a field day today." People in their right mind would avoid like the plague a place where such messages were rife unless they understood their meanings in context!

Since meaning is so intimately related to context, the contexts of messages must be taken into account whether they be the sentences in a book that surround the phrase in question, the occasion at which a speech is delivered, or the place and time of a conversation.

Many significant facets of communication remain to be discussed. We have not explored the critical question of meaning. Up to this point I have said nothing about the significance of culture. I have not said much about respondents, though it is obvious that they are all-important to communication. In fact, "respondents in their respective cultures" might be said to be the subject of this book. We will turn our attention to these and related questions in later chapters. First, however, I will attempt to modify my simple five-point diagram in such a way as to make it more helpful. Omitting the category of culture for the time being, we can now construct a diagram of the essentials of the communication process as it is understood and explicated in this book (see figure 2).[14]

[14]Diagramming the process in this way raises some problems even as it clarifies. For example, since the use of language is a form of behavior, language could be discussed under that rubric. Nevertheless, we will discuss it separately because of its signal importance. Similarly, music and the plastic arts and rituals and drama could be discussed under the topic of behavioral patterns along with silent language and image projection. We will, however, discuss them within the context of the media because they will be more meaningful to most people in that context.

Chapter 5

The Problem of Meaning

Communication has been defined as the transfer of meaning through the use of symbols.[1] At first glance, that definition seems innocent and straightforward. But actually it introduces us to a whole series of questions related to the concept of meaning ranging from "Where is meaning to be found?" to "What is the meaning of 'meaning'?" As a matter of fact, the problem of meaning has been hotly debated from

[1] I take the definition from S. Eldridge, ed., *Fundamentals of Sociology* (New York: Thomas Y. Crowell, 1950), 363. I am aware of the objection against using the word *meaning* in the definition because there is a sense in which meaning is always individual. But the same objection can be raised in regard to definitions of communication such as that of Emery, Ault, and Agee: "Communication is the art of transmitting information, ideas and attitudes from one person to another," in E. Emery, P. H. Ault, and W. K. Agee, *Introduction to Mass Communications*, 3rd ed. (New York: Dodd, 1971), 3. "Meaning" is what we are after, and the objections to using the word do not seem to me to be too devastating. Many semanticists object to the idea of defining communication in terms of the communication of *meaning* as we will see in this chapter. But, as a matter of fact, they themselves have difficulty maintaining consistency at this point and often speak of the "meaning of words" and at times even unguardedly speak of the communication of meaning. Cf. note 2 below.

the time of the Greek philosophers to the present day. Various aspects of it will surface in connection with topics to be discussed later (e.g., cultural context, worldview, and language). Here I will provide a brief overview of some of the more important of these discussions, particularly as they relate to contemporary communication theory.

A THUMBNAIL SKETCH OF SOME DISCUSSIONS ON MEANING

Some of the more significant discussions on the subject of meaning down through history are as follows:

1. Reality as viewed by Plato and Aristotle. Being an idealist, Plato insisted that this world of sensory objects is no more than a dim reflection of the "really real," which exists in a "realm of forms." Only to the extent that human discourse reflects the state of affairs that characterizes the realm of forms does it have real meaning. Aristotle accepted the world of particulars as a real world and based his approach on experience in the sensory world. Conversations concerning things in the unseen world have meaning, not because the participants are somehow able to "glimpse" a "form world," but because things in the invisible world are analogous to things in the visible world. The word *angel* has meaning because angels are in some important respects similar to observed beings that are lower on the "chain of being."

2. Aquinas and William of Occam on universals and absolutes. In the fourteenth century and about the time that Aquinas was developing his proofs for the existence of God, William of Occam insisted that the existence of God could never be proved and, indeed, that all "universals" and "absolutes" are simply mental conveniences. His basic principle was *"Praeter necessitatem non sunt multiplicanda"* (Entities should not be multiplied more than necessary). By application of this principle (known as "Occam's

razor") he proposed to dispense with terms having to do with the nonsensory world and intangible universals. For his part, Aquinas insisted that God does exist, that universals and absolutes are indispensable, and that sound logic leads to these conclusions.

3. The development of the "scientific method." Early proponents of what has come to be known as the scientific method such as Galileo, Bacon, and Newton believed that the regularity of natural laws was assured by virtue of the fact that they were established by the Creator. They believed in the existence of both God and absolutes. However, as time went on, natural law came to have an independent existence and, to use Francis Schaeffer's phrase, supernature was "eaten up." The supernatural lost its meaning. Any proposition that could not be tested empirically was viewed suspiciously. (Among philosophers the logical positivists have been most rigorous in supporting this view, but their fortunes have demonstrated that most people become uneasy when the scientific method is applied too broadly.)

4. Enter the general semanticists and the new rhetoricians. Of course, there are numerous and sharp differences among modern students of communication, language, and meaning. But there is enough agreement on certain basic ideas to constitute a challenge to our thinking and, in some respects, to the communication of a biblical gospel. Whether one reads the likes of Alfred Korzybski, C. K. Ogden, I. A. Richards, Percy W. Bridgeman, or David Berlo, one comes away with an ambivalent impression that the possibility of meaningful missionary communication has been both enhanced and impeded by what they have written. On the one hand, they lead us to a greater appreciation of the fact that meaning is elusive and must be husbanded with great care. On the other hand, their conclusions evidence a profound skepticism as to the existence of absolutes and ultimate meaning. One of the

popularizers of their basic approach, Don Fabun, caps off his discussion of the "problem of 'isness' " with the boldfaced dictum: "Stamp out Isness!"[2] To say the least, that dictum does not sound very "missionary"!

Admittedly sketchy, the above may nevertheless serve as a kind of historical and philosophical framework for the discussion of certain fundamental questions as they relate to the problem of meaning.

WHAT HAPPENS WHEN SYMBOLS "MEAN"?

There have been significant shifts in what we might label the psychological approach to meaning. The *mentalistic view*, which concludes that a word "means" because it elicits an image of its referent in the human mind, was elaborated by Plato and, in modern times, by Titchener among others. This approach has largely been abandoned because of the inability to get at those images in order to compare and analyze them. Pavlov and contemporary exponents of *conditioning views* such as B. F. Skinner contend that meaning is really no more than a response to stimuli and is learned by a pattern of reinforcement. For these theorists, what the organism *does* under certain conditions is quite adequate for a determination of "meaning" from a scientific point of view—in fact, that is all that is adequate. Still others, seeing that the stimulus-response approach is too restricted to account for abstractions such as "reality," "nature," "essence," etc., but still attracted to the stimulus-response interpretation, opt for one or another of the so-called *dispositional views*. For Roger Brown, Charles Stevenson, and Charles Morris, the meaning of a word is in its "response potential." In this view, meaning is thought of as the dispositional property of a "sign" where the stimulus would be the hearing of the sign and the response would consist of psychological processes in a hearer. "Meaning"

[2]Don Fabun, *Communications: The Transfer of Meanings* (New York: Holt, Rinehart and Winston, 1960).

becomes discoverable by creating various contingencies and observing the responses.

It will be apparent in this development that the desire to manage, manipulate, and explain has resulted in limitations (which often are severe) being placed on the meaning of "meaning." I rather believe with Susanne Langer that "all thinking begins with seeing" ("seeing" not only through our eyes but with other senses as well) and that increasingly our perceptions are overlaid with more and more abstractions. Thus the response to linguistic stimuli is ideational as well as practical. Meaning is real even when it is in the mind. Meaning is not rendered nonexistent or inconsequential simply because it is not measurable or discoverable by the tools of science.

Nevertheless, from a missionary point of view, the emphasis of psychologists on something happening in the behavioral pattern of the respondent as well as in his mind is an extremely important one. Missionary communication does aim at response. When the desired response is well thought out and specific, communication will likely be more effective. And when the response can be successfully measured, the communicator is able to adjust his content and goals appropriately.

WHERE IS MEANING TO BE FOUND?

Charles Kraft has placed the answers to this question in three major categories.[3] First, there are those who believe that meaning is to be found in the external world. Meaning is "out there" and waits to be grasped and understood by people. Those who hold to this theory have a great deal of confidence in our ability to understand and report things as they really are. If we are careful observers, we will tend toward the same conclusions about the world. If we reach different conclusions, it is because we are faulty observers or have misinterpreted the way the world really is.

[3]Kraft, *Communication Theory*, 110–15.

Second, there are those who hold that meaning exists in the signs or symbols with which we communicate to one another. Kraft calls this the "boxcar theory of meaning," which

> sees words, gestures, and other symbols invested with meanings in a manner similar to that in which a container is loaded with goods. A skilled interpreter can study the words and/or other symbols from which a message is constructed to discover what the meaning is. The primary task of literary (including biblical) analysis, is, therefore, the impersonal process of studying the history of the words and phrases of which a given text is composed.[4]

Third, there are those who insist that the existence of meaning is related to persons. It contends that meanings do not lie in the external world nor in symbols we use to describe the world, but that they are "attached or even created" in the minds of persons who receive messages. Since this theory is far and away the most widely held understanding among communicologists today, it is well that we elaborate the view of Alfred Korzybski (a pioneer and one of the most influential of the general semanticists).

Writing concerning Korzybski's views, Stuart Chase says,

> Our remote ancestors, when language was in its infancy, gave words to sensations, feelings, emotions. Like small children, they identified those feelings with the outside world, and personified outside events. They made sensations and judgments—"heat," "cold," "bad," "good,"— substantives in the language structure. Though not objects, *they were treated like objects*. The world picture was made anthropomorphic. Sun, moon, trees, were given feelings like men, and a soul was assigned to each. In the old mythologies, gods or demons in human shape made everything with their hands. (The world was created in six days.) These remarkable concepts became rooted in the structure

[4]Ibid., 110.

of language and the structure, if not the myth, remains to plague us today.[5]

In this way we are introduced to Korzybski's understanding of the problems that accrue to our supposed linguistic past and to the study of language and meaning today.[6] Korzybski believes, for example, that since in the structure of almost all languages we are presented with the equating verb "is," we tend to identify the word with the thing. In much the same way, our widespread usage of abstract nouns occasions the mistaken idea that they actually refer to something in space and time. Again, our languages (particularly Indo-European languages) promote the one- or two-valued judgments of Aristotelian logic instead of the multivalued judgments that are in accord with the actual world.

Of course, Korzybski proposes certain solutions for these problems. Consider several of them by way of example.

First, though it is nearly impossible to eliminate the verb *is*, it must be handled with great care, much as we would handle a stick of dynamite. We must always remember that the word is *not* the thing!

Second, the tendency to use generalizations and abstractions can be countered by various means such as finding the referent to which a word refers before ascribing attributes, appending dates to statements to show that new understandings may yet emerge, and using mathematical symbols or "index numbering." He insists that we are less likely to make such misleading statements as "The rich care little for the poor" and "Count on a mother-in-law to mess up a marriage" if we are forced to add numbers to each major term: $rich_1$, $rich_2$, $rich_3$, $rich_4$ . . . ; $mother-in-law_1$, $mother-in-law_2$, $mother-in-law_3$, $mother-in-law_4$. . . . While the terms of classification indicate similarities, the index numbers indicate differences. In other words, not all rich people are alike nor are

---

[5]Stuart Chase, *The Tyranny of Words* (New York: Harcourt and Brace, 1938), 75.

[6]Alfred Korzybski, *Science and Sanity* (Lancaster, Pa.: Science Press, 1932).

all mothers-in-law. Statements that overlook these differences affect both thinking and communication adversely.

Third, Korzybski takes issue with what he calls the "two-valued orientation" that results from Aristotelian logic. Basic to Aristotle's logic were certain laws:
1. The law of identity: A is A.
2. The law of the excluded middle: Everything is either A or non-A.
3. The law of noncontradiction: Nothing is both A and non-A.

When these are "internalized," we tend to think in black and white terms: "I am right and you are wrong"; "The only really trustworthy citizens are Protestants"; and so forth. (Actually, of course, if Aristotelian logic is carried this far, it does result in misunderstanding.) Korzybski and his followers call attention to the fact that other available forms of logic are multivalued (or even infinite-valued), such as symbolic logic and the law of probability. They therefore think of general semantics as non-Aristotelian.[7]

However, I have a problem with Korzybski and those numerous semanticists, rhetoricians, and communicologists who take the same position that he holds. They do make a significant contribution to our understanding of meaning; it is all too easy to assume that the word is the thing, that language and reality are but two sides of the same coin, and that once we have identified a category we have correctly characterized every particular in it. But they are susceptible to the same criticism they level at Aristotle. An "internalization" of "multivalued logics" results in the disintegration of absolutes. Black and white disappear. Everything seems gray. No one is right, and no one is wrong. A person's statements simply represent *that person's* judgment and *his way* of putting his judgment into linguistic symbols. It is no wonder, really, that Korzybski has little interest in the *content* of people's beliefs,

[7]S. I. Hayakawa, *Language in Thought and Action,* 2nd ed. (New York: Harcourt, Brace, and World, 1941), 241–42.

but much interest in the *way* in which they hold them.[8] Korzybski has *internalized* the logic of his system of semantics. (Or, possibly, the logic of his semantics is an externalization of his multivalue system.) The person on the street may know nothing of general semantics. And the student of missionary communication may not be able to identify a single general semanticist. But all will be familiar enough with the popular notion that *what* a person believes is not really important as long as he is sincere. From a Christian point of view, nothing could be more antimissionary!

Let us return, then, to the question with which this particular discussion began, namely, Where *is* meaning to be found? Kraft himself is fully convinced that meaning is not to be found in the world (the interpretation of external phenomena, like beauty, is in the eye of the beholder). It is not to be found in words or symbols (there is divergence in the way various people interpret symbols). Meaning is to be found in persons, in sources and receptors (particularly the latter because that is in keeping with Kraft's "receptor-oriented" approach to communication). Kraft quotes David Berlo approvingly:

> *Meanings are in people,* [They are] covert responses, contained within the human organism. Meanings . . . are personal, our own property. We learn meanings, we add to them, we distort them, forget them, change them. We cannot *find* them. They are in *us*, not in messages. . . .
>
> *Communication does not consist of the transmission of meaning.* Meanings are not transmittable, not transferable. Only messages are transmittable, and meanings are not in the message, they are in the message-users.[9]

We can agree that there are significant insights in this view of meaning and communication. Careful attention to

---

[8]David K. Berlo, *The Process of Communication: An Introduction to Theory and Practice* (New York: Holt, Rinehart and Winston, 1960), 7–10.
[9]Cf. Kraft, *Communication Theory,* 112–13; the quotation is from Berlo, *Process of Communication,* 175.

them will cause us to be much more careful communicators—both when interpreting someone else's message and when authoring our own. But there may be poison in this semantic pot. The cure may be as bad as the disease!

In his book *The Abolition of Man*,[10] C. S. Lewis takes as his starting point a textbook for English school children (he calls it the "Green Book") in which he insists that there is no "right" response to a waterfall. One beholder responds to it by calling it beautiful. Another responds with disgust. Both are describing their own particular feelings. There is nothing in the waterfall itself that allows us to commend one response and condemn the other. Lewis takes off from this and demonstrates that, far from elevating man, an approach that completely relativizes beauty and truth and goodness results in abolishing man!

Where is meaning to be found? What do the Scriptures say? Under divine inspiration, King David looked at the created world and wrote in Psalm 19:1–4:

The heavens are telling of the glory of God;
And their expanse is declaring the work of His hands,
Day to day pours forth speech,
And night to night reveals knowledge.
There is no speech, nor are there words;
Their voice is not heard.
Their line [sound] has gone out through all the earth,
And their utterances to the end of the world.

The apostle Paul built on this idea in Romans 1, and in verses 18–20 he concluded that the idolatrous Gentile world is guilty of disregarding the clear implications of the universe around them:

For the wrath of God is revealed from heaven against all ungodliness and unrighteousness of men, who suppress the truth in unrighteousness, because that which is known

[10]C. S. Lewis, *The Abolition of Man* (New York: Collier, 1962).

about God is evident within them; for God made it evident to them. For since the creation of the world His invisible attributes, His eternal power and divine nature, have been clearly seen, being understood through what has been made, so that they are without excuse.

Turning from the created world to the inspired Word, our Lord said,

Do not think that I came to abolish the Law or the Prophets; I did not come to abolish, but to fulfill. For truly I say to you, until heaven and earth pass away, not the smallest letter or stroke shall pass away from the Law, until all is accomplished (Matt. 5:17–18).

Is meaning to be found in the world? So much so that people are under judgment for misinterpreting or disregarding it! Is meaning to be found in the words of Scripture? So much so that the significance of every letter and marking will be taken into consideration in the fulfillment of them! We can quibble about whether we should speak of the *meaning* of the world and Word or the *message* of the world and Word if we want to. But clearly, the emphasis of Scripture is on the clear and consistent *content* of general revelation in creation and of special revelation in the Bible, not on the prerogative of humanity to interpret it as we think best.

At this point, I offer two proposals that may help us both in the resolution of this problem and in the aiding of the communication process. First, we should distinguish between two kinds of meaning: *inherent* meaning and *imparted* meaning. The world does not have inherent meaning apart from the God who created order out of chaos and who created man with the capacity to decode the significance of the created order. This is meaning that is imparted by the Divine Person. Word symbols do not have inherent meaning (except, perhaps, in the case of an onomatopoeic word like "hiss") apart from persons who impart meaning to them. Words are like paper currency. A ten-dollar bill does not have inherent or intrinsic value, but it does have an imparted or imputed value. Otherwise people would not rob banks! Similarly, words have imparted meaning. I have defined communication in terms of the "transfer of meaning." I see no problem with this. Even general semanticists unguardedly often use phrases like "This word means...." and "The meaning of what I have written is...." But we do need to keep in mind the fact that with a few possible exceptions we are talking about imparted meaning, not inherent meaning!

Second, we should remember that in a profound sense meaning is contractual. Only by agreement on the relationships that exist between linguistic symbols and things can we say anything significant *about* the "thing." And only as we agree on *standards* of right and wrong, truth and error, and good and bad can we make value judgments about any "thing." The fact that agreement in the areas of semantics, grammar, and axiology will always exhibit a certain tentativeness does not rule out a search for standards. Short of agreement on standards, we must determine the degree to which agreement on meaning is attainable on the basis of who is speaking to whom, and where and why, and communicate accordingly. The phrase "God is love," therefore, will be meaningless, less meaningful, more meaningful, or most meaningful, depending on the context and the orientation of the sources and respondents.

THE MEANING OF RELIGIOUS SYMBOLS

As I have intimated above, the meaning of religious symbols presents special problems. There was a time when for all theologians (and most philosophers) religious symbols lent themselves to the most meaningful statements of all. God was God, angels were angels, and heaven was heaven. Even Aristotle with his scientific bent retained these concepts in his epistemology because in his system meaning could be assigned to such words analogically by comparison with things in the sensory world.

The Catholic theologian and philosopher Thomas Aquinas followed Aristotle in much of his thinking. Thomistic philosophy made a careful dichotomy between what we might call "supernature" and "nature" but did not make a complete break between them. Aquinas was convinced that not only the study of Scripture but also the rational pursuit of natural theology would invest the terms *God, angel, heaven,* and so forth, with valid meanings. The reasoning behind his conclusions merits a closer look.

Thomas Aquinas recognized that we do not "name things as they are in themselves but as they are to our minds."[11] He also recognized that the meaning of words or names like *God* may not be easily arrived at. For example, when the pagan says, "The idol is God," and the Christian says, "The idol is not God," it is not immediately apparent that meaningful communication is taking place. On the one hand, it may seem that the word is being used univocally because in using the word *God* the Christian means "something almighty, to be revered above all things" and the pagan means the same thing when he says that his idol is God. On the other hand, it seems that the word "God" is being used equivocally here for two reasons. First, the word is being used of the real God and also of what is thought to be God. Second, since a person cannot mean what he does not understand, the pagan cannot mean the real God of whom the Christian speaks.

Aquinas resolves the difficulty (with help from Aristotle) by concluding that the word "God" in these cases is used neither *univocally* (i.e., with exactly the same meaning in each case) nor *equivocally* (i.e., with entirely different meanings), but *analogically.* A word is used analogically when "its meaning in one sense is to be explained by reference to its meaning in another sense."[12] For example,

> to understand why we call accidents "beings" we have to understand why we call substances beings; and we need to know what it means for a man to be healthy before we can

[11]Thomas Aquinas, *Summa Theologica* IA.13,9.
[12]Ibid., 10.

understand a "healthy" complexion, or a "healthy" diet, for such a complexion is indicative and such a diet is productive of the health that belongs to a man. It is the same with the case we are considering. For we have to refer to the use of "God" to mean the true God in order to explain its use in application to things that share in divinity or which are supposed to be gods. When we say that something is a "god" by sharing in divinity we mean that it shares in the nature of the true God. Similarly when we say that an idol is a god, we take this word to mean something that men suppose to be the true God. Thus it is clear that while "God" is used with different meanings one of these meanings is involved in all the others; the word is therefore used analogically.[13]

Theological language, then, has its ambiguities as does any other kind of language. But it is also capable of objective meaning as are other kinds of language. God exists and reveals himself by creative and redemptive acts and in his prophetic Word. However, as Francis A. Schaeffer has pointed out, after the time of Aquinas and particularly throughout the Renaissance, nature became increasingly dominant until "supernature" (grace, or Schaeffer's "upper story") was "eaten up."[14] The Reformation exposed the error in that way of thinking and pointed the way to a rediscovery of correct meaning at both levels. Meaning was recovered for both supernature and nature by insisting on the *biblical* teaching concerning God and man, and the relationship between God and man and God and the world. In the scientific age that followed, however, propositions that could not be tested empirically were once again subject to suspicion. Knowledge came to be identified more and more with sensory experience.

Because of its scientific orientation, logical positivism became most thoroughgoing in its critique of religious (and, indeed, all metaphysical) language. But the relegation of religious language to an area of limited (or no) significance did

13Ibid.
14Francis Shaeffer, *Escape From Reason* (London: Inter-Varsity, 1968), 13.

not stop with Rudolph Carnap, Percy W. Bridgeman, and the earlier Herbert Feigel. Charles Morris, S. I. Hayakawa, I. A. Richards, and numerous others agree that the meaning of "God is love" and all similar statements is at the very best untestable and therefore hardly worth fighting for. Hayakawa compares such statements with college cheers such as "Rah, rah for our team" and/or a ritual greeting such as "good morning," and Richards categorizes religious statements with poetry. One does not ask the football rooter who shouts "rah, rah" whether or not that is true! Nor does one inquire as to the factualness of a poem!

Taking their cues from Kierkegaard, existentialists have been rather successful in helping to put logical positivism to flight, but they have not rescued *objective* meaning for religious statements or significantly reduced the number of detractors of religious language in other camps. "Christian existentialists," for example, have not been able to disquiet exponents of general semantics and linguistic analysis who assign merely subjective and emotive meaning to religious statements, because they themselves have departed from Reformation and biblical teaching and are left with subjectivity. In their view, the Bible as a mixture of historical truth and falsehood may in any given passage be nonsense historically and meaningful religiously. A passage may be objectively false and subjectively true. Whereas Aquinas may have put too much confidence in reason, neoorthodox theologians forsake reason and verification and urge us to take a leap of faith. From that point it is but a short distance to Paul Tillich's undefined "God behind God." And from there it is but a step to saying that "God (in the traditional, biblical meaning of the term) is dead." When the meaning of "God" is totally subjective, it becomes impossible not only to assert *what* "God" means but *that* "God" means. Both the unbeliever *and* the orthodox Christian may be excused for being unimpressed with this approach.

Orthodox and evangelical Christians hold to a unified universe and epistemology. The world is God's creation and therefore reflects his Person and nature. Human beings are created by God and therefore are capable of knowing God, but they are also fallen creatures and therefore incapable of *fully knowing* God apart from the operation of God's grace in revelation and regeneration. Biblical revelation is personal (i.e., God reveals *himself*), and it is also propositional (i.e., God reveals truth *about* himself and his world). The meaning of biblical revelation must be apprehended objectively by reason and subjectively by faith. In other words, one must *assent* to truth and *commit* himself to truth.[15]

We live in a world in which unity has been broken by sin. But God is still God and it is he who has willed and acted in grace so that the break is neither complete nor final. *Without God*, the meanings that man assigns to God, to nature, and even to himself become less and less significant; existence becomes meaningless because man who thinks and wills is isolated and unaided. *With God*, the world and man, and God himself, take on meaning because man, related to and aided by God, can think God's thoughts after him.

We conclude that naturalism, humanism, existentialism, and any other philosophy that discounts the supernatural order or assigns meaning to it solely on the basis of human reason or will must be incomplete and misleading, no matter how rigorous that viewpoint may be. Consistency without comprehensiveness must of necessity lead to blind alleys. Comprehensiveness without God is impossible and must lead to inconsistency. The dilemma of the naturalist has been expressed well by Susanne Langer:

> That man is an animal I certainly believe; and also, that he has no supernatural essence, "soul" or "entelechy" or "mind-stuff" enclosed in his skin. He is an organism, his substance is chemical, and what he does, suffers, or knows, is just what this sort of chemical structure may do, suffer or know. When the structure goes to pieces it never does, suffers, or knows anything again. . . . It is really no harder

[15]For a more complete discussion see Kenneth S. Kantzer, "The Authority of the Bible," in *The Word for This Century*, ed. Merrill C. Tenney (New York: Oxford University Press, 1960), 34–39.

to imagine that a chemically active body wills, knows, thinks and feels, than that an invisible, intangible something does so. . . .

Now this is a mere declaration of faith, preliminary to a confession of heresy. The heresy is this: that I believe there is a primary need in man, which other creatures probably do not have, and which actuates all his apparently unzoological aims, his wistful fancies, his consciousness of value, his utterly impractical enthusiasms, and his awareness of a "Beyond" filled with holiness. . . .

The basic need, which certainly is obvious only in man, is the *need of symbolization*. This symbol-making function is one of man's primary activities, like eating, looking, or moving about. It is the fundamental process of his mind, and goes on all the time.[16]

I do not believe for a moment that Swedish is the language of heaven or that any historic symbol system is God-given or fixed either for time or eternity. But I do believe that *God* made man a "symbolizing" creature, that he chose to reveal his Word by the use of certain symbol systems, and that he speaks today through that Word as it is communicated by his servants and as his Holy Spirit works in the hearts and minds of the hearers. In other words, I believe that God not only gives meaning to existence but also gives meaning to meaning. The starting point for a full understanding of meaning is the Creator God who reveals himself. Just as history can be studied and a great deal of it mastered without attention to the Lord of history, so communication can be studied and much of its theory mastered without attention to the Lord of communication. But without him, both history and communication will be infinitely poorer!

HOW CAN WE DETERMINE WHAT VERBAL SYMBOLS MEAN?

Our discussion has made it obvious that if we want to know what a verbal symbol means, much more is involved

---

[16]Susanne K. Langer, *Philosophy in a New Key* (New York: New American Library of World Literature, Mentor, 1948), 44–45.

than simply going to a dictionary. In one way or another, *everything* I have said up to this point relates to the determination of meaning, and all that I say in the remainder of this book (and much that I cannot say) relates to the determination of meaning. To say in a few words how meaning can be determined is a hazardous undertaking. But it is clear that meaning must be explored at various levels.

First, the *process of communication* must be understood. Meaning must be encoded, transmitted, and decoded. The language I have used to describe the process may seem altogether too esoteric to some when used in the context of communication. "Feedback," "noise," "encode," and "decode," and even the terms "source" and "respondent," are not immediately recognizable to the uninitiated. But these terms will become very significant as the student comes to realize what happens to verbal symbols during this complicated process and how these various factors impinge on their meaning.

Second, the *nature of verbal symbols* must be considered. As we have seen, at this level we must concern ourselves with the human being as a symbol-using creature, the inherent potential and limitations of verbal symbols, the kind of world to which symbols relate, and the way in which they relate to that world. Our understanding in these areas is important if we are to avoid the fallacy of thinking that a word has only one correct meaning or the erroneous notion that the symbol and its referent are somehow identical.

Third, the *various types of meaning assigned to verbal symbols* need exploration. People make symbols and assign different kinds of meaning to them. As I have indicated, the most common distinction is that which is made between the denotative meaning (also termed extensional meaning and referent function) and connotative meaning (intensional meaning or conceptual function) of verbal symbols. Some confine the former term to labels for objects, events, and states of being in the physical world; others would not be so restrictive. The latter term is used to refer to verbal symbols that label or occasion mental concepts. It is important to know which of these kinds of meaning the source has in mind. For example, in line with what I have already said about S. I. Hayakawa, he insists that the word *angels* has only connotative meaning.[17] In saying that, he does not propose to settle the argument as to whether angels actually exist or not, but rather to serve notice that since we cannot actually point one out there is really no use in arguing about the matter. When one cannot pinpoint even one angel, why argue how many angels can occupy a pinhead? I would insist that the word *angels* has denotative as well as connotative meaning even though the proof for their objective existence is not the "pointing" type of proof. Moreover, when God promises his people that he gives his angels charge over them to keep them in all their ways, the existence of angels is worth arguing about.

Dictionary definitions are nothing more or less than the commonly accepted meanings of verbal symbols as determined from their usage (especially as used by learned and literary people). Hayakawa thinks of dictionary meanings as connotational because they refer to what is "suggested" or "connoted" inside one's head.[18] Robert Hall considers dictionary meanings to be denotational because they refer to those features of a situation that can be described objectively (denoted) and omit the more personal individual overtones of meaning.[19] In either case dictionaries are dated and localized; that is, their meanings will not hold for all times and places. But they do reflect implied agreement as to how words will be used, and without that agreement communication becomes difficult if not impossible.

When one of several possible meanings is assigned to a verbal symbol in order to avoid ambiguity, or when a unique meaning is given to a symbol, we often term it a *stipulated*

[17]S. I. Hayakawa, *Language in Action* (New York: Harcourt, Brace, and World, 1946), 47–48.
[18]Ibid., 46–47.
[19]Robert A. Hall, *Leave Your Language Alone* (Ithaca, N.Y.: Linguistica, 1950), 41–42.

meaning or definition. A stipulated definition is an *invitation* to accept the source's meaning for a word. Dictionary meanings and stipulated meanings leave little room for argument because of their nature.

Fourth, the *meanings that accrue to grammatical construction* must be studied. It is obvious that just as the users of a language must agree on the meanings they will assign to verbal symbols themselves, so they must agree on the meanings that will be assigned to the arrangement in which those symbols are placed. The English sentence "God is love" is composed of three symbols that mean something more than what they would mean separately and something different from what they would mean in any other order. To communicate similar meaning in Greek requires four symbols *(Ho Theos agapē estin)*, as it does in Japanese *(Kami wa ai nari)* . In Greek and Japanese the verbs come last. The meaning that is necessitated solely by word order in English ("Love is God" would be entirely different) is reinforced in both Greek and Japanese by the symbols *ho* and *wa* respectively, but in the case of Greek the subject indicator comes before the subject and in Japanese it comes after the subject. In Japanese the meaning is influenced according to the verb form one chooses out of several grammatically correct options.

Fifth, we must remember that *style affects meaning.* Closely related to the grammatical construction is the stylistic use of symbols. Although style may be difficult to define, its presence and influence is not difficult to detect. As messages change from simple to complex, every language presents an increasing number of options as to how one will encode his message. Every user of verbal symbols, therefore, becomes something of an artist as he selects his symbols and grammatical constructions in such a way as to achieve appropriateness, clarity, and relevancy. The koine Greek language of the New Testament was spoken by the person on the street. When Japanese scholars set about their task of translating the Bible into vernacular Japanese during the 1950s, however, they ran into a number of problems. For many Japanese, the highly literary style of the classical translation seemed far more appropriate for the message of the sacred Scriptures. Moreover, one vernacular form of the copula (the *de aroo* form) in particular introduced an element of tentativeness into many factual statements of Scripture.

Sixth, the *affective use of verbal symbols* should be considered. Symbols possess an almost unlimited potential for influencing others quite apart from the actual information that they convey. People being people, there is a point past which it is all but impossible to move them by simply adding new items of information. Something more is needed. Thus the revolutionist will use certain verbal slogans to whip people into action. The child will intone the word "please" in such a way that his parents find it extremely difficult to refuse his request. Within the connotative area of meaning, certain symbols carry an emotional charge that professional speakers use to great advantage. Examples are "God," "country," "flag," "mother," "home," and "apple pie." With social change, however, there is a corresponding change in audience response to such words. Semantic differential tests are sometimes used to measure reactions to words of this type. Respondents are asked to record their reactions and evaluations (weak-strong, positive-negative, etc.) upon hearing the symbols.

Some verbal symbols have an impact on audiences, not because of their familiar associations, but because of their newness or unpredictability. The word *homoousian* as it was used at the Council of Nicea to describe the Son as being "of the same substance" with the Father may have been such a word. When Christian youth in the late 1960s called Christianity "revolutionary" and referred to conversion as the "ultimate trip" or a "mind-blowing" experience, they were using symbols to achieve impact.[20] Of course, those who use new symbols (or old symbols in new ways) run the risk of

---

[20]"Impact" in the sense in which it is being used here is sometimes called information, but this is a special use of the word *information* that is not widely known. Perhaps another word should have been chosen to avoid ambiguity.

misunderstanding unless they compensate by explaining what they mean in more conventional terms. Too many unique symbols or unique meanings for one symbol may well "overload the circuit" and actually impede communication. On the other hand, too high a degree of predictability results in the loss of impact. The sermon that is simply a series of generalizations capped off with a familiar illustration will not only be soon forgotten, it will probably not be "heard" in the first place. The preacher who simply tells the congregation what they expect to hear will end up communicating little or nothing. This constitutes a special challenge to the missionary because in learning a second language the missionary may be content to learn one way (out of many) of expressing a certain idea. Thereafter the idea becomes a "prisoner" of this one expression. This process is repeated over and over until respondents learn to expect the same patterns of speech in prayer, sermon, and conversation. When that happens, even the results become predictable!

Notice that when God gave the Ten Commandments he injected particulars at certain points: "You shall not covet your neighbor's house; you shall not covet your neighbor's wife or his male servant or his female servant or his ox or his donkey or anything that belongs to your neighbor" (Exod. 20:17). Notice that when our Lord gave the Beatitudes he said that the poor own a kingdom, the meek inherit the earth, the pure in heart see God, and the persecuted can rejoice (Matt. 5:1–12). I am tempted to add still another beatitude: "Blessed is the preacher who does not make the gospel so humdrum that it sounds as if it is neither good nor news!" Remember that high predictability results in low impact and low predictability results in high impact. Kraft is correct when he observes that *"a message has greatest impact if (1) it is not a stereotyped message and (2) if it is presented in very specific life-related fashion"* (italics his).[21]

[21]Charles H. Kraft, *Christianity in Culture: A Study in Dynamic Biblical Theologizing in Cross-Cultural Perspective* (Maryknoll, N.Y.: Orbis, 1979), 153.

Seventh, *meaning as a function of context* merits consideration. *Context* is an elastic word. It can refer to the immediate surroundings in which a given message is encoded. It can also refer to a historical era or cultural area. In effect, Kenneth Burke thinks of context as including every event and all ideas that relate to the specific instance of communication in question, irrespective of where or when those events or ideas might have occurred. Something bordering on omniscience is necessary to satisfy Burke's perspective, but his insights are nevertheless most helpful. It is just as well that the word *context* be left flexible, though I have used it previously to refer to the more immediate surroundings of a communication. From that rather limited circumference, "context" can be stretched by the use of other adjectives. Thus we speak of the "historical" context or the "microcultural" or "macrocultural" contexts, which I will discuss in the next chapter. At any rate, meaning is always determined in terms of who is speaking to whom, and when, and where, and for what reason.

Eighth, the *relationship between the source and the respondent* should be examined. At this level we seek to determine the attitudes that operate between source and respondent, what the source *wants* the receptor to understand by his message, and what the receptor *actually* understands by the message.

Before proceeding, then, it is well to acknowledge the outstanding contributions of semanticists, linguists, anthropologists, and philosophers to our understanding of symbols, symbol systems, and the determination of their functions and meanings. Disagreements are to be expected, but the insights to be gained are many. Missionaries in every geographical area and type of service should grasp them and put them to kingdom service.

Chapter 6

Why Do Missionaries Communicate?

I have indicated that communication is *the missionary problem par excellence. That* missionaries must communicate is hardly subject to question. But when we ask *why* they communicate and *what* they communicate, various questions arise.

Gerald Cooke speaks for a disconcertingly significant number of missionaries when he says:

> One need not contrast the medieval thought-world with our own to demonstrate the extent of the liberal evolution. . . . Think only of the difference in religious and philosophical temper in the days of New England Puritanism and today. We may sing about "that old-time religion" for fun, but the majority of us in Europe and North America cannot seriously affirm that what was good enough for the pioneers in this respect is good enough for us. . . . Yesterday's watchword of "winning souls for Christ" now reads, "raising living standards in 'backward areas'!"
>
> In other words, what was formerly oriented toward the reality and character of God and Christ—theocentric and Christocentric, to use theological terms—is now by and

large man-centered (anthropocentric). Most of us are less concerned with "bringing Christian ideals into action toward all men." We tend to think of lives of Christian service less in terms of pastoral or missionary callings than of medical and educational programs. We are, on the whole, less given to speaking of the Name by which all people must be saved than we are to affirming the value and sufficiency of each person's and each culture's tastes and traditions. The commitment of earlier days that could and often did give rise to intolerance and disparagement of heathen beliefs and practices is widely replaced by an ostensible objectivity that insists each person has a right to his own. The drive to convert others to Christian faith is superseded for many by a "post-Christian" skepticism that finds itself unsure of the traditional claims of Christian faith.[1]

Karl Barth, with his emphasis on the proclamation of the gospel, certainly would not have assented to Cooke's understanding of missionary communication. By making his well-known noetic and ontic distinction, however, Barth gave impetus to a misunderstanding of the intent and content of missionary communication that has appealed to many. Barth held that all people are in the state of having been reconciled to God through Christ (therefore they are reconciled "ontically"), but not all people are in the state of knowing that they have been reconciled (and therefore they are uninformed "noetically"). From this it follows that the missionary task is to announce the fact of their reconciliation to people who are still in ignorance of it so that they may participate in the blessings that attend the "triumph of grace."[2]

The writings of men like Cooke and Barth illustrate why there is much discussion currently as to what constitutes the responsibility of the missionary vis-à-vis the good news vouchsafed to him by God. Is the missionary simply to live

---

[1]Gerald Cooke, *As the Christian Faces Rival Religions* (New York: Association, 1962), 14–15.
[2]Karl Barth, *Die Kirchliche Dogmatik*, II.2, 205.

out the gospel in the respondent culture (so-called "presence evangelism")? Or does his responsibility go on to a speaking forth of that gospel ("proclamation evangelism")? Or, is he to go still further and press his respondents for a verdict—to decide for or against the Christ of the gospel ("persuasion evangelism")?

We have argued for the use of the term "communication" as the basic term with which to describe the missionary task because the missionary's concern is not for the gospel alone but for the whole counsel of God. I will now argue that the early missionaries understood that their commission to make disciples of all nations involved the ultimate in communication—not only reinforcing the Christian message behaviorally, nor simply delivering it verbally in writing or speech, but also persuading men and women to be converted and become faithful and fruitful followers of the Master. (Subsequently we will consider the relationship between persuasive Christian communication and the motivations and value systems of respondents. Here let us briefly examine the case for persuasion evangelism and communication.)

THE NEW TESTAMENT CASE FOR PERSUASION

When one examines the Great Commission in Matthew 28:19–20, he discovers that there is one basic element. It is to "make disciples of all the nations," and the importance of discipling is underscored by the fact that *mathēteusate* (making disciples) is the single imperative in the passage. There are two primary activities that are involved in this process of making disciples, namely, "baptizing them in the name" and "teaching them to observe all that I commanded you." These activities are to be carried on, not successively, but simultaneously. The force of the Greek participle *poreuthentes* translated "Go" is a matter of debate among exegetes, but it is apparent that if the disciples are to be made "of all nations" missionaries must be deployed *in* all nations.

Other statements of the Great Commission are not

identical but, rather, complementary to the statement in Matthew. E.g., Mark emphasizes preaching or proclamation, and Luke emphasizes proclamation and witness (see figure 3).

Figure 3

COMPLEMENTARY STATEMENTS OF THE GREAT COMMISSION

The Statements	The Authority	The Enablement	The Sphere	The Message	The Activities
1. Matt. 28:18–20	The authority given to Christ: all authority in heaven and earth	Christ is with us to the very end of the age	The nations (Gentiles)	All things Christ has commanded	Disciple by baptizing, teaching, and going
2. Mark 16:15			All the world: i.e., all creation	The gospel	Go and preach (proclaim)
3. Luke 24:46–49	In His (Christ's) name	Promise of the Father, i.e., power	All the nations beginning from Jerusalem	Repentance and the forgiveness of sins	Preach (proclaim) and witness
4. John 20:21	Sent by Christ as He was sent by the Father				
5. Acts 1:8		Power of the Holy Spirit	Jerusalem, all Judea, Samaria, and even to the remotest parts of the earth	Christ	Witness

Harry Boer has shown rather conclusively that the disciples did not carry out the Great Commission so much as a result of conscious and calculated obedience as by virtue of the sovereign motivation and direction of the Holy Spirit.[3] It is all the more instructive, therefore, to see how the Holy Spirit led those early disciples in obedience to the command of Christ. *The fact is that he led them to carry out those communication activities which we noted previously (chap. 1) as describing the missionary ministry in the New Testament.* Let us look at the examples of Peter and Paul.

According to the rather literal rendering of the New American Standard Bible in Acts 2, Peter "raised his voice" on the day of Pentecost and said, "Give heed to my words" (v. 14). When he had finished his message and many were "pierced to the heart" (v. 37), he directed them to "repent, and . . . be baptized" (v. 38). And the record is clear that he did not stop at that point but continued his speech and "solemnly testified and kept on exhorting them" to "be saved" (v. 40).

Passing over much that is similarly instructive, we take a brief look at Peter's continuing obedience as it is revealed in his letters. In writing to the believing Jews of the Dispersion, his great concern was that they "grow in the grace and knowledge of our Lord and Savior Jesus Christ" (2 Peter 3:18). With this end in view he *urged* them (1 Peter 2:11; 5:1) and said that his intention was to always *remind* them (2 Peter 1:12) of that which they needed "to make [their] calling and election sure" (v. 10 KJV).

Concerning Paul, Luke says that upon his conversion and the restoration of his sight, he immediately *proclaimed* Jesus in the synagogues of Damascus (Acts 9:20). Moreover, he *confounded* the Jews of Damascus and *proved* that Jesus was the Christ (v. 22). Back in Jerusalem, "speaking out boldly in the name of the Lord" he was "talking and arguing" with the Greeks (Acts 9:28–29).

Bypassing various other similar passages, we proceed to Paul's defense before King Agrippa and Governor Festus (Acts 26). That defense begins with what we might call a witness to what Paul himself experienced. It then moves on to a proclamation of what Moses and the prophets said concerning

[3]Harry R. Boer, *Pentecost and Missions* (Grand Rapids: Eerdmans, 1961).

Christ, and what Christ himself did and said (vv. 22–24). Finally, Paul addresses the king, saying, "King Agrippa, do you believe the Prophets? I know that you do" (v. 27). Was Paul trying to persuade Agrippa to embrace the faith? Agrippa thought so. He replied to Paul, "In a short time you will persuade me [or, 'try to convince me'; cf. NASB margin] to become a Christian" (v. 28).

One of the most revealing passages in the New Testament relating to the missionary is Paul's picture of the missionary as an ambassador (2 Cor. 5). The missionary has been given the message of reconciliation and is God's appointed representative (v. 18). This being the case, he not only delivers the message but does it in such a way as to reveal both the *truth* of God and the *heart* of God, persuading (v. 11), entreating (v. 20), and even begging that people "be reconciled to God" (v. 20).

J. I. Packer does not overlook these references, but nevertheless concludes that these various verbs having to do with missionary communication can be best summed up in the word *teach*:

It is by teaching that the gospel preacher fulfills his ministry. To *teach* the gospel is his first responsibility: to reduce it to its simplest essentials, to analyze it point by point, to fix its meaning by positive and negative definition, to show how each part of the message links up with the rest—and to go on explaining it till he is quite sure that his listeners have grasped it. And therefore when Paul preached the gospel, formally or informally, in the synagogue or in the streets, to Jews or to Gentiles, to a crowd or to one man, what he did was to *teach*—engaging attention, capturing interest, setting out the facts, explaining their significance, solving difficulties, answering objections, and showing how the message bears on life. Luke's regular way of describing Paul's evangelistic ministry is to say that he *disputed*, or *reasoned* (*dialegomai*: RSV renders "argued"), or *taught*, or *persuaded* (*i.e.*, sought to carry his hearers' judgments). And Paul himself refers to his ministry among the Gentiles as primarily a task of instruction: "unto me . . . was this grace given, to preach unto the Gentiles the unsearchable riches of Christ; and *to make all men see* what is the dispensation of the mystery. . .." Clearly, in Paul's view, his first and fundamental job as a preacher of the gospel was to communicate knowledge—to get gospel truth fixed in men's minds. To him, teaching the truth was the basic evangelistic activity; to him, therefore, the only right method of evangelism was the teaching method.[4]

One can understand and appreciate the concern out of which Packer writes (and which A. Duane Litfin echoes[5]). There is always a danger that the Christian communicator will identify too closely the activity and its objective and, believing himself to be successful only to the extent that he actually persuades his listeners, attempt to manipulate them rather than leaving the ultimate issue to the Holy Spirit and them. But one must ask whether we can legitimately attack this problem by soft-pedaling some terms while emphasizing others,[6] or by subsuming terms like "dispute," "reason" and "persuade" under the activity of teaching. (As we will see, from a *communication* point of view, it might be more legitimate to subsume the term "teach" under the activity of persuading.)

No, it would seem to be more true to Scripture to maintain the integrity of "persuade" (and kindred terms). Of course, one *can* translate the present indicative of *peithō* in such passages as Acts 26:28 and 2 Corinthians 5:11 by the phrase "try to persuade." Obviously, to be genuine and effective, persuasion ultimately must be the result of the activity of the Holy Spirit. *He* is the divine "hidden persuader"! For that matter, the same must be said regarding *teaching* the Word of God. Paul makes it clear that the natural

---

[4]J. I. Packer, *Evangelism and the Sovereignty of God* (Chicago: InterVarsity, 1961), 48–49.

[5]A. Duane Litfin, "The Perils of Persuasive Preaching," *Christianity Today* 21 (4 February 1977): 484–87.

[6]For example, in a context in which he refers to 2 Corinthians 5 and its teaching in this regard, Litfin does not mention the use of *peithō* in v. 11. See ibid., 487.

man cannot understand the things of the Spirit apart from the ministry of the Holy Spirit (1 Cor. 2:11–16). The Spirit is the divine "hidden teacher" also! We will discuss some of these issues more fully in chapter 42. But perhaps the foregoing is sufficient to make clear my perspective in the writing of this book. Persuasion evangelism seems objectionable only if, on the one side, the idea of conversion is rejected or if, on the other side, the human activity in any way renders the work of the Holy Spirit ineffective or unimportant.

Finally, one could go on to discuss numerous passages according to which Paul instructed the *converts* in the churches and urged them to continue in devoted discipleship. Just as Paul delivered the gospel to those who were unbelievers and did all within his power to persuade them to avail themselves of God's provision in Christ, so he instructed those who had entered the faith as to the will of God and urged them to continue in the faith. "As ye have therefore received Christ Jesus the Lord, so walk ye in him" (Col. 2:6 KJV). Moreover, he urged his son in the faith, Timothy, to carry on a similar ministry (2 Tim. 3:14).

INSIGHTS FROM COMMUNICATION THEORY

In his book *The Process of Communication: An Introduction to Theory and Practice*, David K. Berlo has written an illuminating section concerning the influence of seventeenth-century faculty psychology on communication theory.[7] Faculty psychology made a clear distinction between the soul and the mind. When this school of thought invaded rhetoric in the eighteenth century, the classical purposes of communication were reinforced accordingly. One purpose was to inform, and this was basically achieved by rational, logical appeals to the mind. A second purpose was to persuade, and it was thought

[7]David K. Berlo, *The Process of Communication: An Introduction to Theory and Practice* (New York: Holt, Rinehart and Winston, 1960), 7–10.

that this was accomplished mainly by emotional appeals to the soul. A third purpose was to entertain.

Contemporary communicologists expand the purposes or functions of communication significantly. In spite of differences, Edward C. Stewart has provided a rather representative list of functions as follows:
1. Referential—transmit information, knowledge
2. Emotive—expressiveness
3. Conative—intensional, motivational
4. Poetic—fusion of concrete perception and abstraction
5. Phatic—belongingness, affiliation
6. Metalingual—communication about communication
7. Metaphysical—worldview[8]

This elaborated taxonomy occasions certain questions even as it clarifies. It is not necessary to explore all the questions here, but it will be helpful to point out some contemporary insights that have a direct bearing on missionary communication.

We have seen that our biblical mandate is conveyed in clear words—preach, teach, witness, proclaim, evangelize, exhort, rebuke, reprove, beseech, warn, persuade. The missionary, therefore, is a witness. He is a bearer of good news. He is a teacher. But he is more than these. Whatever else the missionary is, he is a persuaded man persuading others. Moreover, as most of the world categorizes him, he is a "persuader in religion." Now it just so happens that in the eyes of the world this is the worst kind because a "persuader in religion" is likely to be a "backnumber" *and* a "propagandist"—a curious combination at best and a deadly combination at worst!

The missionary has two options at this point. He can retreat from biblical and existential reality and hang up the shingle of a "teacher only" (or of some other more acceptable professional). Or else he can humbly but determinedly accept

[8]Edward C. Stewart, "Outline of Intercultural Communication," in *Readings in Intercultural Communication*, 3 vols. (Research Council for Intercultural Communication, 1973), 3:22.

his commission and bend every effort to be an effective Christian persuader. *Strangely enough, modern communication theory will assist him if he chooses the latter course!* In the first place, Kenneth Burke and David Berlo (among many others) insist that it is the very nature of communication to be persuasive (conative). They eloquently point out the falsity of interpreting taxonomies in such a way as to make communication functions separate and distinguishable. Burke holds that language is never neutral.[9] From the very beginning it has been an instrument of cooperative action. He believes that if there is meaning there is persuasion, and if there is persuasion there is rhetoric. Ours is a rhetorical world! David Berlo is equally explicit:

> Our basic purpose in communication is to become an affecting agent, to affect others, our physical environment, and ourselves, and to become a determining agent, to have a vote in how things are. In short, we communicate to influence—to affect with intent.[10]

For Berlo, even report language is persuasive in the sense that it focuses attention on the source's interest, underscores what he thinks is important or true, and reflects his view of reality. Thus no statements can be said to be nonpersuasive.[11] The television entertainer does more than entertain. He persuades. The classroom teacher does more than inform. She persuades.

The missionary, therefore, can look at his critic "eyeball to eyeball" and quote not only Peter and Paul but also Burke and Berlo and many others. We are *all* "missionaries"! It is only a matter of degree and direction! And the more one is persuaded himself, the more intent he becomes, and the greater the barriers he is willing to cross in order in influence others. It's as simple as that!

I once participated in a small group discussion on

[9]Burke, *Grammar of Motives.*
[10]Berlo, *Process of Communication*, 12.
[11]Ibid., 10–14, 234.

missionary work around the world. During the course of the discussion an educator suddenly jumped to his feet, faced me, and said, "And who do you think you are, going to those people and telling them that they have to believe as you do?" Instantly Scripture portions came to mind by way of reply, as well as the rhetorical question, "And precisely what do you think *you* are doing right now?" It might have been more effective in that situation simply to quote secular theoreticians!

In the second place, communication experts clearly locate the purpose of any communication in sources and respondents rather than in messages as such. To quote Berlo once again:

> Too often we look to the *message* (speech, manuscript, play, advertisement) in order to determine communicative purposes. From a behaviorist's point of view, it is more useful to define purpose as the goal of a creator or receiver of a message, rather than as the property of the message itself.[12]

Carried to an extreme, this can be misleading (like the statement "Meaning is in persons, not in messages"). But it can be helpful if not pressed too far. Missionary communicators who are not intimidated by contemporary criticism may nevertheless be influenced by it, especially when that influence is in the direction of a very natural tendency. There is a subtle temptation for missionaries to think that they have delivered their soul when they have delivered a faithful message. The gospel itself has an appeal. The Scriptures themselves possess an authority. Therefore it may seem that when God's Word has been declared no more should be required.

There is, of course, a dimension of truth in that position. The truth of it is to be found in the fact that, as we have seen, it is the Holy Spirit who takes the Word and makes it understandable and operative in the hearer. He is, as Harry

---

[12]Ibid., 10.

Boer has called him, the missionary Spirit. But scriptural principles and precedents prevent us from stopping there. One reason why Paul was an effective missionary was that his purpose coincided with that of the Holy Spirit. His purposes reflected the purposes of the Holy Spirit. And those purposes were deep, evident, and specific. Modern persuasion theory insists that effective communication begins here. The communicator must first determine what his precise objectives are in any particular case. If he does not know his objectives, how can his respondents be expected to know? In that case, why communicate at all?

This point should be taken seriously by missionary communicators (indeed, by all Christian communicators). Eugene Nida says that the real purpose of many preachers is "expressive" because they are attempting to impress the audience and acquire prestige.[13] To the extent that Nida is correct, preachers need to reflect and repent. But more than that, they need to determine their specific objectives as a part of their preparation for each communicative act and proceed accordingly. This kind of self-discipline would revolutionize many churches at home and abroad.

In the third place, and closely related to the preceding point, communication experts put the spotlight on audience response. The effective communicator not only knows his specific purpose(s) but also has some method of measuring audience response. Only in this way is he able to ascertain the extent to which he has achieved his purpose(s), i.e., know whether or not he has been truly effective. The instructor whose students as a group never exceed a grade that could be expected on the basis of pure chance should not be rehired! An insurance salesman who has an attractive policy but no buyers should be summarily dismissed! To be sure, it may not be that simple in the case of the missionary. He may have an unresponsive audience. He does not operate in a controlled situation. He may not agree with the behaviorist who says

[13]Eugene A. Nida, *Message and Mission: The Communication of the Christian Faith* (New York: Harper & Row, 1960), 4.

90

that only measurable responses are meaningful. But all the reasons he may adduce in support of the uniqueness of his task do not excuse him from setting goals and measuring results *insofar as this is possible*. Nor should these results simply be in terms of hand-raising or handshaking (in cultures where this is the norm) but in terms of lasting conversions, Christian knowledge and behavior, and church growth.

In the fourth place, with the abandonment of faculty psychology and the reunification of the individual person we can analyze human response more realistically. Humpty-Dumpty has been put together again! We do not speak to people who possess minds only, or souls only, or bodies only. We address people who have faculties of feeling, desire, drives, habits, thought, and will, all in one personality. In the final analysis these are inseparable. Every respondent (and every audience) will be a complex composite of ideas and impulses. To be sure, there will be a great difference between cultures, and between individuals and audiences within cultures. But persuasion will require ethical, emotional, and logical proofs in each instance. We always address those who will make decisions on the basis of that which has captured their attention, merited their consideration, and appealed to them as the right thing to believe or do.

CONCLUSION TO PART I

The missionary task is fundamentally one of communication. In a very real sense the missionary participates in the basic human challenge, for while communication is an elemental human activity, it also constitutes a fundamental human problem—perhaps second only to the problem of his or her Adamic nature! In fact, some theorists insist that in the most ideal relationship between source and respondent *of the same culture*, communication is only about 80 percent effective.[14] What must be the implication of that assertion for *cross-cultural* communication?

[14]Ibid., 76.

I recall giving an hour's lecture on missionary communication some years ago. After the lecture a missionary came up to me and said, "Whew, I'm glad that communication is not that complicated in my area of the world." He was right, of course. Being human, we interact with other humans day in and day out without stopping to analyze all that is involved. This is true even in many cross-cultural situations. And yet we manage to achieve a modicum of understanding and success. But my missionary critic was also wrong. Communication—and especially cross-cultural Christian communication—is far more complex than I had been able to indicate in the one hour allotted to me.

Perhaps an analogy will help us to understand the simplicity and complexity of communication. All of us learn at least one language, our native language, from childhood. The learning and utilization of that language is so natural that we rarely stop to analyze it until one day when, quite far along in formal studies, we are confronted with a required course in our own native tongue—Chinese, Spanish, French, English, or whatever. Very little instruction is required before we meet the complexities of our own "simple" language head-on. The ensuing perspiration and frustration are necessary if we are to understand and appreciate the potential of our native language more fully, to say nothing of developing our capacity to learn still other languages.

Missionary communication is something like that. It is simple *and* it is complex. One can engage in it without studying it. But to study and analyze it is to greatly increase one's potential effectiveness.

Part II

COMMUNICATION AND CULTURE

Chapter 7

The Role of Culture In Communication

The voice of the pilot came over the loudspeaker. It was not easy to understand him above the roar of the jet engines outside, but Ted heard enough to cause him to shake off the drowsiness and make him alert.

"Ladies and gentlemen, we will be landing in approximately forty-five minutes."

It seemed unreal to Ted. There had been just enough time to settle down and get several hours of much-needed sleep since leaving the airport near his home. And yet in a few more minutes they would be back on their mission field with an adopted people whose language and customs still posed quite a challenge, even after almost eight years of living and working among them.

"Alice, we should start getting the children ready. It's going to take a while to . . . ."

THE CULTURAL BARRIER TO MISSIONARY COMMUNICATION

There was a time in the history of humanity (and it was not long ago!) when the barriers between the earth's peoples seemed to be mainly physical. The problem was one of transporting people, messages, and material goods across treacherous seas, towering mountains, and trackless deserts. Missionaries knew all too well how formidable those challenges were. Today, thanks to jumbo jets and towering antennae, those earlier problems have been largely resolved. We can deliver a person, or a Bible, or a sewing machine anywhere on the face of the earth within a matter of hours, and we can transmit a sound or a picture within seconds. This does not end the matter, however. To quote Robert Park:

> One can transport words across cultural boundaries (like bricks) but interpretation will depend on the context which their different interpreters bring to them. And that context will depend more on past experience and present temper of the people to whom the words are addressed than on the good will of the persons who report them.[1]

Park goes on to assert that the traits of material culture are more easily diffused than those of the nonmaterial culture. He illustrates his point by citing the example of the African chief whose immediate response upon seeing a plow in operation was "It's worth as much as ten wives!" One wonders how much prayer and how many hours of study and patient instruction would have been necessary to convince that chief that Christ is infinitely more valuable than plows *or* wives *or* fetishes and false gods! Yes, the barriers are, after all, very real and challenging. But they are no longer essentially geographical—if, indeed, they ever were.

There is a very real danger that, as our technology advances and enables us to cross geographical and national boundaries with singular ease and increasing frequency, we may forget that *it is the cultural barriers that are the most formidable.* The gap between our technological advances and our communication skills is perhaps one of the most challeng-

[1]Robert Park, "Reflections on Communication and Culture," in *Reader in Public Opinion and Communication*, ed. Bernard Berelson and Morris Janowitz, 2nd ed. (New York: Free Press, 1966), 167.

ing aspects of modern civilization. Western diplomats are beginning to realize that they need much more than a knowledge of their message and a good interpreter or English-speaking national. Many educators have come to the position that cross-cultural communication is a *sine qua non* for citizenship in this new world. Missionaries now understand that much more than a microphone and increased volume is involved in penetrating cultural barriers.

"MULTIPLE RHETORICS" AND INTERCULTURAL COMMUNICATION

The newly awakened concern of members of the speech and communication profession for intercultural communication is exemplified in the works of Robert T. Oliver, research professor emeritus of international speech at Pennsylvania State University. From the very beginning of the United States' involvement in World War II he was numbered among those scholars—communication experts, anthropologists, linguists, political scientists, and others—who made signal contributions to international understanding in war and peace. Oliver has demonstrated how American diplomacy is disadvantaged when its overseas representatives take their American approaches to communication and persuasion abroad, and, without careful, studied modification, engage in international discussions. He has analyzed the gargantuan task that faces our diplomats when they accept the assignment to represent their country in the give and take of international politics.[2]

One highly intriguing notion that appears in Oliver's writings is that of "multiple rhetorics." The old rhetoric generally assumed its applicability to all people and situations. The enlargement of concern from which Oliver writes has resulted in the realization that there is not just one

[2]Cf. Robert T. Oliver, *Culture and Communication: The Problem of Penetrating National and Cultural Boundaries* (Springfield, Ill.: Thomas, 1962); idem, *Communication and Culture in Ancient India and China* (Syracuse, N.Y.: Syracuse University Press, 1971).

rhetoric, *there are many rhetorics!* In other words, while *nature* assures us of broad and basic areas of commonality among all people, *nurture* also plays a decisive role. The influences of their respective cultures on two groups of people may be so divergent as to necessitate essentially different rhetorics in the two cultures. For example, Oliver explains how one who is nurtured in the values of traditional American culture must completely reorient his thinking when communicating with avowed Communists because the latter are conditioned by Lenin's ideas of communication as "war," words as weapons, and the insignificance of truth as ordinarily conceived. Or, to take another example, the American may be hard put to deal with representatives of cultures where Hinduism or Buddhism has had a vital role in enculturation. The American is likely to think that in most circumstances any decision is better than none at all. The Indian or citizen of Sri Lanka, on the other hand, is more likely to think that it is better not to choose between alternatives unless one is forced to a decision. For one raised in the Hindu-Buddhistic orbit, neutrality is a kind of way of life that is in harmony with the universe itself.

Oliver, therefore, refuses to confine himself to the changing of a few nuts and bolts in order to adapt to this or that particular culture. Instead, he begins anew as it were, with major cultural systems—Communist, Hindu-Buddhist, Confucian, Taoist, and Shintoist. He urges that communication be more closely allied with cultural anthropology, social psychology, and general linguistics. He advocates that we study the rhetorical process implicit and explicit in any culture, not just in terms of *what* people think but in terms of *how* they think and formulate their ideas.

The validity of this approach to intercultural communication became increasingly apparent to me over a period of years of missionary experience in the Orient. In many ways that experience substantiated the insights of classical theory. Once, for example, a young man who has since become a leader in the Japanese church, returned from a confrontation with his Buddhist father—a confrontation that lasted three days. The avowed purpose of the father was to dissuade his son from entering the Christian ministry. His first argument was, "Son, there are two kinds of things in the world, the possible and the impossible. You have chosen the impossible." When I heard of this later, my first reaction was "The possible and the impossible! Shades of Aristotle!" Robert Burns was right when he wrote, "A man's a man, for a' that!" People *are* people wherever you go.

But that is not the end of the matter. Experience has also shown the incompleteness of classical theory as a basis for cross-cultural communication. The word *rhetoric* itself presents a problem to the Chinese and Japanese. The ambiguity of the word to them is more than a reflection of Western confusion as to whether it refers to delivery, style, argumentation, persuasion, or all of these. Rather, it is the characteristics of rhetoric that grew out of the situation in ancient Greece and Rome (and are closely paralleled in the Western world today) that present the major obstacle to understanding. The directness, the lack of subtlety, the pressing for immediate decision—these are some of the characteristics of rhetoric as we know it, and it is these that disenchant Orientals. It is not that such characteristics are without precedent in their own cultures. It is more the fact that there is always a proper time, place, occasion, and approach for their use. Aristotle did us a great service by focusing our attention on the audience. But his analysis was provincial (and the provinciality of even our jet age should be sufficiently evident to excuse him) and did not take into account the fact that *audiences of different cultures may be so different as to necessitate, not just more education, but reeducation.*

UNDERSTANDING CULTURE

Intercultural communication is as complex as the sum total of human differences. The word *culture* is a very inclusive term. It takes into account linguistic, political, economic, social, psychological, religious, national, racial, and still other differences. A review of relevant literature will show that culture has been defined, described, and categorized in a variety of ways. Nevertheless, there tends to be a consensus on certain basics having to do with what culture is and how it operates. It is imperative that we master some of those basics before we proceed.

First, we need a *definition* of culture. Since "culture" is a very inclusive term that takes into account linguistic, political, economic, social, psychological, religious, national, and other differences, scores of definitions have been offered. Two that are most helpful are those offered by Clyde Kluckhohn and Louis Luzbetak. Kluckhohn says, "Culture is a way of thinking, feeling, believing. It is the group's knowledge stored up for future use."[3] Luzbetak writes:

> Culture is a design for living. It is *a plan according to which society adapts itself to its physical, social, and ideational environment.* A plan for coping with the physical environment would include such matters as food production and all technological knowledge and skill. Political systems, kinships and family organization, and law are examples of social adaptation, a plan according to which one is to interact with his fellows. Man copes with his ideational environment through knowledge, art, magic, science, philosophy, and religion. Cultures are but different answers to essentially the same human problems.[4]

Second, some of the *characteristics* of culture that we should keep in mind include the following:

1. Culture is *learned*—it is not biologically determined or restricted by race.
2. Culture is a *shared* system, and therefore it is held in common by a society.
3. Culture is an *integrated whole*, all the parts of which function in such a way as to affect each other and contribute to the totality.

---

[3]Clyde Kluckhohn, *Mirror for Man* (New York: Whittlesey, 1949), 23.
[4]Louis J. Luzbetak, *The Church and Cultures* (Techny, Ill.: Divine Word, 1963), 60–61.

4. Culture constantly *changes* as a result of innovations, internal pressures, and cross-cultural borrowing.

Third, depending on one's perspective and purposes, the various aspects of culture can be divided up into various *categories* or *types*. As we will see below, G. Linwood Barney thinks in terms of four "layers" of culture. Later in this book we will analyze communication in terms of seven "dimensions" of culture. At a most fundamental level, however, culture can be broken down into three categories that are in accord with Luzbetak's definition above:

1. *Technological* culture includes artifacts and activities designed to manipulate the material world.
2. *Sociological* culture includes those patterns of relationship and behavior that govern interaction between individuals and groups.
3. *Ideological* culture includes the knowledge, beliefs, worldview, and values of a people.

Fourth, we might ask which category of culture is most important. In the final analysis, that question is very difficult to answer because of the wholeness of culture and the interanimation of its parts. But Barney has provided a sort of hierarchy of cultural categories that is helpful to our present understanding. Barney writes:

> By the term, cultural, we refer to that *acquired knowledge* which one uses to *interpret experience* and *generate behavior*. The arrangement of knowledge (categories for classifying reality, hierarchy of categories, "rules" for grammar and behavior, priorities in values, etc.) is reflected in the patterns of behavior, language and even the material artifacts made by man. When a segment of society shares a common configuration of knowledge . . . that [shared knowledge] constitutes a *culture*. Those who share a common knowledge constitute a *society*. Each generation of a given society receives its culture from the passing generation, modifies it, and passes it on to the following generation. Thus a culture is really not static but undergoes change constantly. There are over 3500 ethnic groups in the world and yet no two of them have identical cultural

configurations. Each of these societies has a culture which is systemic and patterned. It can be modeled as a series of layers. The *deepest layer* consists of ideology, cosmology and worldview. A *second layer*, closely related but probably derived from the first, is that of values. Stemming from both of these layers is a *third layer* of institutions (marriage, law, education, etc.). This level of institutions is a bridge to the *surface level* (fourth level) of material artifacts and observable behavior. The artifacts and behavior of the surface level are easily described and even borrowed. Each deeper level is more complex, abstract. It is one thing to describe or share the phenomena of the surface level but it is quite another thing to discover the functional relationship of these to the deeper levels and still more difficult and demanding to decode their meaning at the level of values, ideology, cosmology and worldview.[5]

Barney's model can be diagrammed as in figure 4.

If I understand Barney correctly, then, ideological culture (as in our basic tripartite taxonomy) or worldview, cognitive process, and motivational resources (as in the seven-dimensional approach to be followed in this book) constitute the most important aspects of culture for missionary purposes. But they are also the most difficult to discover, analyze, and modify. Precisely for that reason, missionaries are often tempted to concentrate on surface-level change and let it go at that. Biblical Christianity, however, requires change at the deeper levels of values, beliefs, and worldview.

Fifth, there are no *a*cultural persons. When babies are born into the world, they are at the same time born into one of its cultures. Over a period of time they become *en*culturated into the ways of that particular culture (and, in more complex societies especially, the ways of one or more of its subcultures). In fact, his or her culture is more important than such factors as race, nationality, and gender in determining how

---

[5]G. Linwood Barney, "The Supracultural and the Cultural: Implications for Frontier Missions," unpublished manuscript, n.d., 2. The original version of this manuscript was a chapter by the same title in *The Gospel and Frontier Peoples*, ed. R. Pierce Beaver (Pasadena: William Carey, 1973), 48–55.

that person will think, feel, and act. When a person moves out of the culture in which he or she was enculturated and learns (becomes "at home" in) another culture, we say that he or she has been *ac*culturated into that second culture and is therefore *bi*cultural. Truly bicultural (or multicultural) persons are quite rare because as one becomes older it become more and more difficult to master the complexities of the new language, behavioral patterns, and so on. A good proportion of bicultural people have been introduced to their second culture at an early age.

Figure 4

LAYERS OF CULTURE

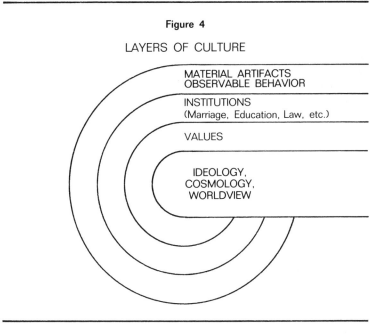

Sixth, deep-level change that is truly Christian involves the introduction of that which is *supracultural* into the respondent culture. In using the term supracultural we refer to anything that has its source outside of culture (and therefore outside of any particular culture). Although the Creator made provision for culture and even commanded it when he told the first man and woman to rule over their environment (Gen. 1:28–30) and when he said to Noah and his sons that they were to establish justice (Gen. 9:5–6), still culture itself is a human product. But it is also the arena of continued divine and Satanic intervention and penetration—God by his Spirit, heavenly agents, and human representatives, and Satan by his demonic forces. It is not difficult to distinguish theoretically between supracultural entities that are divine and those that are demonic if we are sensitive and submissive to the Holy Spirit. The gospel, the Scriptures, the gifts of the Spirit—in short, all that leads to life and godliness—emanate from God. Spiritual darkness, deception, and bondage of all sorts issue from Satan. However, as we will see, it is often difficult for even the most spiritual missionary to maintain a proper distinction between that which is supracultural and that which is cultural at the practical level. Nevertheless that is part of the missionary task. In fact, solutions to some of the most perplexing of all cross-cultural problems such as polygamy, ancestor worship/reverence, and worship forms/styles depend on our ability to analyze and resolve tensions between the supracultural and the cultural.

UNDERSTANDING CULTURES

In the quotation above Luzbetak begins with a definition of *culture* and ends with a reference to *cultures*. The distinction is important. Just as a missionary to the Middle East is concerned with religion, confronts another religious system known as Islam, and in his work deals with persons who are devoted to Islam as they understand and practice it, so the missionary must concern himself with culture, confronts a particular (respondent) cultural system, and in his day-to-day comings and goings deals with people who are enculturated in that respondent cultural system and live it out in their daily lives. It is important, therefore, that the missionary understand culture, but it is equally important that he understand cultures—his own and his respondents'.

After a study of culture, then, a missionary should work to develop cultural self-awareness. That is, he should attempt to understand his own culture. This sounds simple. Actually, it is not simple at all. Try to formulate a significant analysis of the culture into which you have been enculturated—its worldview, value system, behavioral patterns, etc., to see how difficult it really is. And *why* is it so difficult? Because in the enculturation process we seldom stop to analyze what is happening. We do not ask why we speak in a particular way, why we use forks instead of chopsticks, why we place so much importance on individual rights, and why we emphasize competition and winning. If we ask questions of this type at all, we usually postpone them until such time as we enter someone else's culture! Then we want to know why others think and act the way they do. The way we think, feel, and behave is "the way to think, feel, and behave." It is *"the way,"* not *"a way."* This attitude is quite natural to the enculturation process and is the case with almost all of the world's peoples. It is one of the bases of ethnocentrism and a major cause of "cultural overhang," or the tendency to take the ways of our own culture into the new culture and deal with the new culture on that basis. There is a wrong kind of "cultural relativity" that insists that there are no absolutes and that the distinctions between right and wrong, and good and evil, are no more than the dictates of one's culture. But there is also a right kind of "cultural relativity" that says that although there are divinely dictated absolutes of right and wrong, one's own culturally prescribed assumptions of right and wrong will reflect them imperfectly at best and may not reflect them at all. Moreover, many cultural prescriptions are not matters of right and wrong at all but simply matters of utility or taste. Armed with understandings such as these and with an awareness of culturally learned assumptions, values, and behavior the missionary will be enabled to function more effectively in another culture. A variety of games, simulations and exercises have been developed with a view to stimulating this kind of awareness.[6]

I will have more to say about "understanding other cultures" later. In fact, a good share of what follows in this book has to do with that process. Before proceeding, however, let me summarize the ways in which people have gone about learning other cultures. Ted Ward says that there was a time when it was thought that the basis of cross-cultural effectiveness was natural (or supernatural) selection—i.e., a person either had or did not have this ability. After it became apparent that one could *learn* how to function effectively in another culture, various learning approaches were developed:[7]

1. The "informational" (study) approach became prominent in the late 1960s. Indebted to classical learning, those who advocated this approach assumed that if one has enough information about the second culture it will be easier to live and work in it.

2. The "training" (experiential) approach of the 1970s shifted the emphasis to actual involvement. Its adherents said that one can learn about another culture from a distance, but to be effective one needs to begin the acculturation process, and this is made possible by purposefully going into cross-cultural situations (often in groups) and observing, questioning, testing, and analyzing.

3. The "learning" (balanced) approach of the 1980s sought to unify these perspectives and to balance information and skills by learning through intracultural and intercultural activities.[8]

4. The "encounter" (nontechnical) approach that has been most recently proposed by some is really a more

[6]I refer to games such as those that can be found in Appendix A of Ted Ward, *Living Overseas* (New York: Free Press; London: Collier, Macmillan, 1984).

[7]Ibid., 199.

[8]For an instructive explanation of what is involved see Mildred Sikkema and Agnes Niyekawa, *Design for Cross-Cultural Learning* (Yarmouth, Me.: Intercultural, 1987).

radical version of #2 above; it eliminates all technical terms and concepts in favor of developing interpersonal relationships and interpretational skills.

If the encounter approach has any advantage, it is to be found in the fact that the person who has no theoretical knowledge at all is forced to go into a cross-cultural relationship as a learner. If we can put aside any idea that our own culture is a "superior" culture and if we can take the position of a learner despite any theoretical knowledge that we might have, it appears that an approach that balances information and training is best.

A THREE-CULTURE MODEL OF MISSIONARY COMMUNICATION

Eugene Nida has made many important contributions toward an understanding of the communication problems of the missionary. The discussion and diagram in his chapter on "Structure of Communication" furnish the basis for our consideration of a "three-language model" of missionary communication.[9] Although modifications have been made in order to further our present objectives (see figure 5), the reader will greatly benefit by a reading of Nida's text.

Let's take a look at what is involved in faithful and effective missionary communication. The missionary message is the message of the Bible. It was given by God through the apostles and prophets in the languages and cultural contexts of the Bible. For the sake of simplification we may say that "Bible culture" (triangular in our model) includes all cultural contexts in which the message of the Bible was originally given, whether Judah at the time of Ezra, Jerusalem at the time of Christ, or Athens at the time of Paul. In those cultural contexts there were sources (Ezra, our Lord Christ, or Paul), messages, and respondents. The sources of the messages were identified with the cultures I have labeled "Bible culture."

[9]Eugene A. Nida, *God's Word in Man's Language* (New York: Harper & Row, 1952), 45–46.

They encoded the messages in forms that were understandable in those cultures to respondents who were members of those cultures.

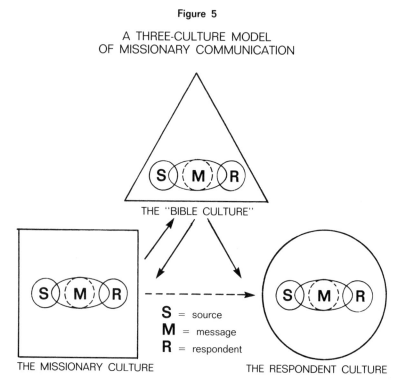

Figure 5

A THREE-CULTURE MODEL
OF MISSIONARY COMMUNICATION

THE "BIBLE CULTURE"

S = source
M = message
R = respondent

THE MISSIONARY CULTURE

THE RESPONDENT CULTURE

The missionary himself is a citizen of a quite different culture, whether his home address is London, Chicago, or Seoul. He has been brought up in his own culture and has been schooled in its language, worldview, and value system. He has likely received the Christian message in the context of that culture as it was communicated by a source (or, sources) who

108

most likely was a citizen of the same culture. (The "missionary's culture" is the square culture in our model.)

The missionary has been sent to a people in still another culture with its own sources, messages, and respondents. We can think of this third culture as the "respondent culture" or the "target culture" (round in our model). In relationship to this respondent culture the missionary has immediate and ultimate objectives. First, he desires to communicate Christ in such a way that the people will understand, repent, and believe the gospel. Second, he wants to commit the message to "faithful men, who will be able to teach others" (2 Tim. 2:2), in culturally relevant terms that only they, in the final analysis, can command.

In a word, then, the missionary task is to attempt to understand/interpret the message intended by the Holy Spirit and human authors of the biblical text and then to explain/communicate that message in a way that is meaningful and persuasive to respondents in the context of their culture. And this must be done with as little intrusion of the missionary's cultural predispositions as possible. (As we will see, aspects of this process have been described in different ways and by the use of various terms—indigenization, inculturation, transculturation, decontextualization/contextualization, the fusion of cultural horizons, and so forth.) Of course, the missionary should also encourage and, insofar as possible, assist nationals in these same endeavors.

Since the major portion of this book will be devoted to cross-cultural communication, I will not expand on that here. However, before proceeding it will be helpful to look at what is involved in biblical interpretation (hermeneutics) with a view to communicating the Bible's message cross-culturally.

With the missionary objective in view, Edward Rommen has explained the hermeneutical problem in terms of certain assumptions and a hermeneutical pattern. In outline form, his approach is as follows:[10]

[10]David J. Hesselgrave and Edward Rommen, *Contextualization: Meanings, Methods, and Models* (Grand Rapids: Baker, 1989), 172–79.

1. Basic hermeneutical assumptions
   a. The gospel has supracultural validity. Of course, this still leaves the question of how to identify supracultural elements of the gospel as over against culturally bound aspects of its biblical formulations. To aid us in this differentiation, Rommen proposes that we make a distinction between two types of validity—categorical and principial.
      1) Categorical validity is nonnegotiable and must be accorded to "those aspects of truth that are necessary for justification by grace such as the sacrificial death of Christ, faith, repentance, and conversion" and to such forms or symbols that cannot be changed significantly without losing their meaning. (For example, sand could not be substituted for water in baptism without losing its biblical meaning, but the symbolism of the bread and wine of the Lord's Supper are not *necessarily* tied to the meaning of Communion.)
      2) Principial validity is ascribed to aspects of revealed truth that are implied in the new life in Christ—explicitly stated and logically necessary implications such as godly living, separation from the world, and keeping the moral law on the one hand, and those implications that are not explicitly stated and therefore allow for more latitude of expression on the other. (For examples of the latter type, consider those parables and analogies that have a distinct connection to Palestinian culture such as the sheepfold. In such cases it is imperative that we determine the principle involved if we are to interpret the analogy correctly and explain it effectively.)
   b. The gospel can be communicated cross-culturally. Cultural gaps can be bridged so that the missionary can understand the biblical text and communicate its intended meanings to people of another culture,

and so that converted and properly instructed persons in that culture can repeat this process. In other words, the task we have described previously is "doable."

2. Basic hermeneutical patterns

In order to determine the meaning of the words in any given text (context) we need to examine and determine three fundamental aspects of meaning.

a. "Public meaning" is "the whole spectrum of meaning of which the text is capable." Every language code involves a "latitude of correctness" of generally accepted meaning. The text must be interpreted within the confines of the generally accepted meaning of the author's time and place unless he clearly indicates otherwise.

b. "User's meaning" is "the specific sense prescribed by [a word's] use in the text." Within the bounds of public meaning, or slightly beyond those bounds, the user/author determines the sense in which he uses words. An honest attempt must be made to arrive at the author's intended meaning. However, since we do not have access to his mind but only to his words, we are not justified in any attempt to discover the meaning "behind the text" or "beneath the letter." To do so is to commit the "intentional fallacy."

c. Meanings are subject to change. Current usage, the "latitude of correctness" and meaning are in a state of flux. Therefore they cannot be dealt with as static givens. For example, the word *repentance* as used in the Scriptures involved a complete reorientation of life and thought. Later it came to involve reparations to the church for religious transgressions. In our contemporary (U.S.) culture it has to do with being sorry for misdeeds. Failure to recognize changes such as these results in the imposition of current meanings into the biblical text.

111

Many and voluminous volumes have been written on hermeneutics. As we have become more and more aware of the nature and influence of culture, questions having to do with cultural context, the supracultural/cultural distinction, and the like occupy more and more space in those volumes. We have done little more than touch on some of the rudimentary principles in the above paragraphs, but perhaps this is sufficient to challenge those who would communicate the gospel "away from home" to remember the importance of doing their "homework."

It is now possible to highlight the missionary communication task by constructing a hypothetical and greatly simplified scenario. Imagine the case of a missionary from New York who goes to Nagoya, Japan. His short-range objective will be to take the truths communicated in such biblical terms as *Theos, hamartia,* and *sōtēria*[11] and communicate them in terms of *Kami, tsumi,* and *sukui.*[12] Ideally he will encode these truths with as little intrusion of the North American cultural accretions attached to the terms "God," "sin," and "salvation" as possible. This is no easy task, for by virtue of his enculturation his understanding of "God," "sin," and "salvation" will tend to be culturally skewed. Only by dint of great effort has he begun to grasp the biblical meaning of *Theos, hamartia,* and *sōtēria.* And, unless he has undertaken special courses in Eastern religions and the Japanese language, he must start from scratch in the attempt to discover what the Japanese understand from the terms *Kami, tsumi,* and *sukui.*

Moreover, his long-range objective must be to encourage Japanese Christian converts to become "sources" and communicate Christ in culturally relevant terms within their own culture and in still other respondent cultures—Javanese culture, for example. In that culture, Japanese missionary "sources" will be called upon to communicate the meaning of *Theos, hamartia,* and *sōtēria* in terms of *Allah, dosa,* and

[11]The Greek words corresponding to God, sin, and salvation.
[12]The Japanese words corresponding to God, sin, and salvation.

keselamaton.[13] The way in which missionaries communicate Christian truth to Japanese in forms available within Japanese culture may have a salutary effect on the way in which Japanese missionaries present these biblical teachings to Javanese Muslims. After all, Allah is defined by the Javanese Muslim in such a way as to make the Incarnation impossible. Sin is defined in such a way as to make the Incarnation unnecessary. And as for salvation, Muslims view God as merciful and sovereign and are quite willing to let it go at that. Whether or not the Japanese missionary is prepared to deal with these cultural differences may well depend on the communication he has received from missionary tutors and models in Japan.

[13]The Javanese words corresponding to God, sin, and salvation.

Chapter 8

Christ and His Communicators Confront Culture

THE TENSION BETWEEN CHRIST AND CULTURE

Whereas, to a certain extent, theologians may enjoy the luxury of *thinking* about the relationship between Christ and culture without *working out* the implications of their conclusions, missionaries find this impossible. If missionaries are to have any influence at all, they will touch upon culture every time they speak and wherever they work. For better or worse (it depends on the viewpoint of the evaluator and the cultural sensitivity of the missionary) they are *agents of cultural change* in accordance with the commands of Christ (Matt. 28:20). It is important, therefore, that they have a biblical view not only of Christ but also of culture. They must recognize that every culture has elements of divine order *and* satanic rebellion; each has potential for the revelation of God's truth *and* for its concealment or mutilation. This merits further elaboration.

H. R. Niebuhr has categorized five views of the relationship between Christ and culture taken by various theologians:[1]

1. Christ *against* culture—i.e., Christ is the sole authority; the claims of culture are to be rejected.
2. The Christ *of* culture—i.e., the Christian system is not different from culture in kind but only in quality; the best of culture should be selected to conform to Christ.
3. Christ *above* culture—i.e., the reception of grace perfects and completes culture though there is not a "smooth curve or continuous line" between them.
4. Christ and culture in *paradox*—i.e., both are authorities to be obeyed and the believer, therefore, lives with this tension.
5. Christ as *Transformer* of culture—i.e., culture reflects the fallen state of humanity; in Christ, humanity is redeemed and culture can be renewed so as to glorify God and promote his purposes.

Neibuhr's analysis is very instructive and helpful if his categories are not taken to be rigid and their representatives are not considered to be antagonistic to one another in every case. The main problem with Neibuhr is that he puts Bible authors and writings at odds with one another. From a biblical point of view there seems to be some value in emphases that fall under categories one, four, and five and, quite possibly, three.

Using Neibuhr's categories and examples, David W. Meyers (then a student of cross-cultural communication at Trinity Evangelical Divinity School) constructed a chart that is helpful in visualizing the spectrum of positions taken vis-à-vis this tension between Christ and culture (see figure 6).

When God created the first man and woman and their environment, he pronounced everything "very good" (Gen. 1:31). God gave Adam and Eve a *cultural mandate*, which entailed rulership over their environment (Gen. 1:26–30). God, however, did not withdraw from the scene. Nor did he

[1]H. Richard Niebuhr, *Christ and Culture* (New York: Harper & Row, Harper Torchbooks, 1956).

116

cease to be God. Rather, he continued to provide for, and fellowship with, his creatures. How long that blissful state continued we do not know, but it was interrupted by the Fall. And the Fall left its mark on creation, creature, and culture (Gen. 3:14–19). Humanity's hope rested on the promise of the "Seed of a woman" who would bruise the Serpent's head.

Subsequently, humanity collectively failed as miserably as Adam and Eve had failed individually, with the result that God pronounced judgment upon man, beast, and land (Gen. 6:6–7). Following the Flood, Noah and his family received promises and a *social mandate* that was to apply to them and their progeny down through the generations (Gen. 8:21–9:17).

The significance of this simple and sublime story in the first chapters of Genesis must be carefully probed but can never be completely fathomed. It forms the basis of a theology of culture that is amplified throughout sacred Scripture. Humanity's relationship to God precedes and prescribes all other relationships. In this sense true religion is prior to culture, not simply a part of it. In listening to the usurper and choosing to disobey God, man invited the impress of sin upon all that he was and all that he touched. The Fall did not result in the eradication of the *imago Dei* in the creature nor in the countermanding of all cultural prerogatives. But it did interpose another and false authority over mankind and it did mar humans and their productions. Only under Christ can man be redeemed and our culture renewed.

The *gospel mandate* (Matt. 28:18–20) requires that missionaries teach other people to observe all that Christ has commanded. In teaching, missionaries touch culture—and happily so—for *all culture needs transformation in motivation if not in content.* If anything at all is apparent in our world, it is that God has *ordained culture* but does not *order man's cultures.* Satan is indeed "the god of this world" (2 Cor. 4:4). Therefore, as Calvin insisted, believers must work to make culture Christian (i.e., under Christ) or at least conducive to (i.e., allowing the maximum opportunity for) Christian living.[2]

Figure 6

CHRIST AND CULTURE*

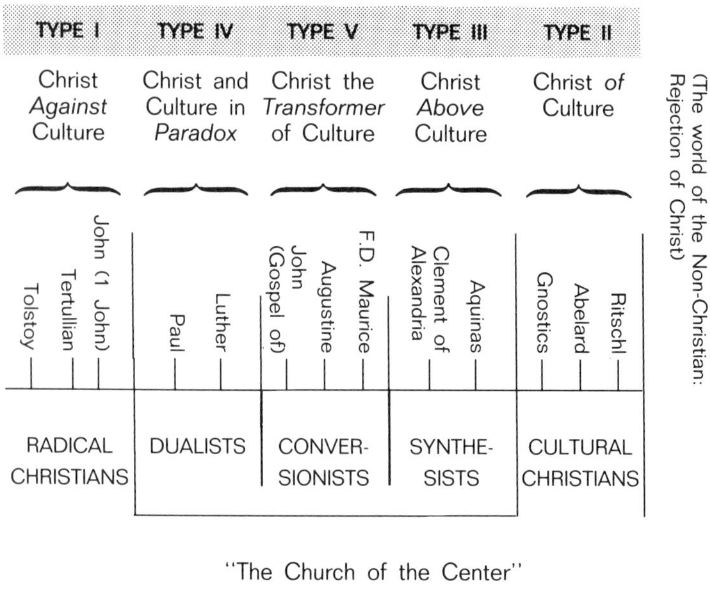

TYPE I	TYPE IV	TYPE V	TYPE III	TYPE II	
Christ Against Culture	Christ and Culture in *Paradox*	Christ the *Transformer* of Culture	Christ *Above* Culture	Christ *of* Culture	(The world of the Non-Christian: Rejection of Christ)

Tolstoy — Tertullian — John (1 John) | Paul — Luther | John (Gospel of) — Augustine — F.D. Maurice | Clement of Alexandria — Aquinas | Gnostics — Abelard — Ritschl

RADICAL CHRISTIANS	DUALISTS	CONVER-SIONISTS	SYNTHE-SISTS	CULTURAL CHRISTIANS

"The Church of the Center"

*Based on H. Richard Niebuhr, *Christ: and Culture,* (New York: Harper & Row Pub., 1956).

The Lausanne Covenant says it well:

Culture must always be tested and judged by Scripture (Mark 7:8, 9, 13). Because man is God's creature, some of his culture is rich in beauty and goodness (Matt. 7:11, Gen. 4:21, 22). Because he is fallen, all of it is tainted with sin

[2] Cf. Henry R. Van Til, *The Calvinistic Concept of Culture* (Philadelphia: Presbyterian and Reformed, 1959).

118

and some of it is demonic. The gospel does not presuppose the superiority of any culture to another, but evaluates all cultures according to its own criteria of truth and righteousness, and insists on moral absolutes in every culture.[3]

The missionary is involved in this process directly and indirectly. He may attempt to stay above the culture line and deal only with matters of the soul. But that effort is as hopeless as is the effort of the social scientist to eliminate God from his world and explain Christianity in cultural terms only. In the first place, the missionary cannot *communicate* without concerning himself with culture because communication is inextricable from culture. Just as Christ became flesh and dwelt among people, so propositional truth must have a cultural incarnation to be meaningful. In the second place, the missionary cannot communicate *Christianity* without concerning himself with culture because, although Christianity is supracultural in its origin and truth, it is cultural in its application.

CULTURE—THE HIGH VIEW

Because culture (not any particular culture, however) is ordained by a holy, all-knowing God, some missiologists take a very high view of culture. Because the various cultures in which they work are the products of sinful and erring humans, some missionaries take a very low view of culture. It is very easy to become imbalanced with respect to the culturally prescribed ways of thinking, feeling, and doing.

Most of Donald A. McGavran's books have had to do with church growth, an area in which he is one of the twentieth century's leading experts. As a result of controversy over the relative value that should be assigned to culture in mission theory, McGavran was motivated to write a book on the subject entitled *The Clash Between Christianity and Cul-*

[3] J. D. Douglas, ed., *Let the Earth Hear His Voice* (Minneapolis: World Wide, 1975), 6–7.

tures. In that book he attempts to resolve the "high-low" debate in a logical and biblical way.

For the Christian, the question comes down to choosing one or another of four possible positions:

1. A high view of the Bible and a low view of culture.
2. A high view of culture and a low view of the Bible.
3. A low view of the Bible and a low view of culture.
4. A high view of the Bible and a high view of culture.

McGavran urges missionaries to take the fourth option: a high view of the Bible and a high view of culture. By "high view of the Bible" McGavran means that the "entire Bible— the canonical Scriptures of the Old and New Testaments—is the Word of God. It is authoritative and demands faith and obedience to all its declarations."[4] By "high view of culture" he means that each culture is *reasonable* given the specific circumstances in which it has developed."[5] He goes on to explain that this does not mean that all the components of a given culture should be regarded as *right* but only that, provided we understand the situation in which they developed, they can be regarded as *reasonable*.

The "clash" to which McGavran is referring, then, is not between Christianity and culture as such, but between Christianity and the components of specific cultures. Taking the cultures of Nagaland in eastern India as an example (the majority of its fourteen tribes are Christians), he estimates that at least 95 percent of their cultural components "came into the Christian faith automatically."[6] The ways in which Nagas grow grain, cook their food, make their beds, settle their quarrels, and do myriads of other tasks represent no problem whatsoever. The 5 percent of the culture remaining divides up into three categories:

1. Some components are welcomed by Christianity as

[4]Donald McGavran, *The Clash Between Christianity and Cultures* (Washington, D.C.: Canon, 1974), 54.
[5]Ibid., 67.
[6]Ibid., 39.

especially wholesome and desirable—e.g., their custom of welcoming guests.
2. Some components Christianity changes or improves—e.g., the "boys' dormitory" used for informal education in tribal ways (enculturation) can be adapted in the new educational system.
3. Some components are unacceptable to God and must be abandoned—e.g., headhunting, and the paraphernalia and practice of idolatry and spirit worship.[7]

All of this is quite clear and straightforward. But, of course, it does not deal specifically with some of the more perplexing aspects of the "clash," such as the elements of the Lord's Supper and polygamy. McGavran does not shy away from these either. Knowing that it is common for those who take a lower view of Scripture and a high view of culture to insist that biblical *forms* can readily be dispensed with, provided the *functions* are retained, McGavran argues that in Communion it may be acceptable to adopt local substitutes for the biblical elements in areas where bread is not eaten and grapes are not grown, but not just any substitute will do (e.g., waving a white lily in a culture where this is part of memorial services) because the form of the elements should convey the idea of the "blood of the new covenant" and the "body broken for you."[8]

Again, knowing that it is common for those who take a lower view of the Bible and a high view of culture to argue that polygamy is not only acceptable but desirable even for Christian leaders in certain cultures (on the grounds that polygamy is found in the Bible and that in certain cultures polygamists are highly respected), McGavran takes issue with this contention. He says that polygamy is not *endorsed* in Scripture and that it is a social evil that could be rationally defended only when large numbers of men have been killed off in war. His solution is that, since there is no biblical proscription against baptizing polygamists, those who have

[7]Ibid., 40–41.
[8]Ibid., 64–65.

taken plural wives *before conversion* could be baptized. But the church should disallow polygamy among Christians. With tens of thousands of Africans (the problem of polygamy has been most pronounced in sub-Saharan Africa) coming into the church, monogamy will be the norm within a generation or so.[9]

These and similar tensions are not easily resolved. McGavran urges Christians to be tolerant of differing opinions concerning them. But at the same time, he insists that resolutions are *Christian* and workable only to the degree that they emanate from a high view of Scripture and a high view of culture. McGavran, of course, is not an anthropologist. He does not approach the problem of the clash between Christianity and cultures with technical precision and therefore is subject to criticism. He does approach the problem on the bases of broad missionary experience, a good deal of common sense, and commitment to an authoritative Bible, however; so his proposals are worthy of consideration.

CULTURAL RELATIVISM

No doubt Christian anthropologists make an important point when they say that the anthropological concept of "cultural relativism" is widely misunderstood among Christians in general and missions people in particular.[10] Anthropologists make a clear distinction between *ethical* or *moral* relativism and *cultural* relativism. Ethical relativism means that a given custom should be judged *only* on the basis of whether or not it makes a contribution to the ongoingness of the culture in question, not on the basis of some exterior standard of right and wrong. Cultural relativism as understood by discerning anthropologists, however, is something quite

[9]Ibid., 79–80.
[10]Cf. Charles H. Kraft, *Christianity in Culture: A Study in Dynamic Biblical Theologizing in Cross-Cultural Perspective* (Maryknoll, N.Y.: Orbis, 1979), 49–51. Kraft cites Marvin K. Mayers (*Christianity Confronts Culture*, Grand Rapids: Zondervan, 1974) for the insight that cultural relativity is at the cultural level while the Golden Rule is at the personal level.

different. It has to do with the validity of a custom in terms of its functional value within a culture and does not stipulate that culture is the sole determinant of what is right and wrong. Charles Kraft writes:

> "Cultural validity" is a doctrine developed by anthropology (ordinarily referred to as "cultural relativism") that maintains that an observer should be careful to evaluate a culture first in terms of its own values, goals, and focuses before venturing to compare it (either positively or negatively) with any other culture.[11]

Understood in this way, the doctrine of cultural relativity is not only defensible, it is also practical. Why? Because there is an almost universal tendency to judge other cultures on the basis of one's own culturally determined predispositions. Ways of thinking, feeling, and behaving in the new culture become good or bad, understandable or incomprehensible, and acceptable or ridiculous, depending on whether they are in accord with "our" (the evaluators') enculturated ways of thinking, feeling, and behaving. If missionaries yield to this tendency, they get off on the wrong foot and jeopardize the missionary enterprise. Judgment should be reserved until considerable effort has been expended with a view to understanding the respondent culture *on its own terms*. That kind of evaluation will be more difficult and time-consuming, but it will be more valid, sensitive, and constructive.

As can be inferred from the foregoing, if taken in its popular sense, the doctrine of cultural relativity is indefensible and unbiblical because it is popularly understood as ethical relativity, and that of a certain kind. C. S. Lewis strenuously opposes it in the following way:

> I know that some people say the idea of a Law of Nature or decent behaviour known to all men is unsound, because different civilizations and different ages have had quite

different moralities. But they haven't. They have only had *slightly* different moralities. Just think what *quite* different morality would mean. Think of a country where people were *admired* for running away in battle, or where a man felt *proud* for double-crossing all the people who had been kindest to him. You might just as well try to imagine a country where two and two made five. Men have differed as regards what people you ought to be unselfish to—whether it was only your own family, or your fellow countrymen, or every one. But they have always agreed that you oughtn't put yourself first. Selfishness has never been admired. Men have differed as to whether you should have one wife or four. But they have always agreed that you mustn't simply have any woman you liked.[12]

Lewis is correct, of course. But it should be noted that he is not dealing with the kind of cultural relativism that is espoused by Kraft and many other anthropologists.

ANALYZING THE RESPONDENT CULTURE

In the previous chapter I said that the best approach to understanding other cultures balances knowledge and experience. Traditionally, that has been the task of the ethnographer. Ethnography is "a method of describing a culture or situation within a culture from the 'emic' or native's point of view, i.e., from the point of view of the cultural actor."[13] This definition builds on a distinction made by the linguist Kenneth Pike between culture as it is seen, understood, and analyzed by an insider (the emic perspective) and culture as it is seen by the outsider who has examined more than one culture and therefore has a more "culture-free" perspective (the etic perspective).[14] Actually, this definition represents a

[12]C. S. Lewis, *The Abolition of Man* (London: Geoffrey Bles, 1946).

[13]Gail L. Nemetz Robinson, *Crosscultural Understanding* (New York: Pergamon, 1985), 73.

[14]Kenneth L. Pike, "Emic and Etic Standpoints of the Description of Behavior" in his *Language in Relation to a Unified Theory of the Structure of Human Behavior, part 1*, preliminary edition (Glendale, Calif.: Summer Institute of Linguistics, 1954), 8–28.

quantum leap forward on the part of ethnographers. It used to be that ethnographers tended to bring their own agenda (mainly in the form of questions) to the particular culture under consideration in order to get answers from within the culture. That that approach was helpful will be evident by reading a very short article that appeared in the 1950s entitled "Ethnographic Questions for Christian Missionaries."[15] In that article author Joseph Grimes proposes that upon entering a new culture missionaries ask questions designed to discover the person-to-person linkages by which news and gossip gets around the community, the ways in which decisions are made, the kind of people who are considered deviant or marginal in the society, and so forth. The relevance of this kind of information will become increasingly clear as we progress in this study. But at this point we should take note of the fact that contemporary ethnographers proceed differently. They say that when we bring our questions to the culture under consideration they are just that: *our* questions. That is, they are the kind of questions that are important to the ethnographer. But they may be quite different from the questions that are being posed *within* the culture. To the extent that this is so the ethnographic analysis will be skewed—i.e., it will reflect the interests and concerns of the ethnographer and his or her culture, but not those of the respondent culture.

The newer ethnographic perspective is reflected in several works now rather widely studied by missiologists, especially those of James P. Spradley.[16] Spradley explains that ethnographers combine formal training and field experience in such a way as to "learn from people" rather than "studying people."[17] Ultimately this means that they learn a culture by face-to-face participation with its members in their daily lives. Of course,

---

[15]Joseph E. Grimes, "Ethnographic Questions for Christian Missionaries," *Practical Anthropology* 6 (November–December 1959): 275–76.

[16]Cf. James P. Spradley, *The Ethnographic Interview* (New York: Holt, Rinehart and Winston, 1979); idem, *Participant Observation* (New York: Holt, Rinehart and Winston, 1980).

[17]Ibid., 3.

the ethnographer must take certain ethnographic tools into the culture in order to make the most of this participation. Spradley provides many of these tools by describing what is involved in contemporary ethnographic research. For example, in collecting data he begins with questions that make broad descriptive observations possible, proceeds to more in-depth and focused observations, and concludes with selective observations that will enable the ethnographer to search out certain "cultural themes." Again, Spradley details four types of analyses that will deepen the ethnographer's understanding of any particular cultural context (domain, taxonomic, componential, and theme analyses).

I highlight the current ethnographic approach, not because every missionary is going to be able to master the tools of the specialist, but because the very knowledge of their existence serves notice that the mere asking of a few questions that interest us (whether in interview, questionnaire, or ordinary conversation), though better than nothing, will yield only very tentative information about a culture. Much more is involved. Spradley himself can be criticized for vagueness when it comes to dealing with foundational culture-integrating entities such as worldview. Ethnographers do not have the last word, but they do have an important word—another word to which missionaries would do well to give ear.

TRANSFORMING CULTURE

Most missiologists/missionaries focus on conversion and changing *people* in the respondent culture. But not a few also focus on changing the culture itself. Some believe that the missionary is to aim at the transformation of people who will then automatically work for the transformation of their culture. But not a few also believe that the missionary is to keep the transformation of the culture itself in clear view while working for the transformation of people.

That cultures will change is not the question here. By virtue of pressures from within and/or without, cultures change as a matter of course. The question has to do with the *direction* of change and the part that missionaries ought to play in that change. Currently, more and more missiologists tend to describe the missionary as an "agent of change" and keep both people and culture in view when they use that phrase:

> . . . when the process of cultural transformation is engaged in by the people of God in partnership with God there is an aim, a direction to the change that is different from that of a transformational change motivated by some other set of factors. This aim is to increase the suitability of the culture to serve as a vehicle for divine-human interaction.[18]

This quotation from Charles Kraft can be fully understood only in the light of his view of contextualization (transculturation, as he terms it), which we will touch on in the next chapter. But it underscores a recurrent idea in missionary literature (also present in theological materials as my previous reference to Calvin attests)—namely, that the missionary should endeavor to make the respondent culture more conducive to Christian values and behavior. That is no small order. How should he or she go about it?

J. H. Bavinck suggests the way of *possessio*, which he describes in the following words:

> Within the framework of the non-Christian life, customs and practices serve idolatrous tendencies and drive a person away from God. The Christian life takes them in hand and turns them in an entirely different direction. Even though in external form there is much that resembles past practices, in reality everything has become new, the old has in essence passed away and the new has come. Christ takes the life of a people in his hands, he renews and reestablishes the distorted and deteriorated; he fills each thing, each word, and each practice with a new meaning and gives it a new direction.[19]

[18]Kraft, *Christianity in Culture*, 1979, 145.
[19]John Herman Bavinck, *An Introduction to the Science of Missions*, trans. David H. Freeman (Grand Rapids: Baker, 1969), 179.

While Kraft agrees with the idea of filling old cultural forms with new meaning, he takes issue with the use of the word "possession" which he believes smacks of the "God-against- culture" position and conveys the idea of approaching the culture from the outside and "capturing" it by force. Rather, missionaries should recognize that God is already at work in the culture; then they should enter the culture and work for change from within it. Something of what he has in mind becomes more clear when we look at his "principles for the outside advocate" (i.e., the missionary). First, missionaries must seek to understand the element to be changed from the point of view of the people. Second, they should encourage a minimal number of critical changes in the worldview rather than concentrating on a larger number of changes at the peripheral levels of culture. Third, they should seek out the opinion of leaders and work with them for change. Fourth, they should recognize the importance of *groups* of people to the change process and encourage "people movements" to Christ. Fifth, they should recognize that considerable time may be required to bring about lasting cultural change.[20]

By returning to the problem of polygamy we can illustrate what Kraft has in mind. In the Old Testament, polygamy was allowed among God's people early on, but by the time of the New Testament era and through a series of cultural changes it had largely given way to monogamous relationships. This becomes a kind of paradigm of cultural change for Kraft. Approached properly by the missionary, today's polygamous society can eventually become monogamous. But this need not occur to the accompaniment of the kind of disequilibrium, misunderstanding, and trauma that occurs when the missionary encourages the disowning of "extra" wives and presents monogamy as a requirement for church membership. Rather, the missionary needs to understand the worldview involved and that *from a polygamous cultural point of view* God is the kind of God who has ordained polygamy as a way of providing for the begetting of children, giving security to women,

[20]Kraft, *Christianity in Culture*, 1979, 360–66.

enhancing productivity, gaining prestige, and so on. The *cultural meaning* of an unthinking forcing of monogamy by insisting on the casting out "extra" wives and requiring monogamous relationships is that the "God of the missionary" is not interested in the begetting of children, the prerogatives and prestige of men, and so forth. In short, the God of the missionary is the "white man's God," who disrupts culture. If, on the other hand, the missionary focuses on the worldview rather than on the peripheral levels of culture and reinforces the fact that the Christian God basically supports the native way of life, favors social stability, enables people to live up to ideals, and wants people of every culture to evaluate their culture in the light of his ideals; if the missionary countenances such things as church membership and even leadership for polygamists at least on a temporary basis; and if the missionary is willing to wait for the "ripple" effect of changed concepts at the basic worldview level—then, change in the direction of God's ideal (monogamy) will ultimately occur. This is "Christian change" and is what is involved in "transforming culture with God."

If Bavinck has opened himself up to the charge of being too beholden to the "God against culture" position on Niebuhr's continuum (and the "low view of culture" in McGavran's schema), it would seem that Kraft has opened himself up to the charge of being too beholden to the "God of culture" and "high view of culture/low view of Scripture" positions. After all, God has now clearly revealed that his will for the church, and one of his requirements for church leadership, is the monogamous relationship (1 Tim. 3:2, 12). The missionary/pastor is charged with the responsibility of "commanding and teaching" this (1 Tim. 4:11 NASB margin). But Kraft is right in insisting that the missionary must "exegete" culture, not just the Bible. Only then can he disciple the nations by "teaching them to observe all that [the Lord] commanded" (Matt. 28:20) in a culture-sensitive way.

Chapter 9

Contextualization— Its Theological Roots

Unlike the meaning of *signs*, the meaning of *symbols* is not bound by their context. Nevertheless, context is very important in determining the meaning of symbols. The ancient rhetoricians were aware of its importance but gave little consideration to *cultural* contexts as such. The apostles were forced to come to terms with cultural differences as soon as the early church began to break out of the cultural and religious cocoon of Judaism. The church fathers were sensitive to it when they met in great ecumenical councils designed to preserve an orthodox faith on the one hand while allowing for a meaningful and persuasive communication of it in the contexts of pagan and unbelieving cultures on the other. Our modern missionary forebears focused on context when they discussed such topics as indigenization, adaptation, and accommodation. Recently, however, a word has been coined that encompasses just about all that our forebears had in mind (and likely more!) and that is constructed from the word *context* itself. That word is *contextualiztion.*

131

WHAT WORD SHALL WE CHOOSE?

There seems to be no ideal term for the process of adapting the Christian message to people of other cultures. J. H. Bavinck disdains the term *accommodation* (and, by implication, *adaptation* also?) because it "connotes something of a denial or a mutilation."[1] Whatever is indigenous to a culture is "rooted in" or "native to" that culture. The word *indigenization*, therefore, is perhaps misleading in that it connotes too much. The gospel, after all, is not native to any culture. *Inculturation*—"the process of disengaging the supracultural elements of the gospel from one culture and contextualizing them within the cultural form and social institutions of another, with at least some degree of transformation of those forms and institutions"[2]—may be a helpful term, but it assumes a common understanding of "contextualizing" and, in any case, has not achieved general usage. Bruce C. E. Fleming objects to the new term *contextualization*. He thinks that the word is so tainted by liberal theological presuppositions that it would be better to adopt the term *context-indigenization*.[3] James O. Buswell III accepts the term *contextualization* but feels that it does not necessarily represent an improvement on the older terms *indigenous, indigeneity,* and *indigenization* in every case.[4]

It seems that a fairly good case can be made for and against almost any word that we might choose. But perhaps we do not have to make a choice. It seems that the choice has been made for us. The word "contextualization" has already become so widely used in missiological and theological literature that we may as well "come to terms" with it! But in coming to terms with it we should know something of its

[1]John Herman Bavinck, *An Introduction to the Science of Missions,* trans. David H. Freeman (Grand Rapids: Baker, 1969), 179.
[2]Ibid., 178
[3]Bruce C. E. Fleming, *Contextualization of Theology: An Evangelical Assessment* (Pasadena, Calif.: William Carey, 1980), 60–67.
[4]James O. Buswell III, "Contextualization: Theory, Tradition, and Method," in David J. Hesselgrave, ed., *Theology and Mission* (Grand Rapids: Baker, 1978), 87–111.

inception and history. In *Contextualization: Meanings, Methods and Models*[5] Edward Rommen and I have attempted to deal with the background of, and approaches to, contextualization in more complete fashion. Here I can do no more than underscore some of the essentials.

THE GENESIS OF A NEW WORD

Whatever may have been the occasion of the very first usage of the word "contextualization," it made its public debut in World Council of Churches (WCC) circles. Back in the late 1950s the International Missionary Council (IMC) launched the Theological Education Fund (TEF) and gave it its first ("advance") mandate, which was to provide aid to certain theological schools around the world in the form of funds, textbooks, and facilities. The IMC became the Division of World Mission and Evangelism (DWME) of the WCC in 1961, and two years later it gave the TEF its second ("re-think") mandate designed to enhance theological education in the Third World by encouraging a reconsideration of culture-sensitive theologizing and communication. Specifically, it attempted to promote "a real encounter between the student and the gospel in terms of his own forms of thought and culture, and a living dialogue between the church and its environment."[6]

Recommendations to initiate and carry out a third ("reform") mandate in the 1970s was approved in 1969. The leaders of the reform mandate program were commissioned to help schools reform their training. What was involved was stated in the official documents:

> The determinant goal of its work is that the gospel be expressed and ministry undertaken in response to:

[5]David J. Hesselgrave and Edward Rommen, *Contextualization: Meaning, Methods and Models* (Grand Rapids: Baker, 1989).
[6]TEF Staff, *Ministry in Context: The Third Mandate Programme of the Theological Education Fund (1970–77)* (Bromley, Kent, England: The Theological Education Fund, 1972).

a) The widespread crisis of faith,
b) the issues of social justice and human development,
c) the dialectic between local cultural and religious situations and a universal technological civilization.[7]

During the 1970s the leaders of the TEF pressed forward toward the realization of this goal.

Meanwhile, much attention in wider WCC circles was given to the significance of the phrase "according to the Scriptures," which had been added to the brief doctrinal confession of the WCC at their meeting in New Delhi in 1961. Questions concerning the unity, authority, and relevance of the Scriptures came to occupy center stage. One such discussion was carried on at a consultation on "Dogmatic or Contextual Theology" held in Bossey, Switzerland, in 1971. In preparation for that consultation its chairman, Nikos A. Nissiotis, circulated a letter noting that the rise of technological society had the effect of leading to

a kind of "contextual or experiential" theology which gives preference, as the point of departure for systematic theological thinking, to the contemporary historical scene over against the biblical tradition and confessional statements constructed on the basis of the biblical texts, taken as a whole and thus used uncritically.[8]

Still another meeting in 1971—the meeting of the Faith and Order Commission (of the WCC) in Louvain, Belgium—wrestled with similar questions concerning the authority and relevancy of the Bible. It attempted to chart a course between a completely authoritative Bible on the one hand, and a Bible devoid of historical integrity on the other. The Louvain position was that by the authority of the Bible "we mean that it makes the Word of God audible and is therefore able to lead men to faith."[9]

[7]Ibid., 17–18.
[8]Quoted in Fleming, *Contextualization of Theology*, 6.
[9]"The Authority of the Bible—The Louvain Report," *The Ecumenical Review* 23 (October 1971), 434.

This very abbreviated historical background is indispensable to an understanding of what the originators of the term "contextualization" had in mind when they got around to define what it involved in the official documents of the TEF. Then the following statement was made:

> The third mandate's strong emphasis on renewal and reform in theological education appears to focus upon a central concept, contextuality, the capacity to respond meaningfully to the Gospel within the framework of one's own situation. Contextualization is not simply a fad or catch-word but a theological necessity demanded by the incarnational nature of the Word. What does the term imply?
>
> It means all that is implied in the familiar term "indigenization" and yet seeks to press beyond. Contextualization has to do with how we assess the peculiarity of third world contexts. Indigenization tends to be used in the sense of responding to the Gospel in terms of a traditional culture. Contextualization, while not ignoring this, takes into account the process of secularity, technology, and the struggle for human justice, which characterize the historical moment of nations in the Third World.
>
> Yet a careful distinction must be made between authentic and false forms of contextualization. False contextualization yields to uncritical accommodation, a form of culture faith. Authentic contextualization is always prophetic, arising always out of a genuine encounter between God's Word and His world, and moves toward the purpose of challenging and changing the situation through rootedness in and commitment to a given historical moment.[10]

SO WHAT DOES "CONTEXTUALIZATION" MEAN?

We must remember that very few words have inherent meaning. Words mean what their users say that they mean. It is apparent that, to its originators, "contextualization" con-

---

[10]*Ministry in Context*, 20.

veyed something new. To them it implied an understanding of the Bible as being, not the inspired Word of God per se, but that which makes the Word of God audible and inspires faith. To them it involved a new point of departure for theologizing—namely, the existential situation in which contemporaries find themselves rather than the Bible and creeds based on the biblical text. To them it meant a new approach to theologizing that involved, not so much wrestling with the text of Scripture to determine its meaning, but entering into the struggles of humanity at any historical moment with a view to discovering what God is doing and saying in that context. To them it meant communicating the gospel, not so much in terms of what God in Christ has done in past history in order to procure our salvation, but more in terms of living out the implications of the "gospel" of whatever we determine that God is saying and doing in our moment of history.

Of course, conservative evangelicals who hold to the position that the Bible is the historically accurate and fully inspired and authoritative Word of God have taken exception to this understanding. *But, for the most part, they have not rejected the concept of contextualization itself. Rather, they have infused it with a different meaning.*

For example, Byang H. Kato writes, "We understand the term to mean making concepts or ideals relevant in a given situation."[11]

Bruce J. Nicholls defines contextualization as "the translation of the unchanging content of the gospel of the kingdom into verbal form meaningful to the peoples in their separate culture and within their particular existential situations."[12]

George W. Peters says, "Contextualization properly applied means to discover *the legitimate implications* of the gospel in a given situation. It goes deeper than application. Application I can make or need not make without doing

[11]Byang H. Kato, "The Gospel, Cultural Context, and Religious Syncretism" in J. D. Douglas, ed., *Let the Earth Hear His Voice* (Minneapolis: World Wide Publications, 1975), 1217.

[12]Bruce J. Nicholls, "Theological Education and Evangelization," in Douglas, *Let the Earth Hear*, 647.

injustice to the text. Implication is *demanded* by a proper exegesis of the text."[13]

Harvie Conn writes that contextualization is "the process of conscientization of the whole people of God to the hermeneutical claims of the gospel."[14]

It is apparent from these definitions that conservative evangelicals have struggled to find a consensus. Certain key words in these definitions—relevant, meaningful, implications, and conscientization—reveal important differences. However, other key words and phrases—unchanging content, exegesis of the text, and hermeneutical claims—serve to underscore the fact that they do enjoy a consensus when it comes to questions concerning the starting point for evangelizing and theologizing, the content of the gospel, and the supreme authority for all matters of faith and practice. All are to be found in the Word of God written.

It is apparent, then, that theological presuppositions will in large measure determine both contextualization definitions and directions, both the meaning and the method of contextualization. Whatever disciplines might inform the way we actually think and go about the contextualization task—whether rhetoric, communication, anthropology, sociology, linguistics, or whatever—the bottom line will be theological. That is, insofar as the contextualization of the *Christian* message is in view, our theology will determine how we understand and go about the contextualization task and how we evaluate the contextualization attempts of others. Biblical theology in and of itself does not yield authentic and effective contextualizations. But *un*biblical theology cannot yield authentic contextualizations in the nature of the case.

[13]George W. Peters, "Issues Confronting Evangelical Missions," in Wade T. Coggins and E. L. Frizen, eds., *Evangelical Missions Tomorrow* (Pasadena, Calif.: William Carey, 1977), 169.

[14]Harvie Conn, "Contextualization: A New Dimension for Cross-Cultural Hermeneutics," *Evangelical Missions Quarterly* 14 (1978): 42.

CONTEXTUALIZATION—A BRIEF THEOLOGICAL ANALYSIS

Although this book is not focused on theology as such, the missionary message with which it is concerned is the *Christian* message. Therefore, all missiological proposals must ultimately be judged on a theological basis. This holds true for every contextualization attempt that claims to be Christian. We have already seen that contextualization as understood by the originators of the term is decidedly different from contextualization as subsequently understood by conservative evangelicals. Before we consider contextualization from a rhetorical perspective, theological differences merit further consideration.

Within theological circles at least four major and distinct schools of theological thought are everywhere recognized. At one end of the continuum is classical or traditional orthodoxy and at the other end is classical or traditional liberalism. Between them we can locate neo-orthodoxy and neo-liberalism.

1. The position of classical or traditional liberalism is that science has antiquated much of the Scriptures, which must now be judged in the light of higher critical studies. Its method is to adopt some current philosophy as a conceptual framework out of which it develops a doctrine of religious experience. It then proceeds to interpret this philosophy in Christian terms, altering Christianity itself in the process. Liberalism accepts all sincere striving after, and expressions of, truth as having validity.[15] Contextualizations growing out of this theological rootage, therefore, will tend to be syncretistic. That is, they will tend to "blunt" any and all claims to exclusive religious truth and "blend" the teachings of the various religions in such a way as to produce a common religious experience. The method that is often employed is interreligious dialogue between representatives of the various

[15]Bernard Ramm, "Liberalism," *Baker's Dictionary of Theology*, ed. E. F. Harrison (Grand Rapids: Baker, 1960), 322.

religions. (Look again at the emphasis on dialogue in the TEF approach to contextualization and know that what is being proposed is not the kind of dialogue one finds in the Scriptures. Biblical dialogue was more of an encounter and often ended in disputation. The dialogue proposed in the TEF document eschews disputation and presupposes some kind of unity from the beginning.)

There are numerous instances of this kind of "dialogical contextualization." One occurred in a WCC-sponsored consultation in Ajaltoun, Lebanon, at about the time when theological discussions that gave birth to the contextualization concept were in progress (March 1970). Called a "Dialogue Between Men of Living Faiths," it brought Christians, Buddhists, Hindus, and Muslims together for ten days of discussion and (voluntary) corporate worship. The outcome as expressed by one member of the consultation was as follows:

> The dialogue, functioning as an internal sign of hope, introduced most of us to a new spirituality, an interfaith spirituality, which I mostly felt in common prayer: who actually led the prayer or meditation, a Christian or a Muslim, or a Hindu, or a Buddhist, did not much matter, what actually was said during prayer was not all important, whether a Muslim would say "amen" after a Christian prayer mentioning the sonship of Christ, was not the question, what we really became aware of was our common human situation before God and in God.[16]

This is certainly a radical type of contextualization, but it is in keeping with its rootage in traditional liberalism. The *context* is an interfaith meeting. The *method* is to pursue (new) truth by nondisputational dialogue. The *result* is a (new) syncretistic "gospel" and a (new) interfaith spirituality.

2. At the other end of the spectrum is classical or traditional orthodoxy. Carl F. H. Henry says the "historical

[16]Stanley J. Samartha, "Dialogue Between Men of Living Faiths, the Ajaltoun Memorandum," in S. J. Samartha, ed., *Dialogue Between Men of Living Faiths* (Geneva: World Council of Churches, 1971), 114.

Christian view" is that "the Bible itself is a form of revelation specially provided for man in sin as an authentic disclosure of the nature and will of God."[17] Orthodoxy identifies the autographs of the canonical Scriptures with revelation. *All* of the Bible is the Word of God and among the world's so-called holy books *only* the Bible is the Word of God. Because of their commitment to this view, orthodox believers adhere to doctrines that are biblical even though unwelcome to the natural mind, such as the lostness of humanity, redemption by the blood of Christ, the necessity of conversion, and so forth. Not only that, such believers are committed to the task of communicating the biblical gospel to the whole world.

One will not have any difficulty in finding biblical examples of contextualization as defined by the conservative evangelicals mentioned above. As the apostles were made more and more aware of the scope of the ministry enjoined by the Lord Jesus in the Great Commission, they became more and more aware of the necessity of cultural adaptation (cf. Acts 15). Of all the apostles, Paul was most expert in this by virtue of his education and biculturalism. Numerous illustrations can be given of his ability to adjust to local cultures, whether in Antioch of Pisidia (Acts 13:41), Lystra (Acts 14:6–17), Athens (Acts 17:22–31), or elsewhere. But in spite of the fact that Peter ministered primarily to the Jews and Paul to the Gentiles, they preached the same gospel (Gal. 2:7–10). And despite the fact that Paul's messages display important cultural adjustments, at the heart of all of them was the one gospel (Gal. 1:11–12).

This kind of contextualization, then, can be called "apostolic." The context is that of (largely) pagan and unbelieving cultures. The method is didactic—"teaching them to observe all that I [the Lord Jesus] commanded you" (Matt. 28:20). It results in spiritual transformation of those who repent and believe so that they live out the implications of the gospel.

---

[17]Carl F. H. Henry, "Revelation, Special," *Baker's Dictionary of Theology*, ed. E. F. Harrison (Grand Rapids: Baker, 1960), 459.

3. For our purposes here we can deal with neo-liberalism and neo-orthodoxy together. This does not mean that the differences between the two schools are inconsequential. Neo-liberalism tends to take the Bible more seriously and judges culture more critically than does classical liberalism but leaves it up to specially perceptive people to approach both the Scripture text and the cultural environment in such a way as to see beyond the deficiencies of both, discover God's *contemporary* word and work, and join him in "saying" and "doing."

Neo-orthodoxy is distinct from liberalism in that it holds that the Bible is more than good or even great literature, and it does not assume a continuity between the human and the divine. It is distinct from orthodoxy because, even though it holds to the uniqueness of Scripture and to some of the important Reformation doctrines, it holds that the Bible contains the Word of God in imperfect form because of its human authorship. It depends on a *contemporary* work of the Spirit—a current and existential "inspiration"—to make the Bible become the Word of God or to make the Word of God in Scripture "audible."

Neo-orthodoxy and neo-liberalism, then, are different in their approaches and can be very different in their conclusions. The former gives more emphasis to the Holy Spirit while the latter emphasizes the "human spirit." But they are similar in that their biblical prototype is the prophet who hears and delivers a word from the Lord vis-à-vis a given historical situation. In the dialectic of human situations the divine Word is discerned and delivered. This is "prophetic contextualization." Its *context* is that of human aspirations and struggles. Its *method* is dialectical. And it *results* in a conjoining of the words and work of God and those of the contextualizer so as to bring about spiritual and/or social change.

Although it is difficult to characterize in a few words the TEF type of definition of contextuality as the "critical assessment of what makes the context really significant in the light of the *missio Dei*," its emphasis on the dialectic between contextuality and contextualization seems to betray either

141

neo-orthodox or neo-liberal rootage.[18] The "liberation theologies" that have sprung up in various parts of the world furnish us with illustrations of "prophetic" contextualizations of this type. Theologically, then, contextualizations can be analyzed in terms of the theological rootages from which they emanate. Although these theological rootages differ in a variety of respects, one of the most important differences has to do with the way in which Scripture is viewed. The Bible is the product of human authorship and divine inspiration. Its contents are both cultural and supracultural. Do the human and cultural elements so permeate that whole as to result in a book that is something less than the very Word of God? Or did God so control the processes of inspiration and inscripturation that the Bible is God's Word and that which is divine and supracultural is not impaired by human authorship and cultural considerations? Those on the liberal end of the continuum believe that the presence of human and cultural elements result in a Bible that is something less than the completely authoritative Word of God. Those on the orthodox end of the continuum believe that such a conclusion is at odds with the testimony of the Bible and of the Lord himself. They believe that, just as Jesus was sinless even though human and divine, so the Bible is errorless (in the autographs) even though "human and divine," cultural and supracultural. How far one goes in either direction on the continuum will to a large extent determine meanings and methods of contextualization (see figure 7).

Before proceeding, then, let me express my understanding of contextualization. In an attempt to give indication of orthodox theological rootage while avoiding what seems to be some of the unnecessary limitations of certain conservative evangelical understandings, I define contextualization as follows:

---

[18]Shoki Coe, "Contextualizing Theology," in G. H. Anderson and T. F. Stransky, eds., *Mission Trends No. 3*, (Grand Rapids: Eerdmans; New York: Paulist, 1976), 21–22.

Figure 7

THE CONTEXTUALIZATION CONTINUUM

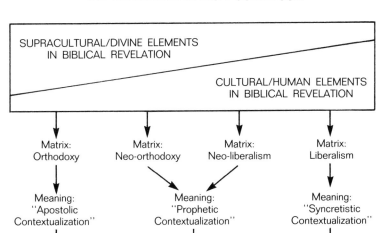

| SUPRACULTURAL/DIVINE ELEMENTS IN BIBLICAL REVELATION |
| CULTURAL/HUMAN ELEMENTS IN BIBLICAL REVELATION |

Matrix: Orthodoxy	Matrix: Neo-orthodoxy	Matrix: Neo-liberalism	Matrix: Liberalism
Meaning: "Apostolic Contextualization"	Meaning: "Prophetic Contextualization"		Meaning: "Syncretistic Contextualization"
Method: Didactic— "Teaching truth"	Method: Dialectic— "Discovering truth"		Method: Dialogic— "Pursuing truth"

David J. Hesselgrave and Edward Rommen, *Contextualization: Meanings, Methods and Models* (Grand Rapids: Baker, 1989), p. 157. Used by permission.

. . .contextualization can be thought of as the attempt to communicate the message of the person, works, word, and will of God in a way that is faithful to God's revelation, especially as it is put forth in the teachings of Holy Scripture, and that is meaningful to respondents in their respective cultural and existential contexts. Contextualization is both verbal and nonverbal and has to do with theologizing; Bible translation, interpretation and applica-

143

tion; incarnational lifestyle; evangelism; Christian instruction; church planting and growth; church organization; worship style—indeed with all of those activities involved in carrying out of the Great Commission.[19]

---

[19]Hesselgrave and Rommen, *Contextualization*, 200.

Chapter 10

Cross-Cultural Communication— Classic Categories and Paradigms

Some very basic concepts have informed communication studies for about 2,500 years and homiletical studies for over 1,500 years. Every student of public speaking and preaching deals with the *speaker* (preacher), *speech* (sermon), *audience*, and many other categories that were bequeathed to us by the ancient rhetoricians of Greece and Rome as a matter of course. Being of necessity much more culture-bound than their twentieth-century counterparts, the ancients nevertheless worked out complex communication strategies that constitute a formidable challenge to both understanding and practice. When a person becomes acquainted with them and then is faced with the challenge of applying them interculturally, he is tempted to throw up his hands and yield to one or another piece of common advice. Either he subscribes to the old cliché "When in Rome do as the Romans do" (as though that is an easy way out!) or he decides to follow Polonius' advice to Hamlet as he was being sent off to another culture: "This above all, to thine own self be true"—in other words, "Just be yourself." There are times when both of these bits of

145

homespun wisdom apply, but as a general approach neither will get one very far unless one is merely sightseeing!

For those crossing cultural boundaries to communicate Christ and the gospel, the best advice is to learn as much of the new culture as possible and apply as much as possible to their communication efforts. Actually, most of what they learned in their own culture will be applicable but it will have to be augmented by new (cross-cultural) understandings. For example, we have already seen how those older categories (speaker, speech, and audience) have given way to cybernetic categories (source, message, and respondent) in this age of mass communication. We have also seen that the older categories have been augmented by (essentially) new terms and concepts such as encoding and decoding. Similarly, when we cross cultural boundaries, familiar categories need to take on new understandings, and new categories and concepts need to be mastered.

The rhetoricians of Greece and Rome focused on some very basic concepts that, as I have said, have informed speech communication studies for 2,500 years and homiletical studies for over 1,500 years. Classical concepts having to do with content, organization, style, argumentation, audience analysis, and so forth are still basic to intracultural and cross-cultural communication studies today. But they do take on new understandings, especially in cross-cultural communication. In this chapter we will deal with some of the basic concepts of classical rhetoric and demonstrate how an updated application of them might inform cross-cultural communication and contextualization. In the next chapter I will introduce an entirely new and expanded paradigm. Then in chapter 12 we will focus on audiences (respondents, receptors) from a cross-cultural perspective. These treatments will not be detailed or complete, but only suggestive and introductory to part 3.

THE *SPEAKER* OR *SOURCE* OF THE MISSIONARY MESSAGE

Let us remember that although missionaries have been commanded by Christ to preach the gospel, they cannot command a hearing. *They must win a hearing by demonstrating that they are people of integrity, credibility, and goodwill.* How do they do this?

First, they demonstrate these characteristics by developing such qualities as empathy, acceptance, and trust. Wayne O. Shabaz of W. Shabaz & Associates, Inc. in Fraser, Michigan, went to Iran as an engineer prepared to make his contribution in the area of engineering technology. As things turned out, he has made a great contribution by training thousands of Americans representing United States multinational companies overseas how to relate to host cultures and nationals. Without the kind of training that Shabaz and his associates provide, overseas Americans often discover that it is impossible to build the kind of interpersonal relationships that are essential to carrying on effective business relationships. Interestingly enough, Shabaz—who is an evangelical Christian—has discovered that the attitudes and qualities that enhance interpersonal relationships are precisely those that Scripture prescribes for the Christian believer. In simple terms, such qualities as love, patience, humility, peaceableness, and so on will go far toward establishing the kind of relationships that make it possible for nationals to really hear our message!

Second—and closely related to the previous point—when appropriate, the missionary should be willing to admit his own spiritual need for mercy and grace. Self-exposure is not out of order. Even the missionary (!) is a sinner saved by grace and subject to the weaknesses and temptations that afflict all sons and daughters of Adam. We must remember that millions of the world's peoples have never seen a "sinner" in the biblical sense of that word. Their own worldview does not really allow for such a category. And when the missionary comes to them, he comes as a "saint" who is somehow better than others. He comes as a "religious person" whose record of past sins has been wiped out and whose present sins are as invisible as the missionary can make them—unless, of course, he assumes the posture of the apostle Paul who wrote, "What then is Apollos? And what is Paul? Servants through whom you believed" (1 Cor. 3:5).

Third, missionaries must be prepared to deal with false systems of religion and philosophy, not primarily at the points of their weaknesses, inconsistencies, and inadequacies but at the points of their strength. Examples of strength are numerous. The contributions of Buddhism to the arts of China and Japan are a matter of record. The attraction of Hindu inclusivism in a divided world is incontrovertible. The fascination with which many view mysticism and transcendental experiences is evident in the West as well as in the East. The fact that adherents of Taoism are much more appreciative of the world around them than are many Christians who ostensibly accept that world as a gift of the Creator is plain to see. We must learn to deal with the best case that the nonChristian can make, not with the weakest case, lest we succeed only in pricking balloons and knocking down straw men. *To deal honestly and sympathetically with the best case that any form of false belief can make, and then show the desperate need that still remains to be met by the true God and his redeeming Son—this is the more excellent way.*

Finally, we should give consideration to the respondent culture and the ways in which it defines such things as integrity, credibility, and goodwill. We may or may not "measure up." We may or may not be able to accommodate it. But in any case we should understand it. From a rhetorical point of view still other considerations are important, however. Note the following paragraph from Condon and Yousef:

As a general principle the ethos of the speaker may universally be the most important factor in persuasiveness. However, what constitutes good *ethos* is not necessarily universal. Again the value orientations will give the best guidance for discovering the ideal ethos of a particular culture. In many societies age will be crucial: The best ethos may accrue to one who is over sixty or under forty. Sex may be crucial: In many societies women are believed to be competent to speak only of women's matters. Family background, achievement, education, relation to the military, religion, and more are likely to be constituents of ethos. As these will differ from culture to culture, their influence in intercultural communication should be obvious.[1]

THE *CONTENT* OF THE MISSIONARY MESSAGE

The Christian message is universal. It is for all people irrespective of race, language, culture, or circumstance. Some have therefore naïvely assumed that this ends the matter. If one knows what the gospel is, all that remains is the motivation to deliver it. There is, of course, "one Lord, one faith, one baptism, one God and Father of all" (Eph. 4:5–6).

But without betraying that unique message in any way, the gospel writer and preachers of the New Testament demonstrated a remarkable variegation in their communication of it.

Return to the examples of Christ, Peter, and Paul. In each case communication included a pointed reference to the basic spiritual need of people in their natural state of sin and alienation from God. In each case, however, this universal need was contextualized somewhat differently. Nicodemus had had but one birth; the Samaritan woman was practicing immorality and false worship; Peter's audience at Pentecost had delivered Christ to be crucified; Cornelius and his friends needed to know that remission of sins was available by believing in the name of Christ; the congregation of the synagogue in Antioch of Pisidia needed to beware lest they refuse the very One of whom the prophets had testified and whom the Father had appointed as Savior; and the Greeks of Athens needed to know that the true God would no longer overlook their ignorant worship now that he had raised Christ from the dead.

We conclude, therefore, that while certain general statements can be made concerning the substance of the gospel

---

[1]John C. Condon and Fathi Yousef, *An Introduction to Intercultural Communication* (Indianapolis: Bobbs-Merrill, 1975), 246.

(e.g., 1 Cor. 15:1–9) and the spiritual need of people as sinners (e.g., Rom. 3:9–18), the communication of these truths in specific situations involves "content contextualization" in terms of definition, selection, organization, and application. 1. *Definition.* One of the disastrous aspects of human sin was that man did not retain God in his knowledge. As a result his understanding has been perverted in precisely those areas where divine revelation is crystal clear. The true God is excluded, but false gods abound. People distinguish between good and evil in some way, but not in accordance with the biblical view. A majority of people believe themselves to be immortal in some sense of the term, but the forms of immortality vary greatly. Geoffrey Bull's reflections on presenting Christ to Tibetan Buddhists illustrates the point well.

The expansion of the Tibetan language came with the growth of Buddhist philosophy; thus words used often represent two distinct concepts. We take up and use a word in Tibetan, unconsciously giving it a Christian content. For them, however, it has a Buddhist content. We speak of God. In our minds this word conveys to us the concept of the supreme and Eternal Spirit, Creator and Sustainer of all things, Whose essence is Love, Whose presence is all holy, and Whose ways are all righteous. For them, the Tibetan word god means nothing of the kind. We speak of prayer, the spiritual communion between God our Father and His children. For them prayer is a repetition of abstruse formulae and mystic phrases handed down from time immemorial. We speak of sin. For them the main emphasis is in the condemnation of killing animals.

When I was at Batang I saw an open-air performance of a Buddhist play. One of the chief sins depicted there was the catching of fish. When I asked the special significance of the "transgression" I was told, "Oh, fishes mustn't be killed, they can't speak," meaning, I presume, that they utter no sound. It is a common sight to see a man, when killing a yak, at the same time muttering his "prayers" furiously. Gross immorality is also condemned by the most thoughtful lamas, but rarely publicly. We speak of the Saviour. They think of Buddha or the Dalai Lama. We speak of God being a Trinity. They will say: "Yes, god the buddha, god the whole canon of Buddhist scripture, and god the whole body of the Buddhist priesthood." We speak of man's spirit being dead in sin and his thus being cut off from God. They cannot understand. A person, they say, is only soul and body. What do you mean by the third concept, a man's spirit? When a man dies, they believe his soul escapes by one of the nine holes in his body; we know nothing of his spirit, they say. We speak of a revelation from God, His own Word which we are commanded to believe, and they know no word but the vast collection of Buddhist sayings, which only one in a thousand even vaguely understands. Those who have studied them believe that only in the exercise of the human intellect, in meditation and contemplation over a very long period, can one begin to enter into the deep things of the "spirit." What "spirit" though, perhaps few of them realize.

We, of course, speak of the Holy Spirit as a gift of God to the believer in Christ. They say, "What nonsense! As if a man could obtain the Holy Spirit as easily as that." Of course, I would point out the other aspect; that it is not so much our possessing the Spirit, as the Spirit possessing us. On acceptance of Christ the believer is born of the Spirit, yet it may be but slowly that He will obtain full sovereignty of the heart and will. This is dismissed as being contrary to the concept of God being a Spirit. We speak of the Almighty power of God and yet of man being responsible to Him, particularly in his acceptance or rejection of His way of salvation. I was told this was a "lower doctrine," cause and effect as a fatalistic law being widely propounded by the lamas.[2]

The missionary who takes the Fall seriously, then, must stop to define his terms. Which terms? Those terms indicated by the distance between divine truth and cultural error. *The definitional process must proceed by comparison and contrast.* If this process seems too painstaking for the Western

[2]Geoffrey Bull, *When Iron Gates Yield* (London: Hodder and Stoughton, 1976), 97–99.

missionary who is used to instant everything—from instant cake to instant coffee—so be it. But he should know that to build Christian conversion on non-Christian foundations is like building skyscrapers on sand. The mission fields are well populated with men and women who have been ushered into the heavenlies without knowing why they got on the elevator. Once back on earth they have no intention of being taken for another ride.

2. *Selection.* On any given occasion, the missionary delivers only a partial message. Christ commanded us to teach people to observe *all* that he commanded (Matt. 28:20), but he did not command us to do it in one sitting! Many evangelists who travel to another culture attempt to communicate all of the essentials of the gospel in a thirty-to-forty-minute message with hardly a clue as to what the audience is actually decoding. For the average adherent of some other religion, this approach results in information overload and may result in a gross *mis*understanding of the gospel. The evangelist has selected too much—and too little!

As we boarded the plane for Bangkok, Thailand, to attend the Consultation on World Evangelization almost a decade ago now, Dr. Saphir Athyal of India handed me the manuscript of a lecture he had prepared for that consultation with the request that I read it and offer suggestions. Feeling inadequate for such an assignment, I was reticent to comply until urged to do so. The lecture was based on Paul's message to the Athenians in Acts 17. As it turned out, my suggestions were minimal and relatively unimportant—except for one. Buried in a footnote that was in mortal danger of being overlooked at Pataya was an all-important statement that deserved a better fate than burial in a footnote!

In that footnote—but later in the body of his address— Dr. Athyal stated his conviction that Bible translators and missionaries make a great mistake when they initially select a single Bible book for translation or choose just any appealing text for use in evangelizing. He emphasized that the Gospel of Mark, for example, can be understood only in the context of the larger revelation and that to grasp the meaning of the gospel one needs to understand its antecedents in the Old Testament. He called attention to the fact that in speaking to the Athenian philosophers Paul painted the larger picture first and then focused on Christ.

Little did Dr. Athyal realize that his would become but one voice in a growing chorus of mission specialists who would call for a significant change in the selection process when it comes to cross-cultural translation, evangelism, and instruction. As we will see in the introductory chapter on worldview, perceptive translators and missionary communicators are now highlighting those texts from Genesis to Revelation that will provide the framework into which individual Bible books and teachings can be placed and appreciated. This approach should be viewed as something of a universal in missionary communication.

Specific cultures will provide special clues for the selection process. For example, in the Hindu-Buddhistic or Taoist contexts, there is little point in attempting to demonstrate the sinfulness of people initially by showing that we are liars. Where all propositional statements (and especially those of a religious nature) are mere approximations, lying becomes *in one sense* a necessary concomitant of communication itself! But selfishness and covetousness are already matters of great concern. Is there any *biblical* ground for labeling these fundamental human weaknesses as sin? There most assuredly is such a basis. Then we can *all* agree that selfishness and covetousness are indeed evil. And we can point out how God looks upon these evils and deals with them.

The missionary does well to answer problems posed but not answered in the false systems. When problems of an otherworldly nature were put to Confucius, he answered very matter-of-factly that he hardly understood this world and should not be expected to know about another world. On the basis of their own worldview, Communists are hard-pressed to give a satisfactory answer as to why extreme sacrifices should be made by the present generation for the generations yet unborn. Many Hindus must recoil in utter despair when faced with the seemingly numberless existences required to effect their final emancipation from the wheel of existence. Christ has real answers for these problems if only his ambassadors will deliver them.

Selection also requires that we answer objections that respondents can be expected to raise vis-à-vis the Christian message. The literature of Nichiren Buddhism, for example, makes much of the point that a person who knows the truth will die peacefully and with happiness apparent in his very facial expression. That Christ died on a cross while raising the anguished cry, "My God, my God, why has thou forsaken me?" (Matt. 27:46 KJV) raises for these Buddhists a serious question as to whether Christ himself knew the truth. A brief apologetic *before* the problem is articulated will go far to disarm the objector.

Finally, the missionary should be alert to watch for special entries ("points of contact," "redemptive analogies," and "eye-openers") to non-Christian systems. When Don Richardson became acquainted with the Sawi "peace child" ritual, he had discovered a "bridge" for gospel communication to the Sawi people.[3] Apart from painstaking teaching, the "hero" of the gospel story would have been Judas because of the value that the Sawi placed on deception and treachery! And without an acquaintance with the larger Bible "story," the story of God's "Peace Child" Jesus most likely would have been squeezed into the mold of their own pagan myth. But a creative use of the Sawi "peace child" ritual opened the door to gospel communication among the Sawi. In attempting to communicate the gospel to those of the Chinese culture, it would be well to remember the words of Confucius and Lao-tzu. Confucius said:

A holy man I shall not live to see; enough could I find a gentleman! A good man I shall not live to see; enough could I find a steadfast one! But when nothing poses as something,

[3]Don Richardson, *Peace Child* (Glendale, Calif.: Regal, 1974).

154

cloud as substance, want as riches, steadfastness must be rare.[4]

Lao-tzu said that "he who bears the sins of the world is fit to rule the world."[5] These quotations furnish the Christian communicator with communication opportunities that should not be overlooked.

3. *Organization*. How does one organize content? How many points are there in a "good" sermon? Should the most important points come first or toward the end? Questions such as these have occupied the attention of rhetoricians and homileticians for centuries. But in cross-cultural communication they are given a new twist.

Condon and Yousef point out that organization is largely a matter of cultural preference.[6] The Anglo-American mode of effective speechmaking is to make a few points (quite often three) and to enumerate these as 1, 2, 3. The pattern of organization will usually be as follows:

I. First conclusion (or generalization)
   A. Reason and support (or proof)
   B. Reason and support
   C. Reason and support
II. Second conclusion (or generalization)
   A. Reason and support
      etc.

A speaker presenting only generalizations and abstractions without specific illustrations and arguments will be thought of as boring and his speech as theoretical and divorced from daily life. A speaker who presents only details and examples will be judged as not "getting to the point." Generalizations and specifics must be in balance, and the former will usually precede the latter.

These authors point out that this type of organization

[4]"Selections from the Analects," in *Readings in Eastern Religious Thought*, ed. Ollie M. Frazier, 3 vols. (Philadelphia: Westminster, 1963), 3:74.
[5]*The Book of Tao*, trans. Frank J. MacHovec (Mt. Vernon, N.Y.: Peter Pauper, 1962), Sutra 78, 17.
[6]Condon and Yousef, *An Introduction*, 240–42.

may be understandable to a Japanese audience but will probably be recognized as foreign. The usual Japanese speech takes one of two forms:

I. Abstraction or Generalization
II. Abstraction or Generalization
III. Abstraction or Generalization
or
I. Specific Point
II. Specific Point
III. Specific Point

This may seem enigmatic to us until we understand the Japanese thought process involved. If the speaker has good ethos and is a recognized authority, specific proofs and support are not needed. And if not everyone understands, maybe so much better. He becomes even more of an authority. If he moves from specific points to generalizations, this may insult the audience because they are expected to make the connection. (It perhaps should be added that this depends somewhat on the makeup of the audience, however.)

Condon and Yousef could have gone on to deal with organization among tribal audiences. Generally speaking, tribal audiences respond better to a limited number of abstractions or generalizations (one may do!) embellished with a number of illustrations or examples (often narratives) that view the main idea from a variety of angles (not so much to *prove* it, however). A typical speech or sermon may take one of the following forms:

Generalization
A. Specific Illustration or Example
B. Specific Illustration or Example
C. Specific Illustration or Example
D. Specific Illustration or Example
or
A. Specific Illustration or Example
B. Specific Illustration or Example
C. Specific Illustration or Example
D. Specific Illustration or Example
Generalization

Too many generalizations will tend toward information overload. But it is almost impossible to provide too many examples! Although unnoticed in most discussions on content, it is still true that "different cultures have preferences and tolerances for different forms of organization and support."[7]

4. *Application.* As is the case in all communication, the missionary message becomes most compelling when it ceases to be general and becomes personal. We are not in the final analysis speaking to worldviews but to the minds and hearts of people of flesh and blood who live out these worldviews in their decisions and actions. Can we make the message of Christ compelling to *them?* We can and we must. It is in application that we say, "Thou art the man" (2 Sam. 12:7 KJV).

For example, depending on one's presuppositions, the strict form of Shankara's illusionist philosophy may be logically unanswerable, but it is practically unreal. All people—including devotees of Shankara's illusionism—live their lives in a real world and can be expected to feel the tension of asserting the unreality of that with which they must come to grips in one way or another every day. Christ dealt with broken bodies, broken hearts, empty stomachs, and empty souls just as Indians would like to deal with them if they had his resources!

Of course, ultimately the Holy Spirit must apply the Word. Geoffrey Bull illustrates that truth in his illustration of a Tibetan Buddhist military governor who refused to be moved by the most obvious refutation of his own faith.

> I was surprised how even a man like the Dege Sey believed in reincarnation. There was rather an amusing incident. He was saying to me how they had to be very careful, for even one of the domestic animals might be his grandmother. I was about to make some mildly humorous comment as to the general treatment of dogs in Tibet, when the words were taken out of my mouth and far more eloquent sounds

[7]Ibid., 241.

fell on our ears. From the courtyard came the piercing squeals of some pitiful canine, which had just been either kicked or battered with a brick bat. The Dege Sey, generally quick to see a joke, sat quite unmoved. Incarnation as a doctrine itself is readily accepted by the Tibetans, but when we assert there is but one incarnation of the Living and True God, "The Word made flesh," it is totally unacceptable to them.[8]

If application is a function of knowledge, it is also a function of faith. It is not according to the usual bent of human nature to admit that one is wrong or to agree with God that we are sinners—especially helpless sinners whose only hope is in divine grace. When God's truth is faithfully and lovingly applied, however, there will be a response throughout Adam's race if that truth is presented intelligently and in dependence on the Spirit.

THE STYLE OF THE MISSIONARY MESSAGE

From their rather limited perspective, the ancients viewed correctness, clarity and appropriateness as primary elements of style. Style can best be thought of as the personal imprint of the source upon his message. Style is that part of missionary communication in which the source's understanding of his respondent culture, his powers of imagination, and his skill in the manipulation of symbols are given rein and can be put to great service for the kingdom.

A few illustrations from the culture the author knows best must suffice. To contemporary Japanese much missionary communication (as reflected not only by missionaries but by national pastors and workers who often simply duplicate Western patterns) must seem to exhibit a great lack of style, though it is not so much a lack of style as a foreignness of style that is at the root of the problem. There are numerous aspects of the Judeo-Christian worldview *as it has come through the Western mold* that must stamp missionary

[8]Bull, *Iron Gates*, 63.

communication as un-Japanese. Some of these would be directness, brusqueness, matter-of-factness, lack of awe, absence of a sense of mystery, oversimplification, narrow scope of interest, aloofness from everyday concerns, and insensitivity to the feelings of the audience.

The Japanese with his multireligious outlook does not admit of easy analysis. He reflects Lao-tzu's feeling that silence best befits true wisdom and that feelings take precedence over facts. Yet he would also concur with Lao-tzu in not opposing speaking out, or even speaking persuasively, provided the speech is suited to the audience and serves the end of peace. He reflects Confucius' interests also: the practical and earthly approach to the questions of life; a tenacious hold to traditional wisdom; and an emphasis on relationships. He reflects Gautama Buddha's conviction that truth is not easily discerned and that nothing is quite as important as the inner vision. And above all he reflects the awe and reverence toward the "*kami*-aspect" (divine aspect) of natural phenomena and the human family that *is* Japan.

I first became intensely aware of much of the above during a series of evangelistic meetings in Urawa, Japan. God's servant during those days was Pastor Ryoun Kamegaya—a converted Buddhist priest who was well known in Japan and an extremely effective communicator of the gospel of Christ. As a small group of us walked down the street and headed out across the rice paddies one day, it became apparent that something within Pastor Kamegaya reached out in profound appreciation for the simple beauties of nature that surrounded us as the sun settled behind the soft clouds in the western sky. The cherry blossoms with their ever-so-delicate pinkness were the special objects of his fascination. Sensing this, one Japanese youth made a move to pick a small branch—something rarely done in that esthetic land. Quickly the *Sensei* raised his hand, saying, "Please . . . let them be." His would-be benefactor stopped short and in an apologetic tone explained that he wanted just a few for the *Sensei*'s room. Pastor Kamegaya smiled, thanked him, and added, "You must understand that they are the gift of my heavenly Father. Since

159

he has given me all things in Christ, they are mine. I prefer to keep my blossoms right there on the tree."

In that moment I inherited what was for me a new insight. Because I was a rather typical American, my esthetic sense required a large bouquet of flowers (the larger the better!) conspicuously placed at the center of some table. Only gradually had I learned to appreciate the beauty of a few flowers in a flower arrangement suggestive of the whole world, or some part of it in its own place in the house. But Kamegaya *Sensei* had taken us beyond that. With him this was indeed his Father's world in an arrestingly practical and yet profound sense. His style in that peripatetic school on the streets of a Japanese city had been, I suddenly realized, his style in the pulpit during those meaningful evangelistic meetings. It was little wonder that he had so effectively communicated the greatness of God, the grace of Christ, and the wealth of true Christians. This was beyond the West and beyond the East. It was biblical Christianity. What made it important was that God had said it. But Kamegaya *Sensei* had repeated it and in a way that most effectively communicated Christ to the Japanese. *That* is style, and *that* is Christian communication.

Chapter 11

Cross-Cultural Communication— Contemporary Categories and Paradigms

Just as electronic models have informed intracultural communication, so a variety of disciplines focused on culture and cultures have informed the categories and paradigms of cross-cultural communication theory. This time the new rhetoric ("comparative rhetoric" and "ethno-rhetoric") has been quick to take advantage of the findings of these various disciplines. Some still think and write from perspectives largely informed by Western culture, albeit Western culture in its larger dimensions. I. A. Richard's approach to literary criticism[1] and Kenneth Burke's "dramatistic paradigm" of rhetorical analysis[2] are examples of this. But Robert Oliver's "idea systems" approach to cross-cultural communication demonstrates a profound familiarity with worldviews and comparative religions.[3] John F. Condon and Fathi Yousef deal

---

[1]I. A. Richards, *A Philosophy of Rhetoric* (New York: Oxford University Press, 1936).

[2]Kenneth Burke, *A Grammar of Motives and a Rhetoric of Motives* (Cleveland: World, Meridian, 1962).

[3]Robert T. Oliver, *Culture and Communication* (Springfield, Ill.: Charles C. Thomas, 1962).

extensively with the implications of anthropological categories such as functions and value systems.[4] Leonard Doob builds on a wide variety of African studies in writing his classic *Communication in Africa*.[5] Karl Potter deals perceptively with the impact of the "self-image" of Asian civilizations on communication with Asians.[6] Many other illustrations could be given of the ways in which modern intercultural theory has been influenced by the theories and findings of the various cultural disciplines. At its best, contemporary intercultural communication theory is informed by all of them but taken captive by none of them.

This brings us to the particular paradigm of cross-cultural communication used in part 3 of this book. Years ago at a time when I was doing doctoral research on Buddhist propagation approaches in Japan, I was struck again with Kenneth Burke's words, "You can persuade a man only insofar as you can talk his language by speech, gesture, tonality, order, image, attitude, idea, identifying your ways with his."[7] Those words had seemed challenging enough when I first came across them in the context of my own culture. Now as I became aware of how well they applied to the propagation materials of Nichiren Shoshu Soka Gakkai Buddhism (at the time, far and away the fastest growing of Japan's numerous "new religions") they became more challenging than ever. It was at that point that, out of years of study and hands-on experience, I began to develop a paradigm and approach to the study and practice of cross-cultural communication that is truly eclectic, incorporating information and insights from a wide variety of disciplines and studies, but always focused on questions having to do with communication.

The approach was first introduced (as far as religious

---

[4]Condon and Yousef, *An Introduction*, passim.

[5] Leonard Doob, *Communication in Africa* (Westport, Conn.: Greenwood, 1979).

[6]Karl Potter, "The Self-Image Approach, " in William Theodore de Bary and Ainslee T. Embree, eds., *Approaches to Asian Civilizations* (New York: Columbia University Press, 1964), 273–75.

[7]Burke, *Grammar of Motives*, 579.

journals are concerned) in *Practical Anthropology*.[8] It is elaborated in part 3 of this book. At this point it is introduced in outline form so the student may get a "handle" on it before dealing with detail.

THE "SEVEN DIMENSIONS" OF CROSS-CULTURAL COMMUNICATION

Let us begin with a diagram designed to help us visualize the cross-cultural communication process (see figure 8).

When the source in "culture X" encodes a message, that message passes through a cultural grid or screen that is largely determinative of the way in which that message will be decoded by the respondent in "culture Y." This grid or screen has seven dimensions that collectively influence the message and the way in which the respondent will decode the message. This grid is like a cake-decorating tool, or the cutting discs in a meat grinder. No message can travel *around* it but only through it. Inevitably it leaves its marks (configurations) on that which passes through it.

Two factors that are determinative of how much of the original message gets through are the respondent's understanding of "culture X" and the source's understanding of "culture Y." In other words, to the extent that the respondent understands the worldview, cognitive process, etc., of the source and decodes the message in terms of that understanding, the original meaning of the message will be preserved. Or, to the extent that the source understands "culture Y" and encodes his message in terms of that culture, the original meaning of the message will likely be preserved in the decoding process.

Since missionaries have undertaken the responsibility of delivering the Christian message across cultural boundaries, the responsibility for achieving cultural understanding and initiating the process of contextualization rests on them. This

[8]David J. Hesselgrave, "Dimensions of Cross-cultural Communication," *Practical Anthropology* 19 (January–February 1972): 1–12.

means that the missionary needs to learn to communicate Christ to respondents in terms of their (the respondents') way of viewing the world, their way of thinking, their way of expressing themselves in language, their way of acting, their response to media, their way of interacting, and their way of deciding future courses of action. These dimensions interpenetrate and impinge upon one another. They are separable for pragmatic purposes, but, of course, combine to form one reality.

Figure 8

DIMENSIONS OF CROSS-CULTURAL COMMUNICATION

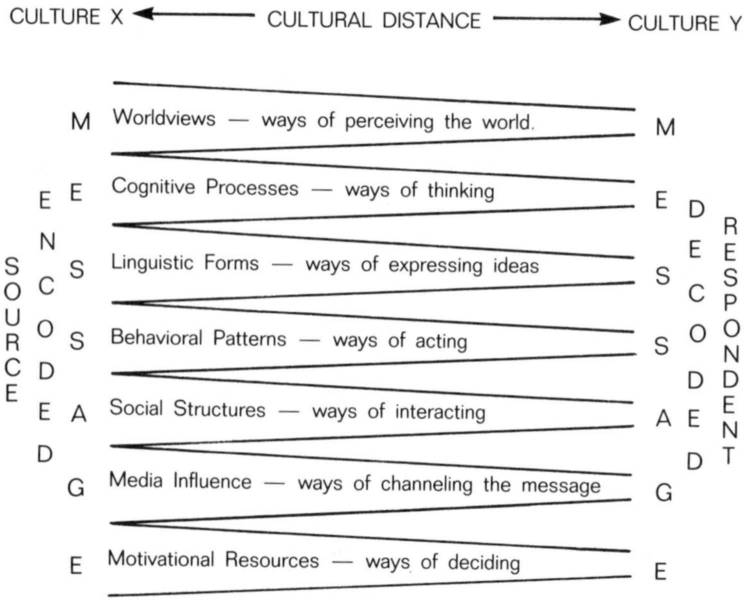

CULTURE X ◄─────── CULTURAL DISTANCE ───────► CULTURE Y

M	Worldviews — ways of perceiving the world.	M
E	Cognitive Processes — ways of thinking	E
S	Linguistic Forms — ways of expressing ideas	S
S	Behavioral Patterns — ways of acting	S
A	Social Structures — ways of interacting	A
G	Media Influence — ways of channeling the message	G
E	Motivational Resources — ways of deciding	E

SOURCE ENCODED

DECODED RESPONDENT

1. Worldviews—ways of perceiving the world. No one sees the world exactly as it is. Each one sees it through the

tinted glasses of his own worldview.[9] Now the fact is that most people neither carefully evaluate their own particular worldview, nor meticulously interpret messages that come to them from sources with other worldviews in terms of those worldviews. In other words, few people take off the glasses of their own worldview to examine them. And perhaps still fewer people decode "cross-worldview" messages in the light of—or by "putting on the glasses of"—the message source. For example, *atman* has been translated into such English words as "soul," "mind," "spirit," and "self." But, in the final analysis, not one of these words correctly conveys the meaning of the word *atman*. Nor do all of them together. One must understand *atman* within the context of the Hindu worldview. The same principle holds when one attempts to convey the Christian meaning of "soul" to Hindus. The word *atman* will not do unless it is explained in the light of the Christian worldview.

Obviously, if *respondents* are not disposed to exchange glasses in order to decode cross-cultural messages correctly, *sources* must assume the responsibility of encoding messages with the worldview of the respondents in mind.

2. Cognitive processes—ways of thinking. Studies show that the ability to think clearly is a function of social and educational opportunity rather than of ethnic origin. All normal people of all cultures have the ability to think. But they think differently. By that I do not mean that they entertain different ideas and arrive at different conclusions, though that is often the case. I mean that people in different cultures tend to arrive at conclusions through differing thought processes.

For example, most missionaries will agree with the Hindu notion that the mystery of divine reality eludes the mystery of speech and symbol. But the fundamental question is not whether there is a sense in which that notion is true. Rather, the question is this: Does true knowledge of God come

[9]Cf. Norman Geisler, "Some Philosophical Perspectives on Missionary Dialogue," in Hesselgrave, *Theology and Mission*, 241–57.

primarily through subjective experience or objective revelation?

Here again, the missionary must do more than *hope* that Indians will understand the ground of Christian truth. He must *help* them understand. But, humanly speaking, that is possible only as he himself takes the Hindu way of thinking into account when communicating Christ.

3. Linguistic forms—ways of expressing ideas. Of all the seven dimensions of cross-cultural communication, language is the one that is the most obvious and the one with which the missionary is best prepared (in terms of awareness) to cope. But language is more important than many missionaries realize.

Languages tend to reflect that which is important in a given culture. For example, European languages reflect the primary importance of time in Euro-American culture. A man was, is, or will be sick. Languages that by virtue of their grammatical structures do not require this distinction between past, present, and future may seem strange to Westerners. But they are instructive at the very point of their strangeness.

"Learning the language," then, means more than learning enough of the receptor language to transliterate English sentences into it. Languages constitute veritable gold mines of information about the people and cultures that employ them.

4. Behavioral patterns—ways of acting. William S. Howell has asserted that "the Ugly American award is won more often by failing to meet expectations of appropriate behavior than by misusing the local language."[10] Whether the newcomer to a neighborhood visits others or waits for them to visit him, the ways in which one receives guests and gifts, public behavior vis-à-vis members of the opposite sex—thousands of such items are matters of cultural definition. Since they are learned informally for the most part, they are seldom pondered and justified. They simply constitute ways in which people "ought" to act.

[10]Class in intercultural communication, University of Minnesota, 1964.

To be sure, as a Christian the missionary cannot accept all the behavior patterns of any given culture. At certain critical points "behaving as a Christian" will mean that one is "behaving incorrectly" according to cultural definition. But there is nothing inherently wrong with the great majority of cultural ways of doing things. "Christian" or "un-Christian," correct or incorrect—an inventory of cultural behavior, therefore, is essential for the missionary who would communicate Christ.

5. Social structures—ways of interacting. Men and women not only have ways of *acting* according to accepted codes of codes of conduct, they also have ways of *interacting* on the basis of where they fit in the social structure. The conventions of social structure dictate which channels of communication are open and which are closed; who talks to whom, in what way, and with what effect; and when one communicates which type of message.

By way of example, consider the familiar story of Jesus and the Samaritan woman in John 4. Given some knowledge of the societal arrangements and relationships in that time and place, we can understand why they met at a well, why the woman expressed surprise when Jesus spoke to her, and why it was particularly unusual that he would ask a favor of her (cf. v. 9). Moreover, we can make some educated guesses as to why the woman went to the men in the city and invited them to investigate the claims of Christ (cf. v. 29).

A "map" of societal arrangements is also a portrayal of communication. Missionaries should no more think of communicating Christ in a society without a societal map than they would think of motoring through a country without a road map!

6. Media influence—ways of channeling the message. In times past the emphases in communication have been on sources and respondents, the contexts in which messages are sent and received, and the messages themselves—their content, organization, and style. Recently we have become increasingly aware of the fact that the media that are used to transmit messages are by no means neutral. First, they affect

the message in the transmission of it. Second, in one sense, they themselves constitute messages.

Take, as an obvious example, the case of a missionary who enters an illiterate society with the objective of reducing the language to writing, teaching literacy, translating the Bible, and establishing a Christian church. Very little imagination is required to realize that the difference between the spoken and the written word will be a major factor in communicating Christ in that culture. But beyond that, think of the tremendous changes that will be set in motion with the introduction of written messages!

Missionaries tend to think of media in simplistic terms such as message availability, audience size, and interest factors. Far more is involved, as we will see.

7. Motivational resources—ways of deciding. The missionary who communicates Christ presses for a verdict as did his first-century counterparts, the apostles. Of course, people of all cultures have to make many decisions. But again, the ways in which people of various cultures think of decision making and the ways in which they arrive at decisions are very diverse.

Think, for example, of the case of the American missionary who presents a Chinese with the opportunity to receive Christ. If the decision is *for* Christ, the missionary will be elated and grateful. But imagine his disappointment when sometime later, the Chinese convert does an about-face and evidences a lapse of faith. The response of the missionary is predictable. But it never occurs to him that his Chinese "disciple in the rough" may be simply reflecting the philosophy of Confucius (not because he is Confucian but because he is Chinese) who said, "The superior man goes through his life without any one preconceived course of action or any taboo. He merely decides for the moment what is the right thing to do."

To point out the problem is not to argue for the correctness of Confucian, or Chinese, or American approaches to decision making. Rather, it constitutes a plea for understanding and preparedness.

CULTURAL DISTANCE

At Lausanne in 1974 Ralph Winter categorized cross-cultural evangelism as being E-1, E-2, and E-3 evangelism.[11] (Later, the category E-0 evangelism was added.) These categories denote differences based on the degree of "cultural distance" between the evangelist or missionary and respondents in another culture. The difficulty encountered in any particular instance of evangelism (or communication more widely conceived) is directly proportional to the degree of difference between the two cultures involved. Winter's idea was both perceptive and important because in these days of rapid transportation and instantaneous communication geography does not present anything like the barrier to communication that culture does.

On our seven-dimension diagram (figure 8), cultural distance is indicated in terms of narrowing "funnels" between the missionary source and the respondent. The greater the cultural distance in any of the dimensions, the greater the impact or impingement on the message, how it should be encoded (contextualized) and how it will be decoded (interpreted).

By expanding Winter's scale and applying the scale to each of the seven dimensions, it is possible to make quantitative as well as qualitative judgment as to the extent of cultural distances between any two cultures. One who has training and experience should be able to investigate differences between culture X and Y and assign values corresponding to the degree of "distance" in each of the seven dimensions. The sum of these values, then, represents the order of difference between the two cultures and serves as an indicator of the degree of difficulty that one might expect to encounter in communicating across that particular cultural boundary (see figure 9).

Take the case of some candidates and furloughing missionaries representing various fields as they sat side by side in

[11]Ralph D. Winter, "The Highest Priority: Cross-cultural Evangelism," in J. D. Douglas, ed., *Let the Earth Hear His Voice* (Minneapolis: World Wide, 1975), 213–25.

a seminar on church planting and development. As the discussions proceeded, it became apparent that two missionaries, one from France (Missionary A) and the other from the Philippines (Missionary B), shared problems occasioned by the cultural difference between France and the Philippines on the one hand, and the United States on the other. Neither missionary had special training in cultural studies or communication before going to the field. Their furlough studies had opened their eyes to many aspects of culture and communication that shed new light on their past experiences. Problems that in the field situation had been but partially understood now came into much clearer focus. Solutions that had not even occurred to them now seemed quite obvious. Together they plotted new approaches and strategies. As they did so, they became increasingly involved in a friendly argument as to who faced the most difficult task.

Missionary A from France worked in a predominantly middle-class small town outside of Paris. The distance was just far enough to discourage commuters, though there were some regular commuters in the town. Almost all of the families in that community were nominal Catholics, but only a small percentage showed much interest in church (or indeed in religion in general) except on "solemn occasions." At first the townspeople had been very distant and seemed suspicious of the uninvited American Protestant missionary who had taken up residence among them. But by dint of a real effort to be friendly and by the persistent use of the French language, the missionary had broken down some of the barriers. Subsequently, a number of young people, two "part families" (both wives), and three whole families had joined the church.

The experience of the missionary to the Philippines was quite different. He had taken up residence in a new section of Manila that could best be described as upper class. Few residents had been in the area for more than four or five years and each week witnessed the arrival of more newcomers. A rather high percentage had ties with the Roman Church, but interest in the American missionary family, their cultural background, and spiritual message had been noticeable from the first. The evangelical church with which Missionary B worked had gained a great deal of strength and now numbered over one hundred members, including ten or fifteen whole families. Missionary B had learned enough Tagalog for ordinary conversation but used English almost exclusively in the church meetings.

Figure 9

CULTURAL DISTANCE

	1	2	3	4	5	6	7	8	9	10
Worldview										
Cognitive Process										
Linguistic Form										
Behavioral Pattern										
Social Structure										
Media Influence										
Motivational Influence										

Total Distance _____

Missionaries A and B defined the *purpose* of missionary communication as the winning of people to faith in Christ and the discipling of converts so that they would be faithful and fruitful members of evangelical churches. Then they compared and contrasted the degree of difficulty their respective

171

target cultures presented to *effective* communication in each of the seven dimensions. When they had completed their comparison by completing the cultural distance scale, it looked like figure 10.

Figure 10

CULTURAL DISTANCE
FRANCE AND THE PHILIPPINES COMPARED

	1	2	3	4	5	6	7	8	9	10
Worldview					B/P			A/F		
Cognitive Process					B/P	A/F				
Linguistic Form			B/P				A/F			
Behavioral Pattern						B/P A/F				
Social Structure					B/P	A/F				
Media Influence						B/P		A/F		
Motivational Resources				B/P				A/F		

TOTAL CULTURAL DISTANCE:

Missionary "A" in France   49

Missionary "B" in Philippines   33

Notice that by adding up the total degrees of distance in the seven dimensions, the cultural distance in the case of Missionary A in France was 49 on the 70-point scale, whereas for Missionary B in the Philippines it was only 33.

It may be objected that this procedure is so general and

subjective as to render it pointless if not misleading. The objection is understandable. Culture and communication being as inclusive as they are, it would certainly be impossible at our present stage of knowledge to propose a standard of comparison that would be completely objective and universally productive. But if the tentative nature of the evaluations is recognized and if a limited number of *particular* cultural contexts are compared in terms of effective communication, the exercise may be profitable.

This can be demonstrated from the case above. The cultural distance in these cases was greatly influenced by the importance of the French language in the French village as over against the relative unimportance of Tagalog in the Manila community. Another factor was the difference between French and Filipinos in openness toward new ideas from the outside. Missionaries and candidates alike were challenged by the idea that missionary communication might be easier in Manila than in Paris. The evaluators benefited by adding item after item to their catalog of relevant factors in cross-cultural communication. All were encouraged to discover that so many diverse factors, which through the long months of study had seemed so unrelated, could be brought together in a meaningful, interrelated whole that was manageable and made sense.

This idea of a quantitative analysis of cultural difference may be premature, though it seems to have potential for the future.[12]

[12]By making this statement I do not mean to disregard the work of George Murdock and others who have pioneered in providing standards for cultural comparisons. All I am saying is that the quantification of the relative difficulty of communicating Christ across cultural boundaries must be tentative.

Chapter 12

Respondents of Other Cultures

It is a truism, of course, that we do not communicate with other *cultures*. We communicate with *persons* (audiences, respondents, receptors) of other cultures. Before rhetoricians have done with their task of discovering the "available means of persuasion"—or evaluating any such attempt—they will have made a careful analysis of the target audience in terms of the degree of their knowledge, interest, hostility, and much else. Among ancient rhetoricians Aristotle analyzed audiences in terms of their character, emotional state, age, and "gifts of fortune." Cicero distinguished various kinds of "hostile" audiences and suggested ways of making audiences receptive.

Experts in missionary communication also emphasize the importance of respondent analysis. James Engel does so in the belief that the audience is "sovereign."[1] We may argue with his choice of words because ultimately the Holy Spirit is sovereign in missionary communication. But the point that Engel is making is a valid one. Charles Kraft says that the "key

---

[1]James F. Engel, *Contemporary Christian Communication: Its Theory and Practice* (Nashville: Thomas Nelson, 1979), 46ff.

participant" in missionary communication is the receptor and that missionary communication should be "receptor-oriented."[2] When we realize that in Kraft's understanding the biblical text *becomes* divine revelation in the existential context of "impactful" communication, we may refrain from following him too far in this direction. Nevertheless, we are instructed by his analysis.

In this chapter, then, I want to underscore the fact that as we proceed to discuss the various dimensions of cross-cultural communication in part 3 we are not simply discussing cultures as such, we are discussing people enculturated in the worldviews, ways of thinking, language, etc., of those cultures. In a real sense, then, as we discuss dimensions of cross-cultural communication, enculturated respondents as well as respondent cultures and communication perspectives are in view. In what follows here we will deal with some aspects of audience analysis that are introductory to part 3: identification with respondents, respondent activities, and respondent response (especially in relationship to gospel communication).

CROSS-CULTURAL IDENTIFICATION

Kenneth Burke proposes that we view our whole world as being engaged in a search for unification. Communication represents the apotheosis of that search. Identification is the means of achieving unification. The philosophical basis of identification is "consubstantiality," by which term Burke means the sharing of "properties" such as sensations, images, ideas, feeling, attitudes, and the like. The strategy of identification is to give signs of consubstantiality (signs indicating that while we are separate individuals, we have a basic oneness) by means of logical, ethical, and emotional proofs, enthymemes, examples, figures of speech, gesture, etc. Insofar as we identify with a person by means of these strategies, we

[2]Charles H. Kraft, *Communication Theory for Christian Witness* (Nashville: Abingdon, 1983), 89ff.

can persuade him. In other words, we can enlist him in a common cause with us. Burke says, "You persuade a man only insofar as you can talk his language by speech, gesture, tonality, order, image, attitude, idea, identifying your ways with his."[3] Paul demonstrated his willingness and ability to adjust to his audiences in his sermons,[4] and he explained the basis for this approach when he wrote to the Corinthians:

> And to the Jews I became as a Jew . . . ; to those who are under the Law, as under the Law . . . ; to those who are without law, as without law . . . ; to the weak I became weak . . . ; I have become all things to all men, that I may by all means save some (1 Cor. 9:20–22).

These classic words are often used by missionaries to justify diverse *methods* of reaching people for Christ. But that is certainly a misinterpretation. Paul was referring to his *one basic method* of communicating the gospel. He put himself in the position of his respondents whether they were Jews or Gentiles, under the law or without law, weak or strong. There was a very real sense in which he could identify with each group, and identify he did!

In our own day Eugene Nida has pointed out that full-orbed missionary communication requires a high degree of identification. He attempts a correlation between degrees of identification and levels of communication as follows:

1. The first level of communication is one in which the message has no significant effect on behavior and the substance of the message is essentially self-validating. For example, if someone says that two and two make four . . . no one is particularly concerned that the source

---

[3]Burke, *Grammar of Motives and a Rhetoric of Motives* (Cleveland: World, Meridian, 1962), 579.

[4]Donald Robert Sunukjian, *Patterns for Preaching—A Rhetorical Analysis of the Sermons of Paul in Acts 13, 17, and 20* (Th.D. dissertation, Dallas Theological Seminary, 1972).

should psychologically identify himself with the receptor. . . .

2. In the second stage of communication, there is a message which, though it has no permanent effect on a man's total value system, does affect significantly his immediate behavior. For example, if a man says that a flood is sweeping down on the town because a dam has broken, the receptors want to make sure that the source identifies himself with his own message—namely, that he also is making preparations to leave town. . . .

3. On the third level of communication, the message not only concerns a large segment of a person's behavior, but also his whole value system. If, for example, someone insists that a man should abandon his carefree way of life, settle down, marry, and raise a family; or if he tries to convince another that he should repent of his sins, become a Christian, and lead an entirely different type of life . . . in addition to identification with his message, he must also demonstrate an identification with the receptor; for the receptor must be convinced that the source understands his, the receptor's, particular background and has respect for his views, even though he may not agree with them. . . .

4. There is, however, still a further and deeper level of communication, namely one in which the message has been so effectively communicated that the receptor feels the same type of communicative urge as that experienced by the source. The receptor then becomes a source of further communication of the message. This level involves "[entrusting a message] to faithful men, who will be able to teach others also" (2 Tim. 2:2). For this level of communication, it is necessary that the receptor be identified in turn with the source. In this last stage of communication the identification is complete.[5]

[5]Nida, *Message and Mission: The Communication of the Christian Faith* (New York: Harper & Row, 1960), 164–66.

The missionary is, of course, engaged in all four levels of communication. But it will be immediately apparent that his main concern is with levels three and four. Theorists and practitioners—both secular and religious—have faced us with a tremendous challenge. To those who might object that a myriad of books could be written on any target audience were such proposals to be followed, we have two reminders. First, the fact that the whole world could not contain all the books that could have been written about Christ did not prevent the evangelists from writing the gospels. Second, the fact that omniscience is unattainable to man is no argument for ignorance. More than any other communicator, the Christian missionary should have the incentive to discover all he can about the people he desires to win for Christ—the way they think, speak, act, evaluate, and decide—and the remote and contemporary background factors that have molded their present state.

RESPONDENT ACTIVITIES

Respondents in other cultures have the "last word" in any communication situation. The are not passive "tablets" on whom the missionary communicator inscribes his message. Rather, they are active interpreters and "responders" to his message. In the final analysis, they will decide whether or not they will listen or read the message; how they will understand it; and what they will do about it. It is understandable therefore that theorists highlight such things as the needs, status, values, and associations of respondent people.

As missionaries prepare to communicate to people of other cultures, Kraft encourages them to keep seven "activities of receptors" in mind:[6]

1. Interpreting. Respondents interpret everything that is said and done as parts of the "message."

2. Constructing meanings. Meaning is constructed by

[6]Kraft, *Communication Theory*, 97–105.

receptors on the basis of their interpretations of words and other communicational symbols.

3. Granting or withholding permission for the communicator to enter their "communicational space." This decision is made on the basis of such things as the range of tolerance to religious messages, the credibility of the missionary, and the acceptability of the language used.

4. Evaluation. Respondents are constantly evaluating every aspect of any given communication event.

5. Maintaining equilibrium. A person's relationship with his or her reference group will often be a major consideration when considering conversion and change. Threats to community solidarity, personal acceptance, security, and other needs will be important factors in receptor reactions.

6. Providing feedback. This respondent activity is always of special importance to the communication source and should be the object of special study in cross-cultural situations where cues may be different. Foreign audiences may be enculturated in such a way that they give outward approval and even commendation while inwardly rejecting the message.

7. Decision making. Having engaged in the foregoing activities, the receptor must ultimately decide what to do about the message.

RESPONDENT RESPONSE

Christ calls for a decision. The gospel presents more than an offer of forgiveness and an invitation to participate in the new life. It also makes demands on its hearers. On Pentecost, when Peter's convicted hearers asked what they should do, the answer was unequivocal: "Repent, and let each of you be baptized in the name of Jesus Christ" (Acts 2:38). As Paul concluded his message to the Athenians he said, "God is now declaring to men that all everywhere should repent" (17:30).

That people must do something in order to take advantage of God's provision of salvation through Christ does no violence to the doctrine of grace. Theologically as well as etymologically there are *two* aspects of *charis* (grace): unmerited provision *and* thankful reception. Faithful to the etymology of the word, we use the word "grace" in English to apply to both aspects. First, we usually define "grace" as "unmerited favor," calling attention to the fact that God's offer of salvation is apart from works of merit on our part. Second, we use the word to refer to the prayer of thanksgiving that precedes the eating of a meal. To "say grace" in this context means to thankfully acknowledge God as the Provider of our food. Thus, grace becomes full-orbed when people repent of sin and in simple faith and obedience gratefully accept God's offer of "so great salvation" (Heb. 2:3). To hear the gospel is a great privilege. It also entails a great responsibility.

I said previously that one of the purposes of missionary communication is to influence or to persuade. Missionaries and evangelists are, as Leighton Ford has put it, "Christian persuaders."[7] When Paul at the Areopagus communicated God's command for repentance, his hearers were faced with an issue that could not be evaded. They knew that Paul wanted—and that the God he represented demanded—repentance for sin and faith in Christ. And some repented and believed. Others, however, sneered. And still others said, "We shall hear you again concerning this" (Acts 17:32). We do not know the final outcome of Paul's visit to Athens. He did not stay there long. Nor do we read of a strong church in that city until a later period. But in Athens as elsewhere, the response to the gospel was mixed. There were those who gladly and gratefully believed. There were those who sneeringly and stonily turned away. And there were many who stood in between—unsure, uncertain, and undecided.

It is customary for Christian persuaders to think in terms of two responses—acceptance and rejection. There is certainly a validity to this, especially in view of the fact that our Lord said, "He who is not with Me is against Me" (Matt. 12:30). In ultimate terms only two responses to the divine message are

[7]Cf. Leighton Ford, *The Christian Persuader* (New York: Harper & Row, 1966).

possible. In immediate terms, however, there are other possibilities. As a matter of fact, in intercultural communication of the gospel it is of the utmost importance that we analyze with some care the various possible responses, because the amount of new information in even a simple message may be so great as to make significant communication in a limited time all but impossible. If but limited adaptation to cultural differences is made in the encoding process, the respondents may easily misunderstand the message.

Generally speaking, Western missionaries (especially short-term missionaries and visiting evangelists) have assumed too much in asking for decisions in non-Western cultures. This observation is in no way intended to place limits on the power of the Holy Spirit. But the number of people in these cultures who have responded in one way or another to a gospel invitation only to return to their former way of life is ample testimony that something is amiss. The answer is often to be found in the fact that they have obeyed the instructions of some missionary or evangelist without having the real understanding required for a "hearing of faith" or an "obeying from the heart" in regard to the Christian gospel.

Let us take a brief look, then, at various types of responses common in the missionary situation.

1. Sincere acceptation. Strictly speaking, respondents can accept—and, for that matter, they can reject—only that message which they understand. Undoubtedly many so-called decisions for Christ are not decisions *for Christ!* Many believe without believing the *gospel!* Many accept something other than salvation. Let us remember that our purpose is not that our hearers simply accept the missionary-evangelist (as a good person), or a better way of life, or peace with God, or heaven as an alternative to hell. No one can simply accept prosperity, peace, and paradise and get Christ as a bonus. But if any of us accepts Christ, then all the promises of God in him are yes and in him amen.

The responsibility of the missionary-evangelist is to make

the gospel of Christ as clear and compelling as possible. It is the responsibility of the Holy Spirit to make converts.

2. Straightforward rejection. Much of what has been said concerning acceptance of the gospel can also be said of its rejection. Strictly speaking, our respondents can reject Christ only when they understand who he is and what he has accomplished for their salvation. Of course, their ability to understand is dependent on what they have done with the *light they already have*. But it is also dependent on the faithfulness of Christ's witnesses in communicating the *light of the gospel*.

No one should ask more of the missionary-evangelist than that his hearers have the opportunity to accept or reject a Christ who has been faithfully and forcefully communicated in accordance with the Scriptures and in reliance on the Holy Spirit. Even the apostles could do no more. That being the case, Paul wrote:

> For we are a fragrance of Christ to God among those who are being saved and among those who are perishing; to the one an aroma from death to death; to the other an aroma from life to life. And who is adequate for these things? For we are not like many, peddling the word of God, but as from sincerity, but as from God, we speak in Christ in the sight of God. (2 Cor. 2:15–17)

Missionaries should resist any human pressure to produce results. They should humbly endeavor before God to faithfully communicate Christ and beseech men to accept him! When Christ has been truly communicated, they are successful as communicators.

3. Situational reformulation. It is natural for people to decode new information in terms of previous experience. This is the basis of the learning process. Of course, the principle applies to Christian information as well. Therefore, when new Christian information is markedly incomplete or when comparisons and contrasts with indigenous beliefs and practices are not made, the new Christian information may be largely

absorbed into the old system. It is absorbed by assigning meanings to the message that are compatible with what is already accepted as true but that are incompatible with Christianity. This phenomenon is variously called "reformulation," "reinterpretation," and "restructuring." Try as he may, the missionary cannot completely avoid some reinterpretation in the decoding process. It is a matter of degree. The goal is to minimize the tendency as much as possible. And one of the steps toward that goal is to understand how it occurs.

Merrill R. Abbey reports an instance of reformulation among the Patuma people of British Guyana.

> Hearers among the Patuma people found certain words used by the missionaries difficult to interpret so they simply used the missionaries' terms—temptation, wicked, Christians, conversion, salvation. Listeners fitted these missionary terms into their pre-Christian experience. Certain "power words" of their animistic religion had been used to call down curses on their enemies. Words they could not encode from the missionaries' message were now regarded as having the force of "powerful words" in the Christian language.
>
> "Now," one Patuma explained, "a person can go to prayer meeting, kneel behind the one he wishes to curse, and while everyone is praying out loud, he can mutter these 'powerful words' and thus destroy the enemy." Needless to say, what the Patuma decoded was not what the missionaries, on the other side of a cultural divide, thought they had encoded![8]

It should be noted that reformulation does not necessarily preclude the possibility of people's accepting Christ. The likelihood is that all of us reinterpret some parts of the Bible message in ways that are culturally compatible to us but, nevertheless, are essentially unbiblical. Reinterpretation or

[8]Merrill R. Abbey, *Man, Media and the Message* (New York: Friendship, 1960), 51–52.

reformulation, however, is particularly damaging when it occurs in relation to the fundamental truths of Scripture.
4. Syncretistic incorporation. Reformulation is generally thought of as a more or less unwitting attempt to assign culturally defined meanings to terms that have much different meanings in their proper Christian (or biblical) context. There is another and somewhat similar response, however, that *may be* more deliberate. When respondents choose parts of the Christian message that appeal to them and, rejecting other parts of the message, incorporate the accepted elements into non-Christian religious systems to make a new whole, the result is a syncretism. The nativistic movements of Africa and numerous other religious systems such as Bahai and Seicho no Ie (House of Growth) are cases in point.

It is well to be aware of the widespread tendency to respond to Christianity in this way, especially in polytheistic societies. Where numerous deities are held in veneration or fear, it is not at all difficult to add one more to the register! In fact, it seems to be the better part of wisdom to make peace with whatever supernatural powers may exist whether in heaven or on earth, or, indeed, under the earth.

The response of an Oriental who had just heard the gospel for the first time is rather typical of this attitude. Bowing deeply and in polite language he said to the evangelist, "I am most grateful to you for coming to my village with this message. This has been a great day for me. I have always believed in our own gods. But tonight when we heard your message we were very moved. We most certainly want to believe in the Christian God also."

Syncretism, East and West, is perhaps best understood as a very natural desire on the part of many people to embrace the most appealing aspects of the various religions. To them it seems unwise if not inconceivable that with so many religious systems in the world one can be expected to opt for one deity, one holy book, and one standard of belief and practice to the exclusion of all others. Missionary communicators will be well advised to be aware of the appeal of this response and to communicate patiently but clearly the uniqueness of Christ and Christian revelation. After all, some of the most exclusivistic claims of all religious literature are to be found in the Old and New Testaments. Ultimately, syncretism is but another form of Christ-rejection.

5. Studied protraction. Notice the response of Paul's hearers in Athens (Acts 17:32–34). Although the response "We shall hear you again concerning this" is far from acceptance, it is not *necessarily* equal to rejection. It is certainly not the same as sneering. We are not justified in concluding that among those who said to Paul, "We will hear you again" that there was not a single one who later became a believer and joined the church at Athens. To argue in that manner would be to argue from silence. Nor are we justified in inferring from the truth "now is the accepted time" (2 Cor. 6:2 KJV) that no one who postpones the decision to accept Christ will listen and believe on another occasion. Those who postpone the decision to accept Christ certainly take a great risk, but who can say that in grace God will not yet grant them space for repentance? Should not honest inquirers be the objects of special concern and prayer? Would this not be a more Christian way?

If a case can be made for giving special consideration to honest inquirers in intracultural evangelism, certainly a case can be made for giving them special consideration in intercultural evangelism. This will become more clear as we consider the newness of the gospel and the way decisions are made in various cultures. Premature "decisions for Christ" may not be, in fact, the decision of the respondents to accept Christ at all, but rather a decision to please the evangelist. While it is true that the knowledge sufficient for an intelligent decision to accept Christ will always be something less than complete knowledge, it is also true that Christ himself urged those who would follow him to count the cost of discipleship. A postponed decision may sometimes be the only genuine "decision," and in some cultural contexts may greatly enhance the discipling of entire families or even larger homogeneous cultural groupings. We should distinguish between *postponement* (delaying the decision) and *procrastination* (unwarranted delay) and, in adopted cultural contexts especially, ask God for wisdom to know how to deal with honest inquirers. 6. Symbiotic resignation. There is yet another response that merits consideration in the missionary situation. The word "symbiosis" is appropriate, for in biology it refers to the living together of two dissimilar organisms.

Respondents may take the position that the new Christian faith is not for themselves while agreeing that others over whom they exercise authority may become Christians. In effect they say to the spouse, son, servant, or subordinate, "As for me, I will not forsake the old ways, but the new way may be good for you even though it is very different. The decision is yours. Do as you will. Let us live and work together in peace."

Nourished on a diet of what someone has called "rugged individualism," many Western missionaries tend to counsel and act in ways that not only do not take advantage of this irenic attitude, but actually antagonize and alienate such persons. Of course our Lord did say,

> Do not think that I came to bring peace on the earth; I did come to bring peace, but a sword. For I came to SET A MAN AGAINST HIS FATHER, AND A DAUGHTER AGAINST HER MOTHER, AND A DAUGHTER-IN-LAW AGAINST HER MOTHER-IN-LAW; and A MAN'S ENEMIES WILL BE THE MEMBERS OF HIS HOUSEHOLD (Matt. 10:34–36).

However, those with experience on the mission field will know that this kind of division results from faithfulness to Christ often enough without our encouraging it by un-Christian attitudes and rash action. We will have more to say about this, but it should be emphasized here that there is a sense in which the respondent who is not against Christ is for him. Others within his sphere of influence, and he himself, may become candidates for conversion if not antagonized unnecessarily.

CONCLUSION TO PART II

Succinctly stated, the missionary task is to communicate Christ cross-culturally. This means that the missionary must interpret the biblical message in terms of the culture(s) in which it was given and, avoiding undue influence from his own culture, transmit that original message in terms that will be informative and persuasive in his respondent culture.

The key word in this section is "culture." Culture is an inclusive concept. It includes all the ways in which people perceive and organize material goods, ideas, and values; it embraces the ways in which people interact in society as well as a person's substitutes for God and his revelation. My concern, however, has not been to attempt a delineation of culture as such. There are numerous books on culture. Nor has it been my concern simply to help the student develop an awareness of cultural differences so that in crossing cultural boundaries he can avoid cultural shock, maintain equilibrium, and develop this ability to function effectively in the new culture. Other books do this. My concern has been to assist present and future missionaries by alerting them to the intimate relationship that exists between culture and the communication of Christ and to introduce the approach to missionary communication that will be taken in this book— the analysis of our communication task in relation to alternative ways of perceiving the world, thinking, expressing ideas, acting, interacting with others, channeling the message, and making decisions.

James Downs writes, "It is on this rock of intercultural communication that the ship of world improvement most frequently runs aground."[9] The "good ship of Christian missions" has often suffered the same fate and on the same rock. How discouraging! The challenge of *intracultural* communication seemed to be quite sufficient to engage our full mental and spiritual faculties, and already we have introduced

[9]James F. Downs, *Cultures in Crisis* (Beverly Hills, Calif.: Glencoe, 1971).

188

the additional challenge of communicating Christ *cross-culturally!* But there are encouragements as well. In the first place, while cultures are radically different from one another, they are not completely so. The worldviews, cognitive processes, languages, behavioral patterns, social structures, media usages, and motivations of people in other cultures have similarities to our own. This means that we already have *some* understanding of the respective respondent cultures. In the second place, most people have great potential for adjusting to the grids of other cultures. Once we have developed an awareness of cultural differences and the ways in which cultures operate, and once we have seriously studied the respondent culture, we can adapt to the new situation and contextualize our message without compromising that message.

In the third place, God the Holy Spirit superintends the work of missions. He is the divine Communicator. Although he places no premium on ignorance, he can and does illumine and convict our hearers in spite of our lack of understanding. While this is no excuse for lethargy in preparation for our task, it is great cause for encouragement to those who have prepared themselves well for their missionary task. Better than others they know how dependent they are on the divine Spirit when they take the message of Christ across cultural boundaries.

189

Part III

WORLDVIEWS—
WAYS OF PERCEIVING
THE WORLD

Figure 11

DIMENSIONS OF CROSS-CULTURAL COMMUNICATION

CULTURE X ◄─────── CULTURAL DISTANCE ───────► CULTURE Y

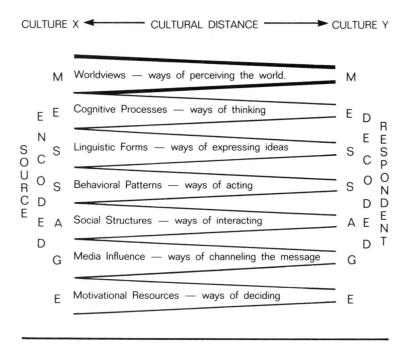

Worldviews — ways of perceiving the world.

Cognitive Processes — ways of thinking

Linguistic Forms — ways of expressing ideas

Behavioral Patterns — ways of acting

Social Structures — ways of interacting

Media Influence — ways of channeling the message

Motivational Resources — ways of deciding

Chapter 13

Worldviews and Cross-Cultural Communication

You have been invited to participate in the discussions of a class in cross-cultural communication at a large midwestern university in the United States. Students represent a variety of cultural backgrounds and interests. The class members reflect maturity and seriousness. They are poring over a paper that has been submitted by one of their number. The problem is to match various possible answers to certain lead questions with the cultures of which they might be representative.

The text of the paper is as follows:

1. "What can explain the origin of the Virgin of Guadalupe in Mexico, an image with a *mestizo* face, a painting which has withstood many attempts at destruction while all around it was destroyed?"
   a. God created the image of Our Lady in this way in order to Christianize the Mexican Indians, and he has protected Her.
   b. Some priest painted the cloth; the stories of miraculous protection are folklore.
   c. There must have been many paintings of Our Lady;

naturally the Indians noticed this one more than the others and so the fame and folklore grew.

    d. Let the historians argue about the origin, and let us put the cloth to an empirical test.

2. "When King Frederick Mutesa, the Kabaka, was forced to flee Uganda, many of the loyal Baganda people began to become sick; some died. Why?"

    a. When the Kabaka left, part of us left, and the life went out of our people. If he remains away we will all die.

    b. For whatever reasons social psychologists can present, the Baganda think that they will die and, lacking a will to live, some do die.

    c. Perhaps an epidemic growing out of the many deaths in the war has spread among the Baganda.

    d. This is a punishment for the Baganda for cooperating with the British colonialists, and profiting at the expense of their African brothers.

    e. The Baganda have been cursed by a witch from another tribe.

3. "Recently a man in England was struck by lightning twice in the same day, yet he lives. Why?"

    a. God has spared him for some purpose.

    b. He was always lucky.

    c. The probabilities of being struck by lightning twice are fantastic, and to live through both—well, this is one for the record books!

    d. A careful examination of all conditions (weather, location, his clothing, etc.) will probably explain both why he was struck twice and at the same time explain why he was not killed.[1]

As the discussion proceeds, the class is struck by the fact that in most cases they can readily agree on the kind of culture suggested by the various answers. In other words, when one

[1]This paper was submitted by a student in a class in intercultural communication conducted by Professor W. S. Howell during the summer session of 1969 at the University of Minnesota.

knows the basic orientation of any cultural group, it seems possible to predict with a significant degree of accuracy just how members of the group will respond to certain kinds of questions.

CULTURE AND WORLDVIEW

Perhaps the foregoing illustration will serve as a cue to a starting point for the study of intercultural communication per se. It illustrates several all-important facts about people in culture. In the first place, people in certain large cultural groupings tend to share certain fundamental commonalities in defining the reality around them. This commonality is a part of culture. Any given culture is made up of folkways, modes and mores, language, human productions, and social structures. It is all of these and more. It is also the larger significance of people and things in relation to which these aspects of culture take on meaning. One might compare culture to a large and intricate tapestry. The tapestry is made up of numberless threads, various colors, larger shadings and lines—all of which go to make up the overall mosaic or pattern, which in turn serves in interpreting any part. *Culture is also this wholeness, this larger reality.*

In the second place, people are born and reared "into" culture. They are *enculturated,* to use the term of the anthropologists. By this process culture is made to be uniquely their own—the *cultural* reality becomes *their* reality over a period of time. As James Downs says,

> Men living in coherent groups . . . define the world around them, deciding what is real and how to react to this reality. Failure to grasp this simple fact about culture—that is, culture, not rocks or trees or other physical surroundings, is the environment of man—dooms any attempt to work in a cross-cultural context.[2]

[2]James F. Downs, *Cultures in Crisis* (Beverly Hills: Glencoe, 1971), 36–37.

195

In the third place, since people of a culture tend to take this culturally determined view of reality with utmost seriousness, the missionary communicator must take it with utmost seriousness also. To fail to do so may render the missionary incapable of effective communication. This does not mean that every way of looking at reality is valid. It is obvious that certain cultural views cancel out certain other cultural views. It is this process of cancellation that fosters the kind of cultural relativism that renders many students of culture incapable of subscribing to *any* view as having universal validity. But the point to be stressed here is that the way of looking at reality that prevails in any respondent culture is valid for the members of that culture. It is *that* validity that must be taken with utmost seriousness by the missionary if he wants to communicate Christ in the respondent culture. Since respondents will decode messages within the framework of a reality provided by their own culture, the missionary must encode his message with that "reality" in mind. To put this in terms of that part of culture with which we are now concerned, the communication of most people is circumscribed by the perspective provided by their own *worldview*. This is true of the missionary also. Moreover, it will be true of him until he makes that herculean effort required to understand the worldview of his respondents in their culture and speaks within that framework. At that point true missionary communication begins.

Norman Geisler correctly contends,

The Christian accepts as axiomatic that his task is to communicate Christ to the world. That sounds simple enough, but in fact it is very complex. It is complex for at least three reasons: first, there are many views of "Christ"; secondly, there are many ways to "communicate"; and thirdly, there are many "worlds" to which Christ must be communicated.[3]

[3]Norman L. Geisler, "Some Philosophical Perspectives on Missionary Dialogue," in David J. Hesselgrave, ed., *Theology and Mission* (Grand Rapids: Baker, 1978), 241.

He then goes on to liken the various worldviews to colored glasses through which people see themselves and the universe around them. Everything is given the "tint" or "hue" of whatever particular "worldview glasses" the person happens to be wearing. Moreover, since the vast majority of people are used to one pair of glasses from the time of their earliest recollections, they are not predisposed—even were they able—to lay those glasses aside (even temporarily) in order to look at the world through another pair of glasses. The analogy is a good one—as we will see!

DEFINING "WORLDVIEW"

The way people see reality can be termed their worldview. It is instructive that in Latin, Greek, Sanscrit, English, and certain other languages, one meaning for the word "see" is "know." A worldview is the way people see or perceive the world, the way they "know" it to be. What people see is in part what is there. It is partly what we are.[4] But these combine to form one reality, one worldview. The concept is not without some degree of vagueness and ambiguity. But like the concepts "culture," "ethos," and "national character," that vagueness stems in part from its comprehensiveness. In spite of comprehensiveness, such concepts are useful, provided we can differentiate between them and point out instances of them.

For our purposes it would be difficult to improve on the observation of Robert Redfield:

> The culture of a people is, then, its total equipment of ideas and institutions and conventionalized activities. The ethos of a people is its organized conceptions of the Ought. The national character of a people, or its personality type, is the kind of human being which, generally speaking, occurs in that society. The "worldview" of a people, yet another of this group of conceptions, is the way a people characteristi-

4Merrill R. Abbey, *Man, Media and the Message* (New York: Friendship, 1960), 54.

cally look outward upon the universe. If "culture" suggests the way a people look to an anthropologist, "worldview" suggests how everything looks to a people, "the designation of the existent as a whole. . . ."

But if there is an emphasized meaning in the phrase "worldview," I think it is in the suggestion it carries of the structure of things as man is aware of them. It is in the way we see ourselves in relation to all else.[5]

In another place, Redfield defines worldview in the following terms:

Of all that is connoted by "culture," "worldview" attends especially to the way a man, in a particular society, sees himself in relation to all else. It is the properties of existence as distinguished from and related to the self. It is, in short, a man's idea of the universe. It is that organization of ideas that answers to a man with the questions: "Where am I? Among what do I move? What are my relations to these things?"[6]

Although there are numerous definitions and descriptions of worldview, most of them tend to reveal a fundamental agreement with Redfield.

Michael Kearney writes, "The worldview of a people is their way of looking at reality. It consists of basic assumptions and images that provide a more or less coherent, though not necessarily accurate, way of thinking about the world."[7]

Paul Hiebert describes worldview as "the basic assumptions about reality which lie behind the beliefs and behavior of a culture."[8]

---

[5]Robert Redfield, *The Primitive World and Its Transformations* (Ithaca, N.Y.: Cornell University Press, 1957), 85–86. Redfield credits Martin Heidegger with the phrase "the designation of the existent as a whole."

[6]Robert Redfield, "The Primitive World View," in *Proceedings of the American Philosophical Society* 96 (1952): 30–36; Anthony F. C. Wallace, *Culture and Personality* (New York: Random, 1961), 100.

[7]Michael Kearney, *World View* (Novato, Calif.: Chandler and Sharp, 1984), 41.

[8]Paul G. Hiebert, *Anthropological Insights for Missionaries* (Grand Rapids: Baker, 1985), 45.

CATEGORIZING WORLDVIEWS

Our worldview, then, is "the way we see ourselves in relation to all else. Conversely, it is the way we see all else in relation to ourselves! Our first reaction to this definition might be, "What could be more simple than that?" But a little reflection will teach us that the simplicity for which we search is not yet within our grasp. In fact, it may appear to be farther away than ever. *Our* worldview, after all, is one thing. The number of *other* worldviews could well be astronomical. In other words, as we begin to study the worldviews of other cultures, the ways in which people see themselves appear to be so numerous that the task to which we have set ourselves seems impossible from the very outset. Moreover, the phrase "in relation to all else" seems to be far too encompassing to be useful. The universe has proved to be a very large place indeed!

Are there any solutions to these complicating factors? Let us look at them more closely. Our first problem is related to the number of "selves" in the world who "see things" differently. It would seem that we are faced with a dilemma very similar to that faced by the irreligious man who, after experiencing his first heart attack, realizes that he has neglected something that may be very important and determines to embrace some kind of religious faith. He has only to settle the problem of which faith he will embrace. He decides that the only defensible approach would be to study all the various religions, and on the basis of an objective comparison, make his final choice. His problems have just begun, however, because the more he investigates the subject of religion, the more profuse and divergent religious views are seen to be. Finally he awakens to the fact that the options are so numerous that he cannot possibly study all of them, particularly in view of his condition and uncertain future. Clearly, an order of priority will have to be established, and, if he is going to embrace one particular faith before it is too late to embrace any, the choice may have to be made rather early in the game. Many persons seeing the dilemma of our imaginary coronary victim decide that the only way out is to refuse to have anything to do with this business of religion, not realizing that they too have made a choice—and that on the basis of even less information.

Now, it will be readily apparent that as students of cross-cultural communication we face much the same problem. For us the question is not one of where we will place our faith, but whether or not the uncommonly large number of possible and actual worldviews can be realistically and objectively reduced to a manageable number. Various authors have already attempted this very kind of reduction process; they have done so, in fact, in relation to Redfield's starting point.

In *The Case for Christianity*, C. S. Lewis begins his discussions (originally given as a series of broadcast talks) with the basic question of the *meaning of the universe*.[9] Using notions of right and wrong as a key to unlocking that meaning for the average man, he proceeds to a discussion of two fundamentally opposing answers (or views) on the subject and also gives some consideration to an "in-between" view. First, there is the *materialist view*, which says that matter and space (and for that matter, the more or less fixed ways in which people behave) just happened, period. Now of course, people find it rather difficult to leave the period there. But if everything is a result of chance, then the universe has no inherent meaning and every attempt to find it is doomed to failure. Second, there is the *religious view* according to which the universe is more like a mind than a machine. In this view, it is proper to talk of purpose and meaning because there is, as Lewis says, "Something behind" everything we know that finds "Its" or "His" reflection in our own purposes and meanings. Third, there is a kind of *in-between view*, which has been variously called Life-Force philosophy, or creative-evolution, or emergent evolution. This is a kind of "eat-your-cake-and-have-it-too" view in which proponents play both ends against the middle. When it suits them to talk about purposes, they speak as though there were a Mind behind the

---

[9]C. S. Lewis, *The Case for Christianity* (New York: Macmillan, 1962).

universe, and they sound like religionists. At other times, they talk as though the universe were simply a machine, and for all the world they sound like materialists. Lewis has little time for this view. A somewhat different and yet closely related approach is taken by Robert Brow in his book *Religion—Origin and Ideas.*[10] Brow first deals with the origin and development of religion. Having dealt with history, he proceeds to philosophy and a discussion of the religious options that present themselves to Western man. By-passing epistemology and science, he proposes to begin with the very practical existential question, "Here I am. What meaning is there in being here?"[11] There are two directions in which one can go from that starting point. First, one can say that there is no inherent meaning to his own existence. That is the position of the atheist and the "egotheist" (Brow's term for the man who wills or determines for himself what that meaning will be).[12] Second, one can say that there is meaning inherent in his existence. That is the position of the theist (whether Jewish, Christian, or Muslim) and the monist (whether of the religious type such as the Hindu and contemporary Buddhist, or the irreligious type such as the Nazi, Communist, or humanist).

It will be apparent that Lewis and Brow are concerned with worldviews. If their starting points are not precisely that of Redfield, they are so close that the difference is hardly worth quibbling about. In any case, the problem posed by the multiplicity of worldviews seems to be solvable.

CHARACTERIZING WORLDVIEWS

There remains a problem implicit in the part of Redfield's definition that says "in relation to all else." How can we possibly deal with "all else" in any way that is satisfactory from a practical point of view? Redfield himself resolves this

[10]Robert Brow, *Religion—Origin and Ideas* (Chicago: InterVarsity, 1966).
[11]Ibid., 76.
[12]Ibid.

problem. He notes that studies undertaken at Yale University reveal there are at least seventy-five elements [now in excess of eighty] common to the worldviews of all cultures. These include humanness, the idea of self, the nuclear family, the notion of a major difference between man and "non-man," nature, spatial and temporal orientation, birth, death, and so forth.[13] But Redfield concludes that all worldviews could probably be related to the elements of one triangle, namely that formed by man, nature, and gods or supernature.[14] That seems to be the case, though one might want to put that triangle in a temporal orientation. A culture's view of time— past, present, and future—is exceedingly important as we will see.

Redfield's conclusion (and, in a sense, Lewis's and Brow's philosophical and theological options) are borne out by Robert Oliver. Oliver's study does not claim to be exhaustive,[15] but it is significant that he describes the salient features of rhetorics that would be applicable to Communist, Taoist, Confucianist, Hindu-Buddhistic, and Shintoist worldviews. These are rather easily subsumed under rubrics similar to those provided by Lewis and Brow. The essentials of most religions are, in point of fact, related to Redfield's triangle of man, nature, and supernature. Thus from perspectives provided by theology, philosophy, anthropology, and communication theory we deduce a way of describing worldviews that suits our purposes here. Since we are concerned in the existential missionary encounter with adherents of other worldviews rather than with philosophical completeness, we can think in terms of the naturalist (I prefer that term to materialist) and the main religious worldviews (omitting the "in-between" category). And we can characterize these worldviews in terms of their basic understanding of supernature, nature, man, and time.

[13]Redfield, *Primitive World*, 90ff.
[14]Ibid.
[15]Robert Oliver, *Culture and Communication* (Springfield, Ill.: Charles C. Thomas, 1962). See also *Communication and Culture in Ancient India and China* (Syracuse: Syracuse University Press, 1971) by the same author.

BIBLICAL THEOLOGY AND THE CHRISTIAN WORLDVIEW

In chapter 7, we described the missionary's communicational tasks in terms of Eugene Nida's three-culture model: i.e., the missionary must divest himself as much as possible from his own "square" culture, interpret the gospel in terms of the "triangular" culture in which it was revealed, and deliver the gospel in a way that will be meaningful to people in the target "round" culture. In chapter 9, we described these tasks as they relate to contextualization; i.e., authentic and effective communication has to do with making the *biblical* gospel meaningful in target culture terms. We noted that the starting point for determining the Christian message must be God's revelation of himself, his will, and his way in the Scriptures. We pointed out that the originators of the term "contextualization" erred to the degree that they chose contemporary existential situations as the starting points for theologizing (or "ethnotheologizing"). But we noted that we also err when we (perhaps unconsciously) allow the results of centuries of contextualizing in the Western world to determine the way in which we (Western missionaries) present the biblical message to our target culture audiences. (Thus the need for "*de*contextualization.") we devoted considerable space in chapter 9 to the former error. In this chapter we will assume a commitment to the complete authority of the Bible and put the emphasis on the latter error—the one of which many of us as evangelicals are guilty.

Fifty-five delegates (and thirty-three observers)—all conservative evangelicals—from Asia, Africa, Latin America, the Caribbean, and the Pacific Islands met in Seoul, Korea, in 1982. Calling attention to a "theological captivity" of the church in their parts of the world, they issued what is known as the Seoul Declaration. In it they highlighted the limitations of Western theology as seen from their non-Western points of view. Among those limitations are the following:

1. Western theology is, by and large, "rationalistic" and

"preoccupied with intellectual concerns, especially those having to do with faith and reason."
2. It is "moulded by Western philosophies."
3. "It has consciously been conformed to the secularistic worldview associated with the Enlightenment."
4. It is captivated by Western individualism.[16]

It should be underlined that these criticisms come from Third World brothers and sisters who believe that the Bible is fully trustworthy. They remind us that, although our theology may be biblical, it is also Western. The criticism is valid. In the first place, it is inevitable that our interpretation of Scripture and our theologizing be "skewed" by the "worldview glasses" of our own culture. In the second place, it is desirable that *in Western cultures* the Scriptures be explained and theologizing be done in ways that are understandable and relevant to the people of Western cultures.

When those theologians at Seoul criticized Western theology, they mainly had Western *systematic theology* in view. After all, there are various kinds of theology. B. B. Warfield said that *systematic theology* is the science that "deals with absolute truth and aims at organizing into a concatenated system all the truth in its sphere" (i.e., truth which we call theological).[17] He also called it the "crown and head" of all other types of theology, and indeed of all sciences.[18] I can agree, but we must also recognize that that which is "crown and head" must have "legs and feet." Warfield recognized that when he reminded us that *exegetical theology* (interpreted Scripture) is exhibited first in *biblical theology* and that biblical theology ". . . is the basis and source of systematics."[19]

[16]"Seoul Declaration: Toward an Evangelical Theology for the Third World," in Bong Rin Ro and Ruth Eshenauer, eds., *The Bible and Theology in Asian Contexts* (Taichung, Taiwan: Asian Theological Association, 1984), 23.
[17]B. B. Warfield, "The Idea of Systematic Theology," in John Jefferson Davis, ed., *The Necessity of Systematic Theology*, 2nd ed., (Grand Rapids: Baker, 1980), 129–30.
[18]Ibid., 142–45.
[19]Ibid., 145.

Now we often use the phrase "biblical theology" to refer to any theology that is true to Scripture. But that is not what Warfield had in mind: he was talking about biblical theology in the technical sense—i.e., theology that maintains the historical framework of the Bible and unfolds God's will and way in that context, dealing with Bible books, persons, events, and truths as God revealed them, beginning with Genesis and ending with Revelation.

If systematic theology as we know it has been one of the great contributions of the Western church to world missions, it has also given rise to one of world missions' greatest problems. Missionaries have tended to use a truncated "systematic theology" type of framework in evangelism (e.g., "Five Things God Wants You to Know") and discipling and theologizing (e.g., studies on God, man, sin, salvation, Christian life, etc.), and have neglected biblical theology. When biblical narratives have been used or a New Testament Gospel translated, seldom have they been put in the context of the "whole story." The Old Testament has often received but little attention even though the New Testament can hardly be understood without it. We have displayed the "crown and head" and covered up the "legs and feet." We have provided the "little pictures" but have not displayed the "big picture" of which they form distinct but separate parts.

Have you ever put together a really complex jigsaw puzzle with perhaps hundreds of pieces? If so, what helped you the most in deciding where each piece fit? Not primarily the coloring, lines, and contours of the individual piece. What was most helpful was the picture of the final product on the cover of the box! It was the "big picture" that was most in helpful in the placing of each individual piece.

Those theologians in Seoul were justified in their criticisms, of course. But what they neglected to say may be even more important. Because today the church worldwide—West as well as East, North as well as South—suffers from an approach that has majored on "little pieces" of biblical truth and Christian experience while neglecting the "big picture" without which the little pieces cannot be fully understood!

The church suffers from an approach that majors on the "little stories" of Scripture without putting them in the "larger story" of God's dealings with, and revelations to, humanity over the centuries. Worldviews can be explained in terms provided by systematic theology, philosophy, and comparative religion. But they are almost always constructed out of stories and myths, history and pseudohistory. The Bible, after all, is not primarily a theological or philosophical textbook. It is primarily the story—the history—of God's dealings with man down through the ages. As mentioned in chapter 10, missionary translators and communicators are gradually coming to realize the significance of that fact. Several examples may serve to indicate what is involved.

1. The first example comes from Luwuk-Banggai, Indonesia—an area missionized by the Dutch Reformed Church.[20] A remote area, it was almost untouched until 1912 when Muslim traders tried to convert some of its 100,000 inhabitants. As a result the Reformed Church sent a missionary to the area. Over the years he baptized thousands but was unable to see to their spiritual nurture. By the end of World War II there were 30,000 nominal Christians in numerous churches, but they were largely nonliterates and without Bibles. Then in 1952, an experienced missionary, H. R. Weber, was sent to instruct them. He was given no money and no helpers except indigenous personnel, who had an average of three years of elementary education. Weber proceeded to hold short five-day Bible courses for these leaders in each of seven districts. They paid for their instruction in money or kind.

Weber's format was simple but profound. Weber stressed the importance of the Bible in the life of the Christian and the congregation. On the first evening he presented a "travel route" through the Scriptures from creation in Genesis to the kingdom of God in Revelation including the Fall, the covenants with Israel, the church, the Second Coming, with Christ at the center of the whole story. The four succeeding days

[20]H. R. Weber, *The Communication of the Gospel to Illiterates* (Madras: Christian Literature Society, 1960).

highlighted Genesis 3:1–19; Exodus 19:1–6; Luke 2:8–14; and Acts 1:6–11. Weber used simple chalk drawings to sketch highlights of the "travel route." Each day time was also spent discussing such topics as baptism, communion, evangelism, and Christian life in a tribal community.

Later Weber and those he instructed used a similar approach in instructing the nonliterates in the congregations. As a result of the total experience, Weber drew some fundamental principles for communicating the Christian message to nonliterates. (We now know that they have a much wider application.)

First, it is a mistake merely to tell Bible stories. All must be set in a complete redemptive history including creation and eschatology, with Christ at the center. All of this must be seen in contrast to the local mythological framework so that the Christian faith can revolutionize all patterns of thought.

Second, it is fundamentally wrong to translate and/or teach only the New Testament or New Testament portions. Jesus the Messiah must not be "de-Judaized" lest he be "de-historicized." Otherwise, Christianity tends to be placed in the same category as local myths.

Third, once the mythological framework has been shattered, the classification and integrating character of "primitive thinking" should be seen as a great gift. The "primitive" is able to cope with any event because it can be absorbed into his myth. The Christian can cope if he knows the beginning, center, and end of history.

2. The second example comes from the New Tribes Mission, especially the experiences and productions of one of its missionaries to the Philippines, Trevor McIlwain.[21] McIlwain's approach arose out of difficulties he experienced in working with the Palawano tribe on Palawan Island. He first tried to teach the Bible topically and later the Gospel of John expositionally, verse by verse. Both methods failed because the Palawanos "had never been taught the basic Old Testa-

---

[21]Cf. Trevor McIlwain, *Notes on the Chronological Approach to Evangelism and Church Planting* (Sanford, Fla.: New Tribes Mission, 1981).

ment historical sequence of events as one complete story."[22]
He looked to Scripture itself for a more logical and practical
method of communicating God's truth. As a result, McIlwain
came up with the following basic ideas:

First, the Bible itself is the outline. The best way to teach
divine truth is to use the literary form and sequence of
progressive historical revelation as unfolded in the Scriptures.
All is "HIS-story." The Old Testament is the preparation for
Christ; the New Testament is the manifestation of Christ.
The latter cannot be understood without the former.

Second, other teaching methods should be used only
when one is teaching people who have a clear panoramic view
of God's dealings with man.

Third, we can learn what to emphasize from the Old
Testament on the basis of what the Holy Spirit taught and
emphasized in the New Testament.

The above is, of course, only bare bones. McIlwain has
been charged by his mission with the responsibility of writing
a whole series of books, which I assume will be used by the
whole mission.[23] All of this becomes even more significant
when we realize that the New Tribes Mission was born with a
passion for reaching new peoples with a "simple gospel" that
required little or no training to communicate.

3. The third example comes from the Lutheran church.
Over a period of time and after much experience in teaching
ministries, the Reverend Harry Wendt devised a method to
facilitate adult Christian education based on the whole of
Scripture and presented at different levels of intensity in a
series of three books: *The Divine Drama I* and *II* and *See
Through the Scriptures*.[24] The method is very similar to those

---

[22]Trevor McIlwain, *Building on Firm Foundations, Vol. 1, Guidelines
for Evangelism and Teaching Believers* (Sanford, Fla.: New Tribes Mission,
1987), 65.

[23]I refer to the series *Building on Firm Foundations* published by New
Tribes Mission in Sanford, Florida.

[24]These and other publications, transparencies, cassettes and video tapes
are available from Crossways International, 7930 Computer Avenue South,
Minneapolis, Minn. 55436.

indicated above, but is accompanied by a long series of elaborate symbolic drawings. Wendt established the Shekinah Foundation in 1982 and through that organization has been promoting his method of instruction in church seminars, the Armed Services, and in a large number of Third World countries. It has been received with enthusiasm world-wide, even by those who have been in the church for many years. Recently, the name of the organization has been changed to Crossways International and headed up by Jack Eichhorst of the Evangelical Lutheran Church in America. Wendt himself is devoting even more time to respond to the flood of invitations to present seminars throughout America and overseas.

Although our treatment has been sketchy, these and other examples point to something of an embryonic revolution in Christian evangelism and instruction. What is involved is a new understanding that God not only inspired the words and truths of Scripture, he also superintended the whole process of revelation and inscripturation in such a way as to provide us with a *model* for discipling the nations—a model that leads to an understanding of what can be termed a Christian world-view.

COMMUNICATING CHRIST IN THE CONTEXTS OF NON-CHRISTIAN WORLDVIEWS

"Well and good," someone says, "but what else is involved in taking that 'large picture,' 'big story' Christian worldview into non-Christian worldview cultures? How can one communicate meaningfully and persuasively to non-Christian respondents who are culturally inclined to 'see' everything through the 'glasses' of a totally different world-view?"

Logically, only three ways are possible.[25]

First, missionaries can invite their non-Christian respondents to lay aside their own worldview and temporarily adopt

[25]Cf. Geisler, "Philosophical Perspectives."

209

the Christian worldview in order to understand the message. But while this approach is theoretically possible, it is highly impractical as we have indicated previously. Why? The reason is that comparatively few non-Christian respondents are *able* to do this. They have never been called on to do so—much less are they prepared to do so. It is as though their glasses have become a part of their eyes. Of the few who by virtue of education or association are able to change glasses, there are only a few of them who are *willing* to do so. Their reticence may be due to pride or disinterest or other causes. Whatever the cause, the result is the same and is in evidence everywhere.

Second, missionaries can temporarily adopt the worldview of their non-Christian respondents. Then, by reexamining their message in the light of the respondent worldview, they can contextualize the message, encoding it in such a way that it will become meaningful to the respondents. This approach is not easy, but it is both possible and practical. Complete communication may not be attainable. Perfection seldom is. But effective communication is possible if missionaries take the initiative and pay the price. And true missionary motivation is to communicate a message, not simply dispense it.

Third, missionaries can invite their respondents to meet them halfway, to exchange one lens and try looking through one eye, so to speak. This has been a rather popular approach to the problem. Traditionally, the study of comparative religion has been undertaken by many missionaries in order to find points of contact or establish common ground between religious worldviews. Many such points and places turn out to be mirages upon closer examination, however. Others seem to have some kind of reality to commend them, but upon close examination the "reality" turns out to be a kind of religious quicksand. That is why Hendrik Kraemer insists that one must have a "totalitarian" understanding of religion. In other words, the separate parts of any religion must be understood in terms of the whole of it.[26] To return to our former analogy, we need *both* lenses. Otherwise we risk distortion.

If we grant limited validity and practicality to possibilities one and three, it seems apparent that possibility two, which involves the attempt to understand the target culture worldview and to contextualize our message in terms of that understanding, is most in keeping with the missionary calling and the realities of culture. We search the Scripture to "perceive the world" as God perceives it. We study the myths, the histories, and the background of the people of target cultures in order to see the world as they see it. Only to the extent that we carry out both of these tasks can we make the kind of comparisons and contrasts that Weber talks about and that he exemplified not only when instructing believers but also when evangelizing pagans. Read his account:

> On our journeyings through the Banggai Archipelago we came to Taulan, a small island consisting of one village only. A number of the inhabitants had been baptized a few years ago.
>
> The village assembled—animals and humans, Christians and non-Christians, babies in arms and old people (among them the heathen priest)—all of them illiterate. . . .
>
> Beginning with the story of the Creation, I illustrated what I said by somewhat clumsy drawings on the blackboard. Then the old heathen priest related the ancient creation legends of the district, and we compared the two reports. Next, the story of the Fall, related and illustrated by "chalk and talk," was contrasted with legends about the origin of evil and the fall of man as they had been handed down in the tribe. It was long after noon before we stopped for lunch, and in the afternoon this unique catechism was continued.[27]

[26]Hendrik Kraemer, *The Christian Message in a Non-Christian World* (Grand Rapids: Kregel, 1963), 135–41.
[27]Weber, *Communication of the Gospel*, 67.

When we communicate Christ cross-culturally, the "heathen priests" and "pagan philosophers" (cf. Acts 17) may or may not be there in person. But we can be sure that the Archenemy of the human soul is there, reminding our respondents of "their way of seeing things," so the process is the same. *In the subsequent chapters in part 3 I will characterize various representative worldviews in some detail and adopt an ethno-rhetorical approach to contextualizing the Christian message for people of those worldviews. In the contextualization sections of each chapter I will use various of the classic categories and subcategories noted in chapter 10 (source, content, style, etc.). In discussing selection of content I will assume that the ideal starting point is the approach of biblical theology, which I have dealt with in this chapter, and highlight other approaches that have been or might be taken.*

Chapter 14

Communicating Christ Into The Naturalist Worldview

CHARACTERIZING THE NATURALIST WORLDVIEW

One would be hard-pressed to improve on C. S. Lewis' way of describing the worldview of those who think the universe is more like a machine than like a mind.

> People who take that view think that matter and space just happen to exist, and always have existed, no one knows why; and that the matter, behaving in certain fixed ways, has just happened, by a sort of fluke, to produce creatures like ourselves who are able to think. By one chance in a thousand something hit our sun and made it produce planets; and by another thousandth chance the chemicals necessary for life, and the right temperature, arose on one of these planets, and so some of the matter on this earth came alive; and then, by a very long series of chances, the living creatures developed into things like us.[1]

[1]C. S. Lewis, *The Case for Christianity* (New York: Macmillan, 1962), 18–19.

The naturalist (or materialist) worldview comes in various guises—sometimes subtle, sometimes not so subtle. Atheism, secularism, scientism, humanism, and "egotheism" all basically belong in this category. Communism, of course, is also naturalistic. Our purpose here is not to construct a case against such a worldview, but to explicate its implications for missionary communication (see figure 12).

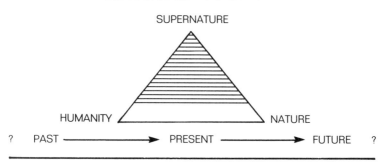

Figure 12

THE NATURALIST WORLDVIEW

SUPERNATURE

HUMANITY   NATURE

?   PAST ⟶ PRESENT ⟶ FUTURE   ?

1. *The supernatural.* As its designation implies, in this worldview the supernatural is disregarded or dismissed as the vestigial notion of some less developed stage of humanity's evolution. While the proponents of this worldview may agree on little else, they seem to be able to agree on this:

> *Let us leave the heavens*
> *To the angels and the sparrows.*[2]

2. *Nature.* Nature may be regarded as providing a generally hospitable, Waldenlike habitat for man. Or it may be seen as an enemy much as Freud saw it: "Nature rises up before us,

[2]Sigmund Freud, *The Future of an Illusion,* trans. W. D. Robson-Scott (New York: Liveright, 1953), 87.

pitiless, inexorable; thus she brings again to mind our weakness and helplessness."[3]

3. *Humanity.* Freud's words also point up the fact that from the time of Copernicus onward, nature became ever more vast, and we became smaller and smaller by comparison. Whereas the psalmist had scanned the sky and asked the question, "What is man, that thou art mindful of him?" (Ps. 8:4 KJV), modern people have been more inclined to ask Plotinus' question, which can be stated like this: "Who in the world are we?" In the naturalist's view it seems that we are no more than some chance collocation of atoms washed ashore on a little planet in a remote corner of a vast universe.

Of course, it does make a difference what *kind* of collocation we turn out to be and the kind of process of which we are a part. Charles Darwin gave impetus to the optimistic notion that we are a developing if not finished product of nature. John Dewey believed that all people are essentially good. He believes that in the past arbitrary and restrictive morality has been imposed by the few on the many, with the result that people conform as a matter of habit and without the conscious intent that true morality requires. Human nature is continuous with the rest of nature. The scientific method holds promise of yielding an ethic that will free people who are good from habits that are bad and guide people into a new and hopeful future.

Others before and after Darwin have tended to put less faith in humanity as a whole and have pinned their hopes on certain select groups or individuals. Marx and Lenin had visions of a utopia that would attend the rise of the proletariat, though in practice it has always been the Party that has been in the ascendancy in the Communist orbit. Friedrich Nietzsche disdained all who put their trust in religious and intellectual approaches to the human problem and was willing to invest all authority with "men of action" who would simply *command* morality. Freud believed that by nature most people are "lazy and unintelligent," with "no love for

---

[3]Ibid., 18.

instinctual renunciation" and are of such a makeup that "arguments are of no avail against their passions."[4] He hoped that a select group of scientists would chart a path into the future.

4. *Time.* The thing naturalists seem to have in plentiful supply is time. History stretches behind us for millions and billions of years to a remote beginning that hardly turns out to be a beginning at all. The most profound complexities of nature are somehow resolved by the mysterious alchemies of time.

The future stretches before us in a similarly endless stretch of time. And just as the enigmas of the present state of affairs are somehow resolved by the copious supply of past time, so the unrealized dreams of the present are continually rekindled by drawing upon the resources of a seemingly endless supply of tomorrows.

Given a generous supply of faith, many naturalists have been able to import various kinds of meaning and purpose into this inexorable rush of time. Since nature and human beings are not without laws that serve to direct if not determine their courses, it is relatively easy to carry out a coronation and declare this or that law—or a kind of sum total of laws—to be reigning over the whole process. Reason dictates, however, that no mindless law can be considered capable of providing purpose to history. Were it not for the fact that people with minds were endowing law with purpose, history could not be considered meaningful. Moreover, in the clash of "lower" and "higher" laws history may well end up being little short of chaotic. Increasingly, as a matter of fact, the naturalist worldview has resulted in a profound sense of pessimism, hopelessness, and meaninglessness. Science threatens us with annihilation. Education is without an axiology. All that resulted from the Soviet revolution and its idealism was the most inhuman and barbarous of governance. Europe has had its "super race" and "superman" and they painted the continent with blood. No wonder that within the naturalist camp there is a rush to irrationalism and worse. No wonder Jean-Paul Sartre insists that individual persons must assert their own meaning. One is reminded of the "hope" held out by the proponents of Zen: "Light your own lamp."

COMMUNICATING INTO A NATURALIST WORLDVIEW

Although naturalism is largely confined to the Western world, it is not exclusively so. The missionary must be prepared to encounter it in any place and at any time. Fortunately, in the Western world we have contemporary Christian models for communicating effectively to this worldview. I have mentioned Lewis and Brow. Francis Schaeffer's approach will also be familiar to many. These men and many others are communicating Christ by starting where the present generation in the West actually finds itself, namely in a world where humanity has drawn an iron lid across the panoply of heaven, locked it, and thrown away the key. Schaeffer therefore calls people to account before the "God who is there." Lewis asks people how they account for their moral nature if human beings are merely machines. Brow points to the only real place where people can find real meaning, if real meaning is what they really want.

In what follows, I can only suggest approaches that are being, or might be, taken.

1. *Source.* One of the greatest obstacles to communicating Christ into a naturalist worldview is the credibility of the missionary source. Few missionaries are highly trained in philosophy, and fewer still are knowledgeable in physical science. Added to that is the fact that most naturalists will automatically impose a negative image on the missionary. This negative image is a product of two primary factors. In the first place, the Christian missionary is perceived as a narrow-minded sort of person. In the second place, the gospel preacher is perceived as a pulpit pounder with an impervious cranium and an Archbishop Ussher chronology.

It is time that missionaries do some reordering of

priorities. Missionaries in service should do some reading and study that will help them understand the position and plight of the tens and hundreds of thousands of naturalists being produced inside and outside of our educational institutions. Missionaries in preparation should avail themselves of the opportunity to study philosophy and apologetics as well as Bible and theology. By so doing they will be in a position to point out that naturalists themselves are at swords' points with each other and that one unbelieving system usually cancels out another. By so doing they will be able to offer an *apologia* or defense of the faith (1 Peter 3:15). By so doing they will be able to declare with a new conviction that the crucified Christ is indeed the wisdom of God (1 Cor. 1:30).

Above all, the missionary should not go beyond his knowledge and abilities in his attempt to communicate Christ. Inaccurate, ill-founded, and illogical arguments will be chalked up against both the communicator *and* the Christian faith. If the kind of studies suggested here do not transform all Christian communicators into successful debaters, they should at least transform them into communicators who are empathetic with the plight of people who find themselves in a world without God and hope.

2. *Content.* If anything is important in the Christian witness to a naturalist worldview, it is that we go behind that gospel to explain those truths that make it good news.

This calls for *definition* of all or most of the major terms, the meaning of which has been taken for granted for too long by too many Christian communicators. Terms like *atonement, redemption,* and *justification* have little or no meaning in the context of naturalism. In fact, the meaning of terms like *God, sin, Satan, evil, righteousness,* and *judgment* will likely be radically distorted.

Similarly, when it comes to the *selection* process, though some naturalists will have studied the Christian worldview before rejecting it, most will have passed it by without serious consideration. In that case, the main lines of the "big picture" become especially important. In a very real sense, no other worldview accounts for all the data of human experience in the way that true Christianity does. C. S. Lewis once said that one reason why he became a believer was that Christianity takes evil (which he saw all around him and even in himself) with utmost seriousness.

People in most societies do not turn to naturalism until they have been exposed to the Christian worldview in one way or another. Therefore, naturalists will most often be encountered in Western societies or in those societies strongly influenced by Western culture. This likely means that the typical Western ways of *organizing* materials into a series of propositions, each one in turn receiving support and elucidation will serve the communicator well.

In the *application* of his message, the missionary might ask the naturalist where he presumes to go in order to procure the "true truth" (to use Schaeffer's phrase) and the "meaningful meaning" for which all thinking people search.

Will he go to science? Science is too circumscribed. That is not to fault science. Science is something like a road map. There probably is no adequate road map of the whole world. There are only road maps of certain specified areas. Let us suppose that we have a road map of Switzerland. No one faults the map-makers for not going beyond the Swiss border. Their task is to chart the roads of Switzerland. No intelligent person expects them to be experts on the road system of Iceland and to provide that information on their map. Rightly conceived, science is like that. The scientist is charged with discovering and charting information about part of God's universe, but there are borders beyond which he cannot go *as a scientist*.

Will he go to philosophy? Perhaps. But he must be careful because naturalist philosophers themselves have come upon difficult days. As a result, many philosophers have confined themselves to "talking about talk" as someone has said. While others are concerned with meaning, many philosophers are hung up on the "meaning of meaning."

Will he go to religion? Then hope is discoverable, but only

after a careful examination of the foundations that distinguish true religion from the systems of pretenders.[5]

Perceptive readers will find at least hints of such apologetic arguments as the cosmological, teleological, and moral arguments in the above. These approaches are not intended in any way to diminish Christology, for Christ, indeed, is the supreme revelation and "argument" of God. In many cases, the missionary may elect to begin with Christ. On the other hand, Christ himself was not sent into our world until the "fullness of the time" (Gal. 4:4).

3. *Style.* I referred previously to the image of the pulpit-pounding preacher. Now that reference needs clarification. I am not against preachers pounding pulpits, provided the right preacher pounds the right pulpit at the right time and before the right audience. But most naturalists perceive pulpit pounding as being the preacher's proxy for a penetrating pondering of profound problems. Only those styles of communication that reflect a true understanding of the plight of modern man and an empathy with his dilemmas will serve the purpose of the Christian communicator who would convince the naturalist that Christ is the answer.

[5]See Robert Brow, *Religion—Origin and Ideas* (Chicago: InterVarsity, 1966), for an example of this approach.

Chapter 15

Communicating Christ Into The Tribal Worldview

Most worldviews presuppose the existence of supernature and can therefore be thought of as religious. The Latin word *religio* means "to link back, or to bind." A religious worldview, therefore, is a worldview that involves a linking (or relinking) of nature, man, and history to the supernatural. The worldviews that we are concerned with in this and subsequent chapters represent attempts to "link back" with the divine.

DEFINING THE TRIBAL WORLDVIEW

Various terms have been used to designate the general worldview that in this chapter is simply called tribal: polytheism (belief in plural deities), animism (belief in spirits—Sir Edward Tylor), animism (belief in impersonal power—R. R. Marett), the primitive apprehension of life (Franz Boas), and so on. It is difficult to settle on a term that will serve adequately and please everyone. John Mbiti, for example, finds fault with just about all of the terms currently being used to identify African religion—polytheism, animism, ancestor worship, primitivism, dynamism, totemism, fetishism, and naturism.[1] And he is probably justified in most of his criticisms. So it is difficult, if not impossible, to find and define a term that will satisfy everyone. I admit that the word *tribal* itself is not altogether acceptable. Not all the peoples whose worldview reflects the characteristics I will describe here have a central authority, are of common stock, and live in primitive or nomadic circumstances—characteristics popularly associated with the word *tribe*. In using the word "tribal" I am merely drawing attention to the fact that the worldview of the people in question does not really correspond to that of any of the *major* religions of the world, though it corresponds to ethnic religions that have stayed at home. Furthermore, it seems to me that to a greater or lesser degree this worldview exhibits characteristics associated with the terms noted above—any one of which may be insufficient as a cover term, but all of which underscore some important aspect or aspects of this worldview.

This tribal worldview often (but not always) transcends the secular-sacred distinction that is so much a part of the thinking of the West. It may be at one and the same time sacred *and* secular. It is preoccupied with gods, spirits, and ghosts, but it is patently anthropocentric (and ethnocentric) in most cases. It brings nature and supernature together in a curious amalgam. It brings space and time together in an inextricable mix. It cements this world and the other world together in a single system. This unity is not that of monism or pantheism, however. It is rather the unity of a continuum on which boundaries between deities, spirits, animals, men, and natural phenomena are more or less obscure and shifting. Some characteristics of this unity are noted by Wallace:

[1]See John S. Mbiti, *African Religions and Philosophy* (Garden City, N.Y.: Doubleday, Anchor Books, 1970); idem, *Concepts of God in Africa* (New York: Praeger, 1969).

1) . . . the distinction between the self and that which the self confronts is blurred so that man tends to see himself as united with nature, rather than standing apart from it; 2) that man participates in maintaining this unitary system of man-in-nature, rather than dominates or changes it; 3) that the universe is morally significant, because all nature is animate and hence man's relationship with nature, like all social relationships, must be moral.[2]

The tribal worldview largely prevails in such widely separated cultures as Sub-Saharan Africa, the Pacific islands, traditional Japan, and various groupings in India, Australia, Southeast Asia, Siberia, and the Americas. Stephen Neill estimates that the worldview of at least 40 percent of the world's population is basically this view and often referred to as "folk religion."[3] While statistics of the major religions of the world may belie this contention, Neill reinforces his conclusion by a reference to India where it is taken for granted by statisticians that all who are not Muslim, Sikh, Jain, Christian, or Parsee are Hindu. Actually the religion of the average citizen of a South Indian village is far removed from classical Hinduism and much closer to the tribal apprehension of life—a state of affairs that finds its parallels in many parts of the world.

CHARACTERIZING THE WORLDVIEW OF SUB-SAHARAN AFRICA

The emergence of Africa into international prominence has resulted in increased attention to its traditional religions. The resultant analyses have complicated the picture while, at the same time, clarifying it. The picture is complicated because analysts often disagree. It is clarified because they supply important insights to our understanding even when they disagree. This can be illustrated by looking briefly at the

---

[2]Anthony F. C. Wallace, *Culture and Personality* (New York: Random, 1961), 100.

[3]Stephen Neill, *Christian Faith and Other Faiths* (Oxford: Oxford University Press, 1970), 125.

ways in which two scholars—one Western and the other African—explain African religion.

Jahnheinz Jahn says that in the African worldview the universe is seen as a network of interacting forces.[4] For Westerners force is an *attribute*—a being has force. For Africans, force is being and being is force. In one tribe the totality of these forces is called *Ntu* or Being. In *Ntu* all individual forces are tied together.

These individual forces can be categorized in four groups and arranged hierarchically:

1. *Muntu* — thinking beings with command over *nomo* (the magic word): *muzima* (living men), *muzimu* (deceased men), *orishas* (deified men, spirits, gods), and *Olorun* (Creator-God).

2. *Kintu* — visible or "congealed" forces such as plants, animals, minerals, and tools, which do nothing of themselves but act in accordance with the *nomo* of *muntu*. (This explains the importance of amulets, talismans, and charms.)

3. *Hantu* — localized forces; place-time as a unity; subject to *muntu* who are to behave so that each "there and then" is brief and full.

4. *Kuntu* — "function forces"; the single set of principles (*nomo* is the highest) governing all cult, social, and environmental behavior such as sorcery, procreation, and farming.

Jahn's analysis helps us understand the fundamental unity that exists for the African—a unity that preserves a hierarchy within the universe, but nevertheless, to a degree, transcends all divisions between supernature, nature, humanity, and time.

[4]See Janheinz Jahn, *Muntu: An Outline of the New African Culture*, trans. Marjorie Green (New York: Grove, 1961).

As I have said, John Mbiti criticizes most of the approaches taken by Western scholars vis-à-vis African religion. He disagrees with Jahn because he feels that in emphasizing force as the key concept Jahn has overstated the case. Mbiti agrees that for Africans the whole of existence is a religious phenomenon. He also agrees that religion is understood ontologically—i.e., as pertaining to existence or being. But in his own analysis he divides African ontology into five categories—all of which are anthropocentric in their orientation:

1. God—the Originator and Sustainer of humanity
2. Spirits—involved in the destiny of humanity
3. Man
4. Animals and plants—part of the environment in which humans live
5. Phenomena and objects without biological life—another part of the environment in which humans live

If this is the way Mbiti categorizes supernature, nature, and humanity and characterizes their interrelationships, what about time? In Mbiti's approach, time is the key to understanding the worldview of sub-Saharan Africa. He insists that Western lineal time with its indefinite past, a present, and an infinite future is foreign to African thinking. For the African, time has two dimensions. It has a past and a present but virtually no future. Actual time moves backward rather than forward, and people focus on what has taken place rather than on the future. Individuals move, not to a future existence, but to join the ancestors of the past. Death moves people to that existence where, if the living remember them and perform the proper rituals, they will achieve a "collective immortality." I will have more to say about this concept of time later on.

Mbiti obviously wants Western students to appreciate the monotheistic perspectives of African religion. He reports the result of a study of nearly three hundred tribal groups from all over sub-Saharan Africa (outside the traditionally Christian and Muslim communities).[5] He failed to discover a single group that does not have a notion of a supreme Being or a Creator-God. In a number of societies this Creator-God is considered to be omniscient (to the Zulu he is "the Wise One," while the Ila say that his "ears are long"); omnipresent (the Bamun name for God means "he who is everywhere"); and omnipotent (the Kiga refer to God as "the one who makes the sun set"). It is not unusual to discover other identifications and descriptions that refer to God as transcendent, immanent, personal, spirit, good, merciful, and as possessing other attributes and characteristics so familiar to monotheists.

Mbiti also insists that the phenomenon that Westerners have called "ancestor worship" is not really worship at all. The acts of giving food and drink to ancestral spirits are symbols of communion, fellowship. and remembrance. To fail to remember the dead in this way is, in effect, to excommunicate them and deprive them of that which is needful for another existence. But to remember them is not to deify them.

If Jahn has overstated his case, Mbiti probably has done the same. Although the African generally believes in a Creator-God, some have all but forgotten him; others say he has gone far away and doesn't care about people; and still others say he is so powerful that one does not dare to mention his name.[6] The Lunda name for him means "the God of the unknown"; the Ngombe name means "the Unexplainable"; and that of the Maasai means "the Unknown."[7] Although Africans do refer to the Creator-God as good, the term usually connotes that he does good things like sending rain and giving harvest. Although they sometimes think of him as holy, his holiness is of the kind that is most offended by failing to obey ritual observances. Although they associate loving acts with him, they do not know him as the Self-giving God. Moreover, for many the concept of a Creator-God does not militate against belief in other deities. This suggests *henotheism*

[5]Mbiti, *African Religions*, 45.
[6]Jahn, *Muntu*, 115.
[7]Mbiti, *African Religions*, 45.

(belief in one God but not to the exclusion of others), if not polytheism.

As for "ancestor-worship," it may be true that the term suggests too much. However, the alternatives seem to suggest too little. More than "honor" and "remembrance" is involved. Like the deities in various polytheistic systems, ancestral spirits that are not remembered are thought to be personally deprived, and may retaliate in kind. Furthermore, the persistence of ancestor practices, even when the true God is known and his teaching concerning the subject is taught, indicates that the practice rivals true worship rather than complementing it. The term "ancestor-devotion" may be a happy compromise for some, but it will probably be too strong for those who insist that the ancestors are not being worshiped, and too weak for those who insist that they are.

A brief look at the worldview—particularly the supernature—of the Mende tribe of Sierra Leone reveals that points made by both Jahn and Mbiti need to be kept in mind if we are to understand them. The supernature of the Mende has been divided into six categories: supreme God, ancestral spirits, nature spirits, mischievous spirits, spirits of the secret societies, and an impersonal power.[8] Among Mende the belief is that the "supreme God" has retired to the netherworld though he sends rainfall to the Earth, which is considered to be his wife. He is thought of as a chief rather than as a Father. The Mende never approach him directly, but go to the ancestors or nature spirits with prayers and rituals to enlist their aid in securing favors from him.

The ancestral spirits are among the most important in Mende religion. They tend to be approachable and beneficent and are therefore the subject of regular and special rites and prayers. The attitude of the people toward these ancestors can be illustrated by the prayer of a Mende who has just selected a site that he will farm for the ensuing year:

[8]Gilbert W. Olson, *Church Growth in Sierra Leone* (Grand Rapids: Eerdmans, 1969), 42ff.

We have come here to make our farm. We have not come in a proud way to annoy you; do not be angry with us. Let not our machetes wound us as we work; let not the big trees fall and hurt us.[9]

Nature spirits are to be found everywhere—in rivers, trees, hills, rocks, and other natural phenomena. They can be approached directly by prayer and ritual but are quite unpredictable and unreliable. Minor evils are usually attributed to these mischievous spirits.

The devils or spirits that ally themselves with secret societies or special individuals among the Mende can be enlisted against opposition from without the group and against defection from within.

Characteristically, tribal peoples have their fetishes, charms, amulets, talismans, and medicines. The Mende are no exception. Perhaps most important among the Mende is *hale* (medicine), which, it is believed, can inhere in any natural object as a result of the will of the supreme deity. It can be used in cursing and in removing a curse, according to the purposes of the one possessing it.

In general terms, then, the worldview of tribalism (and much of folk religion) can be pictured as in figure 13 and summarized as follows:

1. Supernature includes deities and spirit-beings of all kinds, good and evil. They are usually capricious and capable of being cajoled and influenced, especially by those individuals who are privy to the "right" rituals, incantations, and "medicine." The spirits of departed ancestors are of special importance. Quite often a "high god" exists but in spite of his position he is distant and does not receive the attention accorded to the gods and spirits who are closer in daily existence.

2. Nature is populated with spirit beings. More than that, it is animate and possesses its own intrinsic power. It

[9]Kenneth L. Little, "The Mende of Sierra Leone," in Daryll Forde, ed., *African Worlds* (London: Oxford University Press, 1954), 118.

constitutes not only humanity's physical environment but our spiritual and moral environment as well. We must come to terms with it, for there is a very real sense in which we are a part of its existence and it is a part of ours.

3. Humanity is inextricably bound up in this unitary system. We are *in* nature, not *over nature*. And we are, or inevitably will be, *in* supernature, not *apart from* supernature. In that future state the quality of our existence will in part depend on the presence and ministrations of those we leave behind, who therefore are charged with the responsibility of remembering our names and providing for our continuing needs in the spirit world.

4. Time is cyclical in that it has its seasons of growth and decay, of seedtime and harvest. But it is linear in that it stretches back from the present to those important beginnings of the tribe and its myth and in the sense that it does have a distinct future. Several aspects of this understanding of time are important. First, the tribal worldview tends to focus on the past more than on the future. Tribal people "back into the future" while their eyes are fixed on the past because while they are alive they must remember those who have gone before, and when they die, they will "join the ancestors." Present time is valued more in terms of quality than of quantity. In a practical sense, the "future" may be very short, stretching forward only in terms of months or a year or so, though the sense of some kind of utopia in a more distant future is not necessarily uncommon.

COMMUNICATING CHRIST TO PEOPLE WITH A TRIBAL WORLDVIEW

Looking at the Scriptures, we find numerous references which instruct us as to God's attitude toward this worldview. Nor are we without Old Testament and New Testament examples of communication into it. In the very first commandment given at mount Sinai to the children of Israel after their release from Egyptian bondage, God said,

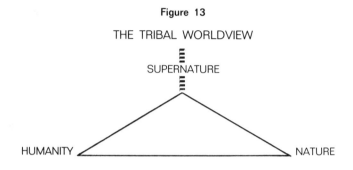

Figure 13

THE TRIBAL WORLDVIEW

SUPERNATURE

HUMANITY   NATURE

PAST ◄————————————————— PRESENT ——► FUTURE

"You shall have no other gods before Me.

"You shall not make for yourself an idol, or any likeness of what is in heaven above or on the earth beneath or in the water under the earth.

"You shall not worship them or serve them" (Exod. 20:3–5).

Isaiah hurled the following challenge at God's idol-prone people:

"Thus says the LORD, the King of Israel

And his Redeemer, the LORD of hosts:

'I am the first and I am the last,

And there is no God besides Me.

'And who is like Me? Let him proclaim and declare it;

Yes, let him recount it to Me in order,

From the time that I established the ancient nation.

And let them declare to them the things that are

coming

And the events that are going to take place.

230

'Do not tremble and do not be afraid;
Have I not long since announced it to you and declared
it?
And you are My witnesses.
Is there any God besides Me,
Or is there any *other* Rock?
I know of none.' "
     Those who fashion a graven image are all of them futile,
and their precious things are of no profit; even their own
witnesses fail to see or know, so that they will be put to
shame (Isa. 44:6–9).

Then the prophet goes on to describe both the process and the
futility of idol-making.
     There are numerous other relevant passages in the New
Testament. But perhaps the passages that are most relevant for
our present purpose are the encounters of Paul with the
heathen of Lystra (Acts 14:6–19) and Athens (chap. 17). I will
refer to these as we proceed.
     1. *The missionary source.* Missionaries are always on trial
in the sense that their respondents want to know what they
are, what they *know*, and what they *do*. It has often been
pointed out that in the context of a tribal worldview *power
encounter* takes precedence over *truth encounter*. In other
words, people want to know what the missionary—or, better,
what the missionary's God—can *do*. This is understandable.
In the early stages of the encounter (in many such cultures),
the power or force issue will be uppermost in the minds of the
people. Quite possibly they will have no indigenous category
for the religious teacher or propagator. The witch doctors,
sorcerers, medicine men, and even priests with whom they are
familiar are more practitioners of religion than they are
instructors and disseminators of it. The Mende, for example,
could be expected to inquire as to the kind of medicine the
missionary brings.
     It was not unusual, therefore, that Paul in Lystra faced the
man who had been lame from birth and, when he saw the

man's response of faith, said in a loud voice, "Stand upright on your feet" (Acts 14:10). The response of the people to the ensuing miracle was also predictable: "The gods have become like men and have come down to us" (v. 11). That did not end the matter, however. Paul and Barnabas were then perceived as deities and had all they could do to restrain the Lystrans from worshiping them! That crisis over, the heathen Lystrans were easily persuaded by Jews from Antioch and Iconium to turn against the apostles. (Remember, deities may have been all but indistinguishable from devils in the Lystran worldview.)

Athens must have been very different from Lystra even though the worldview was generally the same. But as far as the record goes, Paul did no mighty works in Athens. Rather, he appealed to the Athenians' reason, for though his message was not conceived by human ingenuity any more than the response of repentance and faith rested on human power, nevertheless Paul *forcefully demonstrated the fact that the Christian faith is attested to by logicality and history*. And when you go to Athens today, you will discover the message of Paul to the idolatrous Athenians engraved in bronze on the rocky side of Mars' Hill. Paul was that kind of man. And his message was that kind of message!

Folk religions and Satanic cults being as widespread as they are today, the missionary to adherents of all religious worldviews should be prepared to avail himself of the victory over demonic forces that has been assured in Christ's triumph over death and Satan and that is available in his Name.

2. *The content of the missionary message.* Certain aspects of the Christian message contextualized for this type of audience seem abundantly clear. Other aspects are less so.

It is clear from the Scripture that a *definition* of basic terms is in order in such contexts. Everywhere the supposed deities of polytheistic systems are contrasted with the God of heaven. In Lystra, Paul appealed to those who on the strength of one miracle would deify mere men and said, "We . . . preach the gospel to you in order that you should turn from these vain things to a living God, WHO MADE THE HEAVEN AND THE EARTH AND

THE SEA, AND ALL THAT IS IN THEM" (Acts 14:15). In Athens, standing in the very shadow of the Acropolis, he spoke of "the God who made the world and all things in it, . . . Lord of heaven and earth" (17:24). God indeed is known in some sense to all his creatures. But often he is crowded out, pushed back, and shrouded in obscurity. His ambassadors must make it clear of whom, and for whom, they speak. And when the true God is eclipsed by false gods, godlings, and spirits, true perspectives on such things as good and evil, and commandments and duty, are lost. "No-thing" can be taken for granted. All must be defined in terms of the biblical worldview.

Notice also the *selection* of themes that Paul believed to be important to communicating Christ to such people: the creative work of God; the patience of God in overlooking the times of ignorance; and the goodness of God in providing rain and seasons, and food and gladness. One is reminded of the question posed to the missionary by a village headman in Southeast Asia: "Can your God make a rice paddy?" And of the Shintoist (traditional Shintoism essentially embraces a tribal worldview) who asked, "If you want us to understand the Christian way, why do you not open your Holy Book to the beginning and start there?" Both questions are good and valid questions for the missionary to ponder.

At the same time, it is impossible to overlook the "point of entry" that Paul used when he began his Athenian address with references to the inscription, "TO AN UNKNOWN GOD," and his quotation from the Greek poet Aratus who wrote, "For we also are His [God's] offspring" (Acts 17:23, 28). Here were "points of entry" ready-made for the apostle.

Similar points of entry are available today as well. Those familiar with recent missionary literature will recall the beautiful account of Don and Carol Richardson's search for a way to communicate Christ to the Sawi people of West Irian.[10]

---

[10]See Don Richardson, *Peace Child* (Glendale: Regal, 1974). For theological analyses of Richardson's approach from perspectives provided by orthodox and suborthodox Christologies see also Robert A. Evans and Thomas D. Parker, eds., *Christian Theology: A Case Study Approach* (New York: Harper & Row, 1976), 113–32.

At first nothing the missionaries said seemed to occasion interest or understanding. Imagine their discouragement when they discovered that when interest was aroused, it was over the brilliance of Judas. His treachery appealed to the Sawi because for them treachery is a high virtue! Then came the day when a ritual was held to stop the killings and make peace between the Sawi and a rival village. The Richardsons watched in amazement as representatives of the villages approached each other, each with a baby in his arms. Amidst the crying of the women, each in turn held out his own baby son and, giving him into the hands of the other, said, "I give you my son and with him my name." The peace child became the redemptive analogy that the Richardsons needed. Christ could be, and was, communicated to the Sawi after all.

When dealing with the redemptive story of God's dealings with us as Paul seems to have done quite regularly, the narrative itself provides *organization* for the message. In the nature of the case, it may not be legitimate to draw conclusions from a comparison of Paul's address at Lystra with his address at Athens since we have them in such abbreviated form. But insofar as it may be legitimate, it seems that the differences had to do with the increased number of points and the recourse to local productions in the case of his speech to the more sophisticated Athenian inquirers.

Finally, note the *application* in Paul's message to the Athenians, those proud heirs of the *art* of Pheidias and the *wisdom* of Pericles. Paul expressed its negative side when he said, "We ought not to think that the Divine Nature is like gold or silver or stone, an image formed by the *art* and *thought* of man" (Acts 17:29, italics mine). Its positive side was, "God is now declaring to men that all everywhere should repent" (v. 30). (A similar twofold application had been made at Lystra.) Of course, the not-that-but-this application is appropriate no matter what worldview is being countered, but Paul was unequivocal in applying his message to the *specific worldview* of the Athenians with their penchant for fashioning deities of one order or another. When people's worship is wrong, they are culpable. God demands, and the universe awaits, humanity's conversion.

3. *Style*. There are those who believe that Paul's words in 1 Corinthians 2:2, "For I determined to know nothing among you except Jesus Christ, and Him crucified," imply a radical change in the style if not the substance of his communication. They say that Paul at Corinth abandoned the oratorical approach he had taken at Athens (and, perhaps, the public miracle approach he had taken at Lystra?) and resolved to preach a simple gospel, which itself is the wisdom and power of God. This change, they say, was occasioned by the lack of success at Athens.

Perhaps they are correct, but it is doubtful. In the first place, Athens was not Paul's kind of city. He evidently did not go there with the intention of preaching and teaching. In the second place, Paul was in Athens only briefly, whereas, encouraged by a vision, he stayed in Corinth for a year and a half (Acts 18:9–11). In the third place, according to the record, even in Corinth Paul "was *reasoning* in the synagogue every Sabbath and *trying to persuade* Jews and Greeks" (18:4, italics mine).

No, the content and style of Paul's preaching and teaching were essentially the same at Corinth as they had been previously. But he reminded the Corinthians that both his message and his preaching (cf. 1 Cor. 2:4) were very different from those oratorical displays that were so popular at the time. Paul refused to dilute his message with sophistry. He refused to promote Christ's cause by exhibitionism.

Faith built on sophistry and exhibitionism could not stand the tests of the first century, nor can it stand the tests of the twentieth. But faith that rests in the message of the crucified Christ communicated with cogency and conviction, and attended by the work of the Holy Spirit, can be expected to stand the tests of any century. The message may be contextualized as it was in Athens and Corinth. It may be delivered in the style of Paul or Apollos. However, the most important element is that it is a faithful message delivered with conviction and attended by a "demonstration of the

Spirit and of *power*" (1 Cor. 2:4, italics mine). Then *God's work* will be accomplished in the lives of people. (Note that "power" in 1 Corinthians 2:4 does not refer to miracles per se, for that meaning would require the plural form). In the final analysis, it is *that* power that is sorely needed today— certainly among tribalists, but also among all other peoples, whatever their worldview.

Chapter 16

Communicating Christ Into The Hindu-Buddhistic Worldview

Missionaries have been signally successful in communicating Christ into the tribal worldview, particularly in areas of the world where that view has not already been challenged by alternative views. But they have not been nearly as successful in communicating Christ in that part of the world where Hinduism and Buddhism have prevailed over long centuries. One reason for the missionaries' lack of success in those areas may be that they have not given sufficient thought to the Hindu-Buddhistic worldview itself and therefore have not been able to effectively communicate the Christ of the Scriptures.

Hinduism and Buddhism grew out of the same Indian soil. If we were to analyze that soil as it was some four thousand years ago at the time of the Aryan invasions (experts vary as to the date), we would discover that the prevailing worldview was tribalistic. But we would also find certain ideas—some of them originating with the Dravidian invasions one thousand years earlier—that were destined to evolve into a very different worldview. That view has been termed pantheistic— i.e., the universe conceived of as a whole is deity or ultimate reality. As it was developed by some of the most prominent Indian sages, however, it took the form of a particular type of pantheism called monism—i.e., there is but one, unified reality in the universe. Hinduism and Buddhism developed somewhat differently. In fact, there is little of Buddhism left in the land of its birth. Nevertheless, in encountering either faith the missionary will find a twofold commonality. Among ordinary, more or less untutored adherents he will find pervasive folk beliefs and practices resembling those of the early tribalists. Among the more instructed adherents he will find a monism that has permeated much of Asia and now bids for adherents in the West.

THE IDEAS AND DEVELOPMENT OF HINDUISM

Mircea Eliade has written that four "kinetic ideas" form the core of Indian spirituality:[1]

1. The law of *karma*, which binds humanity to the universe and necessitates the round of transmigration.
2. The concept of *maya*, which means that the experienced cosmos is illusory.
3. The idea of the absolute or pure being that lies behind the world of experience viewed as the *atman* (the self or soul), the Brahman (the absolute objectively understood), or nirvana (the highest good, peace, void, and bliss).
4. The means or techniques of gaining liberation called Yoga.

Eliade notes that the Indian quest has not been a search for truth for truth's sake but rather a search for liberation. The quest developed along two main lines: Sankhya and Vedanta. Sankhya exhibited certain dualistic and atheistic tendencies within the larger monistic framework. In Sankhya, matter (*pakriti*) and soul (*purusha*) were separate categories of being.

---

[1]Mircea Eliade, "Two Representative Systems of Hindu Thought," in *Readings in Eastern Religious Thought*, ed., Ollie M. Frazier, 3 vols. (Philadelphia: Westminster, 1963), 1:166–67.

No place was found for a personal deity. Both Mahavira (the founder of Jainism) and Gautama (the founder of Buddhism) were adherents of Sankhya. Vedanta, on the other hand, developed along somewhat different lines and became the more influential school of thought in India. We will deal with Vedanta and then return to consider the Sankhya system as it worked itself out in Buddhism.

Vedanta means "Veda-end" and relates, therefore, to the concluding portion of the Vedas called the Upanishads. The Vedas date to the second millennium B.C. and consist primarily of sacrificial hymns that reflect a polytheistic background. The Upanishads originated between 1000 (some say 800) and 500 B.C. and consist of various texts that develop the ritual and cosmogonic ideas of the Vedas. Together the Vedas and the Upanishads or "Veda-ends" are categorized as *shruti* ("that which is heard," i.e., direct revelation) and are distinguished from secondary scriptures known as *smriti* ("that which is remembered," i.e., memorized tradition). The Vedic literature is held to have been the product of enlightened men who raised themselves to a level of receptivity where they were able to receive divine revelation.

In the Upanishadic and subsequent literature polytheism came to be superseded by a monistic idealism. The Vedic notion of one reality known by many names was elaborated. Brahman became the Real, the One, the Ground of all existence. The Nirguna Brahman (the impersonal Brahman without form) was differentiated from the Saguna Brahman (the personal Brahman with form). Thus, although a place was found for numerous deities beginning with the Hindu Trinity (*Trimurti*) of Brahma, Vishnu, and Shiva, they were all generally held to be the expressions of the one impersonal and indescribable Brahman.

In this view, the world is not believed to be a creation *ex nihilo*. The world of change and appearance that people ordinarily experience is really *maya* or illusion. The "really Real" is behind it. Brahman is "issuing forth." He (It) is "*in*volved" in the world. From the Brahman all has come and to the Brahman all must return. The process requires an almost incalculable amount of time, but behind the world of appearances Brahman has "involved" and all is "evolving" back to him. Why the process at all? All that can be said is that the Brahman delights in going even to the depths and coming back again.

And what about humanity? A person's body and that which he ordinarily calls the "I" is just as unsubstantial as the phenomenal world. But within the person is the *atman* or the divine self, which is really identical with the Brahman. The *atman* equals the Brahman. Therefore it is possible for a person to look into himself or into another person and say, "That art Thou." This likely explains why it is traditional for Indians to greet each other with their hands in a prayer position. It is a salute to the divine within the person.

Linked with these notions of early Indian religion are those of reincarnation and *karma*. Each self goes through a series of births and rebirths that, in the manner of the phenomenal world, is almost endless. One's station and condition in each of these successive existences is determined by his karma. The analogy of a deck of cards is sometimes used to explain this. Having received a hand of cards on the basis of his karma in previous existences, the individual now has the power to play his hand as he will. But he must know that his choices occasion his karma, which in turn determines his next existence.

And how does a person attain to liberation *(moksha)* from this otherwise endless chain of rebirths? The ancients recognized three means: works, wisdom, and devotion. Each of them, however, is linked in one way or another to the overcoming of our fundamental problem of ignorance and the realization of union of the *atman* with Brahman. This calls for a higher consciousness, which may be termed superconsciousness or pure consciousness. This in turn calls for a method—the method of Yoga—which finds its basis in early Indian religious development, the Upanishads, Sankhya, and in the works of Patanjali (A.D. second century).

It was Shankara (A.D. 788–820) who brought Indian nondualism, or *advaita*, to its highest development. His school is sometimes called the school of "illusionist monism." Shankara insisted that only the indescribable Brahman (the Nirguna Brahma) exists. It is ignorance that creates the world of appearances and the various deities. At the same time it is through these appearances that we can see that the *atman* is the Brahman. With this knowledge, ignorance is superseded and illusion is done away. The world, the body, the suffering, the pain, and the striving are all past.

Another important philosopher of Vedanta was a twelfth-century reformer by the name of Ramanuja (1016–1137). He espoused a "qualified nondualism" and attempted to justify Vishnu as the Supreme Being, the sole real being, the Brahman. Here the Nirguna-Saguna distinction is superseded and Brahman is made personal. The phenomenal world and the individual *atman* have some kind of reality, because they are the "body" or "form" through which Vishnu manifests himself. Other supernatural beings are allowable because Vishnu manifests himself through various avatars or incarnations, whether people or animals. Vishnu has his heaven in which he lives and when his followers render to him their devotion *(bhakti)*, they can go to be with him and enjoy his presence.

Ramanuja was still operating within the monistic framework, but in going beyond the strict monism of Shankara he gave impetus to that kind of intense meditation and devotion that currently finds expression among the devotees of Krishna (one of the avatars of Vishnu).

THE IDEAS AND DEVELOPMENT OF BUDDHISM

As has already been suggested, Gautama Buddha (ca. 568–483 B.C.) was oriented to Sankhya philosophy. But he developed his own system. He replaced the Brahman with nirvana, a state where all desire with its attendant suffering is extinguished. The state of nirvana is attainable by anyone of any caste or class who exerts the necessary effort. He replaced the *atman* teaching with the doctrine of *anatta* (no-self, nonego). This is to be distinguished from self-denial or self-mortification, for according to Buddha there is no self to be denied or mortified.

These teachings assured the eventual demise of Buddhism in India. Tension developed between followers who emphasized austerity and a literal interpretation of Gautama Buddha's teachings (Hinayana) and those who espoused more freedom and a more expansive interpretation of his teachings (Mahayana). Still other divergences developed within these larger schools and the resultant variegation within Buddhism is baffling. There are tendencies toward atheism and theism, dualism and monism, enlightenment by faith and enlightenment by works, salvation to a blissful paradise and salvation to the bliss of nothingness. It all depends on how one interprets what Gautama Buddha taught and practiced. To attempt to elucidate a distinctly "Buddhist worldview," therefore, is admittedly a risky business.

At any rate, Buddhists seem to be in basic agreement that humanity lives in a certain kind of universe. This world exists, not as the effect of a single cause, but as a result of multiple causes and conditions. At the same time it is a contributing cause to its own effect and thus helps form its own future. What the world is now is the effect of previous causes. What it will be will be the effect of what it is now. In the same way, a person is what he is in this existence because of what he has been in past existences. And what a person is now will in part determine his future existences. There is no escape from this law of cause and effect *(karma)* short of nirvana. All phenomena in the world, and the world itself, are characterized by impermanence. Nothing—neither human nor beast, neither mountain nor star—has its own separate and distinct existence. All are the results of ever-changing, interrelating *skandhas* (collections or aggregates) that lend present but transitory form to existing phenomena and, in the case of some, consciousness. In this curious alchemy, cause exists but not a First Cause. Misery has a reality that a person does not have. A person is not a separate self but a combination of *skandhas*. What survives is not a soul but a person's karma, which determines the form of his next existence. What beckons him is not immortality but the "emptiness" or "void" or "bliss" of Nirvana.

> *Misery only doth exist; none miserable.*
> *No doer is there; naught but the deed is found.*
> *Nirvana is, but not the man who seeks it,*
> *The path exists, but not the traveler on it.*[2]

A human being has no soul with a separate present existence and a future destiny. A person's problem is not understood in terms of sin but in terms of suffering. Ignorance of the true nature of his present state and the way of deliverance is pandemic and must be dispelled by the preaching of Buddha's message. Whether or not people will undertake to traverse the path to ultimate enlightenment in accordance with the teaching of the manner of the Buddha is for them to decide. A person's destiny is in his own hands.

The *sense* in which a person's destiny is in his own hands is a matter of interpretation. Gautama Buddha's own search started as a solitary quest motivated only by a desire to know the secret of freedom from the chain of births and rebirths. It ended in the solitude of a quiet grove. He described what occurred there as a struggle, but it was *his* struggle. The victory also was his and his alone. He sought no help from deities nor did he receive any. He found the answer to his quest within himself.

There is more to be said, however. For when Buddhist scriptures go on to describe a second struggle in which Buddha despaired of preaching his doctrine for fear that people would not understand or embrace it, none other than Brahma Sahampati, perceiving the Buddha's thoughts, emerged from the Brahma-world to encourage him!

[2]Visuddhimagga XVI as quoted by David Bently-Taylor, "Buddhism," in J. N. D. Anderson, ed., *The World's Religions* (London: Inter-Varsity, 1955), 125.

243

Rise thou, O Hero, Victor in the Battle!
O Leader, Guiltless One, go 'mongst the nations!
The Doctrine let the Buddha teach,
Some will be found to master it.[3]

Nor can we overlook the fact that the new Buddha *took to himself* such names and designations as invited the deepest reverence from his followers. For example, he addressed one of his disciples in these words:

I have no teacher anywhere;
My equal nowhere can be found;
In all the world with all its gods,
No one to rival me exists.

The saintship, verily, I've gained,
I am The Teacher, unsurpassed;
I am The Buddha, sole, supreme;
Lust's fire is quenched, Nirvana gained.[4]

As a result of these and similar statements, Mahayana Buddhism especially has given birth to numerous buddhas and bodhisattvas (savior-beings), and Gautama Buddha himself has been deified. Yet, as in Hinduism, there is in Buddhism one reality behind the universe and these two religions emerge as different pieces of the one cloth. Hinduism and Buddhism share one basic worldview—that of monism. And monism ultimately means that God is impersonal, the world of experience is ephemeral, and a person's gaze must be turned inward.

The monistic worldview that is largely characteristic of Hinduism and Buddhism can be diagrammed as in figure 14.

1. Supernature is that from which all emanates and that to which all aspires. It not only permeates the whole, it

---

[3]"The Summum Bonum" from the Majjhima-Hikaya, and consisting of Sutra 26 in Ollie M. Frazier, ed., *Readings in Eastern Religious Thought*, 3 vols. (Philadelphia: Westminster, 1963), 2:171.
[4]Ibid., 174.

constitutes the "really Real." As such it is beyond such considerations as the personal and the impersonal. It is the Absolute and it is indescribable. Insofar as the myriads of gods, godlings, and spirits that inhabit the universe are real they are expressions of the Absolute.

Figure 14

THE MONISTIC WORLDVIEW

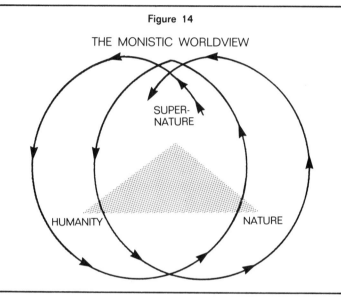

2. Nature represents, not a separate creation, but an emanation from the Absolute. In one sense it is illusory and unworthy of our concern. In another sense it is the setting in which enlightenment occurs and, understood aright, can furnish the occasion for enlightenment.

3. A person does not have individual existence in any ultimate sense. He too issues forth from the Absolute and ultimately returns to It. If he is conceived of as having a "soul," that "soul" is really the Brahman or Absolute within. If he is conceived of as having "no soul," it is because there is no "I" as such to possess one. A person's goal is union with

the Absolute whether that Absolute be thought of as Brahman or Nirvana.

4. Time is cyclical. It is made up of aeons of years (better, a seemingly endless series of existences or transmigrations) during which seekers after enlightenment are emancipated from the bad karma that "weighs them down" and gradually evolve "upward." Ultimately *all* and *everything* returns to the Brahman or the Void from which it emanated. To what purpose the emanations? Why must this great circuitous route be traveled at all? The answers to such questions are shrouded in mystery. No one can really know.

A worldview such as this is all but impossible for the average person to "live out" in everyday life. If it is lived out at all, it tends to be confined to monasteries and mountain retreats. The religion practiced by ordinary Hindus and Buddhists more closely approximates that of tribal and folk religionists. Nevertheless, important elements of the monistic worldview described here will tend to surface again and again; so it is absolutely essential that missionaries in Hindu and Buddhist contexts be familiar with it and be able to respond to it.

COMMUNICATING CHRIST TO HINDUS AND BUDDHISTS

In the light of what has been said, it is understandable that Western missionaries especially find it difficult to communicate Christ into the Hindu-Buddhistic worldview. That view is not only foreign to us but until recently it has been almost "unthinkable" to most of us. In addition, it is characterized by variegated expressions both in terms of philosophical statements of it and also religious expressions of it. Hinduism is not Hinduism (and Buddhism is not Buddhism)!

The Bible does not furnish us with clear illustrations of the encounter with monism. But there is much in the Bible that speaks to the errors and needs of its adherents.

1. *The missionary source.* Missionary sources who would

communicate to Hindus and Buddhists need to take stock. My experiences with these people lead me to believe that they accept most Christian missionaries as people of *goodwill*. But more than goodwill is required. The additional prerequisites are *integrity* and *credibility*.

In the first place, Hindus and Buddhists expect that those who dispense religion will be well versed in religion. Their own lands are well populated with knowledgeable teachers of religion. Theirs is a long religious tradition. If anyone has the audacity to come half way around the world to teach a new faith, he certainly can be expected to have had the good sense to study carefully, not only the faith he would communicate but also the faith he would supplant.

In the second place, there remains a problem that refuses to go away. It is illustrated in a conversation between D. T. Niles and Billy Graham just before the latter went to India for evangelistic meetings.[5] Graham asked Niles if there was anything he would need to understand in order to minister to the people of India. Niles replied, "Yes—there is one thing which you must be aware of. When you are in India, people will expect to see some sign of austerity in your way of life as part of your credentials in claiming to be a man of God." Graham is said to have answered, "That raises one of the unresolved problems of my conscience." And to that answer Niles responds, "He was right. Indeed, the instinct of our people is right when they insist that anyone whose life is not marked by 'renunciation' has not really faced up to the demands of God on his life."

2. *The content of the missionary message.* The "contextualization" required in the context of the Hindu-Buddhistic worldview is so extensive as to make any summary of it border on caricature. If that is admitted and understood, some suggestions of its broad outline may be allowable.

For the Hindu and Buddhist, their worldview colors almost all of the major terms used by the missionary. To the

[5]D. T. Niles, *The Preacher's Task and the Stone of Stumbling* (New York: Harper & Row, 1958), 63–64.

extent that the task of *definition* has not been accomplished by his predecessors, the missionary must proceed by definition, definition, and definition. I do not mean, of course, that missionary communication will be reduced to a lexicon. But by comparison and contrast the missionary must do his best to avoid building the Christian superstructure on a monistic foundation. The members of the Triune Godhead of the Bible must be made to stand out in bold relief against the backdrop of such Hindu ideas as Brahman, and *Trimurti* (the three major deities of Hinduism); and Buddha and *Trikaya* (the three bodies of Buddha). The world of creation must be distinguished from both the materialist world of much of the West and the illusory world of much of the East. Human beings must be seen as creatures of God—not souls in bodies, but whole persons—and their problem as rebellion rather than ignorance. History must be understood as something to be affirmed rather than something to be denied, and as *part* of eternity not just a *prolegomena* to it.

When it comes to *selection*, the above paragraph will give clues, not only to those terms that must be defined but also to those doctrines that must be taught. They are numerous. But where does one begin?

My friend and former faculty colleague, Purushotman Krishna (himself a convert from Hinduism) often reminded me that the Indian is attracted to the person and teaching of Christ, especially such teachings as those contained in the Sermon on the Mount. That is understandable. And it is perhaps a legitimate approach.

George W. Peters reports a conversation that he had with Bakht Singh concerning evangelism and a message for India. The conversation reveals Singh's starting point.

> As we talked about evangelism and a message for India, I asked him: "When you preach in India, what do you emphasize?" "Do you preach to them the *love* of God?"
>
> "No," he said, "not particularly. The Indian mind is so polluted that if you talk to them about love they think

mainly of sex life. You do not talk to them much about the love of God."

"Well," I said, "do you talk to them about the *wrath* of God and the judgment of God?"

"No, this is not my emphasis," he remarked, "they are used to that. All the gods are mad anyway. It makes no difference to them if there is one more who is angry!"

"What do you talk to them about? Do you preach Christ and Him crucified?" I guessed.

"No," he replied. "They would think of Him as a poor martyr who helplessly died."

"What then is your emphasis? Do you talk to them about eternal life?"

"Not so," he said. "If you talk about eternal life, the Indian thinks of transmigration. He wants to get away from it. Don't emphasize eternal life."

"What then is your message?"

"I have never yet failed to get a hearing if I talk to them about forgiveness of sins and peace and rest in your heart. That's the product that sells well. Soon they ask me how they can get it. Having won their hearing I lead them on to the Savior who alone can meet their deepest needs."[6]

Care must be exercised in communicating these truths in the Hindu-Buddhistic context, however. Insofar as India knows of Christ, there is a profound interest in him. But the Hindu tendency is to accept him and give him a home *in Hinduism!* Mahatma Gandhi once said, "I think of Christ as belonging, not to Christianity alone, but to the whole world, to all its people, no matter under what name they may worship."[7] A Hindu friend of D. T. Niles remarked, "We shall put an image of Christ into every Hindu temple and then no Hindu will see the point of becoming a Christian."[8] The Hindu—and, to a lesser extent, the Buddhist—are inclined to

[6]George W. Peters, "Issues Confronting Evangelical Missions," in Wade T. Coggins and E. L. Frizen, eds., *Evangelical Missions Tomorrow* (South Pasadena: William Carey Library, 1977), 167.
[7]Quoted in Niles, *Preacher's Task*, 17.
[8]Ibid.

accept Christ, but on their own terms. And on their terms Christ becomes another avatar or bodhisattva rather than the unique, incarnate Lord and Savior. The latter he is. The former he is not. How can we, and how can they, know? Here again adaptation is necessary. The revelation that we have in the Bible is not that of sages and gurus who experienced some inner vision and then sought to dimly reflect that inner wisdom through the impoverished medium of words. Rather, it is the very Word of God channeled through godly men who spoke and wrote as human instruments of the Holy Spirit.

For that matter, the "forgiveness of sins and peace," which Bakht Singh finds to be a "product which sells well," needs careful packaging. Christians undoubtedly could learn much from Hindu-Buddhistic meditative techniques and passivity. But the rest and peace that Jesus gives come as a result of forgiveness and redemption through Christ's blood and reconciliation with God in Christ, not as a result of self-effort or resignation to the inexorable laws of *karma*.

There is potential in the approaches of Krishna and Singh, of course. This is especially true when one thinks of opening the door to further conversation and dialogue. But the overriding problem in communicating Christ in the Hindu-Buddhistic worldview context boils down to a question of whether or not *any* historical event other than the experience of enlightenment (or "salvation") can be of ultimate importance. All "stories" are significant, but only to the extent that they occasion that experience. However, as we have been reminded, if Christ is "de-Judaized," he is also "de-historicized." That may not be crucial from a monistic point of view, but it is absolutely crucial to the biblical worldview. Therefore it seems essential that, however one approaches the monist, he must fill out the larger "gospel story" and do it in such a way that all other "stories," and especially mythological ones, are seen in contrast to it.

Beyond the *organization* of content that is more or less intrinsic to the approach afforded by biblical theology per se, there are legitimate questions concerning the best way to proceed. On the one hand, an organization of materials into a longer or shorter series of major points, each in turn followed by its logical clarifications and reinforcements seems to be legitimate, especially in India where the British educational system has been so prominent. On the other hand, in a monistic system where laws of Western logic such as the law of noncontradiction do not really hold, the communicator might be tempted to avoid an approach that seems to reduce the "divine mystery" to a brief series of propositions resting on "questionable" logic. The long and short of it seems to be that among monists—and in India especially—the communicator needs to be flexible. Perhaps the dilemma we have just described helps to explain why dialogue has been quite prominent in these contexts. And dialogue itself tends to dictate both the selection of content and its arrangement.

In *applying* the message of Christ, the missionaries may well ask their Hindu and Buddhist friends to face up to the truth question and also to their existential predicament. "True truth" does not admit of self-contradiction. To make a truth claim about ultimate reality, one

> must bow to the law of non-contradiction. No position has the right to claim universal truth, as a worldview does, unless it has some universal test for truth. If the law of non-contradiction is not universally valid, then neither is truth objectively and universally valid. Truth and non-contradiction are co-extensive.[9]

Moreover, "true truth" is narrow, not broad. The authority for that statement is to be found, not only in logicality, but in the assertions of Jesus Christ himself.

When all is said and done, the number of adherents of the Hindu-Buddhistic worldview who will be impressed by reasonable arguments will be small, however. The number who will be impressed by the authority of Christ will be somewhat

---

[9]Norman L. Geisler, "Some Philosophical Perpectives on Missionary Dialogue," in David J. Hesselgrave, ed., *Theology and Mission* (Grand Rapids: Baker, 1978), 241.

greater. But both logicality and Christology should be related to the existential predicament of these people. The Hindu denies the individuality of the self. The Buddhist denies its existence. (The sense of these statements must be understood in their own respective contexts.) But, as Bakht Singh's approach implies, these people are feeling, thinking, willing people. And they are encumbered with *karma*, chained to the wheel of birth and rebirth, and destined to countless existences before achieving some kind of union with an undefinable reality. No wonder that purveyors of an instant enlightenment do a land-office business. (And no wonder that an uncontextualized offer of eternal life does not appeal!) The wonder is that Christ's spokesmen who, true to Christ's promise, offer hope for *this life* and *the life to soon come* (absent from the body, present with the Lord) do not receive a greater hearing (cf. 2 Cor. 5:6).

Consider one more word. Let us remember that India especially has practically drowned in religion. Buddhism originally was a revolt against that religion. Today Buddhist peoples are drowning in the same sea. *The Christian does not offer more religion. He offers the gospel. He offers the Christ.*

3. *The style of communication.* Once more I make mention of my friend, Professor Krishna. I feel that he will forgive my reference to a personal incident in view of the importance of the lesson to be conveyed.

Some years ago we sat together with a chapel audience addressed by an American youth evangelist. The evangelist's leather jacket, festooned with Jesus buttons, constituted a somewhat different attire for a seminary chapel. But it was the message itself that was most unique, punctuated as it was with references to Christ as a "great guy" and "good fellow," and delivered in rapid-fire style with no sense of awe or mystery. After a closing "Amen," I waited for Dr. Krishna to rise, but he just sat there, his head buried in his hands. Aware of his physical problems, I made inquiry. Slowly he lifted his head and, haltingly, said: "I just can't believe it. Is this the way Christians speak of the Lord of the universe?"

I do not recount this experience in order to indict the

evangelist. The cultural contexts involved are different, and that must be taken into account. But Professor Krishna's reaction does point up something that is most important for the *communication* of the Christian faith if not to an *understanding* of it. There is something that we do indeed share with those who espouse the Hindu-Buddhistic worldview. It is that the universe is basically a spiritual universe. "God is spirit, and those who worship Him must worship in *spirit* and truth" (John 4:24, italics mine). That verse needs to be pondered. The message of the Lord of the universe will be communicated into the Hindu-Buddhistic worldview only as its spiritual essence is not lost while making statements about it.

Chapter 17

Communicating Christ Into A Chinese Worldview

Approximately one out of every four or five persons on the face of the earth is Chinese. It is all but impossible to identify a *prevailing* Chinese worldview. It is possible, however, to describe the *traditional* Chinese worldview. And it is likely that in describing it we are describing the basic worldview of the majority of Chinese, wherever they may be found.

THE WORLDVIEW OF ANCIENT CHINA

The three terms used by the Chinese for God—Shang Ti, T'ien, and Shen—go back to the Golden Age referred to in the *Book of History*.[1] (The Golden Age is the age of three of China's greatest emperors—Yao, Shun, and Yu.)

In the twenty-third century B.C. Emperor Shun, on his accession to the throne, is reported to have offered sacrifice to Shang Ti. In addition, he offered a different kind of sacrifice to "six honored ones" and still another sacrifice to the hills and streams.

[1] I am indebted in this section to mimeographed class notes prepared and distributed by my late colleague J. Herbert Kane.

The term T'ien goes back to the same period of Chinese history. Emperor Shun traveled to Tai Shan and in addition to sacrifices to the hills and streams, he offered a burnt offering to T'ien.

The third term for God—Shen—is found in the *Book of History* where Yu is reminded that perfect sincerity moves the Shen.

These three terms are not synonymous. Shang Ti is a personal God, the supreme ruler over all earthly rulers. Throughout history only the Chinese emperors have performed the worship of Shang Ti at the Altar of Heaven in Peking (Beijing). T'ien is the impersonal heaven or providence. All, from the king to the peasant, called on T'ien for help.

Shen is more difficult to analyze. The term was seldom used in the singular. It is the technical term for god; but it also means spirits—good spirits. In contrast, evil spirits are called *kwei*. Shen is the popular name for certain special gods, such as nature gods—the god of wind, fire, and so on. Dr. Kane elucidates other important concepts:

> The core of Chinese religious conviction is the belief that the world of man and the world of nature are inseparable and interdependent, and that beyond and within the mysterious operation of the universe in its relation to human destiny lies an Eternal Order—called *Tao*. Thus man and nature are really one. They have a common origin; they run a similar course; they are subject to the same law.
>
> At the heart of Chinese cosmology is the concept of *Tao*. Literally it means a road, path, way; but in a wider connotation it means law, truth, doctrine, order. *Tao* is the path which the universe follows; and all things and beings evolve from it. *Tao* manifests itself in the dual principles of *Yin* and *Yang*. Out of the alternate actions of *Yin* and *Yang* develop the five primary elements—fire, water, earth, wood and metal. Although *Yin* and *Yang* are diametrically opposed in character, they are equally essential for the existence of the universe.
>
> The *Yin-Yang* system can be traced back to the *Book of Changes*, though the words themselves are not found in the

Confucian classics. The entire *Book of Changes* is built around a symbol, peculiarly Chinese, known as the *pa-kua* [the Eight Trigrams with the Yin and Yang inside—see figure 15]. It is in the *Book of Changes* that the dualistic theory of *Yin* and *Yang* is said to have arisen. It was not until the Sung dynasty that the system took possession of the Chinese in its elaborated form.

The origin of the *pa-kua* is not known. It may have had something to do with the seasons of the year or the directions of the compass. We do know that the Chinese paid great attention to the arranging of the calendar as well as the four seasons. As they observed the complex movements of the heavenly bodies and the innumerable changes in the earth, they came to the conclusion that all natural phenomena operated in accord with and were subject to the control of an Eternal Order, called *Tao*, which functioned in a dualistic manner through the operation of two great opposing forces *Yin* and *Yang*. Accordingly, everything in nature is either *Yin* or *Yang*. Associated with *Yang* are the positive elements, such as heaven, light, heat, masculinity, strength, life, etc. *Yin* includes the opposite elements: earth, darkness, cold, femininity, weakness, death, etc.

This theory of dualism is carried over into the unseen world of the spirit. The atmosphere swarms with spirits, good and bad. The former are known as *shen* and the latter as *kwei*. This led to the development of a "science" which arose out of the *Yin-Yang* idea, known as *feng-shui*—wind and water.

With spirits, good and bad, controlling all parts of nature, it became necessary to do nothing to disturb these unseen powers. Hence an elaborate system of geomancy and necromancy came into existence. Anything likely to disturb the *feng-shui* should be avoided at all costs. The building of a road, or the digging of a grave, the launching of a boat, arranging for a wedding or a funeral, all were potentially dangerous unless beforehand it was determined that the *feng-shui* would be good.

This system of dualism carries over into the moral world. Here *Yang* is identified with virtue and *Yin* with vice. A man full of virtue is also full of *yang* and the *yang* influence of the good man will permeate the whole community. Likewise the *yin* influence of the evil person.[2]

The Chinese have always taken a greater interest in the structure of the world than in its creation. But, for the common people at least, both are probably best understood in terms of Chinese mythology. Although found in rather late literary works, the tale that probably comes closest to a primitive myth is that of P'an-Ku. There are various versions of the myth. According to one account, before heaven and earth existed, chaos looked like an egg. After eighteen thousand years the egg opened. P'an-Ku's body emerged. It was as great as the distance between the earth (formed from *yin* elements) and the sky (formed from *yang* elements). According to certain other versions, upon his death P'an-Ku's body became parts of the world. His head became the four cardinal mountains, his eyes the sun and moon, his hair the plants, and his flesh the rivers and sea.

The myth contains the essence of the Chinese cosmology, though the Chinese developed more sophisticated ways of describing the universe.

THE CONTRIBUTIONS OF LAO-TZU AND CONFUCIUS

Lao-tzu (ca. 604–524 B.C.) and Confucius (ca. 551–479 B.C.) were heirs of, but also contributors to, the traditional Chinese worldview. In the China of their day nature was alive with spirits—the sky, the hills, the roads, the streams, the fields. Most of the spirits were evil or at least capricious and were associated with animals, places, the elements, and so forth. Both the earth and heaven were worshiped. Priestcraft was rife. Ideas of the *Yang* and the *Yin* and the Tao were present and awaited further philosophical development. Lao-tzu and Confucius reacted against the religious and social confusion of their day and, together with their successors, left

[2]Ibid.

an indelible mark on the Chinese view of man, nature, supernature, and time. The difference between Lao-tzu and Confucius was essentially one of emphasis. Lao-tzu emphasized the Tao as manifested in nature. Confucius emphasized humanity and social relationships. Confucius emphasized the past and its wisdom. Lao-tzu emphasized the present experience. Both Taoism and Confucianism began as philosophies and then developed along religious as well as philosophical lines. The worldview of multiplied millions of Chinese over a period of two and one-half millennia has been informed by the ideas of these two great Chinese masters.

The reform that Lao-tzu sought to initiate had to do with the internal state of the worshiper. For him the essential but missing ingredient of true religion and right living had to do with the inmost self and its relation to the Tao. That in essence is the theme of the Tao Te Ching, the book of five thousand Chinese characters ascribed to Lao-tzu. The Tao has been translated into various English words such as God, Nature, Way, Truth, and Ultimate Reality. None of these is adequate. Lao-tzu said that the Tao is indescribable and yet somehow described by Lao-tzu; nameless, yet he gives it a name.

> The Tao described in words is not the real Tao. Words cannot describe it. Nameless it is the source of creation; named it is the mother of all things.[3]
>
> There is something mysterious, without beginning, without end, that existed before the heavens and earth. Unmoving; infinite; standing alone; never changing. It is the mother of all.
>
> I do not know its name. If I must name it I call it Tao and I hail it as supreme.[4]

[3]*The Book of Tao*, trans. Frank J. MacHovec (Mt. Vernon, N.Y.: Peter Pauper, 1962), Sutra, 1.
[4]Ibid., Sutra 25, 6.

The Tao is at once immanent and transcendent; it encompasses both the *Yin* and the *Yang;* it includes and pervades all that exists.

> The great Tao is everywhere, on all sides. Everything derives from it; nothing is rejected by it.[5]
>> It is like a deep, dark pool. I do not know its source. It is like a prelude to nature, a preface to God.[6]

Three adjectives are used to modify Tao. T'ien-Tao, or "the Way of Heaven," can be thought of as roughly equivalent to "Providence." Shen-Tao, or "the way of the gods," is perhaps best thought of as the eternal principle or law by which nature is produced, governed, and supported. Ren-Tao, or "the way of man," focuses attention on the need for a person to reproduce the Tao in himself.

It is the duty of a person to embrace the Tao, to hold to it and thus control himself and his destiny. To do so is to practice *wu-wei* (nonaction). It is to live spontaneously in accordance with nature—not desiring, forcing, or imposing one's will upon nature or other people.

> Hold close to the ancient Tao and be master of your own existence. Knowing the present you mirror the past. This is the clue to Tao.[7]

> One can know the world without leaving the house. One can see Tao without looking out the window. The more you study the less you know. Thus the truly wise know without traveling, perceive without seeing, achieve without doing.[8]

> The highest motive is to be like water: Water is essential to all life, yet it does not demand a fee or proclaim its importance. Rather, it flows humbly to the lowest level, and in so doing it is much like Tao.[9]

[5]Ibid., Sutra 35, 9.
[6]Ibid., Sutra 4, 7.
[7]Ibid., Sutra 14, 8.
[8]Ibid., Sutra 47, 11.
[9]Ibid., Sutra 8, 16.

Whoever knows the Eternal Constant is open-minded. Being open-minded is to be impartial; being impartial is above nations and laws; being above nations and laws is to be in accord with nature; being in accord with nature is to be in accord with Tao; being in accord with Tao is to be eternal. Although the body may die and decay, he shall live forever.[10]

Confucius (Kung Fu-tze; ca. 551–479 B.C.) was well within the Chinese tradition, but disagreed with Lao-tzu. He spoke words that had a ring of practicality, a down-to-earthness that cut through the haze of superstition and the storm of social disintegration that characterized the later Chou dynasty. He was to leave an indelible impression on Chinese life and thought for twenty-five centuries. Confucius' philosophy was preserved by his disciples who composed (in the main) the *Analects*. Although Confucius is not the author, the composers purport to record what he said. We are largely dependent on the *Analects* for the views of Confucius because other sources are later interpretations.

An advocate of utilitarian social reform, Confucius evidently revealed comparatively little of his own view of the supernatural. He sanctioned religious rituals, encouraged children to mourn for three years for deceased parents, and praised a mythical ruler by the name of Yu for being filial toward the spirits. H. G. Creel argues that the most revealing place to look for Confucius' attitude on religious matters is to investigate his reference to T'ien, or heaven.[11] He notes that nowhere in the *Analects* does Confucius use the name Shang Ti, the more personalized name of the same deity. (This may be especially significant in view of the fact that Confucius put a great emphasis on names.) But he did make use of the less personal designation, T'ien (heaven). For Confucius, heaven evidently was a kind of "impersonal ethical force, a cosmic

---

[10]Ibid., Sutra 16, 25.
[11]H. G. Creel, "Confucius, the Philosopher," in Ollie M. Frazier, ed., *Readings in Eastern Religious Thought*, 3 vols. (Philadelphia: Westminster, 1963), 3:42ff.

counterpart of the ethical sense in man, a guarantee that somehow there is sympathy with man's sense of right in the very nature of the universe.[12] He was not antagonistic toward the supernatural. He simply didn't claim to have much understanding of it. And having little understanding and no control of the supernatural, he thought it better to concentrate on other areas. Confucius' attitude is best summed up in the adage, "Let sleeping dogs lie." He felt that absorption in the study of the supernatural militates against an understanding of the social order and therefore is to be deplored.

Nevertheless, Confucius' worldview was grounded in the ultimate nature of things. Heaven and nature bequeathed to humanity a nature that, when properly cultivated, produced thoughtful, well-mannered persons.

> The Master said: "Nature outweighing art begets roughness; art outweighing nature begets pedantry. Art and nature well blended make a gentleman."[13]

As far as humanity is concerned, Tao is the "way to act" and is attested to by reason and experience. However, it is not a code as such, and it does not operate by means of the promise of reward or punishment. Tao is rather a principle of right conduct, which a person can know by virtue of his nature and education. When people adhere to it, they are put in proper relation to each other by virtue of their common relation to Tao. Thus the world becomes a place of harmony and well-being. This importance of the Tao to Confucius is made clear by his well-known saying

> The Master said: "To learn the truth (Tao) at daybreak and die at eve were enough."[14]

Confucius believed that each person had to find the Tao for himself. But this did not prevent him from teaching others

[12]Ibid., 43.
[13]"The Sayings of Confucius," in Frazier, ed., Readings, 3:73.
[14]Ibid., 71.

how they would act if they knew the Tao. His teaching was a mixture of common sense and the wisdom of the ancients. In fact, he glorified the past. He looked to China's past history and saw it as a Golden Age and its emperors as model men and leaders. That is why he concentrated on history and the great teachings of the past rather than on authoring new ones. From the examples and teachings of China's past he propounded the ethic of the Golden Mean. He visualized and portrayed for China the ideal man (*Chun-tzu*—the superior man or gentleman) and the ideal social community. Lao-tzu and Confucius agreed that people are basically good. But they disagreed on how they are kept good. Lao-tzu emphasized *nature* and said that people should retire to a natural environment and learn and practice the Tao. Confucius emphasized the *person in society* and said that people should stay in the social stream and be educated in the truth. In either case, there is something behind and within nature and people that directs them and gives them meaning.

Difficult as it is to characterize a distinctly Chinese worldview (over the centuries China was impacted by Buddhist views as well as those we have reviewed), we might depict it in bold strokes as in figure 15.

1. Supernature is composed of a variety of deities, devils, and spirits. In terms of supernatural personages Shang Ti is the most important though distant and seldom the object of worship on the part of ordinary Chinese. Conceived of in more impersonal terms, Ti'en, or the will of heaven, and the Tao, or all-pervasive principle, are of greatest importance.

2. Nature is the product of the Tao acting through the principles of Yin and Yang. It is the sphere in which the Tao continues to operate through a harmonization of these principles and therefore provides both the context of and configuration for harmonious living. Specially valued is the "good earth" of China itself.

3. People are by nature good and can be kept that way by being in touch with the Tao and by education. Every person has a proper station in society and should conduct himself and relate to others accordingly. A person's spirit outlives his

body. Filial piety extends beyond the grave to proper care of the ancestral spirits.

4. Time. The Chinese look back, not forward, to the Golden Age of China. The spirits of the dead join the ancestors. Therefore history past is extremely important. Nevertheless, the Chinese are very pragmatic as concerns the present and the future. People must take advantage of the present with its opportunities for human achievement and advancement. They can and should plan for the future.

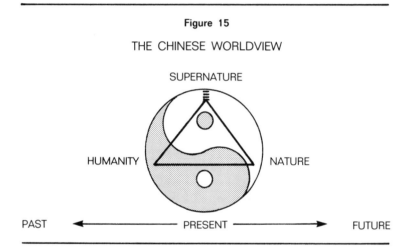

Figure 15

THE CHINESE WORLDVIEW

SUPERNATURE

HUMANITY

NATURE

PAST ◄——————— PRESENT ———————► FUTURE

THE INDIAN AND CHINESE WORLDVIEWS COMPARED

Buddhism entered China quite early and over the centuries had a profound impact on both Chinese religious practice and its worldview. Both worldviews can be described as pantheistic and, in some respects, as panentheistic. Nevertheless, the differences between India and China are apparent to all who study them and become extremely pronounced to all who live and witness in both contexts. While Indian religion and myth resulted in world negation, the pantheism of China

264

entailed a world affirmation—one might almost say an earthiness—that is concerted and unique. People and nature (or people *in* nature) occupy the center of the stage. The Tao is not *concealed* in things. It is *revealed* in things.

Fun Yu-Lan is not altogether happy with this common conclusion, however. He insists that the Chinese worldview should be thought of as "world-*transcending*." By this he means that it is both of this world and of the other world. India venerates the saint, China venerates the sage—one who is at once theoretical and practical. The Chinese describe the ideal man by saying that he is a "sage within and a king without." In other words, he has such a noble spirit that he is worthy of being king. According to Fun Yu-Lan, it is the production of this kind of character that is the goal of Chinese learning. In this view the Tao with which all Chinese philosophers have been concerned is the *synthesis* of the sublime and the common, the inner and the outer, the root and the branches, the theoretical and the practical, *the other world and this world*—in short, the "sageness within and kingliness without."

Like the Indian worldview, therefore, the traditional Chinese worldview is basically pantheistic. But it is not the Indian (monistic) type of pantheism according to which the "really Real" is the Brahman, which (who) is "involving" in an illusory world. Rather it is a pantheism according to which one discovers the Tao (which can be conceived of as both Supreme Spirit and the inner law governing the universe)[15] in a "really real" world—particularly in the history and geography of that part of the world that is China.

That this view has taken its blows in modern China is incontrovertible. How can the Golden Age be in the past? For a Communist, the Golden Age cannot be in the past, ancestor devotion cannot promote progress, and the supreme law cannot be that of the mystical Tao. At the same time, in some respects, the Chinese worldview was susceptible to commu-

---

[15]Cf. Swami Yatiswarananda, *Adventures in Vedanta* (London: Rider, 1961), 216.

nistic interpretation. Point from history to the future; replace the Tao with dialectical materialism; transmute the *Yin* and the *Yang* into thesis and antithesis; and continue to affirm humanity and the world—do this and China will become as materialist in worldview as she is Communist in governance. Whether the masses in China will actually accept the Marxist understanding of the world and history is something that is yet to be determined, however.

THE CHINESE WORLDVIEW AND THE COMMUNICATION OF CHRIST

1. As concerns the missionary source, much of what I have said about the missionary to Indians is also true of the missionary to the Chinese. Of course, integrity and goodwill are important. But the characteristic that may be expected to be lacking most often is that of *credibility*. After all, Chinese culture has much to commend it. China had a developed civilization when our Western forebears were still living in the most primitive conditions. But more than that, Chinese people and culture have exhibited many noble qualities down through the centuries. The famed Catholic missionary to China Matteo Ricci felt that few peoples had been characterized by less grievous moral errors than the Chinese.

The implication of the foregoing is quite clear. From a Chinese point of view, the West has much to offer China in the sphere of science. But when it comes to ethics and religion, it is a different matter. In those areas it might seem to them that Westerners should sit at the feet of the great Chinese sages. If the shoe is to be on the other foot, then the missionary will need to make it clear that: (1) He represents his Christ, not his culture; (2) he really knows Christ and the Bible; and (3) he is schooled in religious matters.

2. If the content of the missionary message is to be contextualized, we must give attention to *definitions*. It will be immediately apparent that fundamental Christian concepts can be rather easily translated into the Chinese languages—concepts of God, heaven, law, duty, right, spirits, soul,

sacrifice, and so forth. However, missionary communication can be broken as well as built on this foundation. Take, for example, the term *Tao*. The Chinese translation of Christ's statement in John 14:6 "I am the way" is "I am the Tao." Now think back on what has been said about the Tao in the context of the Chinese worldview. What concept could be a better bridge to traditional Chinese understanding? And what could be fraught with more potential for reformulation and misunderstanding apart from adequate definition and explanation?

Next, consider *selection*. The Chinese have their *Book of History*. The Christians also have their book of history. It is called the Bible, or, in Chinese, "The Holy Book." Here is to be found the record of the dealings of the true God of heaven and creatures that he created. There indeed was a golden age but it centered in the Garden of Eden. And it was of short duration. Why? The first humans chose to neglect the worship of God; they disobeyed God's clear commandment and joined in the rebellion of Satan. Adam was more than a representative of humanity; he was the representative man. His history is the history of Humanity.

No wonder the earlier missionaries to the Chinese gave so much effort to depicting the past and future of God's dealings with humanity! In a sense the Christian communicator is a bibliographer much as Confucius was. We make available information as to what God has said to, and done for, us.

As I have said previously, there are special entries into the Chinese worldview. As learned as he was, Confucius discouraged questions relating to God and the other world. He deemed it challenging enough to deal with matters relating to humanity and this life! Moreover, for all his emphasis on the superior person and his characteristics, Confucius never claimed to have actually seen such a person. Again, Confucius said that if one hears the Tao in the morning, he can die at peace in the evening. Who could ask for a better invitation to speak of Christ—the One who knew man *and* God; the superior Man; the One who said, and said honestly, "I am the *Tao*"?

The missionary must also adapt his message to a worldview in which filial piety is all but inseparable from ancestor veneration. Chinese filial piety has much to commend it. Aside from its stabilizing influence, it lends itself to an understanding of the new birth into a spiritual family where God is the Father and Christians are brothers and sisters. On the other hand, as Jo Niishima and Hiromachi Kozaki thought, it can be enslaving and tyrannous, keeping individuals from following their own highest aspirations and preventing them from saying yes to Christ.[16] If contextualization involves adapting the message to the particular concerns and understandings of a culture, then one who works with the Chinese must deal with the subject of filial piety.

When it comes to *organization* and *application*, my limited experience with Chinese and Chineselike peoples leads me to hazard what may prove to be some overgeneralizations. Chinese Sunday schools (like many in the non-Western world) are primarily for children. Chinese churches tend to feature special speakers, each of whom selects a topic for consideration and often a topic designed to encourage the hard-pressed believer. Chinese sermons (at least those preached outside of China proper) tend to follow the typical Western pattern. As a result of these factors, Chinese Christians often lack a grasp of Bible history and prophecy, and that in a context where history is crucial and the future is "predictable." If this analysis is at all valid, the Bible approach I have been advocating needs serious consideration. Even topical preaching as such might better follow one of the patterns identified as Japanese or even tribal in chapter 10. After all, the Chinese are very much like the Japanese (or vice versa) when it comes to the deference shown to credible teachers, so little "proof" or "argumentation" may be needed in many situations. And they are very much like tribalists in their appreciation of a "story"—especially when valuable lessons can be derived from it.

In the light of the Chinese predicament in the modern

[16]Cf. Richard Henry Drummond, *A History of Christianity in Japan* (Grand Rapids: Eerdmans, 1971), 185.

world, the topical emphasis on the injunction "comfort ye, comfort ye my people" is understandable. But if overdone it may also be self-defeating. Like all of us, the Chinese also stand indicted before the true God (despite the Chinese view of man) and are confronted with a need to face up to the demands of the gospel. The good news is not really that until the bad news is fully understood and even felt.

3. As concerns style, all that I have said has been motivated by a desire to achieve clarity, correctness, and appropriateness in communicating Christ within a Chinese worldview. But the Western style of communication leaves most to be desired as to its *appropriateness*. It is true that the Chinese are absolutely engrossed in the cultivation of success in this world and in the demands of family and community relationships. But there is still something of Lao-tzu's form of naturism in most Chinese if not in all of them. The world consciousness of the Chinese expressed itself not only in terms of getting an education and being successful but also in terms of an appreciation for the nature that surrounds them. Although it has not been the lot of most Chinese to escape to nature as Lao-tzu is said to have done, still the Chinese ethos is intimately related to the mountains, streams, and soil; and Chinese religion is characterized by geomancy and a variety of ways of divining the way of the *Tao*.

As a consequence, Christian communicators to this worldview need to rethink the world-affirming and world-denying character of Christianity. There is a world that will pass away. But it is also true that the "heavens are telling of the glory of God; and their expanse is declaring the work of His hands" (Ps. 19:1). That is not just theory. It is actuality. The beauty and the laws of nature *do* reflect something of God's power and glory. Just as the missionary to Indians must cultivate anew a sense of reverence before the God of the universe, so the missionary to Chinese must cultivate anew an appreciation for the universe of God.

But, of course, there is more. What is the "more"?

The law *of the Lord is perfect, restoring the soul;*

The testimony *of the Lord is sure, making wise the
simple.*
The precepts *of the Lord are right, rejoicing the heart;*
The commandment *of the Lord is pure, enlightening
the eyes.*
The fear *of the Lord is clean, enduring forever;*
The judgments *of the Lord are true; they are righteous
altogether.*
They are more desirable than gold, yes, than much fine
gold;
*Sweeter also than honey and the drippings of the
honeycomb.*

(Ps. 19:7–10, roman mine)

Chapter 18

Communicating Christ Into Monotheistic Worldviews

Judaism and Christianity share the monotheistic worldview. It is true that in the early centuries of the Christian era a major distinction was made between unbelieving Gentiles, Jews, and Christians—and rightly so. Unconverted Gentiles were called the "first race" because they could accept, or at least respect, one another's gods. The Jews constituted a "second race" because of their system of worship and sacrifice directed to the one Jehovah. Christians constituted a "third race" because they worshiped the "Jewish" God but approached him through Christ and on the merit of his once-for-all sacrifice.[1] Nevertheless, insofar as Jews are Jews and Christians are Christians, they share the same *basic* worldview.

The same can be said for Muslims. In fact, if Muhammad had been acquainted with orthodox Christianity rather than with certain distortions of it (as well as with internecine

[1]Adolf Harnack, *The Mission and Expansion of Christianity in the First Three Centuries*, trans. and ed. James Moffatt (New York: Harper and Brothers, 1961), 266–78.

struggles of Greek Orthodox, Monophysite, and Nestorian Christianity), he may have bequeathed a somewhat different history to the Middle East. Be that as it may, Muslims share a monotheistic worldview with Christians in spite of Muslim objections to the Christian claim to monotheism.

The worldview that we are concerned with has been characterized by Francis Schaeffer in the following words:

> Basically, the biblical perspective is this. First, there is an infinite-personal God who exists and who has created the external universe, not as an extension of his own essence, but out of nothing. Something of the nature of this created universe can be found out by reason because that is the way the infinite-personal God has created it! The universe is neither chaotic nor random, but orderly. Cause and effect is real, but this cause and effect is not in a closed system but rather in an open system—or, to say it in a different way, it is a cause-and-effect system in a limited time span. Although this universe has an objective existence apart from God, it does not operate solely on its own: It is not autonomous. God is not a slave to the cause-and-effect world he has created, but is able to act into the cause-and-effect flow of history.
>
> Second, God has made man in his own image, and this means, among other things, that man too can act into the cause-and-effect flow of history. That is, man cannot be reduced to only a part of the machine; he is not an automaton.
>
> Third, God not only can act into the world, but he is not silent; he has spoken to men in the historic, space-time situation. The Bible and Christ in his office of prophet have given a propositional, verbalized communication to men that is true about God, true about history and true about the cosmos. This should not take us by surprise, for if God has made man in his own image and has made us so that we can propositionally verbalize facts to each other on a horizontal level of communication, then it is natural that the infinite God who is personal would also communicate vertically to man in the same way. Of course, we must be careful to make a distinction here. Although God has not given us

exhaustive knowledge (only he is infinite), he has given us true knowledge (what I have often called true truth)—true knowledge about himself, about history and about the cosmos.

Fourth, the universe as it is now is not normal; that is, it is not now as it was when it was first created. Likewise, man is no longer as he was when first created. Therefore, from God's side, there is the possibility of a qualitative solution to man as he is now and to man's cruelty, without man ceasing to be man.[2]

THE CHALLENGES OF JUDAISM AND ISLAM

It is quite pointless to dwell on the background and basics of Judaism in a book addressed to Christians. Christianity is the fulfillment of the *aspirations* of most of the non-Christian religions. But it is the fulfillment of the *revelation* of only one other religion, and that religion is Judaism. For that reason, when the Christian reads and studies the Old Testament, he is reading and studying about Judaism as well as Christianity. True, there are many divergences within Judaism, and many Jews have departed from the faith completely. The same is true of Christianity. But true Jews and true Christians have much in common. Where they part company is on the person of Christ himself—not on their view of the world.

Islam presents a somewhat different challenge to Christian understanding. The last great world religion to develop was that of the prophet Muhammad. Influenced by Judaism and suborthodox forms of Christianity, Muhammad rebelled against the crude and superstitious polytheism of his native Mecca. Revelations and visions came to him over a long period of time, including a vision of the angel Gabriel. At first Muhammad was unsure of the validity of his revelations, but later he gained confidence through the reassurances of his wife Khadija. Dismayed at the opposition of his countrymen, he took courage from the example of the prophets of the past and

[2]Francis A. Schaeffer, *The Church Before the Watching World* (Downers Grove, Ill.: InterVarsity, 1971), 13–14.

fought on against great odds to a final victory. For history the
results have been decisive. Muslim believers have always been
known for their fanatic devotion. And one of the most
influential books on earth is the Koran—the message of a
tablet in heaven, which the angel Gabriel is said to have
revealed to Muhammad.

> *Praise be to Allah, Lord of the Creation*
> *The Compassionate, the Merciful,*
> *King of the Last Judgment!*
> *You alone we worship, and to You alone*
> *We pray for help.*
>
> *Guide us to the straight path,*
> *The path of those whom You have favoured,*
> *Not of those who have incurred Your wrath,*
> *Nor of those who have gone astray.*[3]

Figure 16

THE MONOTHEISTIC WORLDVIEW

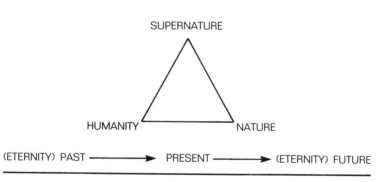

Muhammad's religion begins and ends with Allah. Allah is
described as "One," "Single," and "Eternal." The Creator of

[3]The Koran, trans. N. J. Dawood, rev. ed. (Baltimore: Penguin Books,
1959), Sura 1, 15..

all things and absolute sovereign, he has decreed both good and evil. He is mighty, forgiving, compassionate, all-knowing, wise, and merciful, but he indifferently consigns people to heaven or hell. If these descriptions sound mutually contradictory, there is good reason, because the Allah of the Koran is essentially unknowable. As for the Christian God, it is quite obvious that Muhammad thought that the Christian Trinity was composed of Father; Mary the virgin; and their child, Jesus. It is in the light of this misconception that we must understand the repeated insistence in the Koran on the unity of Allah. Furthermore, Muhammad believed that Christ's prediction of a coming Paraclete was a prophecy about another prophet, Ahmad (another of the prophet Muhammad's names). The force of this transmutation is best understood by reading John 14–16 and inserting Muhammad's name in the place of that of the Third Person of the Trinity

Muhammad, of course, did believe that there are angelic beings, and in orthodox Islam it is infidelity to deny their existence. Between angels and people there are countless beings called *jinn*, some of whom are good and some of whom are bad. Satan is usually thought of by the orthodox as a father angel or a *jinn*. In any case he is the great enemy of humanity. All beings are subject to Allah, however, and, in the final analysis, do his bidding.

From what has already been said, Muhammad's understanding of the world of nature will be quite clear. As the invisible world of spirit beings was created by Allah and does his bidding, so he also created the visible world as a provision of his mercy, and he sustains it by a continual miracle. As such humanity should enjoy it to the full, though always within the bounds of Allah's revealed will. In fact, Muhammad prophesied of a heaven filled with sensual delights, of which the present existence is a foretaste.

Man is the creature of Allah and subject to his will. The Koran is never more inconsistent than at this point. On the one hand people are exhorted to forsake their idols, to believe the truth, and to mend their ways. On the other hand, they have been created weak and are completely and abjectly

275

subject to the will of Allah. "Allah leaves in error whom He will and guides whom He pleases."[4] The difficulty of reconciling divine sovereignty and a person's free will is known to all thinking Christians and in the final analysis cannot be fully explained by man in his finitude. The Muslim and Christian cases are not really parallel, however, for two reasons. First, the Christian God is ever pictured as One who in self-giving love and grace exhausts every possibility of bringing erring, unworthy people to a knowledge of his salvation. One searches the Koran in vain for significant expressions of such *agape* love. Second, the careful balance of the Christian Scriptures is lacking in the Koran. In the latter, the sovereignty of Allah, which leads weak people to destruction, is productive of a fatalism that is pandemic in the Muslim world. Allah has revealed his will through a succession of prophets from Adam, Noah, Abraham, and Moses down to a very human Jesus and a human Muhammad. Let people hear and obey that revealed word—if they can and if they will. And if they cannot or will not, let people know that a day of solemn reckoning is coming when, resurrected, they will face the judgment.

The *summum bonum* of a person's responsibility is contained in Islam's "Five Pillars":
1. The profession of the faith
2. The recital of ritual prayers five times a day
3. The giving of alms
4. Observance of the Fast of Ramadan
5. The pilgrimage to Mecca

Although the requirements of Islam are exacting enough, they have little to do with what we would call morality. This fact, coupled with the fatalism already mentioned, has contributed to a moral and ethical laxity that is recognized both within and without the Islamic world. By many of its own adherents, Islam has been defined as "the easy way."[5]

[4]Ibid., Sura 14, 98.
[5]T. J. P. Warren, *The Muslim Challenge to the Christian Church*, condensed L. B. J. (Birmingham, England: Wakelin, 1960), 14.

Islam is challenged today by the pluralism of modern thought and life. But the Muslim world continues to grow, and it has proved to be most resistant to Christian missions. As in the case of the Jews, however, Christians have much in common with Muslims when it comes to their worldview. Both believe in one God who is personal and holy. Both believe God created the world and people and is concerned about them. Both believe God revealed his will to people and holds them responsible. Finally, both believe God promises a final day of reckoning when accounts must be settled.

COMMUNICATING CHRIST TO MUSLIMS AND JEWS

In spite of the wide divergence between Judaism and Islam, there are those similarities in meaningful Christian approaches to them that grow out of history and a common worldview. I will briefly point out some of those similarities.

1. The overwhelming challenge to the Christian missionary as a source of the message of Christ is that he establish himself as a person of *goodwill*. The Jewish attitude toward Christians in general was conveyed by a most hospitable rabbi with whom I talked at the Western Wall in Jerusalem in 1968.[6] He said, "We Jews will not consider Christ, for we cannot forget the centuries during which we have lived in Christian lands." Add to that problem the impression, widespread among Jews, that Christians have not forgiven the Jews for killing Christ, and you have a monumental obstacle to communication.

Relations with Muslims are no better. In the case of the Muslims, misunderstanding and animosity are not due to the history of the Crusades, Western imperialism, and support of the state of Israel alone. They go back to the antagonism between Ishmael and Isaac and are reflected in the following lines from the Koran:

[6]Cf. David J. Hesselgrave, "Will World Events Change Missions?" *His*, May 1974, 25–27

Believers, do not seek the friendship of the infidels and those who were given the Book before you, who have made of your religion a jest and a pastime. Have fear of Allah, if you are true believers. . . .

Say: "People of the Book, do you hate us for any reason other than that we believe in Allah and in what has been revealed to us and to others before us, and that most of you are evil-doers?"[7]

The difficulty in communicating the Christian faith to Jews and Muslims does not lie in a difference of worldviews, though important differences within these monotheistic views do, in fact, exist. Rather, the difficulty lies in the fact that *Christians, Jews, and Muslims do not meet as strangers, nor do they meet as friends.* To a degree unparalleled in other parts of the world, missionaries to Jews and Muslims must win a hearing by demonstrating Christlike qualities.

2. Next, think of the content of the Christian message to Jews and Muslims. Actually, we share much common ground in that our monotheism entails iconoclasm and antipathy toward all idolatry. Problems relating to the *definitions* of major terms persist, however. *Sin* must be seen as something that is so radical in its consequences that it necessitated the Incarnation and the atoning sacrifice of Christ. *God* must be seen as the kind of God who is holy and yet Self-giving. The Christian concept of the *Trinity* will need definition and explanation—and we may as well admit that it presents problems to the human intellect.

Jew, Muslim, and Christian share the Old Testament. Muslim and Christian share the New Testament. The Muslim alone holds to the Koran. But since we are all people of the Book, it might seem that we could begin the selection process anywhere. The likelihood of raising numerous and somewhat peripheral problems in such an approach looms large, however. Rather, as Chandu Ray says in connection with Muslims, we should begin "where the Spirit begins":

[7]The Koran, ed. Dawood, Sura 5, 381

The Holy Spirit had Matthew put first in the New Testament, and this gospel gives the genealogy of Jesus Christ as the son of Abraham and the son of David, not the son of God. Then immediately it goes on to the Virgin Birth, which Islam accepts, and therefore says Jesus was a holy man and God's wonderful gift to the world. Then it brings in politics, with the account of Herod and the children's deaths. Next comes the reinterpretation of the law in the Sermon on the Mount (and this is not difficult for the Muslim since Muhammad himself came as a reformer). Then the miracles of Jesus Christ show his power in the physical world and how much more he can do in the spiritual world. After that come the parables to make the message specific. Then, only after all that do we see the transfiguration, and Jesus asks, "Who do men say that I am?" The disciples could not have been expected to answer "the son of the living God" any earlier, but we expect every Muslim to believe in the son of God from the word go.[8]

We cannot overlook the fact that Jesus himself and the apostles began with the Old Testament Scriptures and demonstrated to Jews that Jesus was the Christ. And it is also true that, according to the Muslim faith, four of the six prophets are Adam, Noah, Abraham, and Moses. But the history that has intervened between the first and twentieth centuries and the seventh and twentieth centuries makes a difference. Bishop Chandu Ray is correct, but he should have pointed out that Jesus is in the line of Abraham through Jacob, not Ishmael; that Herod was an Idumean (i.e., an Edomite) and Edom was the land of Ishmael and his progeny; and that the character of Christ's kingdom becomes immediately apparent when in the Temptation he rejects the kingdoms of "this world."

Being well schooled in logic and debate, educated Jews and Muslims will tend to approach *organization* and *application* in much the same way as Christian missionaries, though

[8]"Chandu Ray—Asian Strategy for Evangelism," *Christianity Today* 20 (27 August 1976): 1174–77.

Muslims especially often relish debate to a degree that may catch the unwary missionary off guard. It must be remembered, however, that folk Islam is widespread and that at the grassroots level missionaries will often encounter a religious mentality that reflects a faith and practice not unlike the tribalism we described earlier.

3. When it comes to the style of the missionary message, D. T. Niles writes,

> "There may be some use in arguing with the Hindu. There is no use at all in arguing with a Muslim. He needs demonstration as to what it does mean to accept Jesus Christ as Incarnate—God."[9]

"No use at all" may be a little too strong in the Muslim case. As I said, Muslims especially are thoroughly accustomed to vigorous debate and the prepared missionary may gain credibility by engaging in it. Even though, in the eyes of Muslims, he may never be allowed to "win" the debate, he may discover that debate will open the door to individual conversations and dialogues. However, it is certainly true that in dealing with either Jews or Muslims, any display of temper or arrogance *on the part of the Christian communicator* will overshadow any advantage that might be gained. The ultimate question is, What has our faith done for us? And the answer to that question is only revealed in the demeanor of communication and in the attitude of those who confess,

> *When I survey the wondrous cross,*
> *On which the Prince of Glory died;*
> *My richest gain I count but loss,*
> *And pour contempt on all my pride.*[10]

[9]D. T. Niles, *The Preacher's Task and the Stone of Stumbling* (New York: Harper & Row, 1958), 57.
[10]Isaac Watts.

Chapter 19

Communicating Christ Into The Worldviews of Syncretism and Multireligion

As mentioned previously, C. S. Lewis talks about the dualistic worldview of Zoroastrianism and the "in-between" view of G. B. Shaw and Henri Bergson. Since these views have little currency in the Third World, it is probably not important that we deal with them here. However, there are "in-between" views to which I have made implied reference, and these must be dealt with, because most missionaries will encounter them repeatedly.

Man's ability to choose or bend his beliefs in order to make accommodation to the beliefs of others or the apparent practicalities of day-to-day living is almost limitless. This is true of people in the East and the West, in the streets of Cochabamba or the suburbs of Chicago. Such accommodations are often made on a mass scale. They are accomplished in two major ways. First, the beliefs and practices of opposing (or at least, different) systems are modified and accommodated to each other in such a way that they become essentially one new system. This is the method of *syncretism*. Second, the beliefs and practices of opposing systems are accommodated to each other by limiting the sphere in which each will be accorded allegiance and allowed to operate. This is the method of *multireligion.*[1]

SYNCRETISM

Some worldviews are more amenable to syncretism than others. Polytheism lends itself to syncretism by virtue of the fact that new deities can easily be introduced into a pantheon where they find complementary places among their predecessors. When there are myriads of gods, a few more can only enhance the system. The more the better.

Many Hindu monists accomplish a similar syncretism, though in a different manner. If the reality is one, then it follows that a basic unity exists behind all efforts to understand or describe that reality. Thus Hinduism evidences a tolerance vis-à-vis other religious systems that is almost inexplicable to one raised within the orbit of Judeo-Christian theism. In fact, Radhakrishnan asserts that Hinduism is the only truly missionary religion in the world because it is the only religion capable of encompassing the faiths of the other religions.[2] That is hyperbole, of course. Even Hinduism must dictate some terms that are necessitated by its own worldview. But the accommodations possible in Hinduism are nevertheless amazing.

The missionary communicator should be prepared to deal with these phenomena. As we have already seen, the polytheistic worldview still pervades many a society where one or another of the "higher religions" has become prominent. Thus in Latin American "Christo-Paganism," the Christian God is often distant and removed from the effective consciousness of the people much as is the case with the "high god" in polytheistic societies. In the foreground appears the ever-

---

[1]Note that this multireligion is to be distinguished from "symbiotic resignation" mentioned previously. The one has to do with a decision to allow others with whom he is related to be truly Christian without severing or jeopardizing their relationship. The other has to do with the same person or group embracing various religious faiths simultaneously.

[2]Radhakrishnan, *The Hindu View of Life* (New York: Macmillan, 1927), 161–89.

present Virgin who eclipses Christ even as she veils the Father. In this syncretism the saints take on the characteristics of the ancestral spirits. The biblical significance of the Lord's Supper is lost in the mystery of the *force vitale* that somehow resides in the wafer (in much the same way as the Dieri of Australia partake of the flesh of a corpse in order to appropriate the "powers" of the deceased). The Sacred Heart may become a sort of fetish that brings good fortune irrespective of the sins of its owner (in much the same way as the Fox God of Japan is believed to prosper devotees whether they be carpenters or brothel-keepers).

MULTIRELIGION

Japan furnishes us with a classic case of multireligion. In spite of the distinctions made between Shintoism and Buddhism at the time of the Meiji Restoration, and even beyond the centuries-long effort to syncretize the two faiths, there is to be found in Japan the almost universal feeling that if Shintoism and Buddhism are not the same, they are at least compatible and complementary. Millions of Japanese embrace both religions without any qualms whatsoever. As concerns their national life and various festivals and ceremonies having to do with birth, marriage, child rearing, new construction, and so forth, they are Shintoists. As concerns their intellectual pursuits, more private lives, and numerous other festivals and ceremonies relating to death and ancestor worship, they are Buddhists.

In their homes the Shinto god-shelves and the Buddhist god-shelves coexist, each claiming the attention that is appropriate to its domain. And beneath the surface is to be found Confucianism, which supplies not so much ritual or priestly instruction as a spirit and ethic that pervade the Japanese mentality and influence all relationships. To understand the worldview of Japan one must study the main features of polytheism, Shintoism, Mahayana Buddhism, Confucianism, and Taoism. Then one must put the pieces of the jigsaw puzzle together in accordance with the way of the

Japanese. This is the requirement multireligion makes on the missionary communicator.

In much the same fashion, the worldview of most Chinese may best be understood as a kind of multireligion. Chinese speak of the San Chiao or "Three Religions": Ju Chiao (the "religion of the learned," or Confucianism), Tao Chiao (the "religion of the Way, " or Taoism), and Fo Chiao (the "religion of Buddha"). All three lay claim to allegiance because all teach the Tao, the order of the universe in relation to humanity. At the proper time and place, the average Chinese will give proper respect, if not allegiance, to any of the three. More specifically, Taoism contributes to the mystical and idealistic aspects of Chinese thinking and life, Confucianism contributes to the intellectual and ethical aspects, and Buddhism to the philosophic and artistic aspects.[3] Beneath the whole there is the residuum of that early nature worship and spirit worship to which Lao-tzu and Confucius responded. Only the future will reveal the worldview of the new China, but the China we have known and the average Chinese we now encounter in the Orient and elsewhere are steeped in this particular form of multireligion.

It may seem to be a difficult assignment, but for the missionary to this type of people there is no alternative to learning the various components of their overall worldview and communicating Christ accordingly. It may seem incongruous to the missionary heading for São Paulo or Santiago to study tribal religion, but it is doubtful that he will ever really understand Catholicism as it is actually practiced by Brazilians and Chileans—to say nothing of widespread spiritism—until he does. And understanding must precede effective communication.

CONCLUSION TO PART III

There is a tendency to learn a simple formula by which we as Christians can communicate the message of Christ in

---

[3]Cf. Norman Baker, "Confucianism," in J. N. D, Anderson, ed., The World's Religions (London: Inter-Varsity, 1955), 162.

our personal witness. For the preacher there is the closely related tendency to approach his audience with time-worn words and clichés that have become identified with gospel preaching. Certainly new formulae for witness and old phraseology for preaching the gospel are vastly superior to no witness or preaching at all. But there is little warrant for these approaches in the Bible. There we find God's unchanging truth presented by his spokesmen with a remarkable relevance to the background and need of the respondents.

One of the inescapable facts of our time is that we in the West live in a post-Christian age (I disdain the phrase but yield to current usage). When writers like C. S. Lewis and Francis Schaeffer speak to twentieth-century Western people, they do not always assume a monotheistic worldview but rather "begin at the beginning" by differentiating worldviews. In other words, they start by building a foundation rather than by erecting a superstructure on a foundation that is not there.

This should give us a clue. When we cross a cultural boundary, we will most likely find ourselves not simply in a new nation or a new continent or a new hemisphere but in a new *world*. To adequately communicate Christ we must strive to understand that new world and speak in terms of that understanding.

Part IV

COGNITIVE PROCESSES—PROCESSES— WAYS OF THINKING

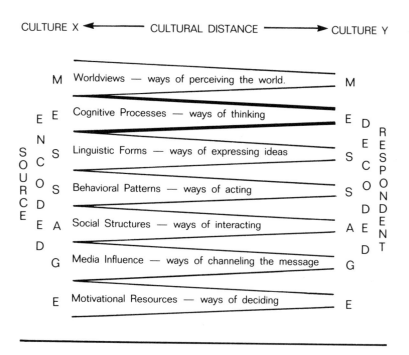

Figure 17

DIMENSIONS OF CROSS-CULTURAL COMMUNICATION

CULTURE X ◄──── CULTURAL DISTANCE ────► CULTURE Y

M Worldviews — ways of perceiving the world. M

E E Cognitive Processes — ways of thinking E

N

S S Linguistic Forms — ways of expressing ideas S

C C

O O S Behavioral Patterns — ways of acting S O

U

R D D

C E A Social Structures — ways of interacting A E

E

D D

G Media Influence — ways of channeling the message G

E Motivational Resources — ways of deciding E

SOURCE / ENCODED MESSAGE / DECODED MESSAGE / RESPONDENT

Chapter 20

The Importance of How We Know What We Know

Behind *what* we know—or think we know—always lurks the question of *how* we came to know what we know. Behind the *assertions* and *affirmations* of Christian doctrine are the *explanations* of *how* those teachings came to be believed in times past and *how* and *why* they should be believed today. Knowing Christ is an ontological state and is intimately related to the spiritual, psychological, and rational processes by which we arrive at the state. Therefore Christian missionaries should not be afraid of, or unprepared for, questions that relate to the *whys* and *hows* of Christian faith any more than they should fear questions that relate to the *what* of the Christian faith.

Some will object to this emphasis on psychological and rational processes. They will insist that the apostles did not put confidence in worldly wisdom. Quite likely they will point to the Corinthian passage I have already referred to and quote Paul who wrote that "the world through its wisdom did not come to know God" (1 Cor. 1:21); that in the church at Corinth there were "not many wise" (v. 26); and that when he proclaimed Christ to the people in that city, he avoided "superiority of speech or of wisdom" (2:1). Moreover, in order to strengthen their argument(!), they may emphasize the fact that this approach was not taken by a man who was circumscribed by a lack of formal education such as the apostle Peter but by one of the most educated and brilliant of the apostles. But how did Paul intend that the Corinthians understand his words?

First, he wanted them to understand that the Christian message is one of divine revelation and not of human origin (1 Cor. 2:9–10). It is not simply that men *could not* have authored it but that they *would not* have authored it. The gospel is *foolishness* to people (1:18). But it is the *wisdom* of God and the *power* of God (v. 24)!

Second, he wanted them to understand that the way in which he communicated the message was in keeping with the nature of the gospel and the purposes of God. He did not want the faith of the Corinthians to rest in his presentation. He wanted their faith to rest in the Spirit's demonstration (1 Cor. 2:1, 4). The precise expressions used in 1 Corinthians 2:4 are instructive in this connection. When Paul wrote that his message and preaching were not in "enticing" (KJV) or "persuasive" words of wisdom, he used the word *peithos*. In context the word most likely referred to the sort of persuasiveness that rests on the appeal of the argument itself. He contrasted that kind of persuasion with the "demonstration" (KJV) *(apodeixis)* of the Spirit. The latter signified a much more rigorous proof, the persuasiveness being occasioned by the factualness of the premises. If the premises were known to be true, the conclusion was not only logical but factually *true*.[1] In other words, the cleverness of argument that must have characterized so many of the philosophical and religious discourses with which the Corinthians were familiar was totally absent from Paul's preaching and teaching. *But the force of arguments that rested*

[1] See Leon Morris, *The First Epistle of Paul to the Corinthians*, Tyndale New Testament Commentaries, ed. R. V. Q. Tasker, 20 vols. (Grand Rapids: Eerdmans, 1955), 5.

on logical validity and historical factualness were very much a part of his preaching and teaching.

From other passages also we know that Paul forcefully and faithfully communicated Christ. Luke says that "he was reasoning . . . and trying to persuade Jews and Greeks" and that he "began devoting himself completely to the word, solemnly testifying . . . that Jesus was the Christ" (Acts 18:4–5). This is reinforced in Colossians 1:28, where Paul says that he preached Christ, 'admonishing every man and teaching every man with all wisdom." But in the first chapters of his Corinthian letter he was emphasizing that in Corinth—famous for its profligacy and logomachies—he wanted to make sure that conversions were based squarely on the most persuasive argument of all. He wanted to make sure that the Corinthian converts *knew* the Holy Spirit's revelation concerning Christ's redemptive acts in history. From that all else flowed in consequence.

Solid conversions and spiritual growth cannot be divorced from sound thinking and right knowing. The Christian missionary is a witness, herald, and servant. He is also a persuader, apologist, polemicist, and teacher. By God's grace and in cooperation with the Holy Spirit, he communicates the *what* and also the *hows* and *whys* of Christianity. And he does so across cultural barriers! If he is not careful, however, he will fall between two chairs. On the one side is the tendency to put too much confidence in the manner of his presentation. On the other side is the tendency to stress dependence on the Holy Spirit but with too little attention to the manner of his presentation. Both tendencies are regrettable. We must indeed depend on the Holy Spirit to make our message understandable and convincing. But if we expect the Holy Spirit to do his homework in the hearts and minds of respondents, then *we should do our homework also.* And that does not mean preaching and teaching as we would at home! It means learning to think God's thoughts after him, learning to think as our respondents think, and communicating accordingly.

"THINKING ABOUT THINKING"

It is significant that the same Aristotle who gave us *The Rhetoric* also bequeathed to us the scientific approach to knowledge that has been so dominant in the West. We of the West, therefore, owe a great debt to Aristotle in two important areas. The first is in the area of the persuasive communication of ideas in contexts of free choice, which is the cornerstone of democracy. The second is in the area of that productive combination of experience and reason that is the foundation of scientific achievement. But by the same token, to this day we are prone to share not only Aristotle's wisdom but also his provincialism. Aristotle indeed was interested, not only in *what* his audience thought, but also *how* they thought. His *topoi* ("commonplaces," or arguments designed to fit into the molds of usual ways of thinking) are ample evidence of this. Implicit in his rhetoric, however, was the notion that *if non-Athenians do not think in the same way that Athenians think, they at least should think in that way!*

The new rhetoricians give serious consideration to, as Condon and Yousef put it, "thinking about thinking." Under that rubric they discuss such things as epistemic structures, cultural variations of argumentation, and rhetorical relativity.[2] Missiologists and missionaries must concern themselves with a similar agenda. The tendency in the past has been to share Aristotle's myopia. When we have made concessions to people of other cultures, it has been in the form of learning something of *what* they think. Not until recently have we given much attention to *how they think and how they formulate their ideas.*

COGNITIVE PROCESS

The word *cognition* requires clarification in this context. Basically, it has a twofold meaning. First, I use it to refer to the

[2]Cf. John C. Condon and Fathi Yousef, *An Introduction to Intercultural Communication* (Indianapolis: Bobbs-Merrill Educational Publishing, 1975), 209–49.

process of knowing. Second, I use it to refer to the *product* of knowing. The one meaning is very close to the philosophical area of epistemology. Epistemology has to do with the bases or foundations of knowledge—with "how we know" what we claim to know. The emphasis here, however, will be more on the process of "coming to know" than on the validation of what we claim to know. And that will be the primary sense in which I use the word. The second meaning has to do with the perceptions, ideas, and notions that arise out of the process of knowing and will be a secondary consideration here.

COGNITIVE MAPS

First coined by Edward Tolman, the term *cognitive map* has come to have a wide and varied usage. In the narrow sense first used by Tolman it has reference to the course of learning that is thought of as something akin to a field map of the environment in which a child grows up.[3] Children of various ages are asked to draw maps of locations visited and certain conclusions about the learning process are made from the results. In passing, it should be noted that the most significant cognitive development studies of this kind have been done by J. Piaget who identified four major periods in the development of intelligence: sensorimotor, preoperational, concrete operational, and formal operational. Most important from a communications perspective is the concrete operational period (ages 7–12 approximately), when the child escapes much of his egocentrism, becomes capable of logical thought, and is able to deal with the viewpoints of others as distinct from his own. At this stage communication begins to be less ambiguous than at the previous stages.[4]

Familiarity with books and articles on cognition reveals that "cognitive map" is also used in a much broader sense. In this sense it becomes more or less synonymous with "percep-

[3]Roger M. Downs and David Stea, eds., *Image and Environment: Cognitive Mapping and Spatial Behavior* (Chicago: Aldine, 1973).

[4]Herbert Ginsburg and Sylvia Opper, *Piaget's Theory of Intellectual Development: An Introduction* (Englewood Cliffs, N.J.: Prentice-Hall, 1969).

tual sets," "mental patterns," "cognitive systems," "cognitive styles," and the "categorization" of experiences in the world. George Psathas, for example, writes,

> In essence, the relationship between the terminological system (the way he talks about the world) and the cognitive system (the way he experiences it) is studied by having the informant make discriminations between a variety of stimuli presented to him and having him name the "things" that he has discriminated, thus presenting the investigator with evidence of how the informant interprets and classifies the world around him.[5]

This broader meaning is more in line with our concerns in subsequent chapters, though we will share the results of one research project that was based on the construction of maps by Western- and non-Western-educated students (p. 331).

THE "MIND OF A PEOPLE"

Perhaps most ambiguous of the relevant terms and phrases is the oft-used designation "mind of a people." In recent years a plethora of titles referring to the "mind" of the Chinese, Japanese, Westerner, "Primitive," etc., have come off the presses. Illustrative is the following paragraph from Harold Lindsell:

> The mind of a people differs from the mind of all other peoples. No two races or groups of people think exactly alike. An understanding of the mind is another prerequisite to effective evangelism. By the mind of a people is meant their thought patterns, the way they themselves reason and react to life in its multiform relationships. Outward actions may be identical, but the mind behind the thought may *differ greatly*. Thus two people coming from different backgrounds may do the same thing but to each the act may

[5]George Psathas, "Ethnoscience and Ethnomethodology," in James P. Spradley, ed., *Culture and Cognition: Rule, Maps, and Plans* (Prospect Heights, Ill.: Waveland, 1987), 209.

have connotations that vary and may arise from a mind set that bears no relationship one to the other. This mind set of people may be seen among oriental peoples who are intensely concerned with "face." They must preserve "face" at all costs, and for the blunt Anglo-Saxon temperament, which is basically opposed to "face" and which is pragmatic and cold in its approach, the mind of the oriental is something of an enigma. But so long as the oriental mind is an enigma to the missionary he is deficient in his effort to present the gospel. The business, then, of the missionary is to bridge this gap by an understanding of the oriental mind (or the mind of the people to whom he goes) for without that understanding his work will be in vain to some degree.[6]

Although somewhat vague, the word "mind" is widely used in the sense in which Lindsell is using it. It is something more than "mind" conceived of as the faculty by which truth or knowledge is grasped (like the Greek word *nous*). It is the *makeup* of the mind. It has reference to the way in which a people think or formulate their ideas and the way they "feel" about things.

The cognitive processes, or the ways of thinking, of various peoples may be a new dimension of communication for many. But it will be an important one, for it is highly unlikely that the people of respondent cultures will think in the same way that Westerners do. Nor is the *Western* way of thinking necessarily superior from a *Christian* point of view. For us as missionaries, one approach to meaningful communication, therefore, will be to familiarize ourselves with the way the members of our target culture think. Our ultimate goal should be to bring them—and ourselves—to a completely Christian way of thinking. *That is missionary communication!*

[6]Harold Lindsell, *Missionary Principles and Practice* (Westwood, N.J.: Revell, 1955), 193.

Chapter 21

Cultural Differences and the Cognitive Process

It must have been the great gulf that divides Eastern and Western ways of thinking that Rudyard Kipling had in mind when he wrote his oft-quoted lines:

> *East is East and West is West*
> *And never the twain shall meet.*[1]

Sir Rabindranath Tagore, on the other hand, was undoubtedly referring to increased intercultural contact and the mutual interdependence of the peoples of the East and West when he wrote that the most important fact of the twentieth century is that the East and the West *have met.*[2]

Both statements are true. And both are false. There have been technological, political, and even religious meetings. That Easterners have learned from the West in these areas has

[1]Rudyard Kipling, "The Ballad of East and West," in *Rudyard Kipling's Verse: Inclusive Edition 1885–1918* (Garden City, N.Y.: Doubleday, 1924), 268–72.

[2]Quoted by Sidney Lewis Gulick, *The East and the West* (Rutland, Vt.: Charles Tuttle, 1962), 17.

been apparent for a considerable period of time. Recently, an increasing number of Westerners have turned to the East for answers that they feel have not been made available to them in their Occidental heritage. Furthermore, we now think of the distance between the Orient and Occident in terms of a few hours instead of the number of miles. And our destinies are indissolubly linked. *Yes, the East and West have met.*

But it would seem that what has occurred between East and West to this point in history might better be expressed in this way: *The East and West are ever meeting, but the East and West have never met.* It is this "ever meeting, never meeting" that we should explore because increased contact will not in and of itself bridge the gulf in the foreseeable future. Neither will the gulf be bridged by those who reject their own cultural heritage in favor of the other. Hope lies rather in the bridging of the chasm by individuals who will stretch their minds and hearts in an attempt to embrace and comprehend—however imperfectly—both East and West. It is regrettable that many missionaries have not really made this attempt. Others in making the attempt have sacrificed much that is basic to historic Christianity. It is those missionaries who have avoided both extremes who furnish inspiration to sending and receiving churches and a challenge to those of the East who are still ignorant or unconvinced of the validity of Christ's claims to their faith and loyalty.

THE BISYSTEMIC APPROACHES OF
S. L. GULICK AND F. C. S. NORTHROP

After the better part of a half century of preparation and during the last ten years of his life, from 1935 to 1945, Sidney Lewis Gulick worked on the manuscript of a book published posthumously under the title *The East and the West*.[3] (Gulick understood the East as including India and the Far East, and the West as including the Near East, Europe, and the Americas.) In his book Gulick dealt with a wide variety of

[3]Ibid.

subjects, among them "thinking and knowing for Occidentals and Orientals." He characterized Occidental thinking (i.e., sustained mental attention) as "scientific, intellectualistic, aggressive."[4] In his understanding, Western thinking proceeds from particulars to general concepts while remembering (usually) that abstractions exist only in the mind of the thinker. It aims at imposing man's will on nature and society.

Oriental thinking, on the other hand, is "mythological, emotional, artistic."[5] It is concerned with meditative introspection and contemplation rather than with logic and induction from observed phenomena. The Oriental wants to *feel* that he has taken hold of the inner significance of the object of contemplation. Thought is more a form of pleasure than a prelude to action. The knowledge thus gained is not so much that of the objective world as it is of the subjective state of consciousness. As a result, in the Orient, knowledge of the natural world has significantly lagged behind that of the West, and only recently is it catching up as a result of a cross-cultural contact.

Gulick was of the opinion that even when the *terms* of religion and philosophy are the same, the differences behind the terms are so great as to render communication exceedingly difficult. He questioned whether Oriental works on religion or philosophy could be accurately translated into the languages of the Occident.[6]

A much better-known and a more influential statement of the differences between Eastern and Western ways of thinking is that of F. C. S. Northrop entitled *The Meeting of East and West*.[7] It is hazardous to attempt to summarize the contribution of Northrop within the scope of a few sentences, but the attempt must be made.

According to Northrop, both Eastern and Western modes of thought begin with sensory experiences such as colors,

[4]Ibid., 128.
[5]Ibid.
[6]Ibid.
[7]F. C. S. Northrop, *The Meeting of East and West* (New York: Macmillan, 1953), especially chs. 8 and 9.

sounds, odors, flavors, pains, pleasures, and so forth. He calls this the "determinate, differentiated, aesthetic continuum." It is a "continuum" because what is apprehended is not merely a disjunctive aggregate of sense but part of an all-embracing whole. It is "aesthetic" because colors, sounds, and odors are the materials of the artist and these are what we actually experience rather than the electrons, neutrons, and positrons of science. It is "determinate" and "differentiated" in the sense that what we experience is localized and selected out of a continuum that at the periphery is indeterminate and undifferentiated. Acknowledging a debt to William James, Northrop notes that this part of human knowledge must be immediately experienced. It cannot be communicated. No verbal description is sufficient to convey the sensed color blue to a person who was born blind, for instance. This is the meaning of "ineffable."

To repeat, the thinking of both East and West begins here. But Western civilization shows itself to be fundamentally theoretical. The West proceeds to form hypotheses about the unobserved components, to propose these hypotheses postulationally and a priori, and to check them indirectly through deductively designated, empirical consequences. This type of theoretical knowledge is quantitatively enormous in the West and the purely empirical, observable component of knowledge is much smaller than most people suppose. When we say that we "know" something, we usually have reference to this comprehensive theoretical system. The corollary of this is that we can never be sure of that portion of religious, moral, or social ideals that is justified only indirectly from inferred, unseen factors. When for any reason the theories do not seem to work out in practice, or when new information dictates, we are ready to dispense with the traditional theory and put a new one in its place. This has happened over and over in the history of the West.

Eastern thinking has been characterized in the West as purely speculative or as the type of thinking that has no designated criteria of verification. Northrop believes this notion to be erroneous. What the Oriental really does is to continue his concentration on the immediately apprehended aesthetic factor rather than proceeding to the speculative hypothesis that is confirmed only indirectly. The Oriental recognizes that which is experienced as the transitory, determinate differentiations within the all-embracing indeterminate aesthetic continuum (which he designates as Tao, Nirvana, Brahman, or Cit). That is, behind the immediate, transitory, sensed data is the unchanging, undifferentiated, and eternal reality. Rather than leave the experienced sensory data in favor of theoretical speculation, the Oriental prefers to take the clues given in even this transitory form and by inward vision arrive at the intuited reality behind it.

Thus in the East, "to know" means to have investigated things in their immediately apprehended aesthetic component and to have grasped the reality behind them. In the West, "to know" means to have gone on to an investigation of the theoretic component. Northrop believes that the consequences of empiricism and positivism are therefore discoverable in the East rather than in the West. For all the emphasis on mysticism, intuition, and emotions in Eastern religions, Orientals are extremely earthly, practical, and matter-of-fact because their knowledge of the divine is linked more directly with the immediately sensed data of human experience. Succinctly put, the Oriental constitutes the nature of the divine directly from the aesthetic as simply an analogical symbol while defining the divine in a postulational way.

One of Northrop's fundamental theses is that both East and West already have a common starting point and that we need to investigate things in *both* their aesthetic and their theoretic components. Since these ways of knowing are complementary, *both East and West* bring a necessary contribution to world philosophy. In this understanding is the inherent *meeting* of East and West.

THE TRISYSTEMIC APPROACH OF F. H. SMITH

Edmund Perry credits F. H. Smith with an elaboration of ways of knowing that goes beyond the East-West distinction of Gulick and Northrop and takes into account the fact that there is a diversity between characteristically Indian and Chinese ways of thinking.[8] Smith espouses, not two, but three cognitive approaches to reality: (1) the conceptual, (2) the intuitional or psychical, and (3) the concrete relational.

Smith's conceptual approach to reality corresponds with the theoretical or postulational thinking that Northrop has identified with the West. The psychological or psychical way of thinking seems to be synonymous with Northrop's Eastern way of thinking in that it emphasizes intuition and the knowledge that emanates from inner experience and vision. In concrete relational thinking, life and reality are seen pictorially in terms of the active emotional relationships present in a concrete situation.[9]

What Smith has done is to differentiate Chinese and Indian thinking in that the former gives greater emphasis to the immediately apprehended concrete experience, while the latter gives more attention to reaching within and beyond them.

Smith also goes on to assert that while one or another of these three ways of thinking is predominant in any given culture, the other two will also be operative. In other words, we are all scientists, mystics, and artists if one chooses to put it this way. Where we differ is in degree, or in the priority given to one approach over another.[10] This insight is perhaps as significant as Smith's three-pronged approach to differences in the cognitive process, for it takes into account both nature

[8]Edmund Perry, *The Gospel in Dispute* (Garden City, N.Y.: Doubleday, 1958), 99–106.

[9]It might be maintained, however, that by emphasizing the determinate and differentiated, as well as the indeterminate and undifferentiated, aspects of the aesthetic continuum, Northrop has also perceived in some sense the "concrete-relational" mode of thought.

[10]Smith would agree with Nida when the latter says that the reasoning processes of various peoples differ in that they proceed from different starting points. He would probably have some misgivings with Nida's notion that this is the only significant difference between ways of thinking and with Nida's incomplete exploration of the subject. Cf. Eugene A. Nida, *Message and Mission: The Communication of the Christian Faith* (New York: Harper & Row, 1960), 89ff.

Figure 18

THREE BASIC COGNITIVE APPROACHES TO REALITY*

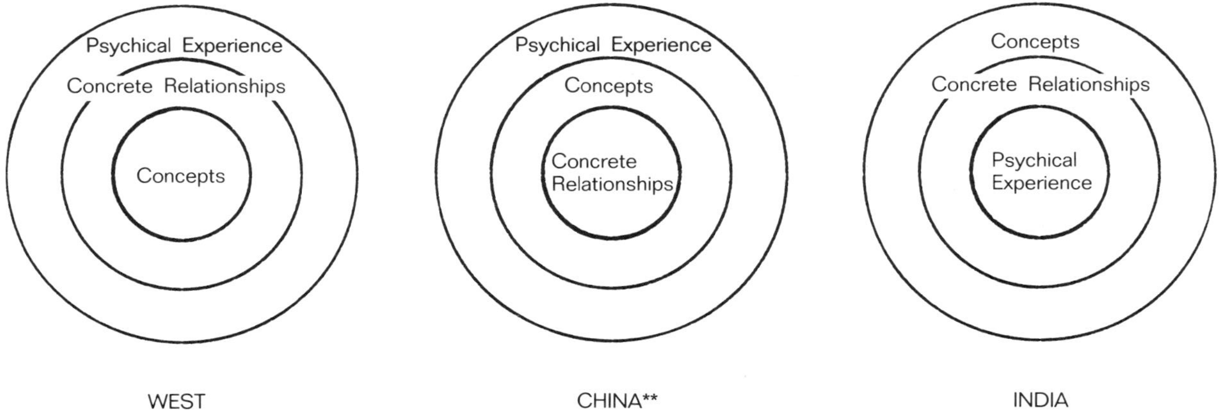

WEST

Psychical Experience
Concrete Relationships
Concepts

CHINA**

Psychical Experience
Concepts
Concrete Relationships

INDIA

Concepts
Concrete Relationships
Psychical Experience

*Edmund Perry, *Gosepl in Dispute*, p. 100.
**As modified by Perry, who in accord with E.R. Hughes, thinks concepts more important than psychical experience in the Chinese way of thinking.

and nurture, and it means that none of the ways of thinking is completely foreign to any to us. By stirring ourselves and stretching ourselves we should be able to make at least a very significant beginning in understanding the "mind" of our respondent cultures.

Smith thinks that the priorities of the cognitive processes in the West, China, and India are as follows:

West: Conceptual, Concrete Relational, Psychical

China: Concrete Relational, Psychical, Conceptual

India: Psychical, Concrete Relational, Conceptual

E. R. Hughes agrees with Smith in the larger dimensions of his analysis but offers what seems to be a more likely order in the case of Chinese thinking, namely that the conceptual takes priority over the psychical mode of thought.[11] If we accept Hughes's order or priority, the three ways of thinking can be diagrammed in the way indicated in figure 18.[12]

[11]Perry, *Gospel in Dispute*, 100.
[12]Ibid.

Chapter 22

Conceptual Thinking and The Western Missionary

It was one morning during Passion Week in the early 1960s. Several days earlier I had discovered that the morning drive required to bring my friendly but skeptical colleague to the university coincided with a certain Christian radio program, and I had encouraged him to listen in. It was evident that morning that he had responded to my invitation and was totally unimpressed. Omitting the usual greeting he began,

> Well, that was circular thinking if I ever heard circular thinking. This morning's message was reducible to a chain argument which, without all the extras, goes thusly: "We must believe in the Resurrection of Christ because the Bible unequivocally teaches it. What the Bible teaches is true. The greatest evidence for the truth of the Bible is the Resurrection of Jesus Christ." Come now, you Christians can certainly do better than that!

To say that I did "better than that" entails no affront to humility. My friend, however, remained unconvinced in spite of the fact that it became quite clear that he accepted much data as historically factual on the basis of considerably less evidence than that which attests to the life, death, and resurrection of our Lord. But, as he reminded me, those data were not claiming the same kind of belief and allegiance either.

This experience illustrates that the process of conceptual or postulational thinking is so much a part of our Western approach to knowledge that we find it difficult to use the word "know" apart from the *kind* of intellection that establishes what is known and could be recalled and communicated in defense of it. We are, in fact, engaged in that kind of thinking right now. We are defining communication, analyzing it, categorizing its separate factors, and relating the parts to the whole—all with a view to putting the resultant knowledge to the practical test to see if our theories work out in practice.

The church is every bit as much a showcase of this conceptual thinking as is the philosophy department or science building of any large Western university. For many, Christianity is true because it is logical (makes sense) or because it is practical (it actually works). The *good* sermon is made up of a series of propositions placed in logical order and attended by some form of application. If a Scripture portion— whether the portion be poetic, wisdom, prophetic, historic, or epistolary—is to be communicated, it must yield itself to logical ordering and analysis. Theology is illustrative of this process in that it takes its primary data from the Scriptures. Then it proceeds to arrange the data into categories such as hamartiology, soteriology, ecclesiology, pneumatology, and Christology. Finally, it posits interrelationships and proposes answers to questions in a systematic fashion, in this way setting our minds at rest.

A. L. Drummond has written that in Germany (the seat of much of the theological erudition and confusion in the world) most people profess some kind of theology "because they cannot tolerate not receiving definite, precise and conclusive answers to all questions."[1] (Drummond calls this love of

---

[1]A. L. Drummond, *German Protestantism Since Luther* (London: Epworth, 1951), 276.

thorough and exact knowledge *Grundlichkeit.*) At the same time, definite answers always elicit new questions. And so the process continues. Drummond believes that a distinction should be made between the German and Anglo-Saxon mind at this point and that the Anglo-Saxon mind on the whole exhibits a more sound judgment. By the same token, the Anglo-Saxon mind is less likely to initiate new theological movements.

The close parallel between the methodology of the scientist and that of the biblically oriented *systematic* theologian is demonstrated by John Warwick Montgomery.[2] He points out that the theologian's craft is to take biblical data, make theological proposals, and proceed to build theological systems and formulate creeds and confessions (see figure 19). This may sound sinister at first. But while holding to general revelation, Montgomery avoids building theology on intuitionism, experientialism, or rationalism. His position is that general revelation must be interpreted in the light of special revelation and that if theology is to be Christian, it must fit the facts of the Bible just as scientific truth fits the data of experience or the shoe fit Cinderella's foot. That we give priority to dedicated reason in interpreting the Bible, rather than interpret it in accord with our intuition or experience, is in accord with the character of that revelation itself.

I concur with Montgomery. Any other kind of *systematic* theologizing is as hopeless as it is un-Christian. But in this process of rigorous theologizing there are incipient dangers also. We can mistake the theology for the revelation. We can go beyond the revelation and insist on our conclusions even where the Bible does not speak plainly. And—most important for our present consideration—we can communicate our theological systems and do so in the manner of our theologizing rather than communicate the message of the Bible itself and in the manner of biblical revelation. When we do so, missionary communication becomes foreign in the Third

[2]Cf. John Warwick Montgomery, "The Theologian's Craft," *Concordia Theological Monthly* 37 (February 1966): 66–98.

World—not foreign because it is Christian, but foreign because it is Western. In other words, missionary communication seems wooden, lifeless, and altogether too theoretical, not because it is biblical, but because it is not biblical enough. The Bible itself is alive and speaks in practical, down-to-earth terms.[3] No wonder those theologians who met in Seoul in 1982 criticized Western theology as being too abstract and removed from their practical concerns.[4]

Figure 19

THE THEOLOGIAN'S CRAFT

	SCIENCE	THEOLOGY
THE DATA (Epistemological certainly presupposed)	NATURE	THE BIBLE
Conceptual Gestalts	Laws	Ecumenical Creeds (e.g., Apostles' Creed) and historic confessions (e.g., Augsburg Confessions)
	Theories	Theological Systems (e.g., Calvin's *Institutes*)
	Hypothesis	Theological proposals (e.g., Aulen's *Christus Victor*)

Let us be clear at this point. I am not inclined to deprecate

[3]For example, see Orlando Costas, *The Church and Its Mission: A Shattering Critique from the Third World* (Wheaton: Tyndale, 1974), 219–32.
[4]"Seoul Declaration: Toward an Evangelical Theology for the Third World" by Bong Rin Ro and Ruth Eshenauer, eds., *The Bible and Theology in Asian Contexts* (Taichung, Taiwan: Asian Theological Association, 1984), 23.

the method of critical thinking and analysis that has been so much a part of Western advancement and the basis of much of the West's contribution to the world. Moreover, the God of the Bible is a God of order who has revealed that orderliness in his creation and in his revelation. In studying the Bible we are thinking God's thoughts after him. Although in times past God revealed his will in various ways, biblical revelation is basically a series of propositions given by God to us; and the particular form in which many of those propositions appear is that of discursive language about righteousness, evil, justification, reconciliation, judgment, and the other concepts of special revelation. Paul seems to rely on the conceptual approach in books like Colossians, Ephesians, and Romans. The book of Romans is perhaps the high point of biblical revelation for Western Christians. Godet called it the "cathedral of the Christian faith." One could make a case for saying that the Bible lays more and more stress on conceptual thinking as the divine message moves through time and from the Semitic to the Hellenistic world.

At the same time, the Bible remains a book of stories, metaphors, similes, symbols, types, parables, allegories, and emblems. It is clear that in biblical times some men and women received communication directly from the Lord. Inner vision was a part of knowing the truth of God from the time of Abraham and Moses to that of Paul and John. Where Western Christian communicators are liable to criticism is at the points of overemphasis on the logical nature of revelation and underdependence on complementary thought processes. This criticism is well taken even in reference to communicating Christ in the West. How much more valid is this criticism, then, of Western missionaries who attempt to communicate Christ to peoples of other cultures? Edmund Perry may be guilty of hyperbole but his words in this connection merit careful consideration. He writes,

> We Western Christians in particular need to be shocked out of our unexamined reverence for logical concepts. There is nothing uniquely Christian or sacrosanct about logical

concepts and we ought to be prepared to explore the possibility of understanding and communicating the Gospel in other than logical conceptual categories.[5]

Agreed. It is to that exploration that we now turn.

[5]Edmund Perry, *The Gospel in Dispute* (Garden City, N.Y.: Doubleday, 1958), 101.

Chapter 23

Communicating Christ in Cultural Areas Where Intuitional Thinking Predominates

MYSTICAL THOUGHT

Hinduism provided the alchemy that ultimately brought the heterogeneous elements (aboriginal tribal peoples, the more cultured Dravidians, and warlike Aryan invaders) of ancient India together. In noting that fact, Radhakrishnan adds that Hinduism is more than a social and cultural phenomenon. It is also a psychological and epistemological phenomenon.[1]

It would be difficult to overemphasize the significance of this. Building on the Upanishadic literature, Vedanta teaches the existence of individual souls *(jivatma)*, which it distinguishes from the Supreme Soul *(Paramatma)*, or Brahman. Vedanta uses the word *atman* to refer to both of these, simply denoting the distinction by the use of lower or upper case letters (i.e., *atman* or *Atman*). *Atman* (upper case) gave birth to all material forms including the human body, and into

---

[1]Radhakrishnan, *The Hindu View of Life* (New York: Macmillan , 1927), 13–14.

311

those bodies enters as the individual soul, the mind, and (subordinate to the mind) the five sense organs of perception and the five sense organs of action. The individual soul is therefore identified with a body; it experiences good and evil, pain and pleasure; and it is entangled in *samsara* (the wheel of rebirth). The mind is the inner organ of deliberation and liberation. If it is untrained and undisciplined, the mind never gets beyond the sensations of the other ten organs. Trained and purified by a study of the scriptures, instruction from a teacher, and the discipline of certain rules, the mind is enabled to transcend sensory experience, scriptures, teachers, and rules, and to attain to a knowledge of the Supreme Soul or the Brahman. The mind, therefore, is a symbol of the Brahman. In fact, *mano vai Brahama*—"the mind is verily Brahman."[2] The earnestness with which some seek this inner vision is demonstrated by the desperate measure of Sur Das who, when he found that his eyes caused his mind to wander, plucked them out in order to better "see" Brahman.[3]

According to Hindu thinking, there are two kinds of knowledge: (1) the higher or perfect knowledge, which is of Brahman, and (2) the lower or relative knowledge including that of mathematics, science, and theology. Philosophizing, theologizing, and dogmatizing come under this second category of lower knowledge. Dogmas, creeds, philosophical systems, and ceremonial rituals have but relative truth. They are but shadows and pointers to absolute truth. If viewed in any other way, they become seducers of the mind. Indians agree with Luther when he said that "reason is the Devil's whore." In the higher knowledge, reason does not intrude with its logic, theories, doctrines, and explanations; and sensory experience does not bind and fetter. In this perfect knowledge the pure mind "sees."

Stephen Neill credits R. O. Zaehner of Oxford with

[2]Swami Nikhilananda, *The Upanishads* (New York: Harper Torchbooks, 1964), 53.
[3]Malcom Pitt, *Introducing Hinduism* (New York: Friendship, 1955), 36.

helping us to understand just what is "seen."[4] Behind the "feeling tone" common to such mystical experiences, Zaehner identifies three "types or fields of mystical support." First, there is what may be called cosmic consciousness or a sense of identification with the whole universe in which the mystic feels a kinship with the largest star of the heavens and the smallest particle of earthly dust. Second, there is the experience of the deeper levels of one's own personality and being in which the encrustations of forgetfulness or casuistry of various kinds are ripped away, enabling the mystic to identify unconscious or forgotten elements of his own development or elements that link him with the whole human race. Yoga techniques, the method of psychoanalysis, and Aldous Huxley's resort to drugs seem especially suited to this type of mystical experience. Third, there is in Hinduism that which seems to be a special type of theophany where the mystic achieves a kind of union with a *personal* god. This is presaged in the Bhagavad-Gita where, after prolonged and involved philosophizing, Krishna reveals himself as the Ultimate Reality and Arjuna bows in devotion. The emphasis on love and devotion to a personal deity is overlaid in Hinduism with monistic interpretations and the idea that knowledge of particular deities is to be placed in the category of lower knowledge.

UNDERSTANDING INTUITIONAL THINKING

Despite certain inconsistencies, then, Indian thinking flows quite naturally from the quest for a higher knowledge that is exceedingly difficult to attain. That higher knowledge has as its object the Ultimate Reality, which is Brahman. When Hajime Nakamura characterizes Indian thinking, he is in effect noting the consequences of this basic commitment in the Indian approach to truth. Nakamura characterizes Indian thinking in the following terms: (1) a stress on the universal,

[4]Stephen Neill, *Christian Faiths and Other Faiths* (London: Oxford University Press, 1961), 91–92.

(2) preference for the negative, (3) a minimizing of individuality and particulars, (4) an emphasis on the unity of all things, (5) the static quality of universality, (6) a subjective comprehension of personality, (7) the supremacy of the universal self over the individual self, (8) a subservience to universals, (9) an alienation from the objective natural world, (10) introspective stance, (11) metaphysical qualities, and (12) a tolerant and conciliatory attitude.[5]

Buddhism, nurtured as it was in Indian soil, takes a similar approach, though there is an overlay of Chinese adaptation in the Mahayana schools of eastern Asia. Zen Buddhism, for example, has been aptly called the "school of Buddha's mind." The Sanskrit root *budh* means both "to wake up" and "to know." C. Humphreys believes that Zen is the "apotheosis of Buddhism" because it makes a "direct assault on the citadel of truth with no reliance on concepts, scripture, ritual or vow."[6] Defending the Hindu-Buddhistic approach as he understands it, Humphreys goes on to assert, "The intellect is admittedly the instrument of proof, but in my experience nothing worth proving can be proved, and the intuition needs no proof by intellect; it knows."[7]

One cannot understand this kind of thinking simply by a "determined act of will. It has to be painfully and slowly fed into the blood stream."[8] We must once and for all divest ourselves of the false notions that Indian-type thinking is the equivalent of what we Westerners have in mind when we speak somewhat disdainfully of a "woman's intuition," and when we think that the Indian "wise man is he who sits all day lost in a stupor of self-hypnosis or perhaps seeking wisdom by meditation on the irregular convexity of his own

[5]Hajime Nakamura, *Ways of Thinking of Eastern Peoples*, ed. Philip P. Wiener (Honolulu: East-West Center, 1964), passim.

[6]Christmas Humphreys, *Buddhism* (Baltimore; Penguin Books, 1951), 179.

[7]Christmas Humphreys, *Zen Buddhism* (New York: Macmillan, 1962), 15.

[8]Robert T. Oliver, *Culture and Communication* (Springfield, Ill.: Charles C. Thomas, 1962), 138.

navel."[9] The thinking of the Indian mystic is every bit as attentive to the everyday world as is the thinking of his Western counterpart. Perhaps more so. And he is certainly no stranger to philosophizing either. In fact, knowledgeable Indians agree that the knowledge of the overwhelming majority of Indians is confined to this lower type of knowledge. Some assert that in all of India not more than ten men can be given credence as possessors of the higher knowledge of Brahman!

The fundamental difference between Western and Indian thinking lies in the fact that the former takes the facts given by experience; links them logically with general statements of a scientific, ethical, or theological nature; and cries, "Eureka, I have found it!" In the vast majority of cases the latter simply finds the same type of knowledge as his Western counterpart. But the Indian thinker does not cry, "Eureka, I have found it!" Rather he thinks of that knowledge as transitory. Reality still eludes him. Higher knowledge is still beyond, and he has not found it.

Christian missionaries should be able to appreciate the Indian way of thinking. First, some scientists in the West such as Professor Polyani and Albert Einstein have emphasized heuristics and intuitive flashes of insight that bridge logical gaps and seemingly represent knowledge of a higher type. Second, a significant part of biblical revelation originally came as a result of inner vision as I have already mentioned. Third, the true Christian insists that the highest knowledge is the knowledge of God through Jesus Christ—not knowledge of his world, or even knowledge *about* God, but knowledge of him, knowing him as a Person, addressing him as Father, and relating to him as Savior and Lord. It is personal knowledge that stems from the ministry of the Holy Spirit, who takes the things of God and makes them real or meaningful. Fourth, missionaries are aware of the persuasive power of the mystical and eclectic thought that the Indian sages offer as a viable alternative to the sometimes stultifying way of thinking that

[9]Ibid., 140.

is characteristic of the West. Although they disagree with his conclusion, they can understand Professor Murti (sic) of Banaras University when he writes:

> There is something inherently secular and unspiritual in any organization. It tends to create vested interests and to breed corruption. In stifling freedom of expression and setting up a norm to dogmas to which the votaries are required to conform, organized religion (the Church) succeeds only in antagonizing other religious groups and creating schisms and heresies within its own fold. What we need is the realization of the spiritual, which is the bedrock of all our endeavor. Only mystical religion, which eminently combines the unity of Ultimate Being with the freedom of different paths for realizing it can hope to unite the world.[10]

Fifth, this kind of thinking has now invaded the Western religious world at every level and has been given the highest respectability. Writing on the "cognitivity of religion," J. Kellenberger says that there are three basic types of response to skeptics who hold that references to a transcendent Reality betray either no cognitive status or a confused cognitivity. The response of the "First Perspective" position held by Neo-Wittgensteinians is that when religious people look within for that reality they come to possess what can be called another kind of cognitivity—an "internal cognitivity." From a "Second Perspective" position others attempt to show that God's existence is a legitimate cognitivity issue because, to a greater or lesser extent, it is an "enquiry issue." Kellenberger himself argues for a Third Perspective position, which he says is a recognizable tradition of religious belief. It does not pursue an investigative methodology of any sort nor does it offer any method of confirmation. But it has a "grammar" and a "logic" that applies to all realization-discoveries. To find the presence of God it invites us to

[10]Quoted in A. C. Bouquet, *Christian Faith and Non-Christian Religions* (London: Nisbet, 1958), 275.

. . . look upon what is already familiar to us: the firmament, the deep, our own lives. And, if we are given new eyes, we shall see what was there to be seen all along.[11]

Kellenberger calls this Third Perspective "realization-cognitivity" and finds it to be a legitimate way of going beyond the kind of understanding that merely attempts to garner more and more information about the world. *The point that I am making here is not that we should convert to Indian-type intuitional thinking. Of course not. The point is that we are surrounded by that way of thinking right here in the Western world as well as by the sterility of the kind of pseudo-Christian thinking that is content to simply pile up information about God without bothering to make that information personal and vital through repentance and faith in Christ. That being the case, we should prepare to communicate Christ in the context of Indian intuitionalism as well as Christian nominalism.*

COMMUNICATING CHRIST TO INTUITIONALISTS

How then can we communicate Christ to those who give high priority to the kind of thinking that has been variously labeled psychological, psychical, intuitional, or mystical whether it be found among the old mystics of India or Japan or the new mystics of the West? For the sake of concreteness let's continue to think in terms of the Indian case.

As Christian communicators we must take with utter seriousness the words of Paul when he exhorts us, "Do not be conformed to this world," but rather "be transformed by the renewing of your mind" (Rom. 12:2).

In the first place, therefore, to effectively communicate Christ to the Indian means becoming more Christian ourselves—more a product of Christ and less a product of our own culture. This involves four factors at the very least:

1. Overintellectualizing must be avoided. Upon reading

[11]J. Kellenberger, *The Cognitivity of Religion: Three Perspectives* (Berkeley: University of California Press, 1985).

the Indian philosophers one might be tempted to inquire whether overintellectualizing is, in fact, possible. The student who has probed the differences between the six philosophic systems of Hinduism or has read the involved arguments that characterize a large part of the Bhagavad-Gita is tempted to conclude that Western philosophy by comparison is less subtle and less abstruse. But the average Indian is as uninformed of these subtle nuances as is the average Westerner. And the informed Indian is unlikely to be impressed by Christianity presented as simply or mainly a philosophical system because as philosophy Hinduism itself has significant appeal. In any case, he is probably searching for something more. The missionary should be prepared to state the Christian case clearly and logically, but that will not be enough. He should remember that Christianity was not thought of as a philosophical system for at least a century after its birth. Only gradually in the second to fourth centuries did it identify itself as a system of philosophy. *In the beginning it was a way of salvation. And this primary identification must be made in the Indian context today. Millions of Indians are on a search for that which they have little hope of attaining through many reincarnations. Christ is the Way.*

2. If overintellectualization is to be avoided, so is oversimplification. Nothing could be so inappropriate to the Indian mind as the presentation of faith as the logical and inescapable conclusion of several simple premises. Such a God is indeed too small to be given credence, and such a faith is too inconsequential to be given consideration. In the final analysis, oversimplification is but another form of overintellectualization.

3. The missionary must communicate a sense of the mystery of knowing God and the awe of approaching him. It would seem unnecessary to state this when the Christian bows before the living Lord of the universe. But nowhere does contemporary evangelical Christianity show itself to be more vulnerable and less worthy of Eastern trust. Christ in us is not a lesser mystery but a greater mystery than Christ enthroned in the heaven of heavens. To feel reverence and awe in the face

of such majestic mystery is to make at least a beginning in communicating Christ to the Indian mentality.

4. Missionaries will have to take with utter seriousness the biblical doctrine of illumination. In opposing Indian intuitional thinking it is all too easy to throw out the baby with the bathwater. The Bible discloses that the Father reveals the truth concerning the Son (Matt. 16:17); the Son reveals the Father (Matt 11:27); the Holy Spirit has been given to lead us into truth (John 16:13); and the Spirit bears witness with our spirit that we are children of God (Rom. 8:16). Are we guilty of taking our methods of presenting the gospel and our arguments for Christian truth more seriously than we take the Spirit's power to teach and convict and assure? Then the Indian mind may be pardoned for objecting. True, human intuition and Spirit illumination are entirely different movements. But the missionary must existentially grasp the mystery and immediacy of the God "who is there" as he penetrates the human mind and heart with the truth of Christ by the power of the Spirit. When he does grasp it, Christian communication is enhanced, and the possibility of the Holy Spirit's ministry to the Indian mind is increased.

In the second place, effective communication to the Indian involves special attention to those aspects of the Christian truth that speak most pointedly to Indian misunderstanding. That there are certain similarities between Christian thinking and Indian thinking is clear. But the similarities are like the tips of an iceberg. Beneath the surface a mountain of differences lies concealed. To underscore these differences will not make Christianity more appealing to the natural mind of the Hindu, but it will make the alternatives clear. After all, the missionary task is not so much to make Christ palatable as it is to make him preeminent. The missionary speaks not so much to a person's taste as to his conscience. And Christ is the truth in a unique way. He stands out in contrast to any human system or personality. Christian truth speaks pointedly to the Indian mind in the following ways:

1. Christian truth contrasts sharply with the Hindu mystic's understanding of the human mind and its capacities.

As marvelous as the mental powers of a person may be, his conclusions are not to be compared with the thoughts of God. The mind of man is God's creation, not his emanation. The natural mind is incapable of comprehending God and, indeed, is at enmity with him. Paul, writing to the Colossians concerning their pre-Christian state, said, "Although you were formerly alienated and hostile in mind, engaged in evil deeds, yet He has now reconciled you in His fleshly body and through death" (Col. 1:21–22). Here Paul correctly links the mind and the body, the thoughts and the deeds. Thinking God's thoughts after him is not simply a matter of discipline. The bodily distractions that frustrate the Indian thinker are as nothing compared to the spiritual disablements and the disaffections of the natural mind. The Indian quest for the divine is in fact a hopeless quest apart from the divine quest for Indians. The divine invitation was never more pointed and needful: "Come to Me, all who are weary and heavy laden, and I will give you rest. Take My yoke upon you, and learn from Me" (Matt. 11:28–29).

2. The cruciality of God's revelation and man's redemption *in history* tears at the vitals of mystical thinking. There is indeed a reality that is *behind* history, but not in the sense that history is an illusion. Rather, God ordained history to achieve his purpose *in history*, and *in history* he discloses his person, purpose, and plan. The Indian (along with the theological liberal who has taken his flight to some kind of suprahistory) must come down to earth because that is precisely what God did in the person of Jesus Christ. As mentioned previously, the Indian mind is attracted to the Christ who taught in the universalistic and sublime terms of, for example, the Beatitudes. Let the Indian mind savor to the full the insights of the master Teacher, for to do so is in accord with his thinking of the best presentment of history. But inevitably he must then come to the uniqueness of Christ's claims, his atoning death, and attesting Resurrection. Here the universals are particularized. The Indian mind may recoil, but in the once-for-allness of redemptive history is to be found God's provision for people individually and collectively.

3. Again, the truth of God is revealed in the propositions of the Old and New Testaments understood in their historical and grammatical senses. Approximately two thousand times in the Bible we find the expression "Thus saith the Lord," or its equivalent. Knowing the fragileness of human language, God nevertheless revealed his truth propositionally to and through prophets and apostles. Why? Evidently it was because the risk of human misinterpretation of truth in the form of verbal propositions is much less than the risk of self-deception inherent in intuited experience! The sacred canon is therefore to be set in sharp contrast to the entire Hindu corpus. The Bible is not the product of holy men who intuited reality and attempted to convey some small measure of truth concerning ineffable experiences by means of inscrutable propositions. Rather, the Bible is the product of holy men whose words were the inbreathed, or inspired, words of God. Nor does the truth of the Bible lie hidden "beneath the letter" (as some Buddhists aver of their scriptures) to be discovered by a mental process as unique as that of unaided intuition itself. The Bible is to be approached by people in precisely those ways in which they would approach any other written document, albeit in dependence on the Holy Spirit to open their minds and hearts to it.

In the third place, the communication of Christ to the Hindu may be enhanced by emphasizing those approaches and methodologies that are familiar to the Hindu. The missionary will certainly take advantage of various avenues of presenting Christ that are available in the context of the Indian mentality.

Two approaches should have abiding appeal, though to suggest them is by no means to intimate that we are confined to them:

1. Hindu thinking invites dialogue. At first glance it may seem that the kind of dialogue that would be culturally appropriate in the Indian case would be inconclusive because of the emphasis on tolerance, the presumed validity of various ways to the truth, the emphasis on neutrality, and so forth. Indian communicators, however, are not famous for their retiring nature or indecision—nor, for that matter, for their

humility. Jawaharlal Nehru, Krishna Menon, and even Indira Gandhi present quite another picture. It would seem that their readiness to speak in an assertive and dogmatic way is only an apparent contradiction. There is in the Indian way of seeking truth a profound emphasis on talking it out and on putting the various sides of a question in bold relief. Moreover, Hinduism allows a place for forcefulness in the "big-fishes-eat-little-fishes" world of business and politics. India's neutrality as proposed by her diplomats is thus a very forceful neutrality, and to foreign observers it has a way of becoming painfully partisan when India's concerns are at stake. There is strong Indian precedent, therefore, for viewing dialogue as something other than simply an eclectic sharing of ideas or a search for the lowest common denominator. Dialogue can be much more profound than that. It can be a determined quest for the higher and better alternative. And in this more profound kind of dialogue true followers of Christ can optimistically participate.

2. Hendrik Kraemer, Malcom Pitt, and many others have noted the potential of the *ashram* for Christian communication. The *ashram* is constituted by a teacher of recognized authority who, in a place apart, gathers learners about him for earnest discussion and instruction. The various churches and missions in India have promoted Christian *ashrams* for many years. Outside the Indian context, a similar type of ministry has been used by missionaries to Buddhists—especially Buddhist students. In some places lodging with a resident missionary or national teacher is provided at reasonable rates, and special opportunities are made for periods of contemplation and times of conversing, with the Scriptures as a point of reference. The weakness in these endeavors often seems to be that they tend to become very low key and overlook the Indian (and Buddhist) precedents for forthright and forceful presentations that we have already noted. The *ashram* model would also seem to lend itself to variations such as the coffeehouse type of ministry, or the house-church approach to church extension.

In communicating Christ in ways that answer to intuitional or psychical thinking, it is imperative that we present the scriptural position vis-à-vis the problems posed by that type of thinking. But it should be remembered that even in the Indian context, thought is not confined to the intuitional level. Therefore communication can be tailored to the Indian mind and still be full-orbed.

Chapter 24

Communicating Christ In Cultural Areas Where Concrete Relational Thinking Predominates

In this chapter we are concerned with people who attempt to discover truth in such a way that "life and reality are seen pictorially in terms of the active emotional relationships present in a concrete situation." In verbal communication, the concrete relational thinker tends to express, inform, and persuade by referring to symbols, stories, events, objects, and so forth, rather than to general propositions and principles. But he is especially prone to rely on nonverbal communication of all types—gesture and sign language, music and the plastic arts, ritual and drama, and image projection. Of these we will have more to say in a subsequent chapter, though it is necessary to presume somewhat on that later discussion.

TRIBAL PEOPLES AS CONCRETE RELATIONAL THINKERS

Chinese thinking has been designated as concrete relational, but it would seem that concrete relational thinking can be observed as readily among the various tribal peoples. The communication of tribal peoples fairly bristles with the

325

myths, parables, aphorisms, fables, analogies, similies, and tribal lore that are part and parcel of concrete relational thinking. Perhaps Lucien Levy-Bruhl makes the gap between the Western and primitive mind greater than it really is. But his words are worth noting:

> The two mentalities which encounter each other here are so foreign to one another, their customs so widely divergent, their methods of expressing themselves so different! Almost unconsciously, the European makes use of abstract thought, and his language has made simple logical processes so easy to him that they entail no effort. With primitives both thought and language are almost exclusively concrete by nature.[1]

Missionaries to tribal peoples (or peoples who have recently emerged from tribal situations) usually become aware of this difference, though they adjust to it, if at all, with some difficulty. Missionary Ted Veer of Ethiopia recounted to me how on one occasion he reprimanded two students who came to class over an hour late. The incident passed without further discussion until the last day of class at which time one of the two students stood to ask a question. One began by telling the story of a horse that had worked hard and then went to a waterhole to drink. Somebody had so muddied the water, however, that is was impossible for the horse to drink it. The student concluded by asking: "Now what should be done about this situation?" To the missionary this way of approaching a problem of interpersonal relationships seemed cumbersome at best and enigmatic at worst. But actually it may be a very superior way. And in any case it was the indigenous way.

Another case in point concerns a correspondence course for Christian pastors in central and southern Africa that met with little response. Some concluded that the pastors lacked the motivation to undertake individual study and that the project should be abandoned. Wiser heads, however, were

---

[1]Lucien Levy-Bruhl, *Primitive Mentality* (Boston: Beacon, 1966), 433.

encouraged to restudy the course materials (which had been prepared mainly by Western missionaries in English and then simply translated into various tribal tongues and distributed). Careful analysis—this time with more native assistance— indicated that the materials were too abstract and theoretical to engage and hold the attention of the pastors. The courses were revised and a number of appropriate drawings included. This time the response was nothing short of overwhelming.

The communication of tribal peoples simply bristles with poignant aphorisms such as the following: "Sin is like a hill; you stand on yours so that you can see another's sin"; "Even monkeys sometimes fall from trees"; and "It is meddlesome for the goat to salute the hyena." Little reflection is required to grasp the messages of these sayings. But more than that, such aphorisms open a window on the tribal mind and thought process. It is not that the peoples of Europe and America do not have similar sayings. What is significant is that thousands of proverbs and aphorisms form an indispensable part of daily communication throughout the cities and villages of Africa and other tribal areas.

I recall the response of an African ecclesiastical leader to the request of a North American board of missions for information on the division of a single church organization into two organizations with separate heads. The core of the answer as it was conveyed in a letter to the board was this: "To respond to your question as to why we now have two churches, the answer should be quite clear to everyone. You yourselves have laid the trap. Now you have caught your animal." The American board puzzled over that for some time until an experienced missionary aided their understanding. The African leader was not trying to be abstruse. Neither was he engaging in recrimination. He was simply calling attention to the fact that the missionary forces, though cooperating in one field organization, had originated from two different denominations, had somewhat different outlooks, and had located in different, though adjacent, areas. The result was predictable.

One might dwell with great profit on the significance of

tribal myths and the attention tribal peoples give to their ritual celebrations. As a matter of fact, concrete relational thinking is evident in almost all of tribal life and lore.

CHINESE PEOPLE AS CONCRETE RELATIONAL THINKERS

Chinese thinking is somewhat more complex. That Chinese thought is basically concrete relational is widely agreed upon. Hajime Nakamura says,

> We can see a distinctive feature of the Chinese way of thinking, i.e., the true way is not to be obtained by words— not through universal propositions—but only through concrete experience.[2]

What complicates the picture are the overlays of religious teachings and philosophies that have been so much a part of Chinese history. Within these various philosophies is discoverable that which is contradictory to this basic Chinese commitment to concreteness and particularity. It seems, however, that in most cases the Chinese have been selective or have made modifications that left their fundamental thought forms intact. For example, Lao-tzu's teaching reinforced the notion that truth is not to be conceived of in terms of logic and reasoning but in terms of feeling and empathy with nature. As we have seen, however, Lao-tzu's mysticism did not develop in the same way as the mysticism of India but in a way compatible with concrete relational thinking.

Confucius' emphasis on tradition, ritual, and social relationships was certainly in accord with concrete relational thinking from the first. Confucius' dependence on tradition and history is apparent in the Chinese challenge to speculative thinking: "Speculate, theorize, as much as you like, but check up on your speculations by finding out what has happened in

[2]Hajime Nakamura, *Ways of Thinking of Eastern Peoples*, Philip P. Wiener, ed. (Honolulu: East-West Center, 1964),197.

the past.[3] In accordance with Confucius' outlook, Chinese ritualism is a way of settling issues before they arise and without resort to deliberation.[4] (The basic idea in the Chinese word "to know" is "to imitate.") As in the case of the famous sage, when it comes to religion, the first thoughts of the Chinese as a whole do not concern human relationship to reality. Instead, the Chinese focus on the relationships between people, particularly within the family. The Chinese think "highly of the art of making it possible for human beings to live together in harmony and happiness."[5] (This is a good description, by the way, of Chinese pragmatism.)

The Chinese imprint on Buddhism is unmistakable. To the extent that Buddhism was reabsorbed into Hinduism in India, it largely acquiesced to the Hindu belief in non-ego. In China it was free to develop as a humanistic religion with an emphasis on individualism and practicality.[6] So Chinese priests developed the Zen school, which retained enlightenment as the *summum bonum* of religious experience, but they also invented objects of concentration and linguistic devices as aids to trigger that experience.

An illuminating story is told of the founder of the Sooji temple (a famous Zen temple) in Tsurumi, Japan.[7] After spending ten years in China in the study of Buddhism, this man returned to Japan. He summarized what he had learned in one phrase, *Ganoh Bichoku*, which means, "The eyes are horizontal and the nose is vertical." Whatever this might have meant, it is obvious that the Chinese master had taught him in terms that were concrete and particular! *This approach to reality uses the concrete to occasion intuitional apprehension. The rational or theoretical is all but omitted.*

[3]Charles Moore, ed., *The Chinese Mind: Essentials of Chinese Philosophy and Culture* (Honolulu: East-West Center, 1967), 78.

[4]Robert T. Oliver, *Culture and Communication* (Springfield, Ill.: Charles C. Thomas, 1962), 114.

[5]H. G. Creel, *Chinese Thought from Confucius to Mao-Tse-Tung* (Chicago: University of Chicago Press, 1953), 2.

[6]Nakamura, *Ways of Thinking*, 235.

[7]Takooki Aikawa and Lynn Leavenworth, *The Mind of Japan—A Christian Perspective* (Valley Forge: Judson, 1967), 53.

The reader will, of course, attempt to relate what I have said to modern China. In some ways the dialectical approach of Hegel and its economic and social interpretation by Karl Marx would seem to be unlikely options for the Chinese. Once again, however, we see the Chinese mentality at work. It is no accident that although Communism was conceived in the West, it perhaps has reached it zenith in China. Robert Oliver believes that Chinese thinking, which lends itself to the subordination of the mind and spirit to official doctrine, led straight to totalitarianism. Although some may question the route by which Oliver arrives at his conclusions, there does seem to have been a preparation for the Chinese Communists' apparently successful effort to reshape Chinese thought and conduct in accordance with official interpretations. In the case of the masses in China, although Communist indoctrination involved a break with that part of classical Confucianism that emphasized familial and ancestral relationships, its leaders have *insisted that the "new" interpretation of history and social responsibility is not really new at all but has long awaited the emergence of leaders capable of articulating and enacting it.* Mao's rhetoric made much of the idea that the source of the new wisdom is really the people who have been held in a kind of bondage by the enemies of the people in the past. Thus the Communist leaders are really the systematizers, interpreters, and articulators of the ideas and aspirations of the people. Mao wrote,

> In all the practical work of our party, all correct leadership is necessarily "from the masses, to the masses." This means: take the ideas of the masses (scattered and unsystematic ideas) and concentrate them (through study turn them into concentrated and systematic ideas), then go to the masses and propagate and explain these ideas until the masses embrace them into action, and test the correctness of these ideas in such action. Then once again concentrate ideas from the masses and once again go to the masses so that the ideas are persevered in and carried through. And so

on, over and over again in more vital and richer concentration each time. Such is the Marxist theory of knowledge.[8]

This is simple and clear. The people's thinking is circumscribed and inchoate. The leaders conceptualize, analyze, and systematize that thinking according to Marxist principles (and in the tradition of the West!) and give the results to the people! The extent to which the Chinese Communists may be successful in this process of reorienting the thinking of a whole nation must await the verdict of history.

UNDERSTANDING CONCRETE RELATIONAL THINKING

A bit of cross-cultural Piaget-type research utilizing "cognitive map-making" may help us to understand something of what is involved in the differences between postulation and concrete relational thinking. It was conducted by P. R. Dasen, who compared a control group of Western-educated students (aged 9–12) to a group of Nepalese students (aged 9–15). Both groups were asked to draw maps of their immediate environment. As compared to the control group, the Nepalese students drew maps that lacked both directional and spatial clues. Typically the route traversed was a line indicating the sequential process of going rather than spatial relationships. Furthermore, the Nepalese drew pictures of their homes and schools on their maps rather than drawing representative symbols.[9] True, one must be careful in drawing conclusions from research such as this. But at the least it may indicate a lack of readiness on the part of the Nepalese for instruction in the Western "scientific-postulational" mode. This, of course, has significant implications for missionary communication in numerous cultures and at various levels.

[8]*Quotations from Mao-Tse-Tsung* (Peking: Foreign Languages, 1972), 128–29.
[9]P. R. Dasen, "Cross-Cultural Piagetian Research: A Summary" in J. W. Berry and P. R. Dasen, eds. *Culture and Cognition: Readings in Cross-Cultural Psychology* (London: Methuen, 1974), 409–23.

The fact that many tribal societies are in the process of rapid change and that China is in the throes of cultural revolution should not blind the missionary to the truth that concrete relational thinking is very much a part of human thought processes and is given high priority in many cultures. The response of many concrete relational cultures to Christianity is almost automatic: It is, for them, too deep, too dogmatic, too definite, and too difficult. It is too abstract, too ideological, too conceptual, too formalistic, too "unnatural," and too "unfeeling."[10] Missionaries may counter that this criticism is superficial and results from misunderstanding. But they would be better advised to adjust their approach. Otherwise the encounter is simply a case of the pot calling the kettle black. An ounce of understanding is worth a pound of recrimination.

Understanding should not be difficult to achieve. The Westerner is certainly no stranger to the concrete relational thinking implicit in the formulae and models of science; the rhetorical and pedagogical value of diagrams, pictures, and illustrations; the current bent toward a situation ethic; and the symbolic mission of various art forms. And he reads a Bible that is chock-full of concrete relational communication. (The Hebrews possessed an unsurpassed genius for making the absolute concrete.) Concretizing is, in fact, the very essence of storytelling, and the Bible—especially the Old Testament—is basically a story, and stories within a story!

SUGGESTIONS FOR COMMUNICATING CHRIST TO CONCRETE RELATIONALISTS

Let me then suggest some steps by which we might better approach those who place a high priority on concrete relational thinking.

In the first place the missionary should consider what *biblical* Christianity says to the *missionary* who is immersed

[10]Cf. Joseph J. Spae, *Christianity Encounters Japan* (Tokyo: Orient Institute for Religious Research, 1968), 71–97.

in Western modes of thought. Recalling what I have already said on this subject, let us take special note of the following:
1. The unfolding of God's revelation to humanity is in a historical context. The Bible is planted in *terra firma*. As J. L. Aranguren writes,

> The transition from the mythical to the historical religions (Jewish-Christian) may be expressed by a play on words as that from *story* to *history*—to those events, or series of unique, real, historical events, on which our Western religion is founded.[11]

Moreover, as the earth yields the treasures of antiquity to the pickaxes and shovels of archaeologists, there is mounting evidence that the Bible is a book of *accurate* history. To appreciate this the missionary should familiarize himself with the mythological or visionary or philosophical nature of most of the sacred corpuses of false religious systems. Then he should turn from the phantasmagoria of non-Christian imaginings; he should put aside (temporarily) the abstractions (however meaningful and true) of Christian theology; and he should review those *events* in which and through which God has disclosed himself and his truth. That exercise complete, let him approach the peoples of the developing nations of Africa, of the island world, and of China and Japan.
2. The Bible is a treasure house of truth communicated indirectly and in concrete thought forms. A catalog of these would require many pages. They include the Old Testament types, the parables and symbolic acts of the prophets, the recounting and interpretation of dreams and visions, the rituals and festivals of worship, the aphorisms of the wisdom literature, the parables of Christ, and so forth. There are classic examples of concrete relational communication such as that of the prophet Nathan delivering his divine message to King David (2 Sam. 12):

[11]José L. Aranguren, *Human Communication*, trans. Frances Partridge (New York: McGraw-Hill, 1967), 81.

Nathan: "the rich man, . . . took the poor man's ewe lamb."

King David: "the man . . . deserves to die."

Nathan: "You are the man!"

Only after David passed judgment on himself in this way did Nathan elaborate the nature and implication of David's sin. Think for a moment of the various figurative representations used in the person and work of the Third Person of the Godhead: dove (Matt. 3:16), seal (Eph. 1:13), oil (Heb. 1:9), fire (Acts 2:3), rain (Zech. 10:1), wind (John 3:8), rivers (John 7:38), dew (Isa. 18:4), clothing (Luke 24:49), and pledge (2 Cor. 1:22).

The Western mind—in theological as well as nontheological pursuits—seems to be on a never-ending quest for more and more encompassing generalizations and higher and higher levels of abstraction. But these tendencies are fraught with danger even in the context of Western literary achievement. The preacher who piles general propositions one upon another and calls the result a sermon gradually leaves his unmoved audience behind. The theologian who seeks to eliminate anthropomorphic language about a "God who is there" in favor of abstractions like Tillich's "Ground of Being" is taking leave of a divine Christ *and* human culture. In the Incarnation the Word became flesh. That is not easy to comprehend for either literary or nonliterary people, but in a special sense nonliterary people at least require a "Word" that is a "he."

The missionary, then, should be able to distinguish and use metaphors (figures of speech in which one object stands for another), similies (figurative language describing one object by its likeness to another), symbols (things that stand for something else), types (objects that prefigure another object), parables (truths illustrated by fictive or factual accounts), allegories (stories that represent or illustrate truth), and emblems (figurative representations). The missionary will find material for this type of concrete communication all around him—in the Book he holds, the life he lives, and the experiences he observes.

3. The ordinances of baptism and the Lord's Supper had a

large part to play in the communication of the faith of the early church. Early Christian worship was understandably quite simple. The church was cradled in the synagogue with its uncomplicated form of worship. There likely was a nascent fear of ostentation and formalism. The gradual development of more formalized patterns and the full flowering of ritual and liturgy in the fourth century demonstrate that the fear was justified. Nevertheless, one could argue that attention given to the ordinances in the early church indicates that the early Christians were more appreciative of the symbolic mission of those ordinances than are many churches and missions today.

Is it inappropriate to suggest that we should recover the witnessing and proclaiming potential of these symbols (Rom. 6:1–4; 1 Cor. 11:26)? Can we not do so without engaging in theological controversy? God certainly knew that there was a risk involved in the presence of such powerful symbols in the church. But evidently the risk to the church and the world that accrues because of their absence is even greater.

In the second place, biblical Christianity should be allowed to correct the misunderstandings that grow out of placing too great a stress on concrete relational thinking. This is the other side of the coin and may be important to prevent some from forsaking one extreme only to embrace another.

1. The *biblical* use of parables provides a corrective to an overemphasis on concrete relational thinking. The word *parable* means a "placing beside"; etymologically this term means that one subject is placed beside another so as to illustrate and explain it. The biblical meaning is somewhat broader than generally thought and is inclusive, for example, of short proverbs. In both Testaments the parable is used to make truth vivid and drive it home to the people. At the same time parables are used to drop a veil around the truth. Jesus employed them in the latter way when his hearers were not really ready or willing to hear more explicit truth (cf. Matt. 13:10–13). The disciples, who were especially desirous of knowing the precise meaning of Jesus' words, often asked for an interpretation of his parables.

We conclude that parables are an aid to the comprehension of truth when the truth they convey also has been made apparent by some other means and when people are spiritually prepared to receive the truth. When these conditions are met, parables promote impact and clarity and aid the memory. But by itself the parable evidences a certain obscurity. We might conjecture that in most cases concrete relational thinking has this defect. Experiences are usually capable of more than one interpretation. In one way or another the Bible clarifies and interprets. Jesus did the same. And when he did so the disciples responded, "Lo, now You are speaking plainly, and are not using a figure of speech" (John 16:29). In the Bible, then, parables, proverbs, and figures of speech do not stand alone.

2. Concrete relational thinking is particularly susceptible to idolatry, though the human tendency toward idolatry is present in all three types of thinking. In the early history of Christianity, conceptual thinking fashioned the *mental* images of Gnosticism which were every bit as offensive to God as the *metal* images of the cult of Diana in Ephesus and were rightly put under the anathema of the early ecumenical councils. Those *mental* images have their counterparts in some theologies of the West and East today.

The tendency to fashion *metal* (and wood and stone) idols is most present today in that citadel of intuitional thought that is India. In spite of the priority given to the spiritual nature of the ultimate reality, the fertile Indian imagination has fashioned a bewildering plethora of multiform idols, each of which is purported to have some symbolic relationship with the reality behind the visible form. The Bible, however, does not make allowance for these fine distinctions: "All the gods of the peoples are idols" (Ps. 96:5).

Very possibly it is concrete relational thinking that provides the entering wedge for idolatry. The mind reaches out for something tangible on which to focus the senses. It somehow captures the divine and localizes God's person, power, or presence. Supposedly, God is somehow presented in this or that particular place or object as in none other.[12] In Christianity God through Christ is present with his people *wherever* they meet in his name, and Christ is *always* with his people even to the very end of the age. True Christianity is the universal religion and has resisted every effort to make God the property of a time, a place, or a symbol. Early Christianity persisted in the Judaistic antipathy toward images of any sort. In fact, as late as the third century, painters and sculptors who presented themselves for baptism were required to change professions because their works could be used in serving the ends of idolatry.[13]

The biblical injunctions against idolatry and incipient idolatry are clear. Idolatry must be resisted wherever found. I recall the advice of a prominent Protestant pastor to those who have difficulty focusing their thoughts during periods of private prayer. This pastor suggested that they place a picture of Sallman's *Head of Christ* in front of themselves as a point of reference. The peril of this innocent counsel is observable throughout Africa, Asia, Latin America, and the island world today. Missionaries must be able to distinguish between simple atmosphere, architecture, and art on the one hand and incipient or overt idolatry on the other. Biblical teaching must be explicitly and patiently communicated. Practices that tend to countenance or perpetuate idolatry must be scrupulously avoided in obedience to God.

God's Word is the final answer to idolatry in all its forms. That answer must be preached and taught even though it will not be palatable to many.

In the third place, and in line with what we have said previously, missionary communication in the context of concrete relational thinking should make full use of legiti-

---

[12]Actually this can be true only in the sense and form in which God begins to thus present himself. Therefore the tabernacle worship of the Old Testament was not idolatrous whereas counterparts devised by heathen imagination were idolatrous.

[13]Cf. M. A. Smith, *From Constantine to Christ* (Downers Grove, Ill.: InterVarsity, 1971), 151.

mate visual forms, the various techniques of storytelling, and the potential inherent in drama and ritual.

1. Christian places of worship should be noted for their cleanliness and orderliness as a matter of Christian testimony. In some areas there is widespread ignorance of what places of corporate worship should be like, though there may be many holy areas associated with natural phenomena such as trees, rocks, mountains, and so forth. In other areas, holy places will be numerous and ornate in the extreme. In and of themselves neither simplicity nor ornateness is essential. What *is* essential is that places of Christian worship provide an atmosphere that speaks of the character of God and true worship.

2. Drama and ritual have special appeal in concrete relational cultures and should be used in missionary communication. (More will be said on this in the chapter on media.) Concrete relational thinkers think dramatistically. Truth is perceived by them in terms of life experiences. Many missionaries will attest to the fact that they find Chinese, Japanese, tribal peoples, and other concrete relational thinkers particularly interested and gifted in pantomime, drama, and ritual. Unfortunately the missionary is often ill at ease with these forms of communication and uninstructed in their use. As a result he does not encourage these interests and gifts, and their potential is not exploited. In the churches such artistic talents tend to gradually wither and die. Perhaps the missionaries of a new generation will be better able to creatively exploit the potential of dramatic forms.

3. Usually, verbal communication—and especially sermonizing—should proceed from the illustration to the principle, not from the principle to the illustration as is characteristic of Western preaching. In a seminary class, missionary Gerald Swank related how during his early days in Nigeria he was instructed by the preaching approach of the senior missionary and Nigerian pastor, both of whom began their messages with Bible passages that conveyed down-to-earth stories; or with references to wildlife, insects, and domestic animals; or with familiar folktales that illustrated the lesson. Before they brought their messages to a close, both missionary

and pastor had communicated timeless spiritual truths that never failed to impress the audience. At first Swank was apprehensive and thought the messages somewhat tedious and juvenile. But when he watched the uninhibited response of the audience, he realized that these preachers were communicating to the African mind.

4. The art of communicating Christian truth by means of, and in conjunction with, diagrams, pictures, and artifacts of various kinds needs much greater development in the training and practice of cross-cultural Christian workers. What a pity that in the West this type of communication is so often thought of as juvenile and appropriate for Sunday schools only! The greater effectiveness of visual as compared with audio communication is well known. How much easier it is to remember the details of a person's appearance than to remember his name! This is especially true in the cases of people who do not write the names or use some system of mnemonics.

Pastor Chiaki Kuzuhara of the Lakeside Japanese Church in Chicago regularly writes a pictorial letter to the members and friends of his congregation. In one of his recent letters he wrote about plans to return to Japan with a series of pictorial sermons and the fact that there are many in that land who report that they still remember pictorial sermons that he preached some twenty-two years ago![14]

CONCLUSION TO PART IV

Missionary communication must take into account the ways in which people think and formulate their ideas. My purpose in this discussion has not been so much to enable the missionary to predict the mind of his respondent culture so he can program his approach. Rather, my purpose has been to familiarize the missionary with *types* of cultural thinking and *priorities* in cultural thinking so the missionary can contextualize his communication to the mind of his respondent

[14]"A Pictorial Letter from Chiaki and Kate Kuzuhara" (Chicago, n.d.).

culture. The missionary *can* adapt because *all* people think postulationally, psychically, and concrete relationally. He *must* adapt because respondents of other cultures have their own priorities in thinking.

Priorities in ways of thinking stem quite naturally from worldviews. Speaking theologically, we may say that when people knew God, they did not honor him as God or thank him. The result was that "they became futile in their speculations" (Rom. 1:21). The Indian mind betrays a desire to return to that primordial status where people knew God and communed with him as did Adam, Enoch, Abraham, Noah, and Moses. But the Indian mind mistakes the mystical, intuited experience for divine revelation and substitutes the machinations of sages for the messages of the prophets.

The Chinese mind betrays a desire to see in creation and circumstances the witness that the Creator has imprinted on all he made, even as the psalmist gained knowledge of the divine Being via the heavens above him and the earth around him (Ps. 19:1–2). But the Chinese mind mistakes the substance for the Sovereign, the rule for the Ruler, and the arrangement for the Artist.

The Western mind betrays an overconfidence in its ability to reconstruct a true picture of reality—both temporal and eternal—by resort to reason. But the Western mind has mistakenly overlooked its own limitations and now finds itself straining to preserve its integrity at home and to demonstrate the flexibility required to communicate abroad

All people stand in dire need of God's self-disclosure in his Word and in his Son. The missionary's opportunity and challenge is to faithfully communicate the biblical revelation that answers to human perversions in ways that make its message understandable. That calls for submission and intercession that God himself will enlighten the minds of those who hear the Word of truth.

Part V

LINGUISTIC FORMS—
WAYS OF EXPRESSING
IDEAS

Figure 20

DIMENSIONS OF CROSS-CULTURAL COMMUNICATION

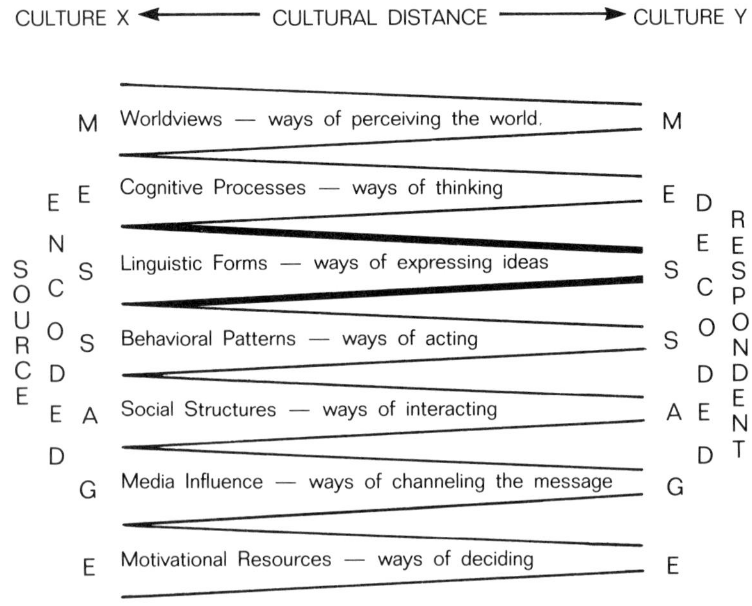

CULTURE X ◄─────── CULTURAL DISTANCE ───────► CULTURE Y

M Worldviews — ways of perceiving the world.   M

E E Cognitive Processes — ways of thinking   E D R
N   E E
S C S Linguistic Forms — ways of expressing ideas   S C S
O   O P
U O S Behavioral Patterns — ways of acting   S D O
R D   E N
C E A Social Structures — ways of interacting   A D D
E D   E
      G Media Influence — ways of channeling the message   G N
                                                                       T
      E Motivational Resources — ways of deciding   E

Chapter 25

The Importance of Language

The ambiguity of one word may have drastically changed the history of the twentieth century.[1] The Japanese word *mokusatsu* has two distinct meanings: (1) to ignore, and (2) to refrain from comment. During July 1945 a significant number of influential Japanese—the emperor among them—were prepared to consider terms for ending the war with the Allies. The Potsdam ultimatum called for a response from Japan but the Japanese wanted more time to discuss terms. A press release announced that the official cabinet policy was one of *mokusatsu*, and the intended meaning of the word was "to refrain from comment." In the process of translation, however, the foreign press overlooked the "no comment" possibility and reported that the Japanese policy was "to ignore" the ultimatum. At that point Japanese psychology came into play. The release could have been recalled and restated. That procedure would have involved admissions that entailed a great loss of face, however, and therefore was really unthink-

---

[1] Stuart Chase, *The Power of Words* (New York: Harcourt, Brace and World, 1954), 4–5.

able to Japanese leaders. The "ignore" meaning was allowed to stand. Consequently, the voices of reason were not heard and the war continued. Had a settlement been made at that time there would have been no Hiroshima, no Nagasaki, no Russian intervention in Manchuria, and (quite possibly) no division of Korea and no Korean War. Tens of thousands of lives might have been saved.

The profound but subtle difference in the meanings of two very similar Greek words became very important in Augustine's controversy with the Pelagians. The Greek word *hamartēma* never meant sinfulness as such, but always referred to sin contemplated in its separate outcroppings and as deeds of disobedience to divine law. In other words, it referred to transgression as the outworking of the evil principle in human actions. *Hamartia*, on the other hand, was (and is) sin in the abstract as well as the concrete. This word reached back to the *quality* of the action, the evil principle from which evil deeds spring. When the Pelagians claimed that Chrysostom agreed with them on the subject of the moral condition of infants, Augustine carried the day by quoting Chrysostom's exact words. He showed that Chrysostom had pronounced infants free from *hamartēma*, the acts and outcropping of sin, not from *hamartia*, sin and the sin principle. Perhaps Augustine was made aware of this distinction by Aristotle's insistence on a similar distinction between the Greek words *adikēma* and *adikia*.[2]

Only fools agree with Faust when he says that "names are sound and smoke." Confucius insisted on the "rectification of names" because he realized that in well-ordered societies "names" (such as "teacher," or "parent," or "friend") dictate appropriate relationships and behavioral patterns. Ralph Waldo Emerson was persuaded that bad rhetoric makes bad people. George Orwell has pointed out that sloppy language

---

[2]Richard C. Trench, *Synonyms of the New Testament* (Marshalton, Del.: The National Foundation for Christian Education, n.d.), 226.

makes for sloppy thought.[3] Language is of the utmost importance to people—psychologically, socially, and spiritually. When we first meet people in the Bible, they have the power of speech. It was an integral part of their entire experience. They received the commands of God, they communed with God, and they were sought out by God—all by means of language. Adam's superiority over the lesser creatures around him was demonstrated in his authority to name them.

Some of the great tragedies of human history have involved the potential for evil inherent in language. The temptation in the Garden of Eden revealed the ability of Satan to raise doubts in the mind of Eve concerning the clear command of God. A common language enabled postdiluvian people in their rebellion against the revealed will of God. And the confusion of speech at Babel aborted that rebellion.

By the same token, some of the great miracles of human history have involved the potential for good inherent in language. One thinks immediately of the miracle of Pentecost when "Jews living in Jerusalem, devout men, from every nation under heaven" were part of a multitude who "were bewildered, because they were each one hearing them [the Christian spokesmen] speak in his own language [or dialect]" (Acts 2:5–6). Of course, this incident is just part of the larger miracle that is God patiently communicating his truth to fallen humanity down through the ages—communicating it through the use of language.

In one sense there are close to six billion "languages" in the world because the language of every individual is as distinct as his fingerprint. Linguists apply the term "idiolect" to this personal language. An idiolect is a "person's total set of language habits."[4] Ordinarily we pay little attention to

---

[3]Quoted in Melvin Maddocks, "The Limitations of Language," *Time*, 8 March 1971, 36–37.

[4]Robert A. Hall, Jr., *New Ways to Learn a Foreign Language* (New York: Bantam, 1966), 44.

personal idiosyncracies though they may become grist for the mills of grammarians, psychologists, and speech therapists. A collection of idiolects with shared commonalities makes a dialect. Peter undoubtedly spoke the Aramaic that was common among his people at the time of Christ, but his Galilean dialect was so pronounced that his speech betrayed him as a follower of the Master (Matt. 26:73). Basic similarities in dialects result in various languages, of which there are over 5,500 in the world. And certain similarities between languages indicate that there are various language families or language stocks. Charles Hockett estimates that one hundred years of separation will result in different dialects and that one thousand years of separation will produce different languages.[5] But, having a common parentage, such languages will still be related. How many language families or language stocks there are in the world is a subject of dispute. A number of scholars believe that there are only six or seven—Indo-European, Afro-Asiatic, Sino-Tibetan, Altaic, Dravidian, Austro-Asiatic, and Finno-Ugric.

Increasingly in the study of foreign languages we have become dependent on the tools provided by such disciplines as phonetics (the study of speech sounds considered as elements of language), descriptive linguistics (the study of the components and structure of languages), and historical linguistics (the changes occurring within languages over a period of time).

In recent times, linguists, psychologists, and anthropologists have also focused attention on the interanimation of language and human behavior within various cultural contexts. The results constitute the materials of the disciplines of ethnolinguistics and psycholinguistics. These disciplines contain many insights for the student of a foreign language.

The naturalistic bias of many scholars in modern times has occasioned, in part, the contemporary interest in the theories of Johanne Herder, Charles Hockett, and others on the origin of speech in the human race (the phylogenesis of

---

[5]Charles Hockett, "The Origin of Speech," *Scientific American* 202 (September 1960), 885.

speech). It also has aroused interest in the theories of people such as O. H. Mowrer and B. F. Skinner relating to the process whereby individuals learn how to use symbols of speech (the ontogenesis of speech). The naturalistic bias is betrayed in many such theories (for example, the "Echoic" theory of Herder, the "Yo-he-ho" theory of Noire, the "Vocal-play" theory of Jespersen, and the "Babble-luck" theory of Thorndike). The naturalists' theories and understandings of speech and symbolization leave much to be desired, however. As Wilbur Marshal Urban has written in an oft-quoted passage, "The mystery, yes even the miracle of language, with the entire marvel of intelligible communication, can be understood only on the basis of transcendental presuppositions."[6] Robert E. Longacre has argued on linguistic grounds that the various languages give evidence of a common substructure and that this fact belies the idea that language is a product of evolution and not a gift of God.[7]

[6]Wilbur Marshall Urban, *Language and Reality: The Philosophy of Language and the Principles of Symbolism* (London: Allen, 1951), 84.
[7]Robert E. Longacre, *An Anatomy of Speech Notions* (Lisse, Netherlands: Peter de Ridder, 1977).

Chapter 26

Why Bother to Learn The Language?

Few national peoples have occasioned more criticism than have contemporary Americans. There are undoubtedly many reasons for this—some good, some bad, and some indifferent—but two factors cannot be overlooked: (1) the tremendously large number of Americans working or traveling abroad, and (2) the unbelievably small number of Americans who have succeeded in learning even the simple "pots and pans" language of the foreign peoples with whom they associate. The truly amazing aspect of this sad state of affairs is that only a small percentage of those who are engaged in the sensitive area of international diplomacy can speak the language of the foreign culture in which they reside. As early as 1958 William Lederer and Eugene Burdick reported in the widely read book *The Ugly American*:

> It would seem a simple fact of life that ambassadors to at least the major nations should speak those languages. Yet in France, Italy, Germany, Belgium, the Netherlands, Norway, and Turkey, our ambassadors cannot speak the native tongue (although our ambassador to Paris can speak Ger-

man and our ambassador to Berlin can speak French). In the whole of the Arabic world—nine nations—only two ambassadors have language qualifications. In Japan, Korea, Burma, Thailand, Vietnam, Indonesia, and elsewhere, our ambassadors must speak and be spoken to through interpreters. In the entire Communist world, only our ambassador to Moscow can speak the native language.[1]

The same authors gave statistics that are most sobering:

In his masterful analysis of the Foreign Service, John Osborne states that the most important element in a good Foreign Service officer is "the faculty of communication." ". . . fifty percent of the entire Foreign Service officer corps do not have a speaking knowledge of any foreign language. Seventy percent of the new men coming into the Foreign Service are in the same state." These figures represent those who can speak no language other than their own—not even French, Spanish, German, or Italian. The number of Americans in the Foreign Service who can speak any of the more difficult languages is minuscule. . . .

On the other hand, an estimated nine out of ten Russians speak, read, and write the language before they arrive on station. It is a prior requirement. The entire functioning staff of Russian embassies in Asia is Russian, and all the Russians—the officials, stenographic help, telephone operators, chauffeurs, servants—speak and write the language of the host country.[2]

Unfortunately there is little to indicate that the situation among American ambassadors and their staff has improved appreciably since 1958.

When we consider the vast throng of service and private American personnel who are totally unprepared to speak to their foreign neighbors except by the medium of their own language, we may expect that Americans will be "ugly." The

[1] William J. Lederer and Eugene Burdick, *The Ugly American* (Greenwich, Conn.: Fawcett, 1958), 230.
[2] Ibid., 231.

same would be true of citizens of any nation that has the economic wherewithal to send great hordes of essentially unprepared citizenry to the other nations of the world.

When it comes to learning the language of their adopted cultures, missionaries would certainly rate high among the various categories of internationals who have learned the language of their host countries. In 1970 Stephen Neill reported that the Bible or parts of it had been printed in 1,392 languages and dialects and that missionaries had been responsible for over 1,000 of them![3] Nevertheless, there is much room for improvement. Every candidate and field missionary faces the issue of whether or not he will learn the language of the respondent culture and *how well he will learn it*. When faced with the challenge of learning an entirely new language certain obstacles and misunderstandings present themselves to the average missionary, however. Let us now turn our attention to some of the most important of them.

LANGUAGE AS A VEHICLE FOR GOSPEL COMMUNICATION

It is rather widely believed that some languages are woefully inadequate vehicles for the propagation of the Christian message. From the fact that the material culture of tribal peoples is very limited, for example, the assumption is often made that their languages are likewise circumscribed. There is a sense, of course, in which every language has limitations. We should not jump to the conclusion that many languages do not have the potential for expressing Christian truth, however. From a limited number of phonemes (sound units) the number of words and phrases that can be constructed is almost limitless. English has forty phonemes. Some languages have more phonemes and some have fewer, but half that number would be sufficient to deal with almost any experience or stimulus linguistically. Similarly, though there

[3]Stephen Neill, *Call to Mission* (Philadelphia: Fortress, 1970), 50. The 1974 total is from the *Bible Society Record*, no. 98, 1975.

are some biblical concepts that will be difficult to convey with the existing lexicon of some languages, the number will not be large. Eugene Nida points out, for example, that *incomplete* dictionaries of the Zulu, Aztec, and Maya languages have 30,000, 27,000, and 20,000 entries respectively. By comparison, the English Bible uses only about 7,200 words.[4] Each language presents its own unique challenges to translators and communicators. But, by the same token, *any* language can be used as a vehicle for conveying God's truth.

ENGLISH AS A LINGUA FRANCA FOR MISSIONARY COMMUNICATION

On the basis of the fact that English is widely used as the language of trade or education in certain cultures, some missionaries are tempted to excuse themselves from the responsibility of learning the native language. When one finds it possible to communicate even imperfectly by using a language in which he is fluent, he finds it more difficult to seriously study a language in which he will be a neophyte for a considerable period of time. He may learn just enough of the native tongue to convince himself (and the uninitiated) that he knows the language, or he may not bother to learn the language at all. But if he stops to analyze his ministry by taking a careful look at those whose lives he has personally influenced for God, he will almost certainly discover that they are nationals who have facility in English. There may be several factors contributing to this limited sphere of influence, but one factor almost certainly will be that only a few of his respondents are capable of the kind of understanding that results in true conversion and Christian growth.

By way of example, there are scores of ethnic groups in the Philippines, all with their own characteristic speech and customs. Spanish was introduced in early colonial times, and English became a primary medium of education and trade

[4]Quoted in Charles Corwin, *Biblical Encounter with Japanese Culture* (Tokyo: Christian Literature Crusade, 1967), 4.

after the Spanish-American War. Recently, Filipino (Tagalog) has been adopted as the national language. In Manila one may hear English, Filipino, Spanish, Ilocano, Visayan, and other languages. The monolingual American will get along fairly well as long as communication is one-way or as long as he confines himself to the business and educational communities. Even in those communities, however, he will soon become aware of limitations in communication.

I once asked a group of graduate Filipino students what cultural adaptation an English-speaking preacher should make if he wanted to be understood by the average *English-speaking* Filipino. Their reaction was immediate and instructive. They said that he should concentrate on (1) speaking slowly, (2) omitting English idioms and non-Filipino cultural references with which the audience could not be expected to be familiar, and (3) learning the Filipino pronunciation of English words! This is no small order. But it is the very least that would be required of the English-speaking missionary if he is to effectively communicate Christ to even the educated people of the Philippines!

No, one has not necessarily solved the language problem when he discovers respondents who speak English! A humorous experience of W. S. Howell comes to mind at this point. In Hawaii during the course of a world tour, Professor Howell met a Dr. Tillmann, who was a former acquaintance of his from Germany. They went out for dinner together. Professor Howell reports the event in the following words:

> In planning his [Dr. Tillmann's] order I asked, "Would you like coffee?" and Dr. Tillmann responded, "Thank you." At this point some recollection of my visits to Germany must have alerted me, for I enquired, "Do you mean yes or no?" Dr. Tillmann said, "I mean no," So I said, "Would you like tea?" He answered, "Thank you." Again I asked, "Do you mean yes or no?" Dr. Tillmann replied, "I mean yes. I've switched to English."[5]

[5]William S. Howell, "The Study of Intercultural Communication in Liberal Education," *Pacific Speech* 2, 4 (1967).

There is still another aspect of the use of English in the modernizing nations that merits our consideration. In earlier stages of their development many of these countries put a great emphasis on the teaching of English as a second language in order to appropriate the scientific learning of the West. Since the late 1950s, however, there has been a significant shift of emphasis back to their local languages in order to preserve their respective national heritages. Some nations have introduced national or regional languages into their primary educational programs, thus giving them precedence over the languages of international communication such as English. Instances of this are Hausa in Nigeria, Amharic in Ethiopia, and Bahasa Indonesia in Indonesia, as well as Filipino in the Philippines. In such countries overdependence on English as the language of Christian communication serves to heighten the feeling that Christianity is a foreign accretion to the indigenous culture. Missionaries from the United States should remember that the Bilingual Education Act of 1963 upholds the right of children to receive their *secular* education in their mother tongue. Do not all the peoples of the world have a right to learn of *Christ* in their primary language?

The missionary should ask himself whether he can in effect say to the people of his respondent culture, "Before you can learn the ways of God from me, you must learn *my* language—and more, you must learn it well." Is this not laying a yoke on respondent peoples that would have been too heavy for us or our fathers to bear?

THE IMPORTANCE OF LEARNING THE LANGUAGE OF THE RECEPTOR CULTURE

Some missionaries are tempted to excuse themselves from language learning by pointing to some missionary who appears to have been eminently successful without having learned the respondent language. Few young people get to the stage of candidacy without having met such individuals. But they should remember that success is not easy to define, especially from the vantage point of another culture. Nor do they know how much more might have been accomplished if the person(s) in question had learned the language. In any case, a catalog of missionaries of unquestioned accomplishment makes it clear not only that they learned a respondent language but also that many of them were outstanding in their mastery of it. A beginning list of such individuals includes Wulfilas (Goths), Carochi (Aztecs), Edwards (Mohicans), Cyrus Byington (Choctaws), Samuel Keinschmidt (Eskimo), David Zeisberger (Onandaga), William Carey (India), and Adoniram Judson (Burma). The list could become very long.

Almost without exception, missionaries will be well advised to learn the language of their respondent culture. Short-term missionaries and some specialists may find that they will have to settle for a limited language-learning experience, but they should not hesitate to make a start. Those who remain unconvinced should recall that when Paul was the center of a great controversy in Jerusalem, he gained the ear of the Roman commander by speaking in Greek and the attention of the large uproarious crowd of Jews by speaking in Hebrew (Acts 21:37, 40; 22:2).

If one wants to communicate Christ to a people, he must know them. The key to that knowledge always has been, and always will be, language. Eugene Nida sums it up:

> Language learning is more than simple mechanical ability to produce acoustic signals so as to buy, sell, and find your way about; it is a process by which we make vital contacts with a new community, a new manner of life, and a new system of thinking. To do this well is the basic requirement of effective missionary endeavor.[6]

---

[6]Eugene A. Nida, Learning a Foreign Language (New York: Friendship, 1957), 8.

Chapter 27

Learning About Language Learning

UNDERSTANDING LANGUAGE AND LANGUAGES

If we grant that something as devastating as war can have at least some positive outcomes, then it becomes apparent that one of the positive results of World War II, especially for Americans, was a new attention to languages and language learning. Some basic aspects of the resulting understanding of language are important for the missionary.[1]

1. Language is first spoken, then written. From the importance of the written language in our own technological culture, we should not infer that there are two equal and parallel kinds of language: the spoken and the written. Actually, fewer than half of the world's population can read and write, but all the peoples of the world have fully developed languages and can speak before they learn to write. The written language, then, is based on the spoken language.

[1]Eugene A. Nida, *Learning a Foreign Language* (New York: Friendship, 1957), 25–48.

2. To learn a language is to learn a complete set of linguistic habits. The interesting thing about habits is that they are habitual! In other words, most of our behavior is so natural to us that we engage in it without thinking and are at a loss to explain how we learned it. Actually we learned it by watching and listening to others in varied situations and by responding in similar situations accordingly. Language is a part of that behavior.

3. Every language constitutes a system. If it were not so, verbal communication would be impossible. Linguistics takes us beyond our traditional understanding of the system of language and demonstrates that the language of each society has a system of its own that correlates with that society's understanding of the world.

4. Language conveys meaning. The meanings of linguistic forms are more elusive than the forms themselves. Semantics is much more complex than, for example, phonemics or syntactics. The greater the cultural distance between source and respondent, the less basis there will be for achieving a commonality of meaning because each linguistic community has different experiences and divides up reality in different ways. However, we do have much in common with all peoples, and we will be in a better position to learn a foreign language if we do the following: (1) remember that meanings are in the users of language and not in the language itself, (2) keep in mind that there is no meaning of a word or construction that is somehow inherently right or valid, and (3) be aware that the meanings people assign to words will vary not only from linguistic community to linguistic community but within the same community with the passage of time.

5. Language is both individual and social in character. Even idiolects are made up of materials given to us by others during the language-learning process; there is comparatively little actual innovation. The important criterion of correctness in language use is social acceptability, and this accounts for the difference between standard and nonstandard,

or formal and informal, usages. To learn a language well is in part the ability to meet the expectations of various audiences. As we saw previously, it is well to think carefully about this newer understanding. Pressed too far, it can lead us to conclusions that are both anti-Christian and antimissionary! For example, in chapter 5 we saw that the notion that meanings are in people and not in language can lead to a misunderstanding of biblical revelation itself. However, generally speaking, missionaries would benefit greatly from a thorough study of language theory as reflected in the principles enumerated above.

First, it would free them from certain widespread myths about language and language learning—myths such as the idea that every word has *a* (one) *correct* meaning; that the *correct* meaning of a word is always the dictionary meaning; and that the *correct* meaning of a word is fixed and permanent. As a matter of fact, most words have more than one meaning and more than one *kind* of meaning (e.g., dictionary, reported, stipulated; denotative, connotative, structural). And meanings change over a period of time by such processes as widening, narrowing, raising, and lowering the meaning.

Second, it would provide new and practical approaches to the mastery of a second language and even one's native language as it changes over a period of time. We will look at language-learning methods in subsequent pages, so let us consider the practicality of applying a Semantic Differential test by way of example.

Back in the late 1950s Charles Osgood and his associates at the University of Illinois developed the Semantic Differential as a means of determining meaning. As is well known, denotative meaning is "pointing" meaning. It depends on a person's seeing a relationship between a symbol (d-o-g) and the referent (the actual animal we call "dog"). It is thought of as being "objective" because the focus is on the object symbolized rather than on the person who is doing the symbolizing. Osgood, however, was concerned with connotative or "inward" meaning—i.e., the internal judgments that are made by the individual. This kind of meaning depends on a person's feelings about the relationship between a symbol, a referent, and himself. It is often thought of as "subjective" because, though denotative meaning is determined by asking "Is this (the referent) a —— (the symbol)?," connotative meaning is much more difficult to determine. So Osgood developed the Semantic Differential test.[2]

David Berlo explains the Semantic Differential in the following words:

> Osgood assembled a large group of polar adjective pairs such as good-bad, fair-unfair, strong-weak, and valuable-worthless. He placed each element of a pair at one end of a seven-interval rating scale, and asked people to place a check mark somewhere along each scale, given a particular term. The answers that people gave for many such terms and scales were submitted to statistical analysis, and three major dimensions were discovered. Osgood called these the three dimensions of connotative meaning. Although later work has raised the possibility of additional dimensions, these three illustrate the general procedure adequately for our purposes.
>
> The three dimensions are (1) evaluation, (2) activity, and (3) potency. The evaluative dimension was indexed most nearly by the scale good-bad; the activity dimension by the scale active-passive, and the potency dimension by the scale strong-weak. By using these and other similar scales, one can use the Semantic Differential to index the internal judgments that people make, given a stimulus. The stimulus may be a word, a phrase, an entire message such as a picture, a name of a person, and so on.[3]

Berlo proceeds to reproduce a sample Semantic Differential as in figure 21.[4] This can be productive in intracultural communication right here at home. For example, a Christian

[2]Cf. Charles E. Osgood, George J. Suei, and Percy Tannenbaum, *The Measurement of Meaning* (Urbana: University of Illinois Press, 1957).

[3]David K. Berlo, *The Process of Communication: An Introduction to Theory and Practice* (New York: Holt, Rinehart and Winston, 1960), 297.

[4]Ibid., 298.

youth worker can gain significant insights into a youth group by using this device to test the response of its members to such words and phrases as "cross," "doctrine," "love," "premarital sex," and so forth. More than that, he can use the responses to initiate studies and dialogues on these topics. Similarly, as one of Osgood's students, Hideya Kumata, demonstrated early on, the intercultural communicator will find that Semantic Differential analyses will open entirely new vistas of understanding and communication.[5]

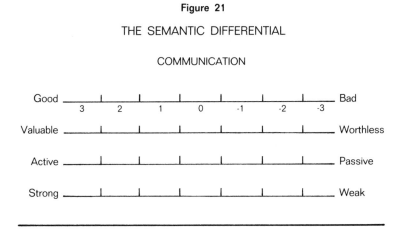

Figure 21

THE SEMANTIC DIFFERENTIAL

COMMUNICATION

APPROACHES TO LANGUAGE LEARNING

Various approaches to language learning have been developed down through the centuries. In the Middle Ages the grammar method was the usual approach to learning Latin. It is still widely used in the study of the so-called dead languages.

[5]Hideya Kumata, "A Factor Analytic Study of Semantic Structures Across Three Selected Cultures," Ph.D. dissertation, University of Illinois, 1958. Cited in Berlo, *Process of Communication*, 297 footnote.

A Frenchman by the name of M. Gouin is credited with having developed the "direct-method" in the 1860s. This method was an effort to reproduce the language-learning experience of the child in the adult. It emphasized continual use of the new language and deemphasized grammar learning to the point of exclusion.

The phonetic method came into vogue after the development of the phonetic alphabet in the first part of this century. This method had the advantage of reproducing the sounds of any language in a single system of written symbols. It emphasized mastery of the sounds of the respondent language and included an approach to grammar that was based on speech rather than on the written language. In placing such a heavy emphasis on sound, however, it appeared to many to be weak in the area of meaning.

In the years between the two world wars, the dominant approach in many schools in the United States was the reading method. It is still widely used and has a validity in many instances, but largely it leaves the student without the ability to communicate with *speakers* of the respondent language.

Just before World War II the American Council of Learned Societies began research in the application of linguistics learning to language study. Out of this research emerged the Army Intensive Language Program in which recruits learned to speak the critical languages of Asia and Africa. The linguistic method borrowed from the phonetics method but augmented it with the new understanding of the nature of language and its functions in society.

In recent years a new dimension has been added to the methodology of language learning. William D. Reyburn put it well in an article containing numerous suggestions that grow out of this contemporary approach:

These suggestions are built around the idea that a *language* is a whole construct which no one really employs except in the business of writing grammars and the like. It does little good to attempt to learn what someone has abstracted into a language system. What the "language learner" really needs is to know what specific utterances can go with what specific situations. The task of "learning a language" is, I feel, a psychological barrier to learning to speak. If we cease to think in terms of learning the abstracted language, with all its idiosyncrasies and illogical ways of behaving, and work to learn an utterance for every situation, we will find that we begin to speak with our first simple phrases and the task of speaking is merely that of expanding the situations and the appropriate phrases.[6]

Reyburn, therefore, is in agreement with Eugene Nida when he writes:

> As long as we maintain a cultural isolation, we cannot expect to learn a foreign language. . . . Linguistic training is of great help but it is no substitute for cultural submersion.[7]

For the sake of simplicity, then, let us call this new approach to language learning the approach of "cultural submersion."

LEARNING A LANGUAGE BY "CULTURAL SUBMERSION"

The philosophy of this approach is quite simple really.[8] It grows out of the linguistics method I have already discussed. Rather than thinking in terms of the "abstracted language" that appears in a grammar book, we should think in terms of the utterances that go with certain situations and the meanings behind them:

[6]William D. Reyburn, "Don't Learn That Language!" *Practical Anthropology* 5 (July-August 1958): 151–78, reprinted in William A. Smalley, ed. *Readings in Missionary Anthropology* (Tarrytown, N.Y.: Practical Anthropology, 1976), 341–58.

[7]Eugene A. Nida, *Customs and Culture* (New York: Harper & Row, 1954), 325.

[8]The following is a summary of the method outlined by Reyburn, "Don't Learn That Language!"

Real communication takes place between two people when each understands the assumptions which lie behind the other's words and phrases. . . . This is tantamount to saying that the purpose of language learning is to be able to handle the language in order to find out what the meanings are. The meanings are not just in the English or French equivalents of the African words but, rather, in the total impression these words make on the *African's thinking.*[9]

Some years ago I visited an African city a short time after the conclusion of an evangelistic crusade by a fairly prominent North American evangelist. In responding to my inquiry as to the success of the crusade, a local leader told of the problem encountered the very first night. It seems that when the evangelist checked in at his hotel he had inadvertently stood too close to a cage of monkeys in the lobby. One monkey reached down and neatly lifted a protruding wallet from the evangelist's pocket. Of course, the incident occasioned a good deal of laughter.

That night in the opening service of the crusade, the evangelist decided to begin his sermon with something humorous, much as he would do in his own culture. He told of his encounter with the monkey and then said, "In my country many wives are like that monkey. They always have their hand on their husband's wallet! Do you have some wives here who are like that monkey, too?"

As the interpreter faithfully interpreted the evangelist's remarks, the stadium began to echo with angry shouts. Soon debris was raining down around the speaker's platform. Police were called in to settle the crowd.

Twenty-four hours later the evangelist was a wiser man. He now knew that in that culture the word for monkey denoted the same animal but had an entirely different connotation and that comparing wives with monkeys was offensive to say the least. But he still was not wise enough. As he began his message he made the mistake to recalling what

[9]Ibid., 343.

he had said the previous night as a prelude to an apology. Before he could get to the apology, the mere reference to the monkey triggered another angry demonstration on the part of the audience.

It is important, then, to approach a language not as "a mountainous mass of material which one must slowly eat away at and digest, but as 'there is an utterance for every situation,'" and then to seek out "as many situations as possible" and to associate "utterances with these specific situations."[10]

Reyburn recommends that the learner begin by training his ear to hear—and his speech organs to reproduce—sounds, rhythms, and timbre (tone color) by the use of phonograph records. (Training in phonetics is helpful.) He says that two things are needed at the very beginning: (1) utterances that make clear the order of "where the actor fits, where the action attaches, and where the word acted on goes" and (2) basic vocabulary used in today's living.[11] He then goes on to indicate four stages in the learning process:

Stage I: The Initial Utterances. At this stage the language learner masters stock utterances by putting himself in imaginary or real situations where they are used. They must be learned by listening to native speakers and rehearsed over and over, much as a child does in speaking to himself while at play. (This is called "inner speech.") Learning is by imitation. No translation from another language is allowable.

Stage II: Real Situations. At the second stage (second month) the student should be ready to take the plunge into real-life situations. The main task at this stage is to learn vocabulary. This is done by careful listening, taking numerous notes, and patient practice—the key being word association. First, the learner establishes an association between the word in the new language and a word in a known language, and then he establishes an association between words in the new language.

[10]Ibid., 345.
[11]Ibid., 348.

Stage III: Consolidation. During the third month one attempts to gain confidence by engaging other persons in conversation on subjects *proposed by the learner.* The student still uses inner speech and word association; he still listens carefully and keeps notes of new words and expressions; but by taking the initiative the student is able to communicate what he knows and elicit a response.

Stage IV: Language in Culture: The Road to Meaning. After about three months the student may move out into a missionary situation. Then comes the real test of language learning. By participation he can become relatively fluent in the language as it is used in that limited context. The question is, Will he go on to put himself in a *variety of situations* so that by continual learning and practice he can gradually achieve mastery of the language and its meaning?

Those who have been exposed to one or more of the difficult languages of Europe or Asia may question Reyburn's timetable. However, use of the techniques of "culture submersion" that he suggests, when undertaken with commitment and carried out as a part of a carefully constructed language-learning program, will yield surprisingly significant results.[12]

[12]For an elaboration of the methods and programs for language learning see Nida, *Learning a Foreign Language.*

Chapter 28

What Can We Learn
From Language?

The closeness of the relationship between language and culture may seem to some to be overstated. But such is not the case. Perhaps our greatest sin against language has been our unwillingness to travel but a short distance down the road along which language would lead us. We have thought of verbal symbols as the packages in which we wrap our ideas in order to export them. We have thought of symbols as simply "descriptors" of the world that we somehow discovered independently. We have sometimes thought of ourselves as sovereign symbol-makers. But the magnitude of our errors is now coming to light. "The limits of my language," Ludwig Wittgenstein has somewhere pointed out, "are the limits of my world."

THE SAPIR-WHORF HYPOTHESIS

In a pioneering work written shortly after the close of World War I, Edward Sapir challenged two common assumptions: (1) that in the use of language we simply report reality as we see and understand it (our worldview), and (2) that language reflects a kind of natural logic that is prior to and independent of language. Sapir said that (1) language is a purely human and noninstinctive method of communicating ideas, emotions, and desires; (2) language systems are voluntarily produced symbol systems; and, in a sense, (3) language is prior to thinking and furnishes the building blocks for thinking. In effect, Sapir was saying that the relationship between language, reality, and logic is much more complex and interdependent than had been assumed. Language is the *means by which we acquire a worldview and logic.* It is, therefore, a determining and defining factor.[1]

Benjamin Lee Whorf amplified and popularized Sapir's ideas.[2] His theory of language and culture is summed up in four generalizations by Franklin Fearing:

1. It is erroneous to say that the cognitive process of all human beings possesses a common logical structure (natural logic) which operates prior to and independently of communication through language.

2. Linguistic patterns themselves determine what man perceives in his world and how he thinks about it.

3. Linguistic patterns vary widely, and thinking and perceiving among different linguistic groups result in basically different worldviews.

4. Language shapes our ideas rather than merely expressing them.[3]

Serious criticisms of these ideas were not long in coming. It was pointed out, for instance, that it is extremely difficult to state these hypotheses in a form that is scientifically testable.

[1]Edward Sapir, *Language: An Introduction to the Study of Speech* (New York: Harcourt, Brace and World, 1921), 207–20.
[2]For an extensive introduction to Whorf's thought, see Benjamin Lee Whorf, *Language, Thought and Reality: Selected Writings of B. L. Whorf,* ed. John B. Carroll (New York: Wiley, 1956).
[3]Franklin Fearing, "An Examination of the Conceptions of Benjamin Whorf in the Light of Theories of Perception and Cognition," in Harry Hoijer, ed., *Language in Culture,* (Chicago: University of Chicago Press, 1954), 47–81.

In a report to a summer seminar on psycholinguistics in 1954, Walker, Jenkins, and Sebeok leveled three primary criticisms at the methodology on which Whorf (and Sapir and others) had based their findings.[4] First, there is a circularity of inference in this reasoning. People in different cultures have different worldviews because their languages differ. How do we know their worldviews differ? Because they use language differently. Second, there is a fallacy involved in translating an utterance from some other language into English and then using the English translation for abstracting a worldview. Yet this is the common procedure. Third, the research has been on crosscultural designs when intracultural designs would be both possible and more defensible.

Perhaps the most telling criticism of the so-called Sapir-Whorf hypothesis and the kind of cultural relativism implicit in it has come from the transformational grammar school of thought, and particularly from one of its chief spokesmen, Noam Chomsky.[5] Chomsky reflects the position of the French structuralist Claude Levi-Strauss, who gathered thousands of myths from various cultures and demonstrated that their similarities outweighed their differences. At the deepest level, Levi-Strauss said the myths revealed a pattern that has not changed since primitive times and is ingrained in the human intellect. Chomsky comes to a similar conclusion with respect to language. He said that all languages draw on universal, context-free rules and logical relationships. He insists that the differences among languages are at the "surface" level. At the "deep structure" level, languages tend to be comparable. By using these universal linguistic principles, the linguist can transform the "surface form" of an expression in one language to a comparable "surface form" in another language. Chomsky, therefore, stresses the similari-

[4]Cf. Charles Osgood and Thomas A. Sebeok, eds, *Psycholinguistics: A Survey of Theory and Research Problems* (Baltimore: Waverly, 1954), 194–95.

[5]See Noam Chomsky, *Aspects of the Theory of Syntax* (Cambridge: MIT, 1965). For a summary of Chomsky's argument, see John C. Condon, Jr., *Interpersonal Communication* (New York: Macmillan, 1977), 75–79.

ties between languages and peoples as language users rather than stressing the differences between them. Robert Longacre, whom I mentioned previously, has built on Chomsky's work. Longacre says that languages reflect a common cognitive-conceptual apparatus and organize data in accordance with causal and implicational relationships that characterize the whole of the human species. He notes that

the evidence is coming in that there are language universals which underlie the surface structure categories of particular languages and that languages differ more in their surface structure than in these underlying categories.[6]

This is what we as Christians would expect, because we hold that all people have their origin in God, and therefore, notwithstanding linguistic differences languages can be expected to exhibit a basic logic and design that are reflections of that common origin. This being the case, languages are not purely human productions that press the world into human molds and radically distort it. Man does not simply impose his rationality on the perceived world. Rather, the world, man, and his languages possess a common rationality imposed by God.

Who are right? Sapir and Whorf? or, Chomsky and Longacre? The argument is a long and involved one, and much of the data is too technical for the nonspecialist to understand and evaluate. But the data, as well as the Judeo-Christian faith, seem to support Chomsky and Longacre.

This should not be construed to mean that the Sapir-Whorf hypothesis has no validity whatsoever. Despite their pointed critique, Walter, Jenkins, and Sebeok do find a certain validity in Whorf's conclusions as I have stated them.[7] They note, in the first place, that there is research to indicate a two-way relationship between language and worldview. Two

[6]Cf. Robert E. Longacre, *An Anatomy of Speech Notions* (Lisse, Netherlands: Peter de Ridder, 1977).
[7]Osgood and Sebeok, *Psycholinguistics*, 196–98.

groups of subjects were faced with the problem of tying together two strings that were suspended from the ceiling and positioned far enough apart so the subjects could not reach both strings at the same time. Subjects who previously had been involved in word association experiences that were totally unrelated to the problem situation but included the words "rope" and "swing" were the first to solve the problem by resorting to making a pendulum out of one string. This would indicate that language does have an effect on the perceptions, thought, and memory processes implicit in a worldview.

They note, in the second place, that another experiment demonstrated the influence of worldview on language. In this experiment two groups of subjects were exposed to a figure in which two circles were connected by a straight line. Linguistically, however, the figure was associated with a dumbbell by one group and with eyeglasses by the other group. After the lapse of a period of time, the two groups were reassembled and asked to reproduce the figure they had seen previously. The results confirmed the hypothesis. The figures of the one group tended to resemble a dumbbell, while the figures of the other group looked strangely like eyeglasses!

Recently some additional data that tends to support the Whorfian argument has come to light. This data conflicts with the belief (quite commonly accepted among psychologists) that the right hemisphere of the brain controls aesthetic and emotive responses (art and music, for example), and the left hemisphere controls cognitive responses (scientific analysis and computation, for example). Research has shown that sounds such as the singing of a bird, the cry of a child, and the snoring of a man stimulate the *left* side of the brain of native speakers of Japanese just as words do. Most native speakers of European languages respond to these sounds in the *right* hemisphere of the brain![8] Even more recent studies by UCLA

[8]Tadanobu Tsunoda, "The Qualitative Differences in Cerebral Dominance for Vowel Sounds Between Japanese and European Languages,"

researchers revealed that different parts of the brains of Hopi Indian children were stimulated depending on whether they were speaking English or Hopi![9] We may conclude that there is a basic similarity in the ways in which people see and think about the world around them. Languages do have a certain validity for the consideration and communication of *facts* concerning that world.

At the same time, as members are enculturated into any linguistic community, they will tend to perceive and think about reality in similar ways, not simply as a result of an inherent human understanding and logic, but also because of the particular language by means of which they "see" and "think." This is so because the various languages divide up experiences differently and store them in very different categories. When from our earliest days we thus share intimately in the total experience of a people, it is only with some difficulty that we are able to comprehend and adopt alternative languages, worldviews, and logical systems. The natural tendency will be to reject or restructure the new material to fit the familiar indigenous linguistic and logical framework, as we have seen previously. A little imagination will therefore enable the missionary to understand what is involved when Yorubas, Samoans, or Moros convert to Christianity.

But by the same token, as missionaries gain an increasingly comprehensive understanding of the respondent *language*, they will be able to vicariously participate in the experiences of the respondent *culture*. To the extent that their prior studies of the worldview and mind of the people have been valid, these will now be corroborated linguistically. And as they proceed with their study of language, they will be enabled to attain entirely new vistas of understanding and empathy, provided they understand and appreciate the nature of language itself.

Medicine and Biology 85 (October 1972): 157–62, cited in Condon, *Interpersonal Communication*, 78.
[9]Ibid., 78–79.

It is to this kind of understanding that careful students of language and culture have been pointing. Let us see how this is so.

LINGUISTIC MIRRORS OF CULTURE

1. *Tribal language and culture.* Few anthropologists have expended more mental energy in an attempt to understand the primitive peoples (I prefer the terms "tribal peoples" and "tribalists") of the world than has Franz Boas. It is helpful, therefore, to note the way he uses language to enhance that understanding.[10] Boas notes that of an unlimited number of possible phonetic elements and sound clusters, which he calls "word-stems" (i.e., vocabulary), each language has a limited number available for the expression of ideas. Of course, to squeeze all experiences and ideas into a limited number of word-stems requires a very careful classification. This being so, the word-stems are in effect an index of culture and aid in its analysis in much the same way as the index of a book indicates what we can expect to find in the text itself.

Boas gives numerous examples. Of the great variety of colors that the human eye can distinguish, the members of any given culture select a given number of word-stems for the designation of colors according to their need and understanding of what is important. One anthropologist concluded that the members of a certain tribe were color-blind because they did not distinguish between green and blue but used one word for both colors. His conclusion was, of course, erroneous. The people in the culture simply had no need for differentiating those two colors.

Another example of the same phenomenon is the parallel that one finds between the importance of water, snow, and seals in the Eskimo language. Eskimos have different words for fresh water and sea water. As concerns snow, one word expresses "snow on the ground," another one, "falling snow,"

[10]Franz Boas, *The Mind of Primitive Man* (New York: Free Press, 1965). See especially chapter 8 "Race, Language and Culture," 137–48.

another one, "drifting snow," and still another one denotes a "snowdrift." Again, there are different words for "seal," such as "seal basking in the sun" and "seal floating on a piece of ice," in addition to a variety of words to designate seals of different ages and sex.

Some may respond by saying that it is of little consequence to them whether there are many or few words for colors, water, snow, seals, and the like. They would "sing another tune," however, were they to learn Tzeltal, which has twenty-five different words for "carry" (carry on one's head, carry by hand, carry by one corner, and so forth); or were they to encounter the different words with which users of the Zulu language describe various kinds of walking—walking pompously, in a crouch, with a swagger, in tight clothes, and so forth; or were they to work with the Malagasy-speaking natives of Madagascar who distinguish more than one hundred colors and two hundred kinds of noises![11] In any case, the real importance of Boas' point will become more apparent as we proceed.

Concerning word-stems and social relationships among primitives, Boas says,

> Thus one term may be used for the mother and all her sisters, or even for the mother and all her cousins of all grades so far as they are derived in the female line from the same female ancestor; or our term "brother" may be divided in another system into groups of elder and younger brothers. In this case also the classes cannot have been formed by intent, but they must either have arisen because of customs that combine or differentiate individuals or they may have helped to crystallize the social relation between the members of the consanguineous and affinal groups.[12]

[11]Cf. Eugene A. Nida, *God's Word in Man's Language* (New York: Harper & Row, 1952), 16. Note that Nida is referring to phrases as well as to single words in this reference.
[12]Boas, *Mind of Primitive Man*, 191.

Boas, of course, does not stop with word-stems. He notes that theoretically one could have a language with one word-stem for every distinguishable experience and idea. Actually, no such language exists. Every language complements its vocabulary with a number of formal elements that together make up the structure of a language. When a language has a large, fixed vocabulary, the number of formal elements may be quite small. Conversely, when the vocabulary is small, the number of formal elements may be large. This also is a matter of selectivity according to understanding and need. As a rule, the formal elements of any language will be very adequate for expressing experiences and ideas that require more than word-stems. They may not, however, closely parallel the formal elements of other languages, and for that reason the experiences and ideas that are easily expressed in one culture may be expressed only with difficulty in the language of another culture. Not only differences in word-stems, but also differences in formal elements, therefore, are an indication of cultural divergencies. Several illustrations may suffice.

First, very different orientations toward *time* may be revealed in language structure.

> Thus in European languages we cannot express any statement without defining its time relation. A man is, was, or is going to be sick. A statement of this type without definition of time cannot be made in English. Only when we extend the meaning of the present over all time, as in the statement, "iron is hard," do we include all aspects of time in one form. By contrast to this we have many languages in which no stress is laid upon the difference between past and present, in which this distinction is *not* obligatory.[13]

Second, the formal elements may mirror the priority given to *location* over time in a given culture.

> Still others substitute the locative idea for the temporal and *require* that it is stated where an action takes place, near

[13]Ibid., 193–94.

375

me, near you, or near him, so that it is impossible according to the grammatical structure to make a statement indefinite as to place.[14]

Third, if the *source of information* is extremely important in a certain culture in order to determine the weight that should be accorded the communication, language structure may reflect this.

Again others may require a statement of the source of knowledge, whether a statement is based on own experience [sic], on evidence or on hearsay.[15]

Among other insights that attend Boas's approach and examples, the reader will be aware that in his exploration of the significance of language, Boas has reenforced what I have said previously about the worldview of the primitive and in particular about the priority given to concrete relational thinking in primitive cultures.

Primitive man, when conversing with his fellow man, is not in the habit of discussing abstract ideas. His interests center around the occupations of his daily life; and where philosophic problems are touched upon, they appear either in relation to definite individuals or in the more or less anthropomorphic forms of religious beliefs. Discourses on qualities without connection with the object to which the qualities belong, or of activities or states disconnected from the idea of the actor or the subject being in a certain state, will hardly occur in primitive speech. Thus the Indian (Kivakiutle) will not speak of goodness as such, although he may very well speak of the goodness of a person. He will not speak of a state of bliss apart from the person who is in such a state. He will not refer to the power of seeing without designating an individual who has such power.[16]

[14]Ibid., 194.
[15]Ibid.
[16]Ibid., 196.

To refer back to a previous discussion, when Janheinz Jahn and John S. Mbiti attempt to assist Westerners in their understanding of African culture, they do so by explaining concepts that they regard as keys to that understanding. Jahn chooses the concept of *force* in the belief that Africans see the whole world in terms of the interaction of various kinds of forces.[17] Mbiti chooses the concept of *time* in the belief that, though the concept does not explain everything, it will nevertheless take the Western student a long way in his understanding of African religion and philosophy.[18] These two authors are not wholly in agreement, therefore, but they do agree that the best way to examine their key concepts is by resorting to *African terms* and putting *African content* into them.

Therefore, by using the linguistic stem *NTU* (universal force) in compounds such as *muntu* (sentient beings) *kintu* (animals, minerals, and the like), *hantu* (the category of time and space), and *kuntu* (modalities such as beauty, speech, etc.), Jahn demonstrates that universals must be concretized. By insisting on terms such as *hantu* and *kuntu*, he makes us put such entities as location and beauty into categories of force as he believes Africans do.

In similar fashion Mbiti requires us to come to grips with the fact that African ideas of past, present, and future do not correspond with ours. By pressing concepts of past, present, and future into the two words *sasa* and *zamani* and explaining these words, he shows that for the traditional African the idea of a distant future is linguistically inexpressible and therefore conceptually *relatively* unthinkable. For the African, endlessness or eternity is something that lies in *zamani*, or past time. After all, Africans, like any other people, must work

[17]Janheinz Jahn, *Muntu: An Outline of the New African Culture*, trans. Marjorie Green (New York: Grove, 1961); cf. also idem, "Value Conceptions in Sub-Saharan Africa," in F. C. S. Northrop and Helen H. Livingston, eds., *Cross Cultural Understanding: Epistemology in Anthropology* (New York: Harper & Row, 1964), 55–69.

[18]John S. Mbiti, *African Religions and Philosophy* (Garden City, N.Y.: Doubleday, Anchor Books, 1970).

377

within the limitations of linguistic categories at their disposal. The implication of this particular limitation for missionaries is crucial. We will explore it at some length later. At present I am simply concerned with pointing out the intimate relationship between the cultural understanding and the language of a people.

The reader must not get the impression that while the languages of tribalists are instructive they are also *necessarily* limiting. Eugene Nida intimates that communication actually may be more meaningful in the picturesque language of primitive peoples than in the prosaic language we are accustomed to. When a Valiente speaks of "hope in God," he says "resting the mind in God."[19] This is a good description of what hope really is. The Navajos use "My mind is killing me" for the word "worry" and thus reveal themselves to be pretty good psychologists.[20] Our first reaction to the Cuicatec (Mexican Indian) word for "worship" may be quite negative because literally it means "to wag the tail before God." But our first reaction would be wrong. The root of their word "worship" is the same root used for a dog wagging his tail, and the pronoun subject, included in the verb, indicates that the reference is to a human and not to an animal. The Cuicatec Indians have recognized that the attitude of worship is similar to that of a dog before his master. When their language is analyzed in this way, the very heart and mind of the Cuicatec begins to open before us and we see in their language a mirror of their cultural experience and understanding.[21]

2. *Chinese language and culture.* Hajime Nakamura uses a very similar approach in his study of Eastern ways of thinking. Nakamura thinks of language as a representation in sound, writing, and gesture of the concepts produced in the operation of thinking.[22] His procedure is to study the linguis-

---

[19]Nida, *God's Word*, 19–20.
[20]Ibid., 23–24.
[21]Ibid.
[22]Hajime Nakamura, *Ways of Thinking of Eastern Peoples: India, China, Tibet, Japan*, ed., Philip P. Weiner, rev. trans. (Honolulu: East-West Center, 1964).

tic forms of expressing judgments and inferences as initial clues to ways of thinking. Then he analyzes these clues in the light of various related cultural phenomena. We should note in passing that this second step is crucial. The linguistic index of any culture is so vast that by selecting data according to his presuppositions and then overgeneralizing, the researcher could easily make a case for a very biased picture of the culture. Language is but one dimension of a culture. Despite its obvious importance, it cannot be studied in isolation.

Nakamura, however, seems justified in his observations of the significance of Chinese language in the understanding of Chinese thought. He finds, for example, that the language reveals the Chinese tendency to passivity or "nonaction" because it is characterized by a poverty of verbal forms. As a matter of fact, the Chinese use uninflected monosyllabic words with little distinction as to parts of speech.

But Nakamura's most interesting observations regarding the Chinese language are in the area of linguistic corroborations of his belief that Chinese thinking gives priority to concreteness. He says that the Chinese language is especially rich in words and phrases that have unparalleled power of concreteness and particularity. He notes that Granet studied the vocabulary of the Book of Odes and found that nearly all its words express *particular* ideas, doing so by *individualization* and *specification* rather than by analysis. Thus he found eighteen different words that mean "mountain" and twenty-three words that mean "horse," but not one word that is parallel to Western words expressing general or abstract ideas. Some examples taken from Granet and Nakamura's own studies aid the Westerner in understanding what is involved.[23]

First, in the expression of attributive qualities the Chinese tend to use concrete numbers rather than abstract terms. A "fast horse" becomes *ts'ien-li-ma*, or "a horse good for a thousand *li*" (one *li* equals 1890 feet). A clairvoyant man becomes *ts'ien-li-yen*, or a man with "thousand *li* vision."

Second, there are also a number of Buddhist terms that

[23]Ibid., 179–81.

express abstract philosophical concepts in a very concrete way. The universe is *shan ho ta-ti*, "Mountains, rivers, and the great earth." A person's ego is *ts'ao-yüan i-ti-shui*, or "a drop of water in the source." One's true nature is *pen-lai mien-mu*, which translates as "original face and eye," or it might be *pen-ti feng-kuang*, which means "the wind and light of one's native place." The Zen terms for "essence" are *yen-mu*, "eye," and *yen-ching*, "the pupil of the eye." The Zen term for itinerant monk is *yun-shui*, which literally means "clouds and water"; and the term for "monastic community" is *ts'ung-lin*, which suggests a thicket where trees and grasses grow together. The Indian words for these latter terms are much less pictorial: "Itinerant monk" is simply *parivrā jaka*, or "traveler"; and the word for a monastic community is *sangha*, or *gana*, which mean "group" or "conglomeration." One most arresting Zen word is *ch'ou-p'i-tai*, which refers to a human body (already a concrete term) in a highly evocative way that underscores Buddhist teaching. It means "stinking bag of skin!" The notion of perfection is often expressed as "round" in Chinese. When the Buddhist scriptures were translated into Chinese, the Indian term for "perfect" became "round and filled." In some systems the perfect doctrine was called "the round doctrine" *(yüan chiao)*. The Indians did use the wheel *(cakra)* symbol, of course, but Nakamura believes that the symbols are quite different. In the case of the Indians, the absolute could not be represented by a concrete symbol. Moreover, the wheel conveys the idea of motion whereas the circle is static.

Nakamura's analysis, therefore, indicates that Chinese thinking, like the thinking of primitives, tends to be concrete relational, and a careful analysis of specific Chinese terms lends insights unavailable to superficial learning.

3. *Semantic change and the "cultural thinking" of the Japanese.* A missionary to Japan, Charles Corwin, has made a careful study of the relationship between language meaning and cultural thinking.[24] Corwin's notion of cultural thinking

[24]Charles Corwin, *Biblical Encounter with Japanese Culture* (Tokyo: Christian Literature Crusade, 1967).

includes the worldview and cognitive process that I have described, and also the value system that will be discussed subsequently. He deals with lexical data but not with the structure of the Japanese language. He chooses 224 general thought categories out of the vast amount of available lexical materials. These general thought categories are determined by a careful examination of Japanese word usage, phraseology, idioms, colloquial expressions, and proverbial sayings. No doubt they reflect the interests of the researcher as well as those of the Japanese, but Corwin insists that in the process of analysis the categories were refined according to Japanese thinking and usage until they became core concepts of distinctly Japanese thought. Out of the large number of words and phrases that were collected in each category Corwin selects one core word for careful analysis. This process results in the selection of such core words as "love," "time," etc. He then analyzes the ways in which these words have been used over a period of time as reflected in Japanese literature and notes the semantic changes that have occurred. In this way he arrives at the cultural thinking of the Japanese.

Corwin's methodology will tend to discourage many missionaries. It is complex and capable of becoming even far more complex and extensive. But most missionaries to Japan, at least, will understand the motivation for his study. As they use certain Japanese "equivalents"—*gi* for "righteousness," *ai* for "love," *kami* for "God," *shinko* for "faith," and so forth— they become aware of the fact that the cultural thinking that surrounds these Japanese words is very different from their own. In a very real sense, therefore, the missionary source and the Japanese respondent will not be thinking about the same thing unless the missionary has come to understand that which Corwin is pointing out.

To take an example that will be familiar to all who are acquainted with Japanese, let us briefly summarize what happens in translating the concept of sin into the Japanese word *tsumi*. In the first place, if we confine ourselves to the New Testament, the Greek words translated as "sin" in English Bibles are the words *hamartia* (sin and the sin principle) and *hamartēma* (the acts and outcroppings of sin) which we have already discussed; but there are other Greek words that cluster around this general concept such as *adikia* (injustice, unrighteousness), *kakia* (malice, wickedness, evil) and *anomia* (lawlessness). It is not strange that various Greek words were used by the Holy Spirit to instruct us concerning evil, for God's revelation must present a diagnosis of our problem before we can appreciate the prescription for its cure. But it is instructive that the *central* word is *hamartia*.

It is likely that in New Testament times alternative words already had more ethical content than this word. Archbishop Trench calls it "the word of largest reach."[25] He goes on to explain that *hamartia* and *hamartēma* were first used simply of natural phenomena as in the case of the warrior who hurled his spear but failed to strike his foe. It was then extended to the intellectual sphere. For example, it was used of the artist who sought to attain results beyond the limits of his art. In still other places it did possess such content of our word "sin" as pagan ethics could conceive. But the word quite obviously lent itself to the New Testament usage because it possessed a greater capacity for conveying the new (Christian) meaning than did the alternatives.

Currently English-speaking Christians use various English counterparts for the related New Testament terms, but the tendency is to resort primarily to the word *sin*. Our failure to give due consideration to the *various* germane biblical words no doubt results in limitations to our understanding. This tendency to narrow down to one primary word is also true in the case of Japan. In Christian usage no term is so widely used in this connection as the word *tsumi*. The cultural thinking that revolves around this word, however, is quite different from that of *either* the New Testament or Western contexts. The Chinese ideograph used by the Japanese for *tsumi* pictures the criminal under a net. And this idea of trapping the criminal is still very much a part of the

---

[25]Richard Chenevix Trench, *Synonyms of the New Testament* (Marshallton, Del.: The National Foundation for Christian Education, n.d.), 224.

Japanese understanding. As Corwin notes, the word *tsumi* is a derivative of the word *tsutsushimi*, which is closer to the English word "imprudent." Acts that are disapproved by men are called *tsumi*. The word does not appear in the classical literature in the sense of moral wrong or of sinning against duty. The fearful thing about *tsumi* is rather the inherent potential of being discovered in the act and therefore shamed for being imprudent. This fear of being out of harmony with society and nature is very much a part of Japanese cultural understanding. It is evident, then, that Christian communicators in Japan are confronted by a problem similar to that faced by early Christian authors, *but by confining themselves almost exclusively to the use of one culturally freighted term to convey the New Testament teaching on this subject, Christian communicators in Japan have probably impeded true communication.*

THE RELATIONSHIP BETWEEN LANGUAGE AND RECEPTIVITY

It may well be that the implications of language systems go even deeper than we have indicated to this point. It seems very clear, for example, that during the early centuries of the Christian era the church was wrestling with the problem of fitting doctrine into the linguistic-logical categories of Greek thought. Thus it became necessary to define the deity of Christ in terms of *homoousios* (the same substance), *homoiousios* (similar substance), *homoios* (like) or *anomoios* (unlike) as compared to the nature of God the Father. And it has been suggested by some that Apollinarius, who accepted the *homoousios* statement of Nicea, later stumbled at the point of defining the relationship between the divine and the human in Jesus partly because of the difficulties occasioned by his linguistic apparatus. The uniqueness of one who was truly God *and* truly Man was difficult to entertain when everything was categorized as absolute or relative, eternal or phenomenal, spirit or material. This posed such a problem to Apollinarius that he was willing to sacrifice Christ's humanity in order to assure his deity.

Stuart Chase suggests something similar in regard to the success of Communism in China.[26] He notes that linguists have emphasized the "multivalued" orientation of the Chinese language. While speakers of English (and Western languages generally) set up such polarities as "right" and "wrong" and "clean" and "dirty" (to which I have several times referred) and tend to ignore various shadings of gray, speakers of Chinese do not ordinarily set up such grim dichotomies. As a result, traditionally the Chinese have been tolerant and not given to the so-called fanatical ideologies of the West.

Russian, on the other hand, is an Indo-European language whose speakers readily accept the necessity of choosing between two—and only two—options. Communism, therefore, meshes with the Russian language. But only a comparatively few Chinese Communists have learned the Russian language and have been indoctrinated in that linguistic medium. What about the hundreds of thousands of Chinese who are more restricted by the Chinese language and way of thinking? Will they ultimately find it difficult to take seriously the central Marxist dialectic? Chase seems to think so.

The implications of the foregoing are far-reaching. If Chase is right, we have an additional understanding into the difficulty of converting large numbers of Chinese to Christ. Perhaps those who have severely criticized missionary methodology in China have been overly zealous in their criticism. The Chinese language itself may constitute an indication that widespread receptivity to the Christian message, *especially as communicated by Western missionaries,* is unlikely. For that matter, perhaps we should rethink our evangelistic approaches in the West where a two-valued orientation seems to be in process of radical change and where it is becoming more and more difficult to use the traditional polar terms "right" and

[26]Cf. Stuart Chase, *The Power of Words* (New York: Harcourt, Brace and World, 1954), 106.

"wrong," "true" and "false," and so forth. Christian communicators in the future may find it helpful to show that the existence and the nature of the God of the Bible *necessitate* absolutes before they can faithfully communicate such biblical concepts as sin and repentance.

As is the case with any dimension of communication, we can go too far in our claims for language. But the time is coming, or now is, when on the basis of linguistic data we may be able to make educated guesses as to the degree of difficulty the people of any language group will experience in understanding the gospel and whether the people are most likely to accept, reject, reinterpret, or syncretize our message. If so, the missionary will be enabled to compensate and adjust in communicating the gospel of Christ. *All the same, the ultimate factor in the receptivity of a people will be whether or not the Holy Spirit of God has been allowed to prepare the hearts of respondent peoples.*

CONCLUSION TO PART V

The use of the respondent language is a part of the credentials of the missionary communicator. It is part of the process of winning a hearing. The missionary who gives due consideration to language will also find that scales will fall from his own eyes as they did from the eyes of Paul in answer to the prayers of Ananias. The importance of language to communication really becomes apparent only as we begin to explore the labyrinths of the relationship between language and the rest of culture. By studying this relationship the missionary will be better able to analyze the respondent culture and proceed to corroborate, augment, and correct conclusions arrived at through other types of inquiry.

Part VI

BEHAVIORAL PATTERNS— PATTERNS— WAYS OF ACTING

Figure 22

DIMENSIONS OF CROSS-CULTURAL COMMUNICATION

CULTURE X ◄─────── CULTURAL DISTANCE ───────► CULTURE Y

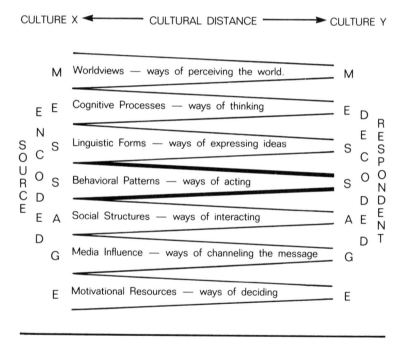

SOURCE ENCODED / M E S S A G E

M Worldviews — ways of perceiving the world.

E Cognitive Processes — ways of thinking

S Linguistic Forms — ways of expressing ideas

S Behavioral Patterns — ways of acting

A Social Structures — ways of interacting

G Media Influence — ways of channeling the message

E Motivational Resources — ways of deciding

M E S S A G E DECODED / RESPONDENT

Chapter 29

From Plato and Aristotle to Edward T. Hall

All communication qualifies as behavior, whether verbal or nonverbal. To quote J. L. Aranguren:

> Behavior takes forms that are in part perceptual and in part kinetic: Not only do we organize our sensations in a perceptual whole, but we organize our movements in an ordered series (walking, playing the piano, typing or writing, carrying out other consecutive articulate actions, grasping, cutting something, and so on). Therefore it would seem a good idea to approach our problems by considering language and communication in general within the general framework of organized behavior.[1]

To this point we have largely concentrated on "organized behavior" (to use Aranguren's phrase) that is verbal and communicative. In this section the focus will be on organized behavior that is *nonverbal* and communicative. In an extensive article on nonverbal behavior Sheila J. Ramsey makes

[1]José L. Aranguren, *Human Communications*, trans. Francis Partridge (New York: McGraw-Hill, 1967), 15–16.

several introductory clarifications that are important to our understanding (the first four points below are made by Ramsey):[2]

First, verbal and nonverbal behaviors are intertwined with each other. It is not just *what* we say that is important. *How* we say it is equally important. It is not just what we *say* that is important. What we *do* is equally important. All are bound up together in the same communication event.

Second, a narrow definition of nonverbal communication would restrict our inquiry to those nonverbal behaviors that are *intended* by the source to be communicative. Out-of-awareness actions that nevertheless occasion some kind of meaning in the respondent would not be included. But this would be an unnecessary and impractical restriction from our point of view. As long as behavior is being interpreted in one way or another and meanings, therefore, are being occasioned in the minds of interactants we had best attempt to discover what those meanings might be. A wide understanding of nonverbal communication, then—and the understanding that we subscribe to here—is that *all* nonverbal behavior is at least potentially communicative. In other words, like verbal behavior, all nonverbal behavior has a potential code capacity and therefore has the potential for being interpreted and given meaning by a respondent. That being the case, we will want to inquire into the communicative significance of nonverbal behavior irrespective of the "actor's" intent.

Third, as Ramsey explains, nonverbal and verbal communication involve different forms of information:

> While the spoken word is exclusively digital, nonverbal behavior is primarily analogic in form. The distinction between the two relates to the characteristics of information flow and use in computers. Digital form involves a precise, abstract, "yes-no/on-off/all-none" relationship between a sign and its referent. Through management of

[2]Sheila J. Ramsey, "Nonverbal Behavior: An Intercultural Perspective," in Molefi Kete Asante, Eileen Newmark, and Cecil A. Blake, eds. *Handbook of Intercultural Communication* (Beverly Hills: Sage, 1979), 106–17.

signs, or syntax, it is possible to represent negative statements and "nothing." Quantities represented in the analogic form are much less precise than those in the digital; they are of the "more-less," "both-and" quality. . . .[3]

Nonverbal analogic communication lacks an expression for "not." That makes for a special difficulty in decoding the meaning of nonverbal behavior. For example, it has been pointed out that tears may be tears of sorrow *or* joy; a smile may signal sympathy *or* contempt. In analogic communication there are no qualifiers to indicate which is in view. Therefore, meaning is much more difficult to pin down. Selective perception, special rules, views on relationships and much more is involved.

Fourth, two levels of communication should be distinguished—the content information level and the relationship information level. The former has to do with facts, events, feelings, and ideas. This kind of information is usually conveyed verbally. The latter has to do with the relationship between source and respondent and is usually conveyed nonverbally. In order to understand meaning, each must be understood within the context of the other.

Fifth, although we generally think of verbal communication as the form of communication that has potential for standing alone (i.e., apart from nonverbal communication), nonverbal communication would seem to possess a commensurate potential. When a policeman raises his hand palm out, when a musician draws his bow from the violin with a flourish, and when an ecclesiastic places his hand on the head of a novitiate—in all such cases nonverbal communication takes place. Nothing *needs to be said;* indeed, at times nothing *can be said.* But there is real communication nonetheless.

Sixth, nonverbal communication is far more significant than usually thought. R. L. Birdwhistell maintains that in the average conversation between two persons (in our culture) less

[3]Ibid., 107–8.

than thirty-five percent of the communication is verbal and more than sixty-five percent is nonverbal.[4]

THE TRADITIONAL APPROACH TO COMMUNICATION BEHAVIOR

Plato evidenced comparatively little concern for the nonlinguistic aspects of communication with one exception: he was insistent that the behavior of the speaker measure up to his speech. For Plato rhetoric had to do with "the *good* man speaking well."

Aristotle was aware of nonlinguistic aspects of communication but his preoccupation with the speechmaking situation prevented him from saying much about them. He did not really emphasize delivery—that area of speech in which his modern counterparts give more or less consideration to gestures, random movements, and so on. As far as ethical proof (*ethos* was Aristotle's word) is concerned, Aristotle's main concern centered on what the speaker said after going to the podium in order to establish his good sense, good character, and good will, not so much on his behavior offstage.

Cicero gave special attention to oratorical practice, including the nonlinguistic aspects of delivery, which he dealt with under the category of *actio*. But although it can be said that modern speech theory owes much to him, it would not be correct to say that he has exerted much influence on contemporary theorists of nonverbal communication.

Augustine underscored Plato's (and Quintilian's) notion of the "good man speaking well," though from a Christian point of view, of course. He also emphasized that students of preaching would greatly benefit by imitating eloquent speakers. Augustine meant more by this than imitating their use of words. He had reference also to their delivery and conduct in the sermonizing situation.

In short, as concerns nonverbal aspects of communica-

---

[4]These findings are attributed to R. L. Birdwhistell and reported in Mark L. Knapp, *Nonverbal Communication in Human Interaction* (New York: Holt, Rinehart and Winston, 1972), 12.

tion, the legacy of the classical rhetoricians is discoverable mainly in the area of speechmaking (and preaching). Textbooks in the speech area reflect this legacy. The Sarretts and W. T. Foster state that action alone reveals the speaker as a person, much as the old silent movies revealed the emotions and attitudes of the players without resorting to words.[5] Alan Monroe defines gestures as any movement of any part of the body used to convey some thought or emotion, or to reinforce oral expression.[6] H. G. Rahskopf emphasizes that although bodily actions may have limited denotative meaning, they nevertheless are rich in connotative meaning. Therefore they make interaction more smooth, complete, and meaningful.[7]

Examples could be multiplied because textbooks on speech are numerous, and almost without exception they emphasize gesture and platform behavior. What they say is important. But at the same time their limited area of focus has perhaps been a large factor in the slowness with which we have become aware of the pervasiveness and importance of the total reach of nonverbal communication. We are now becoming increasingly aware of the fact that it is an unjustifiable and deleterious reductionism to limit our consideration of gestures to the speechmaking situation or our understanding of language to its spoken and written expressions.

THE APPROACH OF EDWARD T. HALL

Perhaps no single individual has done more to cause communication theorists and the layperson alike to think in terms of nonverbal communication than has Edward T. Hall, author of the popular book, *The Silent Language*.[8] Hall's writings are numerous, but it was *The Silent Language* that

[5]L. Sarrett, W. T. Foster, and A. J. Sarrett, *Basic Principles of Speech*, 3rd ed. (Cambridge, Mass.: Riverside, 1958), 324.

[6]Alan H. Monroe, *Principles and Types of Speech* (New York: Scott, Foresman, 1939), 21.

[7]H. G. Rahskopf, *Basic Speech Improvement* (New York: Harper & Row, 1965), 213–17.

[8]Edward T. Hall, *The Silent Language* (Greenwich, Conn.: Fawcett, 1959).

captured the attention of communication people—including numerous missionaries the world over—in the decade of the 1960s. Hall's illustrations especially caught the imagination of his readers. To many, however, his overall approach was complex and obscure. It may not be out of order, therefore, to attempt a brief interpretation of those aspects of Hall's approach that seem most important from a missionary point of view in order to gain perspective for subsequent discussion.

The Silent Language is a book on culture. As defined by many anthropologists, culture seems to be the sum total of an almost infinite number of diverse and disparate elements held together by nothing more than the glue of the word itself. As a result, it sometimes seems that our efforts to understand a given culture consist of a series of probes in which comprehensiveness and interrelatedness elude us. The question that Hall poses, therefore, is quite simple: Is there no integrated approach to the study of culture that will help us to see the wholeness, aid us in possessing the land intellectually, and assist us in introducing changes in other cultures more practically and economically? Hall answers in the affirmative. How can it be done? We can look at culture as communication and proceed scientifically from the simple to the complex in building a unified theory of culture from that perspective.

Hall's building process is based on biological activity that supposedly preceded culture and was later elaborated into culture. He calls this precultural foundation "infraculture." And because the perspective is that of communication, infraculture can be divided into ten "Primary Message Systems" into which all of culture can be categorized. These ten PMSs include the following:

Interaction	Temporality
Association	Learning
Subsistence	Play
Bisexuality	Defense
Territoriality	Exploitation

Several characteristics of these PMSs are particularly important. First, language per se constitutes only one of them—namely, interaction. In other words, they are all message systems but nine of them are basically nonlinguistic. Second, the ten PMSs elaborate into all of culture. Third, these message systems are so constituted that each one reflects all the rest of culture and is itself reflected in the rest of culture. Fourth, each PMS can be broken down into three components: isolates (sounds in the case of language, and soundlike elements of the other systems); sets (words in the case of language, and wordlike combinations in other systems); and patterns (grammar and syntax in the case of language, and similar constructions in the other systems). Fifth, the PMSs are communicated and learned in three ways, or, better, at three levels: the formal level (mistake-correction); the informal level (imitation of models); and the technical level (from a teacher). These three ways or levels of learning are called the Major Triad. Sixth, every PMS is communicated at each of the three levels, and every component can be analyzed at these three levels. Seventh, in learning a new culture it is important to get behind and beyond the formal sets (words, buildings, governments, families, the days, the months, the years) that are so natural and apparent in order to analyze the isolates that go to make them up and the patterns into which they fall. By way of illustration, the Primary Message System of Temporality can be broken down (in our culture) in various ways, including the following (according to my understanding):

Formal Time:
 Isolate— day and night
 Set— a day
 Pattern—days of the week—Sunday the most
    important
Informal Time:
 Isolate— intermittent apologies
 Set— "a while"
 Pattern—agendas, appointment schedules
Technical Time:
 Isolate— equinox and solstice

Set—   solar year (365 days, 5 hours, 48 minutes,
         45.51 seconds plus fraction)
Pattern—years between eclipses, etc.

If one is to learn the message system of Temporality, he must master not only the *formally* learned time sets with their isolates and patterns but also *informally* learned time with its sets, isolates, and patterns. It may or may not be necessary to grapple with technical time, depending on the circumstances.

Finally, I should mention the fundamental assertion of Hall's book before proceeding, though I will elaborate it later. His major contention is that a great part of culture is communicated at the informal level where we learn by the imitation of models. This learning is largely outside our awareness. Like early language learning, it is unthought-out and forms a part of our habitual behavior. This being so, we do not ordinarily think of our way of behaving as being *one* way of behaving among others, but as *the* way to behave or act. By the same token messages learned at the informal level take a firm grip on us and are not easily unlearned. Furthermore— and this is Hall's most important counsel—if we want to introduce change in any of the PMSs of a culture, we must locate the point of change in the informal level of the appropriate message system and introduce the change at that point.

Hall's ideas have been expanded in publications appearing subsequent to *The Silent Language*.[9] Some of his more important contributions will be considered in later chapters. One significant contribution that will not be considered later should be highlighted here because it underscores the importance to intercultural communication of all that Hall said in *The Silent Language*. It has to do with the distinction between what Hall calls "high- and low-context" cultures.[10] In high-

[9]Edward T. Hall, *The Hidden Dimension* (Garden City, N.Y.: Doubleday, 1966; idem, *The Manpower Potential in our Ethnic Groups* (Washington, D.C.: U.S. Department of Labor, 1967); idem, *Beyond Culture* (Garden City, N.Y.: Doubleday/Anchor, 1976).
[10]Hall, *Beyond Culture.*

context cultures people are intensely aware of each other and involved with each other. Nonverbal behavioral patterns and codes are not spelled out but are nevertheless internalized in people's minds and extremely important. In low-context cultures interpersonal awareness and involvement are much less intense and expectations are governed by clearly defined rules and explicit codes for the most part. Hall makes it clear that "although no culture exists exclusively at one end of the scale, some are high while others are low."

Hall places American culture toward the low end of the scale. That means that North Americans will tend to encounter significant problems both in interpreting nonverbal behaviors and in relating to people in high-context cultures such as those that exist in the Middle East and much of Asia, for example. That being the case, a consideration of nonverbal communication becomes all the more important for the North American.

Edward Hall has not been without his detractors, as we would expect. But his works have been avidly studied, and *The Silent Language* especially remains as a classic in the field. Among missionaries it is probably one of the most widely read of the large number of secular books that bear upon effective cross-cultural communication. Before proceeding, therefore, it will be well to point out areas of agreement and disagreement with what he has written.

First, it will be obvious that I concur with Hall in his belief that culture should be carefully studied from the perspective of communication. I agree that "if communication is effective, then understanding grows with collaborative action. If communication is faulty, then no book knowledge of culture can assure effective action."[11]

Second, we agree that the ways in which (or levels at which) the messages of culture are communicated and learned are important in determining how we think about them, the tenacity with which they will be held, and the degree of

[11]Edward T. Hall and William Foote Whyte, "Intercultural Communication: A Guide to Men of Action," *Human Organization* 19 (Spring 1960): 5.

difficulty that will be encountered in changing them. It seems that Hall is correct in concluding that communication that aims at changes in basic beliefs or behavioral patterns, should be introduced (or at least mightily reinforced) at the informal, out-of-awareness level.

However, by studying cross-cultural communication within the framework of the seven dimensions, it will be apparent that I am parting company with Hall. I do this for two reasons. In the first place, although there is positive value in viewing culture as a composite of message systems, the biological foundation and naturalistic orientation of these message systems have resulted in unnecessary restrictions. For example, Hall subsumes religion (along with military defenses, health practices, and so forth) under the message system of Defense. Although this is one way of looking at religion, it is not the only way. That it is not the biblical way goes without saying. By beginning our seven-dimensional approach with the worldview and by defining worldview in religious terms, we have in effect given credence and priority to the religious or spiritual nature of man. In the second place, Hall's system has seemed too complex to be taken over *en toto* by the person of action. To say, for example, that the various message systems *can be* categorized into isolates, sets, and patterns at the various learning levels is not the same as saying that this is the *most advantageous way* of looking at them. For most practitioners his procedure is entirely too esoteric.

TYPES OF "SILENT LANGUAGE" BEHAVIOR

For present purposes it will be convenient to deal with the behavioral dimension of communication under seven rubrics. This division is not arbitrary though the categories are not necessarily all-inclusive nor are they entirely separate and discrete. For example, architecture is often dealt with under the category of proxemics because it has to do with the way space is divided and utilized. Here it is dealt with (briefly) under the category "artifacts and environmental factors" because the emphasis is on form and solidity. It will not be profitable, therefore, to get caught up in a controversy as to whether architecture is best treated under "proxemics" or "artifacts and environmental factors." It can be considered under either or both, depending on the particular emphasis in view.

We will deal briefly in this section with the following seven aspects of the behavioral dimension of cross-cultural communication:[12]

1. Physical Characteristics.

   Includes such factors as physique, body shape, general attractiveness, body and breath odors, height, weight, and skin color or tone.

   Entails information to such questions as, What physical characteristics are admired or disliked? How will the source's physical characteristics be regarded? What part does race play in interpersonal relationships? What effects accrue to differences in the body sizes of source and respondent?

2. Body Motion ("Body Language" or Kinesics).

   Includes such factors as gestures, movements of the body, limbs, hands, feet, legs, facial expressions, eye behavior, posture.

   Entails such information as the equivalents of basic gestures such as pointing, beckoning, refusing, agreeing; how various emotions are expressed; gestures that are considered proper and improper; the degree of and occasions for, eye contact; acceptable postures for men and women.

3. Touching Behavior.

   Includes stroking, hitting, greetings, farewells, holding, guiding another's movements.

   Entails information to such questions as, Is group X a contact or a noncontact group? How are greetings performed? With whom is touch appropriate and in

---

[12]With the exception of the "time talks" aspect of the "silent language," the categories listed are those of Knapp, *Nonverbal Communication.*

what situations (especially in contact between the sexes)?
4. Spatial Relationships (Proxemics).
   Includes such factors as seating arrangements and spatial arrangements as related to leadership, crowding, size and layout of residence, conversational distance, and territoriality.
   Entails information to such questions as, What is a comfortable conversational distance? At what distance can a person be before I must interact? Can the local people feel comfortable in my house?
5. Temporal Relationships.
   Includes such factors as punctuality, duration of meetings, length of conversations, the part of the day or night, special times and seasons.
   Entails information to such questions as, What value does time have? How is it regarded? At what time should meetings be held? At what time would visits in the home be welcome? How much time should be allotted to meetings? When is punctuality important? When would it be considered offensive?
6. Paralanguage.
   Includes such factors as pitch, rhythm, rate of speaking, articulation, resonance, pauses, voice inflection, drawl.
   Entails information on such questions as, How does public address differ from private conversation? Are special types of speaking appropriate for different occasions or for different people? What is effective sermon delivery (in terms of tone of voice, volume, rate of speaking)? How is silence interpreted?
7. Artifacts and Environmental Factors.
   Includes such factors as architectural style, furniture, interior decorating, smells, colors, clothes, missionary outfit, cosmetics, adornment, and material symbols.
   Entails information on such questions as, What is the functional and symbolic significance of indigenous

style? What do colors communicate? What possessions constitute status symbols?

We will consider these various aspects of behavioral communication in order, but first it will be helpful to consider some of the ethical and spiritual implications of behavior.

Chapter 30

The Missionary and Behavioral Norms

Some scholars assign too large a place to culture in determining behavioral norms. Although many of our behavioral patterns are learned at the informal, formal, and technical levels, others are instinctive, or built-in, by the Creator. It has been shown, for example, that facial expressions of sadness, fear, anger, surprise, disgust, interest, and happiness are readily identified by observers from different cultures— even illiterate and remote cultures.[1] More important, C. S. Lewis has argued convincingly against the kind of cultural relativism that says, "Headhunting is not allowed in our culture, but there is a culture in the South Seas islands where it is regularly practiced. Therefore headhunting is wrong in our culture, but right in the South Seas." Lewis readily admits that the circumstances in which killing, lying, or stealing might be allowable vary from culture to culture. But he insists that there is no culture where killing, deceit, thievery,

[1]The findings are those of P. Ekman and his associates and are reported in Mark L. Knapp, *Nonverbal Communication in Human Interaction* (New York: Holt, Rinehart and Winston, 1972).

disloyalty, and cowardice are generally thought to be good and right.[2] God has written his standards in man's conscience as well as in his Word. That standard can be blurred, but it cannot be obliterated. The missionary has a threefold responsibility in regard to behavioral norms. First, he must behave according to the standards revealed by God in the Scriptures and in his own conscience. Second he must accommodate to behavioral patterns considered right or proper within his respondent culture. Third, he must be able to distinguish between supracultural and cultural norms.

Let us look at these more closely.

OBEDIENCE TO THE WILL OF GOD

Those who would speak for Christ must remember that in any context—and perhaps especially in the context of the Third World—their actions must measure up to their doctrine. Sometimes one careless movement, one outburst of temper, or one hypocritical act will undermine the message and destroy a missionary ministry. It is in the light of that fact that one must understand the arresting account of the way in which Paul publicly opposed Peter at Antioch in Galatians 2. Peter, great as he was, had a difficult time divesting himself of old attitudes and habits that conflicted with new truth. In spite of the fact that he had seen God at work in the house of Cornelius and had concurred with the decision of the Jerusalem conference respecting the salvation of the Gentiles, Peter separated himself from the table of the Gentiles in Antioch lest he be criticized by the Jews. And Paul opposed him openly because he saw that Peter was not "walking straight *(orthopodeō)* according to the truth of the gospel" (Gal. 2:14, literal translation). Paul realized immediately that although Peter verbally affirmed the gospel, his conduct nullified the gospel. There is an orthodoxy of lips and also an orthodoxy of life.

[2]Cf. C. S. Lewis, *Mere Christianity* (New York: Macmillan, 1943), 19–20.

Orthodox talking must be accompanied by orthodox walking. Christian communication involves Christian beliefs *and* Christian behavior.

In this connection it is instructive to note what Michael Green says about the believers of the early church generally:

> The link between holy living and effective evangelism could hardly be made more effectively. In particular, Christians stood out for their chastity, their hatred of cruelty, their civil obedience, good citizenship, and payment of taxes (despite the severe suspicion they incurred on this count because they refused to pay the customary civil formality of praying to the emperor and the state gods). They did not expose infants; they did not swear. They refused to have anything to do with idolatry and its byproducts. Such lives made a great impact. Even the heathen opponents of Christianity often admitted as much.[3]

The mission of the church is built first of all upon *people*, not upon programs, strategies, and methodologies. In the face of advancing secularism and the erosion of biblical authority in the West and a rejuvenated and articulate challenge from the non-Christian religions in the East, it is imperative that people see the image of *Christ*—the image that true missionaries bear by virtue of creation and, more especially, by redemption. It is the moral, ethical, and spiritual life of the missionary that makes his message credible and persuasive.

ACCOMMODATION TO CULTURAL NORMS

Astute observers have located a basic cause of culture shock in the area of accommodation to the behavioral patterns of a new culture. When the missionary steps off the boat or out of the plane and is greeted by a cacophonous chorus of conversations being carried on in an unknown tongue, he becomes acutely aware of the fact that he has crossed a

[3]Michael Green, *Evangelism in the Early Church* (Grand Rapids: Eerdmans, 1970), 184.

cultural divide. But this is just the beginning of frustrations as far as the respondent language is concerned, and the missionary has been psychologically prepared for it. The behavioral patterns of the people of the respondent culture will be equally as diverse and confusing as the language. And for this the missionary may not really be prepared at all. With but little formal instruction the missionary has learned in his own culture how "intelligent," and "polite," and "proper" people ought to act. His behavior to date has been dictated to a high degree by what is "proper" and "right" in his own culture. It has been governed by customs and manners, routines and rituals, laws and regulations—in short, by the expectations of his own society. Notions of correct behavior have been internalized and universalized so that in most situations he automatically behaves "correctly."

Of course, the native of the respondent culture has been through a similar process of enculturation. He also knows what is "proper" and "right." And the problem is that the ideas of the missionary and the native as to what is "proper" and "right" do not coincide. In fact, they may be light-years apart! As Ina Corrine Brown has said in an oft-quoted passage:

> Whether you do or do not open a gift in the presence of the giver; whether you should or should not turn the plate over to look at the maker's symbol on the back; whether you put your coat on quietly or as noisily as possible; whether you walk in front of or behind a seated person; whether it is a friendly or an offensive gesture to put your hand on the arm of the person with whom you are talking—these and a thousand other questions are matters of cultural definition. None of them is inherently right or wrong and none is good or bad manners except as a society defines it so.[4]

Moreover, there seems to be a subconscious tendency on the part of all people to reject strange behavior. When behavioral patterns collide, little thoughtful analysis takes

[4]Ina Corrine Brown, *Understanding Other Cultures* (Englewood Cliffs, N.J.: Prentice-Hall, 1963), 86.

place on either side of a cultural boundary. Oh, the missionary goes along with certain quaint customs, but he becomes frustrated at the "inefficiency," the "illogicality," and the downright "untruthfulness" that characterize much indigenous behavior. Determined to make good use of his time and teach the indigenes a thing or two in the process, he builds up an inner reservoir of irritation and antagonism that often spills over in the forms of self-pity, destructive criticism, or even bitterness. One of the obvious vents for his feelings is in his conversation with fellow missionaries who subscribe to the same rules and therefore can be expected to understand how far off base these native people really are.

For their part, the people of the respondent culture go through the same process. When their standards are violated, they dismiss the offending missionary as another ignorant foreigner from whom one does not expect reasonable behavior. Or, if the indigene happens to be attracted to either the missionary or his culture, he may respond by a tacit denial of his own culture (without respect to its desirable aspects) and by this very denial become less effective in ministering to his own people.

In summary, our response to strange behavioral patterns tends to be automatic and unreflective. These responses center in the emotions, and are often subconscious. Cultural shock stems from the fact that we are not well prepared to encounter new ways of acting. And continued frustration results from our failure to analyze and adjust to new ways of doing things. The prognosis is not good unless in one way or another we develop a sensitivity and understanding of what is involved in the process of enculturation.

At this point some will demur. In his study of the face-to-face communication problems of American businessmen overseas, W. S. Howell once told me that he discovered that while some executives thought that cultural orientation in the area of the silent language would be highly beneficial, others thought it largely a waste of time. When one top executive of the Far East operations of a huge American firm read a report that encouraged cultural training for industrial personnel taking overseas assignments, he responded, "Baloney! You can't help men succeed in a different culture by training them. Select sensitive men and let them flounder."

There is something to be said for this point of view. People do have differing degrees of sensitivity and ability to adjust to, and cope with, the unfamiliar. And one way to learn is to throw oneself into the respondent culture and flounder! But we learn behavioral patterns at the same levels at which we learn the other aspects of culture, i.e., the formal, informal, and technical levels. As we have seen, one potential source of problems is that so much of our behavioral pattern is learned at the informal level and without the analysis that attends formal and technical learning. That being so, one way (and perhaps the best way) to ameliorate our difficulties is to bring these behavioral patterns to the formal and even technical levels of learning. This involves careful analysis and evaluation.

The spoken language is a good illustration of how this might work. To a large degree, we learn to speak our native tongue at the informal level. As time goes on, however, and to the extent to which we become students of language, we devote increased attention to formal and technical aspects of language. In so doing, we obtain the understanding and the tools that aid us in gaining a heightened knowledge of our mother tongue and in increasing our ability to master foreign tongues.

It may well be the same with nonverbal communication. I therefore agree with an intracompany report of one corporation with extensive overseas operations:

> If it does not usually seem practical to teach specific cultures, it is possible to teach about cultures and develop cultural awareness. What is known about the distinctiveness of culture and about cultural patterns in general is by itself vital knowledge for the monocultural person who sets out to cross cultural boundaries. Absorbing it will not save him from moving in foreign cultures without being intimate with them. But it will save him from moving in them

as if he were deaf and blind. He will know that there is a silent language, he will be "listening" for it and learn to identify its patterns. He will suspend judgment on observed institutions and behavior until he has learned to relate them to their cultural context rather than to his own. He will be on the lookout for a structural framework into which to fit his isolated experiences, and continually make allowance for the distorting effect of his ignorance of the foreign culture on his understanding and judgments. . . .

Such conditioning for cultural awareness can and should be made an integral part of all executive and management training programs (oriented to overseas service).[5]

Missionaries as well as businessmen and others going abroad would do well to remember the advice that Confucius gave to his disciples: *"Ruh ching wen fu"* (Upon entering a territory inquire about its customs).[6] Some customs may be rather loosely defined and relatively unimportant, and the missionary may be forgiven for ignorance or noncompliance. But other customs will be carefully defined and rigidly adhered to. In this case the erring missionary is less apt to be forgiven. For example, Paul Crane says that protocol is so important to Koreans that by noncompliance the untutored individual can easily become a nonperson in the minds of the people.[7]

The importance of the customs of a people is illustrated by a supposedly true story from the life of Hatem At-Taei of ancient Arabia. Hatem owned one of the fastest and most beautiful horses in the country. The horse was the pride and joy of Hatem's life. One day an unknown visitor stopped by Hatem's tent about dinner time. As was customary, Hatem insisted that his visitor stay for the meal. Afterwards, guest and host got around to the question of the purpose of the visit. Only then did Hatem learn that his guest was a representative

[5]William S. Howell, class notes, communication seminar, University of Minnesota, 1964.
[6]Quoted in J. Herbert Kane, *Winds of Change in the Christian Mission* (Chicago: Moody, 1973), 98.
[7]Paul Crane, *Korean Patterns* (Seoul: Hollym, 1967), 14.

of the king, and that the king had heard so much about the famous horse that he desired to have it if at all possible. Upon hearing this, Hatem let out a cry of anguish and replied that because there had been nothing else available he had just ordered the horse slaughtered and served for the meal. A post-mortem analysis of the story is instructive, for it was at Hatem's insistence that the visitor stayed for dinner; and yet Hatem knew that the price of obedience to the rules of hospitality would be the sacrifice of his prized horse.[8]

An illustration from contemporary life comes from Africa. Among the Ibo of Nigeria a visitor is customarily offered a kola nut and a cup of palm wine. This way of showing hospitality is so much a part of the Ibo pattern that even when many people were facing starvation in Biafra during the final stages of the recent civil war, reporters who visited Ibo huts were extended this traditional courtesy! On their part knowledgeable guests of the Ibo were also expected to give attention to rules of proper behavior. This required that a visitor take chalk and make diagonal marks on the floor and also a ring around his great toe. In this way the visitor identified himself as having peaceful intentions. If, on the other hand, he were to come carrying a palm frond, it would be interpreted as a challenge to fight![9]

Missionaries will not find it difficult to learn a few of the most obvious taboos and conventions of a culture. Then as time goes on they can add to their store of knowledge. It is true that the people of many cultures—especially those who have numerous cross-cultural contacts—will tend to be quite forgiving of foreigners who are not well mannered when judged by their own standards. Nevertheless with the passage of time the missionary will find it greatly to his advantage to learn the rules of proper decorum and to comply whenever

[8]Fathi S. Yousef, "Intercultural Communication: Aspects of Contrastive Social Values between North Americans and Middle Easterners," manuscript prepared for Professor W. S. Howell, University of Minnesota, Fall 1969.

[9]Sonia Bleeker, *The Ibo of Biafra* (New York: Morrow, 1969), 152, 36–37.

possible. In so doing he will free himself from much embarrassment.

WHEN IN ROME AND IN DOUBT

Of course, the following question remains to be answered: What should the missionary do when cultural norms and biblical standards conflict? Or, since the answer to that question is not difficult in the case of the missionary who accepts the Bible as the final authority for faith and practice, perhaps the issue needs a restatement. What should the missionary do when there is a conflict between a cultural norm that is important to the respondents and a biblical injunction that in its application is less than clear to the missionary? It is in these gray areas that the missionary is often found talking to himself!

Cases in point will readily come to the mind of the initiated. What should the missionary do when in a given cultural context it seems necessary to eat food that is (or is likely to be) contaminated? Here there seems to be tension between the local norm and biblical principles growing out of the fact that the Christian's body is the temple of the Holy Spirit (plus some other factors growing out of the missionary's understanding of hygiene). Or, take the case of a culture where people are presumed to be *dis*honest until proven otherwise. In such cultures bribery or double sets of contracts (one for government authorities and one for the parties to the contract) may be the rule instead of the exception. The twin facts that the other party expects this procedure and that the governmental authorities look the other way occasion a tremendous problem for the missionary. Actions usually speak louder than words—and especially in cases such as these. Missionaries encountering such problems must carefully weigh all the factors, but in the end they must trust Christ and let their Christian conscience—not expediency—be their guide.

Consider the following true case. A seminary class in missionary anthropology was assigned to study a chapter in a contemporary evangelical missions textbook. The chapter dealt with the dilemma faced by the teetotaler missionary in a European country where wine with the meal is a common and unquestioned custom. Should the missionary imbibe out of deference to his European host or not? The conviction of the author of the textbook was that in the European context the missionary could well fit into the accepted pattern since the culture seemed to demand it and the New Testament did not prohibit it. At almost the precise time when the class was confronted with this problem, the director of a large mission visited the seminary. As a part of his chapel address the leader told of receiving a phone call at 2:00 A.M. that morning. It concerned a young and brilliant missionary to Europe who had been returned home for treatment. While in Europe he had begun the practice of taking wine with his meals in order to identify with the people of his adopted country. The practice had become habitual, and wine had become his master. Months of treatment had failed. That morning as the director of the mission was speaking, the young missionary was being committed to an institution.

Let the missionary be aware of all the issues involved in such decisions, and, before he *acts*, let the persuader be persuaded in his own mind. The missionary needs saving as well as those who hear him. The life he saves may be his own!

Chapter 31

Seven Aspects of The "Behavioral Dimension"

PHYSICAL CHARACTERISTICS

Some readers may think that I have strayed from the straight and narrow when I introduce the subject of physical characteristics in relation to mission. After all there is only so much that can be done about one's physical appearance. On the other hand, the subject can hardly be avoided in a text of this kind. Too much is at stake.

Preliminary studies reveal that there is a positive correlation in our culture between physical attractiveness and credibility, tallness and success, and skin color and acceptance.[1] The importance of such data should not be pressed too far in the case of missionaries. There is a need for much more research before solid conclusions and cross-cultural comparisons can be made. Moreover, the biblical data seem to suggest that the most successful missionaries of the New Testament did not owe their success to their physical attractiveness. The

---

[1]Mark L. Knapp, *Nonverbal Communication in Human Interaction* (New York: Holt, Rinehart and Winston, 1972), 63–90.

apostle Paul did not pretend to impress his audiences by his physique. Our Lord himself—the only person of history who chose his own body type—did not opt for a handsome profile and soft skin (Isa. 53:2)! And when he died, our Lord had but one garment! In recent times Maharishi Mahesh Yogi, who stands but five feet tall, has achieved a tremendous following in a culture of tall people. He is reported to have said that height should be measured in terms of the distance between the head and the sky—not the head and ground. Napoleon and Bolivar were short men. Obviously there are factors immensely more important than stature and physical appearance.

Nevertheless, something should be said concerning physical characteristics and appearance in view of missions history and current social and racial realities. When the Church of England selected Samuel Crowther as bishop in Africa, it was because ecclesiastics believed that his black skin gave him an entrée with the people. When in the post–World War II era certain missions have attempted to conscript blacks for Africa, *nisei* (second-generation Japanese) for Japan, and teams of internationals, it has been in the hope that missionary communication would be aided by this strategy. Ordinarily one would expect that communication would be enhanced by reducing in any way possible the differences in the physical characteristics of sources and respondents. However, an examination of the record will show that these approaches have not been altogether successful. Why? The reason is that they fail to take other factors into account—factors that may be far more important. The expectations of the respondents can be a factor as well as the missionaries' ability to use the respondent language and adjust to the respondent culture. It does not take much imagination to appreciate the problems confronted by a *nisei* in Japan who *looks* like a Japanese but *talks* like an American! It does not require extensive research to conclude that a black from Chicago will have problems in Zaire if he simply depends on his *blackness* to win him a hearing!

As I have mentioned, perhaps the most important point to be made in relation to physical characteristics is that primary consideration should be given to the expectations of the respondents. Missionaries should not depend on their tallness or skin color or dress to convince their audience; not should they allow shortness or presumed unattractiveness or skin color to obstruct their potential. They should divest themselves of styles that are deemed acceptable or desirable in their native culture but inappropriate in their respondent culture. (Long hair, for example, may be "in" in the West, but it is "out" in much of the Orient. In 1973, it took a presidential decree to get a group of short-term evangelical missionaries into the Philippines because they had long hair!) Missionaries should adopt only those styles of the respondent culture that are encouraged by nationals. Appearance *is* a factor in communication. But God looks past outward appearance to the heart, and multitudes of nationals have developed an uncanny ability to do the same!

"BODY LANGUAGE"

W. LaBarre has said, "Americans are characteristically illiterate in the area of gesture language."[2] Formal instruction in this area has been largely limited to such body signals as are used by athletic officials, Boy Scouts, the Signal Corps, the deaf who use sign language, and the persons who use effective gestures in speechmaking. Currently, however, much attention is being focused on (1) the importance of body movements ("gestures" in an enlarged sense) and their significance in communication and (2) the differences in meanings assigned to various body movements as one crosses cultural boundaries. Body movements that communicate messages are studied under the rubric of kinesics, or body language.

Sigmund Freud wrote, "No mortal can keep a secret. If his lips are silent, he chatters with his fingertips; betrayal oozes out of him at every pore."[3] Ethologists[4] working under the

---

[2] W. LaBarre as quoted in Knapp, *Nonverbal Communication*, 91.

[3] Flora Davis, "How to Read Body Language," *Reader's Digest*, December 1969, 129.

[4] Ethology is the systematic study of the formation of human character.

direction of Michael Chance of Birmingham, England, have isolated and cataloged no fewer than 135 distinct and meaningful gestures and expressions of face, head, and body.[5] As mentioned previously, some of these gestures and expressions are instinctive and are recognizable from culture to culture. Most body language, however, is learned behavior and varies with the culture. G. W. Hews, for example, found that over one thousand different steady body postures are available to man, but he emphasizes the fact that postural choices are determined mainly by cultural differences.[6]

Travelers often become aware of the importance of gestures when for the first time they find themselves in a country where they know nothing whatever of the spoken or written language. Suddenly, the language of gesture becomes all that is available to them. And it usually turns out that they can at least take care of their absolute necessities in this way. In their relief, however, they often conclude too much; namely, that body language is a universal language. That this is not the case they will soon discover if they press their luck too far.

All of us who have lived and worked in various cultures have had experiences that reminded us of the great differences between cultures when it comes to body language. My wife and I, for example, often recall our experience in a hospital in Florence, Italy. Our son had been hospitalized a day or two previously and was, to use his expression, "simply starving." As a last resort we used gestures and a few words from a newly acquired Italian-English dictionary to inquire of the nurses whether we were expected to supply him with food (a rather common practice in some parts of the Orient). Receiving what we interpreted to be a clear green light for the project, we proceeded to buy up enough fruit and delicacies to assure ourselves that the number of our children would not be reduced from three to two because of parental neglect. When we delivered the food to the hospital room, however, the

[5]Reported in *Time*, 13 June 1969, 86.
[6]Cf. Knapp, *Nonverbal Communication*, 97.

hospital ward came alive with words and actions that communicated consternation. Our effort in the "universal" language of gesture had been an abysmal failure. Further investigation revealed that our son had been placed on a diet that was to be strictly observed!

An incident from the experience of Alexander Dumas, author of *The Three Musketeers*, indicates how well some Italians themselves can communicate with each other by means of gesture.[7] Dumas recalls how a musician in the orchestra pit and a visitor in one of the box seats communicated with each other by signs during the intermission of an opera. The visitor was an old friend of the musician but they had not been in contact with each other for three years. The musician decoded the message received from his friend as follows: The friend was married in Naples and subsequently traveled with his wife in Australia and France; he had arrived in Naples the previous day, and he was attending the opera alone because his wife was seasick. Dumas was informed of the message by the musician and then checked out the message with the visitor and found it to be exactly as the visitor had encoded it!

Italians not only *speak* Italian but they *gesture* in Italian! This could be said of any of the world's peoples. To be bilingual means to know two languages of gestures as well as two languages of words. Films that are made in one language and then have another language dubbed in are sometimes incongruous because the gestures cannot be similarly changed. Actually, the differences in gestural patterns within even the same language group will quite likely vary from region to region. North American experts can often identify the part of the United States to which a speaker is native simply by *watching* him speak on film with the sound turned off.

Ray L. Birdwhistell, a specialist in body language, notes a seemingly innate tendency on the part of some people to

[7]Cf. Theodore Brun, *The International Dictionary of Sign Language* (London: Wolfe, 1969), 26.

communicate by means of gestures. In an experiment to determine the number of eye positions with differential meaning that could be encoded and decoded by the subjects, it was demonstrated that there were significant differences between men and women, and between subjects of different nationalities. Of the almost one thousand different positions a high speed camera records in the opening and closing of an eye, Birdwhistell reports that one American male could consciously produce thirty-five different positions, twenty-three of them with different meanings.[8]

In another study, attention was given to the linguistic and nonlinguistic communication that occurred in the interactional chain of a group of nine boys. It was found that the group had two members who exercised leadership. While one of the two was a heavy vocalizer, the other had one of the lowest word count percentages in the group. On the basis of careful analysis the researchers concluded that the leadership of the quieter boy was kinesic; it was based upon his ability to communicate effectively by means of gesture and, though the subject vocalized little, he was known as a good conversationalist![9]

Effective missionary communication involves developing one's sensitivity and understanding in the area of body language. This includes a study of the importance of gesture in the respondent culture. By North American standards, for example, Germans will tend to use gestures that are greatly exaggerated and stylized. To Germans, of course, American gestures will seem undeveloped and uncommunicative. But, more importantly, it also involves a study of the *variations of meaning* assigned to specific gestures in the target culture. "Come here," for example, translates not only into very different words but very different gestures according to culture. North Americans and the Hausa people of Nigeria

[8]Ray L. Birdwhistell, "Kinesics and Communication," 54–64, cited in Marshall McLuhan and Edmund Carpenter, *Explorations in Communication* (Boston: Beacon, 1960), 55.
[9]McLuhan and Carpenter, *Explorations in Communication*, 59.

keep the palm of the hand up while most Filipinos and the Japanese keep the palm down. Americans use a palm-down gesture for "good-bye." If the Japanese used the palm-up, index-finger motion that the American uses for "come here," it would be appropriate when directed to a dog but not to a human being. The Hausa put the palm down and use all fingers in gesturing for a person to come, but only one finger for a goat. Thus the American who remembers to turn the palm down but uses only the index finger can expect to be thoroughly misunderstood. This motion during an evangelistic invitation might divide the sheep from the goats, but not in the best interest of the Christian mission!

What does one do with his eyes during a conversation? It's a matter of culture and context. In the United States, the student who gazes at the floor while being questioned by his high school principal is tacitly admitting his guilt. In much of Latin America the identical situation and gesture would indicate that the student is respectful. In traditional China the focus of the eyes of a younger person listening to an elder was rigidly prescribed. If the elder man was standing, the youth was to look at his feet. If the elder was seated, the gaze was to be directed to his knees.[10] Two Arab men engaging each other in conversation will look one another straight in the eye. Two Hausa men in the same situation will avoid each other's gaze ever so slightly. Two Americans might be expected to look in various directions and look each other in the eye only occasionally and momentarily. If they gazed at each other in the Arab manner, it might well be interpreted as a confrontation over the masculinity of one or both.

James F. Downs writes:

> I . . . cringe to think of all the rupees I have wasted because I always forgot in the early part of a trip to India, that agreement is often indicated by a short shake of the head to the right that very closely approximates our own sign of

[10]Robert Oliver, *Communication and Culture in Ancient India and China* (Syracuse: Syracuse University Press, 1971), 92.

disagreement. When it came to tipping coolies for some personal service, I was uncomfortable like most Americans unaccustomed to dealing with persons in menial positions. Uncertain about exact rates, I would offer what seemed to be a reasonable amount. The coolie would invariably shake his head in agreement. I would invariably interpret it as disagreement and press more money on him. Such an exchange usually left me feeling vaguely exploited and angry because I suspected I had paid too much. It probably left the coolie feeling totally baffled by a crazy man who kept giving him money after he had said he had enough.[11]

Illustrations could be multiplied. In the United States to stick out one's tongue is to show anger or disrespect. In Tibet the same sign indicates a friendly greeting. In the United States the slow handclapping of an audience probably means that they are anxious for the proceedings to begin. In England it most likely means that the audience disapproves of the performance and wants the performer to leave the stage. On the Continent the same slow rhythmic clapping may well indicate a curtain call or the desire for an encore. The American who points at another person communicates disrespect or poor upbringing. Among the Hausa to point directly at someone may well mean that a curse is being put on him. The Hausa case points up the fact that in some cultures ritual power is attached to certain gestures just as a ritual power is attached to certain verbal formulae.

It is too early to attempt anything like a dictionary of the meanings assigned to gestures in the various cultures, though the attempt has been made.[12] It is even difficult to systematize gestural behavior in a meaningful and practical way. The attempt of anthropologist Ray L. Birdwhistell is, however, worthy of mention.[13] Birdwhistell calls this fledgling discipline "kinesics," which he defines as "the study of visual

[11]James F. Downs, *Cultures in Crisis* (Beverly Hills, Calif.: Glencoe, 1971) 152.

[12]See Brun, *International Dictionary*.

[13]Ray Birdwhistell, *An Introduction to Kinesics* (Washington, D.C.: Department of State, Foreign Service Institute, 1952).

aspects of nonverbal and interpersonal communication."[14] He believes that *all* bodily movements have meaning. None is simply random or accidental. But he also advances the theory that no body position or movement in and of itself has a *precise* meaning. (This points up the difficulty of compiling a catalog or dictionary of gestural behavior.)

Perhaps Birdwhistell has made his greatest contribution to future understanding in this area by providing a system for examination of the data. Following a linguistic model, he has studied kinesics under the rubrics of prekinesics, microkinesics, and social kinesics. Prekinesics is concerned with the physiological, precommunicational aspects of body motion such as scratching, shifting, stretching, becoming tense, and so forth. Although prekinesics may have little significance for most missionaries, it remains part of the concern of psychologists who concentrate on ethology because of its psychosomatic implications. When verbal communication breaks down (as in the case of many schizophrenics) prekinesic behavioral patterns assume special importance.

Microkinesics is, however, more directly concerned with communication. Under this category, Birdwhistell deals with isolated positions called "kines" (e.g., of the eyelid), and also various combinations of positions called "kinemorphs" (e.g., raised eyebrow plus squinted eye) by which we communicate. The "kine" therefore, is comparable to the phoneme, and the "kinemorph" is comparable to the morpheme.

Birdwhistell is sure that cross-cultural research will lead to the development of a kinesic syntax in which cross-cultural comparison will yield a priority in various kinds of body movement—of the hands, arm, head, trunk, and so on. He proposes to deal with this syntax under the category "social kinesics."

Birdwhistell's approach goes beyond the practical needs of missionaries. But it does point up the importance of body language.

[14]Birdwhistell, "Kinesics and Communication."

"TOUCHING BEHAVIOR"

Body contact, or "touching behavior," varies significantly with cultures. A. M. Watson and B. T. Graves have made numerous observations of people from various cultures.[15] Since they include such items as direct eye contact, speaking in a loud voice, and body proximity as well as actual touching in their definition of *contact*, the meaning of the term is somewhat more encompassing than our more restricted meaning. It is instructive, however, that they distinguish large cultural groupings on this basis. In their understanding, contact groups include Arabs, Latin Americans, and Southern Europeans. Noncontact groups include North Americans, Asians, Indians, Pakistanis, and Northern Europeans.

Consider the wide variation of contact or noncontact behavior relating to greetings and farewells deemed appropriate in different cultures. Appropriate behavior for the Japanese would be a bow, or a series of bows, while avoiding any physical contact whatsoever. The usual North American gesture is a handshake or possibly an embrace or even a kiss. To the American a bow is quite cold and communicates more respect than is called for in most situations of meeting or parting. (In fact, the fine line between respect and worship as they relate to a Japanese bow has occasioned no small amount of discussion and dissension in Japan itself.) Traveling to another cultural area, the Gururumba of the Eastern Highlands of New Guinea attend their greetings by an extending of the arms, back, and legs and a grasping of the buttocks.[16] It would be difficult to conceive of any gesture of greeting that could be further from the Japanese bow!

An important aspect of touching behavior for the missionary has to do with its sexual overtones. Misunderstandings in this area are occasioned by widely varied and carefully guarded cultural norms.

The sexual revolution in the West has been so complete

---

[15]Knapp, *Nonverbal Communication*, 54.
[16]Philip L. Newman, *Knowing the Gurumba* (New York: Holt, Rinehart and Winston, 1965), 14.

that all but the most intimate physical contact between the sexes is allowable in public, and hand, arm, or waist contact in the case of married people and lovers is expected. To be sure, the sexual revolution has had its repercussions in other parts of the world. But in many (if not most) non-Western countries, body contact between men and women in a public place communicates lack of "culture" or worse. A recent visitor to Thailand said he discovered that the most universally condemned bit of behavior of American soldiers was their practice of embracing or holding hands with Thai girls in public. Another dimension of this type of taboo is the Latin American disapproval of unmarried men and women being alone in a private place for even a short period of time. The same taboo holds in many parts of Africa. (Among some people in Africa there is the additional prohibition that an engaged couple are not allowed to speak together until their wedding day.)

The rationale for the presence or absence of touching may be important. In Latin America people likely feel that men and women left alone cannot be expected to resist giving in to their passions. In cases where certain types of public contact between the sexes is frowned upon, it is quite likely that these contacts are seen as a prelude to further intimacies and people find it difficult to dissociate one from the other. This would mean that even casual contacts communicate something. In the West, prolonged physical contact between men in a public place may very well communicate homosexuality. In some parts of the world, however, it is rather common to see men walking hand in hand, arm in arm, or even with their arms around each other; and this behavior communicates nothing more than friendship. James F. Downs writes about this as follows:

> Over much of Asia, in the Middle East, and elsewhere, two men acquaintances will hold each other's hands while they talk. The sight of two men walking down the street holding hands almost immediately suggests to Americans a taint of effeminacy or homosexuality. In other lands, of course, it is simply a means of maintaining a personal contact with

423

another person while talking. But it is not enough just to tell a prospective overseas worker about this. His reaction to another male holding his hand is visceral; it is part of him. Almost invariably, he will react without thinking, snatch his hand away, and thus offend someone for no reason. I think with pain of my first stroll down the street of a town in northern India holding the hand of a not very likeable minor official who was exploring my presence there to see if he could derive some personal benefit from it. Only with conscious effort could I keep from breaking away. I was certain everyone in town was watching. It was an ordeal. Of course, no one else on the street thought much about it. To them, it was a natural and expected gesture.[17]

Clearly, if missionaries want to maintain rapport with their respondents while giving no occasion for offense to the gospel, they must be as wise as serpents and as harmless as doves in this area of behavior.

SPACE SPEAKS

Place and space constitute another aspect of nonverbal communication. Edward T. Hall has done more than anyone else to focus attention on this aspect of communication. He coined the term *proxemics* (people's use of space) and elaborated some of the fundamental concepts of proxemics as it relates to communication. In *The Silent Language* he dealt with this concern under the Primary Message-System category of "territoriality." His thinking is further clarified in subsequent writings.[18]

[17]Downs, *Cultures in Crisis*, 152.
[18]Cf. Edward T. Hall, "The Language of Space," *Landscape* 10 (Fall 1960): 41–45; idem, "The Maddening Crowd," *Landscape* 12 (Fall 1962): 26–29; idem, "Proxemics—A Study of Man's Spacial Relations," in I. Goldston, ed., *Man's Image in Medicine and Anthropology* (New York: International University Press, 1967); idem, *The Hidden Dimension* (Garden City, N.Y.: Doubleday, 1966). In the latter book (expecially part 3) Hall shows how culture molds our proxemic behavioral patterns by differentiating four zones of behavior: the intimate, the personal, the social, and the public zones.

When God told Adam and Eve to be fruitful and multiply and replenish the earth, he obviously had limits in mind. Today we are wrestling with problems of overpopulation and overcrowding. These problems are very real, but it must be remembered that much more is involved than simply space or the productivity of the earth. If each person were given one square yard of territory, the entire population of the earth could be put into a rectangle forty miles long by thirty miles wide with room to spare. It is apparent that the problem of overpopulation is not simply a problem of *available* space. It is intimately related to people's *attitude* toward space, to their tendency to cluster in large cities, and to the way they exploit the earth's resources. In one sense the only space a person can actually claim as his own is the space that he physically occupies. Beyond his skin there is terrestrial space plus outer space. Who owns what portions of that space and how they own it have been matters of dispute since Adam and Eve said good-bye to the Garden of Eden. Reactions to the way humans use various zones range from private feelings of discomfort in the press of a crowd to mass outrage and war upon the invasion of a nation's territory. Some think that the ability to go to the moon *necessitates* going there. Others find it impossible to believe that any good at all can come of space exploration.

Let us look at some aspects of space and communication.

1. *Private and public space.* How much space around a person can be claimed as his *private* (as opposed to *public*) space? How will it be marked off and defined? Who is allowed to invade it and how close may he come? These are matters of cultural and contextual prescription. Usually a North American does not need a fence in order to promote a feeling of privacy—though he knows precisely where the fence would go if he were to build one. Within his house, however, privacy is maintained by walls and doors. Even interior doors may have locks on them. The Hausa man, on the other hand, promotes privacy—especially on behalf of his wives—by surrounding his compound with some kind of barrier, if not a wall made of mud and brick, then a simple fence of grass or

cornstalk mat. The Japanese likewise prefer fences or walls around their homes if possible. But within their homes doors are flimsy though decorative, and walls often have openings by the ceiling—conveying ideas of privacy that are uniquely Japanese. In the Philippines, one can usually tell whether or not the occupant of a new home will be a Filipino or a Chinese, not simply by the size of the house, but also by the height and thickness of the wall with which the Chinese secures his privacy.

Missionaries from the United States, Canada, England, Germany, and, indeed, most Western countries have difficulty in adjusting to existing ideas of privacy in many other parts of the world. They need windows, walls, and doors at the very least, and they require a modicum of space between themselves and all but their most intimate friends. Arabs, Japanese, Filipinos, and others seem to be able to retreat into themselves or erect psychological walls around themselves and achieve privacy to the degree necessary. In these cases the missionary should learn to recognize and respect those imaginary psychological walls even though he may find it most difficult to build one for himself. For example, the missionary should recognize that when he happens upon a home in Japan where the host is not ready to receive him before changing attire or making other preparations, he should act as though a physical wall were between them whether one is actually there or not. After a bit of practice one becomes quite adept in numerous situations at constructing these psychological walls and fences. In Bacolod City in the Philippines the visitor will find a sign painted on a downtown wall that reads "Do not urinate here." That sign speaks volumes concerning local ideas of privacy and the need for psychological walls.

2. *Interaction distance.* When communicating orally in a face-to-face situation, it is also well to keep in mind that the *interaction distance* may vary considerably from culture to culture. Hall and Whyte give an instructive case in point.[19]

[19]Edward T. Hall and William Foote Whyte, "Intercultural Communication: A Guide to Men of Action," *Human Organization* 19 (Spring 1960): 5–12.

They recount how a Latin and North American began a conversation at one end of a forty-foot hall and ended the conversation some time later at the opposite end of the hall. Both participants had traversed the length of the hall in a series of movements as each attempted to maintain a comfortable conversation distance. The Latin American would close the gap to a distance with which he felt comfortable. At that point the North American would begin feeling uncomfortable and retreat a step or two. And so the process continued until they ran out of space. This illustration is in line with Hall's belief that each person has a "personal distance"—an invisible sphere around him that is off limits to strangers. He also has a "public distance" that is a larger sphere past which personal communication becomes all but impossible. (We may consider these distances as being related to private and public space.) These distances vary from culture to culture. The case of the "retreating conversation" points up the fact that personal distance in Latin America is generally shorter than it is in North America.

The findings of psychologists Stuart Albert and James Dabba, Jr., at the University of Michigan indicate that space may have a special rhetorical significance.[20] In an experiment designed to test the influence of *interaction distance* on persuasion, they varied the distance between sources and respondents from one or two feet to five or six feet and up to about fifteen feet. They hypothesized that the advocates would be most persuasive at the middle distance because, on the one hand, they would not be invading the personal distance of the respondents and thus causing discomfort, and, on the other hand, they would not be losing the respondents' attention due to being located too far apart. To their surprise, the advocates proved to be most persuasive at the greater distance.

We can expect that researchers will continue to work in this dimension of communication and that our information will become more exact from a scientific point of view. We

[20]Cf. "Behavior," *Time*, 7 September 1970, 27.

might even conjecture that science will corroborate the biblical point of view on the importance of preaching with a view to the conversion of people. True, from the word *preach* we cannot infer the necessity of distance between the preacher and his audience. But in a day when preaching—and perhaps evangelistic preaching especially—is under attack in some quarters, it is well to remind ourselves that much preaching in Bible times (as today) of necessity involved an appropriate spacing between the preacher and his audience. There is a time for the more personalized witnessing, counseling, and small-group teaching with which we are so familiar today. But there is also the time for the more public proclamation of the Word of God. We may well discover that the latter is more effective than the former in effecting changes in basic values and living patterns (though we also suspect that there are many exceptions to this, depending on cultural and situational factors).

3. *Positioning.* Closely related to the subject of interaction distance is that of *positioning.* All of us are familiar with the fact that location communicates something. We put VIPs at the head tables in our banquet halls. We reserve certain seats for the speaker, administrators, and faculty members at our commencements. In many homes the father feels somewhat flustered when he sees someone sitting in *his* chair. And every salesman knows how important it is to get his foot in the door.

There are corollaries in every culture. In Japan the visitor must be extremely careful not to sit down until invited to do so, and it is especially important that he not take the place of honor in front of the *tokonoma* (a miniature alcove) until there has been considerable urging. In Korea the guest takes the most inconspicuous seat and advances toward the place of honor only by degrees and at the insistence of his host.

It was in the Orient that for the first time I came across the idea of leaving the middle chair on the sanctuary platform vacant. The empty middle chair conveys the message that Christ is the Lord of the church and therefore no mere man should presume upon that place of honor. This is *somewhat* parallel to the split chancel in some churches and the argument that centers around the question of whether or not it is appropriate for the minister to preach and read Scripture from the same pulpit.

4. *Zones of participation.* Studies on the relationship between classroom shape and size and teacher-student participation in North American culture have shown a positive correlation between these factors. Although there seems to be no difference between open and windowless rooms in respect to student participation behavior, instructors and students seem definitely to prefer open rooms. There is a consistent pattern of increased participative behavior on the part of students sitting in the center of the room. Knapp indicates a *zone of participation* that takes the shape of a triangle from front to back (see figure 23).[21]

Figure 23

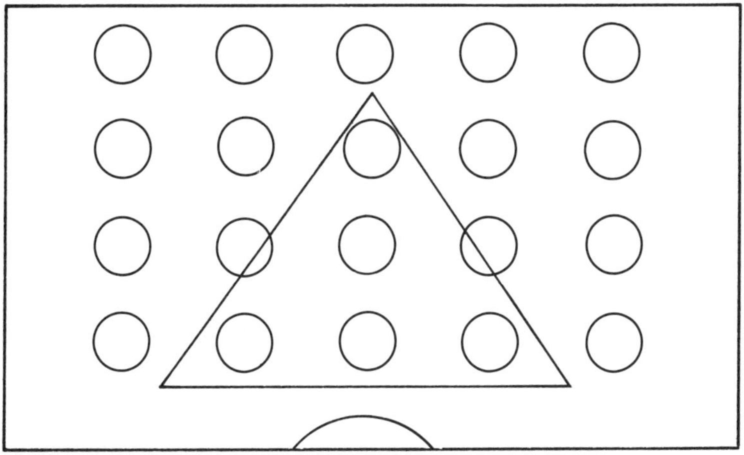

Studies of this type certainly have relevance for the shape

[21]Knapp, *Nonverbal Communication,* 26–27.

of the sanctuaries of American churches—many of which duplicate the narrow and rectangular shape of the typical traditional classroom. If the energy spent in getting the occupants of seats in the rear of the sanctuary to come forward were spent in planning the shape of the sanctuary initially, much good could come of it. The folly, then, of building Western-style churches in the Third World may be more complex than simply erecting Western edifices in non-Western contexts. We may well be promoting something that is not in the best interest of communication in the East or West! In any case, spatial relationship is not a matter of indifference from a communication point of view. Attention should be given to spatial patterns exhibited in respondent culture settings where the purposes most closely parallel those of Christian gatherings.

5. *Functional distance.* There is still another important aspect of proxemics.[22] *Functional distance* has to do with the number of interpersonal contacts encouraged by such factors as the placement and design of housing units. It is apparent that the placement and design of missionary housing and meeting places have an immediate effect on the type and number of contacts that can be made for Christ. A missionary in Caracas, Venezuela, has located his family in a central first-floor apartment of a large housing development. He is assured of numerous personal contacts because he is conveniently located, has a telephone, and usually leaves his door open (an invitation for neighbors to enter). He has secured a similar apartment for Christian meetings. The growth of the congregation has been unusually rapid, and a church building (locally financed) is now under construction. Not all missionary families are able to cope psychologically with so many contacts, however! Nor do all situations and ministries call for it. In such places as India and Korea some missionaries and nationals have had unusually successful ministries by finding locations that appeal to the desire of many to get away from

[22]Ibid., 35.

crowded areas and be closer to nature where they can study and meditate.

It would seem that we cannot do *anything* without communicating *something!* To stand is to stand somewhere. And both the "standing" and the "somewhere" communicate. It is the same with sitting, moving, and even taking up residence. In the final analysis it is impossible for the missionary to do nothing. At the very least he occupies space, and space speaks!

TIME TALKS

The farmer in a rural Philippine barrio may tell the time of day by looking at the sun or the flower of the gourd *(patola)*. At 5:00 in the afternoon the edges of the flower supposedly have a certain bend. Juan M. Flavier relates how on one occasion he determined to test this native ability to tell time. He waited until 4:30 by his Omega watch and then went to the old farmer and announced that it was time to go home. The farmer turned his head toward the gourds and then, shaking his head, said *"Hindi pa ala sinko"* (It is not yet five o'clock). And he continued working.

Unconvinced and undaunted, Flavier decided to play a trick on the old man. He went to the field during the siesta time and picked all the opened flowers. Then at the stroke of five o'clock he invited the man to go home. The farmer looked toward the gourds. Not a single flower was in bloom. Without hesitation he turned his head toward the acacia tree and replied, "Yes, it is five o'clock. Let us go." His explanation was simple: "The acacia trees tell time too. When the leaves start to fold into each other at the midrib, it is five o'clock."

With an attitude of "If he can do it, so can I," Dr. Flavier decided to leave his watch home the next day. Toward the end of the afternoon he went to a lonely spot and sat down under an acacia, his eyes glued to the leaves. After a seemingly interminable length of time his heart leaped. The leaves were beginning to fold! He raced to his home a short distance away and checked with his Omega watch. It was six o'clock!

Perhaps it is more difficult to learn to tell time by the flower of the gourd and the leaves of the acacia than it is to tell time by a watch![23]

Most missionaries would not think of going to their fields of labor without a calendar, an alarm clock, and a watch (preferably with a sweep second hand, date indicator, and alarm), to say nothing of a timetable, a projected daily schedule, and an agenda of things to be accomplished. Of course, they take much more than this with them because within their knowledge and value system they have deeply set ideas as to how these timing devices should be used and about their importance to successful living.

It goes without saying that comparatively few non-Western societies have as highly a developed sense of technical time as we do in the West. High-speed photography, the retrieval of computerized data, the timing of internal-combustion engines, electronic communication, the direction of air traffic—these and many other facets of our culture serve to make us extremely conscious of the need for split-second timing. The calendar (which at first mention seems to be about as far from these illustrations as one could get) also becomes an indicator of the phases of the moon, the placement of the stars, the movement of the planets, and the church year. At the formal level, day and night are likely to be measured by the watch as well as by darkness and light. The days of the week are named after now-forgotten Teutonic gods and fall into a pattern in which one day may be washday, another a day of rest or play, and another a day of worship. As for informal time, the missionary consciously or unconsciously knows how long "a while" is, what constitutes punctuality, when one should bring up the matter at hand, the logical time for meetings, and how much of the schedule must be accomplished if the day is to be a successful one. Therefore if the missionary is so situated that the *gadgets* of time do not

[23]Juan M. Flavier, *Doctor to the Barrios* (Quezon City: New Day, 1970), 28–29.

get him into trouble, he can nevertheless rest assured that his *notions* of time will pose problems.

In discussing worldviews we noted that different peoples see time in various ways. Most Westerners think of time as a valuable commodity to be spent or invested. It is not unusual in the West to hear the phrase "time is money." Although the hands of the clock simply go around in circles, repeating the same cycle over and over again, Westerners are acutely aware of the fact that time is passing, never to be retrieved and never to be relived. The hourglass with the "sands of time running out on us" is an appropriate symbol for our notion of time. In part, Western ideas of time stem from the Judeo-Christian philosophy of history according to which time has a beginning, plus an end, plus purposes to be achieved in the interim. History is lineal. History is moving. Time is marching.

In the Indian view, time is a very different sort of thing. According to Indian philosophy, history is cyclical. It moves continually, but in circles; and the circles themselves move very slowly. Life is bound to the *wheel* of existence. One existence follows upon another. Time is to be endured. The *wheel* is much different from the *watch* or the *hourglass!*

Between these two poles can be located many different attitudes toward time and history. Classical China placed a tremendous value on the past. Modern China—or at least its leaders—reflect the Western parentage of Communism with its emphasis on the future, one-year plans, five-year plans, and so on. Africans characteristically have a long past and an abbreviated future. The present generation of American youth is often called the "now generation" because of their disregard for the past and future in favor of the present moment. Iberian culture as reflected in Latin America and the Philippines seems to exhibit a similar view in many instances, though the grasping may not be so accentuated as in the case of the "turned on" North American youth.

These basic differences in the ways in which the peoples of various cultures view time (plus other cultural factors) result in different behavioral patterns vis-à-vis time. The missionary must remember that the way in which time is interpreted, evaluated, divided, and categorized is largely a matter of culture. Although this does not mean that the missionary must *agree* with the new perspective, it does mean that he must understand it. Otherwise miscommunication and misunderstanding will result. Some examples from various cultures may be in order.

My first illustration comes from Nigeria. The newcomer to Nigeria must learn to adjust to an entirely new way of categorizing time. He will find that the market day is the basic marker that sets off the week. It occurs every four to eight days, depending on the tribe.[24] Among the Ibo people the day will be marked off by three separate gatherings of liquid from the raffia palm with which the Ibo make palm wine. Appointments are made according to the time of the three palm climbings.[25]

The next illustration is from Japan. North American businessmen are frequently frustrated by the time required to do business with the Japanese. Experienced American executives report that it is not unusual for an American representative to go to Japan to conclude a deal with a Japanese firm only to find himself coming to the end of the week or two weeks he has allotted to the negotiations without an agreement having been reached. Often the final agreement will not be forthcoming until he is en route to the airport, or even until he is ready to board his plane to go home. If, however, during the progress of the negotiations his Japanese hosts were prompt in arriving for the various meetings, that was an indication that the final agreement would somehow be reached. If his Japanese hosts were less and less prompt for the various appointments, he could have known that an agreement was most unlikely.

A final illustration is based on a conversation with a missionary in the Philippines several years ago. Let's call him missionary Y. We were at the breakfast table in his home in a outlying province. In answer to my query as to the time of the meeting that morning, he responded, "The announced time is

[24]Margaret Green, *Ibo Village Affairs*, 2nd ed. (London: Cass, 1964), 22.
[25]Ibid., 34.

nine o'clock, but they will not be there. They are never on time." He then went on to relate how in starting Sunday morning worship services in a nearby barrio, he had asked the believers what time the services should begin. Their answer was unequivocal—11:00 A.M. would certainly be the most convenient time if the missionary could make it. Assuring them that he could, he made preparations and arrived at the appointed place shortly before 11:00 the following Sunday morning. The believers gradually came in small groups or singly until there were enough to start the meeting a half hour or more later. After the experience was repeated several times on successive Sundays, missionary Y brought up the matter of their tardiness and asked what time they *really* wanted to begin their service. A discussion ensued and the decision was unanimous that 10:30 would be much more preferable than eleven o'clock. Missionary Y, however, was still doomed to disappointment, because, as he put it that morning at the breakfast table, "They were the ones who set the eleven o'clock starting time originally. And when no one showed up on schedule, they were the ones who changed it to 10:30. They still come late. They're *always* late for services. They are on time when money is involved, but not for the services of the church."

Several things stand out as one reviews the experience of missionary Y and his reaction of frustration. First, punctuality as it relates to religious and social events and as it relates to business is probably interpreted differently in the case of most Filipinos. In much the same way many North Americans make an unwarranted distinction between religious ethics and business ethics. Filipinos simply distinguish religious time from business time. In the Philippines barrio business becomes tied to the urban center, and the urban center, in turn, to international time patterns. Time therefore gradually becomes intimately associated with the hour and minute hands of a clock as far as the business world is concerned. In religious and social gatherings, however, time may still be associated with older patterns when such events were announced according to the general time of day—late morning, early afternoon, evening, and so forth. Eleven o'clock in this case occurs "when everyone has gathered in the later part of the morning." One Philippine national has commented that you can expect Filipinos to be on time only if they are wearing wrist watches!

Second, it is interesting that in changing the starting time of the worship service to 10:30 A.M. the barrio church group had moved in the direction opposite of that which would be normally interpreted from their own behavior. This was likely their way of adjusting to the missionary's disappointment over the fact that they were not beginning the service at eleven o'clock. By advancing the starting time to 10:30, they assured themselves that the service would start about 11:00.

Third, in spite of the fact that by announcing a 10:30 starting hour the original schedule resulted, the missionary and national responses to the new arrangement were most likely very different. We would expect that the nationals were quite satisfied that the change resulted in an eleven o'clock starting time. The missionary, however, was distressed for the simple reason that he felt that Christian religious services merited *the same kind of punctuality* that business requires. Actually for event-minded Filipinos what takes place after the meeting starts is much more important than the time at which the event begins.

Missionaries to the Third World will want to rethink the way in which behavior in respect to time is properly interpreted. It may well be that the Western missionary who subconsciously measures the depth of his commitment by the tightness of his schedule will want to change his pattern of behavior. After finding it difficult to break into the schedule of the missionary, the leader of one Asian church said concerning him, "God loves people but he loves schedules more." That was probably not the case, but it was the message the missionary communicated nonetheless. When it comes right down to it, *people* are more important than *schedules;* and the *quality* of an event is more important than the precise *starting* or *closing times.* Many non−North Americans basically agree with James Stalker in his delightful passage describing the conversion of Saul of Tarsus:

> It would be impossible to exaggerate what took place in the mind of Paul in this single instant. It is but a clumsy way we have of dividing time by the revolution of the clock into minutes and hours, days and years, as if each portion so measured were of the same size as another of equal length. This may suit well enough for the common ends of life, but there are finer measurements for which it is quite misleading. The real size of any space of time is to be measured by the amount it contains of the soul's experience; no one hour is exactly equal to another, and there are single hours that are larger than months. So measured, this one moment of life was perhaps larger than all his previous years. The glare of revelation was so intense that it might well have scorched the eye of reason or burnt out life itself, as the external light dazzled the eyes of his body into blindness.[26]

PARALANGUAGE

We have heard it said many times (and attention has been called to the saying previously in this book) that it is not *what* one says but *how* one says it that is most important. Knapp's way of communicating this is *"how* something is said is frequently *what* is said."[27] By way of illustration he asks his readers to notice the influence of vocal emphases on the meaning of a very simple sentence:

1. *He's* giving this money to Herbie.
   1a. HE is the one giving the money; nobody else.
2. He's *giving* the money to Herbie.
   2a. He is GIVING, not lending, the money.
3. He's giving *this* money to Herbie.
   3a. The money being exchanged is not for another fund or source; it is THIS money.
4. He's giving this *money* to Herbie.

[26]James Stalker, *Life of St. Paul* (Grand Rapids: Zondervan, n.d.), 39.
[27]Knapp, *Nonverbal Communication*, 147.

4a. MONEY is the unit of exchange; not a check or wampum.
5. He's giving this money to *Herbie*.
5a. This recipient is HERBIE, not Lynn or Bill or Rod.[28]

The meaning and importance that attaches to pauses, pitch, inflection, and the other ingredients of paralanguage differ from language to language. Meanings communicated by inflection in one language may be communicated by the grammatical apparatus of another language. For example, the particles *wa* and *ga* in Japanese convey degrees of emphasis that in English would be conveyed by articulation and voice inflection. The particle *ka* communicates that a question is being asked; no rising voice inflection is necessary.

Again, the meaning of a pause or silence (a "prolonged pause" in conversation) may be profoundly different from culture to culture. William Samarin, with a deliberate twist on Hall's phrase "the silent language," writes about "the language of silence."[29] He points out that silence is analogous to the zero in mathematics. It is more than the hiatus that separates words, phrases, clauses, and sentences. And it is more than a form of rhetorical punctuation. It actually *means* something: negation, affirmation, evasion, deception, coyness, and so on. His primary example is the Gbeya of the Central African Republic who seem to place as great a value on silence as we do on speaking ability. Their attitude is summed up in one of their proverbs that says, "Speech is something internal, which when it comes out, attracts flies." They engage in little or no conversation during a meal. They stand by silently when a friend is confined to a sickbed. In one case the North American would interpret silence as disinterest or even hostility. In the other case the North American would probably interpret silence to mean that death is approaching. To the Gbeya silence at the meal probably means that eating

28Ibid., 148.
29William Samarin, "The Language of Silence," *Practical Anthropology* 12 (May–June 1965): 115–19.

is an important business, and at the sickbed it probably says, "We are standing by and wish you well." Anyone who has been asked a question when his mouth was full or been forced into conversation when he would have given anything for peace and quiet will be inclined to applaud Gbeya culture at these points!

The nuances of cross-cultural paralanguage communication are far too complex to be considered here. We simply underscore its presence and importance. It not only affects meaning and thus conveys its own messages, but, as research indicates, it also affects respondent comprehension, retention, persuasion, and the way respondents will judge the emotions, personality, and personal characteristics of the message source.[30]

There were those in Corinth who said that Paul could write up a storm; yet when he was physically present with his hearers, his personal presence to them was unimpressive, and his speech was contemptible (2 Cor. 10:10). Paul wanted all in Corinth to know that there was no difference in his message whether he was personally absent or present. He wanted them to know that he could and would *speak* as plainly, decisively, and authoritatively as he *wrote*. And the Corinthians undoubtedly got the message.

By the grace of God may our respondents in the non-Christian world also get the message. Certainly, we do not measure up to the apostle or speak with the same kind of apostolic authority with which he spoke and wrote. But we are constrained by the same love of Christ, and we do have a sure word of prophecy. May there then be correspondence between *what* we say and the *way* we say it.

ARTIFACTS AND ENVIRONMENT

Those church buildings in Malacca, Malaysia, dating to the nineteenth century bear a remarkable similarity to churches of the same period in England and on the Continent

---

[30]Knapp, *Nonverbal Communication*, 151–68.

and a noticeable dissimilarity to many buildings around them. Church vestments (in churches where they are used) tend to exhibit the same design and colors throughout the world in some communions. Many missionaries are still outfitted with much *impedimenta Americana* even when adequate locally made items are available and a high degree of mobility is desirable. The female missionary who in her own culture made excessive use of cosmetics often continues the practice in the respondent culture.

What is the common factor running through these various illustrations? It is a lack of appreciation for the way in which indigenes interpret architectural styles, special vestments and regalia, mounds of baggage, and multicolored female faces. That important point will be missed if we become defensive and say, "We will proceed in such matters as we like. They are unimportant as relates to our mission." The point will also be missed if we become prematurely prescriptive and say, "We must go native in our dress and lifestyle if we want to reach these people." Hudson Taylor undoubtedly had the correct motivation when he prescribed native dress for missionaries in China. But he did not necessarily have the correct solution to effective communication. Of first priority after any biblical injunction that may apply to the particular case at hand is to ask, "What is the meaning of this item (form, style, color, etc.) to my respondents?" Only when the answer to that question is known—and not until it is known—are we in a position to make valid judgments in such matters. We must know what the item in question means to the respondent people.

By way of illustration of the importance of this area of nonverbal communication let us turn to some research and some personal experiences related to architecture. (Recall that I said earlier that architecture could be subsumed under the topic of proxemics and that subsequently we did consider some aspects of architecture under that heading.)

A student of the cultural ramifications of different house forms, S. Bochner contends that there is a close linkage between the "built environment" and lifestyle.[31] He is particularly concerned about the relationship between house form and such things as privacy, norm reinforcement, and interpersonal relationships. On the basis of cultural studies, he sketches the typical homes in each of six cultures and then hypothesizes as to what changes in basic values and lifestyle would have to be made if indigenes were forced to live in Western-style housing. Bochner's conclusion is that the traditional culture of many foreign peoples could not survive in such an event!

Looking at houses and their furnishings from a missionary perspective, I recall my experience at a conference in Nigeria that featured a daily open forum on missionary and national relationships. On that particular day the attendance reached about eighty and was almost equally divided between missionaries (all were from North America and Europe) and Africans. The discussion became rather animated as Nigerians communicated their desire for a closer fellowship with the missionaries and complained that they were seldom invited to the missionaries' homes. The ensuing discussion made it evident that there were some exceptions and also that the reluctance of some missionaries in this regard was not without some kind of rationale. One missionary stood to his feet and said, "One of the reasons we do not invite you as often as we should is that we are seldom if ever invited to the homes of our African friends." His remark was attended by an approving nodding of missionary heads and noticeable murmurs of agreement. The positive feedback ended rather abruptly, however, when an African with a commanding voice stood to his feet and said, "Missionary brethren, our homes are very humble. There are no carpets on our floors. There are few chairs in which you would be comfortable. Our food is not always so delicious to the Western mouth. Perhaps many of us never understood that you would want an invitation to our

---

[31]S. Bochner, "The House Form as a Cornerstone of Culture," in R. Brislin, ed., *Topics in Culture Learning*, vol. 3., (Honolulu: East-West Center, 1975).

homes." The meeting closed on a high note. But all left wiser than they were when they arrived. If home furnishings and surroundings seem to say "stay out," some adjustment will have to be made. At the very least, both African and missionary will have to find ways to say, "Come in. You are welcome."

The second personal illustration concerns a highly educated Japanese with whom I developed a pastoral relationship over a period of time. Shortly before leaving on a furlough, Dr. _____ came to bid us farewell. Such visits in Japan are usually attended by an air of formality with gift-giving and proper decorum, but it was apparent that Dr. _____ had some special concern. Finally the conversation progressed to a point where he lowered his head and in measured phrases communicated his decision.

"Sensei," he said, "I can never express to you the deep gratitude my wife and I feel for your guidance. We urge you to stay but if you cannot we must tell you that we have decided to attend the _____ church on _____ Street."

"Why would you do that?" I inquired, unsuccessfully attempting to conceal my disappointment.

"As long as you are here our church will remain and grow. But when you leave it will die. Look at the building. One look tells you that it is temporary. But the _____ church will last many lifetimes. Anyone can see that."

I admit that I had not thought in those terms. To me the church was the people. The building was functional. Admittedly our building had little to commend itself from the perspectives of indigenous architecture and apparent permanency, even though it had been locally built and antedated our ministry there. Quite likely more was involved in Dr. RL(5,450'S) decision than the construction materials of our church building. Status may have been one. At any rate it is an encouragement to know that the church of which he despaired continues to the present day under vigorous national leadership. But the incident was a factor in my resolve to give increased attention in my ministry not only to architecture per se, but to the teaching of the biblical truths concerning the true nature of the church of Christ—that church against which the gates of hell will not prevail. Where Christians are a small minority and where economics dictate that church buildings will seldom communicate much of the solidity and permanence of the church that is Christ's "building" (Eph 2:20–22), it seems that it is all the more important to communicate these characteristics in other ways.

The catalog of available illustrations is unending. White may be the absence of color but it is not without its message—nor is black, red, green, or gold. Clothing may cover all but the eyes, hands, and feet, or it may be no more than a loin cloth. But it does more than cover—it communicates sex, status, role, and age. Buildings and furnishings fulfill their functions. But they do more. They occasion envy, pity, the feeling of being at home, or feelings of uneasiness. There is a world of communication at our doorsteps! As we have said, contextualization has to do with more than verbal communication!

Chapter 32

Where The Action Is

It may seem that we have roamed (some may say "strayed!") rather freely over a wide range of material since introducing the present section with references to Aranguren and Hall, Plato and Aristotle, and Paul and Peter. Because we are concerned with any and all aspects of nonverbal communicative behavior, the reaction would not be without some justification. At any rate those references were important for missionary communication. Perhaps their implications will become more clear after we proceed one final step in the discussion of behavioral patterns.

In *The Silent Language*, Edward Hall says that *the message* of his book is this:

> If a person really wants to help introduce culture change he should find out what is happening at the informal level and pinpoint which informal adaptations seem to be the most successful in daily operation. Bring these to the level of awareness.[1]

[1]Edward T. Hall, *The Silent Language* (Greenwich, Conn.: Fawcett, 1959), 91.

Hall's contention is reasonable and fairly bristles with implications for the missionary. His rationale can be simply stated. He believes that significant breakthroughs in culture change are really the result of a series of smaller changes that occur at the informal, out-of-awareness level that is so much a part of daily learning and living. One might argue, for example, that in North America the relaxed moral code as relates to sex, which is implicit in situational ethics and contemporary texts on modes of marriage, is not the result of the new ethic or the new definitions of marriage themselves. Rather, the new ethics resulted from a series of informally accepted changes such as the introduction of the automobile, acceptance of unchaperoned dating, the increase of leisure time, and decreased church attendance, among other factors. Gradually, changes in these areas gave rise to a more or less unthought-out change in patterns of acceptable sexual behavior. Finally, formal and technical-level learning reinforced changes that had already taken place informally. This learning involves new ideas and formal instruction as to the rightness and wrongness of certain kinds of sexual behavior, and, at the technical level, instruction on contraceptives, the legal implications of various types of marriage contracts, the findings of research on sexual behavior, and so on.

It was an awareness of this sequence of change that prompted Mahatma Gandhi to become a model for Indian women by regularly spending some of his time at a spinning wheel. Gandhi saw that if Indian women began to abandon the spinning wheels in their homes in favor of the looms in the factory, a whole set of changes would be set in motion that would ultimately result in a non-Indian philosophy and culture. He believed that without his model behavior, formal and technical instruction of consequences attending women's abandonment of their homes would be unavailing.

It is no easy task to attempt to pinpoint all the implications of these insights for the missionary, but some seem rather obvious and in accord with biblical principles.

First, we are reminded that patterns of missionary living and acting are communication patterns. To pray in the church but not in the home, or to divorce spiritual concerns and business concerns, is to communicate confusion and something less than Christianity. It is rather like verbalizing the word "great" while gesturing with two hands spaced about six inches apart. Specialists call this kind of gesture "meta-incongruent." Paul often noted that his conduct coincided with his creed—that is, his conduct was not meta-incongruent when compared with his behavior. One arresting exhortation was "Be imitators [Greek, *mimētēs;* KJV followers] of me, just as I also am of Christ" (1 Cor. 11:1). In this sense it is not only legitimate but necessary to talk of the "incarnational" aspect of missionary communication. Little wonder that Paul condemned Peter's conduct at Antioch!

Second, the Christian missionary must not guard his privacy too closely. If his home is his castle, the church may well become an ivory tower. It is most natural for indigenes to want to know how this representative of another world furnishes his home, interacts with his wife and children, prepares and eats his food, and even how he sleeps, brushes his teeth, and cares for his person. Taking into account the fact that rules of privacy may be very different, this aspect of missionary life can be most demanding. Lines will have to be drawn somewhere between the conflicting cultural guidelines. But the missionary should remember that when he limits the scrutiny of nationals to his *public* life and refuses to take them into the more intimate associations of heart and home, he has obstructed the channels of communication. The number of the unbelievers in Africa and Asia who have been won to Christ and who have been helped to spiritual maturity by coming into the warmth and love of a Christian missionary's home must be legion.

Third, one of the most potent weapons in the missionary's communications arsenal is the ability to bring the behavioral patterns of pagan cultures to a new level of awareness and open them up to the light of revelation and reason. Many nominal Buddhists, for example, do not know why they celebrate the annual *obon.* It has become an unthought-out way of doing things in July of each year. What may be required is an explanation stemming from a story of Buddha and one of his disciples by the name of Mokuren. Mokuren made an earnest plea to see how his mother was faring in the other world. In answer to his implorations, the Buddha withdrew the veil and allowed Mokuren to see his mother—who was suffering the agony of being crucified upside down! Mokuren secured a temporary reprieve for his mother after which she was obliged to return to her cross in the netherworld. Every year millions of Japanese go through the rituals and festivities associated with inviting the spirits of the departed back to the world of the living for this brief respite—many without knowing or reflecting on the implications of what they are doing. Were they to reflect on these implications, many of them might be inclined to celebrate the death and resurrection of the One who bore our sins in his body on the cross so that we might live eternally!

Finally, proper emphasis on the communicative value of behavioral patterns helps restore the imbalance occasioned by our traditional emphasis on formal and technical instruction. Missionary teaching that relies primarily on dispensing information about God and his will at the formal and technical levels runs the risk of being ineffectual in really changing peoples' basic beliefs and conduct. Theology (whether simple or sophisticated) that is not related to the ways people live, play, work, and worship will fall on deaf ears and on paralyzed hands and feet. By contrast, when cultural behavioral patterns are held up to the light of biblical truth, or when the new biblical patterns are first introduced in the form of model behavior, we can reasonably expect that respondents will experience new impetus to change. This is to argue that all true missionary education is in effect discipleship training and involves teacher and learner in a mutual acting out of Christian doctrine and duty. *And it is to argue that true missionary evangelism is more than delivering new information about God and Christ. It is to demonstrate the implications of the gospel in terms of the behavioral patterns of the respondent culture.* The gospel, then, becomes concrete and practical. Assuming that the Holy Spirit desires changed lives, not just a rearrangement of cortical convolutions, we become better instruments of his purposes by practicing full-orbed communication.

CONCLUSION TO PART VI

If anything, understanding and contextualizing the silent language is more demanding than verbal language. It would be practically impossible to account for all the items of information that are exchanged between parties to any given instance of communication. Fortunately, it is unnecessary to give careful analysis to the vast majority of these items. Our culture has programmed us to care for them unconsciously. To bring them to awareness may in fact be to disrupt the flow of communication. There are times, however, when those whose primary business is communication must bring a good deal of these more or less hidden aspects of communication to the level of awareness. One such time occurs when we cross cultural boundaries to communicate Christ. Of course, it is hoped that conscious and careful attention to these nonverbal factors will ultimately result in an internalization of the behavioral patterns of the new culture and culturally relevant Christian behavior patterns so that the Word and work of Christ may be furthered in the best possible manner.

The materials of this section are not to be summed up in the bit of homespun wisdom often conveyed in the phrase "When in Rome do as the Romans do." It is not that simple. First, that is to imply that we observe all that the Romans are doing but the fact is that we don't. Second, Christ may not at all be pleased with what the Romans are doing! For the sake of testimony (or for the sake of health) the missionary may find it necessary to reject some behavioral patterns that to the members of the target culture are right and proper. This can often be done without arousing resentment by (1) avoiding situations where the objectional practice is likely to occur, (2) proposing culturally acceptable alternatives, or (3) explaining in advance why the missionary cannot participate.

Actually, cases where the missionary will be called on to

participate in inherently objectionable practices or practices that jeopardize health and reputation do not form a large part of the experience of the average missionary. At some place along the line, however, this type of problem will be encountered by almost every missionary. One may find, for example, certain traditional foods or beverages to be unbearable. One missionary who returned to China as soon as possible after World War II found that wherever he went he was treated to century eggs (eggs that are treated and buried for a period of time before serving) so that he developed dysentery and found it necessary to refuse this particular expression of Chinese hospitality in as polite a way as possible. In a case like this, it is wise to warn the host (perhaps through a third person) before the food or drink is actually served.

The missionary should make every effort to understand, adapt, and utilize indigenous behavioral patterns for the cause of Christ. Persons with less lofty ideals than the missionary espouses have recognized the importance of this. It might be well to note the guiding principles of the Philippine Rural Reconstruction Movement of some years ago as given in a book to which I have made reference in this chapter:

> *Go to the people*
> *Live among them*
> *Learn from them*
> *Serve them*
> *Plan with them*
> *Start with what they know*
> *Build on what they have*
> *Not piecemeal but integrated approach*
> *Not showcase but pattern*
> *Not relief but release*
> *Mass education through mass participation*
> *Learn by doing*
> *Teach by showing*[2]

[2]Juan M. Flavier, *Doctor to the Barrios* (Quezon City: New Day, 1970), 12.

Part VII

SOCIAL STRUCTURES—
WAYS OF INTERACTING

Figure 24

DIMENSIONS OF CROSS-CULTURAL COMMUNICATION

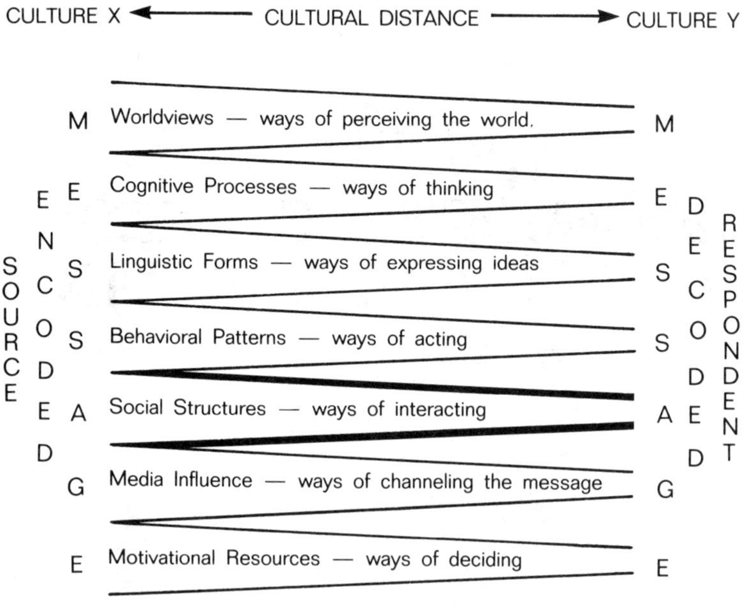

CULTURE X ◄─────── CULTURAL DISTANCE ─────► CULTURE Y

M	Worldviews — ways of perceiving the world.	M
E	Cognitive Processes — ways of thinking	E
S	Linguistic Forms — ways of expressing ideas	S
S	Behavioral Patterns — ways of acting	S
A	Social Structures — ways of interacting	A
G	Media Influence — ways of channeling the message	G
E	Motivational Resources — ways of deciding	E

S O U R C E

E N C O D E D

D E C O D E D

R E S P O N D E N T

Chapter 33

Communication and Societal Orientations

[Andrew] found first his own brother Simon, and said to him. . . (John 1:41).

The Samaritan woman therefore said to Him, "How is it that You, being a Jew, ask me for a drink since I am a Samaritan woman?" (For Jews have no dealings with Samaritans.) (John 4:9).

But Peter, taking his stand with the eleven, raised his voice and declared to them: "Men of Judea, and all you who live in Jerusalem (Acts 2:14).

And when it came about that Peter entered, Cornelius met him, . . . And he (Peter) said to them, "You yourselves know how unlawful it is for a man who is a Jew to associate with a foreigner or to visit him" (Acts 10:25, 28).

The above references are taken from familiar contexts. When Andrew met the Messiah, he gave the news to his brother first. The Samaritan woman was surprised that Jesus, a Jew, would ask a favor of her, a Samaritan. When Peter was filled with the Holy Spirit, he received the courage to speak plainly of Christ. And speak he did—to Jews! Later he preached the gospel to Gentiles in the house of Cornelius—but it took a special vision to make him willing to do that. Those who know the cultural circumstances attending these incidents will say, "What is so unusual . . . ?" or, "Of course, it was natural that . . . ." Precisely. Social factors made it likely that Andrew would speak to Peter and that Peter would first preach to Jews; and social factors make it unlikely that Jesus would speak to the Samaritan woman and that Peter would witness to Cornelius's household. Viewed in this light, the words in Acts 1:8 to the effect that the disciples would be witnesses in Jerusalem, Judea, Samaria, and the uttermost parts of the earth take on *cultural* as well as *geographical* significance. And yet numerous missionaries have entered their respondent cultures without any attention whatsoever to the social structure, evidently assuming that the new culture would be a carbon copy of their own or that the differences would prove to be unimportant.

The importance of the social dimension of communication is based on two fundamental factors. One factor is that we are born into a certain culture with its worldview, ways of thinking, ways of acting, and so on. The other is that we are born into a certain society that has certain expectations of its members, certain ways of interacting, and so on. We undergo two processes as a result: enculturation and socialization. These distinctions are not at all iron-clad. One prominent social anthropologist, Paul Bohannan, disdains the terms "socialized" and "enculturated" as "jargon terms" for "taught the manners and technology of their elders."[1] Nevertheless, he goes on to say that these two processes intertwine and work together in the individual (with "some unknown mixture with his genetic capabilities and inclinations") to form what we call personality:

> The point is that culture, society, and personality are not empirically separable each from the other. In order to have

[1] Paul Bohannan, *Social Anthropology* (New York: Holt, Rinehart and Winston, 1963), 16.

social relationships, we must have culture as the means with which to express them, and we must have personalities that handle the culture and play the roles in the social relationships. No matter with which we begin, the other two are necessary dimensions. Only analytically can a separation be made.[2]

In this process of socialization the individual becomes not so much a subject as an object to himself. In other words, the individual experiences himself, not directly, but indirectly, from the standpoints of individual members of his society or from the generalized standpoint of his social groups as a whole. Accordingly, he learns who he is, where he fits, how he belongs, and what to think, say, and do.

One is tempted to ask, "What happens to my freedom in this process?" Certainly it is easier for the Christian believer to see the sovereignty of God here than it is to see the freedom of the individual. We had nothing to do with any of the accompaniments of our birth. We had nothing to do with the predispositions of the society to prescribe and proscribe our self-understanding and behavior. On the other hand, the Christian faith lends credence to our individuality and freedom, and it assures us that we are subjects and not just objects; it assures us that we are acting and interacting, not simply being acted upon and reacting. By virtue of creation and redemption we possess a freedom that is beyond any freedom that our society or physical environment can afford— namely, the freedom of communication with God and of action within the divine will as he guides us to know that will. In this sense all people are free.

It is this understanding of man that is reflected, however imperfectly, in the traditional Western view of man. Generally speaking, in the West every individual is seen as being of infinite worth and having rights that supersede the claims of this society. Unfortunately, the West has erred in two directions: first, it has forgotten that individual worth is

2Ibid.

rooted in creation; and second, it has overemphasized individual value at the expense of societal values. A member of the U.S. Congress recently made the statement that our government does not exist to protect the rights of society but to protect the rights of the individual. This is entirely in accord with our individualistic and egalitarian orientation. The English language itself reflects an individualistic orientation and egalitarianism. Linguistically, every person has recourse to one and the same symbol with which to express the self as subject: the capital "I." The personal pronoun remains the same irrespective of where and with whom one might interact.

By way of comparison we should note that the Eastern view of humanity as mirrored in Japan is quite different. There it is the responsibility of the individual to submerge himself and promote the ends of the larger group. The self is relative and impermanent while society is constant. Accordingly, in the Japanese language there is no one symbol with which everyone in every situation expresses the self as subject. The form that the pronoun "I" takes is dependent on relationships and circumstances. The appropriate symbol may be *watakushi*, *watashi* (abbreviation), *boku* (used by young men in familiar speech), *atashi* (used by girls in familiar speech), *sessha* (an old expression used in epistolary style by elderly men), or *ore* (used in men's vulgar speech). The differences between these terms are of the essence.[3]

The individualism of the West is also revealed in the way in which people introduce themselves: given name first and then family name. In fact in some places, and especially among the young, it is quite common to introduce oneself simply by the given name. When meeting with a group of North American students in Europe recently, I was struck by the fact that without exception they identified themselves by their given names only. When two or three of the students

---

[3]Unless the foreigner is well-versed in the Japanese language and acculturated to a significant degree he will probably never hear several of these words.

wanted to send greetings to friends in America they were at a loss to recall their surnames!

Idiosyncrasies within the Western context can be expected to sustain this individualistic bias. Robert Evans notes that in Sweden people are identified with their occupations that are given in lieu of first names. Thus in introductions (and even in telephone listings!), it is "Mr. Truckdriver Peterson" or "Mr. Laundryman Larsen." Accordingly, their wives become "Mrs. Truckdriver Peterson" and "Mrs. Laundryman Larsen"! Evans writes of a milkman who identified himself as "Mr. Milk Engineer so-and- so!"[4] This only serves to make Sweden's individualism a little more covert.

By way of contrast turn once again to Japan. When a Japanese introduces himself, it is customary to first mention the larger groups to which he belongs, then his family name and finally his given name. He does not say, "My name is Hiroshi Motoyama." Rather, if he works for the Takashimaya Department Store in Tokyo, he will say, "Takashimaya no Motoyama Hiroshi" ("Takashimaya's Motoyama Hiroshi," i.e., "Motoyama Hiroshi who belongs to Takashimaya"). In an interchurch conference he would most likely introduce himself as "Nihonbashi Kyokai no Motoyama Hiroshi" ("Nihonbashi Church's Motoyama Hiroshi"). In any case, he would first identify himself with his family by announcing his surname (Motoyama) before his given name.

The differences between the United States and Sweden on the one hand and Japan on the other is not simply quaint and superficial. They cut to the very sinews of our social orders and reveal that basic tension between the prerogatives of the individual as over against those of the social group to which he belongs. We all feel this tension, but we attempt to resolve it in very different ways.

When it comes to communication, in full accord with our bias toward individualism, we Westerners expect open channels of communication in every direction and greatly deplore the gaps that exist in our society. More and more we tend to

[4]Robert Evans, Let Europe Hear (Chicago: Moody, 1963), 452.

shy away from those forms of address that indicate differences of status. And individuals are often urged to make decisions independent of consideration for even the primary groupings to which they belong. *How very different we are when compared to great portions of that Third World in which most missionaries are called to communicate Christ!*

It is good to see both sides of the coin from a Christian perspective. On one side is discoverable the imprimatur of the *imago Dei* with its endorsement of the uniqueness and value of the individual. On the other side is clearly discernable the divine sanction for society and its authority, for the same God who said, "It is not good for the man to be alone" (Gen. 2:18), placed men in society and gave society certain rights over its individual members.

The ramifications of the foregoing for missionary communication are numerous and of great consequence. Individuals are citizens or aliens vis-à-vis any particular society. They live in free or totalitarian states, or in the bustling city or the quiet village. They belong to families—nuclear and extended—to which they give varying degrees of loyalty. They communicate with some people every day and many times a day. With others they do not communicate at all. They communicate "upward" to some people, "downward" to others, and "across" to still others. Such are the arrangements of society. Within the will of God it is society that in large measure determines who will speak to whom, in what way, at what time, and with what effect.

The ancients took note of these factors. They did so when they remarked that it is not difficult to "praise Athenians *among Athenians!*" They did so when they emphasized that effective persuasion is related to a knowledge of the particular *laws* that govern a people. The Bible writers also took note of these societal arrangements as we have already seen. But it has remained for us in the twentieth century to explore the significance of these factors more fully. Although much research remains to be done, we can now speak with some confidence concerning the ways in which societal arrangements affect communication.

Chapter 34

Status and Role

Fundamental to our present consideration are the twin concepts of status and role. Status is essentially the social position assigned to (or achieved by) an individual—his or her place on the social ladder, so to speak. To a person's status certain expectations, beliefs, and sentiments are attached; and these determine the role of the individual. Role is an action term and is perhaps best defined as the "acting out of one's status." No matter what the society, every member has his status and role in that society. Or, it might be more accurate to say that every member has his *statuses* and *roles*. For example, a man may be a son, a husband, a father, a teacher, an employee, a citizen, and so on. Almost unconsciously his communication undergoes subtle—or not so subtle—changes as he acts out the roles proper to his statuses in the family, company, and community.

Few cultures ever delineated a more clear-cut definition of statuses and roles than that which Confucius bequeathed to China. As we noted previously, he selected five of the most important relationships in society and then went on to prescribe the attitudes and behavior (roles) that were suitable to the ten resultant statuses. By defining the "Fivefold Relationships" in this way, Confucius in effect solved many communication problems before they arose. The whole pattern of communication (whether by silent deed or spoken word) between a superior and inferior, for example, reflected the subject's knowledge of the expectation of Chinese society. The same was true in the case of father and son, friend and friend, and so on. To fail to communicate according to status was to fail, not only as a superior, or father, or son, but *as a Chinese.*

The Chinese case is instructive not only because statuses and roles were so clearly defined but also because the system played such an important part in that society for many centuries. But to varying degrees, what was true of China is true of all societies. For that reason one is obliged to ask two basic questions when he crosses *any* cultural boundary as a missionary communicator: (1) Who am I in relation to my respondents? (2) Who are my respondents in relation to other members of their society?

THE STATUS AND ROLE OF THE MISSIONARY COMMUNICATOR

When Jesus was in Caesarea Philippi, he inquired of his disciples, "Who do people say that the Son of Man is?" Upon hearing their answers, he said, "But who do you say that I am?" (Matt. 16:13, 15). The answers of unbelief are one thing; the answers of faith are quite another.

Similarly, we have previously considered the question, "Who is a missionary?" That question should be answered in the light of biblical evidence and before the candidate leaves his homeland. When the missionary arrives in his respondent culture (if not before), he should ask, "Who do *these people* say that I am?" In addition to being an ambassador of Christ, he will then realize that he has the statuses of foreigner, alien, outsider, guest, intruder, and man—to say nothing of husband, father, friend, chairman, committeeman, and so forth. Let us look at several important statuses in some detail.

460

1. When Paul preached in Athens, he did so as a *foreigner.* The local Epicureans and Stoics encountered him. Some said, "What will this babbler say?" Others said, "He seemeth to be a setter forth of strange gods" (Acts 17:18 KJV). Although it may have been easy to praise Athenians among Athenians, it obviously was not easy to convince Athenians that they were sinners and in need of salvation, especially when they were in an audience composed of *other Athenians!* And that task must have been doubly difficult for a non-Athenian preacher.

The missionary may well find that his foreignness is at once an asset and a liability, but he should never forget that it sets him apart. He is on trial. His message is from the outside. In a very real sense the missionary is *persona non grata* until he proves himself worthy of a hearing. Many a preacher in the homeland has as a motto, "Sir, we would see Jesus" (John 12:21 KJV). As missionary communicators, let us take that motto with us to our respondent cultures in order to be continually reminded of God's expectations in sending us: "For we do not preach ourselves but Christ Jesus as Lord" (2 Cor. 4:5). As a reminder of what our audiences in the respondent culture will be thinking as they listen to our speech, it might be well to remember the reaction of the Athenians to the apostle Paul's: "What will this babbler say?" (Acts 17:18 KJV).

2. The missionary is also a *guest.* He lives and moves in the new culture not only by the grace of God but also by the forbearance of its citizens. That does not necessarily mean that his coming was in response to their invitation. Nor does it mean that he dare not preach that which, while true to Scripture, might offend them. But as is the case with any ambassador of any government on earth, as long as he lives in his adopted society he will be a guest in a host country. And for good or ill he will be so regarded. In the Middle East he will likely find an ambivalent reception that results from the extreme cordiality those cultures reserve for a guest on the one hand, and the extreme suspicion with which a Western Christian missionary is regarded on the other. In the East, the missionary may find that many respondents will receive him

461

as a guest and praise him for his attainments (small though they may be); they will agree with his message and even follow his instructions in taking the first steps of faith. Later he will discover that this positive response in many cases was as ephemeral as morning mist. In evaluating this reaction he should not overlook the distinct possibility that the respondents were simply acting in accordance with cultural dictums that bite rather deeply into Western notions of ethicality! After all (from their point of view) what kind of host is he who would invite the embarrassment of his guest by contributing to his failure?

3. The missionary is an *expert in religion*. The reader may demure upon reading that statement. In the so-called sending nations, we tend to think of missionaries more as witnesses, not so much as experts; they are more proclaimers of the faith than professional teachers of religion. And certainly where there has been widespread contact with missionaries in the Third World, there has been an attendant diminishing of expectations on this score!

The words of a Japanese Buddhist remain with me, however. After expressing disappointment with the fact that a visiting missionary speaker seemed to have no appreciation of the kind of questions Japanese were asking of Christians, he queried, "Is he actually an expert in religion?" I tried to explain that in the West it is not always considered essential that missionaries be well trained in Christian theology or culture of the people to whom they are sent and that other considerations are sometimes given priority. My answer evidently failed to satisfy him. He replied, "I can only say that if we Buddhists send someone to another country to train the people in Buddhism, it is first required that they be experts themselves." He may have been overstating his case, but the curriculum and regimen of a Buddhist school for training missionaries to be sent to North America (located just a short distance from our place of conversation) certainly supported his argument.

The more one thinks of the concept of an "expert in religion," the more one realizes that there is some validity to the expectation of respondent peoples. They believe the one who is sent halfway around the world to convert them from religious systems that have commanded their faith for many centuries should know whereof he speaks and be able to communicate alternatives intelligently and clearly. We would certainly expect that also. Moreover, it is only natural that national Christians expect sound instruction from the missionary on Christian faith and life. And it is right that national workers and pastors expect helpful information from the missionary in the areas of Christian service and church practice. The vistas of available and important knowledge are so broad that we are encouraged to be very humble about our expertise as missionaries in any case. But honest questions deserve educated answers. By and large the missionary can expect to be successful as a communicator of Christ only so long as he provides good responses.

It would be profitable to discuss still other statuses and roles that emerge in the missionary situation. Recall Robert Burns's words:

> O wad some power the giftie gie us
> To see oursel's as ithers see us!
> It wad frae monie a blunder free us,
> and foolish notion.[1]

But if such a gift would be profitable, it is not very likely to come as a gift! Let the thoughtful missionary *analyze* his status in each context and then look to God for wisdom and strength to play out his role in a manner pleasing to his Lord.

WHO ARE MY RESPONDENTS IN RELATION TO OTHER MEMBERS OF THEIR SOCIETY?

As important as is the question "Who am I (to them)?" the consideration of "Who are they (to others)?" must not be

[1]Robert Burns, "To a Louse, On Seeing One on a Lady's Bonnet at Church," *The Complete Poetical Works of Robert Burns*, Cambridge Edition (Boston: Houghton Mifflin, 1897).

overlooked. Rarely, and only in the case of small, isolated tribal societies, will the missionary address the entire membership of a society. The great majority of audiences represent but a part of the larger whole. And audiences are made up of people who belong to families, clans, and tribes. In audiences are people identified with the upper, middle, or lower strata of society, as well as people from the village, town, or city. It is this fact that has occasioned this discussion. Before looking at the large ramifications of these societal associations, however, it may be well to think of certain types of respondents who relate to other members of their society in special ways that make them important to the missionary communicator.

1. *Marginals* are people who, for one reason or another, stand on the fringe of their society without enjoying the privileges of acceptance as full members.

A recent book on church growth in the Philippines takes note of the fact that a certain local church was born in circumstances that had many of the earmarks of a small people movement.[2] This promising work flourished briefly only to wither and die. Having a special interest in this particular case, I sought out one of the original members of the church to inquire as to its beginnings and demise. The full story can now be told.

Included in the original missionary contacts in that village was a man who was looked upon with great suspicion by other members of his community because of his opportunistic business dealings. This man made a profession of faith and, with remarkable ability for deception, won the complete confidence of the missionary. But his profession carried the seeds of distrust in the community much as summer winds bear aloft the seeds of thistles and dandelions. It was not long before those seeds bore their bitter fruit and a promising work for Christ was choked out. The weakness of the present Christian witness in that community is a testimony to the danger (especially in a new work) of not recognizing who the

[2]A. L. Tuggy and R. Toliver, *Seeing the Church in the Philippines* (Manila: O. M. F., 1972), 98.

respondents are in the eyes of the other members of their society and then acting accordingly.

Gerald Swank, who for many years has served as Sudan Interior Mission missionary in Nigeria, relates that there are two outstanding examples of the same phenomenon in the work among the Muslim Hausa.[3] First, missionaries have worked with the lepers with no little success. The leprosaria ministries have resulted in good relations with government officials and, in many cases, in the arresting of the disease and the restoration of lepers to their families. Many lepers have returned to their villages as new people in Christ. Not a few have become evangelists. A problem has arisen, however, because these lepers are still marginals in the eyes of the majority of the villagers. Because these sources of Christian communication are suspect, their message is not given serious consideration by many.

Second, missionaries among the Hausa have also done yeoman service in ministering to the blind. Many sightless Hausa have had their spiritual eyes opened to the truth of God in Christ and have prepared themselves as evangelists. But again, though their fellow Hausas often marvel at the ability of these blind evangelists to read with their fingers, they still place them on the fringe of society, where the sightless long have been relegated in that land. This makes the evangelization of the Muslim Hausa—already fraught with formidable obstacles—that much more difficult.

I am not saying, of course, that the disadvantaged should not be helped and won to Christ. Nor am I saying that they should not be challenged to witness and trained to serve as pastors and evangelists. The point I am making is that missionaries and national leaders should be aware of the effect that a *primary approach* to marginals of any type will have on the larger work of Christ. The leaders should prayerfully devise an overall strategy that will not require the *average* Hausa to change his attitude toward the leper and the blind,

[3]This information was given to me by Mr. Swank in a personal conversation.

for example, *before* he gives attention to the Christian gospel. Every effort should be made to win and train Hausa who are in the mainstream of their society.

Two considerations may serve as blinders, preventing the missionary from seeing the consequences of a primary contact with, and dependence on, marginals of a society. In the first place, it is obvious that our Lord ministered to many such people with the result that great throngs came to see and hear the Miracle-Worker from Nazareth. In this connection we must be reminded of three facts: (1) miracles assumed a place of special importance in the ministry of our Lord as an authentication of his messianic claims; (2) the Lord Jesus disclaimed the kind of hearing and faith that accrued to his miracles among extraordinary people who did not evidence an understanding of his basic message and purpose; and (3) none of the Twelve on whom Christ relied for the proclamation of the gospel and the building of his church could be said to have been a marginal (with the possible exception of Matthew the tax gatherer).

In the second place, we may be overly impressed by the fact that in our own society it is often the converted marginal—the former drug addict or the ex-convict—who commands the largest audience. Often in our society, the greater the convert's alienation from the Christian community before conversion, the greater the attention he receives subsequently. Once again, however, we must be reminded of other pertinent information: (1) our society is perhaps unusual both in the acceptance of the exceptional individual and the attention given to him; (2) the churches in most Western communities are already established and their members are in the mainstream of society; and (3) it is one thing to gain the temporary attention of an audience to a marginal's testimony, while it is quite another thing to build a lasting *church* testimony on the witness of such individuals.

These warnings concerning marginals should not be construed to mean that the gospel should be withheld from anyone. As someone has commented on Luke 19:10, the Lord Jesus came to save the last, the least, and the lost. The church at Philippi probably included a slave girl whose conversion and healing from demon possession had excited no little attention and opposition in that city. The great church among the Karens in Burma started with the witness of Ko Tha Byu, an unlettered, converted criminal who served as a servant in the home of Adoniram Judson. A remarkable movement to Christ among the Chuhra in India began with the testimony of a dark, lame, little man by the name of Ditt, who by patience and persistence won relatives and friends in his village of Mirali. Within a generation all but a few hundred of the Chuhra caste had been converted to Christ.[4] Undoubtedly examples could be multiplied.

But it should not be forgotten that although both Ko Tha Byu and Ditt were "marginal" to the larger society in which they lived, they were not so to the people among whom they ministered. Ko Tha Byu ministered among his Karen people, not among the Burmese who despised them. Ditt ministered to fellow outcast people, not to the castes. Nor should it be forgotten that the church in Philippi included a prison warden, a business woman named Lydia, and a slave-owner named Epaphroditus. After careful investigation, E. A. Judge concludes that the earliest churches did not flourish among the depressed sections of society nor among those who protested the existing social order. Rather, "the Christians were dominated by a socially pretentious section of the population of the big cities."[5] He adds that sixty years later Pliny noted that Christians represented a cross-section of society and he noted what was to Pliny the ominous fact that the new religion was spreading from the cities to the countryside. "Until then however we may safely regard Christianity as a socially well-backed movement of the great Hellenistic cities."[6]

2. All societies seem to have certain *influential individuals* who are especially important to communication. These

[4]Cf. Stephen Neill, *A History of Christian Missions* (Grand Rapids: Eerdmans, 1965), 294, 365.

[5]E. A. Judge, *The Social Pattern of the Christian Groups in the First Century* (London: Tyndale Press, 1960), 60.

[6]Ibid., 61.

individuals have an important role in the processes of informing the other members of society, instituting opinion and behavior change, and reinforcing group values and norms. Influence of this kind has been identified as of two primary types—prestige and personal. *Prestige influence* is gained by the occupation of a key position of prominence and power in the community; in developed societies it tends to be exerted through the mass media and the more formal channels of communication flow. *Personal influence* is the product of access to information and also of personal characteristics such as force of personality, competency, and communication ability. It is more or less independent of one's position in the hierarchical ranking of the society and is usually exerted through face-to-face contacts.

Individuals who possess prestige influence are often identified as *formal leaders*, while those who exercise personal influence are called *opinion leaders*.[7] The distinction is an important one, but it should not be pressed too far. In traditional societies especially, formal leaders are apt to be opinion leaders as well.

Perhaps because prestige (vertical) communication does not possess the persuasive potential of personal (horizontal) communication, research in Western societies has largely focused on the role of opinion leaders as a factor in persuasive communication. Typically, opinion leaders tend to be very much like the people they influence and may well belong to the same primary groups of family, co-workers, and friends. But they are what Joseph Klapper calls "super representatives" of their groups. In other words, although they are like everyone else in the group in regard to norms, they personify the values of the group. They are people of sound judgment. More often than not, opinion leaders are influential in certain specialized—whether medicine, politics, religion, or whatever—not across the board. They can be counted on to

[7]Stanley K. Bigman, "Prestige, Personal Influence and Opinion," in Wilbur Schramm, ed., *The Process and Effects of Mass Communication* (Urbana: University of Illinois Press, 1954), 401–10.

reinforce group opinion as well as facilitate change and therefore have a double significance for missionary communication.[8]

One of the classic calculated attempts to win and utilize influential individuals in kingdom service was that of Ludwig Nommensen (1834–1918) and his colleagues of the Rhenish Mission (Lutheran) in their work among the Bataks on Sumatra. The Christian message was delivered to the local chiefs who were recognized by the church and given ecclesiastical responsibilities. In addition, the missionaries broke with Western patterns and appointed elders who were responsible for church organization, discipline, and funds. They also appointed native assistants who were Christian counterparts to the teacher-preacher so well known to Indonesian society. From the ranks of the native assistants, pastors were later chosen on the basis of performance and, though they were without full academic training, they were nevertheless given authority as pastors of the churches. It goes without saying that the chiefs were the formal leaders of Batak society and that the missionaries' objective was to use their prestige in the process of Christianization. We can only hypothesize that the native assistants were, in many cases, natural opinion leaders whose emergence as able communicators of the gospel was made possible by the innovative strategy of the Rhenish missionaries.

The Batak experiment has been variously evaluated, though if one were to judge by size alone he would be compelled to conclude that it was highly successful. By the middle of the twentieth century the Christian community among the Bataks numbered more than one-half million souls.[9] Many other factors must be taken into consideration for a proper evaluation, but Peter Beyerhaus indicates that there were real strengths that accrued to the recognition of the

[8]Joseph T. Klapper, *The Effect of Mass Communication* (New York: Free Press, 1960), 32–37.

[9]Peter Beyerhaus and Henry Lefever, *The Responsible Church and the Foreign Mission* (Grand Rapids: Eerdmans, 1964), 85.

chiefs (though few proved fit for ecclesiastical responsibility) and the utilization of the native assistants (though they were too few and too much under the control of the missionaries).[10] That Christian leaders tend to overlook the status and role of natural leaders—particularly the elders—is apparent in Charles Kraft's search for a culturally appropriate preaching form in Nigeria.

> In attempting to discover a dynamically equivalent form of preaching, I once asked a group of Nigerian church leaders how they would present the Christian message to the village council. They replied, "We would choose the oldest, most respected man in the group and ask him a question. He would discourse at length and then become silent, whereupon we would ask another question. As he talked, others would comment as well. But eventually the discussion would lessen and the leader would talk more. In this way we would develop our message so it would become the topic for discussion of the whole village." I asked them why they didn't employ this approach in church. "Why, we've been taught that monologue is the Christian way," they replied. "Can this be why no old men come to church?" I asked. "Of course—we have alienated them by not showing them due respect in public meeting," was their reply. Thus it is that a preaching form that may (or may not) be appropriate (dynamic equivalent) in American culture—loses its equivalence when exported to another culture, and is counter productive rather than facilitative with respect to the function such a form is intended to fulfill.[11]

3. The statuses accorded *good speakers* or orators in society have not been overlooked by social scientists. In some tribal societies, it is the orator who in fact rules. He does so not by the devious routes of modern democratic processes, but simply by engaging his rivals in a winner-take-all debating contest. Although orator societies in this sense are not

[10]Ibid., 74–89.
[11]Charles H. Kraft, "Dynamic Equivalence Churches," *Missiology* 1 (January 1973): 50–51.

numerous, almost all societies have a special place for the individual who can speak persuasively. In commenting on the high statuses that the French give to good speakers, for example, a former professor of mine once made the interesting observation that all over the world people hold the gifted speaker in higher regard than the gifted doer.

In New Testament times the people were so impressed by both powerful words and wondrous deeds that they associated them with the deities. Thus Paul in Lystra was called Mercurius (the god of eloquence) and Barnabas was called Jupiter (from his commanding mien, according to Chrysostom) (Acts 14:12 KJV). Herod had a great ability to use words to move men, but he failed to give glory to God for the ability and was judged accordingly (Acts 12:21–23). Apollos, on the other hand, was eloquent in expounding the Scriptures and used his ability to extend the kingdom (Acts 18:24–28). So far from being depreciated in the Scriptures, eloquence gets a high rating—not as something to be depended on in and of itself, but as something to be used in God's service.

He is an unusual missionary who achieves the kind of mastery in a second language that enables him to achieve the status and persuasiveness of native orators. But even the missionary who does not achieve this ability can recognize, encourage, and help in the training of such persons and thus advance the cause of Christ. The church of Christ in India would be poorer without the contribution of the persuasive Sundar Singh. The church in Japan would be weaker today had it not known the eloquent Joseph Niishima. The church in Ubangi would not have achieved its present place of influence without a powerful preacher like Pelendo. Eloquent orators are not numerous in the nature of the case. And orators who are candidates for salvation and Christian service may be few indeed. The future of the church does not rest in the eloquence of people any more than it rests on resources of earthly wealth or human wisdom (1 Cor. 2:1). But the number of missionaries who have been used of God in the salvation, calling, and education of greatly gifted preachers, and the number of nations and tribes that have been mightily blessed by the ministry of such preachers, constitute ample testimony to the value of prayer and alertness so that God might raise up such men and use them to His greater glory.

4. The role of the *sponsor* is important in certain societies—especially those that are face-to-face or tend to be traditional or closed to outsiders. Eugene Nida notes that the successful missionary to Peru John Ritchie entered only those villages where he could find a sponsor who would invite him to come and preach his message. As a result people listened to the foreigner and a certain credence was given to what he said. Ritchie was undoubtedly one of the most successful missionaries ever to go to South America, and was largely responsible for beginning over two hundred churches![12]

Alan Tippett has indicated that missionaries to the tribal villages in the South Sea Islands found it necessary to first approach the chief and secure his favor before speaking to the people. Missionary James Luckman in Ethiopia enjoyed an open door to most areas of that country because he made it a practice to introduce himself to royalty and government officials and secure their understanding and good offices. Paul himself was no stranger to this approach. He first visited synagogues—probably for practical as well as theological reasons. But whether there was a synagogue or not (perhaps there was none in Philippi, for example), he found those who would open hearts and homes to his apostolic band. Lydia and Jason thus became sponsors of Christian communication in their communities in Philippi and Thessalonica (Acts 16, 17).

Sponsors have statuses and roles that are formal or informal, well defined or ill defined, depending on the society. In some cases they are absolutely essential to missionary communication. In other cases, they simply aid the flow of communication by enlarging the audience, providing a platform, or lending credibility to the messenger and his message.

5. Like the sponsor, the *mediator* stands between the missionary and his respondents, but, unlike the sponsor, the

[12]Eugene A. Nida, *Message and Mission: The Communication of the Christian Faith* (New York: Harper & Row, 1960), 110.

mediator aids communication by actually delivering or interpreting the missionary's motive and message. Most societies find a place for mediators, at least in certain situations. But some cultures can be called "mediator cultures." In such societies communication would be drastically reduced and impaired if suddenly by fiat decree some autocrat were to insist that the role of mediators be immediately abolished. Business, politics, and government, and even affairs of love and marriage would come to an abrupt standstill, though we could probably count on human ingenuity to find ways of circumventing old communication patterns in order to carry on the business of living and loving!

To most Western minds the resort to mediators may seem a waste of time and an invitation to misunderstanding, if not an evidence of cowardice. The more delicate the situation and the more important the message, the greater the likelihood that we would react with disdain toward the person who employs a mediator. "Why doesn't he tell me (them) himself?" might well be our response. On the other hand, in certain areas of human interaction the Westerner is content to put his case in the hands of a mediator such as a lawyer or real estate agent, not simply because he lacks knowledge, but also because he desires to avoid personal confrontation.

When one becomes familiar with the advantages of mediators in such cases as the arrangement of marriages and the presentment of personal requests (in other cultures), one is better prepared, as the adage goes, to do as the Romans do when in Rome. In a society where people would be shamed by refusing a request in face-to-face communication, it is certainly easier to ascertain the true response of an individual by employing the good offices of a mediator. Even in the case of courtship there are advantages to receiving from a mediator the answer, "No, she's not interested," rather than a direct "No" from the girl of one's dreams!

Depending on the cultural patterns, wise missionaries will make good use of mediators and wise national Christian leaders will not be overly influenced by the direct communication approach that is so characteristic of the West.

Chapter 35

Kinship: Kindred and Lineage

In 1955 Donald McGavran published a book that he entitled *The Bridges of God*. The main thesis of that book is that the early church did not span the gulf between Jewish and Gentile societies and spread through Asia Minor and into Europe as a result of helter-skelter preaching and willy-nilly witnessing. McGavran believes that when Paul was in Antioch he discovered the key to the conversion of great multitudes of people in the Mediterranean world: preach to those who were prepared to listen by virtue of the fact that they were related to those who had already become Christians, or by virtue of the fact that in being related to the synagogues they would give the gospel a ready hearing.

While Paul worked with that Greek-Hebrew Antioch community for a year, he must have come to know hundreds of relatives of Christians and to hear of thousands more. Some of these relatives from Cyprus, Pisidia, Iconium, Lystra and Derbe had quite possibly come to Antioch during Paul's year there and had joined in his hours of instruction. According to the record some of the Christians who had first spoken of the faith to Greeks in Antioch had come from Cyprus. They probably belonged to families who had connections on both the island and the mainland. Having won their relatives in Antioch, it was natural for them to think of winning their unconverted relatives, Jews and Greeks, in Cyprus. . . .

How . . . did Paul choose fields of labour? To be accurate we must say that *he did not choose fields. He followed up groups of people who had living relations in the People Movement to Christ.* . . . Pisidia (Acts 13:14–50) is typical. . . . On the Sabbath Paul and his companions went to the synagogue. . . . The first messages of Paul were clearly messages for the Jews. . . . So after his first messages . . . "Jews and devout converts" followed him home, he then taught of the universality of Messiah. . . .

As far as Gentiles were concerned, his messages appealed mainly if not solely to those "on the bridge." The synagogue community was composed of Jews of the Hebrew race, Jews of the Greek race, and a fringe of believing but uncircumcised Greeks. It was thus a bridge into the Gentile community which Paul recognized and used. His message brought conviction to those on "the bridge." . . . Missionary labours of the early Church, headed by Paul, were devoted in large measure deliberately to following responsive peoples and to expanding existing impulses to Christ in the hearts of people.[1]

In these paragraphs are discoverable the concepts of people movements and responsive peoples—concepts that were elaborated at length by McGavran in subsequent publications. Our present concern is with his thesis that Paul's strategy was to follow up people who had "living relations in the 'People Movement to Christ.' " Contemporary missionary methodology does not adequately exploit these communication channels. Living relations do not receive enough attention at the practical level. Why? Some will fault our preoccupation with mass evangelism and its attendant weakness of

[1]Donald McGavran, *The Bridges of God: A Study in the Strategy of Missions* (New York: Friendship, 1955).

impersonal follow-up. One probably has to dig deeper for the real reasons, however. The family (nuclear or extended) is the basic social group in human societies. But as Francis L. K. Hsu has noted, "Though the family as the first human grouping is universally important, its importance to the individual varies enormously from society to society."[2] In old China the family was most important, in India it is somewhat less important, and in America the family is of still less importance. The difference becomes even more pronounced, however, when we examine the interaction patterns in consanguineal and affinal groupings that extend out from the family in the various societies.

Peter Hammond and others make a significant distinction at this point, i.e., the distinction between "kindred" and "lineage."[3] The term *kindred* is applied to that group of people to whom an individual (ego) can establish a genealogical bond through his parents and with whom he is reciprocally bound by certain conventions and obligations. Note that the kindred is "ego-focused" and that the composition of the kindred group which is important to ego and with whom relationships are living and vital will vary according to his age, situation, and interests. (See figure 25.)

The term *lineage* is applied to a group composed of all consanguineal kinsmen to whom an individual is related through one or the other of his parents and with whom he is bound in a system of conventions and obligations. The lineage is "ancestor-focused." All descendants of an ancestor become members of the lineage upon their birth and grow into a set of relationships with (and responsibilities toward) other members, and this set is predetermined and constant. The composition of the group does not change according to the needs and wishes of an ego, but only as new members are born into the group and as the older members die. Even in case of death, it is

[2]Francis L. K. Hsu, *Clan, Caste and Club* (Princeton, N.J.: Van Nostrand, 1963), 6.
[3]Peter B. Hammond, *An Introduction to Cultural and Social Anthropology* (New York: Macmillan, 1971), 169–721.

likely that the departed ancestor will continue to occupy an important place in the lineage grouping and will remain bound to the living in a very real sense. (See figure 26.)

Figure 25

THE KINDRED KINSHIP SYSTEM

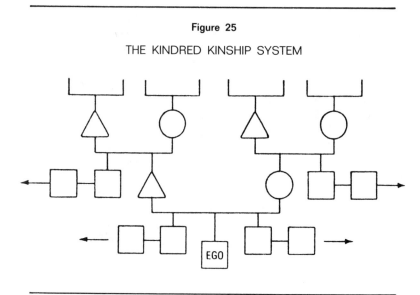

Kindred Kinship is based upon a relationship to "ego" through either parent (squares indicate persons of either sex) (adapted from Peter B. Hammond, *An Introduction to Cultural and Social Anthrolopology* [New York: The Macmillan Company, 1971], p. 170). Copyright © 1978 by Peter B. Hammond. Used by Permission.

The social system of the United States is basically of the kindred type. The kin of both parents are included among our relatives. Only rarely, however, do we give consideration to those who are more distant than second cousins. The term *relative* is vague for two primary reasons. First, since it is ego-focused, its composition varies for all members except full siblings. Second, its composition changes for ego himself according to his age and situation. When he is a child, he relates to his nuclear family and such other kinfolk as are important to his parents (proximity being a key factor). As he grows older, he may become interested in establishing a relationship with various other kin, especially at times of childbirths, christenings, graduations, weddings, funerals, and so on. When ego grows old, the composition of the kindred grouping may change dramatically due to the death of others in his own generation, the multiplication of descendants, and, in many cases in our society, by a rather general disregard for the very old.

Figure 26

THE LINEAGE KINSHIP SYSTEM

Common Ancestor
(often mythical)

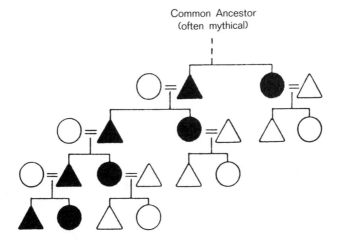

Kinsmen think of themselves as descended from a common ancestor through the male line (adapted from Peter B. Hammond, *An Introduction to Cultural and Social Anthropology* [New York: The Macmillan Company, 1971], p. 177). Copyright © 1978 by Peter B. Hammond. Used by permission.

The lineage groupings of old China and literally hundreds of tribal societies are at the other end of the continuum. In those societies the bloodline (either of the father or the mother, but not both) may well determine an individual's entire life pattern—education, vocation, marriage, care of elders and younger members of the lineage, religious obligations, and much more. Ego has comparatively little to say. Lineage members are bound together not simply for the sake of convenience and fellowship, but in order to sustain life, secure the good of every member, and perpetuate the ancestral line.

There are, of course, many variations of kindred and lineage relationships, but the basic distinction I have made here throws new light on the apparent inability of many Western missionaries to see the fundamental importance of the natural bridges to the unreached afforded by living relationships of blood and marriage. In the missionaries' own social system these bridges may be nonexistent or may have fallen into disuse and disrepair. Blood may be little thicker than water. Missionaries may be separated from aunts, uncles, cousins, and other kin, not only by hundreds or thousands of miles, but by infrequent contact and differing interests. The circle of relatives who maintain vital communication with the missionary may be small indeed. The circle is widened somewhat only in case of a family reunion or other affairs arranged at the discretion and initiative of someone who is a relative. Ancestors are soon forgotten. No wonder missionaries have been so ill prepared to recognize and properly evaluate the systems of other cultures where contact between kinfolk is not only carefully maintained but where kinfolk are interdependent to a degree that puts kinship interests above personal desires and ambition!

A good illustration of the importance of kinship factors to missionary communication is provided by Marian Cowan's report of a movement to Christ in Mexico.[4] Miss Cowan relates how the gospel entered the Tzotzil Indian tribe in Mexico through the "chance" meeting of a Tzeltal Christian and an unbelieving Tzotzil. She shows how the gospel spread

[4]Marian Cowan, "A Christian Movement in Mexico," *Practical Anthropology* 9 (September–October 1962): 193–204.

through the extended family and then to another family that held membership in the same economic cooperative group. In tabulating the instances of effective gospel communication among the Tzotzil (i.e., persons who became Christians), she notes that out of a total of eighty cases, thirty-nine occurred between consanguineal kin, thirty-eight occurred between affinal kin, and only three occurred between people who were unrelated by blood or marriage. She also records that of the eighty cases, seventy-five were from males to females! Among the Tzotzil and Tzeltal Indians kinship ties became natural bridges for the communication of the gospel. It is as though one member (especially an older, trusted, male member) of the family became a Christian and the whole extended family "plugged in" and waited to hear about Christ.

Chapter 36

Nonkinship Groupings

There are, of course, numerous groupings of people in which membership is determined on bases other than kinship. Although birth or marriage into a family of blue bloods in Boston may enable one to move within a certain social set, membership in that set will not likely be confined to the offspring of one ancestor and their spouses, nor will it be automatic. Good breeding means more than blood relationship in this case. Education, occupation, accomplishment, wealth—these and other factors are important and may, in fact, be paramount.

Nonkinship groups exist in all societies with the possible exception of extremely simple ones such as those of the Bushman or Eskimo. They are so pervasive and variegated that anthropologists and sociologists differ greatly in their approaches to the study of these groups. The British anthropologist Raymond Firth sees many of them as fulfilling the same overall function as the kinship groups and subsumes all of these under the category of *social structure.*[1] Within this

---

[1] Raymond Firth, *Elements of Social Organization* (Boston: Beacon, 1963), 29–40.

category he sees basic relationships arising from such considerations as position in a kinship system, the possession of ritual knowledge, status in regard to political superiors, and relation to the soil. Thus social structure includes such divergent groupings as family, clan, caste, age-sets, and certain secret societies. The crucial criterion for identifying components of social structure is that the relationships growing out of them are of such critical importance to the behavior of the members that the larger society would be significantly different apart from their existence. Their presence, therefore, is determinative of the form of society and tends to perpetuate that form.

The study of social structure alone, however, would not account for social change. In the existential situation, forces of constancy and continuity are buffeted by the forces of adaptation and change. Groupings that harness and direct the forces of change are categorized as *social organizations* by Firth. In social organizations people come together in order to evaluate alternative courses of belief and action, set future goals, and initiate change. While structures place a high priority on a steady state in society and are therefore more or less static, organizations accentuate ways and means of change and tend to be more dynamic. They include such diverse groupings as the Maryknoll Fathers, Rotarians, Parent-Teacher Associations, Red Cross, Young Republicans, and the National Association for the Advancement of Colored People—to name just a few from our society. Various covering terms have been applied to them such as voluntary associations, institutions, and sodalities. As an inclusive term each has utility, and each has limitations. By whatever name, social organizations abound in the West and are discoverable in most societies around the world.

The distinction we are making between social structure and social organization relates to the *gemeinschaft-gesellschaft* (community-association) contrast. Generally speaking, in traditional non-Western agrarian societies the emphasis is placed on the larger community and its primary groupings or collectivities of people. The social structure predominates, and change comes more slowly because individual initiative is more restricted. In Western industrial societies more emphasis is placed on secondary groupings, and individuals are more free to establish associations that meet common needs and are directed toward common goals.

In the New Testament the distinction is evident at various levels but in a uniquely significant way in the household community (oikonomia) on the one hand, and the unofficial associations of Christians (koinonia) on the other.[2] Especially in the Roman republic, the government allowed the pater familias to have almost complete control over his personal household composed of both bond and free individuals. Most households had their clientila including freedmen who retained a linkage with households in which they had formerly been slaves and others who associated with the household for mutual benefit. The oikonomia relationship entailed significant obligations on everyone connected with it. Its continuity was ensured by arranged and strategic marriages and, if the regular succession failed, by adoption. Its solidarity was expressed in a common religion—a fact that helps to explain the baptism of entire households in the New Testament.

One of the features of the Roman system that weakened the domination of the household or family in Greek society was the allowance for spontaneous associations or koinonia. Provided that no law was infringed, individuals could join together for common purposes. Some of these were officially recognized and some were not. The concern of the government seems to have been that they not cause disruption. Economic interests were sometimes an important consideration as in the case of the silversmiths at Ephesus (Acts 19:24, 27), but convivial gatherings seem to have been a most common feature. Since these often centered around one or another deity, Christians often found them to be embarrassing (cf. 1 Cor. 8:10). Of course, both Jews and Christians took

[2]E. A. Judge, The Social Pattern of the Christian Groups in the First Century (London: Tyndale Press, 1960), 30–48.

advantage of this kind of associational relationship. Although Christians met in various households, the composition of the church meetings was obviously wider than the household itself. And their common meals and activities paralleled those of other associations in many ways.

From a missionary perspective, all social groupings are important because they enable us to identify and evaluate the communication process in a given culture. The particular importance of the structure-organization differentiation is that it provides us with models of communication calculated to *maintain traditional beliefs and behavioral patterns* (primarily) when structures are operative, and to *initiate and accelerate change* when organizations are in view. Having already considered kinship groups independently, we will proceed to consider class in the Philippines as an example of nonkinship *structures*, and the neighborhood association of Japan as an example of social organizations.[3]

CLASS IN THE PHILIPPINES

Numerous developed societies are class societies. There are, however, wide divergencies in class structure from society to society as concerns the relative size of the various classes, the relationship between classes, and the possibility and means of mobility by which membership in one class is exchanged for membership in another. For example, in terms of mobility certain representative societies have been placed on a continuum (cf. figure 27).

Influenced by the relatively closed class system of Spain and the open system of the United States, Philippine society is located in a central position on the continuum and will serve as a good illustration of the interrelationship between class membership and communication patterns.

In an effort to understand Philippine society better, the leadership of an evangelical mission secured the services of anthropologist Marvin Mayers in the late 1960s. Mayers's

[3]By definition, social organizations are nonkinship groupings.

analysis was later published, and a part of his report is especially instructive concerning the relationship between class and communication.

Figure 27

OPEN AND CLOSED CLASS SOCIETIES

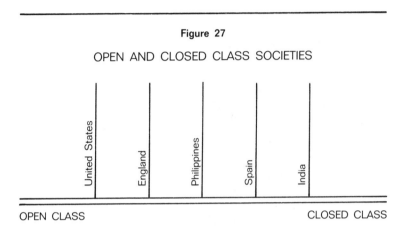

OPEN CLASS   CLOSED CLASS

There is an interpenetrating social class and status system operating in Philippine society. From an impersonal, general point of reference there are three social classes—upper, middle, and lower. These classes are determined primarily on the basis of behavioral expectations. A few examples of this behavior pattern are given below.

Upper class behavior is characterized by exceptional wealth, use of helpers such as driver, yard man, house girls (two or more), the use of English, wearing imported clothes, a brusqueness characterizing interaction (does not imply lack of concern), a potential for travel (especially to the U.S.), ownership of a vehicle for personal transportation, and a more formal garden plan than that characterizing the other two classes. Upper class occupations include plantation owners, managers of corporations, highly paid doctors, judges, etc.

Characteristics of middle class behavior include a regular income of 400 pesos or more (some say 250 pesos); one or two helpers in the house (with the helper doing the marketing), certain characteristics of clothing, including a better quality of clothing than most though not necessarily imported, the use by the women of shoes rather than slippers when in public, a neat garden but not as formal as the upper class (the woman responsible for the garden), a characteristic house decoration involving pictures (whereas lower class people use calendars and magazines). The playing of chess is generally a middle class activity, and they may own land averaging twenty hectares. Middle class occupations include those of lawyers, dentists, professors, small businessmen, pilots, government employees, inspectors and supervisors, higher-rank military, and some teachers and pastors.

Lower class people earn less than 400 (or 250) pesos a month, are generally involved in crafts and services, will tend to discuss issues of the day on street corners, and play dama (a game with twelve stones). Their occupations include jeepney, tricycle and bus drivers, laborers, carpenters, gardeners, masons, the average military personnel, most pastors, and farmers.

Upper, middle, and lower class designations are referred to generally within conversation. When respondents are pressed to indicate on what class level a person falls, he will generally indicate this with a certain amount of reluctance though his indication is confirmed by others. One can get insight into the class system through an understanding of that which is operating in North America. However, to assume that this is all that is going on within the society is to ignore a very vital part of the social mechanism operating in the Philippines. . . . Superimposed upon the class system is a status system with status ranking from a personal, specific point of reference. Everyone in the society knows those that are above them and below them in status. Members of an alliance group . . . share the same status as its head. Within the status system a person wishes to associate only with those who are on the same level of status as he, or above. At the same time, because of the restrictions imposed by a rank . . . system, the only ones that he really can associate with are those on the same status level and below. The outcome of such an associational relationship is that though you might wish to influence someone above you in statuses, you are in effect only able to influence those below you. Each person, upon meeting another, attempts to establish as accurately as possible the status of the other person. This will be the intent of his conversation unless he already knows by some previous acquaintance all about him. A new person coming into the society or moving into a different region within the country has a period of one to three years to establish his status. Those encountering the individual or institution will decide on a status ranking in terms of the consistency with which one follows the expected behavior patterns for a given class/status.

A large percentage of the people living in a society with a status system attempt to move up in status with every opportunity that comes to them and they may even make opportunity to move. There are five primary means to move up: (1) by an increase in salary; (2) by education up through the high school level that makes a student potential for a higher status level than that enjoyed by his family. Provincial college outside of Manila, college or university in Manila, and finally overseas education will each move a person further up the ladder. Education makes an individual potential for a higher salary. If he gains this higher salary, he can live on the level of his new status; (3) by having a number of higher status compadre/comadres; (4) by marriage, which is particularly useful for girls. Whenever a boy of lower status marries a girl of higher status a certain prearranged sum of money changes hands in order to more nearly balance the status level; and (5) by receiving a windfall or winning a lottery and investing all or part of this money that gives him potential for a higher status. In reality this is a most difficult thing to accomplish because of the reciprocal obligation pattern.

One can move down the status system through bad judgment (e.g., in continued losses in gambling), or bad luck (e.g., when accident wipes out the finances of a family), or a combination of the two (e.g., when someone continues to overplant during a drought period).

Security within the status system is achieved by having an extensive association through the alliance system with one's peer group; extensive contact with higher statuses through the mechanism of ritual extension of the family, i.e., the compadre relationship; and by having an extensive network of mutual obligation within statuses lower than one's own.[4]

With this background, and confining ourselves to the North American missionary for purposes of illustration, the missionary to the Philippines would do well to give special attention to several new factors and to their ramifications for the communication of Christ.

1. The missionary will most likely establish a new class identification in Filipino society. In most situations his North American origin will lend him a certain prestige. Economically, the average missionary income will probably be equal to those in the upper classes, though this will vary greatly with the area. Educationally, he will be among the more advantaged. The fact that he is English-speaking will also enhance his social standing. The net result of these factors may well be membership in a class in the Philippines that is relatively higher than that to which the missionary belonged in North America. If the missionary had been a member of the middle or lower middle class in Iowa City, he will be (or has the potential to be) a member of the upper middle or lower upper class in Cebu City. This can be visualized (cf. figure 28).

This should not be interpreted to mean that now that the missionary has a chance to join the more elite of a society he should jump at it. What we are saying is that the missionary is entering a new social situation in which he is not shut up to membership in, or identification with, the class to which he belonged in his home culture. Many factors enter into the new situation, some of which relate to the personality and abilities of the missionary himself. These may well serve to restrict his options. He certainly does not have a *carte blanche* enabling him to write his own ticket in the new society. But he does

[4]Marvin K. Mayers, *Background Notes on Christian Outreach in a Philippine Community* (Pasadena: William Carey Library, 1970), 4–6.

have new and exciting possibilities with some important missionary implications.

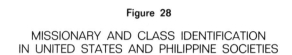

Figure 28

MISSIONARY AND CLASS IDENTIFICATION
IN UNITED STATES AND PHILIPPINE SOCIETIES

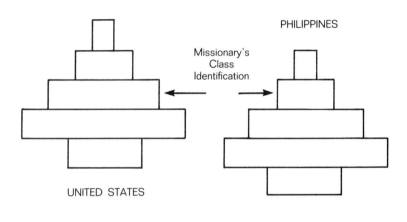

PHILIPPINES

Missionary's
Class
Identification

UNITED STATES

First, the missionary should be sensitive to the problem of class identification both in his own background and as an important consideration in missionary strategy in the Philippines. For example, if he is from a middle-class background, he should not allow that fact to dictate that he work only, initially, or mainly with middle-class Filipinos.

C. Peter Wagner writes that middle-class missionaries have often theorized that by winning members of the middle class in their respondent cultures, they would eventually reach members of the lower classes.[5] This is probably true. But

[5]C. Peter Wagner, *Look Out! The Pentecostals Are Coming* (Carol Stream, Ill.: Creation, 1973).

491

it should be added that in many (if not most) cases, middle-class missionaries have not worked with middle-class respondents as a result of carefully laid strategy to reach members of the lower classes. Rather, being members of the middle class in their native society, they have identified with the middle class in their respondent culture *as a matter of course.* In so doing, they rather uncritically have entertained the hope that this would ultimately eventuate in the conversion of some of the elite and many poorer people—a hope that in most cases has not been realized. As a matter of fact, missionaries from lower-class backgrounds who rather naturally have identified with the masses in the Philippines have had a certain advantage due to the propagation potential of the lower class.

Figure 29

HORIZONTAL AND VERTICAL COMMUNICATION COMPARED

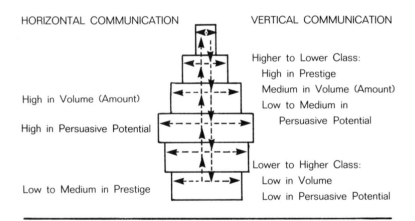

HORIZONTAL COMMUNICATION

High in Volume (Amount)

High in Persuasive Potential

Low to Medium in Prestige

VERTICAL COMMUNICATION

Higher to Lower Class:
High in Prestige
Medium in Volume (Amount)
Low to Medium in Persuasive Potential

Lower to Higher Class:
Low in Volume
Low in Persuasive Potential

Second, the missionary to the Philippines should consider seriously his new potential for communicating the gospel to the elite. This possibility takes on great significance when one stops to realize that the average Filipino pastor-evangelist finds it extremely difficult to establish lines of communication with those above on the socioeconomic scale. It is important, therefore, that missionaries exploit this potential. One of the key ideas in Mayers's proposed strategy for outreach in the Philippines is that missionaries cultivate contacts with the elite. Noting that Americans come into Filipino society at a high level of status, he suggests that they endeavor to maintain that level in order to assure penetration into all parts of the society. He feels that this approach can open up the entire country to the gospel.[6]

Third, the missionary may have a special responsibility to reach the lower classes in the Philippines. There are pitfalls, of course. People are often attracted to the missionary for purposes of self-aggrandizement. Rice Christians are still a very real possibility in the Philippines. One missionary on one of the southern islands has attracted great throngs to the services of his church by giving free meals and handsomely rewarding people who bring newcomers. Although it is noble to feed the hungry, such a program is questionable from several standpoints. But identification with people in need is certainly Christian. And unlike his Filipino counterpart, the missionary can identify with the masses without a significant threat to his own status. If he can learn to "speak their language" and is able to win their confidence, he may be greatly used to win many of the common people—members of that same class who in the first century heard Christ gladly.

2. The future course of Christianity in any given area will be greatly affected by the class membership of the people who initially hear and respond to the Christian gospel. This is so because of the nature of communication and interaction between classes. Normally, horizontal communication within a class is quantitatively greater and qualitatively more persuasive than is vertical communication; communication from sources in the higher classes to respondents in the lower classes is, of course, *prestigious*, but is not necessarily *persuasive* on that account. Vertical communication from members of lower classes to those of the higher classes is

[6]Mayers, *Background Notes*, 16.

infrequent and the least persuasive of all (unless members of the lower classes band together and establish some kind of a power base from which to speak). While the information given in figure 29 would have to be validated in any particular cultural context, it may be valuable for comparative purposes and in furnishing hypotheses as a starting point for study.

Churches as well as other institutions reflect sociological facts of life. Early on, it was clearly demonstrated, for example, that American churches are basically class churches. P. E. Kraemer drew on recognized sources in the following ranking of U.S. denominations:

Upper class:	Episcopalian and Unitarian
Upper middle class:	Presbyterian, Congregational, and Reformed
Middle class:	Methodist, Lutheran, Baptist, Disciples, Evangelical Reformed, and Christian Reformed
Lower class:	"Sects"[7]

The same phenomenon can be observed around the world. On any given Sunday, a visitor to Bombay, India, would be able to attend three Protestant churches that are located within a stone's throw of each other—one low class, one middle class, and one upper class. (Think of caste as "congealed class.") A visit to these churches would convince the thoughtful observer that their class character makes it highly unlikely that any of the three will cross social barriers and have an effective ministry to those of another class. However, it is much more likely that the high-class Indian could minister to those of the lower classes than it is that a member of the lower classes could minister to those above him.

[7]Cf. Joel H. Nederhood, *The Church's Mission to the Educated American* (Grand Rapids: Eerdmans, 1960), 31. The denominational identifications reflect the ecclesiastical situation at the time of the study.

Turning once again to the Philippines, since Philippine society is typically a class society, the missionary communicator can safely hypothesize the following:

First, missionaries will usually find it advantageous to contact members of the upper classes initially. If members of the upper classes become Christian, their conversion may aid (or, at least will not hinder) the evangelization of the middle and lower classes. If members of the upper class are unresponsive, their rejection of Christ is not likely to deter members of the other classes from entering the faith.

Second, the great potential for propagating Christianity in Philippine society that exists among the members of the lower classes should not be overlooked by missionary strategists. George Foster says that most changes occur among the upper classes and then spread downward to the lower classes and outward from the city to the countryside.[8] Foster's conclusion, however, may possess greater validity in the case of technological innovation than in the case of religious conversion. In C. Peter Wagner's discussion of class and church growth in Latin America, he contends that religious movements in general move from the lower classes upward, not only in Latin America, but throughout the world.[9] Foster's position may seem to be more in accord with what I have said about vertical communication, while Wagner's contention may seem to be out of keeping with the rather low value I have placed on suasive communication moving upward from the proletariat. This is not necessarily the case, however, because Wagner goes on to defend his conclusion by explaining the phenomenon of upward social mobility in Latin America. Redeemed lower-class people live more moral and industrious lives and tend to rise on the social ladder. As they rise, they communicate the gospel horizontally to higher-class peoples in accordance with their newly achieved status. Thus the gospel

[8]George M. Foster, *Traditional Cultures: and the Impact of Technological Change* (New York: Harper & Row, 1962), 29.
[9]Wagner, *Look Out!* 71.

permeates the society upward as members of the lower classes are won to Christ.

Third, once there is a movement Christward within any class in a Philippine community, a concerted effort should be made *within that class* to bring as many as possible to faith in Christ and into the fellowship of a local church. Donald McGavran refers to this as "discipling to the fringes" and applies it to every homogeneous grouping of people. Simultaneous and indiscriminate missionizing cannot be expected to be as fruitful as missionizing that concentrates on people who understand one another and "speak the same language." Many local churches in the Philippines (as well as elsewhere) do have representatives from more than one class. But in the typical church the members of one or another class tend to predominate. In any case, we are not advocating that all churches be exclusive classwise, but rather that the membership be deployed in a concerted effort to take the gospel to those with whom they will naturally be able to communicate most intelligently and persuasively.

3. As would be the case in numerous developing societies where education is a significant means of upward mobility, missionaries in the Philippines must be aware of the problems connected with "educating out of class." Just as a new potential for evangelism accompanies the rise of Christians on the social scale, so a new danger appears also. Christians may lose contact with (and even the ability to communicate with) members of the class they leave behind. This phenomenon can occur at two levels. First, *an entire church* may be educated out of class by virtue of the fact that mission aid, increased productivity, new opportunities for education, and other factors result in this upward mobility. Second, *church workers* may be educated out of class with the result that it becomes difficult for them to communicate with their own people and unlikely that they will be able to raise up responsible churches within the class of their origin (cf. figure 30).

Certainly it is desirable for Filipino Christians to better their lot. Better sanitation, more wholesome food, increased literacy—these and many other benefits can be expected to attend a knowledge of the Creator and Savior of us all. But the fact remains that as the people of God better their position in society they are often cut off from previous contacts. Old social ties are broken as Christians move to better areas, attain new positions in their occupations, and communicate in new and unfamiliar terms. Relationships in the higher classes to which progressive Filipinos aspire may not be easy to attain at first due to the reluctance of members of higher classes to receive newcomers as equals. Christian leaders and church members need to be made aware of what is happening and be guided in their outreach. There is always the danger, despite the great opportunity Christians have to reach the entire society, that the churches may become islands in middle- and upper-class communities with a minimum of living relationships that can be used to advantage in Christian communication.

Figure 30

EDUCATING OUT OF CLASS

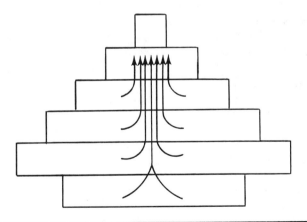

Furthermore, though Philippine churches desperately need quality leadership, they do not have either a great number of ready-made positions for highly trained leaders or the support base to compensate such leaders adequately. There is a rather widespread feeling that many Filipinos who have gone to the West (principally to the United States) for graduate-level training have not returned to the Philippines because of a lack of positions with challenge and compensation commensurate with their educational attainments. To the extent to which this is true there is, of course, a spiritual side to the problem. But an understanding of the social factors involved must be gained before missionaries and nationals can really come to grips with the problem in its larger dimensions. Education gives young Filipinos the credentials for identification with the higher stratas of society and affords the skills that enable them to successfully fill roles associated with higher statuses. At the same time, the Protestant pastor, qua pastor, is not accorded a very high status. If the educated minister has a low-class origin, therefore, he may find himself in a peculiar position in which he is out of phase with his society. Depending on the criterion employed, he could be identified with various classes. He may find himself without a class home.

For example, a young man from a plantation laborer's family is converted. Over a period of time he manages to secure a good secular and theological education in Manila. On entering the ministry in, say, Bacolod City, he finds himself in the anomalous situation confronted by a significant number of Filipino pastors. His education is equal to the education of the higher classes. His image as a Protestant pastor pegs him as a member of the middle class. But his income as a pastor allows him to live at a level not much higher than that of a common laborer. And he still retains many of the marks of his low class origin (cf. figure 31). The result is an identity crisis that, for good or ill, profoundly affects his ability (and willingness) to communicate the message of Christ.

The pastor with upper-middle- or upper-class background may have a similar problem because the image and salary of the average Protestant pastor do not allow him to maintain the higher status to which he may otherwise be entitled (cf. figure 32).

Figure 31

POTENTIAL CLASS IDENTIFICATION OF A
FILIPINO PASTOR OF LOWER-CLASS ORIGIN

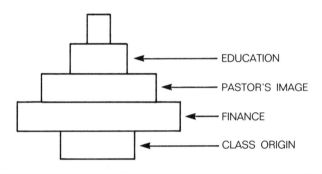

EDUCATION

PASTOR'S IMAGE

FINANCE

CLASS ORIGIN

The diagrams are, or course impressionistic but may be valuable in pointing up the tensions that many Protestant pastors experience in finding a status and role that enable them to be at home in their own society. Instead of communicating horizontally, they "speak up" (or up and down simultaneously) to their respondents, depending on the criterion (criteria) employed in judging their status.

Missionaries must be willing to encourage Filipinos to step into such leadership roles as are available and now occupied by missionaries and also to work to enhance the image and effectiveness of pastors so that promising young men will aspire to the ministry and churches will more adequately support their pastors. Above all, sensitivity to their problems is required. Viable solutions can be built only on an understanding of what is involved.

Figure 32

POTENTIAL CLASS IDENTIFICATION OF A
FILIPINO PASTOR OF UPPER-CLASS ORIGIN

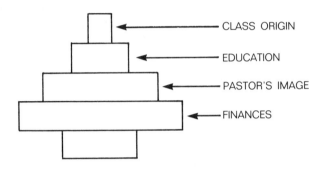

CLASS ORIGIN

EDUCATION

PASTOR'S IMAGE

FINANCES

NEIGHBORHOOD ASSOCIATIONS IN JAPAN

While social structures tend toward the preservation of traditional benefits and values, most societies also have social organizations in which members voluntarily come together in order to accomplish ends not entertained by the larger society or toward which the larger society moves too slowly or uncertainly. These groups—especially those that are indigenous to the target culture—provide the missionary with ready-made patterns of the ways in which indigenes communicate and interact with each other when proposed changes or necessary tasks call for special cooperation by concerned members of the society. From the countless social organizations that exist in societies around the world, we will take the *tonarigumi* (neighborhood association) of Japan by way of illustration to point up the importance of these phenomena to missions.

The *tonarigumi* is another instance of the selective

cultural borrowing that has characterized Japan's development. Leaders of the Taika Reform in the seventh century took a cue from the Chinese Tang government and formed every fifty families into a *sato*, and each *sato* into groups of five called *goho*, each with a responsible elder.[10] The system met important needs for a considerable period of time but gradually fell into disuse.

When, however, rigid control over the citizenry became the policy of the government in Tokugawa times (1607–1867), these neighborhood associations were revived in a modified form and made into effective instruments again. They collected revenues, imposed sanctions, and defended local communities against marauding bandits.

The Meiji Restoration of the late nineteenth century uprooted the Tokugawa system and the neighborhood associations were officially abandoned. By that time, however, this method of organizing at the local level to fulfill community needs was so ingrained in Japanese society that the *tonarigumi* persisted on a wide scale as a result of voluntary initiative. Used to the advantage of the militarists during the period leading up to and including World War II, they were banned again by the terms of surrender in 1945. Not a few perceptive analysts of postwar SCAP policies view its opposition to neighborhood associations as a case of bad judgment because of their potential for communicating the ideals of democracy.

In any case, neighborhood associations have once again proved their viability and persistency in the postwar period. All over Japan these groups have been revived. As early as 1955 they had been revived in 32 percent of all block units of housing in Tokyo and in 66 percent of outlying neighborhoods.[11] If the family is the basic unit of social structure in Japan, the *tonarigumi* is the basic unit of social organization. Almost everyone in a given *buraku* (neighborhood) belongs to several organizations or associations such as the Funeral

---

[10]Cf. Joseph J. Spae, *Neighborhood Associations: A Catholic Way for Japan* (Himeji, Japan: Committee of the Apostolate, c/o Catholic Church, 1956).

[11]Ibid., 30–31.

Association, the Fire Association, the Young Peoples' Association, the Farmers' Cooperative Association, or the Parent-Teachers' Association. But their primary identification will most likely be made with the Neighborhood Association that many of these other organizations are patterned after and to which many of them are related. Its members meet regularly (usually monthly), but special meetings may be called to deal with extraordinary problems. Its members maintain the community hall, and the shrine and temple grounds. They conduct local festivals. They may be called on to act as a kind of community court in order to settle local disputes, thus avoiding the embarrassment and expense of formal litigation.

The association serves as a means of communication by circulating a *kairamban* or informal bulletin that is signed by a member of each household as it is circulated through the community. When members come together for meetings, a spirit of camaraderie is fostered. The peculiar feeling of Japanese vis-à-vis the meetings is revealed in expressions that are often used to describe them: *kojo* (close fellowship), *jita-fuji no kyo* (the state where there is no distinction between you and me), *sogo-shinai* (mutual love), *shinrai* (confidence), *kyodo* (collaboration), and *rentaisekininkan* (sharing of responsibility).[12]

Father Joseph Spae agrees with C. R. Boxer that it was the potential for this type of communication, cooperation, and sense of community that enabled Catholic Christianity to survive during the early persecutions. Boxer says:

> It was this organization which was the means of preserving Christianity in secret for more than two centuries in southwest Kyushu, without the presence of any foreign missionaries, and cut off from all communication with the outer world.[13]

[12]Ibid., 31, 100.
[13]Ibid., 34.

Another indication of the viability of neighborhood associationlike organization in Japan is the importance that the so-called new religions have given to community groupings. The Soka Gakkai, for example, turned to the *zadankai* (discussion meeting) as its primary instrument of propagation during the mid-1950s. The *zadankai* exhibits most of the important features of the neighborhood associations. They are neighborhood-oriented. They meet regularly in the home of a believer. Notice of extraordinary meetings is easily communicated. The *zadankai* fosters a strong sense of belonging. It serves as a primary agency for passing on information from Soka Gakkai headquarters while winning new converts and instructing believers. The ability to recognize and utilize the communication potential of the *zadankai* is certainly one of the secrets of the astounding success of Soka Gakkai in Japan in growing from about five thousand adherents in 1950 to over fifteen million at the present time.

Unfortunately, most Christian missions and churches have been slow to learn from either secular or non-Christian religious organizations, not only in Japan, but generally throughout the world. It is time to correct this myopia of the ecclesia. When we carefully examine organizations such as the neighborhood associations (and the Soka Gakkai *zadankai*) of Japan, we receive important clues about the way indigenes communicate and relate to each other when they voluntarily join together to accomplish common objectives. Father Spae has suggested that the impersonal, one-way communication characteristic of the Catholic mass, for example, is insufficient for Japan and that Catholic neighborhood associations are needed to provide opportunity for more intimate, participative communication in the context of small groups.

The same conclusion could be drawn in relation to Protestant evangelistic and worship services. Astute observers agree that mass evangelism in Japan must be augmented by more personal approaches. And it is well known that Protestant churches tend to stop growing when the membership reaches about thirty or forty. It seems rather obvious that in Japan, at least, effective evangelism and church growth must come to grips with the pattern of communication inherent in the interrelationships of the neighborhood associations. Until the local churches grow to the outer limits of small group size, the entire membership can quite easily relate to each other in a satisfying manner. As they grow larger, however, special attention must be given to fulfilling the need for belongingness and participation that characterizes the *tonarigumi*.

From the perspective of communication, neighborhood associations (and similar organizations) demonstrate the importance of augmenting vertical communication with effective horizontal communication in Japan. They also illustrate ways in which this can be done as Christian leaders learn from these models.

1. The place of meeting should be in a home or other appropriate neutral place in the community where the members reside. This facilitates communication and encourages the attendance of prospective members.

2. A group leader should be chosen. Ideally he would be an older, married man, an opinion leader, and one who is skilled in guiding small-group discussion. His responsibilities would include the maintaining of regular communication with the members, directing the activities of the group, and leading the meetings and discussions. From the standpoint of communication, he can best be viewed as one who receives and assimilates the message received vertically from God through his Word, the great teachers of the Word, and the local missionary or pastor. He then redirects that message horizontally by means of face-to-face, participative discussion at the community level.

3. Meetings should be kept informal and should include Scripture reading and prayer, Bible study, testimonies, sharing of problems, singing, the announcements of scheduled meetings and activities, discussion of ways and means to fulfill the purposes of the group, games, and so forth. Everyone should be encouraged to participate. The atmosphere must be warm and cordial.

4. The members should be encouraged to keep open channels of communication on all important matters relating

to other members and also between members and their nonmember friends and relatives. By communicating concern in cases of illness or bereavement, and congratulations in cases of baptism, marriage, births, and special achievement, members achieve a sense of belongingness. By encouraging group participation in community projects that do not entail a compromise of Christian principles, the group may achieve an acceptance that churches seldom achieve in the context of Japanese culture.

Throughout the world there are numerous illustrations of religious organizations that have achieved great success in propagating their teachings within their respective cultures. Often their success is due in large measure to the fact that they have learned from indigenous models of social organization. To the degree that Western missions have influenced the practice of the Christian churches in these lands, the churches often seem foreign, not only in the content of their teachings, but (more importantly) in the ways in which they propagate their teachings and indoctrinate believers.

The Japanese churches are cases in point. The neighborhood associations may well provide the key for effectively communicating Christ in a new area. More than that, they may provide the key to continued growth in existing churches. By establishing neighborhood groups *along Japanese lines* local churches can accelerate their own growth and begin new churches. In the case of unbelievers this pattern could result in a new awareness of the Christian message and a realization that they could actually receive it as their own faith. In the case of believers it could result in a new strength with which to face the tests and difficulties that inevitably attend conversion. It could also produce a new sense of belongingness that is so necessary to continuation and growth in the Christian faith.

Chapter 37

Urban and Rural Societies

CITY SOCIETIES

To the unreflective observer the city is different from the countryside simply because it has crowds of people, tall buildings, lots of excitement, and increased economic opportunity. But the differences are, of course, much deeper and more important. Cities and villages may represent entirely different sets of problems and potentialities—to the missionary as well as to any other advocate of change. Years ago Leonard Reissman wrote,

> For better or worse, the world is on its way to becoming massively urban, and the quaint peasant societies and primitive cultures still hidden in the backwaters and untouched for centuries are now, for the most part, doomed. The nations of the West have long since been transformed and those on other continents are soon to be. Walden Pond is a chimera, a bit of nostalgia that represents for some an imaginary retreat from the city and the world pressures of the moment. We have come to the stage where Walden is only to be reached by a super-highway, through the televi-

sion-antenna forest, and directed all the way by road signs. Urbanism is inundating all areas of the world and its force is a testament to the nature of man himself and the potency of the product he has created.[1]

Harvey Cox agreed and concluded that historians of the future may look back on the twentieth century as that century when the world became "one vast city."[2]

A trek through the jungles and grasslands of central Africa would lead one to believe that these statements are somewhat overdrawn. But statistics lend credence to them. By the year 2000 more than half of the world's projected population of 6.2 billion will probably live in cities of one hundred thousand people or more.[3] Moreover, the swiftest pace of urban growth has shifted from advanced nations to the less developed nations such as those of South America and Africa.[4]

This trend is in accord with the plan of God for his people, for in spite of the ills of man's cities, God will ultimately establish a new Jerusalem as the perfect environment for his redeemed ones. Thus man who was created in a garden will find his home in a city when he is recreated. Commenting on this, Jacques Ellul says that God chooses the city because man has chosen it. What man has always built but never perfected, the Creator will give to him as a perfect work.[5]

The city is therefore of special importance to missions simply because it is there—a growing phenomenon with a large place in the future whether that future is thought of as man's future or God's! It is important for at least two other compelling reasons. First, God has always seen to it that his message was sent to the cities. The major missionary book in

---

[1]Leonard Reissman, *The Urban Process: Cities in Industrial Societies* (New York: Free Press, 1964), 9–10.

[2]Cf. Harvey Cox, "Mission in a World of Cities," *International Review of Missions* 55 (July 1966): 273.

[3]David B. Barrett, "Annual Statistical Table on Global Mission: 1988," *International Bulletin of Missionary Research* 12,1 (January 1988): 16–17.

[4]Ibid., 44.

[5]Jacques Ellul, *The Meaning of the City* (Grand Rapids: Eerdmans, 1970), 174.

the Old Testament records God's concern that his prophet Jonah preach to Nineveh, "that great city" (Jonah 1:2 KJV). The obvious strategy of the great missionary strategist of the New Testament, the apostle Paul, was to reach the important cities. Second, cities are focal points of change. When anthropologist George Foster writes that most changes occur in the city among the upper classes and spread downward to the lower classes and outward to the countryside, he is referring specifically to social and economic changes.[6] Nevertheless, even in the case of religious change, a visit to Bombay, Bangkok, Tokyo, and Manila, or to Nairobi, Kinshasa, and Ibadan will convince one that there is a tremendous concentration of potential for Christian evangelism and growth in the cities.

Over two decades ago, sociologist Louis Wirth defined the city in a way that was generally acceptable at that time: "a relatively large, dense, and permanent settlement of socially heterogeneous peoples."[7] From a communication perspective, some important characteristics of Wirth's understanding were as follows:

Large size:

There are many face-to-face contacts in the city, but they are impersonal, superficial, transitory, segmental, and utilitarian. A city-dweller tends to be free from the control of intimate groups, but loses the capacity for self-expression, and a sense of participation, and has a lowered morale. Mass communication is paramount.

Density:

City populations tend to be patterned ecologically in concentric circles or zones with a business district in the center enveloped by a transitional zone, the area of working men's homes, a zone of better homes, and then the suburbs or commuter zone that rings large cities. Competition is

---

[6]George M. Foster, *Traditional Cultures: and the Impact of Technological Change* (New York: Harper & Row, 1962), 29.

[7]Louis Wirth, "Urbanism As a Way of life," in Sylvia Fava, *Urbanism in the World Perspective: A Reader* (New York: Crowell, 1968), 49.

keen, exploitation prominent, and a secular approach to life is dominant. City-dwellers become isolated and lonely (Emile Durkheim used the word "anomie"), and experience friction and frustration. Caste lines are broken. Traditional bases of social solidarity are undermined.

Heterogeneity:

Class structure is complicated. Social organizations (associations) assume vital importance to the individual, but no single group has undivided allegiance of its members and membership is fluid. Mass media communication tends to level society.

This more or less classic view of the city has subsequently been challenged, however. On the basis of his experiences in Asian cities where he has lived (Rangoon, Bangkok, Djakarta, and Calcutta), Phillip M. Hauser concludes that they evidence more of the characteristics of folk society as set forth by Robert Redfield.[8] Some of the most important of these as concerns communication are: nonliteracy, homogeneous groups, strong family ties, pronounced group solidarity, conventional behavioral patterns, strong emphasis on status, lack of systematic knowledge, and an orientation toward the sacred. Hauser's criticism of Wirth and the classic view of the city is well taken. Ethnic minorities such as the Chinese emigrants in many Asian cities maintain strong family and clan ties, and they perpetuate traditional values. P. C. Lloyd has demonstrated that town relationships tend to be continued as Africans move into the larger cities.[9]

Certainly there is a great difference between cities, and particularly between industrial and preindustrial cities. Preindustrial cities tended to remain rather isolated from the countryside. They still exhibit many of the societal arrangements of the rural areas. Much of the wealth and power

[8]Philip M. Hauser, "Application of Ideal-Type Constructs to the Metropolis in the Economically Less-Advantaged Areas," in Fava, *Urbanism*, 93–97.

[9]Cf. P. C. Lloyd, *Africa in Social Change: West African Societies in Transition* (New York: Praeger, 1968).

remains outside the city with the great landowners. The preindustrial city does not possess the means of communication and transportation for effectively influencing rural populations. But technology changes all that. With industrialization the center of economic power shifts to the city, the labor force gathers, and a new middle class emerges with the urge and inventiveness to innovate and change. The result tends to be a critical change in class structure, kinship ties, education, and traditional value and belief systems. These changes seem to be in the direction of the classic sociological view of the city as represented by Wirth—a view that, after all, grew out of the study of industrialized cities in the West. The process and technical contents of industrialization may be diverse, but the social consequences are often the same, as Wirth and his colleagues have noted.[10] It is imperative, therefore, that we distinguish between industrial and preindustrial cities. At the same time, there is still the danger of overgeneralization. In the final analysis, cities are of many diverse types.

Missionary communicators make a grave mistake if they think of their target cities in the Third World as sociological hodgepodges and engage only in undifferentiated mass communication. Ibadan is populated by Yoruba, Hausa, and other tribespeople, and these people are very different, as civil strife in Nigeria in the 1960s made evident. Mandarin-speaking Chinese in Hong Kong tend to be more entrepreneurial and amenable to change than are most other Chinese. Moreover, the inhabitants of the well-known resettlement projects in Hong Kong have a living pattern that makes evangelism and follow-up by conventional means exceedingly difficult. In addition, the higher classes often live behind locked gates and doors and are attended by servants—a combination that complicates the task of Christian communicators. The *danchi* (housing complexes) in Tokyo and other large cities in Japan call for new approaches in evangelism and indoctrination. They cannot be overlooked because they are the wave of the future. In ten or twenty years some of them will house

[10]Reissman, *The Urban Process*, 179.

populations greater than those of some of the old prefectural capitals. They are of different types, however, with age-level, family-size, and class identification largely determined by the type of housing and rental requirements. They therefore require special study and selective strategies.

Missionaries to cities who want to be good stewards of the gospel must stop to investigate and evaluate. They must find out where the various classes live, what included ethnic groups are present, where newcomers tend to locate, and other demographic data. They must discover the relative importance of nuclear and extended-family ties as over against free-associational ties. They need to know the kinds of concerns that are entertained by the various groups. They must determine what ties are maintained with rural populations. Only when this information is available to the missionary is he equipped to devise communication strategies.

PEASANT AND TRIBAL SOCIETIES

Rapid urbanization should not blind us to the fact that more than half of the world's population presently (about one-half billion more) live outside the cities.[11] Rural areas have commanded the attention and energies of missionaries throughout the period of modern missions and will continue to do so.

It is important to distinguish two fundamentally different types of rural societies. One type is tied to the city in the sense that the city is the source of much of the community's resources, whether of finance, material goods, or new ideas and values. The other type is isolated and self-contained. It views the city from afar, if at all. The first type of rural society is variously designated as folk, village, traditional, or peasant society. The words *primitive* and *tribal* are usually applied to the second type (cf. figure 33).

Peasant and tribal societies have much in common when compared to the city. They tend to be more homogeneous and

[11]Barrett, "Annual Statistical Table," 16–17.

more traditional in their lifestyle and value systems, present considerable resistance to change, and may take a negative attitude toward outsiders who come to tell them what to do. The social structure tends to flatten out with less distance from top to bottom and increased possibilities for face-to-face communication between those of high and low status. Leadership is therefore in closer touch with those at the grass roots of society. The structures of society in general—and kinship groups in particular—tend to predominate, and social organizations are of somewhat lesser import. Since everyone seems to know everyone else, individuals are hesitant to make major decisions on their own. Decisions are likely to be group decisions, whether arrived at through formal or informal processes. Time is therefore required to initiate change. The general cultural orientation is sacred, and the sacred-secular distinction is often obliterated with a blending of religious and social activities and even of religion and technology.

Figure 33

THE CITY-PEASANT-TRIBAL CONTINUUM

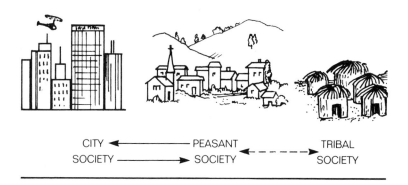

CITY ◄———————— PEASANT ———————► TRIBAL
SOCIETY ————————► SOCIETY ◄— — — —► SOCIETY

It would be a mistake, however, to think that peasant and tribal societies share these characteristics to the same degree or evidence them in the same ways. By virtue of their history of interaction with the city, inhabitants of the peasant community are less naïve in selecting from city ways and city ideas. On the other hand, many of the decisions affecting peasant village life are actually made in the city—a fact that sometimes results in uncritical acceptance of the inevitable and a type of fatalism. Cohesion and homogeneity are bombarded not only from without but also from within as certain members of the peasant village are attracted to the city and disdain the status of country bumpkins.

Tribal groups are more closely banded together under their leaders, who may be the only ones who can make decisions. On the other hand, leaders may be much less free to initiate change than appearances would indicate. Tribal chiefs and elders may be extremely sensitive to the desires of the members of the tribe, who therefore exercise a great influence even though they would not hazard a decision independent of the leadership. When contact with the outside world results in dissatisfaction with the deprivations of primitive living, the decision to adopt new ways may be abrupt and dramatic.

After emphasizing the distinction between peasant and primitive societies as indicated above (which, of course, is elaborated at much greater length in anthropological literature on the topic), Eugene Nida suggested four basic principles by which missionary communication to these face-to-face communities should be governed:

1. Effective communication must be based on personal friendship.
2. The initial approach should be to those who can effectively pass on communication within their family grouping.
3. Time must be allowed for the internal diffusion of new ideas.
4. The challenge for any change of belief or action must be addressed to the persons or groups socially capable of making such decisions.[12]

[12]Eugene A. Nida, *Message and Mission: The Communication of the Christian Faith* (New York: Harper & Row, 1960), 110.

A rationale and field experience can be marshaled in support of each of these principles. Some of the most critical issues in communicating the gospel to peasant and primitive societies are related to *ethos*. Specifically, there is often a lack of confidence and trust in the character and purpose of the missionary communicator on the part of respondents. To barge in unknown and unannounced, preach a gospel (which has exceeding great and precious promises but also requires radical change) to anyone who will listen, and ask for an immediate decision is an approach that is hardly well calculated to win large numbers of inhabitants of these societies to an abiding faith in Christ.

Even more deliberate approaches may leave the problems of communication unsolved, depending on the circumstances. Missionaries working out of Manila have found that the house-to-house survey method of making contacts for evangelistic campaigns, a method that has been relatively successful in Manila, meets considerable resistance in outlying villages. City-dwellers are more used to doorbell-ringers and their rather prying questions. Village-dwellers are suspicious of the motives of strangers who invade their quiet communities asking personal questions and inviting them to meetings sponsored by outsiders. On the other hand, missionaries have found that the villagers are often responsive when local friendships are established and utilized, identity and purposes are clarified, and the message is given by precept upon precept over a period of time.

The key to effectively evangelizing many village communities is to be found in those transformed individuals who by virtue of kinship, friendship, or business relationships are links between the city and village and who can become natural bridges to the village community. It is highly probable that Paul viewed such believers as the bridges over which the message that he so eloquently and persuasively preached and taught in the cities would reach the surrounding countryside. And in this he was not disappointed because he could write to the Thessalonians, "For the word of the Lord has sounded forth from you, not only in Macedonia and Achaia, but also in every place your faith toward God has gone forth, so that we have no need to say anything" (1 Thess. 1:8).

Perhaps the most critical issue in winning tribal peoples to Christ is that of timing. Primitive peoples do not remain primitive. It is virtually impossible for tribal societies to maintain their isolation in the twentieth century. As contacts with the outside world commence and increase in frequency and depth, pressure mounts within the tribe to adopt ways that have resulted in increased material goods and other advantages. Depending on the degree of isolation and the quality of initial contacts, fear and suspicion may force a delay in this change process. But the time for radical change will come. And when it does, agents of change have a golden opportunity to introduce an entirely new worldview consistent with the obvious results of technology and education. The process that has been called modernization can in the providence of God become a process of Christianization.

Comparatively few truly isolated tribes remain in the world. Most of these are located in West Irian and along the mighty Amazon in South America. There are, however, numerous tribes or parts of tribes from Oceania to African forests that are still in the initial stages of modernization and still responsive. It is the glorious responsibility and opportunity of a church under the authority of Christ to see to it that his emissaries are there at these strategic times in the history of these *ethnē*. And it is the responsibility and opportunity of these emissaries to be prepared, not only to introduce the benefits of modern education, medicine, and agriculture, but to communicate the transforming gospel of Christ. Resisting the forces of syncretism, Christ's emissaries are to teach all things that he commanded.

Chapter 38

Free and Totalitarian Societies

The language of rhetoric implies a society of free individuals where people are allowed to contemplate alternative beliefs and courses of action and choose between them. The implication exists also that persuaders on all sides of an issue are at liberty to attempt to influence those decisions in an atmosphere of openness. The language of the Bible has similar overtones: "Choose you this day whom ye will serve" (Josh. 24:15 KJV); "Come now, and let us reason together, saith the Lord" (Isa. 1:18 KJV); "Whosoever will, let him take" (Rev. 22:17 KJV). Both the early rhetoricians and the Bible writers contemplated other states of affairs, however. And Bible writers insisted that one ought to obey God rather than human authority in the event of a clash between Caesar and conscience.

Christian missions now face a world in which vast populations cannot hear the gospel or worship God and live for Christ in an atmosphere of freedom. According to the *World Christian Encyclopedia*, the facts are that when we entered the 1980s seventy-four countries were politically free, eighty-one were partially fee, and sixty-eight were not free. In seventy-nine countries where there were constitutional guarantees of religious freedom 2.2 billion people nevertheless lived under de facto restrictions on their religious freedom.[1] Rulers rise and fall, and governments come and go. The political fortunes of modern humanity are not at all clear. Advocates of modernization like Ward Hunt Goodenough warn that community development will have to be undertaken and accomplished in a context of revolution.[2] If, then, the future of missions is dependent on the existence of stable contexts of freedom in which missionary communicators and their respondents are at liberty to preach, hear, and believe the Christian gospel and live out its implications, the future is not without shadows. If that future is dependent on the person, power, and promises of Christ—and it is—we can move forward with confidence.

Before making some observations concerning missionary communication in the context of totalitarianism, it would be well to characterize forms of totalitarianism as they impinge on the communication process. It is in the nature of totalitarianism to control both the channels and the content of communication. Communication—vertical and horizontal—is controlled by, and put to the purposes of, the ruling elite insofar as this is possible and practicable. Obviously vertical communication downward from those in power to the masses is of primary importance. Nevertheless, vertical communication upward from the masses to the elite is by no means overlooked. However, whereas it is true in democratic societies that communication from people to the leaders is determinative of their course of action and even of their continuing in a position of leadership, it is to the extent that a regime is totalitarian that the leaders themselves determine the uses to which that communication will be put.

[1]David B. Barrett, ed. *World Christian Encyclopedia: A Comparative Study of Churches and Religions in the Modern World* A.D. 1900–2000 (Oxford: Oxford University Press, 1982), 5.

[2]Ward Hunt Goodenough, *Cooperation in Change: An Anthropological Approach to Community Development* (New York: John Wiley, Science Editions, 1966), 286.

Mao Tse-Tung looked at Western democracy and called it "ultra-democracy" precisely because it weakens centralist power and weakens or undermines the ability to wage war.[3] Since "political power grows out of the barrel of a gun"[4] and "war is the highest form of struggle for resolving contradictions . . . between classes, nations, states or political groups,"[5] vertical communication traveling upward must be selected, interpreted, and put to uniquely communist ends by the Party. Mao made it completely clear what this involves: First, only those who support the "social construction" are "people"—all others are enemies.[6] Communist government is "people's government" and a "democracy" in the sense that it is responsive and responsible to the "people" only. Second, it is the task of Party leadership to take the "ideas of the masses," interpret and systematize them according to communist philosophy, and then propagate and explain these ideas to the masses until they "embrace them as their own."[7]

As far as horizontal communication in a totalitarian society is concerned, it is both encouraged and controlled. Everyone is free to speak out. It is by speaking one's true thoughts that peers among the "people" are reinforced in their beliefs and encouraged to act on behalf of socialist construction, and also that "enemies" are exposed and singled out for "teaching."

The effectiveness of the methods of Mao not only in communication control but also in thought control can be appreciated by those standing at a distance only by reading such books as Edward Hunter's *Brain-Washing in China*[8] and Geoffrey Bull's *When Iron Gates Yield*.[9] At the same time, it

[3]Mao Tse-Tung, *Quotations From Chairman Mao Tse-Tung* (Peking: Foreign Languages, 1972), 162–63.
[4]Ibid., 61.
[5]Ibid., 58.
[6]Ibid., 45–46.
[7]Ibid., 128.
[8]Cf. Edward Hunter, *Brain-Washing in Red China* (New York: Vanguard, 1953).
[9]Cf. Geoffrey Bull, *When Iron Gates Yield* (London: Hodder and Stoughton, 1967).

is encouraging to realize that during the repressive days of Mao's rule and up to the present moment the Christian church (particularly the house church) in China has grown at an unprecedented rate. It is estimated that the number of Christians in China has grown from perhaps 3 million at the time of Mao's takeover to some 40 to 50 million today, and some estimates go even higher! Truly, the Word of God is not bound!

The Roman Catholic Church traditionally has been totalitarian in that church structures and procedures ensured that correct doctrine and important decisions were made at top levels and then disseminated downward through the membership, who were obliged to accept them, endure discipline, or voluntarily leave the church. Moreover, there has been an effort to control communication and prevent the dissemination of competing ideas by giving approval to certain publications or media, publishing blacklists, and practicing suppression at the local level. Only recently has Catholic totalitarianism given way to a larger measure of democratization and openness.

It should be noted that Protestant groups—especially missionary ones—are also denominated as totalitarian by many. Ward Hunt Goodenough concludes that early Christianity, the Puritan movement, and the missionary efforts of the more "militant Christian denominations" of today are no less uncompromising and totalitarian than modern communism.[10] Goodenough, however, is using the word "totalitarian" in the sense of "wholeness," i.e., concerned with the total pattern of thinking and living. Biblical Christianity certainly *is* concerned with wholeness in this sense. Christians not only admit this but insist on it. What is odious and misleading to Christians is the comparison to communism and the double-entendre of contemporary witticisms like "the Puritans insisted that they should worship God according to their own conscience—and that every one else do the same." It is of the very essence of Protestantism that *all people* are equal before

[10]Goodenough, *Cooperation in Change*, 306.

God and that everyone should be free to accept—or reject—the revelation that God has given in Christ and the Scriptures. Furthermore, in the Protestant view all believers are priests having direct access to God, responsibility in the church, and a ministry to the world of lost people. Believers do not continue in the church by the good graces of the hierarchy. Vertical communication is characterized by a genuine mutuality.

In free societies, the emissaries of historic Protestant Christianity ask no more than access to a free and open marketplace of ideas, trusting the Holy Spirit to enable them to present the claims of Christ in the manner of Stephen—of whose audience it is recorded that "they were unable to cope with the wisdom and the Spirit with which he was speaking" (Acts 6:10).

Because of the very nature of totalitarian societies, missionaries and their target audiences in the twentieth century face actual or potential restrictions on their communication as Christians did in the first centuries. Cross-cultural missionary communication should be guided by certain principles and guidelines:

1. It is the will of God that all people have the opportunity to hear the gospel, repent, believe, and be saved.

2. Governmental authority is ordained by God, and its leaders are his ministers irrespective of whether or not they recognize him.

3. When the laws of God and the laws of human government clash, believers are obliged to obey God rather than people.

4. Primary responsibility for communicating Christ in any given society belongs to Christians who are members or citizens of that society.

5. Missionary agencies operating from a base outside a target totalitarian society have an obligation to encourage and strengthen the witness of that society's Christians and to avoid activities that would make their task more difficult. It should not be forgotten that communication with God in prayer is a vital missionary ministry. Christians are never put in the place where they can only look on and do nothing.

6. Since man proposes and God disposes, and human governments rise and fall, it is incumbent on mission leaders in free societies to pray and plan for the day when totalitarian societies will open to the gospel, and, having learned from the past, be prepared to participate in an expected harvest. Currently the Philippines is a case in point. A large majority of Filipinos are Roman Catholics. In the past Protestant missionaries were being openly opposed at the local level, their Bibles and literature were blacklisted, and their potential audiences frightened away by the threats of ecclesiastics. For a time the problem was compounded by near social chaos. Today post–Vatican II openness in Catholicism have resulted in the kind of opportunity for which missionaries in the past must have earnestly prayed. It remains to be seen whether evangelicals are prepared to take advantage of their new opportunities.

7. Much more attention needs to be given to a study of the ways and means of communicating Christ in totalitarian societies. By and large, the study of missionary communication and strategy has presupposed freedom of speech and the press. The world, on the other hand, is only partially free. The time has come for students of missionary communication to deal with problems of communication in an underground church and responsible ways of communicating Christ cross-culturally in those parts of the world that are no longer free.

CONCLUSION TO PART VII

Human societies represent a mosaic in which all the various stands and variegated colors combine to make a meaningful whole. The rugmakers among the Navajos in the southwestern United States or among the Chinese in the New Territories north of Hong Kong, the weavers of silk in Japan or Thailand, and the artists whose products can be found on the streets of Kinshasa or the galleries of the Ufizzi all have the ability to make visible certain patterns that can be appreciated by connoisseurs and laymen alike. Similarly, all human societies have implicit and explicit patterns of interaction with certain cross-cultural similarities and differences. In a day when societies are insisting on the validity and integrity of their own forms, it is imperative that missionary communicators become connoisseurs of their "art," fully appreciating the forms and significance of these similarities and differences. Perhaps the most practical way to conclude this discussion, then, is to summarize some (by no means all!) of the principles growing out of the way people interact in society that apply to missionary communication. Since there is a certain tentativeness about some of these principles, let us call them working hypotheses (i.e., statements that will likely be true often enough for the missionary to give serious consideration to them).

Hypothesis number one: The more closely communication follows the patterns of the prevailing social structure, the more effective it will be.

Hypothesis number two: People communicate more to others of their own class; i.e., interpersonal communication is usually horizontal.

Hypothesis number three: Interpersonal, horizontal communication lends itself best to effecting voluntary changes of attitude and behavior.

Hypotheses number four: Prestigious communication is from upper to lower classes.

Hypothesis number five: Prestigious, vertical communication is best suited to effecting social control.

Hypothesis number six: The degree of difficulty in achieving effective communication is positively correlated with the degree of social distance on the socioeconomic scale.

Hypothesis number seven: The degree of difficulty in achieving effective communication is positively correlated with the degree of compatibility of social systems (e.g., those from modern urban societies will have more difficulty in communicating with those from tribal societies than with those from folk societies).

Hypothesis number eight: The more face-to-face the society, the more difficult it becomes for the outsider to establish effective communication (and, therefore, the more important it is that communication be based on personal friendship).

Hypothesis number nine: In all societies, the initial communication of the gospel should be to responsible, accepted members of the community who are, therefore, good potential channels of communication.

Hypothesis number ten: The more heterogeneous the society, the more flexible and variegated the communicative approach to its included groups must be.

Hypothesis number eleven: In face-to-face societies, consideration should be given to communicating the gospel first to someone at the top (or someone near the top) who is more capable of making decisions and presenting the gospel to the larger group.

Hypothesis number twelve: The more cohesive, homogeneous and face-to-face the society, the more likely it is that communication will be along established group (probably familial) lines and that decisions will be collective.

Hypothesis number thirteen: The more cohesive, homogeneous and face-to-face the society, the more time-conscious the communicator must be if he is to effect lasting change.

Part VIII

MEDIA INFLUENCE—
WAYS OF
CHANNELING THE
MESSAGE

Figure 34

DIMENSIONS OF CROSS-CULTURAL COMMUNICATION

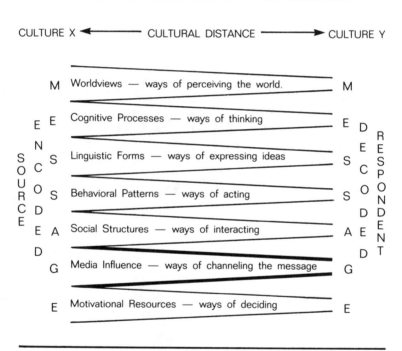

Chapter 39

Media Have Their Own "Messages"

It seems that some delusions will never die. One such delusion is the notion that messages can be put into any available medium of transmission at one end and come out the other end as the same message—unscathed, untainted, untouched. The idea has no basis in fact. It has been dealt severe wounds that should have proved fatal. But it lingers on with no indication of an imminent demise. No less an authority than David Sarnoff nourishes it by saying, "We are too prone to make technological instruments the scapegoats for the sins of those who wield them. The products of modern science are not in themselves good or bad; it is the way they are used that determines their value."[1]

Sarnoff's reference is to the mass media, of course. And little wonder. Not only have mass media commanded his energies and thinking as the head of a major media corporation, but they concern us all, for we cannot escape them—and would not if we could. The mass media are such an important

[1]Quoted in Marshall McLuhan, *Understanding Media: The Extensions of Man* (New York: McGraw-Hill, 1964), 11.

part of contemporary communication that they will constitute the primary (but not sole) focus of our attention in the next few chapters.

In the act of encoding a message, the source puts his message into spoken or written words or into one of the nonlinguistic codes. Words spoken with the unaided human voice will be audible to a comparatively few respondents at best and will be lost to listening ears in a moment of time. But those same spoken words can be amplified for the world to hear and recorded for posterity. Words inscribed on sand, or even papyrus or paper, are fragile and limited. But those same words set in type and printed in books can simultaneously traverse oceans and continents. Similarly, gestures of all types, musical scores, shapes and colors, or ritual forms can be limited and even ephemeral, or they can be amplified by means of molds, photostatic copies, film, orchestration, and so on.

Thinking now of the various channels as media or conveyers of messages, can we subscribe to the notion that it really makes no difference whether they are simple or syndetic, whether the voice goes out by radio or television, whether the words are handwritten or printed, whether the gesture is on stage or on film, or whether the music is "live" or "canned"? That, after all, is the issue. If the media are neither good nor bad, appropriate nor inappropriate, effective nor ineffective—then they are neutral and our total concentration can be on the message and the various codes that are available. But if the message can be affected once it has been encoded, then the media are not neutral and attention must be given to them also. Otherwise, the tables will be turned upon us, and instead of people being users of the media, the media will become users of people.

No one has done more to encourage the demise of the illusion that the media are innocent adjuncts of human communication and life than has Marshall McLuhan, the late, Canadian-born Catholic professor of English literature and philosopher of communication. His philosophy of the media does not admit of simple explanation, but it is important that communicators understand his basic contentions.

"MEDIA" AND "MESSAGE" ACCORDING TO MCLUHAN

McLuhan sees the "media" (a term stretched to include electric lights, automobiles, and computers) as extensions of the human person—whether of his body, his nervous system, or his consciousness and cognition. To put it concisely, "All media are extensions of some human faculty—psychic or physical."[2] Thus the wheel is an extension of the foot, and the motorcar a greater extension. Radio and television represent an extension, not so much of the body, but of the central nervous system. Via electronic media we instantaneously become aware of—and feel with—other people far removed from us geographically. A final phase of this overall development is rapidly approaching. It will entail an extension of consciousness by which the whole of society will corporately and collectively experience the "creative process of knowing"—whether for good or ill!

An important aspect of this understanding of the media is that extension implies amputation. That is, before the wheel and then the automobile could become extensions of the foot, the foot had to be amputated. Pain is involved—a kind of mutilation of the body. The "old" feet are lost and have to be "recovered" by reminders that walking and running are crucial to health and well-being. In similar fashion, radio and television lay bare our central nervous system and expose the nerve endings to the predicaments of people the world over. Only by a natural numbing process can sanity be preserved. One at first cries and lashes out to somehow help the situation or relieve the pain, and then, reaching a point of nervous exhaustion, one becomes insensitive to the stimuli.

McLuhan distinguishes the "content" of any "medium"

[2]Marshall McLuhan and Quenten Fiore, *The Medium Is the Message: An Inventory of Effects* (New York: Bantam, 1967), 26.

and its "message." *"Message" in this sense has to do with impact.* To use McLuhan's words, "The 'message' of any medium or technology is the change of scale or pace or pattern that it introduces into human affairs."[3] Max Lerner explains that according to McLuhan, "Each of the media has its own brand of vibrancy, personal impact, social consequence."[4]

In this chapter "media" and "message" in the McLuhan sense of the words will be used with quotation marks to distinguish these new meanings from the more usual meanings of these words.

TYPES OF "MEDIA" AND THEIR "MESSAGES"

What, then, have been some of the important "messages" of the media throughout history and down to the present day? Consider what happened when people became literate. In preliterate societies people reacted firsthand with their environment and social communities. One language bound the various societies together, and the necessity of communicating by the spoken word ensured face-to-face relationships between their members. Writing changed that—especially phonetic writing. The ideographs and hieroglyphs of the Chinese, Babylonian, and Mayan cultures served primarily single cultures and were not so decisively divisive. But the phonetic alphabet was suited especially to obtaining, considering, and storing up information from within and without a culture while avoiding personal involvement. A great portion of the achievements of human civilization is attributable to that potential of the written word. But McLuhan says that those accomplishments were purchased at a price. Literate people were free to go their own way, responding to *written messages* and *written codes of law* rather than to the *human sources of knowledge and law.*

This potential for noninvolvement and separateness was greatly accentuated by the invention of moveable type about

[3]McLuhan, *Understanding Media*, 8.
[4]Max Lerner, "Private and Public Sexuality," *Pacific Stars and Stripes* (13 March 1973), 10.

530

A.D. 1500. The printing press is the archetype of all mechanization. It introduced a galaxy of changes in the consciousness of Western man. It put an end, once and for all, to parochialism in both space and time. It brought the ancient and medieval worlds into fusion and was the harbinger of the modern world. It issued in nationalism, industrialism, mass markets, education, and a much higher level of literacy. It heightened the ability of people to collect information and cogitate while detached from one another and from events by both space and time.

Electricity has changed all of that. In the electric age we are involved once again—and on a global basis. The whole world is now a village. The concern that a primitive person felt for a fellow villager is now felt by us on a world scale, thanks to radio and television.

Automation technology has also played a part. It differs from machine technology. The machine by its very nature was fragmentary, superficial, and centralist in the patterning of human relationships. Automation is integral, decentralist and depth-oriented. The machine was characterized by sequential relationships. Now everything has been made "instant." As a result we not only seek to encompass the whole world, but we also want to know whole persons—persons in their totality—with everything disclosed at once and nothing concealed. Modern education is programed for discovery—an immediate grasping of the whole rather than a sequential mastering of the parts.

McLuhan does not suppose for a minute that all the "media" of a given stage of human development are the same in their effects. *Traditional* tribalism collapses when assaulted by any medium that is mechanical, uniform, and repetitive. Money, the wheel, and writing speeded up exchange and information. They tended to fragment tribal structure. A much greater speed-up, such as occurs with the electronic "media," however, may result in retribalization. In other words, they may restore the intense involvement of the tribal pattern. This took place with the introduction of the radio in Europe and is taking place as a result of television in America.

McLuhan is not easy to follow at this point, but one key to understanding him is to keep in mind his distinction between "hotness" and "coolness."

"Hot media" (the phonetic alphabet, photographs, radio) have high definition, i.e., they are well supplied with information. "Cool media" (ideographs, cartoons, and television images) have low definition, i.e., they have gaps and require the participation of the respondent in order to fill those gaps. The television image, for example, is made up of numerous dots in a kind of mesh mosaic. As an extension of the sense of touch (think of the nervous system surfacing in the skin), the "coolness" of the television image invites us to reach out and feelingly supply whatever is necessary to complete the picture. It short-circuits sequential thinking and dims distant goals; it appeals to the senses to become involved in all-inclusive "now or neverness." The TV child has little concern for pedagogic techniques, the curriculum, or a specialist *job* in the future. He is a citizen of the world; he wants a *role*, and he wants it now. As far as McLuhan is concerned, this change is fraught with possibilities for good and ill. In either case, he is extremely doubtful that Western civilization as we know it can withstand the impact of the electronic media any more than primitive society was prepared to withstand the impact of literacy. In fact, backward countries may be better able to confront electronic media than is the West! Why? The reason is that they are "cool" cultures and have never gone through the "heating up" connected with mechanization and specialist culture. Therefore the change of pace or impact of electronic media is not as great as in the West. "Hotness" and "coolness" therefore, have reference to culture types and to the reversal of procedures and values in moving from one type of age to another (e.g., mechanical to electronic), as well as to the impact of different kinds of media in any given age.

LEARNING FROM MCLUHAN

As mentioned previously, Marshall McLuhan is not easily understood. Very possibly his position cannot be summarized in a few paragraphs. George P. Elliot is confident that it cannot and for two reasons: (1) The attitude and tone of his writings are as important as the ideas themselves, and (2) his writing is deliberately antilogical.[5] In fact, Elliot is fearful of the consequences of McLuhan's own refusal to submit to the rules of logic and the requirements of systematizing. He knows that McLuhan may be just probing when he "substitutes . . . electricity for divine grace."[6] He knows that McLuhan may be just exploring when he talks about by-passing languages and using computers to achieve a "general cosmic consciousness—a Pentecostal condition of universal understanding and unity."[7] He knows. But he fears this kind of mindless, unthought-out, contentless kind of harmony to be achieved by electronic technology. And he fears that McLuhan may be serious when he espouses it. Or, at least, that *others* may take him seriously when he espouses it.

Explaining, exploring, or prescribing, McLuhan is worth careful consideration. He explains as well as anyone, and better than most, the current shift from *precept* to *percept*— why the young especially tend to be impatient with doctrinal concepts; why they want to *be*, to *experience*, to *feel*; why they want a Christianity that works; why they are prepared to pass up institutional Christianity in order to experience personal Christianity. In fact, it is this state of affairs that causes McLuhan to go on to predict both the demise of Christianity and the advent of a very religious age—religious, of course, on *his* terms as per the above.

Western evangelicals, committed as they are to biblical *doctrine* and dedicated to being co-laborers with Christ in the building of his church, should inquire as to the correctness and import of McLuhan's analysis. The stakes are particularly high for evangelicals in mission.

In the first place, let us note well that the repeated

---

[5]George P. Elliot, "McLuhan's Teaching Is Radical, New, Capable of Moving People to Social Action. If He Is Wrong, It Matters," in Gerald E. Stern, ed., *McLuhan Hot and Cool* (New York: Diel, 1967), 67.

[6]Ibid.

[7]Ibid.

warnings against communicating Western forms of Christianity rather than the biblical form of Christianity now take on new dimension. If in the past we have erred in the direction of transplanting Western churches rather than planting biblical churches, we now are in danger of erring in the direction of "introducing Christ" while not planting churches at all. And this is by the same process of taking excess cultural baggage to the mission field! If the old error was bad—and it was—the new error could be even worse. the East needs very little encouragement from the West to base its religion on personal experience at the expense of doctrine and creed. And potential converts from non-Christian or sub-Christian sectors of Eastern populations need little encouragement to "believe in Christ" while remaining outside of, or becoming only superficially identified with, local expressions of Christ's universal church! A recent bulletin of an evangelical church in a Far Eastern country noted that over thirty people had "received Christ" that week. Yet when the pastor asked these new "converts" to introduce themselves, it was discovered that not one was in attendance at the worship service. A campus missionary in that same country recently reported that over a period of several months, nine out of ten students to whom he had witnessed concerning Christ on a face-to-face basis had accepted Christ as Savior. When asked how many of them had become members of evangelical churches in the area, he could not name one! If Bible-believing churches in any respondent culture are the real hope for the continuing evangelization of that culture, self-examination in missions is called for. Are we communicating the whole counsel of God or a truncated Christianity originating not in the still, small voice of the Spirit of God but in the overpowering sounds of modern electronic technology?

In the second place, the missionary should be aware of the "message" of his innovations in underdeveloped societies. Missionaries are exporting media with *their* "messages" as well as taking Christ and *his* message past cultural boundaries! President Sukarno of Indonesia once made some visiting American film executives prick up their ears by calling them "the most important revolutionaries in history."[8] His logic was impeccable. By creating and distributing films that showed ordinary people driving cars, storing their food in refrigerators, and listening to radios, members of the film industry had created a desire for these goods throughout Southeast Asia. After all, Asian viewers are ordinary people also.

Sukarno may have overlooked other "revolutionaries" in his speech, because it was the *missionaries* who introduced writing, medicine, and new material goods as well as the Bible. Their part in initiating the so-called "revolution of rising expectations" can hardly be gainsaid. To be aware of the impact of innovations which set great changes in motion—and to feel some trepidation at the prospect—is not to subscribe to the fiction of the noble and happy savage. It is rather to understand how rapidly we export the savage and senseless aspects of our own civilization! When far removed from respondent cultures by time or space, missionary recruits may not really sense the problem. But neither anthropologists nor missiologists are insensitive to it.

When anthropologist Edmund Carpenter was employed by Australian administrators of Papua, New Guinea to conduct studies and advise them about ways of communicating with the natives, he recommended that the government use electronic media only with great restraint. The recommendation grew out of his own experience with isolated peoples located between the Sepik River and the Highlands of New Guinea in 1969. As a result of his contacts, housing, clothing, and demeanor changed during the span of six short months. But of even more importance to Carpenter was the self-awareness that had resulted from the introduction of mirrors, photographs, recorders, and motion pictures. The "cohesive village had become a collection of separate, private individuals. . . . Our actions had produced instant alienation. They had destroyed the natives' old, strictly tribal self-concept."[9]

[8]Merrill Abbey, *Man, Media and the Message* (New York: Friendship, 1960), 39.

[9]Edmund Carpenter, "Television Meets the Stone Age," *T.V. Guide* (16 January, 1971), 16.

The missionary also is an agent of change. He wants to see men and women transformed into citizens of Christ's kingdom with all that that implies. No change could be more profound and hopeful. But missionary-initiated change is not confined to that spiritual regeneration. The missionary is the bearer of a message—a bearer of the greatest story ever told. But the missionary-borne message is not confined to the gospel of Christ. For better or worse, the very media by which the missionary conveys the Christian message will carry their own "messages" and promote their own changes. Only as the missionary understands this fact will he be able partially to control this extra-Christian change process and assist his respondents as they experience it.

Timothy Yu is not especially enamored with the works of McLuhan, but he says,

Among the many things Marshall McLuhan has said, he is right at least in one point. We are in a new world, and our techniques are such that we have given ourselves a new form of communication, but we have not figured out yet the right way to use it. We use television but without knowing what we do.[10]

Yu concludes,

Our task as Christian communicators is to find out the right and effective ways to use of the different form [sic] of communication for our task: world evangelism.[11]

---

[10]Timothy Yu, "If the Body Were All Eye—A Note on Mass Media Coordination," *Asia Focus* 6 (third quarter 1971).
[11]Ibid., 28.

Chapter 40

Using Simple Media

It is not just *who* says *what* to *whom*, but *how* the message is channeled to the respondents that determines how the message will be decoded. Language is basic to communication, but language does not stand alone. As we have said, words are augmented by pictures, actions, sounds, silence, smells, and objects. Words can be spoken or written; pictures can be drawn on canvas or projected on a screen; and actions can be part of sign language for the deaf or part of a stage play. In addition, any of these media can be used more or less singly and simply or they can be used syndetically—in combination and extended in time and space.

One of the most exciting challenges facing missionary communicators is the challenge to use indigenous simple media such as dramas, diagrams, and drawings more imaginatively and more often. Simple media are especially important in cultures where concrete-relational thinking predominates and where mechanical and electronic media are more difficult to reproduce and comprehend. For the missionary, simple media have great and largely untapped potential in most cultures and therefore should not be overlooked.

Those who were present at the large international Congress on World Evangelism held in 1980 in Pattaya, Thailand, can witness to that potential. Included in the program was a presentation by a Thai Christian drama group entitled "The Prodigal Daughter." The presentation featured a converted professional Thai actress who played the part of a Thai girl who conspires with her boyfriend to get money from her father and go to Bangkok. Bereft of friends, money and reputation, she finally returns to her father who receives her with forgiveness and joy despite the angry protestations of her older sister. The presentation was attended by numerous difficulties ("noise" in technical jargon). The auditorium had no stage facilities. The script was in Thai and therefore understood by only a small minority of the audience. A floodlight exploded and scattered glass over a large part of the "stage." But when the final curtain fell there were few dry eyes in that audience of hundreds despite the fact that they came from a wide variety of ethnic and cultural backgrounds. If a survey were to be conducted today it would probably reveal that few attendees recall much of what was communicated in the numerous "high-powered" addresses that crowded the conference program. But the impact and message of "The Prodigal Daughter" would still be etched on everyone's memory!

THE POTENTIAL OF AURAL MEDIA

The percentage of nonliterates in the population of many countries of our contemporary world is astounding. Of those over fifteen years of age the figure in Benin is 83.5 percent; in Burkina Faso, 91.2 percent; in Ethiopia, 95.8 percent; in the Central African Republic, 73 percent. In fact, only a few countries in Africa have an adult literacy rate of over 50 percent. The picture in many other parts of the world is not much brighter.[1] Given the relatively high literacy rate of most

[1]Cf. *Statistical Yearbook, 1988* (Paris: United Nations' Educational, Scientific and Cultural Organization, 1988), 1–15.

missionary-sending nations and the importance that Christians place on the Bible as the written Word of God, it is to be expected that literacy, Bible translation, and the printing of Bibles become linked with Christian mission. The dedication of the members of Wycliffe Bible Translators and other missions to the Word of God written is legendary. It was not without encountering a degree of resistance, then, that Herbert Klem reminded missions people that more indigenous oral-audio media have a far greater potential than their use would suggest.[2]

Klem reports his experience among the Yoruba people of Nigeria. He had the Epistle to the Hebrews translated in a style of Yoruba that could be sung in a traditional Yoruba music style. Bible lessons were then taught both with and without written materials. He found that it was most effective to use both books and songs. However, those who studied the Bible with only the songs learned just as much as those who used books. Moreover, the use of songs in teaching aroused the most interest and attracted the most visitors. Klem writes,

> These indigenous oral communications systems are at the very heart of the indigenous social order. They have great social significance vital to the ethnic identity of the people and the survival of ethnic cohesion. It appears that at the very core of the conflict of cultures in Africa today is the question of which kind of communication the people will use—western printed media, or more indigenous oral-audio (aural) media. Perhaps even the survival of the indigenous social order is at stake. My findings indicate that considerable resistance to the teachings of the Bible is needlessly engendered by our heavy dependence upon written materials in segments of societies accustomed to communicating orally.[3]

[2]Herbert V. Klem, *Oral Communication of the Scripture: Insights from African Oral Art* (Pasadena: William Carey Library, 1982).
[3]Ibid., xix.

Klem, of course, is not opposed to the introduction of literacy and Bible translation. What he argues against is an understanding of evangelization and mission that makes them absolutely dependent upon literacy. He would take issue, for example, with at least one aspect of the otherwise ingenious instructional approach of Mexican tribal church leaders as reported to the author by George Cowan (then president of Wycliffe Bible Translators). On Sundays the Christians gathered for worship and instruction. During the instructional period literate or semiliterate church leaders taught the basics of Christian truth to believers who were divided into classes according to their level of understanding. Individual members stayed in a class until they had mastered the lesson being communicated in that particular class. Then they were allowed to enter the next class in the series. Class members proved their mastery of the lesson by quoting verbatim from the newly translated Scriptures in answer to certain carefully devised questions. When they could not read the Scriptures, they were required to *point to the place in the Bible where the quoted passage could be found!* In addition, they were asked to produce two or three witnesses who could attest to the fact that they were living out the lessons in their daily lives!

Klem would point out that although there is considerable merit in such a system of instruction, it betrays the kind of over-emphasis on literacy that has resulted in leaving the potential of indigenous media largely untapped.

If we do not choose one emphasis to the exclusion of the other, both are valid and helpful. We should not overlook the fact that the authority for our message rests in the Word of God as it was written in the autographs of the Old and New Testaments and is now translated into over thirteen hundred languages and dialects and appears in multiplied millions of printed Bibles and Bible portions all around the world. If we think of the worldwide missionary effort as a great battle, there is a very real sense in which it is a battle for the Book. Let us remember that the missionary is only a secondary source in that his message is not his own but comes from God. As J. I. Packer has pointed out, the central issue in the great encounter between belief and unbelief is that of authority.[4] By what authority do we say and do these things? The answer of historic Christianity is clear: Our authority is to be found in the God and Father of Jesus Christ and in his Spirit-inspired Book, the Bible. If the acids of modernity are allowed to eat into the authority of the Bible, the mission of the church stands in jeopardy. More than one missionary to Islam has been turned back with the statement, "We have a book that every follower of the Prophet accepts as the very word of Allah, while among Christians themselves many cannot agree as to the veracity of the Christian Bible. How then can you expect us to forsake the Koran and embrace your Bible?" Those who for one reason or another have undermined the authority of the Old and New Testament Scriptures have incurred a debt of which few of them are aware. They have set aside their own credentials and in the forums of the world stand as simple purveyors of opinion. The ultimate authority of the true missionary is not what he has in his head, or even in his heart, but what he has in his hand—the written Word of the living God!

From this fact certain conclusions follow and others do not. It should not be inferred that only literate people can be good Christians. The reasoning for this false conclusion goes something like this: The Word of God is essential for understanding the will of God; understanding the will of God is essential to spiritual growth; therefore, we must make people literate so they can read the Word of God for themselves. The conclusion is, of course, a *non sequitur*. Thousands of Christians in the first century must have become stalwart Christians with but limited access to written copies of even the Old Testament, and other thousands without the ability to read what was available. Their faith and maturity rested on the Word of God even though they did not have access to written copies of that Word; and if copies had been available, they would have lacked ability to read them. It

[4]Cf. J. I. Packer, *"Fundamentalism" and the Word of God: Some Evangelical Principles* (London: Inter-Varsity, 1958).

is certainly important today that languages of primitive peoples be reduced to writing, that the Scriptures be translated into their languages, and that some of them at least be taught to read and write. A new day is dawning for tribal peoples everywhere—a day in which not only mechanical but also electronic media will pierce the darkness of tribal night like the shafts of the morning sun that reach through the boughs of giant trees to the jungle floors. But we must not overlook the potential for communicating Christian truth that exists in indigenous media. Some primitive peoples have passed on their tribal lore for centuries by means of chants and rituals, or by appointing certain members as repositories of tribal knowledge.

TALK AND CHALK

One of the most interesting accounts of the awakening of a missionary to the possibility of visual communication of a simple sort is that recorded by H. R. Weber to whom I made reference previously. In his account of how he was sent to Luwuk-Banggai in Indonesia to work among thousands of nonliterate and semiliterate Christians largely bereft of Christian instruction, Weber tells of his attempt to communicate the "larger story" of God's dealings with humanity. In the process he resorted to what he calls "talk and chalk":

> On our journeyings through the Banggai Archipelago we came to Taulan, a small island consisting of one village only. A number of the inhabitants had been baptized a few years ago.
>
> The village assembled—animals and humans, Christians and non-Christians, babies in arms and old men (among them the heathen priest)—all of them illiterate. A few planks served as blackboard; my imagination and powers of expression are too impoverished to follow the example of the illiterate and make the Bible message come alive in words only. So we decided to make use of simple drawings.
>
> Beginning with the story of the Creation, I illustrated what I said by somewhat clumsy drawings on the black-

board. Then the old heathen priest related the ancient creation legends of the district, and we compared the two reports. Next, the story of the Fall, related and illustrated by "talk and chalk," was contrasted with legends about the origin of evil and the fall of man as they had been handed down in the tribe. It was long after noon before we stopped for lunch, and in the afternoon this unique catechism was continued.

We were not concerned about the fact that our drawings were clumsy and over-simplified. We knew that the illiterate's vivid imagination would enliven and animate our sketches, and that the best colour film would not have served our purpose as well as simple drawings did.

Encouraged by our experiences, we invited some people from Taulan to attend a Bible course for illiterates, and repeated this experiment in other villages. Everywhere we encountered increasing enthusiasm and unbounded zeal for learning.

The Bible course for illiterates was constructed in the same way as the one described earlier, but in the light of our experiences we laid much more stress on the picturesque and dramatic element. Study was done in groups again, the leader of each illiterate group being a literate who was able to read the questions and the text to which they referred. The study method, however, was auditive. The result of such work with illiterates was usually much better than study with literates or semi-literates who, after all, had great difficulty in reading the text they were studying. In introductions and summaries we made full use of "talk and chalk" and dramatization.

It was only later, during my missionary work in Java and Bali, in a world of religious symbols and dances, that I began to see the significance of the use of Christian symbols in evangelism. And so, in later Bible courses, we added to "talk and chalk" by dramatizing the frequent use of Christian symbols, like the Buddhist zoetrope, the Taostic sign, hammer and sickle, etc., with that of Christian symbols, above all the various signs of the cross—cross and crown, cross as sword over the serpent's head, cross and anchor, etc.

Figure 35

WEBER'S "HISTORY OF THE PEOPLE OF ISRAEL"

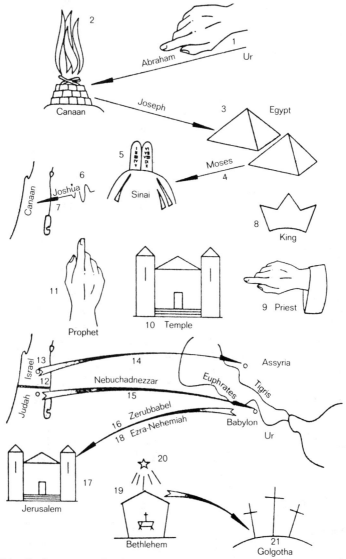

H.R. Weber, *The Communication of the Gospel to Illiterates* (London: SCM, 1957), 85. Used by permission

As a result of the Bible courses in the Banggai Archipelago the "equipment" was revised and changed into "directions for the religious instruction of illiterates and semi-literates," with all necessary drawings, Bible studies, and instructions for "talk and chalk," drama and group work.[5]

Note that Weber's pictures and diagrams are quite simple and relatively easy to construct and explain (see figure 35). Seeing a desperate need for instructing adult Christians of the Western world (!) in the larger story of Scripture, a Lutheran theologian, Henry Wendt, founded Shekinah Foundation, Inc. (now Crossways International)[6]. For over thirty years he has worked to produce study materials (called "The Divine Drama") for use in his native Australia, in the United States, and throughout the world. Wendt became so convinced that the visual word must be married to the spoken word that he engaged the services of two top-rank illustrators who worked over a four-year period to produce the visuals that accompany the instructional materials. The resultant symbols are quite "culturally freighted" and would be difficult (if not impossible) for the average teacher to reproduce on a blackboard (see figure 36). For that reason Crossways International reproduces the illustrations that accompany "The Divine Drama" in manuals and in 182 full-color overhead transparencies. (In this form they become "syndetic" in our categorization and therefore would normally be discussed in the following chapter.) Wendt insists that the symbols are readily understood in the cultures in which he has used them (primarily cultures already significantly impacted by Western culture).

Still another form of "talk and chalk" has been widely used by missionary Marilyn Steiner with a high degree of success. Although its use is limited to audiences that are literate or becoming literate, it can be used with almost any

[5]H. R. Weber, *The Communication of the Gospel to Illiterates* (Madras: Christian Literature Society, 1960), 67.

[6]Crossways International, 7930 Computer Avenue S., Bloomington, MN 55435.

written language. It consists of providing the audience with a written outline of the study lesson in the form of "part-letter" words (and simple drawings) on a blackboard as in figure 37. The method is effective with a wide range of audiences because it is simple to replicate, requires no special equipment, and involves the audience in dialogical communication (the audience assists in filling in the missing strokes).

Figure 36

"DIVINE DRAMA" ILLUSTRATION

© H.N. Wendt 1987

Adult Talk (Winter, 1988–89), p. 4. Published by Crossways International, 7930 Computer Ave., So., Minneapolis, Minn. 55432.

Pictures, diagrams and symbols on a blackboard or some other material—all of these have communication potential

Figure 37

STEINER'S "TALK & DRAW"

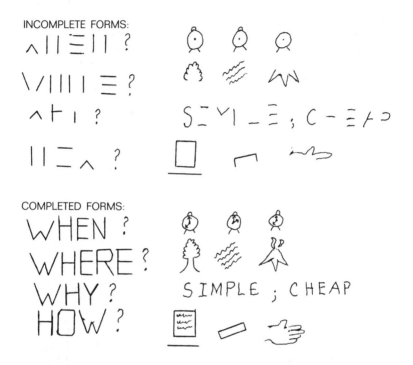

INCOMPLETE FORMS:

COMPLETED FORMS:

WHEN ?
WHERE ?
WHY ?
HOW ?

SIMPLE ; CHEAP

EXPLANATION:

To use "chalk and draw" the teacher begins with an incomplete form which outlines and illustrates the lesson. The teacher completes the words and drawings as he/she proceeds through the lesson, asking members of the class/audience to help in identifying the words and pictures.

that needs to be exploited. Once we have become aware of that potential, however, we must not jump to the conclusion that the more simple media are always and everywhere similar in their acceptability and effect. That is *simply* not the case! Psychologist J. B. Deregowski, for example, distinguishes between two kinds of perceptual ability: the *epitomic* and the *eidolic*. Epitomic ability is the ability to see that differently pigmented areas of a flat surface represent three-dimensional objects on one or another of two bases—either on the basis of a third dimension that is implicit in the pigmentation or on the basis that the thing being represented is reminiscent of a three-dimensional object. Eidolic ability has to do with the ability to see something in a picture that is independent of the picture's meaning.[7] Consider the response of a tribal people in Nyasaland (now Malawi) when confronted with a picture as recorded by a Scottish missionary at the end of the nineteenth century.

> Take a picture in black-and-white, and the natives cannot see it. You may tell the natives: "This is a picture of an ox and a dog"; and the people will look at you and that look says that they consider you a liar. Perhaps you say again, "Yes, this is a picture of an ox and a dog." Well, perhaps they will tell you what they think this time! If there are boys about, you say: "This is really a picture of an ox and a dog. Look at the horn of the ox, and there is his tail!" And the boy will say, "Oh! yes and there is the dog's nose and eyes and ears!" Then the old people will look again and clap their hands and say "Oh! yes, it is a dog."[8]

Again, consider the recent research of Bruce L. Cook of the David C. Cook Foundation in Papua, New Guinea.[9] Cook researched the question, "What kind of pictures communicate most effectively with illiterates?" Using pictures to communicate a simple story of a man chopping wood, Cook presented the story using five types of pictures: (1) stick figure drawings, (2) faceless outline drawings, (3) detailed black-and-white drawings, (4) detailed black-and-white drawings with water-

---

[7]J. B. Deregowski, "Pictures as a Means of Communication: A Psychologist's View," *Educational Broadcasting International* (March 1978), 8–9.
[8]Ibid., 8.
[9]Bruce L. Cook, *Understanding Pictures in Papua, New Guinea* (Elgin, Ill.: David C. Cook, 1981).

color wash, and (5) black-and-white photographs. On the basis of his findings, Cook provides nine "rules of thumb" for those using pictures among nonliterates (note that numbers 1 to 3 have to do with content and numbers 4 to 6 have to do with style):

1. Sociological and educational differences have the most effect on picture understanding.
2. Pictures of people should be used because they are easily understood.
3. Picture content affects understanding more than art style.
4. Art style does affect preference.
5. No single art style is best for nonliterate people.
6. If an artist had to choose art style on the basis of this study, realistic art (detailed black-and-white line drawings) would seem best.
7. Publication and distribution of comic book pictures can help develop understanding.
8. Avoid using a single picture to depict a lapse of time.
9. Do not assume that viewers automatically recognize a cause and effect relationship between two pictures.[10]

Cook also provides rules of thumb that are based on other research that call into question such approaches as the use of abstract symbols among nonliterates.[11] Rules of thumb such as these are not iron-clad, but they are worthy of consideration.

DRAMA, RITUAL, MUSIC, AND DANCE

I have already mentioned the impact of the Thai drama, "The Prodigal Daughter" on an international audience. One might think that Christian communicators in general, and cross-cultural communicators in particular, would make greater use of media such as the powerful *wayang* or dance-drama that is so popular in much of Asia. Especially so when

[10]Ibid., 79–83.
[11]Ibid., 84–85.

they become aware of the fact that drama (and the ritual, music and dance that accompanied it and made it a syndetic medium) was a primary means by which religion and culture flowed throughout Asia. In fact, in ancient China music was believed to possess a power of its own; dance became an official part of Confucian ceremonies in A.D. 485, and multiplied millions learned Confucian teachings and Taoist aphorisms by means of the Chinese opera.[12] In India, dance was regarded as a special gift of Brahma and therefore became a part of religious ritual. Since the Ramayana and Mahabharata epics and, later the Jataka Tales or birth stories of Buddha provided much of the content, dance and drama served to propagate the teachings of both Hinduism and Buddhism. The rest of Asia as well as large parts of Africa and many other regions provide similar data on the importance of drama, ritual, music, and dance. More often than not, these art forms are much more than forms of entertainment. They are

> preoccupied with questions people ask about the seen and unseen worlds; the mysteries of origin, birth, disease, death, drought and catastrophe, poverty and riches, good and evil, truth and beauty.[13]

Understandably, Christians have felt a profound tension when considering the use of these powerful media. On the one hand, it is obvious that they possess tremendous potential for the communication of the gospel. On the other hand, in many if not most Third World contexts they are intimately associated with heathen ideas and practices—and sometimes with the grossest of immorality and evil. In India, for example, dance-drama fell into the hands of temple girls who were "slaves of the gods" but gained a reputation as prostitutes. Nevertheless, seasoned and discriminating national leaders

[12]Chandu Ray, "The Use of Dance-Drama in Evangelism," *Effective Evangelism* 1,1 (April 1971): 6.
[13]Ibid., 8.

and missionaries encourage careful use of these indigenous media.

Bishop Chandu Ray of India notes that there are biblical and historical precedents for their use and suggests that adapting them to the communication of the gospel would help us get on the "wave-length" of the people.[14] Kathleen Nicholls (also from India) says that drama becomes Christian when Christian values are applied to real-life situations and conflicts. She insists that it can be reformed and claimed for kingdom service in India and elsewhere.[15]

Finally, Robert Bolton of Taiwan urges that Christians go even further in making use not only of drama but also of a wide variety of "celebrations of festivity" that are so much a part of Chinese life. This can be done by enhancing Christian "celebrations" and rituals such as those connected with Easter, Christmas, baptisms, weddings, and so forth, but also by seizing upon opportunities presented by Chinese celebrations and rituals such as the placing of inscriptions written on red paper on doorposts during the Chinese New Year season. By participating in such a ritual but infusing it with Christian content, Christians can draw attention to a different message on *their* red paper hangings—for example, "God Is Lord of My Family," or "Jesus Is My Benefactor of Grace."[16]

We may conclude that, upon entering a new culture or reassessing communication media use in one's own culture, it would be beneficial to inquire into the potential of indigenous media for the communication of Christ.

---

[14]Ibid., 11–14.

[15]Cf., Kathleen Nicholls, *The Prodigal Returns: A Christian Approach to Drama* (India: Traci, 1977), 1–18.

[16]Robert Bolton, "Celebrations of Festivity: A Potential Means of Effective Communication to Further Advance the Gospel Among the Taiwanese," a paper submitted to the School of World Mission and Evangelism, Trinity Evangelical Divinity School, for the course Advanced Problems in Cross-Cultural Communication, March 17, 1989.

Chapter 41

Using Syndetic Media

Depending on the circumstances, it is often easier to use syndetic media than simple media. It is easier to turn on a projector than it is to draw on a blackboard. It is easier to send a gospel tract than it is to write a personal appeal. But if it is easier to use syndetic media, their use is also more complex. Extending the message in time and space usually separates the source from the respondent and introduces new factors into the equation—factors that may be overlooked.

Edmund Carpenter recounts what happened when the Australian government attempted to communicate with underdeveloped native populations by means of large printed posters. The posters said, "Protect Our Rare Birdwing Butterflies" and carried a picture of the birdwing butterfly along with a warning: "$200 fine for collecting." The poster had an effect that was exactly opposite of that intended. Natives embarked on a campaign to capture the butterflies and then took them to the government offices for payment![1] *The*

[1]Edmund Carpenter, "Television Meets the Stone Age," *T.V. Guide* (16 January 1971), 15.

terseness and brevity that is the hallmark of printed signs or posters left too much information to be supplied by the native reader.

A very similar case of misunderstanding occurred among these same people in connection with a campaign by missionaries of the London Missionary Society against beer drinking. A large advertisement showed a picture of a glass of beer and carried the slogan, "Be specific, say South Pacific." To counteract the influence of this ad, missionaries printed and circulated posters that were identical except that they said, "Say No." The result must have been both frustrating and embarrassing for the missionaries—sales of No Beer skyrocketed![2]

Dayton and Fraser chronicle how a program designed to send a New Testament to every Pakistani whose name appeared in the telephone directory boomeranged. Many addresses had changed by the time the packet arrived in the post office. Some Pakistanis refused to accept unsolicited Christian Scriptures. Tons of New Testaments piled up in post offices and were auctioned off as "waste paper." Muslims could not understand why Christians would contribute to such desecration of a Holy Book![3]

Note that the *intention* of communicators is not in question in any of the foregoing cases. The problem in each case was that the assumptions were wrong.

SEPARATING FACT FROM FICTION

I have already referred to the fact that certain misconceptions often come into play when it comes to media use. This is especially true when using syndetic media, so it will be useful to separate some facts from fiction at this point:

1. The notion that any medium is acceptable provided one is sending a worthy message is fiction. The fact is that media

[2]Ibid.
[3]See Edward R. Dayton and David A. Fraser, *Planning Strategies for World Evangelization* (Grand Rapids: Eerdmans, 1980), 116. The authors quote one Frank S. Khair-Ullah.

themselves are variously judged as worthy or unworthy and appropriate or inappropriate depending on a variety of factors. Some examples will help to illustrate what I have in mind.

Example one: Mass media expert Malcolm Muggeridge insists that television is not an appropriate medium for Christian communication because it is basically a "fantasy" medium. The source must accommodate the television medium by abbreviating the message, sharpening the source "image," and so forth. Muggeridge concludes that, had television been available in the first century, Jesus would have refused television coverage of his ministry![4] Although it is obvious that many media people do not agree with Muggeridge, a reading of Virginia Stem Owens's *The Total Image: Selling Jesus in the Modern Age*[5] will enable one to understand why he thinks as he does.

Example two: There is some disagreement as to whether or not *manga* (cartoons) are suitable for gospel communication in Japan. The fact that Japanese *manga* so often carry indecent messages may reflect negatively on the gospel message itself.

Example three: The use of "magic" (in both simple and syndetic forms) to convey Christian messages in an animistic culture is questionable at best. That which cannot be explained (and much that can be explained!) is likely to be attributed to the *power* of the "magician" or the spirits.

2. The notion that the media are of more or less equal value in "spreading the gospel" is fiction. The fact is that each medium lends itself to certain objectives better than others. It is apparent that when it comes to the *speed* at which communication travels, radio and television are at the top of the list. Then come magazines, films, and books—in that order. If, however, we are thinking of *permanence*, the order changes: books, films, magazines, radio and television—the reverse of the previous order! Again, if our objective is to

[4]Malcolm Muggeridge, *Christ and the Media* (Grand Rapids: Eerdmans, 1977), 37–42.

[5]Virginia Stem Owens, *The Total Image: or Selling Jesus in the Modern Age* (Grand Rapids: Eerdmans, 1980).

teach, media of low speed, low participation, and greater permanence get a superior rating. If, on the other hand, our purpose it to *report* and *persuade*, media of high speed, high participation, and less permanence are superior.
3. The idea that if a medium is appropriate and effective in one context it will be equally appropriate and effective in another context is fiction. The fact is that "culture defines the language of the media, and the social structure defines the situation."[6] As Viggo Søgaard says,

> In one culture television is used mainly for entertainment totally financed by commercial enterprises. In another, it is used primarily as a news and educational source; and in a third culture, television is utilized mainly for propaganda. All of these variables influence people's attitudes toward a particular media channel, and in turn influence its effectiveness in persuasive communication.[7]

One survey taken a number of years ago failed to reveal a single person in the rural areas of the Philippines who did not regularly listen to radio.[8] Those who did not have their own radio made it a practice to listen to the radio of a neighbor at least once a week. (It is the common practice of Filipinos who own radios, television sets, or record players to accommodate less fortunate neighbors by turning up the volume and allowing them to congregate in or around their homes.) In urban areas 90 percent of the sample listened to radio programs every day. By contrast, print made a poor showing. Of literate people in the rural areas, 70 percent had read nothing in the previous week, and 60 percent had read nothing in the previous month. Even among urban college graduates,

---

[6]Viggo B. Søgaard, *Everything You Need to Know for a Cassette Ministry: Cassettes in the Context of a Total Christian Communication Program* (Minneapolis: Bethany Fellowship, 1975), 40.
[7]Ibid.
[8]Merrill Abbey, *Man, Media and the Message* (New York: Friendship, 1960), 88–89.

80 percent had read nothing in the three-day period prior to the interview except what was necessitated by their work. In Western Europe women listen to radio and read magazines more than men do. But due to the very different status of women in Arab countries and southeast Asia, women listen to radio and read magazines much less frequently than men do.[9] Obviously this difference is of great importance to communicators.

4. The idea that the best way to evangelize the world is by radio or satellite television is fiction. The facts are that the potential of mass media is somewhat limited and that mass media need to be complemented by interpersonal communication. Wilbur Schramm writes,

> The mass media can help only indirectly to change strongly held attitudes or valued practices. Mass communication has never proved very effective in attacking attitudes, values, or social customs that are deep-set or strongly held.[10]

G. Ralph Milton agrees and adds another dimension that is very important to Christian communicators:

> Enough research has been done . . . to enable us to be certain that a person's communication with family and friends is more significant in terms of attitude change and formation than any or all of the media. In fact, this result is reported with almost monotonous regularity. This is especially true of deep rooted attitudes and beliefs, such as religious conviction.[11]

We can be heartened by the commitment of three great missionary broadcasting organizations—Trans World Radio, Far East Broadcasting Company, and World Radio Missionary Fellowship (HCJB)—to evangelize the world by radio within

[9]Wilbur Schramm, *Mass Media and National Development* (Stanford: Stanford University Press, 1964), 82–83.

[10]Ibid., 132.

[11]G. Ralph Milton, "Media Integration—A Fad and a Fact: The Church and the Media," *Asia Focus* 6 (third quarter 1971), 41.

the next few years. But we should not let that blind us to the need of sending missionaries and going ourselves. Joe Bayly reminded us of this in his little classic *The Gospel Blimp*.[12] Virginia Stem Owens warns us of "the dangers of the disembodied message."[13] Our Lord commanded us to go and to send, not just the message, but *messengers*.

Turning now to an examination of specific syndetic media, we will examine print, electronic, and various other media. (Readers are referred to an important work by James F. Engel for a more detailed analysis of these media.[14])

THE PRINT MEDIA

It is commonly believed that print media are not only the oldest mass media but also the most effective. For example, there are some indications that, in the United States at least, the printed page is more believable than either radio or television.[15] However, one must take into account the high degree of illiteracy in many parts of the world, a situation I alluded to in the preceding chapter. In addition to illiteracy per se, a significant percentage of the people who are categorized as literate are *functionally* illiterate. And still others who *can* read *do not* read very much, if at all, as in the Philippines. In some countries it may not be realistic to expect that even 10 percent of the population can be reached by print media.[16] Nevertheless, the various types of literature are very important to that part of any population who can and will read.

1. *Books.* Christianity is the religion of "The Book," the Bible. There can be no question as to the importance of the Bible in evangelism and Christian instruction. Worldwide (all sources), close to 50 million Bibles and over 73 million New

---

[12]Joe Bayly, *The Gospel Blimp* (Havertown, Pa.: Windward, 1960).

[13]Owens, *Total Image*, 77ff.

[14]James F. Engel, *Contemporary Christian Communications: Its Theory and Practice* (Nashville: Thomas Nelson, 1979), especially 135–58.

[15]Cf. Joseph T. Klapper, *The Effects of Mass Communication* (Glencoe, Ill.: Free Press, 1960), 110–12.

[16]Søgaard, *Cassette Ministry*, 49.

Testaments are distributed each year.[17] Our task now must be to promote the best possible use of these Bibles in promoting the kingdom cause.

Some years ago I opened a desk drawer in my hotel room in Kyoto, Japan, and found two religious books—the *Holy Bible* and *The Message of Buddha*. The latter had an attractive, multicolored jacket, an extensive and helpful index, a glossary of important terms, an explanation of basic Buddhism and a list of the contents of the book in addition to the basic text. The former had a very abbreviated topical index to certain Bible passages, a list of Old and New Testament books, and the text. It became immediately apparent that we as Christians need to give attention, not only to the truth and power of the Bible and its message, but also to the way that we "package," distribute, and otherwise promote its reading, study, and understanding.

Again, thinking in terms of Christian books of all kinds and using the UNESCO definition of "book" (over forty-nine pages), almost 65,000 new titles now appear worldwide each year.[18] This too is impressive. Books are more or less permanent. They can be referred to over and over. Although the number of people who come to Christ on the basis of a single reading of one title may not be large, the number of readers who are motivated in that direction and who are confirmed and instructed in Christian faith must be great indeed. With that in mind Christian communicators should put more emphasis on pre-evangelistic titles, on Christian novels, on books that highlight contemporary issues, and on encouraging the production of more books by competent national authors in non-Western nations.

2. *Magazines and journals.* As literacy, education, and income increase in any nation, the readership of magazines will increase. Although their number has actually been decreasing somewhat until very recently, some 22,700 Chris-

[17]David B. Barrett, "Annual Statistical Table on Global Mission: 1989," *International Bulletin of Missionary Research* 13,1 (January 1989), 20–21.
[18]Ibid.

tian periodicals are now being published around the world.[19] Perhaps the greatest advantage of magazines and journals is that they can be made to appeal to general audiences; thoughtful preparation and marketing, as with *Breakthrough* in Hong Kong and *Yo no Hikari* (Light of the World) in Japan, can result in significant appeal to general audiences. Care should be taken to ascertain the need and readership potential before undertaking costly ventures, however.

3. *Booklets and tracts.* The emphasis in the United States on the *number* of tracts and booklets distributed overseas needs to be balanced with an emphasis on *content* and *quality.* Tens of thousands of gospel tracts and gospel portions have been unceremoniously put to the torch overseas. Why? Because the tracts (translated from English) were entirely embarrassing to national Christians and therefore went unused and because the gospel portions were distributed day after day at the same city centers and therefore to essentially the same people. The locals were too courteous to refuse a "gift" and therefore dispensed with them upon arriving at the office or home. We should remember that booklets and pamphlets are of very limited value unless they are attention-getting, related to felt needs, and have local appeal. Even then, people generally do not value that for which they pay nothing. For that reason, until postwar days, missionaries in Korea made it a general policy to *sell* tracts and Scripture portions if only for a very small amount.

THE ELECTRONIC MEDIA

David Barrett projects that the present number of Christian radio/TV stations (1,900) will more than double to 4,000 by the year 2000 and that the total number of monthly listener/viewers of all Christian programs (on Christian and secular stations) will increase from a present 1,291,582,000 to 2,150,000,000![20] Truly radio and television are the characteris-

[19]Ibid.
[20]Ibid.

tic media of our day. We are reaching almost total media access.

1. *Radio.* There are a number of advantages that accrue to radio communication: it is the most widely used mass medium; it is easy to listen to and encounters less resistance that most media; it may result in greater retention, at least among uneducated people; and it is much less costly than television. But it also has some disadvantages in that it appeals to but one sense; it offers little opportunity for re-exposure; and accessibility to Christian broadcasts may be limited. All things considered, radio may be the best medium for *mass* evangelism. However, some changes may be in order before its potential can be fully exploited. For example, research indicates that a large part of the listening audience of evangelistic broadcasts is actually Christian. Broadcasters need to think more in terms of meeting the real needs of believers worldwide. Where pastors and established churches are few, it would be most helpful to instruct believers in ways of coming together to form believing groups. Where oppression is significant it is important to lead listening believers in Bible studies that build toward maturity rather than just repeat the basic gospel truths. If unbelieving audiences are to be attracted to a gospel message, it may be necessary to change the format. For example, the "Lutheran Hour" of the Lutheran Church–Missouri Synod is now broadcast in many languages around the world. As a result of careful study and implementation, the format has been changed in many areas from the sermonic one so familiar to North American listeners to drama, documentary, storytelling, and music with commentary formats. With these more viable culturally adapted formats, the "Lutheran Hour" is "bringing Christ to the nations."[21]

2. *Television.* Some feel that television has the greatest potential as a communication medium.[22] It appeals to both the

[21]Abbey, *Man, Media,* 97.
[22]Søgaard, *Cassette Ministry,* 44.

eye and the ear. It has attracted huge audiences of all ages and for extended periods of time in those nations where the technology allows for this. But at the same time, it is a very costly medium; its use requires multiple communications skills; and users usually must appeal to the lowest common denominator because of the nature of the television audience. Recent episodes involving the ministries of Jim Bakker and the PTL, Jimmy Swaggart, and others give indication of the tremendous pressures that attend television communication even when by some measurements the programming is successful. Perhaps more than any other medium, television will present the greatest challenge to Christian ingenuity, stewardship, and integrity in the future.

PLATFORM MEDIA

1. *Mass evangelistic crusades or rallies.* Although waning in their appeal somewhat, mass evangelistic meetings still attract large audiences and likely will continue to do so. There is something appealing about the festive atmosphere. Of course, the popularity of the evangelist is an important factor also. Mass meetings can be effective in bringing those who have had previous exposure to the church and the gospel to the place of decision. Perhaps the most crucial factor in mass evangelistic meetings has to do with the way in which "seekers" are dealt with and followed up.

2. *Film.* The popularity of such films as the *Jesus* film both on TV and in platform showings, both in intracultural and intercultural Christian communication, would seem to indicate that film constitutes a universally accepted and understood medium. Such is not the case.

There are some illuminating and "moving" paragraphs in McLuhan's *Understanding Media* that "show" us up for the naïve communicators we often are in this regard.[23] McLuhan

[23] Marshall McLuhan, *Understanding Media: The Extensions of Man* (New York: McGraw-Hill, 1964), 284ff.

asserts that movies assume a high level of literacy in the viewer and are likely to baffle the nonliterate.

> Movies as a nonverbal form of experience are like photography, a form of statement with syntax. In fact, however, like the print and the photo, movies assume a high level of literacy in their users and prove baffling to the nonliterate. Our literate acceptance of the mere movement of the camera eye as it follows or drops a figure from view is not acceptable to an African film audience. If somebody disappears off the side of the film, the African wants to know what happened to him. A literate audience, however, accustomed to following printed imagery line by line without questioning the logic of lineality, will accept film sequence without protest.[24]

John Wilson of London University's African Institute tried for years to teach Africans their letters by film. Then he discovered that it was easier to teach them letters as a means to understanding film.[25]

Sidney Cook, a friend of mine, tells how he convinced some communication experts in South Africa that certain black Africans were not "tracking" film messages. He did it by taking them to theaters where the feature film was "cut" (because of curfew) before the plot was resolved. The audience exited without any indication at all that they were frustrated or wondered how the film ended!

Film offers many of the advantages of television without some of television's advantages. However, Christian communicators should not expect too much from its use. The reports of great numbers of people who "made a decision for Christ" upon seeing this or that Christian film should be taken with a grain of salt. A careful study of the results of one showing of the *Jesus* film to the Gwembe Tonga in Zambia, for example, reveals positive results but also alerts us to the need for careful use. One viewing was followed by significantly differ-

[24]Ibid., 285–86.
[25]Ibid., 286–87.

ent knowledge and attitude mean scores. Knowledge was generally increased. The attitude toward Jesus of some Tonga became more positive (although, curiously enough, the attitude of a lesser number became more negative). The researcher, Cathy Lee Mansfield, concludes that whether or not the *Jesus* film makes a positive contribution among people like the Gwembe Tonga depends on a variety of factors and especially on how the film is used. "One isolated film showing is not likely to be followed by permanent impact, unless succeeded by careful teaching about God's entire plan of salvation from the Bible."[26]

OTHER MEDIA

A wide variety of syndetic media (some of which might well be included in the categories dealt with above) merit much more consideration than can be given to them here. For that matter, they merit more consideration than is given to them in many a mission and church. We will briefly mention a few of them before concluding the present discussion.

1. *Group dialogue.* A variety of media can be used in combination and within the context of a group (usually a small group) in order to secure active participation of members of the group in two-way communication. Some of the fastest-growing religious movements in the world—both Christian and non-Christian—capitalize on the educational and persuasive potential of small-group discussion.[27] As a matter of fact, small cell groups really constitute the growing edge of many rapidly growing local congregations, such as Paul Yonggi Cho's Full Gospel Assembly in Seoul with a membership of over 500,000.

2. *Records and audio cassettes.* Gospel Recordings has

[26]Cathy Lee Mansfield, "Cognitive and Attitudinal Changes Following Viewing of the Jesus Film Among the Gwembe Tonga of Zambia," M.A. thesis, Trinity Evangelical Divinity School, 1984, 72.

[27]Cf. David J. Hesselgrave, *Dynamic Religious Movements: Case Studies in Rapidly Growing Religious Movements Around the World* (Grand Rapids: Baker, 1980), passim.

done an outstanding job of preparing and distributing recordings for hundreds of language groups worldwide. In fact, an ingenious hand-powered record player that costs only a few cents to produce has been made available for people in areas where electricity and modern technology are completely unknown. Once again, the critical factor has to do with the way these media are used.[28]

3. *Video cassettes.* On the surface, the video cassette may appear to be the same as television. In reality it is a quite different medium with a potential for pre-evangelism, evangelism, and Christian education that is just beginning to be tapped in cross-cultural ministries.

4. *Slides.* Often overlooked after the rise in popularity of the motion picture film, slides should still be considered by the Christian evangelist and teacher. Not a few communicators have gone back to the use of slides as an effective tool, especially for teaching.

5. *The telephone.* Anyone who has watched numerous lights go on signaling that callers on a number of telephone lines are simultaneously listening to a recorded Christian message will be impressed as to the potential of "dial-a-devotion" and similar approaches to telephone ministries.

6. *The computer.* So far, Christian computer use has largely been restricted to the sharing of information among Christians and Christian groups. The time will come when computers will be used to a much greater extent than today in sharing both pre-evangelistic information and the gospel message itself with unbelievers on a worldwide basis.

7. *Direct mail.* In the United States, direct mail ranks third, behind newspapers and television, as an advertising medium.[29] Obviously, direct mail does not have equal potential in all countries. But in that it can be used to reach a highly selective audience, its possible use should be considered in many situations.

[28]Cf. Søgaard, *Cassette Ministry*, 50–51.
[29]Engel, *Contemporary Christian Communications*, 157.

MIXING AND MATCHING MEDIA

It is axiomatic that in the vast majority of cases a multimedia approach is the most effective. Media should be mixed and matched in accordance with communication objectives and with media, message, and audience characteristics.

1. *Choose media on the basis of communication objectives.* Søgaard writes,

> During the decoding, or reception process, each message that reaches a person must first pass through a "filter," a conscious and unconscious selectivity that a person engages as the message reaches him. It consists of exposure, attention, comprehension, and retention. This selective filter is active for all kinds of communications, but the degree of use may vary on the media, program content and format, as well as on stored information and personality.[30]

This filtering process can be diagrammed as in figure 38. If the right media mix is used, one can fulfill all four objectives. If only one medium is used, other changes such as a change in format or style will be necessary.

2. *Choose on the basis of audience preferences.* In the Philippines the order of audience preference seems to be radio, television, magazines, books. In Japan it seems to be magazines, television, books, radio. In the early 1960s the Kenyan government switched from films to filmstrips for instructing rural people concerning government programs. Previous exposure to films had the effect of rendering filmstrips less interesting to the people, with the result that audiences became smaller and smaller. It became necessary to switch back to films.

3. *Choose on the basis of media characteristics.* All else being equal, the order of media in terms of speed of delivery would be radio, television, magazines, films, and books. In terms of permanence the order would be books, films,

magazines, radio, and television. As we have noted, low-speed, low-participation media lend themselves to instruction. High speed and high participation are better for reporting and persuasion.

Figure 38

SELECTIVE FILTERING PROCESS

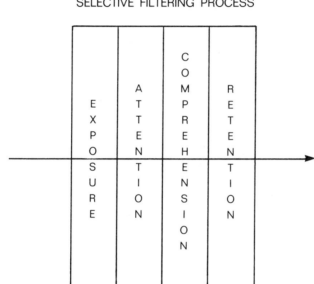

Viggo B. Søgaard *Cassette Ministry: Cassettes in the Context of a Total Christian Communication Program* (Minneapolis: Bethany Fellowship, Inc.), 38.

---

4. *Choose on the basis of "reach," "frequency," and "cost" considerations.* Writing from a marketing perspective, James Engel explains that "reach" indicates the percentage of homes in an area that are exposed to a medium over a period of time, whereas "frequency" indicates the number of times

the average home is reached.[31] Depending on the objective and cost, the communicator will often make a trade-off of one for the other. The cost of the various media can be compared through a cost per thousand (CPM) formula and can be computed as follows:

$$\frac{\text{Space or time rate} \times 1000}{\text{audience reached}}$$

In the case of newspapers the "milline rate" is often used. It is computed as follows:

$$\frac{\text{cost per line} \times 1,000,000}{\text{readers reached}}$$

THE IMPORTANCE OF INTERPERSONAL COMMUNICATION

It must always be borne in mind that media communication needs to be conjoined with interpersonal communication. Early on, certain media specialists put forth the principle of "two-step flow": ideas and influence flow from the mass media to opinion leaders, who, in turn, pass on the ideas and influence more passive members of society.[32] More recently, experts have tended toward a "multistep flow" theory, according to which interaction between opinion leaders and nonopinion leaders result in the reinforcement of mass media–communicated ideas and influence.[33] From a Christian point of view, the important thing to remember is that *people* are important in the communication process, not only as respondents but also in relaying and reinforcing syndetically commu-

[31]Engel, Contemporary Christian Communications, 168–72.
[32]Paul F. Lazarsfeld, Bernard R. Berelson, and Hazel Gaudet, The People's Choice (New York: Columbia University Press, 1949), 151; cf. also Klapper, 32.
[33]Engel, Contemporary Christian Communications, 162.

nicated Christian messages, especially those of the mass-media variety.

To put it another way, there is abundant evidence to support the contention that the primary role of the mass media in persuasion is a *contributory* role. As we have noted, the mass media tend to stimulate interest and heighten awareness and, in that way, contribute to decision making. But they do not play a *decisive* role in decision making, especially when basic attitudinal changes are involved. *For that reason, mass and interpersonal witness should be integrated.*

The importance of this principle has been corroborated in my own experience in several years of broadcasting within the context of a foreign culture. It has been corroborated in numerous other cases as well. For example, a well-known gospel radio program (originating in North America) that is also aired in a number of foreign countries was deemed to be almost totally ineffective in terms of adding believers to evangelical churches in Colombia until a portion of the air time was given to Colombian pastors. Once the program was identified with certain local churches and pastors, its message was reinforced by local believers and it became possible for interested listeners to be counseled and instructed locally. The result was that many more listeners were converted and added to the churches. (Of course, in very hostile environments it may be advisable to confine follow-up to letter writing.)

CONCLUSION TO PART VIII

In the office of RAVEMCCO in New York there is displayed a photograph that has caught the attention of many a visitor. It is a picture of a Filipino farmer plowing his field with a buffalo and plow reminiscent of the Iron Age. To one horn of the buffalo is attached a transistor radio!

The world is in the midst of a communications revolution of which we may have witnessed only the beginnings. Christian missions cannot afford to be left behind in this "brave new world" of tomorrow. But neither can they afford to be trampled underfoot by the relentless surge of technological advance. In the rush to keep up with the times and get the Word out, they will experience an even greater temptation to pull out all the stops and get on with the task while neglecting cultural adaptations—a neglect that has already made Christianity seem too Western to much of the world. When technological skill and impatience override cultural adaptation, the result is sometimes lamentable.

This often occurs, for example, when books written within and for Western cultures are translated into languages of other cultures and then printed and distributed. Messages prepared by Western authors in Western idiom for Western audiences are hastily translated, printed, and distributed in Latin America, Africa, and Asia. It is really no wonder that intelligent nationals keep insisting that Christianity is a Western religion in spite of its Eastern origins. Over and over they are required to decode the Christian message in terms of their understanding (or misunderstanding) of Western cultural forms—a strange kind of reversal of the missionary program. If print, therefore, presents a great opportunity, it also presents a significant challenge. People are more inclined to overlook the weaknesses of oral presentations than the weaknesses of the printed tract or book. Something similar can be said about other media.

With all the emphasis on the importance of the media we should never forget that the gospel message itself is even more important. The biblical gospel must be faithfully preserved and carefully contextualized. As someone has remarked, "The Greeks could not *broadcast* an Aeschylean tragedy but they could *write* it!" Just so, those first-century apostles could not *televise* the Christian gospel, but they *communicated* it!

Part IX

MOTIVATIONAL RESOURCES— WAYS OF DECIDING

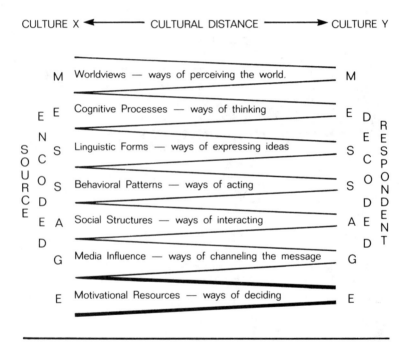

Figure 39

DIMENSIONS OF CROSS-CULTURAL COMMUNICATION

CULTURE X ◄——— CULTURAL DISTANCE ———► CULTURE Y

M Worldviews — ways of perceiving the world. M

E Cognitive Processes — ways of thinking E

S Linguistic Forms — ways of expressing ideas S

S Behavioral Patterns — ways of acting S

A Social Structures — ways of interacting A

G Media Influence — ways of channeling the message G

E Motivational Resources — ways of deciding E

SOURCE ENCODED MESSAGE

DECODED MESSAGE RESPONDENT

Chapter 42

From Persuasion to Elenctics

Ghulam Susil Ram had just finished reading Sadhu Sundar Singh's *With and Without Christ*.[1] He was deeply moved by the faith and devotion of this man who had pushed through the dense undergrowth of Indian religiosity and had embraced the Christ. He too was attracted to the great Teacher. But could any teacher take him to loftier planes than those ancients who bequeathed the Upanishads to his native India? He wondered.

Manuel Osmenas stood quietly but not unmoved. He had known nothing but disappointments and hardship in recent times. Life in Manila was just as unrewarding as life had been in the backward barrio he still called home. The new life promised by the evangelist was certainly appealing. But what of his family and friends? What would their reaction be? He did not know.

Jean Omodo had been persuaded by one of his wives to attend the big Sunday meeting with her. Such meetings were not uncommon in that part of the Cameroons, but they were

---

[1]Sundhar Singh, *With and Without Christ* (New York: Harper, 1929).

special in any case. Now the crowd that numbered in the hundreds was breaking up. Many gathered in small groups outside the thatch-roofed church. Others were already climbing into decrepit, crowded buses and trucks. He motioned his wife to hurry as he started down the dusty road. Why had he invited the pastor to visit his home? Why had he done so? Why, if not for the fact that he was impressed by his favorite wife's changed life and the message he had just heard from the preacher? But what would he say to the pastor? To contemplate forsaking the gods of his ancestors was difficult indeed. What would be the reaction of his brothers and his other wives? He felt a twinge of fear as he walked along.

Viewed from the perspective of our respondents—whether Indian, Filipino, or African—the ultimate issue in missionary communication can be rather succinctly stated in the form of a simple question. It is this: "Why should I forsake the traditional ways of my people and, repenting for what I have been and what I have done and left undone, give my full trust and allegiance to this Jesus Christ?

Viewed from the perspective of the missionary, the ultimate issues can be rather succinctly stated in the form of three questions. The first is, "Do I have the responsibility to persuade people to forsake traditional ways and convert to Christ?" The second is, "Do I have the right to do so?" The third is, "Do I have the resources to do so?"

In this chapter we will focus on the missionary. (Having examined the question of persuasion and mission in Chapter 6 we will confine our discussion here to issues having to do with the missionary's rights and resources.) In ensuing chapters we will examine respondent motivations.

HAVE WE THE RIGHT?

Logically, this problem must be considered in a context wider than that of Christian mission. In its larger dimensions the philosophers of Greece faced the same problem head-on.

Embracing Socrates as his paragon of virtue and the philosopher-king as his ideal, Plato was not the rhetorician's best friend. He insisted that rhetoric could not make people good. Moreover, he disdained the ability of orators to make an unjust cause *seem* right and good. Only with great reluctance did he allow for a *proper* kind of rhetoric for democratic states (and there only because citizens of democratic states restlessly strive to better their condition). In the *Phaedrus* he characterized that rhetoric as consisting of truth plus its artful presentation, with good as the object. Logically, he said, one cannot justify the "moving of another man's soul." Practically, however, the discipline can pass muster if its practitioner possesses the truth and persuades toward the good. Richard Weaver summarizes Plato's position well.

> Rhetoric moves the soul with a movement which cannot finally be justified logically. In can only be valued analogically with reference to some supreme image. Therefore when the rhetorician encounters some soul "sinking beneath the double load of forgetfulness and vice," he seeks to reanimate it by holding up to its sight the order of presumptive goods. This order is necessarily a hierarchy leading to the ultimate Good. All of the terms in a rhetorical vocabulary are like links in a chain stretching up to some master link which transmits its influence down through the linkages. It is impossible to talk about rhetoric as effective expression without having as a term giving intelligibility to the whole discourse, the Good. Of course, inferior concepts of the Good may be and often are placed in this ultimate position; and there is nothing to keep a base lover from inverting the proper order and saying, "Evil, be thou my good." Yet the fact remains that in any piece of rhetorical discourse, one term overcomes another rhetorical term only by being nearer to the term which stands ultimate. There is some ground for calling rhetorical education necessarily an aristocratic education in that the rhetorician has to deal with an aristocracy of notions, to say nothing of supplementing his logical and pathetic proofs with an ethical proof.[2]

[2]Richard Weaver, *The Ethics of Rhetoric* (Chicago: Regnery, 1953), 23.

Plato's transcendental idealism came in such large doses that it was not easily swallowed by a great many ancient philosophers—Aristotle among them. Aristotle was an idealist in a quite different sense. He thought that truth and goodness possess a kind of natural tendency to prevail over their opposites. If people can think clearly and speak well, they will not obstruct this natural tendency. That being the case, he believed that virtue and justice would result if dialectic and rhetoric were widely taught.

Can we not say that the disagreement between these two famous pedagogues of Greece exhibits many of the elements of the great warfare between religion and science that, however badly fought, has raged in Western society for several centuries?

In his book *Religion and the Modern Mind*, W. T. Stace dwells at length on the evolution of human thought from the general conviction that the world is a moral order to the widespread belief that people are "moral orderers." He argues that this drastic change was not due to logical prescription but to psychological reaction. He writes,

Thus the train of thought which has led from the prescientific belief that the world is a moral order to the modern belief that it is not may be summarized thus:

If morality is grounded in divine or cosmic purpose, it is objective. The world is a moral order.

Newtonian science caused a loss of effective belief in divine or cosmic purpose. . . .

Hence morality could no longer be grounded in divine or cosmic purpose.

If divine and cosmic purpose are eliminated, the only remaining alternative is human purpose.

Therefore moral values must now be made dependent upon human purposes.

But this, by definition, is subjectivism and is the view that the world is not a moral order. This is no more than a schema, a naked skeleton of human thought—not the full flesh of any human thinking.[3]

Therefore, as Stace points out, "loss of religious faith necessitates the substitution of a secular ethics based on human purposes for an ethics grounded in religious conceptions."[4] Tragically, Stace's analysis is all too true. In this post-Christian age Western society searches vainly for the secular ethic. Meanwhile, it is deemed legitimate to teach students to think clearly so they can arrive at valid opinions. It is legitimate to teach them to speak eloquently so they can communicate those opinions. It is legitimate to form lobbies in order to effect legislation that transmutes the opinions of pressure groups into law. But we have abandoned the good and true and right that transcend our opinions, feelings, desires, proclivities, and even our laws, and which eventually will sit in judgment on all of them. Plato was right. Rhetoric has no inherent absolutes. Nor does it have the power to make people good. Truth and goodness transcend man himself. They *are* in the *logos*, but—and here Plato was wrong—they are not in the *logos* of the philosopher but in the *Logos* of God, the Christ of the Bible.

Few passages more clearly portray the dilemma of one who perceives our modern problem while still hoping against hope for a secular solution than does this lament over modern education written by Donald Lemen Clark, professor emeritus of rhetoric at Columbia University:

> We might also learn from Greek and Roman teaching of rhetoric that the teaching of the arts of speaking and writing was in antiquity and can be at all times an agent for the teaching of morality. And we are beginning to realize what floods of barbarism are let loose when morality is not taught. The phrase "original sin" may seem old fashioned,

[3]W. T. Stace, *Religion and the Modern Mind* (Philadelphia: Lippincott, 1952), 107.
[4]Ibid., 108.

but sin is not. It is a commonplace of universal observation that children by natural impulse are liars, thieves, and vandals. Only if some rudiments of morality are inculcated by parents and teachers will the little savages acquire some semblance of civilized conduct. Now all ancient teachers believed that rhetoric should teach virtue and justice. Plato was indignant because he recognized that rhetoric cannot make people just. But Isocrates, Cicero, and Quintilian pointed out in many passages which I have quoted that training in rhetoric can and does contribute to civilizing young people. "When anyone elects to speak or write discourses which are worthy of praise and honor, it is not conceivable that he will support causes which are unjust and petty," says Isocrates. After his father, in the *De partitione*, had given an account of the rhetorical principles of awarding praise and blame, "which have power not only to teach us to speak well, but also to live honorably," Cicero Junior says: "You have taught me, not only how to praise others, but also how to be worthy of praise myself." Quintilian sums up the theme that the orator must be a good man, doing and speaking no evil. Training in rhetoric cannot alone, or with other educational helps, make a youth prudent, temperate, courageous, and just, but it fails in its traditional educational duty if it does not throw its weight in favor of these cardinal virtues. Teachers may be assured that some measure of success will follow.[5]

Although it betrays a naturalistic bias, Clark's admonition is worthy of careful consideration at a time when Western society faces moral bankruptcy.

Some of the best of ancient (and modern) thinkers, then, have realized that human societies need teachers who will prepare themselves to make the strongest possible case for truth, justice, and goodness. Woe to those societies that fill their curricula with courses in speech, communication, language, critical thinking, and persuasion and then neglect to

[5]Donald Lemen Clark, *Rhetoric in Greco-Roman Education* (New York: Columbia University Press, 1957), 264–65.

balance these studies with courses in ethics (by whatever name).

Now if we admit that there are any people at all who are qualified to persuade others toward that which is true and good, perhaps Christian missionaries can be excused for submitting their credentials for our examination. They believe that such time-honored standards as the Ten Commandments, the Beatitudes, and the Golden Rule are quite impossible to improve upon, and at that point good men have almost universally agreed. They believe that in all too many cases people do not order their lives according to these standards but that, insofar as possible, they *should* do so—and here too there is widespread agreement. They recognize their own imperfections but set out on a mission to teach, persuade, and help people to promote love and justice at all levels of their existence. Most would agree that, though their aims are utopian, those who undertake such a mission are to be encouraged and admired. Those who would demur would probably do so on the ground that we have no right to interfere with the lives of citizens of *other cultures*. But missionaries cannot afford to wait for cultural Rip Van Winkles to awaken to twentieth-century reality in which cultural differences and geographical distances neither insulate nor isolate societies from one another. Since the bad and deplorable cannot be put into quarantine, we jolly well better not shut up those ideas that are good and desirable.

But my argument entails more than the proposition that it is justifiable to send missionaries as do-gooders persuading people to behave and otherwise helping them in the process. Were that my intent, I could rest my case with Plato and Aristotle (and Quintilian *et al*). Or I could clinch it by insisting that Christians have every bit as much right to persuade people toward that which we believe to be right as those who disagree with us have the right to persuade us to refrain from so doing! Our argument, however, entails the further assertion that *the* truth (and goodness and grace!) came by Jesus Christ. The implications of that fact transport people

of faith to holy ground where Christ's followers must walk
without shoes and unbelievers cannot walk at all.
It must seem incredible to the naturalist when, for
example, we insist that seemingly *good* people need to be
converted. And it evidently seems incongruous, to some
Christians at least, when we insist that a sovereign God
requires that his frail children "do the converting"! To get the
naturalist to see the biblical truth that all people (including
good Hindus, Buddhists, and Muslims, among others) are lost
spiritually and need to be converted to Christ is almost
tantamount to conversion itself! And, as far as the professing
Christian who is skeptical at this point is concerned, to do
more for him than call to his attention the multitude of
Scriptures that witness to these truths is, in effect, to deal
with him as a naturalist. In the final analysis, we know that
all people need to come to Christ for salvation for precisely
the same reason that we know that *we* needed to come to
Christ for salvation. And we know that we must urge people
everywhere to come to Christ for precisely the same reason
that someone urged *us* to come to Christ. We know these
things because God has told us so in his eternal Word!
Conversion, after all, is a good New Testament word.
Bishop Stephen Neill has written,

> It is constantly said that old ideas of mission must be
> completely replaced by those that are new and relevant.
> This is a statement that needs elucidation, and much useful
> discussion can arise out of it. But I wonder whether the
> heart has not gone out of the missionary enterprise in all
> the mainline Churches for another and deeper reason.
>
> If we put the plain question, "Do we want people to be
> converted?" from many of our contemporary ecumenical
> theologians the answer will be a resounding "No." If we are
> evangelicals, must not the answer the a resounding "Yes"?
>
> For years I have been looking for a word which will take
> the place of the now very unpopular word "conversion" and
> have not found it. I am well aware of all the possible
> objections to the word. But I have an uneasy feeling that

those who hesitate to use the word are also rejecting the thing.[6]

HAVE WE THE RESOURCES?

As I mentioned, the notion has been advanced by some that while they are not against conversion per se, they are opposed to the idea that missionaries (being ordinary mortals, as most people will now grant) should do the converting. Conversion, they say, is God's work.

Granted. Conversion is God's work. But it is also man's work. The Bible is unequivocal at that point. The angel's prophecy concerning John the Baptist was to the effect that John would "turn back many of the sons of Israel to the Lord their God" (Luke 1:16). Paul told Agrippa that he had been commissioned to go to the Gentiles "to open their eyes, and to turn them from darkness to light, and from the power of Satan unto God" (Acts 26:18 KJV).

Admittedly, the Bible does not seem to speak unequivocally on such problems as how God can be responsible for the consummation of his plan for the world and yet hold people responsible to carry out that plan; and how God causes people to turn to himself in repentance and faith while commissioning his (sometimes disobedient) children to actually do the converting. These seemingly contradictory teachings of Scripture are called antinomies. They entail apparently mutually contradictory conclusions but no actual contradictions. They will be fully understood when we know even as we are known, but they do give us pause as long as we only "see through a glass, darkly" (1 Cor. 13:12 KJV).

These questions are pursued in elenctics—a neglected subject in contemporary theology.

One of the finest brief explanations of the subject of elenctics to be found anywhere comes from the pen of the Dutch missionary and theologian John Herman Bavinck:

[6]Stephen Neill, "Conversion," cited in *Church Growth Bulletin* 7 (May 1971): 145.

The term "elenctic" is derived from the Greek verb *elengchein*. In Homer the verb has the meaning of "to bring to shame." It is connected with the word *elengchos* that signifies shame. In later Attic Greek the significance of the term underwent a certain change so that the emphasis fell more upon the conviction of guilt, the demonstration of guilt. It is this latter significance that it has in the New Testament. Its meaning is entirely ethical and religious.

In the New Testament the verb *elengchein* appears in various places. It is used together with various subjects.

a. The Lord in his final judgment. Thus, in Jude (vss. 14, 15 KJV), "Behold, the Lord cometh with ten thousands of his saints, to execute judgment upon all and to convince all that are ungodly among them . . ."

b. The Lord in his daily care for the congregation. Thus in Revelation 3:19 (KJV) where we read: "As many as I love, I rebuke *(elengcho)* and chasten."

c. The Holy Spirit. Thus, in John 16:8 (KJV) "and when he is come he will reprove *(elengxei)* the world of sin, and of righteousness, and of judgment."

d. An elder in relation to those who err in the congregation. This occurs in I Timothy 5:20 (KJV), which states: "Them that sin rebuke *(elengche)* before all."

e. One brother trespassing against another brother. Thus, in Matthew 18:15 (KJV), Jesus says, "Moreover if thy brother shall trespass against thee, go and tell him his fault *(elengxon)* between thee and him alone."

From these texts it is clear that the word in the New Testament is regularly translated as rebuking, but then in the sense that it includes the conviction of sin and a call to repentance.

When we speak of *elenctics* we do well to understand it in the sense that it has in John 16:8. The Holy Spirit will convince the world of sin. The Holy Spirit is actually the only conceivable subject of this verb, for the conviction of sin exceeds all human ability. Only the Holy Spirit can do this, even though he can and will use us as instruments in his hand. Taken in this sense, elenctics is the science which is concerned with the conviction of sin. In a special sense then it is the science which unmasks to heathendom all false religions as sin against God, and it calls heathendom to a knowledge of the only true God. To be able to do this well and truthfully it is necessary to have a responsible knowledge of false religions, but one must also be able to lay bare the deepest motifs which are therein expressed. This can actually occur only if one recognizes and unmasks these same undercurrents within himself. Elenctics is possible only on the basis of a veritable self-knowledge, which is kindled in our hearts by the Holy Spirit.[7]

Bavinck inquires into the question of whether reason can be of service as a basis for elenctics. The early Christian apologists, of course, were convinced that it could. They put great store in the power of reason to unmask heathenism with its fantastic myths and degrading practices. Connecting the *logos* of Socrates, Plato, and later Greek philosophy with the *Logos* of the apostle John, they were confident that reason could lead from the one to the other. This approach reached a certain zenith in Thomas Aquinas' *Summa Contra Gentiles*. Aquinas thought it possible to convince pagans of the existence of one God, justice, and life after death by the use of reason. His approach is summarized by Bavinck:

> If we proceed in this manner, one can thus say that reason is necessarily the original standpoint or basis of elenctics. The latter employs reason as an opening wedge, or as a level. Pagans neither recognize nor believe in the Bible, so that every appeal to it simply beats the air. Reason is compelling. Well-chosen arguments open a broad field of possibilities. After the ground is broken and a certain level of light attained, the revelation of God, as recorded in the doctrine of the church, can then afford a second base of operation.[8]

John Calvin (and the Reformation in general) broke with this method. Calvin made a clear distinction between the *logos* of Greek philosophy and the *Logos* of John, between the

[7]John Herman Bavinck, *An Introduction to the Science of Missions*, trans. David H. Freeman (Grand Rapids: Baker, 1960), 221–22.
[8]Ibid., 225.

god of the philosopher and the God incarnate in the person of Jesus Christ. In Calvin's understanding, it is one thing to point out the foolishness of pagan superstitions. It is quite another thing to convince the heathen that their superstitions are an affront to the one true God and a sign of their rebellion against him. It is one thing to get pagans to appreciate the *idea* of a God who does not share in the vagaries and the vulgarities of the false gods of pagan machinations. It is quite another thing to get them to forsake (indeed, to repent of) false gods and embrace, not simply the *notion* of a high god, but God himself revealed in Jesus Christ.

I believe that, insofar as we can unravel the mystery before us, we can do so only by recourse to the biblical teaching that missionaries and evangelists are instruments of the Holy Spirit. Reason plays a part because all truth is God's truth. Uplifting emotions and strivings play a part because the human psyche still bears the imprint of the *imago Dei*. But neither fact nor feeling, neither logic nor passion, can constitute the *sine qua non* of repentance and faith. Writing to the Corinthian Christians Paul gave them the following reminder:

> And my message and my preaching were not in persuasive words of wisdom, but in demonstration of the Spirit and of power, that your faith should not rest on the wisdom of men, but on the power of God. (1 Cor. 2:4–5)

And so it must always be.

> For our struggle is not against flesh and blood, but against the rulers, against the powers, against the world forces of this darkness, against the spiritual forces of wickedness in the heavenly places. (Eph. 6:12)

Unaided by the Spirit, no Christian is equal to such a struggle! That's why our Lord promised to send the Paraclete, the Holy Spirit, to stand by us and accomplish that which, left to our own resources, we could not do. Notice John 16:8–10 again: "And He, when He comes, will convict [*elengchein* =

convict, convince, reprove, rebuke] the world concerning sin, and righteousness, and judgment." Specifically, concerning what sin? *The sin of not believing in Christ* (v. 9). By sheer logic and with an assist from conscience it may be possible to convince our hearers that lying, stealing, and murder are sins. But try to convince them that not to believe in Christ is sin, to say nothing of being the kind of sin that will seal their fate for eternity. Only the Holy Spirit can do that! And specifically, concerning what righteousness? *The perfect righteousness exhibited in Christ* (v. 10). People compare themselves with their neighbors and on that basis feel pretty good about themselves. However, when the people of Nazareth compared themselves with *their* Neighbor, the Lord Jesus, they came far from measuring up. But he returned to heaven. Who will convince men and women that they need this kind of (better, *his*) righteousness? Only the Holy Spirit can do that! And specifically, what judgment? *The judgment of the ruler of this age, Satan, at the cross of Christ* (v. 11). Try to convince people that Satan and his evil hosts have already been defeated; that the cross was a triumph; that God is in control and Jesus Christ is Lord *even today*. When we look around us that seems to defy logic. But it is true. and the Holy Spirit has the power to convince men and women that it is true.

When all is said and done, Christ's representatives are engaged in a great truth and power encounter. At certain times in history and in certain cultures one or another may seem in the ascendancy. In the first century when those first missionaries (the apostles) went forth and while the words of the New Testament (the new covenant) were in process of being written and circulated, demonstrations of divine *power* were singularly important. Today, in those cultures where the worldview and value system accentuates power, the power encounter is especially important. In cultures such as our own, the truth encounter takes on special significance. *But always and everywhere both truth and power are required. And the Holy Spirit supplies both, working in concert with Christ's representatives—with those who, like Paul, will both preach and pray—teach and trust—and give God the glory for all that might be accomplished for the kingdom.*[9]

The missionary persuader, then, must recognize three basic facts that underlie his or her ministry of reconciliation. First, the Triune God is sovereignly active in the task of missionizing. With him all things are possible. Without him we can do nothing. He created us in his image. He concerned himself with human beings when they became hellbent (I use the term advisedly) on self-destruction. He convicts people of sin and causes them to turn (return) to himself.

Second, the missionary is the servant of God. True, he is but a human being, and a sinful one at that! For that reason he can identify with his respondents in their willfulness and weakness. But he is also a servant of God. For that reason he can depend on God to use his explanations, arguments, and pleadings (insofar as they reflect God's will and Word) to the conversion of people and the building of his church.

Third, though people are sinners, they still bear the marks of the *imago Dei* in their reason, conscience, aspirations, inclinations, strivings, hopes, feelings, fears, values, and desires. (Our inclusive term for these concepts in this context is "motive," which Gordon Allport has defined as "any internal condition in the person that induces action or thought.")[10] These ingredients of our humanity exhibit the scars of sin. But they also bear the imprimatur of the Divine. And as Augustine, that great knower of the heart and ways of humanity, knew so well, when the Holy Spirit broods over people as he once did over the primal deeps of our world, men and women will find rest in their Creator.

[9]For a more theologically oriented explanation of the conversion process see my *Planting Churches Cross-Culturally* (Grand Rapids: Baker, 1980), 231–36.

[10]Gordon Allport, *Pattern and Growth in Personality* (New York: Holt, Rinehart and Winston, 1961), 196.

Chapter 43

Psychology, Ethnopsychology, and Mission

Modern psychology has been shaped to a significant degree by three major forces: Freudian psychoanalysis, which gave birth to clinical psychology; Watsonian behaviorism, which gave rise to experimental psychology; and the recent humanistic psychology of Abraham Maslow and others. Gary R. Collins notes that there is a widespread ferment in the field of psychology growing out of the conviction that much of the psychological theory emanating from these forces is irrelevant, and much of the resultant methodology simply does not work.[1] He insists that the root cause of this irrelevance is discoverable in the underlying assumptions of modern psychology, which he identifies as (1) naturalism, (2) determinism, and (3) optimism (man is basically good). He believes that the future for a Bible-based, believing psychology is bright, but he underscores the fact that Christian psycholo-

---

[1]Cf. Gary R. Collins, "Psychology on a New Foundation: A Proposal for the Future," *Journal of Psychology and Theology* 1 (January 1973): 19–27.

gists must demonstrate that such a psychology "really works."[2]

It is instructive that to a large extent the high-powered theories of psychology ultimately are reduced to one basic, simple test: Do they work? That certainly gives incentive to the nonprofessional to enter the psychologist's store, peruse the merchandise, and buy whatever seems to suit his purposes. In fact, that is precisely what many are doing, and that with no little danger to a public that is only vaguely aware of how it is being manipulated to the ends of others.

The Christian persuader, however, has three strictures that apply in his selection and use of the insights of psychologists. First, those insights must not be in conflict with the teaching of the Word of God. Second, they must be used in accordance with divine purposes and ends. Third, they must be used in subjection to biblical principles and the direction of the Spirit of God. Attention to these strictures will prevent the Christian persuader from relying on the pragmatic test mainly or alone.

For example, before me is a large advertisement for a "Christian" meeting. The text says,

Success and Prosperity
can be yours . . .
right here and
right NOW!

Surround yourself with
all the good you desire. . . .

Health—Happiness—Love
Success—Prosperity—Money. . . .

Message:
"How to be Rich in Every Way!"

[2]Ibid., 26.

In my opinion, this is the approach, not of a Christian persuader, but of a charlatan. It is in accord with contemporary interests to be sure. One study made some years ago indicated that 80 percent of Americans were more serious about living comfortably in this life than they were about life after death.[3] But it is a travesty if one gives attention to more than a few biblical texts removed from their contexts. It is a carbon copy of the appeals of many a cargo cult of Melanesia, the nativistic movements of Africa, and "new religions" of eastern Asia.

Attention to the aforementioned strictures will also prevent the Christian persuader from avoiding certain themes simply because they are unpopular and seemingly unproductive. Take, for example, the theme of judgment. Research indicates that in America, at least, appeals to fear and the need to prevent the results of certain courses of action (or inaction) have issued in decidedly different results, depending on the situation. In one study, fear-threat messages on the dangers of improper dental hygiene actually had a boomerang effect. The high school students who received the strongest fear-threat message demonstrated lesser compliance with the preventive program than those who received the weakest fear-threat message.[4] As concerns fear of divine judgment, one survey taken in America as early as a generation ago indicated that 73 percent of our population at that time believed in an afterlife, with God as a Judge, but "only 5 percent [had] any fear, not to say expectation, of going [to hell]."[5] There is little ground for thinking that the situation has improved.

It may well be that in view of such findings, contemporary preachers will choose not to take the approach of Jonathan Edwards in his sermon "Sinners in the Hands of an Angry God." Obviously, Edwards' audience was very unlike audiences today, and adaptation is called for. But *compromise*

[3]Cited in Will Herberg, *Protestant, Catholic and Jew* (Garden City, N.Y.: Doubleday, Anchor, rev. ed., 1960), 73.
[4]Melvin L. DeFleur, *Theories of Mass Communication* (New York: McKay, 1966), 124–25.
[5]Herberg, *Protestant, Catholic and Jew*, 73.

is not called for! And it is compromise or worse that occasions the almost total lack of preaching on topics like judgment, hell, and repentance today. One evangelical preacher remarked, "What good does it do to preach on hell? One cannot frighten people into conversion these days!" That may be true but, nevertheless, the preacher was in error. The *valid* reason for preaching about hell has never been to frighten people but to deliver the whole counsel of God!

Certain strictures and reservations in the use of psychology, therefore, are entirely in order. But when they are observed, the missionary can study the conclusions of the psychologists and the psychological make-up of his respondents with great benefit. The various motivational theories—whether those theories be of the homeostatic (e.g., Maslow), hedonic (Thorndike), personality (Freud, Adler, Allport), gestalt (Lewin, Festinger), or stimulus-response (Skinner) varieties—are beneficial in understanding why people decide and behave as they do, even though the theories conflict with the Bible and even with each other at important junctures.

The various concepts of ethnopsychologists and anthropologists (Riesman, Hsu, Benedict, Barnett, Wallace, et al.) also lend insights into the similarities and differences that exist in the motivational patterns of various cultures and the motivational factors that are operative as cultures change internally. It is with some of the insights gleaned from these fields that much of the remainder of this chapter is concerned.

MOTIVATION AND CULTURAL PATTERNS

In recent years no little attention has been devoted to the broad differences in values and motives that result from differences in the processes of enculturation and socialization. Perhaps it is best to reduce to simple explanations and schemas some of the ways in which these differences have been described so that the reader may quickly familiarize himself or herself with them. Then an evaluation can be made and some practical lessons drawn.

1. *Gemeinschaft* and *gesellschaft* cultural patterns. One

of the best-known and relevant distinctions bearing the relationship between culture and motivation is the *gemeinschaft-gesellschaft* (community-association) differentiation made by Ferdinand Tonnies and, following him, numerous other prominent sociologists. The distinction is usually related to the social changes that occur in the development from agrarian to industrial-urban orientations. But whether thought of in terms of the change within one culture or the differences between two cultures, the distinction is important for our present consideration. It pinpoints a fundamental difference in the relationship of an individual to his group, and therefore in his motivations, values, and decisions.

Tetsunao Yamamori and E. LeRoy Lawson[6] have succinctly summarized the important characteristics of these cultural orientations in the way indicated in figure 40.

2. *Dionysian and Apollonian cultures.* Building on Friedrich Nietzche's analysis of Greek tragedies, Ruth Benedict in one of her earlier works made a clear distinction between the Pueblo Indians of southwestern United States and other North American Indians.[7] The conclusions of Nietzsche and Benedict are briefly summarized in figure 41.

3. *Guilt and shame cultures.* Later in particular reference to the difference between Japanese and American cultures, Benedict made a distinction that has been most significant in cultural studies.[8] She noted that the behavior of Japanese in a time of war, for example, could be so different from that which American observers would expect as to render that behavior absolutely baffling and incongruous. She related the problem to the fundamental distinction between guilt and shame orientations. See figure 42 for these distinctions.

4. *Repression cultures and suppression cultures.* Edmund Perry believes that Francis L. K. Hsu has pressed beyond

[6]Tetsunao Yamamori and E. LeRoy Lawson, *Introducing Church Growth: A Textbook in Missions* (Cincinnati: Standard, 1975), 81.

[7]Ruth Benedict, *Patterns of Culture* (Boston: Houghton Mifflin, 1934), 78–79.

[8]Ruth Benedict, *Chrysanthemum and the Sword: Patterns of Japanese Culture* (Boston: Houghton Mifflin, 1946).

Benedict's guilt-shame differentiation.[9] Hsu shows that guilt-shame feelings are only symptomatic of the chief "mechanisms of socialization," which he identifies as "repression" and "suppression." Hsu uses "repression" in the Freudian sense of excluding from the consciousness that which is socially taboo so that it becomes deeply buried in the subconscious. By "suppression" he means a restraint from certain actions because of external circumstances but with no attempt to exclude them from the consciousness. In a study of four cultures he notes that both mechanisms are operative in all four, but because of emphasis he identifies Germany and America as "repression cultures" and China and Japan as "suppression cultures." His conclusions are summarized in figure 43.

5. *Tradition-directed, inner-directed, and other-directed cultures.* In a popular work in which he took a long look at ancient Greece and Rome and at contemporary societies (particularly the United States), David Riesman differentiated three types of societal orientations to life.[10] Riesman focused on those changes in our own society that have grave implications for us all. In so doing he called our attention to the fact that important distinctions are to be made not only between various societies but within the same society over a period of time. Riesman's trifurcation is summarized in figure 44 somewhat more fully than is seen in the distinctions we have explored previously.

There are obvious areas of overlap, agreement, and disagreement when one compares the schemas of Tonnies, the earlier and later Benedict, Hsu, and Riesman. In some ways Riesman's approach seems to have more explanatory potential; yet in the light of Benedict's work, he perhaps does not give enough emphasis to the difference between societies where a high value is placed on objective standards (e.g., the

[9]Cf. Edmund Perry, *The Gospel in Dispute* (Garden City, N.Y.: Doubleday, 1958), 101–3.

[10]David Reisman, *The Lonely Crowd* (New Haven: Yale University Press, 1961).

Puritan's dependence on the Bible) and those that value the subjective vision more highly (e.g., most North American Indians). Furthermore, by making "other-direction" a more or less unique category, he obscures the fact that there is a remarkable similarity between "other-directed" and "tradition-directed" societies. It will be apparent, for example, that the change toward peer-group orientation in the United States is attended by a greatly increased interest in a type of communal living and in community values that are strangely reminiscent of folk societies. It may well be that "other-direction" is simply a half-way station en route back to a (new) "tradition-directed" society.

Figure 40

GEMEINSCHAFT AND GESELLSCHAFT
CULTURAL PATTERNS

GEMEINSCHAFT (community)	GESELLSCHAFT (association)
Primary Group relations	Secondary group relations
Face-to-face, total relationships with each other (as in the family and village)	A set of relations with the participants presenting only one specialized part of their social personalities (roles) to each other
More rural	More urban
Preindustrial	Industrial
The individual swallowed up in group life where the communal principle dominates social relationships	The individual free to choose
Emphasis on collectivity-orientations	Emphasis on self-orientations
Non-Western societies	Western societies

All categorizations have their limitations because socie-

Figure 41

DIONYSIAN AND APOLLONIAN
CULTURAL PATTERNS

	Dionysian Cultures	Apollonian Cultures
Nietzsche's analysis of Greek tragedies	Pursues values through "the annihilation of the ordinary bounds and limits of existence"	Has little idea of the nature of such experiences; finds means of outlawing them
	Seeks to escape boundaries imposed by his five senses; to break into another order of experience	Limits oneself to tradition; keeps to "the middle of the road"; stays within the "known map"
	In personal experience or ritual the object is to press through it to a certain psychological state; analogous to drunkenness.	
Benedict's application to American Indians	In spite of many differences, American Indians (other than the Southwest Pueblos) tended to seek supernatural power in a dream or vision. Grown men often went to the cemeteries where they stood motionless, or staked out a tiny spot from which they would not move until they received their "blessing." Some sought it by torture, in which case they would employ a helper. The most prized technique was concentration.	Southwest Pueblos carried traditionalism farther than it was taken in Greece. Any influence that went against tradition was uncongenial and unwelcome. In particular, there was a great distrust of the individualism implied in Dionysian institutions.

ties combine important elements of the various categories. As Hsu explains, what is primary in the socialization process of one culture is secondary or tertiary in the socialization process of another.[11] Perhaps more important than the designations for the archetypes is the similarity of themes that occur over and over again in the writings of these authors (as well as those of Robert Redfield, J. J. Honigman, H. Ian Hogbin, George Foster, Robert Oliver, et al.). My own typology, therefore, is reminiscent of the conclusions of these various writers, but it puts more emphasis on the psychosociological development of a people. It is only partially original, the archcategories being suggested by Susumu Akahoshi. He uses the terms "collectivistic-dependency" and "individualistic-independency."[12] By adding subcategories suggested by our study to this point, I come up with the schema shown in figure 45.

The importance of giving close attention to these concepts in missionary efforts can hardly be overestimated. The applied anthropology of such authors as H. G. Barnett and George Foster is witness to this. Barnett insists that while all cultural changes are initiated by individuals, "cultural constructs" external to those individuals and independent of their personalities, as well as predispositions and abilities, are vital to change.[13] With his interest in the betterment of underdeveloped societies in mind, Foster writes,

> It appears as if *the most important* categories of culture that should be more or less completely understood to carry out successful health and hygiene programs are *local ideas* about health, welfare, illness, their causes and treatments.[14]

The seriousness with which Foster has taken Barnett's and his own dictum is apparent in his *Traditional Cultures and the Impact of Technological Change.*[15] There he talks about such

[11]Cf. Perry, *Gospel in Dispute,* 101–3.
[12]Susumu Akahoshi, "Japanese and Western Religiosity," in Kenneth J. Dale, ed., *Circle of Harmony: A Case Study in Popular Japanese Buddhism* (Pasadena: William Carey, 1975), 170–90.
[13]H. G. Barnett, *Innovation: The Basis of Cultural Change* (New York: McGraw-Hill, 1953), 39.
[14]Quoted in Guillermo Bonfil Batalla, "Conservative Thought in Applied Anthropology: A Critique," *Human Organization* 25 (Summer 1966): 89–92.
[15]George M. Foster, *Traditional Cultures and the Impact of Technological Change* (New York: Harper & Row, 1962).

culture-based attitudinal barriers to change as tradition, fatalism, ethnocentricity, pride, and dignity; such stimulants to change as the desire for prestige, economic gain, competition, friendship obligations, curiosity, and religious appeal; and the problems of "fit," timing, and meeting felt needs. All of these are, of course, to be determined and defined in terms of the respondent culture's motivational and value orientation.

Figure 42

THE GUILT-SHAME DIFFERENTIATION
IN CULTURAL PATTERNS

GUILT AXIS	SHAME AXIS
Concerned with each separate, discrete act	Concerned with the overall self
Involves transgression of a specific code; violation of a specific taboo	Involves falling short; failure to reach an ideal
Involves an additive process; advance to healthy personality by deleting wrong acts and substituting right acts	Involves a total response that includes insight, something more than can be reached by addition
Emphasis on decision making; any decision is better than none	Emphasis on the ability to live with some indecisiveness (multiple possibilities) and anxiety
Emphasis on the content of experience in work, leisure, and personal relations	Emphasis on the quality of experience more than on its content
The surmounting of guilt leads to righteousness . . .	The transcending of shame may lead to a sense of identity and freedom. . . .

POINTS OF CONTACT

It is a commonplace of communication theory that the source must identify with his audience by establishing some point of contact (common ground, eye-opener, redemptive analogy, etc.). Traditionally, missionaries have located points of contact in two primary areas: the *religious beliefs* and the *felt needs* of people in the respondent cultures. These kinds of points of contact have a certain validity, but not as they have been generally understood. Let us examine them more closely.

Figure 43

THE REPRESSION-SUPPRESSION DIFFERENTIATION
IN CULTURAL PATTERNS

REPRESSION CULTURES: GERMANY AND THE UNITED STATES	SUPPRESSION CULTURES: CHINA AND JAPAN
Internal controls more important	External controls more important
The pattern of life is individual-centered.	The pattern of life is situation-centered.
Religions emphasize the search of individual souls for the inner meaning of life, and stress one religion and the worship of one God.	Religions stress satisfactory adjustment with every power, an emphasis that results in polytheism and polytholatry.

---

1. *Religious teachings as points of contact.* As a science, comparative religion has benefited greatly by the interest and input of missionaries who have been anxious to discover similarities and differences between the Christian and non-Christian faiths. These missionaries widely believed that by comparing the teachings of Christianity with those of other religions, they could appeal to reason and show the superiority of the Christian faith. This approach has been largely abandoned for at least three reasons. First, it is *philosophically* suspect. By what standard do we judge one faith to be better than another? Reason has been, and may be, appealed to. But it must be remembered that reason is not the final standard. It is not true to Christianity itself to presuppose a standard higher

than the Christian faith by which it and all other faiths are to be judged. Well, then, is it fair to those of other religions to ask them to judge the validity of their faiths by standards provided by a Christian revelation that they have not yet accepted? Again, the answer must be at least a qualified no. Second, the approach is *psychologically* suspect. Whatever reasons people may adduce for their faith, the heart has reasons the head does not know. Third, the approach is *scientifically* suspect. Students of the world religions know that seeming similarities between faiths usually touch only the tip of the iceberg. Beneath the surface the similarity rapidly disappears, as we have already discovered in our discussion of worldviews.

Supposed similarities between Christianity and other religions, therefore, yield points of contact that must be used only with extreme caution lest the door be opened to misunderstandings of the most dangerous sort. For example, Hinduism, Islam, and Christianity all put great store in authoritative revelations. But the *kind* of authority and the *nature* of the revelation to be found in the Vedas, the Koran, and the Bible respectively are very diverse. Again, some schools of Buddhism and historical Protestantism place great emphasis on salvation by faith. But as one probes into the respective teachings, the understandings of both salvation and faith in Buddhism and Christianity are so diverse as to constitute a difference in kind.

Points of contact in the area of religion per se can be made. But they should be attempted only by those who are prepared for dialogue at these deeper levels.

2. *Felt needs as points of contact.* With their manifest concern for the welfare of others, missionaries have quite naturally found valuable points of contact with their respondents by addressing themselves in word and deed to felt needs. *Felt needs* should be distinguished from *basic needs*, however. Felt needs are not always basic, though they may be. Basic needs arise out of what a person is by virtue of his creation. Created a biological organism, a human being needs food, rest, sleep, exercise, and so forth. Created a sentient being, he requires reasons for his choices, reasons that are grounded in

Figure 44

DAVID RIESMAN'S ORIENTATIONS OF SOCIETIES TOWARD LIFE

	TRADITION-DIRECTED (e.g., Primitive and Folk societies, and Thailand, Burma, etc.)	INNER-DIRECTED (e.g., United States, 1776– 1945?)	OTHER-DIRECTED (e.g., United States, present day)
GENERAL			
Outlook:	"We have always done it this way."	"We ought to do it this way—it is right."	"Everyone is doing it; therefore it is O.K."
Type:	"Beaten path"	"Gyroscope" (built-in conscience)	"Radar" (watching others)
COMMUNICATION MODIFIERS			
Guiding principle:	Tradition	Conscience	Contemporaries
Population and Birth Rate:	Static population, stable birth rate	Increasing population, rising birth rate	Leveling population, birth rate tapering off
Primary Consideration:	Maintain and adjust to world as it is	Expand frontiers; discover, adjust, improve world	Run the machine; adjust within the society
PLOTTING COURSE			
Source of Guidance:	Clan	Family	Peers
Nature of Guidance:	Distinct—living out role	Purposeful—acquiring better role	Indistinct, conflicting— finding a goal
Follow:	Culture heroes	Pioneers	Soap opera actors
Avoid:	Shame (when caught violating tradition)	Guilt (if violating conscience, whether apprehended or not)	Failure (diffuses— other-centered)
Text:	Myth	Sermons	Counseling, psychiatric interviews
RELIGIOUS CONTEXT			
Sanctions:	Supernatural sanctions. (ancestral spirits; society-conserving gods or God)	Punishment (here or here-after, from personal devil or a conscience-supporting God)	Social ostracism (worries are only psychosomatic)
Focus:	They (forefathers)	I	We

his intelligence or feeling of well-being. Created a social being, he needs fellowship with, and the approval of, other people. Created a spiritual being, he needs fellowship with God. Understanding this, the missionary, in the very nature of his calling, must give attention to the basic needs of the whole person, and especially to essential spiritual needs.

Felt needs, then, may well serve as points of contact, but they should not be confused with basic needs nor should they be allowed to divert the missionary from ministering to basic needs or delivering the whole counsel of God.

> Without deliberately omitting any aspect of Christ's mission and teaching, the missioner appreciating the principle of felt-needs would seek a *starting-point* in his instruction that would be most in accord with the existing felt-needs. To a non-Christian society that feels no sense of guilt the work of Redemption as a starting-point or a point of emphasis would not be very meaningful. On the other hand, the *person* of Christ would contain many values highly appreciated by the non-Christian. . . . Thus a missionary could lead his flock from an appreciation of the *person* of Christ to the culturally more-difficult and less-appealing aspects of Christiology.[16]

3. *The disposition and attitude of the missionary as a point of contact.* Our discussion has brought us to the contention of the perceptive Hendrik Kraemer. He insists on the indispensability of a point of contact and emphasizes the difficulties of establishing contact on the basis of supposed similarities between the religions. Then he comes to a conclusion that deserves to be called a classic statement on the subject:

> If the word is not misunderstood, the missionary has to be a religious artist. Here we approach the pastoral aspect of our problem, and enter the field of psychology, of pedagogy

[16]Louis J. Luzbetak, *The Church and Cultures* (Techny, Ill.: Divine Word, 1963), 67–68.

and of knowledge of the human heart. But it is a regenerated and purified psychology, pedagogy and knowledge of human nature, because baptized into a sense of the conditions of all men by the Spirit of Christ.

One might state this important aspect of the problem of concrete points of contact in this somewhat unusual way: that there is only one point of contact, and if that one point really exists, then there are many points of contact. This one point of contact is the disposition and the attitude of the missionary. It seems rather upsetting to make the missionary the point of contact. Nevertheless it is true, as practice teaches. *The strategic and absolutely dominant point in this whole important problem, when it has to be discussed in general terms, is the missionary worker himself.* Such is the golden rule, or, if one prefers, the iron law, in this whole matter. The way to live up to this rule is to have an untiring and genuine interest in the religion, the ideas, the sentiments, the institutions—in short, in the whole range of life of the people among whom one works, *for Christ's sake and for the sake of those people.* Whosoever disobeys this rule does not find any real point of contact. Whosoever obeys it becomes one with his environment, and has and finds contacts. Obedience to it is implied in the prime missionary obligation and passion, to wit, preparing the way for Christ and being by God's grace a pointer to Him. Only a genuine and continuous interest in the people as they are creates real points of contact, because man everywhere intuitively knows that, only when his actual being is the object of humane interest and love, is he looked upon in actual fact, and not theoretically, as a fellow-man. As long as a man feels that he is the object of interest only for reasons of intellectual curiosity or for purposes of conversion, and not because of himself as he is in his total empirical reality, there cannot arise that humane natural contact which is the indispensable condition of all real religious meeting of man with man. In these conditions the door to such a man and to the world he lives in remains locked, and the love of Christ remains for him remote and abstract. It needs translation by the manifestation of the missionary's genuine interest in the whole life of the people to whom he goes.[17]

MISSIONARY APPEALS

The apostle Paul wrote, "Therefore, we are ambassadors for Christ, as though God were entreating [parakaleō] you through us; we beg [deomai] you on behalf of Christ, be reconciled to God" (2 Cor. 5:20). What a powerful appeal! But notice that it is wholly spiritual. How does one reconcile it with the conclusion of Augustine? He wrote that a person is moved

> if what you promise is what he [the respondent] likes, if the danger of which you speak appears real, if your censures are directed against something he hates, if your recommendations are in harmony with what he embraces, if he regrets what you say is regrettable, if he rejoices over what you claim is a reason for joy, if his heart is sympathetic toward those whose misery you describe, if he avoids those who you advise should be avoided . . . not merely imparting knowledge about things that ought to be done but rather moving them to do that which they already know must be done.[18]

The answer is twofold. First, our message must be given in terms that are meaningful and appealing in the respondent culture. Second, our message must press on to make it apparent that we are messengers of *Christ* and that, in the Christian message, *we speak that which must be heard, understood, and heeded by all his creatures.*

God-given needs are met in ways that are, in measure, culturally determined. All humans need nourishment, and therefore they provide, prepare, and eat food. The average American, however, does not find seaweed, snake flesh, ants,

---

[17]Hendrik Kraemer, *The Christian Message in a Non-Christian World* (Grand Rapids: Kregel, 1963), 140–41.

[18]Augustine, *On Christian Doctrine* IV.12. Quoted in Luzbetak, *Church and Cultures*, 67.

Figure 45

COLLECTIVISTIC-DEPENDENCY CULTURES AND INDIVIDUALISTIC-INDEPENDENCY CULTURES

	COLLECTIVISTIC-DEPENDENCY CULTURES		INDIVIDUALISTIC-INDEPENDENCY CULTURES	
	ANCESTOR ORIENTATION	PEER-GROUP ORIENTATION	SUBJECTIVITY ORIENTATION	OBJECTIVITY ORIENTATION
Values	Traditional: "It has always been done this way."	Popular: "Everyone is doing it."	Intuitional: "Follow the gleam."	Lawful: "It is written. . . ." "The evidence shows. . . ."
Avoidance Goal	Shame of dishonoring the ancestors	Shame of disappointing the peer group	Guilt of disregarding the "vision"	Guilt of disobeying the "laws"
Attainment Goals	Acquiescence to the will of the ancestors leads to harmony.	Conformance to the expectations of peers leads to acceptance.	Attention to inner self leads to identity.	Obedience to requirements leads to reconcilation.
Models	"Great men" of the tribe or clan	"Good guys" of the gang or club	Gurus and "tycoons"	Lawmakers and prophets
Media	Myths and legends	Interviews and opinion polls	Arts, poetry, reports of "visions" or success	Lawbooks, sermons, and scientific treatises
Decision Type	Group decision expected rather than individual	Group decision or individual decision expected to reflect group expectations	Individual decisions expected	Individual decisions expected
Decision Timing	Time is required for either group or individual.	Time may be required to ascertain "group mind."	Time may be required. Decisions should be immediate when the way becomes known.	The time for decision is now. The way is known. Any decision is better than none.
Decision Strength	Group decision is binding; individual decision tends to be risky and tentative	Group decision binding, but both group and individual decisions subject to change with mood or fashion	Group decision regarded with some suspicion; individual decision binding but subject to change with new "light"	Group decision regarded with some suspicion; individual decision expected to be followed through
Example	China	Modern United States	India	United States in the past

or grubs very appealing. On the other hand, Muslims find pork inedible, orthodox Hindus would never think of eating beef, and Chinese students have been known to become ill at first seeing Westerners drink milk. To hungry people the world over, food is appealing. But one look at the menu of another culture may be enough to cause one to lose his appetite, or worse!

Now people's spiritual needs are the same all around the world. Just as people need their daily bread, so they need the Bread of Life. We can count on that and appeal to it. But what further steps can we take to encourage them to recognize the living Bread and to "taste and see that the Lord is good?" (Ps. 34:8 KJV). For that matter, *Christians* around the world need the "sincere milk of the Word" and solid spiritual food (1 Peter 2:2 KJV). But how shall they be helped to drink *deeply* and to nourish themselves *daily*? The answer is obvious. We do it by making God's provision palatable—not changing its substance but by preparing and serving it in accordance with local taste. But more must be said. The following paragraphs represent an effort to stimulate meaningful deliberation on the problem. The ideas will be more helpful if related to the distinctions and concepts noted in figure 40.

1. *The appeal to selfhood.* In the West, motivation is intimately related to (one might almost say synonymous with) self-interest. Children of the West are encouraged to excel and to rise above their peers. Young people are urged to find out who they are and to be true to themselves. In the business world, self-preservation and self-advancement are the rules of the game, and the watchword is "watch out for number one." At the apex of the Maslowan "motivational pyramid" is "self-actualization."[19]

In much of the rest of the world things are quite different. Often, the non-Western child is taught to think first of his family, clan, community, and country. He is encouraged to improve his lot, not at the expense of, but in concert with, his

[19]Cf. Abraham Maslow, *Motivation and Personality*, 2nd ed. (New York: Harper & Row, 1970).

fellows. As he grows older, the web of responsible relationships grows until every major decision must take the concerns of others into account. At the apex of the "motivational pyramid" one is likely to find "social harmony." Christian evangelism the world over tends to betray its Western moorings. People are told, "If there were no sinner in the world other than you, Christ still would have died for you." Evangelists encourage the members of their audience to blot everything and everyone from their consciousnesses and to think only of their own personal relationship with God. New converts are urged to prepare themselves for misunderstanding and even persecution by trusting Christ and being true to their own convictions no matter what opposition they may face. As a matter of fact, the more one thinks about Christian communication worldwide, the more one becomes convinced that it is almost totally permeated by the Western orientation to "individualistic-independency," to use Akahoshi's term.

As a matter of fact, every missionary will be familiar with the "three-self" (self-supporting, self-governing, self-propagating) formula for the indigenous church. This formula has been the announced goal of most Protestant missions since the time of Henry Venn and Rufus Anderson in the middle of the nineteenth century. Peter Beyerhaus has taken issue with this understanding of the indigenous church.[20] He does not object to the goal of establishing churches that will learn not to lean on their respective missions for support and direction. Rather, he objects to the emphasis on *autonomy* and *self* when rightly the churches should be *Christonomous* and responsible to Christ as the Head of the church! The more one thinks about Beyerhaus's contention, the more one is forced to agree that overemphasis on *autonomy* is a throwback to the orientation of Western culture and that, while it has some validity in compensating for the non-Western collectivistic-dependency orientation, it has at the same time encouraged the younger

[20]Cf. Peter Beyerhaus and Henry Lefever, *The Responsible Church and the Foreign Mission* (Grand Rapids: Eerdmans, 1964).

churches to become *self-satisfied* when they have become self-supporting and self-governing and (usually to a far lesser extent) self-propagating. To be *self*-satisfied and to be *Christ*-satisfied, after all, are very different.

Now I hasten to say that far from being bad, *individualism* has aspects that are biblical and good. Each person is God's unique creation, loved by him, and responsible before him to live a life of faith, obedience, and fruitfulness. The Bible is replete with texts and teachings that reinforce individualism. It is *Western individualism* that is the problem. That is what helps missionary communicators (and, in many instances, indigenous, non-Western communicators who learn from them) to see clearly those biblical texts that support individualism while partially blinding them to texts that teach family loyalty, brotherly responsibility, self-denial, and submission to others.

Let us be clear, then. The Scriptures emphasize *both* self-interest and self-abnegation, *both* individualism and communalism. For that matter, *both* forms of motivation are present in both the West and the East. The problem is one of emphasis (or overemphasis). In areas of Chinese influence, for example, why not make the appeal that the Christian family is the harmonious family—at peace with God and one another? Why not urge the new convert to return to his father, mother, sisters, and brothers and, instead of *occasioning* or *inviting* opposition, say to them, "I am sorry that I have not been a dutiful son (faithful father, brother, etc.). But something wonderful has happened to me. I have become a Christian. With God's help I will be a better son." This approach is not as Western, but it is no less biblical than the usual one. And in most of Asia, at least, it can be expected to be much more productive.

Louis Luzbetak has proposed a similar appeal to the collectivity-oriented Middle Wahgi of New Guinea.[21] Since the Middle Wahgi define right and wrong, security and success in terms provided by the living and departed members of the

---

[21]Luzbetak, *Church and Cultures*, 164–68.

clan, he advises missionaries to build their work on *group* concepts and *group* values. The Christian message can easily be put in these terms. Clan rights were foolishly thrown away by our first parents. Sin was, and is, a betrayal of the heavenly Father and puts us under a usurper, Satan. But our new clan Head, Jesus Christ, who always lives in harmony with the heavenly Father, has provided a way whereby full clan privileges can be restored. Christ's clan is the church. This is an approach that has every expectation of being understood and appreciated by the Middle Wahgi.

2. *The appeal to authority.* In the United States, respect for authority has eroded to the point where the Bible itself—long the basis of that country's ethics and value system—has been barred from tax-supported schools and relegated by many to the shelves of antiquity. True, the United States has its so-called Bible belt. But even there one suspects that when the preacher raises his hand and shouts, "The Bible says—" the traditional ring of authority is no longer there for many people. And in many of the community Bible-study classes so popular in some parts of the United States, the leadership function is largely confined to soliciting various opinions on what the biblical text might mean to group members and conferring a certain value on all or most interpretations.

All of this is indicative of the shift from authoritarianism to egalitarianism in America. Wherever it started, it has now permeated most of the institutions of American society from the home through the public schools, government agencies, and churches. It has given a new face even to that bastion of traditional religious authority, the Catholic Church. When the decision to discontinue meatless Fridays was announced at a New York mass some years ago, one parishioner turned to his neighbor and said, "Meat on Fridays? Not on your life! I'm going to be a good Catholic whether the Pope wants to be one or not!"

A most instructive commentary on the importance of the appeal to religious authority in non-Western contexts comes from the research of Kenneth Dale on Rissho Koseikai.[22] Rissho Koseikai is one of the flourishing new religions in Japan. Dale's research centers on the group counseling sessions that are held daily in the large Great Sacred Hall *(Daiseido)* in Tokyo. In fact, he attended, recorded, and analyzed as many of fifty such sessions.

Group counseling meetings *(hoza)* constitute one of Rissho Koseikai's chief means of making new converts and confirming the faith of believers. Members of the groups meet in the balconies that surround the large worship hall (which seats some thirty thousand people). They squat on *tatami* mat floors, arranging themselves in circles with group leaders— their hand luggage being placed in the middle. Children run in and out and play on the *tatami* floor with no apparent disturbance to the groups. Members come and go at their convenience. Groups range in size from twelve to twenty or twenty-five. Discussions include testimonies of believers, problems and questions of converts and nonconverts alike, and the teachings of Rissho Koseikai Buddhism.

For our purposes, the important factor in these sessions is the manner in which the Rissho Koseikai message comes across to participants.

Dale explains that in either individual or group counseling in the West, the counselor struggles to empathize with the clients and elicit their feelings and thinking. In respect for their integrity as individuals, he tries to assist them in making wise choices and living by them. But the choices are theirs. The counselor is careful not to simply put forth solutions and evaluate what is right and wrong for other people.

The Rissho Koseikai *hoza*, however, fits the Japanese pattern of "collectivity-dependency." First, they use language that appeals to the members as a *group* rather than as a collection of individuals; and they treat problems as symptoms of universal problems rather than as individual problems. Second, the counselors give *authoritative solutions* to

[22]Cf. Kenneth J. Dale, ed. *Circle of Harmony: A Case Study in Popular Japanese Buddhism* (Pasadena: William Carey, 1975), especially chapter 8.

problems—solutions the members feel they can depend on because they come from an expert. An example of the Rissho Koseikai approach follows:

> *Mrs. B:* My two children both have aches and pains in their legs. And the other day one of them got a very bad nosebleed. What is wrong with them?
>
> *L:* The cause of this condition is lustful thinking. Trouble in the legs always points to a problem of sexual lustfulness. You yourself probably have a problem with this, don't you?
>
> *Mrs. B:* (With embarrassment) Yes, I do. I am a person of very strong passions, but my husband is even more that way. We've had so much trouble between us. (She tells the story of her marriage.) But today my husband is at an RK retreat seeking spiritual help.
>
> *L:* Oh, how obvious the nature of your trouble is! A wife should be the first one to apologize and repent, but here we have the opposite happening. Your husband has gone to the spiritual retreat before you have. He is the first to repent, but his religious exercises won't do him any good if you don't humble yourself before him right away. Go meet him today when they return from the retreat, and immediately apologize to him and do everything you can for him from now on.
>
> *Mrs. B:* (Weeping) Oh yes, I will surely do that! I see now where I have been wrong.
>
> (Everyone joined in telling Mrs. B that she must be more meek, and that today offers an especially crucial opportunity for their marital life to take a turn for the better, and that the Buddha has prepared the way for a new life in their family.)[23]

3. *The appeal to reason and logicality.* It is only partially true that some cultures place a high value on reason and logic while other cultures place little value on them. All cultures adduce reasons for their beliefs and actions, but some reasons are more reasonable than others! And all cultures have their logic, but sometimes the logic of one is the illogic of another.

[23]Ibid., 88.

In my study of Soka Gakkai Buddhists, I point out that they appeal to rational proofs for the truth of their faith, but that their apologetic is fragile and breaks down at critical junctures.[24] The brittle apologetic is seemingly of no great consequence to their respondents, however, for their respondents require no more than a pseudo-logic for religious faith. Another illustration of this phenomenon comes from the African experience cited in Chapter 41. The programmed textbooks that have become so popular, especially in theological education by extension efforts in the Third World, are based in significant measure on Skinnerian stimulus-response motivational theory and his so-called learning machine. As might have been anticipated, the haste and enthusiasm with which American missionaries introduced programmed textbooks to respondents of other cultures meant that they were destined to encounter real difficulties and misunderstandings as well as some significant successes. Some of the problems were located precisely at the point under discussion. In one African case, for example, the whole educational process implicit in programming was aborted because the students insisted on referring to the answers provided in the textbooks *before* devising their own answers to the problems. Instructors attempted to explain that the procedures outlined in the manuals were essential to the learning process and that it was imperative that they first work out their own answers to the various questions. To the Africans what was being required of them simply did not make sense! Why would any person in his right mind expend time and mental energy working out solutions that are already available!

4. *The appeal to shame and guilt.* Shame motivation has been discounted by many missionaries in "shame" cultures. As has been mentioned, the meaning of the word "elenctics" shifted from "to bring to shame" in Homer to "to bring to guilt" in Attic and New Testament Greek. The real mischief in the understanding of many shame cultures, however, is not

---

[24]David J. Hesselgrave, *A Propagation Profile of the Soka Gakkai* (Ph.D. dissertation, University of Minnesota, 1965), 276.

so much in the concept of shame itself as it is in the notion that there is no need for shame unless one is caught in his shameful behavior! A culture without shame is as culpable before God as a culture without guilt. As a matter of fact, *both concepts* are important in dealing with the basic motivations having to do with one's relationship to God and one's relationship to fellow human beings!

One could proceed to demonstrate the importance that the various concepts in our typology of cultures have for missionary appeals. There is much more that merits reflection. Serious students of mission should study the various concepts carefully and add to the list of applications.

Before I close this chapter it is important to remind ourselves that the missionary message must relate God's Word *per se* to respondent cultural constructs. As we evaluate Christian communication, certain questions are in order:

> Is this way of presenting Christ calculated to impress on people that the gospel is *a word from God?* Is it calculated to divert their attention from man and all things merely human to God and his truth? Or is its tendency rather to distract attention from the Author and authority of the message to the person and performance of the messenger? Does it make the gospel sound like a human idea, a preacher's plaything, or like a divine revelation, before which the human messenger himself stands in awe? Does this way of presenting Christ savour of human cleverness and showmanship? Does it tend thereby to exalt man? Or does it embody rather the straightforward, unaffected simplicity of the messenger whose sole concern is to deliver his message, and who has no wish to call attention to himself, and who desires so far as he can to blot himself out and hide, as it were, behind his message, fearing nothing so much as that men should admire and applaud him when they ought to be bowing down and humbling themselves before the mighty Lord whom he represents?[25]

[25]J. I. Packer, *Evangelism and the Sovereignty of God* (Chicago: InterVarsity, 1961), 87.

Chapter 44

Motivation, Decision Making, and Conversion

It is one thing to appeal to people to repent, believe the gospel, and "grow up in all aspects into Him, who is the head, even Christ" (Eph. 4:15). However, it is quite another thing to succeed in getting them to do it. The decision is theirs. As has been noted, however, the ways in which societies look upon decision making and are predisposed actually to make decisions vary widely from culture to culture. In the nature of the case, Christian evangelists and missionaries are required to emphasize the necessity of making a decision. Unfortunately, it has not been required that they study the philosophy and methodology of decision making from a cultural perspective. In chapter 11, we examined the various decisions encountered in missionary work. In this chapter we will discuss the decision process itself.

DECISION AND NONDECISION ORIENTATIONS

Some cultures place a great value on decisiveness and "making up one's mind" as soon as possible. *Any* decision is deemed to be better than *no* decision. Deliberations are

613

expected to end in *closure*. Indecisiveness is thought to be a flaw in one's character.

Other cultures place a high value on the ability to live with a degree of indecisiveness. To people in these cultures, when options are not clear-cut or when the situation does not demand a decision, it seems better to make *no* decision than to risk making the *wrong* decision. Decisions may be put off as long as possible and deliberations often end in a certain open-endedness. To these people, tentativeness and open-endedness are aspects of wisdom.

Moreover, in decision-oriented societies decisions are usually thought of as having a binding and lasting quality. Where indecisiveness is the norm, decisions once made are apt to be looked upon as subject to change with changing conditions.

It is a lack of appreciation for this difference that occasions Northrop's contention that missionaries to the Chinese have misjudged Chinese character.[1] The Chinese are encouraged to postpone as long as possible any decision regarding a future course of action. When they do make such a decision, it will usually be with a high degree of tentativeness. To the Chinese it is wise to keep one's options open in case the situation changes. It is *virtuous* to change one's mind if the situation does change! The Chinese, therefore, are not two-faced or wishy-washy. They are simply Chinese. The missionary to Chinese and similar peoples, therefore, should be slow to condemn, willing to learn, and ready to gear evangelistic appeals and pastoral ministries to this very divergent understanding of decision making.

GROUP CONVERSION AND CONSENSUS DECISION MAKING

Missionary G. Linwood Barney and a national evangelist were once invited to present the gospel to a Meo village in

[1] F. C. S. Northrop, *The Meeting of East and West: An Enquiry Concerning World Understanding* (New York: Macmillan, 1953), 381.

northern Laos.[2] After the presentation the village chief stepped forward to announce that the entire community wanted to become Christian!

To many this kind of a decision raises questions. Actually, however, it may have more validity than the decisions of a large number of heterogeneous individuals responding to the invitation in a mass meeting in Chicago or New York. In order to appreciate that fact, however, one needs an understanding of the background of this "village conversion" and an insight into the way such group decisions are made.

For some months prior to the time when Barney and his companion were invited to the Meo village, formal discussions had been carried on among the villagers. Contacts had been made with Christian relatives and believers in other villages. Unanimously, the village had decided to invite the evangelists to come and present the gospel. After their arrival runners had been sent throughout the village. Only after everyone was present had the evangelists been asked to begin their presentation.

The presentation (with time allowed for questions) lasted for four hours. It summarized the biblical redemptive narrative, starting with the Creation and ending with Pentecost. After the presentation the villagers assembled in household groups in which they animatedly discussed what they had heard. When the groups had quieted down, the chief asked for further questions and gave the evangelists an opportunity to respond. He then polled each household. One after another the heads of households announced their decision to follow Jesus. Only then did the chief make the formal announcement.

For the next two days Barney and his national colleague visited in the village, helping in the burning of fetishes and instructing the people in the faith.

As a result of this kind of experience and the study of nine tribal societies in the area between eastern India and Kalimantan, Indonesia, Barney concludes that decision making by

[2]G. Linwood Barney, "Is Decision by Consensus Valid?" *The Alliance Witness* (20 January 1971), 9–10.

consensus is not only valid but a key principle to understanding these cultures.

There is, of course, a great variety in societies as to the ways in which decisions are made, who may be qualified to make decisions, and the kind of decisions that can be made. There can be no doubt that even in our society where each individual is encouraged to weigh all the factors involved and make his own decision, numerous factors such as age, family counsel, peer pressure, and mass psychology are very important. Overlooking such factors in individual decisions in our own culture (e.g., the psychological reinforcement of numerous counselors and others going forward at a large crusade), many American Christians are suspicious of consensus decisions in other cultures. Partly for this reason Donald McGavran introduced the term "multi-individual conversion." However, his church-growth theory still underscores the importance of "group conversion" and "people movements to Christ." McGavran insists that this is the way a majority of our Christian forebears became Christian and that a strategy that encourages whole tribes, sub-tribes, clans, families, and extended families to come to Christ is the kind of strategy that will win great portions of humanity to the Christian faith today.[3]

The term used is relatively unimportant, though some terms are obviously better than others. What is important is that missionaries give attention to the way in which decisions are made in their respondent societies, and who is qualified (in societal understanding) to make decisions. This does not mean, of course, that missionaries will be bound by societal norms. But it does mean that missionaries should avoid raising unnecessary obstacles to conversion by disregarding the social role of decision-makers. Missionaries should not make *initial* gospel presentations to those who are "not qualified" to respond, and they should not unduly obstruct the

[3] Cf. Donald A. McGavran, *Understanding Church Growth*, rev. ed., (Grand Rapids: Eerdmans, 1980), chaps. 16–17.

decision-making process by refusing to allow ample time for deliberation by individuals and responsible groups.

CONVERSION AND DECISION MAKING AS POINT AND PROCESS

Traditionally, missionaries have thought of decisions as occurring at a point in time. There is a good deal of biblical and common-sense support for this view. The Bible talks about the acceptable time as being "now," and "now" as being the day of salvation (2 Cor. 6:2). Becoming a Christian is spoken of in terms of a new birth. In fact, the Bible consistently speaks of conversion and salvation in radical terms that imply urgency and instantaneous change. Obviously one is either justified or he is not, a member of the family of God or not, a citizen of heaven or not. Logically, there is no room for an intermediate state where one is neither a nonbeliever nor a believer! That is one side of the picture.

But there is another side as well. It is this. The *Lord* can distinguish between the wheat and the tares, but *we* may not be able to do so. The Lord knows the precise moment at which each of his children came into the heavenly family, but we are often unsure of the moment at which he accepts them. Listen to the testimony of many genuine saints. It sometimes seems as though they became Christians by virtue of a *series* of decisions. To force them to identify the moment of *decisive* decision would be to require them to play some kind of game. They simply do not know!

Let us agree, then, that in individual and group conversions, both point and process are involved. While we urge our respondents to be decisive, to "make [their] calling and election sure" (2 Peter 1:10 KJV), and not to unduly delay the ultimate decision, we also recognize that to be genuine a decision requires both preparation and follow-through. Since in the missionary context particularly it is often difficult for the missionary to put his finger on the *point* of conversion, it is important that he recognize the stages in the conversion *process* so he can give encouragement along the way.

As an aid to understanding what happens (from a human point of view) when an individual "turns to God from idols to serve a living and true God" (1 Thess. 1:9), missiologists have attempted to describe what happens in this kind of a decision-making process. (The group conversion process bears some similarity to individual decision making but also has its own unique features as we have seen in the case of the Meo.)

Figure 46

STAGES IN THE CONVERSION PROCESS

Stage	Label	Definition
One	Discovery	There is a person called Christ whom the true God is said to have sent into the world to be the Savior and Lord of mankind.
Two	Deliberation	There is a possibility that I (we) should forsake the old ways and follow Christ.
Three	Determination	I (we) will repent and believe in Christ.
Four	Dissonance	Shall I (we) resist the forces that draw me (us) back to the old ways, and continue to follow Christ in spite of present difficulties?
Five	Discipline	I (we) will identify with the people of Christ in His church and live in submission to His lordship and church discipline.

One of the first to draw attention to this process was Alan Tippett.[4] Drawing on innovation theory, Tippett influenced a number of missiologists to give more attention to the conversion process.[5] Although Tippett's nomenclature is different,

[4]Cf. A. R. Tippett, *Verdict Theology in Missionary Theory* (Lincoln, Ill.: Lincoln Christian College Press, 1969), 122–25.

[5]One of the most notable of the various publications on conversion that reflects Tippett's views is Hans Kasdorf, *Christian Conversion in Context* (Scottsdale, Pa.: Herald, 1980).

his influence is reflected in the five stages of the conversion process as diagramed in figures 46 and 47 and explained below. (Still another, and more elaborate, description of the process has been undertaken by James F. Engel who has adapted the Martin Fishbein Marketing model into a spiritual decision process model.[6])

Figure 47

DECISION AS POINT AND PROCESS

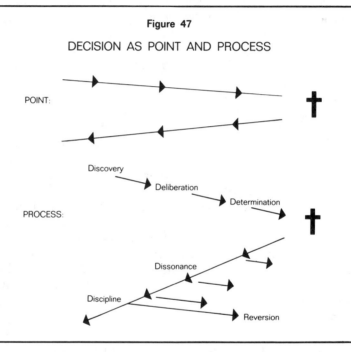

---

1. Currently, missionary literature—especially of the evangelical variety—does not give much attention to preevangelism and the stages of *discovery* and *deliberation* in decision making. This is unfortunate. The oversight has resulted in a short-circuiting of the decision-making process and in multiplied thousands of premature determinations to "believe in

[6]James F. Engel, *Contemporary Christian Communication: Its Theory and Practice* (Nashville: Thomas Nelson, 1979), 183.

Christ." Many a twentieth-century evangelist or missionary, if put in the place of Philip when he accosted the Ethiopian eunuch (Acts 8:26–40), would have asked him, "Will you believe?" But Philip's question was, "Do you understand what you are reading?" (Acts 8:30). It is absolutely essential that communicators of the gospel grasp the fact that although the *decision point* may be precipitated by prematurely closing off further deliberation, the *decision process* will go through its successive stages. Humanly speaking, there is simply no rhetorical way by which we can circumvent the struggle implicit in stages one and two by catapulting our respondents to stage three! The fact that there is a vast number of people in the Third World who say that they "tried Christianity and found it didn't work" speaks volumes about our evangelistic *methods*. But it says nothing about Christ! People must have time to think, time to understand, and time to weigh the issues. My experience indicates that the majority of converts who have come out of the large evangelistic crusades in the Orient and continued in the faith are those who had previous exposure to Christian teachings in the churches. Of course, we may also infer from this that leaders in the local churches err in the direction of not providing occasions for the unconverted to act on their knowledge by actually repenting and believing in Christ. Evangelism that focuses on the decision point to the exclusion of the decision process is regrettable. But evangelism that seldom gets around to asking those who have heard and understand the gospel to make a choice represents no improvement.

2. Another concept in the decision-making process that needs clarification is that of *dissonance*. This stage has been most clearly described by Leon Festinger who has developed the theory of cognitive dissonance.[7] Briefly stated, it refers to the state of unsettledness that occurs after a certain course of action has been taken. For example, X has a choice between two kinds of automobiles. Both are appealing to him, but after

---

[7]Leon Festinger, *A Theory of Cognitive Dissonance* (Evanston, Ill.: Row, Peterson, 1957).

deliberation he settles on one, signs the papers, and drives it home. There follows a period of time during which X experiences the shortcomings built into his new car—rattles that cannot be located, poor gas mileage, and so forth. Naturally, he thinks back to the automobile he *did not buy*. Perhaps it would have performed better. Why did he not choose the other make? If he would have done so, perhaps he would not have these problems! Put in these terms, we can empathize with X immediately. All of us have experienced cognitive dissonance times without number!

Applied to the conversion process, dissonance refers to that period during which the new convert encounters the various difficulties that accrue to following Christ in the cultural contexts of non-Christian traditions. In those contexts, too often the peace and joy that comes with knowing Christ is challenged by opposition in the family or community. Group conversion, of course, lessens the likelihood and severity of these difficulties, but even in group conversion some dissonance can be expected. If rain does not fall, or sickness occurs, or an abnormal child is born, there is always the temptation to interpret these experiences as being caused by vengeful gods, spirits, or unhappy ancestors. In fact, the imaginations of Satan and the natural mind share an uncanny ability to come up with false but appealing reasons for such misfortunes.

In the missionary situation, the first forty-eight hours following an individual's determination to receive Christ may be some of the most important hours of his entire lifetime. (In the case of a group, the dissonance crisis may be delayed somewhat.) If evangelism has been perfunctory and follow-up is haphazard or (as is often the case) too little and too late, the new convert may yield to the temptation to return to the old ways rather than take up his cross and follow Christ. It is absolutely imperative that Christian missionaries and nationals pray and go out of their way to communicate the love and concern of Christ during this crucial period. Some of the most embittered enemies of Christ in the Third World are those who have taken important steps in the direction of discipleship only to be abandoned by those who have preached to them. *No aspect of the Christian mission calls for more soul-searching on the part of missionary strategists than does this.*

3. *Discipline* is essential to conversion. When one decides to become a soldier or sailor, or when one decides to become a fraternity brother or sorority sister, it is taken for granted that there will be an initiation into the new group and submission to a new set of regulations. One does not find soldiers without serial numbers, insignia, rank, unit membership, and orders. Yet there seems to be a general impression among evangelicals that belief in Christ is imperative for salvation, but after that everything is more or less optional. The new Christian can be a member of a church, or of a parachurch organization, or of no organization at all. He can be baptized sooner, or later, or not at all. He can subject himself to the discipline of a church, or determine for himself the discipline that he deems acceptable, or refuse any discipline whatsoever.

It is not difficult to adduce reasons for this state of affairs in evangelicalism. Christianity *is much more* than simply becoming a member of a local church, participating in a ritual, or subscribing to a set of rules. To that we must agree. But Christianity *is not less than this* even in a laissez faire "Christian" society where discipleship seems to be considered an elective course after one has passed the required course of salvation.

Confusion on these issues is sometimes lessened on the mission field. At other times it is accentuated. Missions and the younger churches vary widely as to methods and content of indoctrination programs, the time of baptism, requirements for participation in communion, policies on church membership, and the application of discipline. No attempt can be made to resolve these complex issues here. Two pertinent observations are in order, however.

First, conversion should be understood and communicated as involving incorporation into the church of Christ (not just the "universal church" but a local expression of it) and submission to the discipline of Christ. We need not be apologetic about this. It is in accord with biblical teachings and the dictates of human experience. We err when we promote churches that are not New Testament churches and when we substitute purely human rules for divine requirements. But we do not err when we instruct new believers to become members of true churches, learn Christian doctrine, serve Christ and his church faithfully, and submit to Christian discipline. In fact, new believers expect this. One of the most successful evangelists in the Philippines in terms of actually gaining converts and establishing new churches has said that one of the foremost questions in the minds of Filipinos when they hear the Christian gospel is "If I accept this gospel, with what group will I be identified?"

Second, the symbolic *formal* aspects of discipline—incorporation into the church, participation in church life, and submission to authority—must be accompanied by *informal* practical aspects of these acts to be biblical and meaningful. One mission, for example, decided to baptize converts coming out of their large evangelistic campaigns immediately upon confession of faith rather than waiting to baptize them after a period of instruction. In this way they hoped to reduce the number of such converts who reverted within the first few months or year after their profession of faith. The mission discovered that simply changing the time of baptism made no difference whatever in the number of reversions. Obviously, factors other than the rituals *per se* (as important as the ritual may be) must be considered. Respondents must be made aware of the life-changing implications of the gospel. Believers must wholeheartedly accept new converts to the point of helping them in practical ways with their problems, patronizing their business establishments, and so forth. Pagan concepts must be exchanged for Bible doctrines. Unless the foregoing occur, mere formal rituals will not greatly assist the convert through the stages of the decision-making process.

PROFIT EQUALS REWARD MINUS COST

I have defined "motive" but have used the term "value" without stopping to define it. In some ways values are complementary to a people's worldview because the kind of universe they conceive themselves to be a part of will largely determine *the comparative worth they assign to ideas, objects, and actions.* For the Christian, these values are, or should be, determined in accordance with God's revelation to man. But in anthropological terms, value scales must be seen in relation to cultural context. *Explicit values* will find their expression in ethical rules and opinions. *Implicit values* must be located in the premises that underlie a course of action.

In a chapter entitled "The Voluntary Acceptance of Change," H. Ian Hogbin asserts that individuals adopt change voluntarily only in terms of reward—a reward that must be worth the cost.[8]

Sociologist George Homans says something very similar.[9] In a study of decision-making small groups, Homans concludes that the process can best be understood as an exchange of material and nonmaterial goods. Decisions are made on the basis of the difference between the reward received for a certain type of behavior and the cost of that behavior to the individual. The difference is "profit." The upshot is that the motivation to adopt or reject a certain line of behavior can be studied, and even "predicted," on the basis of a simple equation from economics:

$$\text{Profit} = \text{Reward} - \text{Cost}$$

At first glance this type of an analysis of decision making may seem altogether too simple and crass to be considered by missionaries and missiologists. Homans acknowledges as much in regard to sociologists who might be expected to be even more suspicious of such simple constructs. It is significant, therefore, that as one of America's leading sociologists, Homans concludes,

---

[8]H. Ian Hogbin, *Social Change* (London: Watts, 1958), 57.
[9]George Homans, "Social Behavior as Exchange," *American Journal of Sociology* 63 (May 1958): 597–606.

In our unguarded moments we sociologists find words like "rewards" and "cost" slipping into what we say. Human nature will break in upon even our most elaborate theories. But we seldom let it have its way with us and follow up systematically what these words imply. Of all of our many "approaches" to social behavior, the one that sees it as an economy is the most neglected, and yet it is the one we use every moment of our lives—except when we write sociology.[10]

Perhaps it is even more enlightening to note that our Lord spoke in a similar vein when he said, "For what shall it profit a man, if he shall gain the whole world, and lose his own soul? Or what shall a man give in exchange for his soul?" (Mark 8:36–37 KJV). A model that at first glance may seem to be simplistic, upon closer examination turns out to be profound—especially when spiritual and cross-cultural considerations are taken into account.

Hogbin uses this model to analyze the decision of many Pacific Islanders to accept Christianity.[11] He says that although missionaries offered security to them, natives initially were unstirred. Yet today practically all who are below middle age and who have had ten or more years of contact with Christianity have decided to become Christians. Why? Hogbin believes that the decision has been made without proof of Christianity's truth claims and often with disruptive social consequences. But it has been made because contemporary missions can now deliver at precisely that point where they could not do so initially. Positively, missions can offer equality with whites, education for the young, social standing for the elders, and so forth. Negatively, they can offer the avoidance of certain burdensome traditional observances because missionaries have told them that these observances could be neglected without ill consequences.

This type of analysis is not altogether flattering to missions. One could wish that more anthropologists were in a

[10]Ibid., 606.
[11]Hogbin, *Social Change*, 72–74.

position to take into account the various spiritual factors involved in conversion to Christ. On the other hand, one could also wish that more missionaries were prepared to take the nonspiritual factors into account. Security, prestige, and similar motivations are not necessarily evil. When these and other motivations are involved in the decision to accept Christ, the missionary should be the first to recognize them in order to make appropriate adjustments in his appeals and then more effectively and wisely counsel his respondents.

THE CORRELATION BETWEEN MOTIVATION FOR CONVERSION AND CHRISTIAN ATTAINMENT

There are three parties to the conversion process in the context of mission—the missionary, the respondent(s), and God. Each of these parties has his reasons for conversion. God's motives are absolutely pure. He loves people with an *agapē* love that desires only that which is good for his creatures. Even his desire to be worshiped and glorified by people is an expression, not of divine egoism, but of that same *agapē* love, for only when God is God to his creatures can the universe be put back on its true center.

Missionary and respondent motivation, on the other hand, may be mixed. It may well be that in some cases criticism of the missionary to the effect that he is not seeking the welfare of the people to whom he ministers but rather is desirous of personal prestige and self-satisfaction is justified. Perhaps ulterior missionary motivation for the conversion of large numbers of non-Christians is one reason for faulty missionary methodology. On the other hand, the overall missionary record of altruism is a most impressive one. And for that matter, in what other undertaking are feelings of satisfaction and a sense of accomplishment construed to be ulterior motivations?

It is the motivation of the convert, however, that we are concerned with here. Why do Indians, Pacific Islanders, Latin Americans, or Africans become Christians? Perhaps one of the most monumental missionary studies ever undertaken attempted to answer that question. It was initiated in 1928 in order to study the Christian mass movements in India and was published in 1933 under the editorship of J. Waskom Pickett.[12] The researchers fully recognized the difficulties inherent in making a study relating to the psychology of religion, particularly of ascertaining the real motives for the conversion of people (some of whom had been Christians for many years) simply by inquiring after those motives. If I remember correctly, however, Abraham Maslow at one time criticized his fellow psychologists for *not* asking people about their motivations rather than simply trying to deduce those motivations by a study of rats and chimpanzees! In any case, the informants in the India study were asked, not to analyze their motives for becoming Christians, but for the primary reason for their conversion. While admitting that informants sometimes seemed to have forgotten the real reasons and at other times exhibited a tendency to rationalize, the researchers were fully persuaded that the results were basically accurate and very significant.

The great majority of the almost four thousand informants were able to locate their primary reason for conversion among forty standardized replies noted on the interview schedule, though some two hundred responses were recorded in their own words. The motives were classified into four groups:

In Group 1 (Spiritual Motives) are placed all answers that had been recorded under the heads: "seeking salvation," and "convinced by the preacher," and also all such answers as "to know God," "to find peace," "because of faith in Jesus," "because of the love of God," etc.

In Group 2 (Secular Motives) are placed all answers that had been recorded as "sought help of the missionaries," "in hope of education for the children," "for improved social standing," "had agricultural service," and "had medical

[12]J. Waskom Pickett, *Christian Mass Movements in India* (New York: Abingdon, 1933).

service," and also all answers that revealed a hope of personal gain not definitely spiritual, such as "to marry a Christian girl," "because the landowners oppressed us," etc.

In Group 3 (Social Reasons) we put all answers checked as "family was being baptized," and "brotherhood was being baptized," and all such answers as "I didn't want to remain a Hindu when my relatives were Christians," or "My people told me to do so."

Group 4 (Natal Influences) is composed of those whose replies were entered as "child of Christian parents." Their parents were Christians when they were born or became Christians while they were quite young, so that they were brought up in the Christian faith.[13]

Before noting the results, it should be explained that informants who mentioned reasons that fell into more than one of the above classifications were recorded in each category for which their answers qualified them. When this question on motivation was not answered, or the answer could not be confidently interpreted by the researcher, no entry was made. The classified answers totaled 3,947, which broke down in accordance with the table in figure 48.[14]

The study went on to examine the relationship between motivation for conversion and Christian attainment measured in terms of membership and loyalty to the churches, abstinence, "memoriter work," and so forth. (Incidence of reversion as such was not a part of the study—a fact that detracts somewhat from its value.) Results showed that there was a relationship between the motive claimed and the measure of attainment.[15] Those whose motives were classified as spiritual or natal showed higher attainment than those with secular or social motives.

The result that the researchers considered most important for the consideration of the churches, however, was the smallness of the margin on the scale of attainment between

[13]Ibid., 164–65.
[14]Ibid., 165.
[15]Ibid., 165–68.

those who became Christians for secular or social reasons and those in the spiritual-motive group.[16]

Figure 48

MOTIVES FOR CONVERSION
ACCORDING TO A STUDY IN INDIA

TYPE OF MOTIVE	NUMBER OF INFORMANTS	PERCENTAGE OF WHOLE NUMBER
Spiritual	1,371	34.8%
Secular	322	8.1%
Social	885	22.4%
Natal Influences	1,369	34.7%

Christian communicators should give priority to the spiritual aim. There can be no question about this in view of the fact that our Lord said, "But seek *first* His kingdom and His righteousness" (Matt. 6:33). No little mischief results from giving priority to temporal concerns. Missionaries ministering to the masses in one area of India sought to help the people raise their levels of education and living *preliminary* to helping them spiritually. "Schools were opened, co-operative societies organized, and medical work inaugurated. Many became literate, economic conditions were improved, and many diseases were cured."[17] Then, and only then, did the missionaries begin to preach Christ and urge the people to believe the gospel. The response of the people must have been shattering. They said, "You are experts in running schools, co-operative societies, and hospitals. What do you know about religion? For advice on religion we will go to the priests who make that their business."[18] Discouraged, the missionaries left

[16]Ibid., 168.
[17]Ibid., 347.
[18]Ibid.

the area. Within a short time the people slipped back into poverty and unsanitary living.

Pickett, however, concludes that there should be no hesitancy on the part of missionaries to minister to temporal needs if there is a *simultaneous* effort to give the primary place to spiritual motivations for conversions.[19] It should be remembered that Christ fed the hungry and healed the sick. Furthermore, it certainly is not unchristian for people to desire health, a better standard of living, a sense of worth, justice, and hope for their children's future. The important thing is to minister to the whole person while placing priority on his or her soul. We must continue our spiritual ministry to those who may be motivated to come to Christ for other than spiritual reasons in the realization that they too can be led by the Spirit to spiritual understanding and attainment.

[19]Ibid., 346.

Chapter 45

Receptivity and Missionary Response

When Jonah preached what would normally be considered an unpopular message on the judgment of God in Nineveh, the unexpected occurred—all from king to commoner repented and judgment was averted. When Jesus did some of his mightiest works in Bethsaida, Chorazin, and Capernaum, the people turned away. But if those same miracles had been done in Tyre, Sidon, and Sodom they would have repented (Matt. 11:21–24). When Paul and Barnabas preached in Lystra, there was an overwhelming reception until Jews came from Antioch (in Pisidia) and Iconium and persuaded the masses in the opposite direction. Thereupon Paul was stoned, dragged from the city, and left for dead (Acts 14:8–20).

TIMING

Most students of mission are familiar with the great changes in response to the gospel that have occurred in the era of modern missions. Although there were but 10 million Christians in Africa in 1900, the 1970 census reported 130 million African Christians.[1] (I report those figures without further comment simply to point out the fact of changed receptivity). Whereas there were only fifty thousand Protestants in Latin America at the beginning of the twentieth century, there are probably more than twenty million today. While there had been remarkable turnings to Christ among the certain groups in Indonesia as early as a century ago, Indonesian Muslims remained unresponsive and hostile until an abortive coup in the 1950s. Since that time there has been a general revival, and more Muslims have turned to Christ in Indonesia than in any other nation. When I first visited the Philippines in the 1960s, there was a general apathy, if not antipathy, toward the gospel message. Less than a decade later I returned to find widespread interest in what the Bible teaches, greatly increased attendance in Protestant churches, and numerous home Bible studies in most of the urban centers.

It should be remembered that the changing circumstances that so vitally affect the receptivity of populations are all under the control of a sovereign God. He allows the contact with primitive cultures that opens them up to the possibility of embracing his Christ. He allows great civilizations to be built on foundations of sand that ultimately cannot bear the weight that has been entrusted to them. He allows national cataclysms that cause whole populations to grasp for new hope and values. He anonymously superintends human councils, where doors are closed and opened to the preaching of the gospel.

There are many Scriptures that support this high view of a God who condescends to become man to provide a way of reconciliation for erring people while nevertheless refusing to be less than God in guiding all things toward their divinely appointed consummation. In fact, the "fullness of time" (Gal. 4:4 KJV) represented just that confluence of circumstances that

[1]David Barrett, "History's Most Massive Influx in the Churches," in Alan R. Tippett, ed., God, Man and Church Growth (Grand Rapids: Eerdmans, 1973), 396–413.

brought Christ into the world, facilitated the communication of that gospel throughout the Mediterranean world, and encouraged its acceptance by great masses of people. Enough has been written about the Roman hegemony and roads, and the Greek language and thought, that played their parts in that culminating tragedy and triumph of history. But Kenneth Scott Latourette's words should perhaps be recalled to complete the picture:

> In the Graeco-Roman world cultural disintegration had set in before Christianity attracted more than a minority. It was largely because the established civilization was dissolving, weakened by many other factors than the attack of Christianity, that the faith was able to win.[2]

Those words help us understand the impact of the Christian message on the pagan world of the first century. And they send a ray of light piercing through the darkness of the neopagan world of the West in this twentieth century.

Receptiveness, then, is first of all a matter of God's sovereign direction in the affairs of people. "He . . . opens and no one will shut, and . . . shuts and no one opens" (Rev. 3:7). The demise of indigenous religions, the disintegration of cultures, the conquests of nations, the freedom from longstanding controls, the migration of peoples—these and numerous other factors that often facilitate receptivity can, for the most part, be only indirectly affected by Christians committed to mission. I say indirectly because we have a responsibility to pray that doors will be opened for communicating Christ (Col. 4:3) and that the gospel will spread rapidly (2 Thess. 3:1). But along with this goes the responsibility to recognize the times and seasons, to locate responsive peoples, and to communicate Christ to them in a way that will promote continued receptivity and church growth.

At the same time, there are strong arguments for main-

[2]Kenneth Scott Latourette, *A History of the Expansion of Christianity*, 7 vols. (New York: Harper and Brothers, 1937), 1:7.

taining a missionary witness among unresponsive peoples (where that is possible). In the first place, one can argue that obedience to Christ demands such a witness. In the second place, one can argue that it will ensure the presence of missionary communicators who can identify with the people of the respondent culture when and if they become responsive. When a people become responsive, far more is involved than simply rushing in with a large number of hastily recruited volunteers and large quantities of material resources.

Still fresh in my memory is a lengthy interview with two prominent leaders of the Indonesian revival at its very height in the 1960s (one of whom was my long-time associate in missionary work in the Orient). They told of preaching up to ten times a day to crowds of people who walked for days to hear the message. But at the same time they urged great care in the recruitment of workers. In essence they said:

> We already have occasion to fear an influx of Christian workers who will squelch the revival. The people are ready to listen to Christian witnesses who understand and love them. But missionary opportunists who simply preach, take pictures, and write articles for publications in the West will do more harm than good. We need, not just more missionaries, but more missionaries who are men and women of God and who understand how to communicate Christ in our culture.

This reaction of seasoned, non-Caucasian church leaders working in one of the responsive fields in modern missions deserves our consideration, and requires no further comment.

SEQUENCE

Another important consideration in communicating Christ to a newly responsive or potentially responsive society is sequence. I have previously mentioned the problem occasioned by missionaries in India who attempted to cultivate responsiveness by programs in education and welfare, and then when they anticipated a welcome hearing for the gospel, they were rebuffed by the response "You are experts in education and medicine, but when we want advice in religion we will go to our priests."

From his perspective as an applied anthropologist, George Foster notes that although literacy and adult education programs are often thought to be basic in community education programs, this notion is a mistake.[3] In peasant societies people do not usually look upon literacy as an abstract thing that is good per se. In support of this contention, he reports the finding of I. C. Jackson in Nigeria.[4] During World War II an adult literacy program carried on in that country was extremely successful. Surprisingly, after the war ended it ground to a sudden halt. Why? Because the people had received no significant satisfaction from the ability to read and write. Rather, they had only wanted to communicate with their young men who had left for military service. When the servicemen returned, the need for literacy lessened and responsiveness to the program diminished.

Such examples become invaluable to missionary communicators. I have found that, taken as a whole, evangelical communication strategy is often no less defensible than at times and places of great responsiveness. With but limited consultation and forethought, missionary groups and individuals—each with his own specialties and approaches—descend upon the situation to take advantage of the opportunity. Priorities in welfare, literacy, education, literature distribution, preaching to the masses, etc., are then determined on the basis of the interests of the missionary sources rather than the needs that occasioned the responsiveness of the respondents.

This approach is regrettable. Prayerful study and discernment are essential. When the people are ready to understand and receive the gospel itself, priority should not be given to philanthropic service that in other cases may be required to help secure true spiritual responsiveness. In an unresponsive

[3]George M. Foster, Traditional Cultures: And the Impact of Technological Change (New York: Harper & Row, 1962), 167–68.
[4]Ibid., 168.

field, Bible translation and distribution may be important to prepare the way for widespread teaching and preaching. In a responsive field, widespread teaching and preaching may arouse the felt need for literacy and the Bible. Consideration of the kind, extent, and degree of responsiveness is essential to communication strategy.

RELEVANCE

Finally (and closely related to our previous points), communication itself must be made relevant *in terms of the antecedent causes of responsiveness* if missionaries are to capitalize on the situation. Barnett's way of saying this is that what is being proposed to people must be "associable."[5] Receptive peoples sometimes may seem to *respond to any new system of beliefs and values* that are communicated to them along with the promise of a better future. But they will likely *retain* only that which is meaningful in terms of those experiences and longings that occasioned their responsiveness in the first place.

Postwar Japan furnishes what may be a classic example of this. The vast majority of that large number of missionaries who went to Japan within a decade after that country's humiliating defeat in 1945 went in the belief that the Japanese people felt forsaken by their gods and misdirected by their leaders. In his providence, God was giving Japan another opportunity to hear his truth and follow his Son. And the Christian missionaries were heaven-appointed ambassadors, privileged to declare the message to multiplied thousands at that time of history when the Japanese were most receptive to the Christian message.

What happened is now a matter of record. In terms of meetings held, sermons preached, Bible portions and pieces of literature distributed, media utilized, *and decisions for Christ recorded*, the postwar evangelistic effort in Japan must rank

---

[5]H. G. Barnett, *Innovation: The Basis of Cultural Change* (New York: McGraw-Hill, 1953), 334.

with one of the most concentrated efforts to evangelize a nation in the annals of Christian missions. Yet, after a generation, the number of Christians per capita in Japan is little more than one-half of one percent—a figure that represents no appreciable increase over the last thirty years! Certainly no knowledgeable person would suggest that any one simple answer explains the disparity between the promise and the product in Japan. But one very important clue may be provided by Susumu Akahoshi in his comparison of Japanese (and to some extent of all Oriental) and Western religiosity—i.e., the "collectivistic-dependency" versus the "individualistic-independency" religiosities to which I have already referred. Regarding the "spiritual lostness" of modern Japan, Akahoshi says,

> Japan's "spiritual lostness" has not come about because a fundamental sense of individual responsibility has been lost—such a sense never existed in Japanese mentality—but because *the group to depend on has been lost* [italics mine].[6]

Now let every communicator of Christianity in postwar Japan reflect on the expenditure of effort and the message to which hundreds of thousands responded by taking some initial steps on the Christian way. From well-planned rallies in halls, theater, and stadia—complete with films, musical productions, and fervent preaching—"converts" were often directed (if directed at all!) to small churches or simple rooms in out-of-the-way places where they met comparatively few Christians whom they probably had little prospect of meeting again until the next scheduled meeting. That the Christian *meeting* had something to commend it in spite of the Western form in which it was (usually) communicated was apparent, because they came. That the Christian *group* did not commend itself as *the group to depend on* was apparent because (usually) they

[6]Susumu Akahoshi, "Japanese and Western Religiosity," in Kenneth J. Dale, ed., *Circle of Harmony: A Case Study in Popular Japanese Buddhism* (Pasadena: William Carey, 1975), 182.

did not stay. In far too many cases the Christianity communicated to postwar Japanese was not relevant to the *kind* of lostness that occasioned their responsiveness. Religious groups that have prospered in contemporary Japan have, without exception, answered to the need for belonging to, and depending on, local groups of adherents as well as the larger national constituencies.

CONCLUSION TO PART IX

It is not only permissible for people to persuade others, it is essential to the betterment of society that they be free to do so. More important than this, however, is the fact that the missionary mandate requires persuasion because it involves a call for conversion and conformity to Jesus Christ. From a theological point of view, elenctics must be considered in relation to this process because the Holy Spirit works in and with and through the missionary to bring unbelievers to repentance and faith. Both the sciences and elenctics are important, therefore, but the mission of the church is God's mission. Since conversion is ultimately the work of the Holy Spirit, science must take its place as a handmaid of elenctics.

Humanly speaking, people are persuaded for *their* reasons, not *ours*. Missionary persuasion, therefore, is concerned with differences in motivational patterns and value systems occasioned by differences in the enculturation processes of the various cultures. For that reason I have characterized and analyzed broad cultural differences. I have noted some of their implications for such areas of communication as points of contact, missionary appeals, decision making, the conversion process, and the missionary response to receptive peoples.

The implementation of knowledge in these areas greatly enhances the prospect that the missionary will be successful in converting his hearers and in assisting believers to continue and mature in the faith. *When the missionary is successful, his respondents are greatly enriched, for Christ is Lord of all.*

BIBLIOGRAPHY

Abbey, Merrill R. *Man, Media and the Message*. New York: Friendship, 1960.

Aikawa, Takaaki and Lynn Leavenworth. *The Mind of Japan—A Christian Perspective*. Valley Forge: Judson, 1967.

Akahoshi, Susumu. "Japanese and Western Religiosity." In *Circle of Harmony: A Case Study in Popular Japanese Buddhism*, edited by Kenneth J. Dale. Pasadena: William Carey, 1975.

Aquinas, St. Thomas. *Summa Theologica*, Vol. I, Articles 9 & 10 Question 13. Translated by the Father of the English Dominican Province. New York: Benzinger Brothers, 1947.

Allport, Gordon. *Pattern and Growth in Personality*. New York: Holt, Rinehart and Winston, 1961.

Aranguren, José L. *Human Communication*. Translated by Francis Partridge. New York: McGraw-Hill, 1967.

Augustine. *On Christian Doctrine*. Translated by D. W. Robertson, Jr. New York: Liberal Arts, 1958.

Baker, Norman. "Confucianism." In *The World's Religions*, edited by J. N. D. Anderson. Rochester, England: Staples, 1950, 161–89.

Barnett, H. G. *Innovation: The Basis of Cultural Change*. New York: McGraw Hill, 1953.

Barney, G. Linwood. "Is Decision by Consensus Valid?" *The Alliance Witness* (January 20, 1971), 9–10.

_____. "The Supracultural and the Cultural: Implications for Frontier Missions" n.d. The original version of this manuscript was a chapter by the same title in *The Gospel and Frontier Peoples*, edited by R. Pierce Beaver, 48–55. Pasadena: William Carey, 1973.

Barrett, David B. "History's Most Massive Influx in the Churches." In *God, Man and Church Growth*, edited by Alan R. Tippett. Grand Rapids: Eerdmans, 1973.

_____. "Annual Statistical Table on Global Mission: 1989." *International Bulletin of Missionary Research* 13, 1 (January 1989): 20–21.

————. "Annual Statistical Table on Global Mission: 1988." *International Bulletin of Missionary Research* 12, 1 (January 1988): 16–17.

Barrett, David B., ed. *World Christian Encyclopedia: A Comparative Study of Churches and Religions in the Modern World A.D. 1900–2000.* Oxford: Oxford University Press, 1982.

Batalla, Guillermo Bonfil. "Conservative Thought in Applied Anthropology: A Critique." *Human Organization* 25 (Summer 1966): 89–92.

Bavinck, John Herman. *An Introduction to the Science of Missions.* Translated by David H. Freeman. Grand Rapids: Baker, 1969.

Bayly, Joe. *The Gospel Blimp.* Havertown, Pa.: Windward, 1960.

Behavior. "Distant Persuasion." *Time,* 7 September 1970, 27.

Behavior. "The Body." *Time,* 13 June 1969, 86.

Benedict, Ruth. *Chrysanthemum and the Sword: Patterns of Japanese Culture.* Boston: Houghton Mifflin, 1946.

————. *Patterns of Culture.* Boston: Houghton Mifflin, 1934.

Bently-Taylor, David. "Buddhism." In *The World's Religions,* edited by J. N. D. Anderson. Rochester, England: Staples, 1950, 118–35.

Berlo, David K. *The Process of Communication: An Introduction to Theory and Practice.* New York: Holt, Rinehart and Winston, 1960.

Berndt, Manfred Helmuth. "The Diakonia Function of the Church in Hong Kong." Ph.D. Dissertation, Concordia Seminary, 1970.

Berne, Eric. *Games People Play.* New York: Grove, 1964.

Beyerhaus, Peter and Henry Lefever. *The Responsible Church and the Foreign Mission.* Grand Rapids: Eerdmans, 1964.

Bigman, Stanley. "Prestige, Personal Influence and Opinion." In *The Process and Effects of Mass Communication,* edited by Wilbur Schramm. Urbana: University of Illinois Press, 1954.

Birdwhistell, Ray. *An Introduction to Kinesics.* Washington, D.C.: Department of State, Foreign Service Institute, 1952.

————. "Kinesics and Communication." In McLuhan, Marshall and Edmund Carpenter. *Explorations in Communication.* Boston: Beacon, 1960.

Blake, Cecil A. "Rhetoric and Intercultural Communication." In *Handbook of Intercultural Communication,* edited by Molefi Kete Asante, Eileen Newmar, and Cecil A. Blake. Beverly Hills: Sage Publications, 1979, 86.

Bleeker, Sonia. *The Ibo of Biafra.* New York: Morrow, 1969.

Boas, Franz. *The Mind of Primitive Man.* New York: Free Press, 1965.

Bibliography

Bochner, S. "The House Form as a Cornerstone of Culture." In Brislin, R., ed. *Topics in Culture Learning*. Vol. 3. Honolulu: East-West Center, 1975.

Boer, Harry R. *Pentecost and Missions*. Grand Rapids: Eerdmans, 1961.

Bohannan, Paul. *Social Anthropology*. New York: Holt, Rinehart and Winston, 1963.

Bolton, Robert. "Celebrations of Festivity: A Potential Means of Effective Communication to Further Advance the Gospel Among the Taiwanese." A paper submitted to the School of World Mission and Evangelism, Trinity Evangelical Divinity School, for the course Advanced Problems in Cross-Cultural Communication, March 17, 1989.

Bouquet, A. C. *Christian Faith and Non-Christian Religions*. London: Nisbet, 1958.

Bramer, George R. "Right Rhetoric: Classical Roots for Contemporary Aims in Writing." In *Rhetoric and Praxis: The Contribution of Classical Rhetoric to Practical Reasoning*, edited by Jean Dietz Moss. Washington, D.C.: The Catholic University of America Press, 1986, 135–56.

Brewster, E. Thomas, and Elizabeth S. Brewster. *Language Acquisition Made Practical*. Colorado Springs, Colo.: Lingua, 1977.

_____. "Involvement as a Means of Second Culture Learning," *Practical Anthropology* 19, 1 (1972): 27–44.

Brow, Robert. *Religion—Origin and Ideas*. Chicago: InterVarsity, 1966.

Brown, Harrison. *The Challenge of Man's Future*. New York: Viking, 1954.

Brown, Ina Corrine. *Understanding Other Cultures*. Englewood Cliffs, N.J.: Prentice-Hall, 1963.

Brun, Theodore. *The International Dictionary of Sign Language*. London: Wolfe, 1969.

Bryant, Donald C. "Rhetoric: Its Function and Scope." *Quarterly Journal of Speech* (1953).

Bull, Geoffrey T. *When Iron Gates Yield*. London: Hodder and Stoughton, 1967.

Bunkowske, Eugene W., and Richard French. *God's Communicators in Mission*. Fullerton, Calif.: Great Commission Resource Library, 1988.

Burke, Kenneth. *A Grammar of Motives and a Rhetoric of Motives*. Cleveland: World, Meridian, 1962.

Burns, Robert. "To a Louse, On Seeing One on a Lady's Bonnet at Church." In *The Complete Poetical Works of Robert Burns*. Cambridge Edition. Boston: Houghton, Mifflin, 1897.

Buswell, James Oliver, III, "Contextualization: Theory, Tradition and Method," and Ericson, Norman R. "Implications from the New Testament for Contextualization." In *Theology and Mission*, edited by David J. Hesselgrave, Grand Rapids: Baker, 1978, 71–111.

Carpenter, Edmund. "Television Meets the Stone Age." *T.V. Guide* (January 16, 1971), 16.

Chase, Stuart. *The Power of Words*. New York: Harcourt, Brace and World, 1954.

Chomsky, Noam. *Aspects of the Theory of Syntax*. Cambridge: MIT, 1965.

Clark, Donald Lemen. *Rhetoric in Greco-Roman Education*. New York: Columbia University Press, 1957.

Coe, Shoki. *Contextualizing Theology*. Mission Trends No. 3, edited by G. H. Anderson and T. F. Stransky. Grand Rapids: Eerdmans; New York: Paulist Press, 1976.

Coggins, Wade T. and E. L. Frizen, Jr. *Evangelical Missions Tomorrow*. Pasadena: William Carey, 1977.

Collins, Gary R. "Psychology on a New Foundation: A Proposal for the Future." *Journal of Psychology and Theology* 1 (January 1973): 19–27.

Condon, John C., Jr. *Interpersonal Communication*. New York: Macmillan, 1977.

Condon, John C., Jr., and Fathi Yousef. *An Introduction to Intercultural Communication*. Indianapolis, Ind.: Bobbs-Merrill, 1975.

Conn, Harvie. "Contextualization: A New Dimension for Cross-Cultural Hermeneutics." *Evangelical Missions Quarterly* 14 (1978): 42.

Cook, Bruce L. *Understanding Pictures in Papua, New Guinea*. Elgin, Ill.: David C. Cook, 1981.

Cooke, Gerald. *As the Christian Faces Rival Religions*. New York: Association, 1962.

Corwin, Charles. *Biblical Encounter with Japanese Culture*. Tokyo: Christian Literature Crusade, 1967.

Costas, Orlando. *The Church and Its Mission: A Shattering Critique from the Third World*. Wheaton: Tyndale, 1974.

Cowan, Marian. "A Christian Movement in Mexico." *Practical Anthropology* 9, 5 (1962): 193–204.

Cox, Harvey. "Mission in a World of Cities." *International Review of Missions* 55 (July 1966): 273.

Bibliography

Crane, Paul. *Korean Patterns.* Seoul: Hollym, 1967.

Creel, H. G. "Confucius, the Philosopher"; "The Sayings of Confucius." In *Readings in Eastern Religious Thought: Chinese and Japanese Religions.* Vol. 3. Edited by Ollie M. Frazier. Philadelphia: Westminster, n.d., 35–89.

_____. *Chinese Thought from Confucius to Mao-Tse-Tung.* Chicago: University of Chicago Press, 1953.

Daily American (Rome) 36 (8 January 1977): 1.

Dale, Kenneth J., ed. *Circle of Harmony: A Case Study in Popular Japanese Buddhism.* Pasadena: William Carey, 1975.

Dasen, P. R. "Cross-Cultural Piagetian Research: A Summary." In *Culture and Cognition: Readings in Cross-Cultural Psychology,* edited by J. W. Berry and P. R. Dasen. London: Methuen, 1974.

Davis, Flora. "How to Read Body Language." *Reader's Digest* December 1969, 129.

Davis, Kingsley. "The Urbanization of the Human Population." In *Urbanism in World Perspective: A Reader,* edited by Sylvia Fava. New York: Crowell, 1968.

Dayton, Edward R., and David A. Fraser. *Planning Strategies for World Evangelization.* Grand Rapids: Eerdmans, 1980.

DeFleur, Melvin L. *Theories of Mass Communication.* 2nd ed. New York: McKay, 1970.

Deregowski, J. B. "Pictures As a Means of Communication: A Psychologist's View." *Educational Broadcasting International* (March 1978), 8–9.

Doob, Leonard. *Communication in Africa.* Westport, Connecticut: Greenwood, 1979.

Downs, James F. *Cultures in Crisis.* Beverly Hills, Calif.: Glencoe, 1971.

Downs, Roger M., and David Stea, eds. *Image and Environment: Cognitive Mapping and Spatial Behavior.* Chicago: Aldine, 1973.

Drummond, A. L. *German Protestantism Since Luther.* London: Epworth, 1951.

Drummond, Richard Henry. *A History of Christianity in Japan.* Grand Rapids: Eerdmans, 1971.

Eliade, Mircea. "Two Representative Systems of Hindu Thought." In *Readings in Eastern Religious Thought: Hinduism.* Vol. 1. Edited by Ollie M. Frazier. Philadelphia: Westminster, n.d., 169–94.

Elliot, George P. "McLuhans's Teaching Is Radical, New, Capable of Moving People to Social Action. If He is Wrong, It Matters." In

McLuhan Hot and Cool, edited by Gerald E. Stern. New York: Diel, 1967.

Ellul, Jacques. *The Meaning of the City.* Grand Rapids: Eerdmans, 1970.

Elridge, S. ed. *Fundamentals of Sociology.* New York: Crowell, 1950.

Engel, James F. *Contemporary Christian Communications: Its Theory and Practice.* Nashville: Thomas Nelson, 1979.

Engel, James F. and Wilbert H. Norton. *What's Gone Wrong With the Harvest? A Communication Strategy for the Church and World Evangelism.* Grand Rapids: Zondervan, 1975.

Engel, James F., Hugh G. Wales, and Martin R. Warshaw. *Promotional Strategy.* Rev. Ed. Homewood, Ill.: Irwin, 1971.

Evans, Robert A. *Let Europe Hear.* Chicago: Moody, 1963.

Evans, Robert A., and Thomas D. Parker, eds. *Christian Theology: A Case Study Approach.* New York: Harper & Row, 1976.

Fabun, Don. *Communications: The Transfer of Meaning.* Belmont, Calif.: Glencoe, 1968.

Fava, Sylvia, ed. *Urbanism in the World Perspective: A Reader.* New York: Crowell, 1968.

Fearing, Franklin. "An Examination of the Conceptions of Benjamin Whorf in the Light of Theories of Perception and Cognition." In *Language in Culture,* edited by Harry Hoijer. Chicago: University of Chicago Press, 1954, 47–81.

Festinger, Leon. *A Theory of Cognitive Dissonance.* Evanston, Ill.: Row, Peterson, 1957.

Firth, Raymond. *Elements of Social Organization.* Boston: Beacon, 1963.

Flavier, Juan M. *Doctor to the Barrios.* Quezon City: New Day, 1970.

Fleming, Bruce C. E. *Contextualization of Theology: An Evangelical Assessment.* Pasadena, Calif.: William Carey, 1980.

Fleming, Daniel J. *What Would You Do?* New York: Friendship, 1949.

Ford, Leighton. *The Christian Persuader.* New York: Harper & Row, 1966.

Foster, George. *Traditional Cultures: And the Impact of Technological Change.* New York: Harper & Row, 1962.

Freud, Sigmund. *The Future of an Illusion.* Translated by W. D. Robson-Scott. New York: Liveright, 1953.

Gay, John, and Michael Cole. *The New Mathematics and an Old Culture: A Study of Learning Among the Kpelle of Liberia.* New York: Holt, Rinehart and Winston, 1967.

Geisler, Norman. "Some Philosophical Perspectives on Missionary Dialogue." In *Theology and Mission,* edited by David Hesselgrave, Grand Rapids: Baker, 1978, 241–57.

Bibliography

Ginsburg, Herbert, and Sylvia Opper. *Piaget's Theory of Intellectual Development: An Introduction.* Englewood Cliffs, N.J.: Prentice-Hall, 1969.

Goodenough, Ward Hunt. *Cooperation in Change: An Anthropological Approach to Community Development.* New York: Wiley, Science Editions, 1966.

Green, Michael. *Evangelism in the Early Church.* Grand Rapids: Eerdmans, 1970.

Green, Margaret. *Ibo Village Affairs.* 2nd ed. London: Cass, 1964.

Grimes, Joseph E. "Ethnoghraphic Questions for Christian Missionaries." *Practical Anthropology* 6 (November-December 1959): 275–76.

Gulick, Sidney Lewis. *The East and the West.* Rutland, Vt.: Tuttle, 1962.

Hall, Edward T. *Beyond Culture.* Garden City, N.Y.: Doubleday, Anchor, 1977.

_____. "Proxemics—A Study of Man's Spacial Relations." In *Man's Image in Medicine and Anthropology,* edited by I. Goldston. New York: International University Press, 1967.

_____. *The Hidden Dimension.* Garden City, N.Y.: Doubleday, 1966.

_____. "The Language of Space." *Landscape* 10 (Fall 1960): 41–45.

_____. "The Maddening Crowd." *Landscape* 12 (Fall 1962): 26–29.

_____. *The Manpower Potential in Our Ethnic Groups.* Washington, D.C.: U.S. Department of Labor, 1967.

_____. *The Silent Language.* Greenwich, Conn.: Fawcett, 1959.

Hall, Edward T., and William Whyte. "Intercultural Communication: A Guide to Men of Action." *Human Organization* 19 (Spring 1960): 5–12.

Hammond, Peter B. *An Introduction to Cultural and Social Anthropology.* New York: Macmillan, 1971.

Harnack, Adolf. *The Mission and Expansion of Christianity in the First Three Centuries.* Translated and edited by James Moffat. New York: Harper and Brothers, 1961.

Haskins, J. B. "How to Evaluate Mass Communication." A monograph published by the Advertising Research Foundation, 1968.

Hauser, Philip M. "Application of Ideal-Type Constructs to the Metropolis in the Economically Less-Advanced Areas." In *Urbanism in World Perspective: A Reader,* edited by Sylvia Fava. New York: Crowell, 1968.

Hausman, Louis. "Measured View: The Public's Attitude Toward Television and the Other Media." A talk delivered to The

Television and Advertising Club of Philadelphia, February 8, 1962.

————. *Language in Action*. New York: Harcourt, Brace, 1946.

————. *Language in Thought and Action*. 2nd ed. New York: Harcourt, Brace, and World, 1941.

Henry, Carl F. H. "Revelation, Special." In *Baker's Dictionary of Theology*, edited by E. F. Harrison, 459. Grand Rapids: Baker, 1960.

Herberg, Will. *Protestant, Catholic and Jew*, rev. ed. Garden City, N.Y.: Doubleday, Anchor, 1960.

Hesselgrave, David J. "A Propagation Profile of the Soka Gakkai." Ph.D. dissertation. University of Minnesota, 1965.

————. "Dimensions of Cross-Cultural Communication." *Practical Anthropology* 19 (January-February 1972): 1–12.

————. *Dynamic Religious Movements: Case Studies in Rapidly Growing Religious Movements Around the World*. Grand Rapids: Baker, 1980.

————. "Identification—Key to Missionary Communication." *Evangelical Missions Quarterly* 9 (Summer 1973): 216–22.

————. "Interreligious Dialogue—Biblical and Contemporary Perspectives." In *Theology and Mission*, edited by David J. Hesselgrave. Grand Rapids: Baker, 1978, 227–40.

————. *Planting Churches Cross-Culturally: A Guide for Home and Foreign Missions*. Grand Rapids: Baker, 1980.

————. "Will World Events Change Missions?" *His*, May 1974, 25–27.

Hesselgrave, David J., ed. *Dynamic Religious Movements: Case Studies in Growing Religious Movements in Various Cultures*. Grand Rapids: Baker, 1978.

Hesselgrave, David J., and Edward Rommen. *Contextualization: Meanings, Methods, and Models*. Grand Rapids: Baker, 1989.

Hiebert, Paul. G. *Anthropological Insights for Missionaries*. Grand Rapids: Baker, 1985.

Hile, Pat. "Communicating the Gospel in Terms of Felt Needs." *Missiology* 5, 4 (October, 1977): 499–506.

Hockett, Charles. "The Origin of Speech." *Scientific American* 202 (September 1960): 885.

Hogbin, H. Ian. *Social Change*. London: Watts, 1958.

Homans, George. "Social Behavior as Exchange." *American Journal of Sociology* 63 (May 1958): 597–606.

Hovland, Carl I., and Walter Weiss. "The Influence of Source Credibility on Communication Effectiveness." In *The Process and Effects of Mass Communication*, edited by Wilbur Schramm. Urbana: University of Illinois Press, 1955.

Howell, William S. Class notes, communication seminar. University of Minnesota, 1964.

_____. "The Study of Intercultural Communication in Liberal Education." In *Pacific Speech* 2, 4 (1967).

Hsu, Francis L. K. *Clan, Caste and Club*. Princeton, N.J.: Van Nostrand, 1963.

Humphreys, Christmas. *Buddhism*. Baltimore: Penguin, 1951.

_____. *Zen Buddhism*. New York: Macmillan, 1962.

Hunter, Edward. *Brain-Washing in Red China*. New York: Vanguard, 1953.

Inch, Morris A. *Doing Theology Across Cultures*. Grand Rapids: Baker, 1982.

Jahn, Janheinz. *Muntu: An Outline of the New African Culture*. Translated by Marjorie Green. New York: Grove, 1961.

_____. "Value Conceptions in Sub-Saharan Africa." In *Cross Cultural Understanding: Epistemology in Anthropology*, edited by F. C. S. Northrop and Helen H. Livingston. New York: Harper & Row, 1964.

Jorgensen, Knud. "Models of Communication in the New Testament." *Missiology* 4, 4 (October 1976): 465–84.

Judge, E. A. *The Social Pattern of the Christian Groups in the First Century*. London: Tyndale, 1960.

Kane, Herbert J. *Winds of Change in the Christian Mission*. Chicago: Moody, 1973.

Kantzer, Kenneth S. "The Authority of the Bible." in *The Word for This Century*, edited by Merrill C. Tenney. New York: Oxford University Press, 1960, 34–39.

Kasdorf, Hans. *Christian Conversion in Context*. Scottsdale, Pa.: Herald, 1980.

Kato, Byang H. "The Gospel, Cultural Context, and Religious Syncretism." In *Let the Earth Hear His Voice*, edited by J. D. Douglas, 12–17. Minneapolis: World Wide, 1975.

Kearney, Michael. *World View*. Novato, Calif.: Chandler and Sharp, 1984.

Keesing, Felix M. *Cultural Anthropology: The Science of Custom*. New York: Holt, Rinehart and Winston, 1958.

Kellenberger, J. *The Cognitivity of Religion: Three Perspectives*. Berkeley: University of California Press, 1985.

Kelly, D. P. *Destroying the Barriers: Receptor Oriented Communication of the Gospel*. Vernon, British Columbia: Laurel, 1982.

Kipling, Rudyard. *The Ballad of the East and the West.* In *Rudyard Kipling's Verse: Inclusive Edition 1885–1918.* Garden City, N.Y.: Doubleday, Page, 1924.

Klapper, Joseph T. *The Effects of Mass Communication.* New York: Free Press, 1960.

Klem, Herbert V. *Oral Communication of the Scripture: Insights from African Oral Art.* Pasadena, Calif.: William Carey, 1982.

Kluckhohn, Clyde. *Mirror for Man.* New York: Whittlesey, 1949.

Knapp, Mark L. *Nonverbal Communication in Human Interaction.* New York: Holt, Rinehart and Winston, 1972.

Korzybski, Alfred. *Science and Sanity.* Lancaster, Pa.: Science, 1933.

Kraemer, Hendrik. *The Christian Message in a Non-Christian World.* Grand Rapids: Kregel, 1963.

————. *The Communication of the Christian Faith.* Philadelphia: Westminster, 1956.

Kraft, Charles H. *Christianity in Culture: A Study in Dynamic Biblical Theologizing in Cross-Cultural Perspective.* Maryknoll, N.Y.: Orbis, 1979.

————. *Communication Theory for Christian Witness.* Nashville: Abingdon, 1983.

————. "Dynamic Equivalence Churches." *Missiology* 1:1 (January 1973): 39–57.

Kumata, Hideya. "A Factor Analytic Study of Semantic Structures Across Three Selected Cultures." Unpublished Ph.D. dissertation, University of Illinois, 1958. In David K. Berlo, *The Process of Communication: An Introduction to Theory and Practice.* New York: Holt, Rinehart and Winston, 1960.

Kuzuhara, Kate and Chiaki. "A Pictorial Letter from Chiaki and Kate Kuzuhara." Chicago: n.p., n.d.

Langer, Susanne K. *Philosophy in a New Key.* New York: New American Library of World Literature, Mentor, 1948.

Larson, Donald N., and William A. Smalley. *Becoming Bilingual: A Guide to Language Learning.* New Canaan, Conn.: Practical Anthropology, 1972.

Latourette, Kenneth Scott. *A History of the Expansion of Christianity,* 7 vols. New York: Harper and Brothers, 1937.

Lazarsfeld, Paul F., Bernard R. Berelson, and Hazel Gaudet. *The People's Choice.* New York: Columbia University Press, 1949.

Lederer, William J., and Eugene Burdick. *The Ugly American.* Greenwich, Conn.: Fawcett, 1958,

Lerner, Max. "Private and Public Sexuality." *Pacific Stars and Stripes* (March 13, 1973), 10.

Bibliography

Levy-Bruhl, Lucien. *Primitive Mentality*. Boston: Beacon, 1966.

Lewis, C. S. *The Abolition of Man*. New York: Crowell-Collier, Collier Books, 1962.

————. *The Case for Christianity*. New York: Macmillan, 1962.

Lindsell, Harold. *Missionary Principles and Practice*. Westwood, N.J.: Revell, 1955.

Lingenfelter, Sherwood G., and Marvin K. Mayers. *Ministering Cross-Culturally: An Incarnational Model for Personal Relationships*. Grand Rapids: Baker, 1986.

Litfin, A. Duane. "The Perils of Persuasive Preaching." *Christianity Today Magazine*, 4 February 1977, 21.

Little, Kenneth L. "The Mende of Sierra Leone." In *African World*, edited by Daryll Forde. London: Oxford University Press, 1954.

Lloyd, P. C. *Africa in Social Change: West African Societies in Transition*. New York: Praeger, 1968.

Loewen, Jacob. "Self-exposure: Bridge to Fellowship." *Practical Anthropology* 12 (March-April 1965): 56.

Longacre, Robert E. *An Anatomy of Speech Notions*. Lisse, Netherlands: Peter de Ridder, 1977.

Luzbetak, Louis J. *The Church and Cultures*. Techny, Ill.: Divine Word, 1963.

McGavran, Donald A. *The Bridges of God*. New York: Friendship, 1955.

————. *The Clash Between Christianity and Cultures*. Washington, D.C.: Canon, 1974.

————. *Understanding Church Growth*, rev. ed. Grand Rapids: Eerdmans, 1980.

McIlwain, Trevor. *Building on Firm Foundations*. Vol. 1. *Guidelines for Evangelism and Teaching Believers*. Sanford, Fla.: New Tribes Mission, 1987.

————. *Notes on the Chronological Approach to Evangelism and Church Planting*. Sanford, Fla.: New Tribes Mission, 1981.

McLuhan, Marshall. *Understanding Media: The Extensions of Man*. New York: McGraw-Hill, 1964.

McLuhan, Marshall, and Edmund Carpenter. *Explorations in Communication*. Boston: Beacon, 1960.

McLuhan, Marshall, and Quenten Fiore. *The Medium is the Message: An Inventory of Effects*. New York: Bantam Books, 1967.

Maddocks, Melvin. "The Limitations of Language." *Time*, 8 March 1971, 36–37.

Mansfield, Cathy Lee. "Cognitive and Attitudinal Changes Following Viewing of the Jesus Film Among the Gwembe Tonga of

Zambia." M.A. thesis, Trinity Evangelical Divinity School, 1984.

Maslow, Abraham. *Motivation and Personality*, 2nd ed. New York: Harper & Row, 1970.

Mawby, Sir Maurice. "Austria and Asia." *The Asia Magazine*, 24 September 1972, 26.

Mayers, Marvin K. *Background Notes on Christian Outreach in a Philippine Community*. Pasadena: William Carey, 1970.

————. *Christianity Confronts Culture: A Strategy for Crosscultural Evangelism*. Grand Rapids: Zondervan, 1974.

Mbiti, John S. *African Religions and Philosophy*. Garden City, N.Y.: Doubleday, Anchor, 1970.

————. *Concepts of God in Africa*. New York: Praeger, 1969.

Milton, G. Ralph. "Media Integration—A Fad and a Fact: The Church and the Media." *Asia Focus* 6 (third quarter 1971): 37.

Monroe, Alan H. *Principles and Types of Speech*. New York: Scott, Foresman, 1939.

Montgomery, John Warwick. "The Theologian's Craft." *Concordia Theological Monthly* 37 (February 1966); 66–98.

Moore, Charles, ed. *The Chinese Mind: Essentials of Chinese Philosophy and Culture*. Honolulu: East-West Center, 1967.

Morris, Leon. *The First Epistle of Paul to the Corinthians*. Tyndale New Testament Commentaries. 20 vols. Edited by R. V. Q. Tasker. Grand Rapids: Eerdmans, 1955.

Moss. Jean Dietz, ed. *Rhetoric and Praxis: The Contribution of Classical Rhetoric to Practical Reasoning*. Washington, D. C.: The Catholic University of America Press, 1986.

Motoori, Morinaga. "The Religions of Japan." In *Readings in Eastern Religious Thought: Chinese and Japanese Religions*. Vol. 3. Edited by Ollie M. Frazier. Philadelphia, Pa.: Westminster Press, n.d., 177–87.

Muggeridge, Malcolm. *Christ and the Media*. Grand Rapids: Eerdmans, 1977.

Murphy, James J. "Augustine and the Debate About a Christian Rhetoric." *Quarterly Journal of Speech* 46 (December 1960): 408.

Makamura, Hajime. *Ways of Thinking of Eastern Peoples*, edited by Philip P. Wiener. Honolulu: East-West Center, 1964.

Nederhood, Joel H. *The Church's Mission to the Educated American*. Grand Rapids: Eerdmans, 1960.

Neill, Stephen. *A History of Christian Missions*. Grand Rapids: Eerdmans, 1965.

_____. *Call to Mission*. Philadelphia: Fortress, 1970.

_____. *Christian Faith and Other Faiths*. Oxford: Oxford University Press, 1970.

_____. "Conversion." *Church Growth Bulletin* 7 (May 1971): 145.

Newman, Philip L. *Knowing the Gurumba*. New York: Holt, Rinehart and Winston, 1965.

Nicholls, Bruce J. "Theological Education and Evangelization." In *Let the Earth Hear His Voice*, edited by J. D. Douglas. Minneapolis: World Wide, 1975, 647.

Nicholls, Kathleen. *The Prodigal Returns: A Christian Approach to Drama*. India: Traci Publications, 1977.

Nida, Eugene A. *Customs and Cultures*. New York: Harper & Row, 1954.

_____. *God's Word in Man's Language*. New York: Harper & Row, 1952.

_____. *Learning A Foreign Language*. New York: Friendship, 1957.

_____. *Message and Mission: The Communication of the Christian Faith*. New York: Harper & Row, 1960.

Nida, Eugene A., and William D. Reyburn. *Meaning Across Cultures*. Maryknoll, N.Y.: Orbis, 1981.

Niebuhr, H. Richard. *Christ and Culture*. New York: Harper & Row, Harper Torch Books, 1956.

Nikhilananda, Swami. *The Upanishads*. New York: Harper & Row, Harper Torchbooks, 1964.

Niles, D. T. *The Preacher's Task and the Stone of Stumbling*. New York: Harper & Row, 1958.

Northrop, F. C. S. *The Meeting of East and West: An Enquiry Concerning World Understanding*. New York: Macmillan, 1953.

Oliver, Robert T. *Communication and Culture in Ancient India and China*. Syracuse, N.Y.: Syracuse University Press, 1971.

_____. *Culture and Communication: The Problem of Penetrating National and Cultural Boundaries*. Springfield, Ill.: Thomas, 1962.

Olson, Gilbert W. *Church Growth in Sierra Leone*. Grand Rapids: Eerdmans, 1969.

Osgood, Charles and Thomas A. Sebeok, eds. *Psycholinguistics: A Survey of Theory and Research Problems*. Baltimore: Waverly, 1954.

Osgood, Charles E., George J. Suei, and Percy Tannenbaum. *The Measurement of Meaning*. Urbana: University of Illinois Press, 1957.

Owens, Virginia Stem. *The Total Image: Or Selling Jesus in the Modern Age*. Grand Rapids: Eerdmans, 1980.

Packer, J. I. *Evangelism and the Sovereignty of God.* Chicago: InterVarsity, 1961.

————. *"Fundamentalism" and the Word of God: Some Evangelical Principles.* London: Inter-Varsity, 1958.

Parks, Robert. "Reflections on Communication and Culture." In *Reader in Public Opinion and Communication,* edited by Bernard Berelson and Morris Janowitz. 2nd ed. New York: Free Press, 1966, 167.

Patterson, George. "Communication—The Last Revolution." *Interlit* (June 1970), 2, 14–16.

Perry, Edmund. *The Gospel in Dispute.* Garden City, N.Y.: Doubleday, 1958.

Perry, Lloyd. "Trends and Emphases in the Philosophy, Materials and Methodology of American Protestant Homiletical Education as Established by a Study of Selected Trade and Textbooks Published Between 1834–1954." Ph.D. dissertation, Northwestern University, 1961.

Peters, George W. "Issues Confronting Evangelical Missions." In *Evangelical Missions Tomorrow,* edited by Wade T. Coggins and E. L. Frizen, 169. Pasadena, Calif.: William Carey, 1977.

Pickett, J. Waskom. *Christian Mass Movements in India.* New York: Abingdon, 1933.

Pike, Kenneth L. "Emic and Etic Standpoints of the Description of Behavior." In his *Language in Relation to a Unified Theory of the Science of Human Behavior.* Part I, prel. ed. Glendale, Calif.: Summer Institute of Linguistics, 1954, 8–28.

Pitt, Malcom. *Introducing Hinduism.* New York: Friendship, 1955.

Potter, Karl. "The Self-Image Approach." In *Approaches to Asian Civilizations,* edited by William Theodore De Bary and Ainslee T. Embree. New York: Columbia University Press, 1964, 273–75.

Psathas, George. "Ethnoscience and Ethnomethodology." In James P. Spradley, *Culture and Cognition: Rule, Maps, and Plans.* Prospect Heights, Ill.: Waveland, 1987.

Pye, Lucian W. "Communication Operation in Non-Western Societies." *Reader in Public Opinion and Communication,* edited by Bernard Berelson and Morris Janowitz, 2nd ed. New York: Free Press, 1967.

Quotations from Mao-Tse-Tung. Peking: Foreign Languages, 1972.

Radhakrishnan. *The Hindu View of Life.* New York: Macmillan, 1927.

Rahskopf, H. G. *Basic Speech Improvement.* New York: Harper & Row, 1965.

Bibliography

Ramm, Bernard. "Liberalism." In *Baker's Dictionary of Theology*, edited by E. F. Harrison. Grand Rapids: Baker, 1960.

Ramsey, Sheila J. "Nonverbal Behavior: An Intercultural Perspective." In Molefi Kete Asante, Eileen Newmark, and Cecil A. Blake, eds. *Handbook of Intercultural Communication.* Beverly Hills: Sage Publications, 1979.

Ray, Chandu. "Asian Strategy for Evangelism." *Christianity Today.* 20 (27 August 1976): 1174–77.

_____. "The Use of Dance-Drama in Evangelism." *Effective Evangelism* 1, 1 (April 1971): 6.

Redfield, Robert. *The Primitive World and Its Transformations.* Ithaca, N.Y.: Cornell University Press, 1957.

_____. "The Primitive World View." *Proceedings of the American Philosophical Society* 96 (1952): 30–36.

Reissman, Leonard. *The Urban Process: Cities in Industrial Societies.* New York: Free Press, 1964.

Reyburn, William D. "Don't Learn That Language!" *Practical Anthropology* 5 (July-August 1958): 151–78; reprinted in William A. Smalley, ed. *Readings in Missionary Anthropology.* Tarrytown, N.Y.: Practical Anthropology, 1967.

Rhetoric and the Poetics of Aristotle. Translated by Rhys Roberts and Ingram Bewater. New York: Malen Library, 1954.

Richards, I. A. *A Philosophy of Rhetoric.* New York: Oxford University Press, 1936.

Richardson, Don. *Peace Child.* Glendale, Calif.: Regal, 1974.

Riesman, David. *The Lonely Crowd.* New Haven: Yale University Press, 1961.

Rin Ro, Bong, and Ruth Eshenauer, eds. *The Bible and Theology in Asian Contexts.* Taichung, Taiwan: Asian Theological Association, 1984.

Robinson, Gail L. Nemetz. *Crosscultural Understanding.* New York: Pergamon, 1985.

Samarin, William. "The Language of Silence." *Practical Anthropology* 12 (May-June 1965): 115–19.

Samartha, Stanley J. "Dialogue Between Men of Living Faiths, the Ajaltoun Memorandum." In *Dialogue Between Men of Living Faiths*, edited by S. J. Samartha. Geneva: World Council of Churches, 1971, 114.

Samovar, Larry A., Richard E. Porter, and Nemi C. Jain. *Understanding Intercultural Communication.* Belmont, Calif.: Wadsworth, 1981.

Sapir, Edward. *Language: An Introduction to the Study of Speech.* New York: Harcourt, Brace and World, 1921.

Sarrett, L., W. T. Foster, and A. J. Sarrett. *Basic Principles of Speech.* 3rd ed. Cambridge, Mass.: Riverside, 1958.

Schaeffer, Francis A. *The Church Before the Watching World.* Downers Grove, Ill.: InterVarsity, 1971.

Schramm, Wilbur. *Mass Media and National Development.* Stanford: Stanford University Press, 1964.

"Selections from the Analects." In *Readings in Eastern Religious Thought.* 3 vols. Edited by Ollie M. Frazier. Philadelphia: Westminster, 1963, 3:74.

Schaeffer, Francis. *Escape From Reason.* London: InterVarsity, 1968.

Shannon, Claude E., and Warren Weaver. *The Mathematical Theory of Communication.* Urbana: University of Illinois Press, 1949.

Shaw, R. Daniel. *Transculturation: The Cultural Factor in Translation and Other Communication Tasks.* Pasadena, Calif.: William Carey, 1988.

Show Business. "Video Cartridges: A Promise of Future Shock." *Time,* 10 August 1970, 41.

Sikkema, Mildred, and Agnes Niyekawa. *Design for Cross-Cultural Learning.* Yarmouth, Maine: Intercultural, 1987.

Singh, Sundhar. *With and Without Christ.* New York: Harper, 1929.

Smith, M. A. *From Constantine to Christ.* Downers Grove, Ill.: InterVarsity, 1971.

Smith, Alfred G., ed. *Communication and Culture: Readings in the Codes of Human Interaction.* New York: Holt, Rinehart and Winston, 1966.

Søgaard, Viggo. *Everything You Need to Know for a Cassette Ministry: Cassettes in the Context of a Total Christian Communication Program.* Minneapolis: Bethany Fellowship, 1975.

Solmsen, Friedrich, ed. *The Rhetoric and the Politics of Aristotle.* New York: Random House, 1954.

Spae, Joseph J. *Christianity Encounters Japan.* Tokyo: Oriens Institute for Religious Research, 1968.

————. *Neighborhood Associations: A Catholic Way for Japan.* Himeji, Japan: Committee of the Apostolate, c/o Catholic Church, 1956.

Spradley, James P. *Participant Observation.* New York: Holt, Rinehart and Winston, 1980.

————. *The Ethnographic Interview.* New York: Holt, Rinehart and Winston, 1979.

Stace, W. T. *Religion and the Modern Mind.* Philadelphia: Lippincott, 1952.

Stalker, James. *Life of St. Paul.* Grand Rapids: Zondervan, n.d.

Statistical Yearbook, 1988. Paris: United Nations' Educational, Scientific and Cultural Organization, 1988.

Stewart, Edward C. "Outline of Intercultural Communication." In *Readings in Intercultural Communication*, vol. 3. Research Council for Intercultural Communication, 1973.

Stuart, Chase. *The Tyranny of Words.* New York: Harcourt, Brace, 1938.

Sunukjian, Donald Robert. "Patterns for Preaching—A Rhetorical Analysis of the Sermons of Paul in Acts 13, 17, and 20." Th.D. dissertation, Dallas Theological Seminary, 1972.

Taylor, John. *The Growth of the Church in Buganda.* London: SCM, 1958.

"The Summum Bonum" from the Majjhima-Hikaya, and Consisting of Sutra 26. In *Readings in Eastern Religious Thought: Buddhism*, Vol. 2. Edited by Ollie M. Frazier. Philadelphia: Westminster, n.d., 109–80.

The Book of Tao. Translated by Frank J. MacHovec. Mount Vernon, N.Y.: Peter Pauper, 1962.

The Koran, translated by N. J. Dawood. Rev. ed. Baltimore: Penguin, 1959.

The Authority of the Bible—The Louvain Report." *The Ecumenical Review* 23 (October 1971): 419–37.

Theological Education Fund (TEF Staff). *Ministry in Context: The Third Mandate Programme of the Theological Education Fund (1970–77).* Bromley, Kent, England: The Theological Education Fund, 1972.

Tippett, A. R. *Verdict Theology in Missionary Theory.* Lincoln, Ill.: Lincoln Christian College Press, 1969.

Trench, Richard Chenevix. *Synonyms of the New Testament.* Marshallton, Del.: The National Foundation for Christian Education, n.d.

Tse-Tung, Mao. *Quotations From Mao Tse-Tung.* Peking: Foreign Languages, 1972.

Tsunoda, Tadanobu. "The Qualitative Differences in Cerebral Dominance for Vowel Sounds Between Japanese and European Languages." *Medicine and Biology* 85 (October 1972): 157–62. In John C. Condon, Jr. *Interpersonal Communication.* New York: Macmillan, 1977.

Tuggy, A. L., and R. Toliver. *Seeing the Church in the Philippines.* Manila: O. M. F., 1972.

Urban, Wilbur Marshall. *Language and Reality: The Philosophy of Language and the Principles of Symbolism.* London: G. Allen, 1951.

Van Til, Henry R. *The Calvinistic Concept of Culture*. Philadelphia: Presbyterian and Reformed, 1959.

Wagner, Peter. *Look Out! The Pentecostals Are Coming*. Carol Stream, Ill.: Creation, 1973.

Wallace, Anthony F. C. *Culture and Personality*. New York: Random, 1961.

Ward, Ted. *Living Overseas*. New York: Free Press; London: Collier, Macmillan, 1984.

Warren, T. J. P. *The Muslim Challenge to the Christian Church*. Condensed by L. B. J. Birmingham, England: Wakelin, 1960.

Weaver, Richard. *The Ethics of Rhetoric*. Chicago: Regnery, 1953.

Weber, H. R. *The Communication of the Gospel to Illiterates*. Madras: Christian Literature Society, 1960.

Whorf, Benjamin Lee. *Language, Thought and Reality: Selected Writings of B. L. Whorf*, edited by John B. Carroll. New York: Wiley, 1956.

Wiener, Norbert. *The Human Use of Human Beings*. Boston: Houghton Mifflin, 1954.

Winter, Ralph. "The Highest Priority: Cross-Cultural Evangelism." In *Let the Earth Hear His Voice*, edited by J. D. Douglas. Minneapolis: World Wide, 1975, 213–25.

Wirth, Louis. "Urbanism As A Way of Life." In *Urbanism in World Perspective: A Reader*, edited by Sylvia Fava. New York: Crowell, 1968.

Yammamori, Tetsunao and LeRoy Lawson. *Introducing Church Growth: A Textbook in Missions*. Cincinnati: Standard, 1975.

Yatiswarananda, Swami. *Adventures in Vedanta*. London: Rider, 1961.

Young, Richard E., Alton L. Becker, and Kenneth Pike. *Rhetoric: Discovery and Change*. New York: Harcourt, Brace and World, 1970.

Yousef, Fathi S. "Intercultural Communication: Aspects of Contrastive Social Values Between North Americans and Middle Easterners." Manuscript prepared for Professor W. S. Howell, University of Minnesota, Fall 1969.

Yu, Timothy. "If the Body Were All Eye—A Note on Mass Media Coordination." *Asia Focus* 6 (third quarter 1971).

Yu-Lan, Fun. "The Spirit of Chinese Philosophy." In *Readings in Eastern Religious Thought: Chinese and Japanese Religions*, Vol. 3. Edited by Ollie M. Frazier. Philadelphia: Westminster, n.d., 30–34.

INDEX OF PERSONS

Index of Persons

INDEX OF
PLACES AND PEOPLES

INDEX OF SUBJECTS

SCRIPTURE INDEX